About the author

Alan Watkins

Alan is the CEO and founder of Complete – a consultancy that specialises in developing exceptional leadership through individual and team development.

Alan is unusual in that he advises completely different businesses in totally different market sectors, in different geographies, and works with many different types of businesses from innovative tech start-ups to FTSE 100 giants. He consults with them on how to grow their revenues, transform their strategy, step change their leadership capability using the Change Wheel in this book and how to develop their culture. He is a disruptive thinker and a modern business innovator. He can take complex global concepts from multiple market sectors, integrate his own ideas with the wisdom of the crowd and come up with novel answers that have proven extremely helpful to the 100 different companies that constitute his client base.

Alan has written several books including *Innovation Sucks! Time to Think Differently*, co-authored with Simon May (Routledge, 2021) and *HR (R)Evolution: Change the Workplace, Change the World*, co-authored with Nick Dalton (Routledge, 2020). Alan is based in the UK and has recently been appointed as a Visiting Professor at Kingston Business School, London.

Step Change

No one likes change. Too often it's viewed as something that must be endured; something to 'get through' as fast as possible so that everything can 'return to normal'. We need to change our view of change and see it for the opportunity it really is. *Step Change: The Leader's Journey* helps leaders to become gifted and skilful at moving through the change process gracefully and productively.

Based on Joseph Campbell's 'hero's journey', *Step Change: The Leader's Journey* offers a universal road map of change from step-1 (comfort zone) through to step-12 (post-delivery inspiration). The journey travels through four distinct phases of 'discover', 'decide', 'develop' and 'deliver'. *Step Change* provides a proven formula for change, both personal and organisational, which allows us to know where we are on the Change Wheel and what to expect from each step, including what it looks and feels like at each step. By identifying what causes change to fail at each step as well as tools to navigate past the pitfalls and dead ends that leave us stuck at a particular step or retreating to the comfort zone, the change cycle can be understood and mastered.

The book provides the ideal structure for senior managers, human resource managers, coaches and business leaders to follow in order to embed change across their teams and organisation.

Alan Watkins is the CEO and founder of Complete, a consultancy specialising in developing exceptional leadership through individual and team development. Alan is unusual in that he advises completely different businesses in totally different market sectors, in different geographies, and works with many different types of businesses from innovative start-ups to FTSE 100 giants. He is the author of several successful books including *Innovation Sucks!*, co-authored with Simon May, and *HR (R)Evolution: Change the Workplace, Change the World*, co-authored with Nick Dalton.

Step Change

The Leader's Journey

Alan Watkins

Routledge
Taylor & Francis Group

LONDON AND NEW YORK

First published 2022
by Routledge
2 Park Square, Milton Park, Abingdon, Oxon OX14 4RN

and by Routledge
605 Third Avenue, New York, NY 10158

Routledge is an imprint of the Taylor & Francis Group, an informa business

British Library Cataloguing-in-Publication Data
A catalogue record for this book is available from the British Library

Library of Congress Cataloging-in-Publication Data
A catalog record has been requested for this book

ISBN: 978-0-367-77236-9 (hbk)
ISBN: 978-0-367-77238-3 (pbk)
ISBN: 978-1-003-17040-2 (ebk)

DOI: 10.4324/9781003170402

Typeset in Joanna
by Newgen Publishing UK

Printed in the UK by Severn, Gloucester on responsibly sourced paper

Contents

Acknowledgements   xi

Introduction   1
The hero's journey 2
Change and stress 7
The leader's journey 8

1. Step-1: Comfort zone   11
    How do I know if I'm at step-1? 11
    How does it feel to be in step-1? 14
        The trap of narcissism 15
    Cultural metaphors 16
    The transition from step-1 to step-2 18
        Questions to ask yourself 19

2. Step-2: Challenge to reality   21
    How do I know if I'm at step-2? 21
        Value-based wake-up call 22
    How does it feel to be in step-2? 26
        The biological consequences of being stuck at step-2 29
        The mental health consequences of being stuck at step-2 30
        Victimhood 33
    Cultural metaphors 37
    Transition from step-2 to step-3 39
        Questions to ask yourself 39

3. Step-3: Resistance to change   43
    How do I know if I'm at step-3? 43
        Vertical development 45
    How does it feel to be in step-3? 47
        The expert mindset 50
        Assessing the helper 51

Cultural metaphors 53
Transition from step-3 to step-4 54
Questions to ask yourself 55

4. Step-4: Overcoming resistance   57
How do I know if I'm at step-4? 57
How does it feel to be in step-4? 59
Doubt 61
The accountability compass 63
Cultural metaphors 67
The transition from step-4 to step-5 69
Questions to ask yourself 70

5. Step-5: Commitment   73
How do I know if I'm at step-5? 73
Rites of passage 75
How does it feel to be at step-5? 77
State change vs level change 78
Cultural metaphors 80
The transition from step-5 to step-6 82
Questions to ask yourself 83

6. Step-6: Prepare for change   85
How do I know if I'm at step-6? 86
Behaviours needed to master step-6 86
How does it feel to be at step-6? 89
Appreciation 89
Appreciation skill 90
Cultural metaphors 92
The transition from step-6 to step-7 94
Questions to ask yourself 94

7. Step-7: Trials and tribulations   95
How do I know if I'm at step-7? 96
Start from where you are 97
Start where the biggest impact can be made 100
Charting our progress 102
How does it feel to be at step-7? 103
Lack of diligence 104
Cultural metaphors 106
The transition from step-7 to step-8 108
Questions to ask yourself 109

8. Step-8: Deep work   111
How do I know if I'm at step-8? 112
Albert Pesso's five basic needs 115
Fixing the faulty code 122

How does it feel to be at step-8? 125
  Fear 126
  Delusion and pseudo-enlightenment 127
Cultural metaphors 128
The transition from step-8 to step-9 130
  Questions to ask yourself 131

9. Step-9: Embodying the change   133
How do I know if I'm at step-9? 134
  Embodiment 135
  Purpose 137
  The 'story of you' 138
How does it feel to be at step-9? 138
  Complacency 139
Cultural metaphors 140
The transition from step-9 to step-10 141
  Questions to ask yourself 142

10. Step-10: Return   143
How do I know if I'm at step-10? 143
  Working with your purpose 145
How does it feel to be at step-10? 148
  Failure to mark the return and disillusionment 148
Cultural metaphors 149
The transition from step-10 to step-11 151
  Questions to ask yourself 152

11. Step-11: Delivery at the new level   153
How do I know if I'm at step-11? 153
How does it feel to be at step-11? 158
  Satisfaction 159
Cultural metaphors 159
The transition from step-11 to step-12 161
  Questions to ask yourself 161

Step-12: Inspire   163
How do I know if I'm at step-12? 163
How does it feel to be at step-12? 165
  As good as it gets 166
Cultural metaphors 166
The transition to a new change cycle 169
  Questions to ask yourself 169

13. The leader as coach   171
Step-1: Comfort zone 172
Step-2: Challenge to reality 175
  Archetypes at step-2 176

Step-3: Resistance to change 177
    Resistance revisited 178
    Archetypes at step-3 179
Step-4: Overcoming resistance 179
    Coach's resistance 180
    Archetypes at step-4 181
Step-5: Commitment 181
    Archetypes at step-5 182
Step-6: Prepare for change 182
    Archetypes at step-6 183
Step-7: Trials and tribulations 183
    Archetypes at step-7 184
Step-8: Deep work 185
    Archetypes at step-8 186
Step-9: Embodying the change 186
    Archetypes at step-9 187
Step-10: Return 187
    Archetypes at steps-10 to -12 188
Step-11: Delivery at the new level 188
Step-12: Inspire 189

Index   191

Acknowledgements

This is a book I have been wanting to write for some time. Joseph Campbell is a hero of mine. One of my four sons is named Joseph in his honour. Without Campbell's genius and inspiration this book would never have been written. I am also indebted to the many storytellers over the years who have kept Campbell's legacy alive through their own work, be it in film or through other cultural work.

I am also deeply indebted to the many CEOs and leaders I have worked with over the years who have listened to me tell stories of heroes and journeys and who have been prepared to let me guide them on their own leader's journey. It has been a deep pleasure to be the Samwise to your Frodo, the Morpheus to your Neo. I only hope you got as much treasure from your journey as I did as your companion.

Finally, as always, I acknowledge my companions at Complete, my allies at Routledge and Karen McCreadie who has been my Samwise on this book. I must mention my wonderful sons, my great friends Anthony and Rachel in Australia and my many other friends around the world. Principal companion amongst all these companions is my beautiful wife, Sarah. We have travelled many revolutions of the Change Wheel together, and I could not ask for a better partner. The revolutions continue, and many more adventures await us. Let's travel well, travel light and enjoy every moment.

Introduction

No-one likes change. As a species we prefer things just the way they are. We are much more comfortable with consistency, secure with stability and positive about permanence. Our need to curb change seems to hold true regardless of culture, geography, education or background. And nowhere is our relationship to change more tortured than in business.

Most leaders ask for 'no surprises' from their team. Markets abhor an unexpected gain almost as much as a loss. Why? Because unpredicted profit suggests a potential fragility, a poor understanding of the market or the economy or that some form of instability is at play. All these things are warning signs of future losses. Often, far greater problems are created by our collective discomfort and distrust of change than the change itself. During team meetings, many leaders recite the cliché that 'change is the only constant', and yet they and their team remain reluctant to embrace this truth – personally or professionally.

This ambivalence is a real paradox given we change significantly throughout our lives, not least physically. Even though we are constantly changing, we never really develop change competency. We don't talk about change in a sophisticated way; we don't understand its anatomy, its physiology or its real purpose. Instead, change is frequently perceived as a negative or, at the very least, an inconvenience. Something that must be endured, something we have to 'get through' as fast as possible so that everything can 'return to normal'.

For most of us, our first conscious experience of significant change is puberty. The physical and psychological transformation is literally life changing. How these challenges are handled often determines our view of change for the rest of our lives. If we fail to understand the scope of what's actually happening during this tumultuous period, our whole perspective on change can narrow, reducing our view of change to a purely physical phenomenon with a dash of emotion thrown in.

In reality, as we grow up, we start to see the world differently and wake up for the first time. But we still don't consider how we are changing as human beings, even though these changes extend well beyond our physical body. Through our early teenage years our value systems, or what we consider important, changes dramatically. Our ego-centricity shifts, or at least it should if we are ever to mature into a fully-functioning adult. Our cognitive capabilities expand and hopefully our emotional and social intelligence steps up a level. But we rarely stop to consider

DOI: 10.4324/9781003170402-1

these critical changes to our interior landscape or consciously facilitate and encourage them.

Beyond the personal upheaval, we also experience dramatic changes in all our relationships as teenagers. But we don't necessarily explore or identify the connections between our individual change and how our relationships change. We never take a step back from the shifting interpersonal dynamics to ponder some of the rules that dictate the evolution of our relationships at these critical moments. And if we don't make the connections in our teenage years, we are unlikely to make those connections later in our lives. We simply become embroiled in our relationships without any deep evaluation of how our personal transformation affects the evolution of those relationships. If we don't appreciate the impact of who we are on who we connect with and why, it's hardly surprising that divorce rates are at record highs in most developed countries, not to mention the fragility in our relationships with family, friends and work colleagues.

Whether personal change, relationship change or business change, change shouldn't be this hard. It shouldn't cause this much angst. What should we do to avoid the agony of change? The simple answer is study. We need to become students of change. We need to see change for what it really is and become gifted and skilful at moving through the change process gracefully and productively. This is especially true for leaders and senior C-suite executives charged with moving a business forward in an ever changing, fast-paced business and economic environment.

Luckily, we have a road map – thanks largely to the work of Joseph Campbell.

The hero's journey

Campbell was the American professor of literature who introduced the world to the hero's journey – essentially a road map for human development and change. Raised in an upper-middle class Irish Catholic family, he developed a fascination with Native American culture that would hint at his future life's work. In 1925 he received his degree in English literature and two years later his Master's in medieval literature from Columbia University. His interest spread across comparative mythology and comparative religion, and his encounters with different cultures, stories, myths, legends and cultural rites of passage eventually led him to theorise that all myths, from Native American to Hindu to Aboriginal to German fairy tales, are the products of the human psyche. Artists such as Pablo Picasso and writers such as John Steinbeck or James Joyce were culture's mythmakers. All mythologies, regardless of source, were essentially creative manifestations of humankind's universal need to explain psychological, social, cosmological and spiritual realities.

In 1949, Campbell's seminal work, *The Hero with a Thousand Faces*, was published. It is essentially the study of myths from around the world. Campbell suggests the existence of what he originally referred to as a monomyth (a phrase he borrowed from James Joyce). This monomyth, which would later become known more commonly as the hero's journey, described a universal pattern common to heroic tales in *every* culture. As well as drawing the reader's attention to the basic phases of this mythic cycle, Campbell also explored the common variations in the hero's journey.

The journey begins in the *ordinary world*. The hero receives a *call to adventure* to leave the familiar known world. *Threshold guardians* may appear to prevent the departure or a *mentor* might appear to help the hero *cross the threshold*, leading him to an *unknown world*, where familiar laws no longer apply. There, the hero will embark on a *road of trials*, where he is tested. *Allies* may appear to help the hero face their ordeal and, once they rise to the challenge, the hero will receive a reward or *boon*. The hero must then return with this *boon* to the *ordinary world* and face more trials on *the road back*. Upon the hero's return, the boon or gift may be used to improve the hero's ordinary world, in what Campbell calls the *application of the boon*.

In essence, there are three general phases: 'departure' (sometimes called *separation*), 'initiation' and 'return'. 'Departure' deals with the hero venturing forth on the quest, including the *call to adventure*. 'Initiation' refers to the hero's adventures, where they are tested along the way. And finally, the 'return', which follows the hero's journey home. Of course, the hero is now forever changed by the journey. It's worth pointing out that hero in this context has nothing to do with gender − heroes or heroines, we all embark on some form of the hero's journey in our lifetime − often many times.

On the journey from departure to return, the hero will meet and interact with various archetypes or characters who will help or hinder that journey. When we recognise these characters in our work or personal lives and the roles people play, it can help signpost and accelerate the change process. There are many archetypes that we may encounter in our lives, but the most common are:

- *Threshold guardians*: These are the people who actively try and prevent change or seek to maintain the status quo. Their role is to test the hero or leader's worthiness to cross the threshold. In most stories, they are typically the henchmen of the villain, but they can be neutral or even a secret helper, ensuring the hero/ leader is equipped for the journey ahead. Often, they prevent the hero from crossing the threshold and embarking on change. Occasionally they can be the hero's own fears, or show up as an inanimate object, an animal or a force of nature.
- *Mentor*: These are the helpers, often viewed in story as the wise old man or woman, sage or guide who helps the hero make positive change. The mentor is a source of wisdom, a gift giver or, for mature heroes, their conscience or code of honour. They can motivate the hero to overcome fear or act as teacher. In life, mentors might be a parent, doctor, consultant or coach who will help us face the need for change and support us along the path.
- *Herald*: The herald arrives to signal change and invite the hero to answer the call to adventure. Their job is to motivate the hero/leader to action, throwing down the gauntlet and provoking engagement. Heralds can be people, events, objects or acts of nature. They can be positive, negative or neutral. The arrival of a baby is a positive herald, for example, whereas a profit warning or redundancy is a negative herald.
- *Shapeshifter*: These people are hard to pin down. They bring uncertainty and tension to a story. Shapeshifters may switch roles from mentor to trickster to

villain and back again, changing appearance, mood or behaviour. Their job is to dazzle, confuse, lie to or, occasionally, help the hero. The hero is never quite sure if the shapeshifter is on their side or plotting against them and must spend time figuring this out. Often, shapeshifters are there to teach the hero the importance of diversity and develop wisdom by integrating multiple perspectives. In life, a shapeshifter may be that colleague who appears to be helping but plotting in side bar meetings. They may be the friend who turns out to be disloyal. Sometimes in business, shapeshifters can be a strongly positive force providing disruption, new ideas or new perspectives on existing problems.

- *Shadow*: Most often the shadow is the dark side of the hero, containing all the things about the hero they don't like about themselves. These aspects of Self may show up for them during the journey. Occasionally, the shadow may be a side of the hero that they simply can't see yet, a worthy opponent or the hero's own doubt. In life, the shadow is what we learn about ourselves on the journey; external shadows are exposed, defeated or disempowered and internal shadows can be faced or transformed.
- *Ally*: The hero normally recruits or co-opts several allies on their journey. They are normally friends and supporters of the hero, a companion or sparring partner that can also provide comic relief. The ally usually starts the journey in a fairly undifferentiated role but can gain in prominence and can also morph into other archetypes such as the lover, the maiden warrior, the trickster, the mentor, the shapeshifter or anything that helps the hero to keep going. In life, allies are friends or team members who work together to deliver objectives and make progress. A high performing leadership team should be full of allies.
- *Trickster*: These are the mischief makers who are great at bringing heroes down to size. In stories, they are often the hero's sidekick or a more subtle troublemaker. They can provide moments of humour or light relief after periods of intensity, but they are mainly catalysts or accelerants for the story because they hate the status quo. In life, these are the mavericks, clowns and troublemakers that cause trouble and alleviate tension in equal measure.

With the exception of the threshold guardians, these archetypes can show up at any point on the Change Wheel. We see them show up in film, and I'll flag their arrival in the cultural metaphor section of each chapter to help you better appreciate their role. I will also mention the archetypes again in the final coaching chapter. Whether going through change yourself or coaching others, learning how to recognise these archetypes can accelerate and smooth out the change process.

Since the publication of *The Hero with a Thousand Faces*, Campbell's theory has been consciously applied by writers, artists and filmmakers to tap into this universal story that resonates so strongly within us all. For example, filmmaker George Lucas purposefully changed the story of Star Wars to align more closely to the hero's journey. We will return to well-known cultural touch points, including films such as Star Wars, as we explore the various steps on the leader's journey.

Campbell demonstrated that these myths are not simply entertaining stories passed down at the campfire from generation to generation. They are practical guides and operational metaphors to enable us to successfully navigate the changing nature of life. Campbell believed that "Myths are clues to the spiritual potentialities of the human life." And, if we understand these clues through the universal metaphor, we are better able to reach those potentialities and self-actualise. In addition, understanding the nature of change allows us to better manage the inevitable ups and downs of life, not just for us individually but collectively within cultures as well.

What Campbell did was assimilate an extraordinary amount of information. For example, during the Great Depression, when he was unable to find work, he spent five years engaged in intensive self-study in a shack in Woodstock, New York. He would divide the day into four four-hour periods and read for three of them, thus reading for nine hours a day for five years. Such dedication, on top of a lifetime of self-study and enquiry, allowed him to pull the context from the content. In other words, he was able to see the underlying meta-frame or story architecture that existed within all the myths. This, in turn, offered us a universal map of the journey we all take as we grow, develop and change as adult human beings.

Such meta-frames are profoundly useful.

The best maps or meta-frames help us navigate our own lives more successfully and explain how things evolve. My mentor, and another great American intellectual, Ken Wilber, is also well known for his prodigious research, reading and map making. This is not a coincidence. When Wilber first started, he read everything from all the great psychologists, philosophers, theorists and thinkers. As such, he was able to grasp the full extent of all the various ideas which then allowed him, like Campbell, to see the links and patterns that revealed an underlying narrative or architecture. Wilber is responsible for some of the most profoundly useful meta-models ever created. One that is especially pertinent to this discussion is the notion that everything evolves through three distinct phases: emergence, differentiation and integration.

In this case, emergence refers to the emergence of the stories and myths of various cultures and religions from around the world. The Upanishads, The Hindu Vedas, the Buddhist Sutras, the books of the Bible, the texts of the Quran, the Egyptians' Hermetica, The Samurais' Hagakure, The Tao Te Ching, The Analects of Confucianism, The Emerald Tablets of Thoth, The Tibetan Tantras, The Gnostic Gospels, The Book of Enoch and The Torah are all cultural attempts to create allegorical guidance for their respective communities or congregations.

They emerged into existence over thousands of years. Campbell then sought to differentiate one myth from the other, and in doing so was able to spot the similarities and the differences. Finally, Campbell was able to assimilate that knowledge into an integrated map that gives all of us confidence about the process and what we can expect on the journey. As such, we can lay down our innate fear, distrust and discomfort of change and embrace it as part and parcel of being human. As Wilber said, and he could have been talking directly about Campbell's contribution:

> *To understand the whole, it is necessary to understand the parts. To understand the parts, it is necessary to understand the whole. Such is the circle of understanding. We move from part to whole and back again, and in that dance of comprehension, in that amazing circle of understanding, we come alive to meaning, to value, and to vision: the very circle of understanding guides our way, weaving together the pieces, healing the fractures, mending the torn and tortured fragments, lighting the way ahead—this extraordinary movement from part to whole and back again, with healing the hallmark of each and every step, and grace the tender reward.*[1]

Campbell's contribution identified the universal nature of individual and collective change while also giving us clearly identifiable signposts of that process. Like many, I was enthralled by the series of interviews between Joseph Campbell and Bill Moyers on PBS in 1988, which was released after Campbell's death a year earlier.[2]

One of the things that really struck me was that every single culture has created a fantastic array of stories that dealt with the different aspects of life which are in effect that culture's view of change. Campbell's spellbinding accounts drew on his personal study of the thousands, possibly hundreds of thousands, of stories from multiple cultures and countries around the world. Whether fairy tales or mythology, they talk about the human condition and how it changes. Too often, we get distracted by the surface details – the animations around the campfire – and we lose the underlying meta-frame or message. And that's the gift that Campbell gave to the world. He brought the underlying meta-frame or architecture to the surface to remind us that our stories and myths are not just nice stories but clues and guides to our best future, the legacy left by our ancestors.

The true gift is in understanding that structure because when we do, we get a much more profound appreciation for the story and, more importantly, how it might help our own lives. When we can clearly see the phases and how the journey progresses, we can embrace and learn so much more from those phases and the variety that exists within them.

For example, how a certain archetype shows up might differ depending on the stage of the story, but if we can recognise these archetypes in our own life, it can be transformative. Such characters act as reference points and remind us we are on the right track. However, if we have no understanding of the underlying structure of our journey and don't or can't recognise the archetypes as they appear to us, then they can hinder change and confuse us. If we don't recognise the shapeshifter as someone who sows confusion, we can get lost in the confusion. If we don't recognise the mentor as someone who can help, we may ignore the help. If we don't recognise the trickster, we can become distracted and all this can derail, slow or stop the change. Without this recognition of the steps of the journey and the role that archetypes play at the various steps, we can very easily get lost, confused and fearful as we muddle through the change.

This is one of the reasons why so many of us find change so challenging and why we have such an ambivalent relationship to change. We simply don't acknowledge and appreciate the steps of the leader's journey meta-frame that guides this normal, natural and essential part of our own evolution and development. Instead, we get sucked into the noise and drama. We become bewitched by the characters of the change process rather than seeing them as the signposts that they really are.

Campbell's meta-frame is basically an allegory of the human condition. Knowing that there will *always* be trials and tribulations is strangely comforting. Knowing there is always a way through can be liberating.

Campbell's meta-frame is supremely relevant to corporate leaders who must deliver successful change time and time again or suffer the consequences. Without understanding the underlying structure of the journey, leaders can easily get lost in the details of the business, the KPIs, the targets, the budgets, the numbers and all manner of surface noise. Leaders may then struggle to find their way through whatever they are facing and lurch from one fire to the next because they don't appreciate that they are simply at a specific stage on the hero's journey.

Once the leader can see that journey and recognise where they are, they literally have a road map that can take them successfully through *any* change. Without the recognition of the phases, they can very easily end up going round in circles or getting stuck forever. They are not making any real progress if they are simply stuck at step-2. The story may change, and that changing story may trick them into believing they are making progress. But drop down into the meta-frame or structure of the journey, and they can immediately see that nothing significant has changed at all. This is why suffering happens. Leaders are stuck but they don't realise they are stuck. This book is, I hope, an antidote to that. It is about liberating leaders so they can become unstuck and reduce their suffering and help others to do the same.

We are all called to make these hero's journeys whether we like it or not. We are called to make them in business, at home, in our families and personal relationships; we can't avoid them. As such, we must understand them, recognise where we are and consciously engage with the steps of change to achieve the outcomes we need and foster our own development as adult human beings. That's it. That's our job – regardless of our formal job title.

Change and stress

Whilst change is inevitable it is not synonymous with stress. To prosper, we must develop a far more constructive and deliberate relationship with change. One of the reasons we mistakenly believe change is stressful is the enduring story created in the 1960s by psychiatrists Thomas Holmes and Richard Rahe. They examined the medical records of over 5,000 patients to assess whether stressful events might cause illness. Their finding took on a life of their own far beyond the original confines of the research. Their work even spawned the Holmes and Rahe Stress Scale, which assigns 'Life Change Units' to various life events such as the death of a partner, divorce, redundancy, etc. The story was that if someone has too many units, they are more likely to get ill.

Having experienced some pretty turbulent pre- and post-pubertal changes during adolescence, many then heard the story that Holmes and Rahe could quantify just how destructive change is using their Stress Scale. In time this story was completely discredited, but by the time that occurred it had already passed into sci-entific folklore and the damage was done. When it was pointed out that there were plenty of people who scored very highly in the Holmes and Rahe Stress Scale who never become ill, there was no scientific retraction, no apology for misleading us all. The good news that Holmes and Rahe got it wrong was just not as compelling as the bad news that we were all doomed if we had too much change in our lives.

Subsequent to the mythology that life events make us ill, other researchers, such as Aaron Antonovsky[3] and later Suzanne Kobasa,[4] identified a series of 'resistance resources' that protect us from the damage that change can create. They discovered something they called hardiness or what is now called resilience. Kobasa suggested that our psychological hardiness or lack of it determines our health and success, and hardiness has three components or the 3Cs: Commitment, Control and Challenge. If we can understand change and recognise the phases of change, we can take more control of the process and commit to the challenge ahead. If we do, we develop change competency or hardiness. Such resilience can turn change into oppor-tunity, change our destiny from post-traumatic stress to post-traumatic growth. We may even develop the ability to enjoy the process of change and help others to do the same.

Change is constant, unrelenting and indiscriminate. We either learn to harness it or we may be crushed by it – personally and professionally. Given that the world is accelerating, we need a proven path more than ever. Campbell illuminated the way.

But Campbell's map of the hero's journey is now over 70 years old. It has been adapted, reworked and elaborated on. Many of these maps have lost their definition, scale and meaning. For example, some identify anything from 6 to 17 steps. Many have lost touch with the original meta-frame embedded in the map, and this deep code that is the key. This code was the purpose of Campbell's work.

The leader's journey

Being a lifelong Campbell fan (one of my four sons is called Joseph) this book aims to restore Campbell's code. In order to do so, we looked at everything that had emerged since Campbell's original work and sought to differentiate those new versions. What we are now proposing is an integrated, updated version for those in positions of responsibility – hence the leader's journey. This research saw 12 steps and four phases emerge to form the Change Wheel (see Figure 0.1).

Standing on the shoulders of a giant (Campbell), adding in the phases gives more precision. There are three steps in each of the four phases of discover, decide, develop and deliver.

These four phases correspond to the process of human development. The first phase in the process of evolution requires awareness. We must 'wake up' and dis-cover our current situation is not as we thought. We must realise that the control and power we thought we had is largely an illusion. Secondly, we must 'own up' to how we are co-creating the problems we face. We must own up and admit to our-selves how we are resisting change. We must also take ownership of the parts of our nature that we may dislike. This ownership leads us to make a decision about the

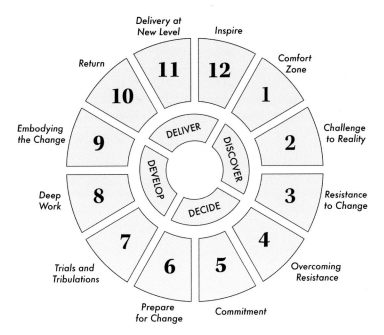

Figure 0.1 The Change Wheel.

need to change. If we don't own up, we never really decide or commit to the process of change and, therefore, the change never really occurs or sustains.

The third phase is where we develop. This is where the work occurs and we 'grow up'. Growing up can never occur if we haven't first woken up and owned up to the need for change and committed to that change. If the work of growing up is successful and we develop, then we can enter the deliver phase and 'show up' very differently, armed with new insights, new more sophisticated ways of being that demonstrate greater wisdom and maturity. The person who shows up in phase four is literally a different person to the one who started the change journey.

When we 'wake up', 'own up' and 'grow up', this evolution alone can make a dramatic difference to how we 'show up' as a leader which, in turn, can help us and the business develop still further. If we refuse or fail to make this personal journey, then we simply stagnate and in time become obsolete.

We must evolve. All of us. Each revolution of the Change Wheel, through all four phases and 12 steps of the leader's journey, alters us profoundly. With each revolution we become more sophisticated, more inclusive, more creative, more adaptable and more capable. We become change champions, and we can successfully harness and utilise the increasing complexity, intensity and disruption in business, rather than be debilitated by it.

If we want to succeed long term in an accelerating, turbulent and uncertain world and build an enduring legacy, the only way forward is to develop ourselves.

Something new is always emerging, but with enhanced change capability, change is not only possible but planned for and successfully navigated for the betterment of all the stakeholders.

Forensically defining four phases and the 12 steps of change has taken something brilliant and insightful, that emerged in 1949, and created a modern map of change. It signposts the journey and provides structure for those seeking to navigate change successfully, in business and beyond. Chapter 1 to Chapter 12 explore each step on the leader's journey, and Chapter 13 outlines how to use the leader's journey to coach others through the change process.

Notes

1   Wilber, K., (2001). *The eye of spirit: An integral vision for a world gone slightly mad*. (3rd Ed.). Boston and London: Shambhala.
2   Moyers, B. and Campbell, J., (1988). *The power of myth*. (Audio and transcript of interview) Available from: www.billmoyers.com
3   Antonovsky, A., (1979). *Health, stress and coping*. New York: Jossey-Bass.
4   Maddi, S. and Kobasa, S., (1984). *The Hardy Executive: Health under stress*. London: Irwin.

1 Step-1

Comfort zone

The hero's journey always begins with the call. One way or another, a guide must come to say, 'Look, you're in Sleepy Land. Wake. Come on a trip. There is a whole aspect of your consciousness, your being, that's not been touched. So, you're at home here? Well, there's not enough of you there.' And so, it starts.

(Joseph Campbell)

One of the reasons that change is viewed negatively by so many people is because it creates an inevitable departure from our comfort zone. Like leaving a warm bed on a bitterly cold winter's morning, few people enjoy the shock and dislocation. Our departure from comfort can create a sense of dis-ease and a desire to stay exactly where we are. But if we don't depart, we may never develop as adult human beings, and we will not fulfil our potential.

When we talk about being in our comfort zone, the implicit assumption is that the comfort zone is a good, safe and happy place to be. For those living outside their comfort zone, it looks like the perfect destination, a worthwhile goal. Many see it as a haven from the difficulties of life. The comfort zone is imbued with magical properties; a womb-like sanctuary to which we can return. But this is a myth and a dangerous one at that.

How do I know if I'm at step-1?

Everyone has experience of being in the comfort zone, nestled nicely in the familiarity of their known world. It's where every journey of change starts. Unfortunately, too many people have taken up permanent residence there because they have bought into the mythology of the comfort zone. They have privileged survival over development.

The illusion of the comfort zone has arisen largely because few people develop the level of change competence needed to successfully leave. This is despite the multiple opportunities that show up as the years stack up on our journey from infants to adults. When the train to transformation appears, we retreat, we shy away and we fail to board. Each voluntary or involuntary opportunity for change from infant to junior school, from senior school to university, from first job to each successive promotion creates turbulence. In the face of this turbulence and without change

DOI: 10.4324/9781003170402-2

competence we mistakenly believe our primary goal is to stay where we are, sta-bilise our position and return to our comfort zone. If we experience any slight change at all, we are immediately compelled to establish a new comfort zone in our new environment as quickly as possible.

But why have we become so addicted to the need for comfort? To understand this, we must take a step back and look deeply into who we are, how we are constructed and what drives us.

All living things have two fundamental drives, but human beings have developed three. The first motivational drive for all living organisms is survival. We are wired to detect novelty because our safety, growth and navigation depend on it. We con-stantly compare what we know and what is familiar with what is new and different. Such pattern recognition is our brain's core operating programme. We must detect threats and protect ourselves against excessive change. In order to do this, we map our inner and outer worlds. The fundamental difference between these maps gives birth to our identity.

Briefly, the maps we make of our external world are awash with change and var-iety. In contrast, our interior maps are incredibly stable with little variance. We are perpetually mapping our physical existence, and these maps hardly change at all. Our blood pressure, pH, oxygen levels, heart rate, breath rate and muscle tone are all controlled very tightly. We come to understand that these stable, invariant patterns are who we are. Our physical identity is formed. We are the thing that doesn't change. We are the fixed point in this sea of external hypervariability. This is why we are, at our core, more comfortable with no change. It is who we are. Our most fundamental drive to survive is about maintaining the integrity of that stability, the comfort of no change. But there's a catch.

If we survive, protect ourselves, feel comfortable and satiate our primary drive by not changing, we create a stable platform. In this non-threatened world of physical and psychological safety, a second motivational drive is activated. And this second drive changes everything.

The second drive is for exploration. It's our desire to look for more resources that takes us beyond survival and towards a new, more expanded future. At the core of that future is reproduction. If we find the resources we seek, which at the most basic level means nutrients (oxygen, food and water) plus security or shelter, we can meet our second drive. This second reproductive drive transcends and includes the primary drive. It drives us to search, to connect and to reproduce so we can con-tinue as a species. To do this successfully, we must become comfortable with change. To explore, we must venture out. The more advanced or complex the organism, the greater the adventure and the more developed our change competence must become.

The exploratory reproductive system is where the journey ends for most of the biosphere, but not us. Human beings have developed a third motivational system, which goes beyond the exploratory reproductive drive of most organisms, and that is the conscious desire to evolve. This consciousness transcends and includes the two previous innate systems. In fact, the third system emerges to inhibit the first two systems to enable us to adapt and flourish as complex beings in an increasingly complex world.

It's this third system that is failing us now. It's not kicking in because many people continue to over prioritise system one and privilege comfort while under-valuing change. This is why many people's relationship with comfort and change has become fickle. Our primary motivational system has become too dominant. Our secondary exploratory motivational system is shut down, and our third motivational system has not even fired up and so can't deliver the abilities we need in a rapidly accelerating world.

When our primary system is dominant, we become trapped in our cage of comfort, just surviving. We lose the opportunity to experience some of the most beautiful and inspiring moments in life; we don't encounter the exquisite freshness of novelty. The experience of something new is what keeps our brain (and us) young, fresh and alive. People get bored when nothing is changing. When we privilege our primary system and 'no change', we put ourselves on the slippery slope to senescence and decay. In our comfort zone, we stick to our unconscious bias for stability. And in a world that is accelerating, this bias is massively impairing our ability to grow, develop and succeed.

Some people spend their entire lives at step-1. But what are the warning signs that you may inadvertently be living out your days in the cage of comfort? The clues that you might be in step-1 include:

- You believe everything is 'fine' right now.
- Conditions are stable and there is no need for change.
- Everything is just ticking along quite nicely – no crisis, no burning platform.
- Things feel good or at least manageable.

Step-1 is soporific, there are no surprises. Everything is functioning well. We are operating in 'business as usual' mode. We know exactly what is expected of us and what we need to do to maintain the status quo.

In a relationship, we might find ourselves in the comfort zone after several years together and a couple of children. We know each other well enough to have moved past the early expectation of perfection. We are liberated from idealism and have surrendered the idea of what could have been and replaced it with what is. In this trance, we have not noticed the infection of complacency, comfort and the erosion of ambition. The partnership is functional and stable, and that's fine. As parents, we know our roles and get on with our tasks and responsibilities. There may not be fireworks, but there are rarely any nasty surprises either. It's nice.

Professionally, the picture is similar. Everything looks normal, and our career and the business might be ticking along. Results are stable – not stellar, but not terrible either. It's all a bit stale, and there is often little urgency. We don't expect to be stretched or challenged and can simply 'go through the motions' of our work. It's predictable – we have no desire to rock the boat, and neither, it seems, does anyone else. There are very few curve balls which can give us a false sense of control. We are generally oblivious of the need for change. This operational blindness can mean that even if a few red flags start to appear or subtle indications that change might be imminent or needed, we miss them. This is not deliberate; it's not that we see these danger signals and ignore them at step-1; often we just don't see them. The boat is either becalmed, drifting, or a storm is brewing, but either way no action is taken. We're not especially engaged or excited by our work anymore, but we don't hate it either. We can get stuck in this limbo existence because it's not bad enough to leave. At step-1, we're not really aware of the need for change. We're 'asleep'. We may even buy into the ultimate fallacy of step-1 that 'ignorance is bliss': it isn't. Ignorance is just ignorance. Bliss is a completely different place that can't be mistaken for step-1. If you have ever been to the planet of Bliss, there is no confusion.

In this state of stasis, we urgently need to change our set point. We need to activate our third motivational system and swing the pendulum back to adventure. We need to wake up. The journey of our life awaits. If we become alive to this quest, embrace our innate curiosity, then we can change our view of change. The opportunity that lies within our grasp is to use change as a stepping-stone to a better, more productive, creative and wonderful future. One where we can become a more enlightened leader, live large, sacrifice ourselves to something beyond ourselves – this is the hero's journey, and it starts with the realisation that we are stuck at step-1, too comfortable in our complacency.

How does it feel to be in step-1?

Primarily we feel alright, we are comfortable in step-1, and in some cases that comfort is warranted. There may genuinely be nothing wrong and nothing to fix or improve. We are not stressed, there is no drama and no chaos. Of course, even if that's true, it can still feel dull, humdrum and, at times, boring, ironically because there is no stress, no drama and no chaos!

But business is business. Markets change. Economic conditions alter. Pandemics propagate. Political fortunes reverse. Customers demand something new or better. Employees come and go. Supply chains have challenges. Technology disrupts demand. Business needs change. It's unlikely that we can remain in the comfort zone forever – regardless of the type of business we may lead.

What tends to emerge when the occasional red flag appears is dismissive complacency, wilful ignorance, rationalisation, self-justification or insularity. It may be that the numbers are down in a particular department, there is a production issue that no one can seem to get to the bottom of or a new appointment is causing problems, but we are reluctant to wake up to warning signs and underlying issues.

In our insularity, we lack sensitivity to market forces, we refute external advice, we ignore the signals and continue to reject the need for change. Instead, we dismiss the red flags as just the small or short-term ups and downs of business. We convince ourselves that the poor numbers are a blip or that the production issue is minor or that the new recruit is just finding their feet. There is often an absence of curiosity. We will often make up our mind about issues with very little data, external input or verifiable fact – hence the insularity. This type of insularity and refusal to heed any warning signs is probably why the first sign of heart disease in many men is death! Sadly, ignoring the flashing lights or various symptoms of impending doom doesn't alter the outcome.

When we are in the comfort zone of step-1, we may actively seek to ignore the facts and cling to the story. This is certainly understandable in business, where the share price is linked to the narrative of the business rather than the facts. When things go wrong, the short-term focus of most public companies means they are invested in ignoring the issue or at the very least glossing over the problem to make sure they don't spook the analysts, the market or the media. Leaders may, similarly, want to paint a somewhat idealised picture to ensure staff remain motivated. It is a small step from overly optimistic narratives to convincing ourselves things are better than they really are. If leaders succumb to this comfortable story, then trouble won't be far behind.

At step-1, we are 'asleep'. This is a metaphor for walking through life with a lack of awareness and a lack of recognition that anything needs to change. Such somnolence has many parents:

1   Immaturity – our perceptiveness is unsophisticated; we don't realise that change is brewing.
2   Naivety – wishful thinking and idealism may blind us to the reality.
3   Wilful ignorance – we may have a sense something is happening, but we stick our 'head in the sand'.
4   Denial – flat out rejection of any facts that would indicate that change is needed.
5   Invincibility – we may have a misplaced certainty that the current success is unassailable.

The trap of narcissism

At every step of the leader's journey there are traits or behaviours that the leader can exhibit that will actively stop the leader's journey in its tracks and prevent progress. In step-1, one of the commonest traps is narcissism. Unchecked, narcissism can create a sense of invincibility and keep us stuck in the comfort zone.

The psychology of narcissism means there is often a very low level of change competence. When we've cycled through the Change Wheel a few times, it's almost impossible to be that self-absorbed. With experience and maturity, we come to realise that we are never really in control. Contrary to whatever story we construct to keep us in the comfort zone, we are not omnipotent. Leaders stuck in narcissism often operate with a delusional attachment to the idea that they are in control. Such narcissistic control freakery is common in the C-suite, and it is part of the 'shadow' of many leaders stuck at step-1.

Narcissism is a very powerful and seductive behavioural trap because there is often a very thin line between this and its slightly more functional alter ego, wilful insistence. The latter can make things happen and inadvertently reinforce a sense of control and invincibility. Success that flows from wilfulness can, therefore, obscure an underlying narcissism. The shadow can be exacerbated by the fact that many leaders have learnt to mask their more narcissistic tendencies.

Part of the narcissist's operating model is that they are attracted to the latest 'shiny object' or rising star. Initially, many people feel the warmth of their charismatic energy. But it can turn very frosty, very fast for those who fall out of favour with a narcissist.

Narcissists are often unconsciously driven by their need to prove themselves superior, and they can subtly or overtly undermine those around them.

The key characteristics of narcissism are:

1   Need to be seen positively – narcissists often talk endlessly to show others how brilliant they are. Often, they are unaware how grandiose they may appear or simply don't care if they are coming across as self-important. Regardless of whether they have achieved anything significant or not, they expect to be acknowledged as superior. They are often preoccupied with fantasies of incredible success, particularly material success. Unfortunately, they can also feel their failures are much greater than others, and they can become quite explosive and vindictive to anyone who they believe slighted them or contributed to the failure or loss of face. They often set expectations that are unreasonably high, although they also have a sense of entitlement, paradoxically on minor issues.

2   Superficial relationship – narcissists are often somewhat insensitive to the real needs of others. Instead, they tend to focus on how relationships can help their agenda. Narcissists like to have an audience but don't seem very interested in listening to others, often making others feel like they have nothing worth listening to. They want people to pay them attention but are not really interested in reciprocating.

3   Antagonistic – because of their feeling of superiority, narcissists can often come across as condescending. Their style suggests that their views are important and yours are not.

4   Persistent bad behaviour – their need for success and approval often drives them on to achievement but often at the expense of others. They will frequently leave a trail of broken relationships, and it is never their fault that these relationships failed. Their bad behaviour can take many forms from subtle undermining to bullying and verbal abuse.

Cultural metaphors

What makes the hero's journey such an enduringly useful map to guide us on our way is that the steps of the journey remain true regardless of culture, geography or time. As cultures around the world evolve, so do their descriptions of each step, but the steps themselves always remain the same. Each step of the journey can be clearly seen in the cultural metaphor that resonate globally, particularly in film.

Step-1 is normally depicted by showing the central character of the film innocently wandering around in their 'known world', either happily or unhappily. We start with the known world because it creates psychological safety for the audience as a place most of us recognise for its ordinariness. The humdrum start enables the story to establish its cultural reference points and the qualities of the central character. Filmmakers seek to make the central character relatable so the audience will go on a journey with the character as the story progresses. It can really help if the director makes the audience feel like they are a small step ahead of the main character.

In film, if not in life, the known world often takes one of two forms: the peaceful kingdom, where the hero or central character must save the world from impending doom, or the wasteland, where the hero must restore order or hope to his known world.

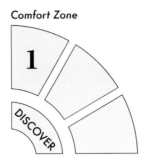

Comfort Zone

The Matrix: We first encounter the hero, Neo, played by Keanu Reeves, in his boring commercial cubicle, living out his days as Thomas Anderson, a restless computer programmer at 'MetaCortex'. The company name is itself a hint to the journey's sub-text – 'meta' suggests there may be a bigger picture available, and 'cortex' suggests this could be accessed through the mind. Anderson's alter ego 'Neo' suggests the journey of awareness will be into the neocortex – the executive part of our brain. By night, Anderson becomes the hacker known as 'Neo'. There is a scene near the start of the film where he is being reprimanded for being late. His manager suggests that he has a problem with authority, adding, "The time has come to make a choice, Mr Anderson. Either you choose to be at your desk on time from this day forward, or you choose to find yourself another job." This is a familiar conversation to many in the audience; Neo is experiencing the corporate boredom of his ordinary world and, like many others, Neo is clearly dissatisfied by it.

The Lord of the Rings: We meet the hero, Frodo Baggins, happy and contented in his known ordinary world of the Shire. Frodo's parents had died in a boating accident when he was 12 years old, but Frodo wasn't adopted by Bilbo Baggins until the age of 21. When Frodo comes of age at 21, Bilbo leaves the Shire, bequeathing Frodo the ring, which Frodo keeps hidden for the next 17 years until Gandalf appears to warn him. Frodo's name comes from the Old English word Fróda, meaning wise by experience, implying that a journey lies ahead.

Star Wars: In *Star Wars*, we first encounter our hero, Luke Skywalker, as a boy at home in the relative comfort of his known world of Tatooine. Jawa traders have incapacitated R2D2 and taken him for scrap. Luke's uncle buys C3PO and R2D2 and asks Luke to fix the droids. Luke is bored and frustrated working on his aunt and uncle's farm in the middle of nowhere. While fixing R2D2, a hologram message appears from Princess Leia, where she says, "Help me Obi-Wan Kenobi. You're my only hope."

Harry Potter: When we meet Harry Potter for the first time in the *Philosopher's Stone*, he is living an ordinary life with the Dursleys at 4 Privet Drive. He is clearly unwanted by his aunt, uncle and cousin, and his bedroom is a cupboard under the stairs. Harry knows nothing about his wizarding pedigree and what lies ahead; we just identify with his dissatisfaction – surely there is something more to life than this?

The Wizard of Oz: The hero in *The Wizard of Oz* is Dorothy Gale, and we meet her for the first time when she is in the ordinary world of her farm in Kansas with her trusty dog Toto. Even Dorothy's surname is a deliberate irony for change – Gale, as in the winds of change. Dorothy lives with her Auntie Em and Uncle Henry. She's comfortable enough but bored. The farm is run down and shown in black and white to represent the struggle and humdrum of her existence. Her guardians and the farmhands are kind and loving, but she longs for something else – excitement over the rainbow.

Implicit in all these depictions of the known world is that while the hero is safe at home, something beyond the ordinary world awaits them, and this is how all journeys begin.

The transition from step-1 to step-2

The way we talk about step-1 facilitates a sense of 'being stuck' or 'treading water'. This comfortable incapacitation is how step-1 is almost always portrayed in movies. The comfort zone is safe but frustrating – a little like the global lockdown many people experienced during the COVID pandemic.

Being stuck can cause varying degrees of dissonance depending on how the comfort zone and the reality of life at step-1 are portrayed. The absence of change in our comfort zone ultimately turns out not to be the great place it was originally thought to be. Many people eventually realise that when living at step-1 there is a big difference between comfort and happiness or fulfilment. Eventually, we experience a growing sense of disquiet that something is not quite right, something is missing. This disquiet is often portrayed in film and sets the scene for change.

In addition to feeling vaguely uneasy despite being comfortable, we may even experience guilt and stress because of the gap between our expectations for our life and the reality we are living. If "everything is fine and we are ticking along, why am I not happy?"

As the restlessness builds, we are approaching the transition between step-1 and step-2. Therefore, the dis-ease should be viewed positively. It is really a sign of momentum that has yet to take hold. Our weariness with step-1 is a recognition that, actually, the comfort zone is not that fabulous, and perhaps it's time for us to move along on our journey. While step-1 can be portrayed as dull, boring and uninspiring, it can also be viewed as a safe harbour to which we return momentarily before we launch again. In the harbour, we have time to refuel and recuperate. We may drop anchor, but we should not moor up permanently. When we recognise that the comfort zone is no longer that comfortable, we can move past complacency, wilful ignorance or narcissism, and we are now open and receptive to heed the call of step-2.

Questions to ask yourself

If you are unsure if you are in step-1, it can be helpful to ask some questions. There is little doubt that the comfort zone is well named. It is safe and uncomplicated, but if you want to step change yourself, your team or your organisation and start the leader's journey to step-2, ask yourself:

- Am I missing something?
- Am I really open to ideas?
- Is there something that people aren't telling me?
- Am I stuck in a rut?
- Am I sure I am right and others are wrong?
- Am I actually open to change?

By answering these questions, we get to probe our receptivity to step-2: challenge to reality.

2 Step-2

Challenge to reality

The call to adventure signifies that destiny has summoned the hero.

(Joseph Campbell)

Sometimes, whether we want to leave the comfort zone or not we are forced out. Something happens that demands our attention and changes our view of where we are and what is happening. In many ways, step-2 is where the leadership development journey really begins. While we are cocooned in the comfort zone, nothing much is changing at all. We are attached to the status quo. Even if we get glimpses of something else, a hint of some future destiny or something better, we tend to nullify or smother it with rationality and reminders not to rock the boat.

Step-2, the challenge to reality, is that moment when the data can no longer be ignored. Campbell called this step the 'call to adventure', but call to adventure implies a positive, exciting initiation to the impending change. Most of us do not feel positive or excited about the prospect of change – especially when it has been forced upon us. We certainly don't see it as an adventure. Instead, it is most often seen as a threat to our stability, our comfort or even our life as we know it.

Either way, when we are at step-2 we cannot ignore the evidence, whether this is data, pain, or some type of sign. We may look away, but when we look back it's still there. This evidence may make us question who we are, where we are or what we are doing. Something is wrong, and we know it. The comfort zone is no longer an option. We are called to face this new reality and decide what we are going to do about it.

How do I know if I'm at step-2?

Towards the end of step-1, we may have suspected something was brewing. Step-2 confirms that. If we didn't notice the storm clouds gathering, then the jolt into step-2 can feel like an ambush, an unwelcome surprise, a bombshell. We may experience step-2 as a crisis or a challenge to reality. Something has happened or is happening that we didn't expect, and it's often upsetting or distressing. Indications that you might be in step-2 include:

DOI: 10.4324/9781003170402-3

- A realisation that you are in pain or out of your comfort zone.
- Something is not right, but you don't know what it is.
- Someone has said something (or provided data) that has shaken you.
- A realisation that you are suffering mental health issues such as anxiety, depression, exhaustion or disillusionment.
- Engaging in too many distraction techniques such as drinking too much.

In step-2 we experience some sort of 'wake-up call' that shakes our foundations and demands our attention. It's rarely welcome.

In our personal life, the wake-up call may be the break down in a friendship, redundancy, learning about a partner's infidelity, a separation or even a divorce. Ironically, many of the life events identified by Holmes and Rahe in their stress test are the types of challenges to reality experienced in step-2. They act like hand grenades: the pin is pulled, and they are lobbed into the middle of our life. What often follows is carnage and confusion as we scramble to put the pieces back together again. And therein lies the biggest hurdle – our first thought is often to 'get back to normal'. But we can't go back. We are in pain, and the equilibrium of the comfort zone is not so easily restored.

We often experience these wake-up calls as unfair. In our confusion, we vacillate between blaming ourselves and blaming others. We may see the pain as a punishment for our past behaviour. More often than not we prefer to blame others for our distress. In blaming someone else, we mistakenly believe this gets us off the hook. Unfortunately, it does the exact opposite. Blaming others for our predicament sustains our pain. It disables us from being able to do anything about our pain, because if someone else is to blame then we can cling to the delusion that *they* will have to fix the problem. Of course, *they* rarely do, so we remain in pain. This basically traps us in the position of the victim (more of that later).

In business, the wake-up call can be anything from high staff turnover to the loss of a key customer, a dip in sales or a sudden drop in market share, EBITDA or profits. The underlying cause for this pain may not be obvious. Perhaps the strategy, which may have served the business well initially, is starting to fail. Maybe the new appointment is not panning out and is proving toxic to the culture. Perhaps a change in regulations have significantly impaired operational flexibility and are now posing a serious threat to future growth.

As the leader, we may be tempted to cast around for someone or something to blame, but blame will not move the dial. Business change is only possible if we recognise the signals and messages we are receiving from multiple objective data sources and do something about them. And we only act if the pain we are experiencing is damaging something that really matters to us. Even if the signal creates significant damage to something close to our heart, we may still not heed the wake up. We may still fail to drive change.

Value-based wake-up call

For a wake-up call to work and trigger a review, the signs that something is wrong must point to something that is important to us. To determine the likely success of a wake-up call, we must first understand what motivates us. We explained in step-1 that all living organisms have three motivational drives. The primary drive is for survival, and once this is achieved the second drive is for growth and reproduction. But human beings have developed a third motivational drive that transcends and includes the first two but can also override them and replace them with something more nuanced – evolution and development.

Over the years, many academics have explored this third motivational drive of human beings and identified a set of specific value systems that themselves develop over time. But it was the pioneering work of Professor Clare Graves that allowed us to appreciate the evolutionary nature of values and how they emerge over time. He emphasised that these motivational drives or values systems are not just variations of each other but genuine evolutions. This is profoundly important.

If we mistakenly see different value systems as variations not evolutions, then we effectively remove the possibility of progress and we kill the entire journey.

Think of it this way. Running is not a variation of walking and walking is not a variation of standing. Standing evolves into walking, as any parent will tell you. Walking doesn't exist without standing. Likewise, once a toddler is proficient at walking, they gradually develop the ability to speed up and, eventually, the ability to run evolves. You will never see a child that can run but cannot walk. There is a natural and healthy hierarchical relationship between standing, walking and running. Each new ability transcends and includes the previous ability. Such healthy hierarchies are called 'holarchies'. Another example would be letters. Letters are in a holarchical relationship to words, which are in a holarchical relationship to sentences, which are, themselves, in a relationship with paragraphs, chapters and a book itself. Each new level is more sophisticated than the previous level in that it gives more options and nuance of, in the case of words, expression. If we remove the 'sentences' level, we are left with the level of 'words' and 'letters', but without access to sentences our options are limited.

Value systems also evolve, as Graves pointed out. Graves saw the first two motivational drives that we talked about in Chapter 1 as part of our species drive for survival. The seven value systems he identified as having evolved after the survival drive was met can all be seen as increasingly sophisticated variations of the third motivational drive we mentioned in step-1. All seven value systems can override the first two drives, which in Graves' model were merged as the drive for survival. Each of Graves' value systems transcends and includes its predecessor, and each value system was subsequently given a specific colour to help people remember where they were on their evolutionary journey. As we have said, all organisms start at the survival level of beige, but only more complex organisms evolve to purple then to red, to blue, to orange, to green, to yellow and ultimately to turquoise. More recently, some authors have suggested we should refer to blue as amber and yellow as teal. We have labelled each level below with the organisational dynamic most commonly associated with that level (see Figure 2.1).[1]

Each value system cannot exist without its predecessor, and with each new value system the focus shifts from the individual to the collective and back again in a never-ending evolution of increased sophistication. This evolutionary holarchy is a

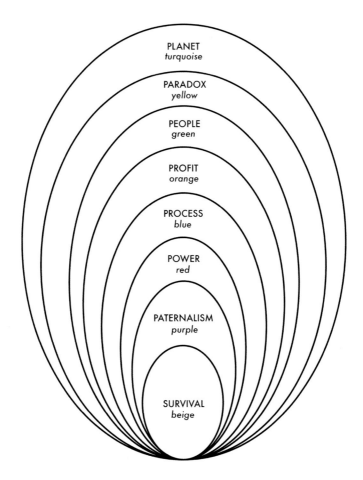

Figure 2.1 Values Holarchies.

fascinating field of study, and I have written extensively about these value systems and their implications for individuals, teams and organisations in my earlier books.[2]

In the context of step-2 and the leader's journey, they are illuminating because they help us to understand why some wake-up calls trigger action and others are ignored. People operating at the beige level of survival will most likely respond to wake-up calls that threaten their survival, their very existence or their ability to mate. They are unlikely to be woken up by the sort of existential threats that may be relevant to someone who has evolved to the blue value system, where process is the driver.

People operating from the purple value system will respond to wake-up calls that threaten their family or tribe (paternalism) as well as threats to all earlier value systems (survival and reproduction). People operating at the red value system may respond to survival or family threats, but they can also be woken up by threats to their power, status, authority or ability to enjoy themselves.

At the blue value system, meaning emerges significantly as a motivational drive along with rules and process. People operating from the earlier red value system are often too busy making things happen or driving things forward to spend too much time contemplating the meaning of life. So, the wake-up call for people who have reached the blue value system is often a crisis of meaning (more of this later). They can also be triggered by threats to their integrity, principles or illegal attacks that contravene the 'rules' they operate to. The discovery of bonded labour or unethical practice somewhere in their supply chain can also ignite action very successfully.

At the orange value system, the primary wake-up call is the threat to profit, wealth and their sense of achievement. People operating from the orange value system like to win. If they perceive that someone else might beat them to a deal, this can cause them to stop in their tracks and re-evaluate everything. Failure to deliver on their targets or a realisation that 'the numbers' are off and the profit or their bonus might be threatened is also highly effective at triggering a crisis of confidence.

Given that people operating from the green value system prize people and their relationships, they are often triggered by poor engagement scores, high staff turn-over stats or terrible ratings on the glass door; alternatively, low customer satisfaction scores or low net promoter scores can galvanise them into action. People who are driven by the orange value system may also be triggered by this but more often because they are competitive. Given the green value system is more environmentally aware, people at this level may also be triggered by pollution data or data that goes right to the heart of the corporate social responsibility agenda. Evidence of discrimination or exclusion of minority groups is also a powerful wake-up call to those operating from the green value system.

For those operating at the yellow value system, the wake-up call tends to come in the shape of some type of paradox, a threat to the future or their ability to solve a problem. And finally, at turquoise, the wake-up call comes in the form of a threat to the planet, humanity, the biosphere or the harmony of all things. You can review the most common types of wake-up call for each value system in Figure 2.2.

It is really surprising how often people miss their wake-up call and remain stuck in step-1 or step-2 for much longer than necessary. I remember coaching a very senior CEO, well known in his industry. From his language and posturing, it was very clear that he was a red leader. Red leaders can be very egotistical, and certainly he spent most of our meeting telling me how he was considered the darling of his industry. Fortunately, prior to the meeting we had already measured his physiology for 24 hours. The data we collect can accurately quantify how much energy a leader really has and what is going on for that person in terms of their ability to create impact in their organisation. This CEO's biology was at the 3rd centile, so worse than 97 per cent of leaders in our global benchmark of 2,000 leaders.

Having listened to his story about how good he was, I said "let's assume that is true. My only question is: if your story is true, why is your data worse than virtually

WHAT WAKES US UP		
Planet	Threats to humanity, the biosphere, the harmony of all things	
Paradox	Threat to the future or ability to solve the problem	

People	Being excluded or threats to engagement, retention, fairness and equality, customer satisfaction or environment	
Profit	Pay cuts or insufficient remuneration or threats to wealth, goals or possibility of winning	
Process	Threat to belief structure, integrity, principles or illegal rule contraventions	
Power	Threat to status, authority or control or ability to enjoy ourself	
Paternalism	Threats to our family, tribe or nation	
Survival	Threats to our personal survival	

Figure 2.2 Wake-Up Calls by Value System.

everyone on our database?" This stopped him in his tracks and caused him, for the first time, to sit and reflect. As it turned out, our coaching programme improved his biology by 30 per cent but strangely that didn't seem to matter to him. It may have been because the information remained confidential and there was neither a loss of status from his pre-coaching data or a boost in status when he regained the energy he had ten years ago. If we had anonymously published his data alongside ten of his peers and he had moved from the bottom of the table to the top three, I am sure he would have been the first person to tell everyone that he was the person that shifted so massively. For him, the wake-up call stopped him momentarily but didn't create a permanent shift.

For the wake-up call to be most effective, it must be attuned to our value systems; otherwise, it is likely to fall on deaf ears.

How does it feel to be in step-2?

How we might feel in step-2 depends largely on the type of wake-up call we receive.

There are essentially three categories of wake-up experience at step-2:

- Prolonged discomfort
- Observable pain in others
- Personal pain

Prolonged discomfort

The least common type of wake-up call is the growing awareness of prolonged discomfort. It's less wake-up call and more nagging noise from somewhere, but we are not sure where. We might recognise that something is wrong, but it's not a disaster. It's not ideal, either, but it's not yet bad enough to warrant much action. It can be personal or professional, and while it may demand our attention it's not a crisis. Such a wake-up call tends to be less intense; it triggers discomfort rather than outright pain. We are much more likely to see options but may not be suitably motivated to action any of those options. Change can be ignored because there is no burning platform. Curiosity rather than pain is much more common as a pre-cursor to this type of wake-up call. We are more likely to engage in honest reflection and seek answers to questions we might ask ourselves about what is not working and why. This type of wake-up call may indeed feel more like a call to adventure because it is less acute and probably more positively nuanced.

We may be inspired or excited to pursue something else rather than be driven to change or get away from something painful.

Observable pain in others

The second wake-up call is often initiated through observed pain, not personal pain. Again, this wake-up call is less intense and, therefore, affords us enough distance to consider options. It is possible for us to learn from another person's pain, but it is equally easy to ignore. We can rationalise the pain away on the basis that "it won't happen to me". We might have a moment of pause if we see a peer fired suddenly for poor revenue performance. We may even fully appreciate the parallels between their situation and our commercial struggle, but on its own it's unlikely to trigger a strategic or operational review or change to what we are doing.

It is interesting to note that many of the best leaders have experienced this observed pain early in their life. They may not have been beaten up by an abusive mother or alcoholic father, but their early experiences of discomfort caused them to wake up earlier than most. They became acutely aware that things were not right, and this meant they started to notice things about their life and environment that would otherwise have passed them by. This early observation started them on a journey of development and played a significant role in their commercial ascent to the C-suite. As a child, part of their waking up was their difficult family life or witnessing their parents' suffering. But if there is insufficient reflection on this early life trauma then the lessons may be lost over time.

While observed pain, struggle and hardship can drive change, its impact may subside. This is partly because such early lessons may also bring negative association of change and inadvertently create resistance and an avoidance stance as an adult. When we observe pain later in life, we see change as a negative not as a stepping-stone to help us towards an opportunity. The observed pain of childhood could also train us in the art of victimhood, particularly if our parents were experts in victimhood having largely lived their lives stuck at step-2 (more on that later).

This observed wake-up call may be more powerful if the pain is being experienced by someone we love, or if we have a particular empathic connection with the type of pain they are experiencing. Since we are not directly feeling the pain ourselves, we may be better placed to see this as a call to adventure rather than something to be avoided.

The problem is, both the first and second type of wake-up call are rare. Very rare.

Personal pain

The most common and effective wake-up call is one that is personally felt. Something has happened that stops us in our tracks. The intensity might vary from deeply painful and upsetting to moderately challenging. Either way, the signal is personal. It can be immediate and often overwhelming. It is very hard to view such pain positively and therefore to imagine this experience as some type of exciting call to adventure. More likely, it is a challenge to reality. Something about the way we see the world, what we believed about someone or what we imagined our life to be has been broken or altered in some way.

When we experience this personal pain, all we can think about is the pain. We can't plan or plot a course out of the pain because the pain can be all consuming. In fairness to those in pain, it's difficult to see past the pain. It narrows our time horizons dramatically, so all we really think about is the pain we are in right now. All the focus is on getting through this moment and then the next. When such pain arises, it can keep us stuck at step-2.

That's why people can remain in pain for extended periods of time, sometimes their entire life, because they just can't get past it. Whether the pain is physical pain, grief or a sense of loss of something, it can become all consuming.

We forget that pain is just a signal telling us something is wrong and encouraging us to make changes, but because it is all consuming the commonest response when we are in pain is to try to anaesthetise or distract ourselves from it.

The classic anaesthetics we use to mask our pain and change how we feel, if only for a few hours, are alcohol and drugs, whether illicit or prescription. Millions of people rely on a glass of wine or three or a few stiff gin and tonics to blot out the frustrations of the day. Millions of prescriptions are written each year for anti-anxiety medication or anti-depressants, and countless people may have swapped cigarettes for vapes, but the distraction is still active.

For those in pain, anaesthetic and distraction may seem like perfectly legitimate strategies, but they are, at best, temporary fixes. If we are not anesthetising ourselves, getting 'wasted' and risking drifting onto the slippery slope of alcoholism or drug addiction, then we are probably trying to manage by getting stuck into a whole range of distraction strategies. Everyone has their own personal favourite.

Retail therapy is the distraction favoured by many. Some become dependent on this pick me up, because while we are comparing prices, trying things on or looking for that fashionable item we momentarily forget our pain. An unfortunate few become addicted as shopaholics. Some prefer the distraction of the gym. While they are pumping iron or going for the burn, they can forget the problems and the pain of their life. But even if we manage to divert our attention for an hour or two, when we get home from the gym or return with our shopping bags the problems or pain from which we are trying to escape are still there.

If a pair of Jimmy Choos or a Zumba class doesn't appeal, you might enjoy a flutter. Some people become embroiled in gambling, which can easily spiral into an addiction. If you don't wager your wages, then you may succumb to the classic distraction, especially in mid-life, the affair.

Many of these addictive distractions create their own unique form of pain and have necessitated their own treatment programmes. In an attempt to escape we may get lost again, sometimes for years, in drug detox, Alcoholics Anonymous, Gamblers Anonymous, sex addiction treatment programmes or marital therapy.

More recently, many have added new ways to distract themselves with a rash of social media platforms all vying for our eyeballs. And who's to say that a four hour a day 'habit' on these social platforms is not an addiction? If none of these have caught you out, just check you haven't been consumed by the more mundane workaholism, particularly now the boundaries between home and work have been dissolved by a global pandemic.

All of these anaesthetics or distractions simply keep you stuck at step-2. They don't solve the underlying problem: they merely serve to perpetuate your pain.

The biological consequences of being stuck at step-2

Remember, pain is a signal. If we heed the signal, we can move forward and escape the pain. But if we don't heed the signal, or worse try and blot it out with anaesthetics or distractions, then things tend to get much worse. Being stuck in the pain of step-2 has real biological consequences that can take us down the path towards real physical or mental health problems.

Staying too long at step-2 means we pump out high levels of the stress hormone cortisol, plus a whole range of other 'catabolic' hormones. These hormones are designed to break our body down. The chaos that ensues comes in two forms, depending on whether we have also activated either our fight/flight or flee response. The biological patterns created at this moment of the journey have been understood for years and were originally beautifully described by Professor James P Henry of McMaster University in Toronto.[3,4]

If we fight the pain, we activate our sympathetic nervous system and pump out high levels of adrenaline, which when added to cortisol significantly increase our risk of high blood pressure, heart disease and cancer as well as agitated depression or anxiety. If we surrender, the consequences may be worse. We activate our para-sympathetic nervous system, which pours acetylcholine into the tides of cortisol leading us into helplessness, hopelessness, impaired immunity and the risk of profound depression and even catatonia. There are real dangers in both outcomes. In fact, nearly all of the diseases we could possibly suffer from await us if we linger too long at step-2. We simply don't realise the peril we are in. Our difficulty is compounded because the catabolic hormones create vicious cycles and downward spirals of negativity.[5]

It's vital that we break free of the victimhood and catabolic whirlpools of step-2 that serve to draw us deeper into danger. This is why we must fiercely guard against distractions and anaesthetic, which blunt our senses and keep us trapped.

There is good news in all this. There is an escape route, but we must take it. There are calmer waters. There are virtuous cycles, that can lift us out of the pain. We can soar on the thermals of health and happiness, fuelled by anabolic hormones such as dehydroepiandrosterone (DHEA). DHEA is the 'performance' hormone and our body's natural antidote to cortisol. It is the molecule that makes testosterone in men and oestrogen in women. If we can escape step-2, we can discover the temples of bliss and fulfilment and the secrets of the universe. But all this comes later on our journey.

The mental health consequences of being stuck at step-2

People who get stuck at step-2 are either causing themselves real biological damage or damaging their mental health. Prolonged episodes of feeling sad, tired, unhappy, angry, irritable, frustrated, anxious, restless, worried, distracted, guilty, helpless or exhausted are considered mental health issues. Indeed, suffering from mental health issues is often considered as evidence that someone is stuck at step-2. Currently, one in six people suffer from mental health problems at work. Roughly 300,000 people quit work every year as a result, with a cost to employers of between £33 billion and £42 billion.[6]

Despite the increased recognition and awareness of mental health issues, all the evidence suggests the problem is getting worse. There is now an urgent need to step change the narrative on mental health. This starts with acknowledging that the problem is not 'mental' and it's not 'health'.[7] The misdiagnosis of the issue as mental is causing stigma. A whopping 90 per cent of people with a 'mental' health issue say they face stigma and discrimination, and 60 per cent say this is worse than the mental health issue itself!

And yet, the mental processes of the person experiencing these states is normal most of the time. The content may be darker or more agitated than the next person, but the way they think and the actual mental processes are normal. Schizophrenia is a 'mental' problem because normal cognitive processes are disordered. For example, timelines can be disrupted, and logical sequences can be impaired. The mental processes of most of the 'conditions' currently lumped under the banner of mental health are normal. Calling them 'mental health' problems simply creates stigma and exacerbates the problem. 'Mental' is the wrong word.

'Health' is also the wrong word. Repeated negative emotions can lead to health issues, but in and of themselves they are not health problems. Sadness is not a health issue. Anxiety is not a health issue. Frustration is not a health issue. These are emotions, and we need to develop the ability to regulate them effectively. Developing emotional competence is a critical skill that everyone needs. To some extent, we naturally develop a small amount of emotional competence as we emerge from infancy, but this development often stops. If, as children, we fail to develop beyond the most basic level of emotional competence, we are easily overwhelmed later in life when these powerful negative emotions are triggered. Our inability to manage anxiety, fear, worry or depression is a developmental problem not a health problem. It is a profound error to medicalise normal development and think of this as a pathology or an illness. It is not, it's a failure of development – which is why it's not mental 'health' or mental 'illness', although it can lead to illness if developmental capability is not restored. It would be much more accurate, and frankly significantly more helpful, to consider such challenges as emotional development issues not 'mental illness' or 'mental health' issues. Remember, we must stop medicalising normal development.

The reason we mistakenly call anxiety, depression and many related disturbances a 'mental' health issue is because we have way too simplistic a view of the human system. There are five levels to the human system, but most clinicians only recognise two: thinking and behaviour. We rarely look beyond behaviour (level one) and cognition (level two). This is why we assume the problem is mental, and one of the primary treatments is cognitive behavioural therapy.

However, in the human system there are three levels below cognition that we must acknowledge, and these deeper levels determine what and how we think. Immediately below the thinking level is the level that determines what we feel (level three). What we feel is, itself, determined by the next level down, which is our emotions (level four), or energy-in-motion; hence, e-motion. Our e-motions are, in turn, composed of the raw physiological signals generated by our bodily systems (level five).

Most people's approach stops at level two, and they collapse the bottom three levels and lump them in with level two. Given this, it is very easy to see why many people mistakenly assume anxiety or depression is a 'mental' problem, because if we've ignored or don't recognise the deeper emotional and physiological levels, the only phenomenon below behaviour *is* mental.

When we understand there are three levels below cognition, then it becomes obvious that the real problem in 'mental health' exists in the bottom levels (i.e., levels three, four and five) with level two, cognition (mental), being perfectly normal in most cases.

As we said, the problem is not a health issue, rather it is one of development. People who suffer with anxiety, depression or many other unhelpful emotional states are unable to turn on and sustain more positive emotional states. This is not their fault. No one has taught them how to do this. They have yet to develop this skill.

Being unable to turn on a more productive emotion, such as resilience, determination or compassion, often leaves people stuck on the negative side of the 'Universe of Emotion' – largely of their own making. This universe contains thousands of emotions or planets, and if they stay stuck on the 'planet' of 'depression' for too long, they start to believe this is who they are – depression becomes part of their identity. They say, "I am depressed". Of course, the truth is who they really are is much larger than just a single emotional state. This again is a failure of development.

If their identity has become synonymous with a single emotional state, it becomes very hard to escape from this trap. The trap is made even harder because depression increases cortisol levels, which create more negativity and, hence, a vicious cycle. The cortisol makes them feel negative, they label this negativity and that then becomes part of their identity and how they see themselves. Unfortunately, such an unhelpful view is reinforced by a well-intentioned mental health campaign at work, to talk about the fact that they 'have' a mental health problem. This inadvertently reinforces their narrow and negative identity issue and keeps them stuck at step-2 in their victimhood, which further increases their cortisol levels, locking in the emotion of depression. But depression is not who they are; they need to develop emotional regulation, and with practice they can develop the ability to change how they feel and move to a more helpful emotion or planet. We are very rarely taught how to do this at school, yet it is a skill as important as reading or writing.

We must stop medicalising what is a normal developmental challenge as a 'health' issue. Every person would benefit from developing the ability to regulate their inner emotions. Failure to do so is a failure of development, not a failure of the individual. Such people are certainly not 'mental'. They do not have a 'condition' called 'mental health'. They are not helpless victims.

We must get off the 'mental health bandwagon' and start actually helping people develop. They are wonderful human beings who need support to develop their self-regulation capabilities, their maturity, their identity and their wisdom.

What's ironic is that the drug companies have obviously spotted this misdiagnosis because their drugs don't treat mental processes, they seek to treat emotion. But for many people such drugs don't work so the treatment is largely ineffective, albeit extremely lucrative. And drugs should certainly not be considered a long-term option, although many people take these medications for years! Altering emotional valance with drugs is not development, and it may keep people stuck and dependent by stopping them from developing the emotional competence that they really need.

Besides, why are we prescribing mood altering drugs if it's a mental illness? The answer is, sadly, money. But that's not the worst of it. Using drugs as a solution to a development problem can actually make it a mental problem. Haloperidol, informally known in medical circles as a 'liquid cosh', is given to some people for depression. It is an anti-psychotic. Prozac or other SSRIs (selective serotonin reuptake inhibitors) can actually slow down our mental processes. This means we are treating the problem of impaired mental processes – that doesn't actually exist – and then delivering a treatment that then creates that exact problem. This makes no sense. These drugs can flatten people. Sure, the person taking the drug doesn't feel anxious or depressed any more but that's because they don't feel *anything* anymore.

No joy, no peace, no frustration, no contentment – nothing. These drugs may create more mental problems, not less!

We are human beings, and as such we have access to a vast array of emotional experience. Some of them feel good, and some of them don't. When we don't feel good and we are in some sort of pain, this is always a signal. We are not meant to live trapped by such pain or negative emotions.

But if we can understand the signal that the painful emotion brings us, assess our situation, pay attention to the wake-up call and do something about the situation that is causing the distress, then we can change our future. Day to day, we need to strengthen our ability to emotionally regulate so we can move out of sadness or frustration or anxiety faster and move to positive, pleasurable emotions and live there.

We certainly shouldn't feel bad about struggling with our emotions; it's a normal part of life, but we are at risk of developing genuine health problems if we don't develop some form of emotional self-regulation. If we continue to just label our symptoms as a 'mental health' issue, we don't move into solution mode. Instead, our label becomes who we are, and we get stuck there. We are meant to get better at emotional self-regulation as we grow up and develop from child to adult and adult to mature adult. We develop, we struggle and develop some more and get better at managing our emotions. At some point, we stop throwing ourselves on the floor in the supermarket aisle and thrashing our arms and legs around because our mum didn't let us get a chocolate egg.

In adult life, we decide that the sadness we feel is holding us back, so we lean into that sadness, feel it fully, seek to understand its message and let it go, while shifting to a more useful emotion like compassion or patience. Using emotional self-management techniques, we are able to nudge ourselves into a more constructive and useful emotional state on demand.

The real badge of honour, in my view, is when we can see the developmental journey required to take us from the supermarket tantrum to an elevated level of emotional resilience. We are human beings, and we can develop far greater control than we realise over what that means and how we feel as a result. That's real progress and far more effective than the short-term, occasionally necessary, chemical manipulation that drugs offer or hiding behind the now acceptable face of mental health. Any single emotion is not a final destination we should pursue. We should not aim to set up camp and live on a single emotional 'planet'. They are signals and transitory stops on our journey of life.

Victimhood

In step-1, narcissism is a major block that prevents people from recognising the need to wake-up. In step-2, victimhood is the primary obstacle that prevents progress so they can escape from their pain. Victimhood deafens us to the wake-up call of step-2.

The world is full of people who have consciously or unconsciously made a career out of their victimhood. Many people, often through a profound absence of self-worth and self-efficacy, don't believe they can exert any control over their own destiny. When we feel that we have no control or power or way to change our life, then the only option is to point the finger of blame elsewhere and exteriorise the pain. The source of many people's ire may be their boss, partner, government, the weather or any number of possible reasons for their predicament, none of which involve them.

To be fair, taking the victim stance makes sense if we believe we have no control, but we always have choices. Viktor Frankl, a respected neurologist and psychiatrist before the Second World War, is a testimony to this. Frankl and his wife and parents were initially deported to the Nazi ghetto, and in 1944 he and his wife were transported to Auschwitz. Before falling foul of the Nazis for being Jewish, he had finished his life's work and had sewn it into the lining of his coat in an effort to preserve it. Unfortunately, it was discovered, and even though he pleaded with the guards, they destroyed it in front of him. But the Nazis destroyed much more. His wife, mother and brother were all killed. Of his entire family, only he and his sister survived. But even amongst all the horror, Frankl realised something profound. The Nazis could take everything he loved and valued, but they could not take his mind or his ability to find and choose a higher meaning for himself. That's exactly what he did, and when the war was over and the camp was liberated, he went on to write one of the most famous books of all time – *Man's Search for Meaning*. As Frankl said, "Between stimulus and response, there is a space. In that space is our power to choose our response. In our response lies our growth and our freedom."

We all have a choice. Do we stay a victim, stuck in step-2 and believing we must endure the pain? Or do we recognise that, whilst this pain may not be our fault, we can change our response? We can enable a different future. In fact, it is our response-ability to find a way out.

Psychologist Martin Seligman has written extensively about victimhood, although he refers to it as learned helplessness. He demonstrated that helplessness is mainly a learned behaviour. He discovered this by administering electric shocks to dogs and watching what happened. Over time, the dogs simply gave up trying to escape from the shock. Even when the door to their enclosure was left open and they were encouraged to get out of the environment that was causing them pain – they stayed. They learned to be helpless and give up. Human beings do the same thing – hence victimhood.

There is some very interesting research that suggests that the amount of cortisol we produce in response to a threat is dependent on how our mother managed stress when we were in the womb, and then this set point becomes reinforced in our early years, depending on how well we were nurtured.[8] If we consider cortisol as nature's built-in alarm system, whether or not we were properly nurtured can set that alarm system very early in life. This is hardly surprising considering how helpless and vulnerable an infant human being is. Babies are entirely dependent on a primary care giver, usually the mother. If that adult is not particularly doting or attentive, the baby's survival alarm system may be triggered relatively easily, establishing a cortisol set point. British psychologist John Bowlby proposed attachment theory to explain how much the parent's relationship with the child influences development.[9] Bowlby believed that the only difference between a secure child, one that would grow up more optimistic and resilient, and an insecure child, who might skew more toward pessimism and victimhood, was the type of early care that child received, and over 3,000 published empirical studies have proven his theory correct.[10] Without an emotionally engaged, consistently present primary care provider in the early phases of life, a child can develop an easily triggered cortisol set point. Once the alarm is triggered, cortisol production can create vicious cycles of self-perpetuated negativity, keeping that individual stuck in a more negative frame of mind, making victimhood an easier place to inhabit.

That said, David Lykken, a researcher from the University of Minnesota, determined that it is still possible for experience to modify our tendency to respond negatively to painful threats. By studying 4,000 sets of twins, including twins separated at birth, he concluded that 50 per cent of our innate positivity or negativity is down to genetics (some of which may actually be down to epigenetic effects in pregnancy rather than hard genetic wiring), 8 per cent is affected by circumstantial factors such as income, marital status and education and the remaining 42 per cent is down to life experiences. That means that, regardless of our early life experiences, we can still significantly change the outcome and decide to play the role of victim or not. If our cortisol set point and how we respond in life is largely learned, it can also be unlearned.

Seligman suggests that victimhood or learned helplessness consists of three P's that makes up our 'Explanatory Style' or how we explain things to ourselves and others. Knowing what they are gives us an insight into how we can free ourselves from the clutches of victimhood. They are:

- Permanence
- Pervasiveness
- Personalisation

Permanence

Those that wallow in victimhood tend to view negative life events as permanent and will use phrases such as "this stuff *always* happens to me" or "I can *never* catch a break" or "*everything* always goes wrong". As such, they extend the duration of the challenge. In many cases, it is assumed that the negative events are caused by some personal defect that will have permanent repercussions in that person's life.

Those who are able to muster greater self-efficacy and optimism tend to see the negative situation as temporary; all things pass. One event does not foretell a future of misery.

Moving your mindset from permanent to temporary can help to dial down the victimhood.

Pervasiveness

A victim will assume that a challenging situation in one area of their life will automatically pollute everything else. A missed promotion, a failed exam or a lacklustre performance review is the prelude to relationship breakdown and ill health. The victim can be so caught up in their own misery that they completely fail to see any glimmers of hope or positive events or simply dismiss them as irrelevant if they do.

If victimhood is not a persona we embody, we are much more likely to see a negative event or situation as an isolated incident that has no bearing on our ability or opportunities elsewhere.

We can practise seeing challenges for what they are – isolated to a particular area. There is no reason that one piece of bad luck or poor fortune should impact any other area of our life.

Personalisation

People stuck in victimhood prefer to blame others for their ills. However, when victimhood becomes advanced there is often a deeper-rooted fear that they are the problem. Seligman suggests that victimhood or learned helplessness is amplified when someone internalises the blame for something going wrong. If an individual gets stuck in this more pernicious belief, it locks them into their victimhood; because their self-worth is so low they can never get out of this guilt-infested trap. People who are not stuck in victimhood tend to see that bad things happen for a whole variety of reasons, some of which may or may not be to do with them.

One of the ways to get out of the black hole of blame is to differentiate blame from responsibility. Forget about blaming anyone – ourselves or someone else or an external event or situation. Instead, focus on what we can do to change the situation. As Victor Frankl advises, change your response to what is happening, don't stay stuck.

Interestingly, we can consider Seligman's three Ps and Kolbasa's three Cs together. Kolbasa described the qualities of hardiness, which require a positive emotional stance, whereas Seligman described the qualities of victimhood, which all have a negative emotionally valence (see Figure 2.3).

Figure 2.3 is essentially an emotional map of victimhood and its antidote. Not only can we employ Seligman's optimistic frame and reverse the Ps, viewing our situation as temporary, localised and our responsibility but not necessarily our fault, but we can also employ Kolbasa's insights on psychological hardiness to move even further away from the debilitating state of victimhood.

Projection

Victimhood may come with an additional P – Projection. Projection is common in people stuck at step-2. When victims are trapped in a negative emotional state, they can lose perceptual awareness and accuse others of doing the very thing they themselves are doing. For example, they may be angry about something, but because they don't recognise their own anger they project it onto others and then complain about other people's anger. Freud popularised the term in the mid-1890s and believed that it was a defence mechanism used to avoid the pain that would be caused by acknowledging the weaknesses or faults as our own. Jung added to this

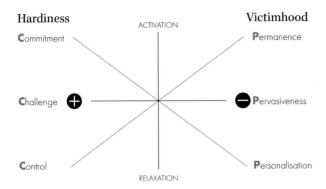

Figure 2.3 Hardiness Vs Helplessness.

idea by suggesting that becoming aware of and overcoming our own projection is an important part of development.

Projections can reveal our unconscious biases or provide us with an awareness of traits in our unconscious that may be holding us back. If we can see projection for what it is, a sign that we need to address that very same issue we are complaining about, then we can use it constructively to move through change. The secret to working with projections and turning them into development opportunities is to take ownership of them, which ironically is the primary escape route from victimhood, moving from a victim to an owner. We will cover more of this shadow work in step-8.

Of all the steps in the Change Wheel and mini-steps within some of the twelve main steps, the shift from victim to owner is the single most important move on the entire journey.

Cultural metaphors

Step-2, the challenge to reality, is the invitation to change. In films and books, the central character's ordinary world is challenged in some way, and the message is often brought or reinforced by what Campbell called the herald archetype. The herald character in stories, as in life, issue challenges to inform the hero of impending and significant change. The appearance of the herald is often the catalyst for genuine change. They will either challenge the hero or encourage them to break free of their coping mechanisms and defence mechanisms in order to start to embrace real change. Whether the hero is willing or not, the herald often brings the situation to a head.

The Matrix: Neo's first challenge to reality comes before we know very much about him or his ordinary world. We meet him for the first time when he is asleep at his desk in his apartment. A message flashes on his computer screen: "Wake up, Neo … the matrix has you …". Of course, this message is meant literally and metaphorically.

Initially, he's confused and thinks the message is a mistake. He tries to exit the programme. A further message arrives on his computer: "Follow the white rabbit.", and finally, "Knock, Knock, Neo". A second later, there is a knock on his door. It's his contact, Gordon, with some friends. Neo asks, "Do you ever have that feeling when you're not sure if you are awake or still dreaming?" Gordon suggests he takes a break and comes with them to a club. Neo refuses, as he has work in the morning, but changes his mind when the girl Gordon is with momentarily turns to reveal a tattoo of a white rabbit (itself a refence to Alice in Wonderland, which is another story about human consciousness). He agrees and meets Trinity. Trinity plays the role of the ally in the movie. The ally can play many roles: companion, conscience or sparring partner, or provide comic relief. In this case she is Neo's companion and eventually his love interest. As such, she brings an extra dimension and human-ness to his character. When they first meet in person at the club, Trinity warns him that he is in danger: "they" are watching him. She senses his disquiet and seems to understand he is searching for answers. Does he know the question? Neo answers, "What is the matrix?"

The Lord of the Rings: Gandalf plays the role of the herald when he visits the Shire for Bilbo Baggins 111th birthday party. Bilbo has already shown the ring to Frodo and has behaved very strangely. Frodo is concerned, but it is only when Gandalf arrives and realises what the ring is and what it represents that Frodo begins to grasp his call to adventure. Change is coming whether he likes it or not, and he is charged with saving his beloved Shire and beyond.

Star Wars: Darth Vader is the herald in Star Wars, and his capture of Princess Leia heralds something is wrong before Luke, the hero, even appears. Later, R2D2 plays a portion of a holographic message from Princess Leia calling for help.

Harry Potter: Harry has been living in ignorance with his aunt and uncle. Although he has already had a number of experiences that hint at the fact that he might be different, he doesn't understand them. For example, Harry visits a zoo and realises he can somehow communicate with snakes, but he shrugs it off as wishful thinking or an active imagination. It's only when a letter arrives from Hogwarts along with Hagrid (both the letter and Hagrid act as heralds) that he realises that his life is never going to be the same again.

The Wizard of Oz: Dorothy's first challenge to reality comes in the form of Miss Gulch, their irate neighbour and landowner. Miss Gulch threatens to have Toto put down for digging up her garden and snatches the dog, with Auntie Em and Uncle Henry powerless to do anything about it. Toto escapes and runs home. This is what triggers Dorothy to embark on her quest. She runs away to save Toto and get him away from the nasty Miss Gulch.

Transition from step-2 to step-3

When we enter step-2, the challenge that heralds the journey ahead may come in many forms or from a variety of sources. In film, that may include a message on a computer screen, a visit from an elderly wizard, a video message from a damsel in distress or a letter from a kindly professor, delivered by owl. In real life, the wake-up call is often a little less exciting. Whatever form the wake-up message takes, we are often not ready to listen, particularly if the message implies significant change. For most people, the wake-up call must be intense and personal enough to create pain that may trigger the desire for forward momentum and change. It must jolt us forward and prevent a retreat to the safety of the comfort zone in step-1. But the risk is that if the pain is too great then people may reach for the anaesthetics or draw down from a long list of possible distractions. While such mind numbing may offer temporary relief, it doesn't remove the pain. Sooner or later, we must acknowledge that something is wrong. To solve the problem, we must take another step forward and change ourselves. There is no change without awareness, and all change must start by facing the brutal truth, no matter how unpalatable.

But even if we are honest with ourselves about the fact that change needs to happen, we are still a long way away from being able to effect change. All that is happening at step-2 is a waking up and a discovery of the need for change. We normally can't get there on our own; we usually need a guide, coach, mentor, companion, wise elder or helper. But when such allies greet us in step-3, our first response is to reject their help. Such resistance is, in fact, a step itself. It is processing the need to change. We are still in the discovery phase – we are still working out if the change we face is something we want to embrace or not.

Questions to ask yourself

If you are unsure if you are at step-2, ask yourself the following questions:

- Do I understand what is really going on here?
- Am I blinded by the pain or discomfort?
- Am I missing the message? Am I stuck in my pain?
- Am I open to the possibility of change?
- Am I holding onto the past?
- Why me? What is happening?
- What does this really mean? What else could it mean?
- Am I in victimhood, blaming everyone else for my woes?

It's inevitable that we answer these questions from our current world view or value system. Remember, the only way for the wake-up call to work and to trigger forward momentum is if it occurs at the level of our own development. The wake-up message has to speak to our current value system and what we believe is most important. If the wake-up call is too sophisticated, it won't work. As the Oracle says to Neo in the second of the Matrix trilogy: "We can never see past the choices we don't understand."

If the wake-up call doesn't create meaning in our current value system, then we are probably going to permanently reject it or remain confused. If we can't make sense of the message being transmitted in our own value system, or we misinterpret the message, then we are not going to make any progress. Only when we understand the meaning of the wake-up call and see it as a challenge can we move to step-3 and experience the inevitable resistance.

Notes

1   Watkins, A. and Dalton, N., (2020). *HR revolution: Change the workplace, change the world.* London: Routledge.
2   Watkins, A., (2014). *Coherence: Secret science of brilliant leadership.* London: Kogan Page.
    Watkins, A., (2016). *4D leadership: Competitive advantage through vertical leadership development.* London: Kogan Page.
    Watkins, A., (2021). *Coherence: The science of exceptional leadership and performance.* 2nd ed. London: Kogan Page.
3   Henry, J.P., (1982). The relation of social to biological processes in disease. *Social Science & Medicine.* **16**(4), 369–380.
4   Henry, J.P., Stephens, P.M. and Ely, D.L., (1986). Psychosocial hypertension and the defence and defeat reactions. *Journal of Hypertension.* **4**(6), 687–697.
5   Watkins, A., (2014). *Coherence: Secret science of brilliant leadership.* London: Kogan Page.
    Watkins, A., (2016). *4D leadership.* London: Kogan Page.
6   Farmer, P. and Stevenson, D., (2017). Thriving at work: The Stevenson/Farmer review of mental health and employers. *UK Govt Website.* Available from: http://publishing.service.gov.uk [Accessed 29 March 2021].
7   Watkins, A., (2020). Why HR should stop talking about mental health and act. *HRD Connect.* Available from: www.hrdconnect.com/2020/05/27/why-hr-should-stop-talking-about-mental-health-and-act/.
8   Hompes, T. et al., (2012). The influence of maternal cortisol and emotional state during pregnancy on fetal intrauterine growth. *Pediatric Research.* Available from: www.nature.com/articles/pr201270.

Buss, C., Entringer, S. and Wadhwa, P.D., (2012). Fetal programming of brain development: intrauterine stress and susceptibility to psychopathology. *Science signaling*. Available from: www.ncbi.nlm.nih.gov/pmc/articles/PMC3837231/.

9 Holmes, J., (2014). *John Bowlby and attachment theory (makers of modern psychotherapy)*. East Sussex: Routledge.

10 James, O., (2007). *Affluenza: How to be successful and stay sane*. London: Vermillion.

3 Step-3

Resistance to change

Your life is the fruit of your own doing. You have no one to blame but yourself.

(Joseph Campbell)

The natural inclination when we receive a call to adventure, or more likely a challenge to our reality, is to refuse, refute or resist it. We may avoid the message or attack the messenger. Or we may simply remain inactive and continue to tread water. We may fake nostalgia to justify a desire to return to the comfort zone. But all of this is futile. What consolidates us in step-3, and makes it different from step-2, is the appearance of a guide or mentor, some type of genuine help. There can be a certain amount of resistance in step-2, but it tends to be internal. In step-2 we may recognise that something is wrong, but we are either seeking to solve the issue ourselves or we are busy ignoring it via various forms of anaesthetic or distraction.

In step-3, we know that such rouses are not working but we are still not ready to change. That's why a helper appears. Our helper may take the form of a consultant or coach who challenges us to do something about the pain we are experiencing. Of course, some of us don't want to be helped or we are adamant that we don't need help. Such a stance puts us firmly in step-3, where the internal resistance we may have experienced in step-2 manifests itself, often against the helper.

How do I know if I'm at step-3?

This step is characterised by resistance. The arrival of the guide or mentor makes it harder, but certainly not impossible for us to avoid, deny or dismiss our challenge to reality. Indications that you might be stuck in step-3 include:

- Fighting to maintain the status quo.
- Trying to return to what is familiar or comfortable, resisting change.
- Believing that you don't need help or guidance and irritation at the implication or suggestion that you do.
- Operating from an "I'm alright" mentality. Such a stance means change may occur around us because of us or despite us. There may indeed be nothing wrong with you or no need for you to personally change that much, but your

DOI: 10.4324/9781003170402-4

business and environment has changed profoundly and that still needs your attention.

In our personal lives, when we are resisting change, we have a tendency to justify and distract. If there is a problem in a friendship, we will brush it under the carpet and hope that it spontaneously improves in time. If our partner seems distant, we put it down to the alignment of the stars or come up with some story that allows us to abdicate responsibility for seeking to rectify that distance. If our doctor tells us that we really need to take our health seriously and get more active, we decide that taking the stairs once a week will do the trick, even if we eat a Mars bar on route. We justify that doctors are always erring on the side of caution, and we probably just have to lay off the takeaways for a week or two. The message is always diluted or simply ignored and rationalised.

In our professional lives, we may do the same and will also add more busyness to the mix. The potentially damaging distractions and anaesthetic tactics we employed in step-2 are replaced by healthier alternatives. Instead of relying on booze or cigarettes, a resisting leader might decide that their stress levels or pain can be better served by doing more at work and becoming even more of a workaholic or by joining a gym. Certainly, spending time on our health is smart, but too much can be counterproductive. In most businesses, being considered a workaholic is held up as a necessity for career advancement. Such obsessions are obviously not as damaging as alcohol or drugs, but they are still distractions from our own development and moving through the Change Wheel. Executives who point to such practices as evidence of change or progress would not fool an experienced coach or helper.

The other common tactic is disinterest. This can manifest as pseudo-authenticity, where someone in pain acknowledges their pain. They may even admit to their part in the problem, as though such a confession is somehow enough to warrant its dismissal. A close relative to this fake admission of guilt is the 'what you see is what you get' (WYSIWYG) approach. The false bravado that comes from those who know they are causing problems or being intolerable but believe they are being authentic in that dysfunction: "Yes, I know I'm and arsehole, I'm fine with that. I know who I am."

They take pride in their difficulty or confrontational stance as though it's a badge of honour. They often believe they are the tellers of truth amongst a barrage of 'politically correct nonsense'. Being proud of their own limitations, and often their own ignorance and stupidity, is just another form of resistance that is saying, "I don't need to change. I like who I am; this is me – deal with it." Underneath, however, is usually suppressed pain or unconscious fear. Sometimes this is a fear that they actually don't know how not to be an arsehole anymore!

If we want to make progress, we have to see this behaviour for what it is – a distraction from the challenge to reality we are experiencing. This can be confusing, because we might look like we are changing on the outside and certainly we might be getting fitter and healthier, which is definitely positive, but it's doing nothing for the inner development journey. And thus, it's not going to get us out of pain. Needless to say, rationalising our addiction and distraction is extremely common in step-3. The risk is that rationalisation and justification together with busyness keeps us locked in resistance. Some individuals are so skilled at resisting change there is almost no point in trying to help them. They are proudly immune to change, stubbornly digging in almost as a matter of principle.

Vertical development

When it comes to actualising potential, vertical development is the only game in town. Most businesses with more than, say, 250 employees have a Learning and Development (L&D) department. The role of L&D is to design and implement people development initiatives. Everyone in the business is knocking on their door requesting programmes on everything from how to tackle mental health issues in the workplace to how to increase productivity to how to increase employee engagement. But there are actually two types of learning and development – horizontal and vertical. Or, more accurately, there is horizontal learning and vertical development. Horizontal learning is the acquisition of skills, knowledge and experience. This covers everything we currently consider as 'learning'. Learning is clearly important because leaders and senior executives need technical skills relevant to their role, they need to be knowledgeable about a variety of factors or business issues and they need to be skilful in a number of areas. But learning is NOT development.

Development psychologist Robert Kegan likens adult development to filling a glass with water: horizontal learning is about filling the vessel while vertical development expands the glass itself.[1] Vertical development is the systematic deployment of those new skills that, in turn, change the human being. It's a little like 'levelling up' in a computer game. Horizontal learning delivers more capability at the same level, like adding another weapon in a first-person shooter game. Vertical development takes the player to a new level where a completely different set of phenomena exist that were not accessible at the previous level. Some of the problems that were encountered at the previous level actually disappear completely.

What's ironic is that most L&D departments are all 'L' and no 'D'. This is not a slight on L&D departments or the hard-working professionals within them; it's simply an observation of the way L&D departments have evolved within most businesses.[2] Most L&D departments have tended to focus on the more readily deliverable 'L' without much, if any, attention to the much more challenging 'D'.

Skills, knowledge and experience are very important to productivity, performance, engagement and all the other metrics that are so critical in business, but they do not drive verticality across the three dimensions of 'I', 'WE' and 'IT' or 'being', 'relating' and 'doing'. These three dimensions relate to the three aspects of human experience. Our lives exist only in these three dimensions. This was originally pointed out by Ken Wilber and has proven a game changer in every organisation where we have introduced it. Wilber pointed out that what's going on for the individual inside ('I' or 'being') is connected to what is going on for the collective inside ('WE' or 'relating'), and both of these are connected to the individual's observable actions on the outside ('IT') and the systems and structure people create ('ITS'). The world of 'IT'/'ITS' is simplified as 'doing'. Everything you and I and everyone else ever thinks, feels and does in life falls into one of those three dimensions. The fourth dimension is the sophistication of our 'I', the sophistication of our 'WE' and the sophistication of our 'IT'.[3]

In business, we talk at length about executives needing to get up the 'learning curve' and acquire the skills they need to be effective in their new job. For example, when appointing a new CFO, we may explore whether the candidate has the requisite Investor Relations experience or has sufficient international experience or media skills to be able to succeed. Is their knowledge of the market strong enough? All of these things are enormously important.

But what we rarely assess is how mature or emotionally developed the leader is. This would necessitate us measuring aspects of their 'being' or 'I', such as ego maturity, empathy or trust building capability, or their social and emotional intelligence. We are more interested in *what* they know than *how* they know. Furthermore, their ability to convert learning into development is not part of the executive assessment process. And this is primarily because it's much easier to measure knowledge, skill and experience. Determining a leader's values, emotional sovereignty, energy levels, or level of ego maturity and, therefore, how effectively they deploy that learning is much trickier.

And yet, all those and several other internal lines of development are crucial for leaders who want to thrive in our rapidly changing world. It's vertical development, not horizontal learning, that will give us the true competitive advantage by allowing us to expand our capacity and increase our altitude or verticality across each of the three dimensions of 'I', 'WE' and 'IT'. Vertical development takes performance to a new level. It is profoundly different from learning, and the two terms should not be used interchangeably. Horizontal learning may allow us to become more proficient, but vertical development unlocks significantly higher levels of capability that can step change performance. Horizontal learning adds more 'Apps', vertical development upgrades our operating system.

Perhaps the best way to think about the difference between the two is to consider the life of a six-year-old child. If you ask a six-year-old the question: "If $4x = 16$, what does x equal?" they don't even understand the question. This is because their frontal cortex is not fully developed yet. They think in concrete literal terms, and they are unable to think in abstract terms. However, if you ask a 12-year-old child they will probably be able to tell you that $x = 4$. The frontal cortex is much more fully developed at 12, and this development unlocks abstract processing at speed. As a result, the child's ability to understand algebra has come 'online'. The older child has a level of capability and sophistication that didn't exist at six. Vertical development offers that kind of quantum leap forward for leaders. There is no reason that the kind of development we see in children cannot continue into adulthood to enable us to thrive in today's complex world. Unfortunately, very few leaders ever 'upgrade their own personal operating system' because:

- they are too busy;
- they don't know they can;

- they don't appreciate the relevance and the impact it can have; and
- even if they did, they don't know how to do it.

Most leaders and senior executives are very good the 'doing' (the 'IT' dimension). They wouldn't be in the positions they have risen to without an ability to get stuff done and meet targets. But once they enter the C-suite, the rules of the game change and it's no longer about skills, knowledge and experience but more about nuance, subtlety and sophistication. The skills they need now are much more focused on 'being' and 'relating' than 'doing'. There is, therefore, a subtle but significant shift from the 'IT' dimension to the 'I' and 'WE' dimensions. In our work, we have found that there are eight lines of development that make a significant commercial difference to a leader's ability to deliver sustainable success across these three critical dimensions (see Figure 3.1).

Change is always easier with a guide, mentor or coach. But without this type of deeper understanding of what really makes the difference to a leader, it can be easy to hire the wrong help (more on that later in this chapter). Marrying these lines of development up with the immediate need of the leader can deliver maximum impact and develop the all-important change capability that leaders must master to thrive in an accelerating world.

How does it feel to be in step-3?

The driving emotion at step-3 is fear. But because most individuals stuck at this level rationalise and self-justify their resistance, this underlying fear is often not conscious. The guide or helper may have arrived to facilitate or encourage change, but they are still reluctant to embrace help or accept the necessity for change. Fear of failure or fear of the unknown holds them back.

Such resistance is natural. We are essentially being invited or encouraged into an unknown world, where we may have to learn new things and adapt our ways. This can be daunting, regardless of our surface bravado or self-confidence. We are all wary of the unknown; it's a human survival mechanism that has evolved over thousands of years, we are never going to be able to turn it off completely. But we can manage it.

Of course, in the C-suite, fear is rarely expressed as fear. The more common demonstration of fear is hubris, arrogance and dismissiveness. The ego bubbles to the surface and expresses dismay at anyone who suggests that something is genuinely wrong. There is a lot of messenger shooting at step-3.

The hubris suggests there can't possibly be anything wrong because the leader is in charge and the leader knows what they are doing. This can very easily morph into insularity. We have seen numerous CEOs and C-suite leaders who have pressed on, head down, refusing help, believing that they are doing well enough, only to discover within the year that they have been removed from post, usually for under performance. In fact, we have seen this phenomenon so often we started to keep a 'watch list' of executives who have been resistant to input. We stopped when the

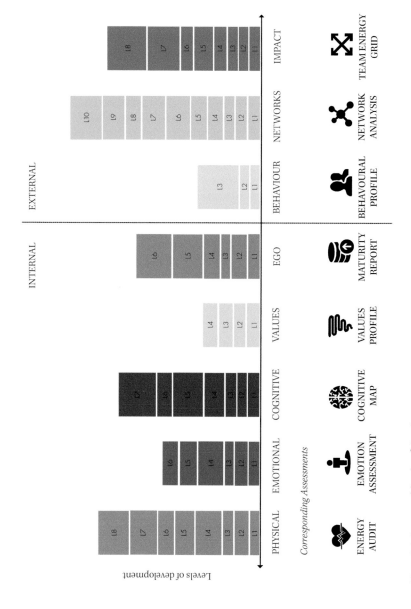

Figure 3.1 Lines and levels of development.

list passed 30 about five years ago. These individuals were people who had been introduced to us over the preceding 8–10 years. They had either refused our offer of help or said, "not just yet", and within a year they were sacked, sometimes very publicly. Insularity can be fatal.

The leader's resistance may be caused by their hubris or the belief that accepting coaching guidance is a sign of weakness. Such resistance is often exacerbated because many leaders *have* opened themselves up to help but been profoundly disappointed when their chosen help hasn't delivered a real ROI or has fallen well short of expectation. As a result, leaders mistakenly assume that all corporate coaching and leadership development programmes are a waste of time and money.

It could be argued that a good Chairman or the non-Executive Directors (NEDs) should provide this sort of guidance for the CEO or C-suite leaders in a business. Sometimes they do. But in our experience, running a large multi-national business today is now so complicated and pressurised that it is very difficult for most leaders to manage the multiple layers and levels of complexity across so many different dimensions. Robert Kegan has suggested that many leaders are "in over their heads". For these reasons, it is imperative that leaders find a high-quality, experienced developmental coach independent of the business who can provide the requisite challenge to thinking and who also has the ability to actually drive that leader's *development*, not just teach them skills.

The problem is that finding a coach that can do this is much easier said than done. Coaching qualifications from the organisations that have set themselves up as the 'professional bodies' in corporate coaching are no guide to quality. A coach's track record can help sort good coaches from poor ones. Breadth of coaching experience is also a good indicator. Level of seniority of experience can also help, as there is no doubt that more senior leaders are often more demanding.

The main point is that if leaders want to be able to sustain their success and last longer than the average premiership football manager, they need to become less insular. If anyone or any organisation thinks they know it all, then they are very likely to fail. If they become too obsessed with themselves and too enamoured with their own brand, they are rarely open to feedback. They believe they know it all and start to think they are invincible.

The irony of this insularity is that we are all defined by relationships, whether we like it or not. Relationships require us to interact and get out of our echo chambers. When we disconnect from the world, from others and their feedback, we begin to know less. Every company is defined by its relationship with customers, and each human being is defined by their relationships with the people around them. It is only when we meet other people that we realise we might not be the genius we think we are.

Leaders need to become much more curious about their own development and hunt down a high-quality corporate coach with the skill and capability to really develop them and their fellow leaders within the business. Such a person is rare and should be seen as a critical resource for any organisation.

The expert mindset

Whereas narcissism is a major block in step-1 and victimhood is a major block in step-2, the expert mindset is the major stumbling block in step-3.

Our lauding of experts is a consequence of our emphasis on learning rather than development. In primary school, children get one generalist teacher who teaches them everything on their curriculum including reading, writing and simple maths. By the time the child enters high school, the generalist has been replaced by a specialist. Each subject has its own specialist teacher. If the child studies for A-levels, they will get a super-expert teacher whose knowledge of that subject is even more detailed and precise. When they go to university, the child will specialise even more, until finally they arrive in a position that fosters the expert mindset. Our society cultivates the idea that becoming an expert is a pinnacle of achievement. Children become adults and rise through the ranks, whether that is academia, business, sport or public sector, based on the quality of their expertise. All is well.

When we enter the C-suite, where we must successfully lead others, our expertise is no longer enough. In the C-suite, leaders fail because the expertise that put them in the role is not enough to allow them to flourish and succeed in that role. What's needed are a very different set of capabilities from the skills, knowledge and expertise they cultivated to get them to the C-suite. This happens everywhere from teaching to medicine to law and beyond.

We trust experts, but they tend to take a very narrow and definite approach to any issue. The old joke is you can always tell an expert, but you can't tell them much. Many experts also believe that because they are an expert in one area, they are naturally an authority in many other areas, even if they haven't put the study in to become one. This is a very common shadow in experts, and it makes them very difficult to coach and guide. In fact, experts will often tell you how to do your job even when they have not been trained to do your job.

An expert is usually deeply trained to have a clear and singular perspective on any issue. Therein lies the problem. They may have very deep knowledge on the topic in question but, almost by definition, they lack the breadth and experience to be able to see beyond their own area of expertise. Such a narrow focus means they are poorly equipped to integrate multiple perspectives or see the issue from an unrelated standpoint. When it comes to any pain they may be feeling at step-3 or any uncertainty about what to do about their pain, those locked in an expert mindset are often so busy being right and being an expert that they close themselves off to potential solutions.

I have, over the years, met many leaders who took the view "what can someone else possibly know or say that could help me?" This mindset is often underpinned by a degree of arrogance. How dare you? Who are you to question me? I think you'll find I'm the expert here. I am the one in charge. I am the one who knows!

Usually, what lies behind the expression of indignation is fear. The implication is if something is wrong and I don't know what it is or how to fix it or what to change to make a difference, then perhaps I don't know. If I don't know, I'm not an expert, and if I am not an expert then what am I?

Being an expert in an area is a genuine advantage but only if we can recognise that while we know a lot of stuff about that area, we might not see the whole picture and, therefore, a mentor, guide or coach with a different perspective might be able to break the deadlock and move us, the team or the business forward.

The expert mindset is often a defence mechanism because the emergence of the helper, mentor or coach is viewed as a threat to their validity. It is somehow suggesting they don't know rather than seeing that person for what they really are – a useful guide through the change process.

Assessing the helper

Leaders need to become much more discerning about their chosen help, coach or consultant. Not only can a good coach help to dial down the fear and navigate the expert mindset, but they can open up avenues for exploration that the leader may never have considered.

There is often a faulty assumption that the more expensive the help, the better it is. This is often why people hire the brand name consultants like Bain, BCG or McKinsey. No one has ever been fired for hiring McKinsey. The problem is that they are often insanely expensive and deliver very little in terms of tangible change or performance improvement. The late Clayton Christensen of Harvard Business School gave one of the best explanations of the triumph of these types of 'solution shops'. Essentially, clients don't know what they are getting in advance, because they are looking for knowledge that they don't have. They can't determine effectiveness based on results either, because outside factors, such as the quality of execution, influence the outcome of the consultant's recommendations. So instead, they rely on "educational pedigrees, eloquence, and demeanour" as some form of proxy for tangible results. Hardly surprising that they frequently contain the smuggest guys in the room not the smartest.[4] These brand name helpers are consultants. They arrive with pre-packaged black box solutions that they roll out to multiple companies regardless of the type of help that's needed. Often these are system or process changes that focus on what the business is doing in the 'IT' dimension.

A good coaching organisation will work with the leader so that they can find their own bespoke solutions while focusing on individual vertical development. A good coach may indeed look at what someone or a business is doing ('IT'), but that is secondary to how the people in the business are being ('I') and relating to each other ('WE'). Develop the being and the relating, and the doing will often look after itself. Focus only on the doing, and those expensive 'solutions' almost always fail.

Hiring the name is logical but it rarely works. They are a little like fund managers. The behaviour of fund managers is pretty consistent despite claims of differentiation. They are following the crowd, safe in the knowledge that if it doesn't work, they can justify the loss. However, if they step outside the norm and it doesn't work, they will struggle to justify that loss. Both options result in loss, but one is considered recoverable and the other isn't.

Corporate coaching or the use of consultants follows the same herd mentality. Everyone knows that most of it is pretty ordinary and doesn't work. But, as long as it can be explained or justified, they keep hiring the big names, keep spending a fortune and keep getting disappointing results.

If you really want to know whether you have got the best help available, you can apply the simple '4 A's filter'. Leaders should be looking for help that is assessed against these criteria:

1   **Aptitude** – what evidence is there of skill sets? How many different theories or models does the helper use? Is the helper attached to a single model, or do they integrate multiple perspectives and a range of practices? Their ability to integrate multiple views testifies to the sophistication of their ability. A quality helper will come with an extensive kit bag, a back catalogue of experiences that suggest they may have a very broad range of capabilities that they can bring to bear. But the critical factor is not that he or she can tick lots of experiential boxes, rather that they can make nuanced use of such skills and experiences by integrating them into a coherent narrative that is useful to the collective and can move the leader and the business through the Change Wheel.

2   **Amplitude** – what scale has the helper worked at? Have they worked all over the world in multiple markets and multiple geographies? Have they experienced several economic scenarios and market conditions? Can they work with the C-suite and the factory floor? Are they equally comfortable with a diversity of cultural values, financial backgrounds, age ranges, sexual orientations, etc.? Or have they been restricted to coaching just one or two types of people? Working across multiple fields is not a checklist. What matters is why the coach was working across multiple fields and whether they've compared the insights from these multiple fields to more deeply understand the nature of variance to create a more powerful ability to transition from A to B successfully. A coach who flourishes in diverse environments is more likely to have a greater amplitude.

3   **Attitude** – how good are the social skills of the helper? Are they emotionally intelligent, literate and well managed? Are they easy to get on with? Do they radiate warmth and enthusiasm? Would you enjoy spending time with them away from the developmental journey they are taking you on? Are they interested in the individuals in the business as human beings, or do they see people as assets or resources in the business? This dimension comes with a warning. It is easy to be fooled by a veneer of niceness and sociability. Many a company has been taken in by a socially skilled coach with little behind the façade. Look deeper for evidence of genuine concern and proof of compassion and emotional depth.

4   **Altitude** – what level of sophistication do they bring? If you had to weigh the 4 A's then this would be the most heavily weighted. Has the coach got real depth, or are they just re-telling a well-known story they have taken off others? Do they have something fresh to say about the human condition and how to effect a positive change? Most importantly, do they understand the difference between vertical development and horizontal learning? And can they operationalise this difference? What distinctions do they make and what level of nuance do they work with? Do they understand multi-dimensionality across

the quadrants of 'being' ('I'), doing ('IT') and 'relating' ('WE')? Altitude takes a leader beyond simple description of phenomena to the ability to transform the future.[5]

The capacity to embrace change and become a change champion largely comes down to vertical development. A change champion is someone who doesn't shy away from change but who assesses objectively whether change is needed. They dive into the unknown again and again, armed with the skills and mindset to navigate the inevitable challenges. As a result of multiple cycles of the Change Wheel, change champions have returned to the known world a changed person on more than one occasion. They have direct first-hand experience of what better, more capable, more empathetic, more sophisticated and innovative leadership looks like. They know that learning will only ever take us so far. The real step change comes from vertical development of the human being doing the learning so they can deploy the knowledge in a more sophisticated way. And most of that growth potential is in the 'I' (being) and 'WE' (relating) dimensions. It is the source of our power, and accessing it is only possible with a coach who appreciates the distinction.

Cultural metaphors

Step-3, resistance of change, is where the hero resists the call to adventure. Fear, uncertainty or disbelief arises about the journey into the unknown. This often inhibits the hero from moving forward. Initially there is a 'refusal of the call'. The hero doesn't want to or can't believe what his heart or the herald is telling him. The helper arrives to encourage the hero to start the journey.

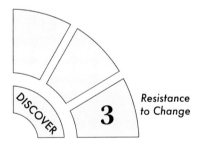

The Matrix: It is clear from the opening scenes that Neo is searching. He's unhappy, dissatisfied and tortured. While Trinity seemed to recognise how he was feeling at the club and he is certainly unhappy at work, he doesn't really believe anyone is after him. After being reprimanded for being late, we see Neo at his desk where he receives a delivery – a mobile phone. The phone rings and it's Morpheus. Morpheus is his guide or mentor, and he tells him that they are coming for him. Neo looks over his cubicle to see agents, including Agent Smith. Morpheus guides him to an empty office where he must climb out the window onto scaffolding to escape. Neo refuses. Morpheus says, "There are two ways out of this building, one is that scaffolding, the other is in their custody." Neo is resisting the call – he believes it's insane. Although he does climb out, he gets scared and climbs back in and is taken into custody.

The Lord of the Rings: As Gandalf explains to Frodo what he must do, Frodo is sure he's made a mistake and is refusing the call. Gandalf realises that Frodo's friend Samwise Gamgee (Sam) is hiding outside the house and listening to the conversation. The task ahead seems a little less daunting for Frodo with Sam, his ally, by his side.

Star Wars: Luke finds and talks to Obi-Wan Kenobi and is thrilled to hear that his father was a Jedi. The idea of helping save Princess Leia is appealing. "You must learn the ways of the force if you are to come with me to Alderaan", says Obi-Wan, to which Luke replies, "I'm not going to Alderaan. There's nothing I can do about it right now." Deep-down, Luke is starting to recognise that his destiny lies with Obi-Wan, but he feels obligated to stay and help his aunt and uncle on the farm.

Harry Potter: Harry is whisked away to the castle, where Hagrid tells him more about his wizarding heritage, but he doesn't believe it. He tells Hagrid, "I think you must have made a mistake. I don't think I can be a wizard."

The Wizard of Oz: Dorothy meets Professor Marvel, who tells her that Auntie Em is seriously ill. It's not by chance that he's called Professor Marvel. A challenge to reality can be marvellous, but there's also a more common, painful version of a challenge. Dorothy loves her family and decides to return home. While understandable, her choice is also her resistance to change and a refusal of the call to adventure.

Transition from step-3 to step-4

At step-3, the guide, coach or mentor has arrived to encourage the leader to face the truth, accept the facts, face the music and take a 'spoonful of medicine' in some way. The arrival of this helper is rarely accidental, especially in a business setting. The leader has perhaps been stuck in step-2 for too long and recognises that a new perspective may help them get out of their pain. But the helper is rarely welcome. Often, even if the leader recognises the need for the helper, they are hugely resistant and often resentful of the helper's presence. Even in the movies, there is an almost whimsical, albeit fleeting, regret for leaving the comfort zone.

Resistance to change can last a few days, months or years. In the worse cases, it can last a lifetime! But usually, even the most resistant leader will accept that something needs to change and become more open to the idea that change is inevitable, and it might even be positive.

It may be that the leader has to invite several helpers into the fold before a breakthrough is possible. Better the devil you know will almost always become untenable. Resistance to change is the last step of the discovery phase. The evidence is in, there is no way to dispute it. The only question is, are we going back or are we pushing forward?

The big question is whether you are going to be

able to say a hearty 'yes' to your adventure.

(Joseph Campbell)

Questions to ask yourself

If you are unsure if you are in step-3, it can be helpful to ask yourself some questions:

- What am I scared of?
- What is my fear?
- What is stopping me developing?
- Am I holding onto the past?
- Am I struggling to let go?
- Am I rejecting offers to help?

Use the answers to these questions to gain confidence about your location on the Change Wheel and use that knowledge constructively to move forward and not retreat to the comfort zone or languish in the pain and uncertainty of step-2. The only way out is to press on: seek out a guide that can help you.

Notes

1 Petrie, N., (2011). *A white paper: Future trends in leadership development.* Centre of Creative Leadership. Available from: https://leanconstruction.org/media/learning_laboratory/Leadership/Future_Trends_in_Leadership_Development.pdf.
2 Watkins, A. and Dalton, N., (2020). *HR revolution: Change the workplace, change the world.* London: Routledge.
3 Watkins, A., (2016). *4D leadership: Competitive advantage through vertical leadership development.* London: Kogan Page.
4 Schumpeter, (2021). McKinsey's partners suffer from collective self-delusion. *The Economist.* Available from: www.economist.com/business/2021/03/03/mckinseys-partners-suffer-from-collective-self-delusion.
5 Kegan, R. and Laskow Lahey, L., (2016). *An everyone culture: Becoming a deliberately developmental organization.* Boston: Harvard Business Review Press.

4 Step-4

Overcoming resistance

Opportunities to find deeper powers within ourselves
come when life seems most challenging.

(Joseph Campbell)

Step-4, and the move from the discovery phase to the decision phase, often emerges gradually as the defences against change erode over time. Despite the considerable resistance at step-3, and weeks, months or even years of assurances that the leader is on top of the problem, eventually there is a dawning realisation that they are not on top of the problem and are, in fact, stuck. Resistance is futile because despite the posturing, claims of progress, distraction, deception and all manner of ploys to prevent progress, either deliberately or unconsciously, there is no improvement. The pain hasn't subsided, the data haven't improved and the failure is obvious for all to see.

Having moved to step-4, the leader has completed the discovery phase and is now having to admit, at least to themselves, the truth of the situation they find themselves in. The big insight is that theory isn't practice. Knowledge alone doesn't deliver a thing if it isn't implemented and used to drive change. Learning isn't development. It's necessary but insufficient to effect change.

Step-4 isn't just a drift from step-3 down a gentle off ramp to the moment of truth that awaits at step-5. Nor is step-4 just a half-way house between the full-blown technicolour resistance of step-3 and the full-steam-ahead commitment of step-5. There are still critical dynamics to understand before a leader can exit step-4, so it's importance should not be underestimated. Step-4 is absolutely critical to the active process of engaged, conscious change.

How do I know if I'm at step-4?

In step-4, resistance starts to subside. The intensity and certainty that nothing much is wrong, characteristic of step-3, begins to fracture. Indications that you might be in step-4 include:

DOI: 10.4324/9781003170402-5

- Working hard but not getting very far.
- Recognition that something is still holding you back.
- Things may be moving, but they are moving very slowly.
- Humiliation.
- Scepticism.

When we are overcoming resistance in our personal lives, there may be moments of clarity where we see ourselves as others see us. We appreciate, if only for a moment, that our actions and behaviour may have something to do with the challenge we face. We may realise that our actions contributed to the breakdown of a relationship or friendship. These insights are rarely fully formed, but there is enough of a glimpse to recognise that we played our part, and the certainty that we are right, so central in step-3, begins to slip. We haven't reached a point of decision yet, but we are likely to experience mini moments of truth in step-4 along with the realisation that defending our previous position, our status, our ego or our role is not helping.

The pain of step-2 that gave way to the self-justification and hubris of step-3 is now replaced by a mixed bag of emotions, which can range from guilt to depression as we enter the realisation that no matter how much we exercised the muscles of victimhood or the expert mindset, our life hasn't improved and we might just have something to do with that.

At step-4, we are often at a low ebb because we are having to face the reality that maybe we're not as smart as we thought we were. We can't solve the problem on our own. This can be humiliating to someone who believed they were an all-powerful expert. Even if we start to admit, at least to ourselves, that we need help, we are still somewhat sceptical about accepting that help. Such scepticism is really cynicism's more amenable cousin. When scepticism appears, it's actually a positive sign of progress that indicates the last stand of the expert mindset and energy. Scepticism is a psychological play that reveals that a leader may be ready to admit that they don't know but they are still not quite ready to concede that someone else may know.

Initially, as our resistance subsides in step-4, we may find ourselves working harder and harder on the challenge with nothing much to show for it. Why? Because we are still applying our current thinking to the challenge, and it's proving much more stubborn than we expected. Our assurances to the Board that the poor numbers were just a blip is increasingly untenable. Something else is clearly going on, but we are still pretending that the numbers will bounce back. Even if some progress is made, it's likely to be far too slow to quieten the discontent. All of this can fuel a growing sense of impatience and frustration that things are not going as planned. We begin to accept that something must be done and that the current way of operating is simply not working.

In some people, the pain of step-2 is mirrored by the low mood of step-4. There is a futility or even meaninglessness to step-4. In truth this has been brewing since step-2, but it was largely obfuscated by pain (step-2) and resistance (step-3). As the resistance begins to crumble, the meaninglessness and despondency become more apparent. For example, I've seen countless leaders who faithfully followed the corporate rules and dedicated themselves to climbing the corporate ladder only to 'arrive' in the C-suite and wonder, "is this it?" The sense of victory or achievement they felt sure they would experience doesn't materialise or, if it does, it's so fleeting to be almost non-existent. This can really suck.

They feel despondent because they kept their side of the bargain. In their personal and professional life, they were a dutiful husband/wife, father/mother, leader, worker, friend and colleague, and it still didn't work out. They feel cheated. They followed the rules and played their part, but the promised rewards never quite arrived. I have seen this sense of injustice so often in business. It often occurs during a merger or acquisition where one side feels they have been hard done by or when one side isn't 'playing by the rules'. It also occurs when someone is suddenly made redundant after 25 years of loyal service. They didn't quite make it to the board-room and were then just cast aside. This experience often comes as a terrible shock, and yet we hear stories all the time of people being marched out of the building by security guards as soon as they become surplus to the new requirements.

Step-4 is the step that demands some soul searching. And it is that soul searching that is so crucial to forward momentum. The decision phase, of which step-4 is the first step, is part of the owning-up process of development. Sooner or later, we must all 'own up' to our own part in the challenging situations we face as well as 'own up' to the parts of our nature that we may dislike or hold us back. We are all human. We make mistakes, but when we refuse to learn from those mistakes, we can get stuck in step-3. Step-4 represents a positive and significant shift forward because we begin to recognise our own role in the drama, and our resistance to change finally begins to falter.

How does it feel to be in step-4?

The transition emotion from step-3 to step-4 may be an overwhelming sense of boredom. There really are only so many times we can repeat the same distraction tactic before we recognise its futility. Another affair with a junior employee, another expensive watch to add to the other 27 expensive watches in the collection. Another stinking hangover. None of it helps. None of the game playing makes any difference. None of it makes us any better or any happier. Dante, in his allegorical tale the Divine Comedy, alludes to this as he wakes up in the middle of his life and wonders how he got to this point.

Something happens at step-4 that facilitates a letting go or surrender of some sort. Rock bottom has been hit and often thoroughly explored. But, more importantly, rock bottom is now accompanied by a recognition that no one is coming to help. There will be no white knight on a majestic steed to gallop in and save the day.

We finally realise that our parents aren't going to fix our problem; our boss isn't going to make things any better; society or the government isn't going to solve our woes. It's down to us and us alone to fix things. At this point, we finally take ownership of the situation – often for the very first time. Sometimes step-4 is referred to as the 'long-dark night', a metaphor for the darkness that precedes the emergence of a new day and ownership of what lies ahead.

At this point of the journey, we are forced to turn our attention from the outside to the inside. We finally realise that the blame and recrimination we have directed towards other people, situations or events has not helped to change the situation. Instead, it has just kept us stuck. As a result, we finally let go of the idea that someone else is to blame or someone else will solve our problems and take ownership to solve them ourselves. This shift in ownership from outside to inside is absolutely crucial for the progression to step-5 where we, in Campbell's terminology, will "cross the threshold" and commit to real change.

The only way we can get to step-5 and commitment to change is to first recognise that the narrative that we are running isn't getting us anywhere. If the archetype of the mentor or helper has not turned up yet, or we have already dismissed them, we are forced to consider that we are the thing that is preventing our progress. We start to question ourselves. Is the expert mindset we clung too so desperately in step-3 actually blinding us to some other potential solution or way forward? If a helper is present, then we may start to wonder if they can actually help. Our guides may reassure us that it's going to be okay, and we may even be tempted to trust them, but we are not fully committed yet. That said, once the doom of step-4 subsides, the green shoots of hope and optimism start to emerge. We move into the realm of possibility.

Something is drawing us forward and we may not know what that is. Of course, it's the same call to adventure we ignored at step-2 and step-3, but it's just louder and more obvious. But rather than fearing the change, curiosity starts to emerge along with a developing openness to what the future might hold.

This openness is almost the antithesis of the expert mindset of the previous step.

Prior to the London 2012 Olympics, I was thrilled when I was invited to work with the GB rowing squad. They were attempting to beat their best ever result at the Beijing Olympics, where they won six medals. Rowing was my sport, and London my home Olympics, so the request for help felt like all my Christmases had come at once.

I went to speak to all 15 GB rowing crews, including their respective coaches, and outlined what I could do to support their preparation in the three-month run-up to the games. What was fascinating was that seven of the coaches were open to me working with them, and eight felt that their crews didn't need any help.

Of the seven crews I worked with, six won medals compared to only three medals from the remaining eight crews I didn't work with. I'm not for one second suggesting that they won because of my input (although I'd like to think I helped a bit) but rather that openness is imperative for success. World-class performers are always receptive and open to new ideas for improvement. They are always seeking more insight and looking for ways to improve.

I remember the first time I ever met Katheryn Granger. I had just watched her race. We got chatting afterwards, and I suggested that while the performance was impressive, if she did that in the Olympic final she wouldn't even win Bronze. I'll never forget her face; without any language her facial expression was clearly saying, "And who the fuck are you anyway?!"

Part of what made Katheryn an exceptional champion was her openness and her willingness to question everything and constantly push for better. She had the good grace to carry on chatting to me, and we explored what else I could add to her considerable skill to ensure she was unbeatable. Katheryn went on to win Olympic Gold in the double sculls with Anna Watkins, after breaking the Olympic record in the qualifying phases. She then took a two-year break, came back with a new partner, Victoria Thornley, and won Silver at the Rio Olympics in 2016, probably an even greater achievement given that the crew was not even selected to go three months before Rio started.

Kathryn is a shining example of the fact that the best people are always open to the possibility of improving and will pursue every avenue to find even the slightest advantage. At elite sport levels, even tiny improvements can make the difference between Gold and Silver or medalling at all. In fact, I would go so far as to say that openness to input is one of the defining characteristics of world class anything. People who are truly world class normally have the humility to realise that they do not know everything, and they realise that there is always another level of brilliance they have yet to achieve. As a consequence, they are curious and constantly on the lookout for things inside and outside their area of expertise that could give them an additional competitive edge.

Doubt

One of the biggest stumbling blocks to overcoming the rampant resistance of step-3 is doubt. At step-4, there is still a significant amount of doubt to be resolved. As the resistance starts to subside at step-4 while we may sense that we are not repeating the same old mistakes, there is still comfort in the devil we know. We may have finally realised that we can't go back, but we are still doubtful if going forward is a legitimate option. In this limbo-land, doubt is the slippery slope back to the resistance of step-3. We may acknowledge we must let go of the rules of the old world, but we haven't yet discovered the rules of the new world. In this discomfort, we can create a vacuum that sucks us into a regression, and we end up taking backward steps. To move forwards we must let go of our doubt and start looking to what lies ahead.

This letting go must be differentiated from the giving up of learned helplessness that is common in step-3 or the surrender borne of victimhood in step-2. This letting go is a conscious relinquishing of control, where we renounce old patterns, old hurt or injury as well as our rationalisations, justifications and excuses and instead willingly embrace the need for change. This requires some courage and faith because we're often being asked to let go of the old before the new has even partially emerged. It is perfectly normal to feel mixed emotions at this time.

Embracing these mixed emotions and having faith that we can genuinely overcome our resistance is absolutely crucial to the success of any change of direction. If we jump into step-5 with some doubt in our heart, the change is unlikely to work; the door back to old habits remains ajar.

One of the reasons I decided to write about the Change Wheel is our experience trying to help global leaders develop. We coach executives, leaders and teams and teach them practical tools that can transform their lives and results. However, even though they intellectually acknowledged the benefits of what they learned, there was often insufficient application. These great tools didn't really bite or make a measurable difference. Most of those involved in the coaching enjoyed it and looked forward to the sessions because they were learning new and interesting things, but without application nothing much would change.

I reflected deeply on what was preventing progress. It became clear that those individuals and teams that were struggling had never overcome their resistance. They had just jumped into participation, either because they thought that was what was expected of them or their boss or team was asking them to make certain changes, but they hadn't truly let go of their resistance or decided to change.

With hindsight, we were underestimating the importance of the decide phase of the journey, and step-4 in particular. We often discussed the commercial challenges leaders and teams were facing. In fact, this was usually the reason they were talking to us. We mapped the range of problems they were facing, but it became clear that there was a huge desire to rush to solution mode, often completely overlooking steps 3 to 6. This rush was driven by most clients' bias for action. Action often preceded an appropriate understanding of the issues.

Over time, it gradually dawned on us that without sufficient clarity of the issues the client was seeking to change, including a sophisticated understanding of the reasons for their resistance, the brilliant tools we were giving them wouldn't deliver sustainable improvements. This doesn't necessarily need to take a lot of time, but a forensic dissection of the problem and its causes always helped. Such a dissection needed to include helping the executive overcome their resistance. If we didn't clarify the specific issue and the reason for resistance, then clients would never fully close the back door to their old habits. If we didn't address their resistance and doubt effectively, then as soon as any changes became uncomfortable the executive would simply retreat to the comfort of old habits and old ways of thinking, undoing all their efforts in one regressive step.

The doubt we feel at step-4 is just the last remnants of resistance, but it must be vanquished before we can make the commitments we need to make at step-5. A proper commitment needs to burn the bridges so there can be no going back. Doubt stops that and pulls us back. Faith will help us move forward.

Of course, I mean faith in the most general terms, not religious faith. I mean faith in Self, faith in the universe, faith in life, humanity, faith that we can no longer tolerate or ignore the signs. Action is needed, and we need faith that once we commit, things will work out.

Overcoming resistance is about resolving the arguments for 'no change' so we can aspire for something better. None of us are perfect in all areas of our life all the time. But when we realise that the current situation is untenable, we must actively slay the dragon of inertia, overcome our resistance and step forward towards the moment of truth. We must reach a point where our doubt has gone, and we are ready to go 'all in'. This will likely be challenging. But faith will take us forward, and doubt will keep us stuck.

Sometimes our internal battle between the two poles of doubt and faith can rage for a long time. Our inner dialogue is between all the voices that want to maintain the status quo or pull us backwards, such as doubt, fear, anxiety and scepticism, and the voices that are encouraging us forward, such as faith and curiosity. This is a significant battle, and the helper should never rush this step. We need to understand and acknowledge the competing forces at play on both sides. We may want something desperately, but if we don't believe we can have it or change it we create cognitive dissonance, and this dissonance itself can become part of our resistance, leading us to dismiss what we really want, thus denying that potential outcome.

The act of overcoming resistance may require us to desire change but fail to follow through a few times before we fully overcome our resistance. At the core of this inner battle, we are laying the foundations for a new version of us to emerge once we embrace step-5 and really commit to the adventure that lies ahead.

There is a great line in the movie *Rocketman*, the Elton John biopic, where Elton is wondering about changing his name, and someone says to him, "You've got to kill the person you were in order to become the person you want to be."

This is what we are aiming for in step-4: a psychological death where we are purposefully and consciously letting go of the current version of our Self in order to create the space for something better to emerge in its place.

In overcoming the resistance, we are starting to build some energy for the critical moment at step-5 where we will need to cross the threshold and commit.

The accountability compass

The danger in step-4 is that we simply go through the motions of change, without ever changing. We game the change. We may understand the theory and fully recognise the need for change. We may acknowledge that the expert mindset we clung onto in step-3 is holding us back, and we may even start to listen to the helper archetype in whatever form they show up. But if all remaining resistance is to be swept aside in preparation for commitment, we must take ownership for our change. We must be accountable for our own progress. To help leaders and teams deal effectively with this struggle, we built the accountability compass. It defines the top five reasons that prevent them reaching step-5 (see Figure 4.1).

The accountability compass explains why people don't change and don't cross the threshold. We've all had the experience of asking someone to do something and discovering that they've done nothing. Why don't people do what we ask? The answer can always be found on the accountability compass, and it's as applicable to meeting sales targets as it is to driving change initiatives or getting stuff done at home.

Imagine I'm in the south of France on holiday with my family, and I say to one of my sons, "Your mum and I are going out for the day. Can you nip into town and get some bread for dinner?" When we come back at the end of the day, we discover

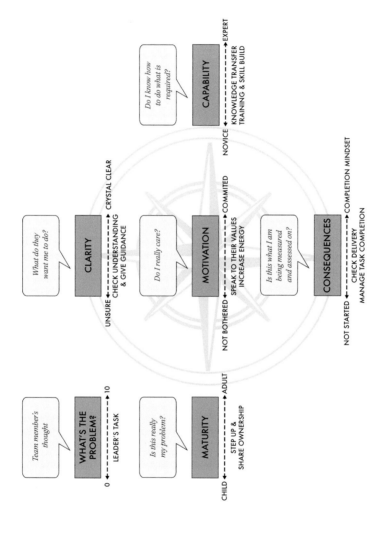

Figure 4.1 The Accountability Compass.

there's no bread. Why? There are only five reasons, as illustrated by the account-ability compass:

North: clarity

When I ask my son why he didn't go to town and get bread, he says: "Oh, I didn't think you meant today. I thought you meant when we were next in town." Or, if he did know I wanted the bread today, he might not have done the task because he got there and wasn't clear on what type of bread we wanted, and he didn't want to get the wrong sort of bread. Or he may have known what type of bread, but he wasn't clear where the boulangerie was because every other time we had got bread we have driven there, and he couldn't remember how to get there – so he didn't even go to town.

He didn't get the bread because something about the instruction was not clear enough. Lack of clarity can cause resistance, because even if we embrace the need for change, if we are not clear about exactly what is wanted and why then the resist-ance is likely to persist. Leaders often assume their broadcasted instructions were crystal clear, but they rarely check what has actually been received by their audience. The assumption is that 100 per cent of what was transmitted has been received and understood. This is rarely the case.

If we are unclear about what needs to change, then change is unlikely to happen. It can be very helpful to explore what part of us we're seeking to change and why. What is it costing us, and what are we likely to gain if we can execute the change we are considering? The goal here is to move from foggy, undefined outcomes to crystal clear outcomes.

East: skill

Assuming my son knows we want the bread today, how to get to the boulangerie and that we want one sourdough loaf and one granary loaf, we should get our bread. And yet we get home and there's still no bread.

When I ask my son, it becomes obvious that despite all this clarity the task hasn't been completed because he can't speak French. The task failed because of a simple lack of skill.

Sometimes, we don't action tasks or embrace change because we don't have the skill needed to execute. Even if we are clear about what we want to do or change, we still need the skills to make that happen. These may be technical skills like speaking French, computer literacy or change competency. Avoiding this reason for failure is usually a simple matter of training. The goal is to ensure the person has the correct level of ability to deliver the outcome.

South: follow up

Let's assume my son had the clarity and the skill to get the bread, but when we returned there was still no bread. Follow up might be the issue. This often happens in busy organisations. Leaders give clear instructions to capable people, but if the leader doesn't check up to see if the task has been done then the failure is down to poor performance management. It may be that the team member hears all sorts of requests from the leader and if most of them aren't checked up on over time, they learn that they don't need to action all the requests. Besides, they can't be that important because no one ever checks on progress or completion.

Sometimes, we may resist change because we get all enthusiastic at the start and then the energy fizzles out. We know that no one is going to follow up and check that the change has been successful, so we don't do it. Again, this can be a simple problem to solve. With a small amount of discipline and a little checking, we can remove this reason for failure. It may necessitate some rewards and punishments for action and inaction, or a sunset clause so everyone is clear on what by when. The goal here is to move from hiding within the turbulence of change or simply surviving the requests with low levels of proactivity and helping everyone to participate in a more robust performance management culture and becoming much more self-directed and proactive.

Centre: motivation

Let's assume my son knows what bread to buy, has the skill to secure the bread and is very sure that I'll ask about the bread when I return. But when I do get home, the bread is still not on the table. What happened this time? Then the likely reason is motivation. My son was more interested in playing in the pool, sunbathing and having a good time with his brothers, and he doesn't even like bread. The problem here is that I failed to understand his motivation or what was needed to make sure he followed though. Maybe if I'd offered an incentive, the outcome would have been different. My son may be able to make a very good case for not getting the bread because he wanted pizza instead.

We may resist the change we are considering because we lack the motivation to make it happen. Something else trumps the desire to please or appease the parents, boss, co-worker or friend. The resistance lies in the fact that whatever is being asked for is just not important enough for us. In order to avoid failure due to motivation, it is necessary to understand the eight value systems that drives behaviour and realise that what motivates us may not necessarily be what motivates others. The change may fail to happen because our colleagues believe the change suggested is the wrong change. And by that, they mean the change advocated is not motivational to them. In order to avoid failure due to poor motivation, we have to define what our own and other people's value systems are in order to move them from disengaged to committed.

West: maturity

If my son is crystal clear about what bread and how to get it, he has the skill needed to secure the bread, he has the will or desire to do it and the certainty that I will be checking, then there can only be one reason that the bread is still not on the table after our day out and that is my son's lack of maturity.

This might manifest with my son saying something like: "Why should I go and get bread? You're the parents; surely that's your job not mine."

The final piece of resistance that must subside or be overcome at step-4 is maturity. If the person involved has abdicated responsibility for making the change happen because they can't be bothered, then that is a basic maturity problem. They are not refusing because they are poorly motivated, they are refusing to take action because there is a lack of ownership of the problem or the need to deliver an outcome. If we are fully functioning adults, we must recognise that even if something isn't our fault it may still be our responsibility to change that situation. No one else is going to change it. Adults step up to the plate without waiting to be asked. Adolescents are much less likely to do this. The work in this scenario is to cultivate a more adult stance and help those around you to move from immaturity to maturity.

The only way we will ever truly overcome resistance in step-4 is if we dive deeply into the change that we are considering and investigate our willingness to change from each of these five points of the compass.

It's easier to overcome resistance when we are clear about the changes we want to make and why. It greatly helps if we know how to make progress and have at least some of the skills needed to execute the change. Do we have any experience of change? As a leader, we need to become skilful at change in all three domains of 'I', 'WE' and 'IT'. We need to understand the psychology, inter-personal dynamics and the practical processes of change. And we need to know that the change will be measured, monitored and followed up on rather than announced and ignored! We need a framework to determine if we are making progress to monitor performance along the way and check in on those milestones consistently. We need to be honest about our motivation and better define the motivation of others. Is this change something we genuinely want or something we feel obligated to do? Does the required outcome align with our values? And finally, we need to take responsibility for the change in order to cast off the last remnants of resistance.

Cultural metaphors

Step-4, overcoming resistance, is an active, ongoing process. It's rarely an on/off phenomenon – especially not in the movies, where the resistance to change and the overcoming of that resistance play an important role in the narrative and drama. As such, there are often several calls to adventure, of various importance, as well as various resistance tactics deployed until eventually the hero reaches the point of decision and must choose.

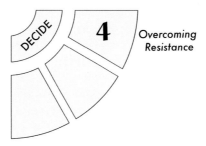

The Matrix: Neo meets Trinity and gets into her car. But he doesn't trust her, not helped by the fact that one of her colleagues has a gun on him. He decides to leave and opens the car door to leave. Trinity implores Neo to trust her. "Why?" he asks. Trinity explains: "Because you've been down that road. You know exactly where it ends. And I know that's not where you want to be." He closes the door and stays in the car. Overcoming resistance is as much a recognition that our current known world is no longer working and our rationalisations, self-justifications and lies to ourselves aren't either. We're approaching the moment when we will need to make a deliberate and conscious move to something else. Trinity's words hit home to Neo because he knows she's right. If he gets out of the car, he's back to square one: his dull life in the ordinary world in his soulless cubical at MetaCortex.

The Lord of the Rings: Frodo overcomes resistance with the help of Sam, and together they leave the Shire. On route, they meet Pippin and Merry who are running away from a farmer after stealing some vegetables. Pippin and Merry alternate between the role of ally and trickster throughout the film. They are all excited about the idea of an adventure, but none of them really appreciates what they are up against yet.

Star Wars: Luke returns home after speaking to Obi-Wan to find stormtroopers have burned their home down and both his uncle and aunt are dead. There is very little emotion from Luke in this scene; he simple looks away for a moment, perhaps sensing his destiny as a Jedi and the future adventure that awaits him. His resistance is overcome because he has no other choice.

Harry Potter: Hagrid encourages Harry to remember times where odd things have happened so he can recognise what he's telling him is the truth – he is a wizard. But Harry's still reluctant to accept the news, even though he desperately wants it to be true.

The Wizard of Oz: Dorothy's emotions and her desire for a different life, as well as the real threat to Toto, are powerful and are represented in the movie by the tornado which causes so much damage. She returns to an empty house. She's gone back even though she knew she probably shouldn't. There is still some resistance to her journey.

Often the guide, mentor or other archetype portrayed in film asks the hero to look within for the truth. And that truth is that the winds of change are blowing and a different future awaits.

The transition from step-4 to step-5

Overcoming resistance can happen in a heartbeat. It can result from a moment of clarity. Such a moment commonly occurs for people after they have hit rock bottom. Or it can be a gradual awakening after a series of signs or moments of synchronicity. In the movies, it tends to be the more dramatic, rock bottom, or explosive events that sweep away any lingering resistance. In real life, it is more commonly a gradual process. This awakening is different from the waking up at step-2 when news arrives that something is wrong. The awakening at step-4 is about the need to make a decision, not just understand the problem or accept that something is wrong. It is about ownership. Hence, once we have woken up at step-2, we now need to own up in step-4. We can't just meditate on the problem, think about things, reflect or acknowledge. That time has passed. We are now alive to the nature of change itself.

At step-4, we must own up to whether we understand what change is really about. We must look for clues. We may find that while we have overcome resistance to the principle of change, we can't actually point to any examples of where or when we deliberately change ourselves on the inside. Change may have happened as a result of circumstances, external to us. Or we may have changed something we are doing at work, in the 'IT' world of task and targets. But can we honestly identify something we have changed about who we are as a human being in the 'I' dimension?

If we can't, then we may have overcome resistance in theory but not practice. And to paraphrase Yogi Berra, "In theory, there is no difference between theory and practice; in practice there is."

In order to change anything, we must overcome resistance and commit to change. Taking the time to identify an example from our life where we deliberately changed ourselves can help to build our change confidence and the belief that we can change in practice.

Of course, part of the challenge with the transition from step-4 to step-5 may be status. If a leader has already reached the C-suite, they can argue that they are already successful. Such success can perpetuate or cement the expert mindset of step-3, where they already consider that they have 'made it'. If a leader is already successful, why should they bother changing anything? It's a good question. But in an accelerating world that is changing exponentially, the argument for 'business as usual' or no change is much less common now than it was even five years ago. Nowadays, the resistance is rarely theoretical: it's usually practical. And that usually means the resistance is attributed to time, timing or change capability.

Part of the challenge of change capability is a leader's 'IT' addiction. When we talk to leaders about change, they are often very quick to point out the things they are doing differently compared to a year ago. When we ask them to explain in what way their relationships have changed, they will cite examples of how they do different things with customers or with their staff. All of which are still in the 'IT' domain. If you look for genuine changes in the 'WE' dimension, such as levels of trust within the company, changes in culture or improvements in the strength of relationship bonds within the leadership team, they are much harder to come by. A leader's conceptualisation of change is 'IT' dominated. 'WE' change is much rarer.

This is interesting when we consider things like The Harvard Study of Adult Development, which has followed the lives of 724 men since 1938. Half of the subjects were sophomores at Harvard and the other half were from the most troubled and disadvantaged families in Boston's poorest neighbourhoods. Each year they would be interviewed about their work, home lives and health, and their health would be tested. Studies like this are extremely rare because of their longevity. And yet the results are conclusive: what makes a good life is not money or fame or an impressive job title or even good health – it is the quality of our relationships. Good relationships keep us healthier and happier, and yet this critical component of life is often dismissed in the clamour for the top job or the bigger house.[1]

If we press leaders for examples of their personal inner 'I' change and disallow changes in what they are doing in the 'IT' world, then we usually can't find much in this dimension either. In fact, bizarrely many leaders wear 'no-change' as a badge of honour. Such lack of change is often repackaged and sold as 'consistency' or even 'authenticity', when it's really a failure to develop. As philosopher Alain de Botton rightly points out, "If you're not embarrassed by who you were 12 months ago, you didn't learn enough." I would go further and say you've not developed enough.

Success is every bit as much about happiness as it is about wealth or any of the other 'IT' measures. And happiness is an 'I' and 'WE' phenomenon. There is a reason the trappings of success are called trappings! And it's the reason so many people who look successful on the outside feel trapped and are unable to push through change that could also make them happier and give their life more joy and meaning. They are not connected to their interior. If they are aware of their interior, they may not have a yardstick of how to measure progress. And even if they do have a yardstick, they don't have a playbook to help them move from one level to another.

Leaders have to become expert in the phenomenon of change in all three dimensions of 'I', 'WE' and 'IT', and a big part of that is how to overcome the inevitable and very natural resistance we all feel when we are being asked or expected to step off the cliff into the unknown world. Our reticence is inevitable because we are human. But change is also inevitable. We can either fear it and fight it, or we can embrace it and get proficient at it.

Questions to ask yourself

If you are unsure if you are in step-4, it can be helpful to ask yourself some questions:

- What will help me move faster?
- How well have I really let go?
- Do I really want to change?
- What is still holding me back?
- Am I really listening to my guide or coach?
- Am I really curious enough?

Gaining clarity on these questions can nudge you further and further toward step-5 and one of the most important moments on the entire journey – the moment of truth.

Note

1 Waldinger, R., (2015). *What makes a good life? Life lessons from the longest study on happiness.* TED Talk. Available from: www.ted.com/talks/robert_waldinger_what_makes_a_good_life_lessons_from_the_longest_study_on_happiness#t-171.

5   Step-5

Commitment

We must let go of the life we have planned,
so as to accept the one that is waiting for us.

(Joseph Campbell)

If we can successfully let go of fear and doubt and all the other phase one energies that are subsiding but still holding us at step-4, we eventually arrive at step-5,
the 'moment of truth'. This is the turning point in all journeys and a big deal for
everyone. This is the moment when a person finally commits to real change. If
they don't commit, they almost immediately regress to an earlier step. As Abraham
Maslow once said, "*In any given moment we have two options: to step forward into growth or to step
back into safety.*" Step-5 commitment is the step forward into growth.

Having overcome any remnants of resistance at step-4, we are in the heart of
the discovery phase. Everything was leading to this moment. The momentum we
gained as the resistance subsided in step-4 now slows as we reach the point of decision. We are clear about what needs to happen and why, we are fully aware of the
consequences should we retreat and so we now need to commit or, in Campbell's
language, "cross the threshold". This is the moment where an internal shift must
precede any real exterior change.

How do I know if I'm at step-5?

At step-5, there is a solid recognition that something has to change and, perhaps
more importantly, that we must drive that change. We must jump off the mountain
in our squirrel suit or go home. I like the metaphor of the squirrel suit because it
testifies to the courage you need at this moment. Once you jump off the mountain
into fresh air, everything changes. You are no longer on solid ground, and there is
literally no going back. Many people claim they have jumped but what they have
done is jump up and down whilst remaining on the mountainside. Indications that
you might be in step-5, ready to jump, include:

DOI: 10.4324/9781003170402-6

- A realisation that you are at a point of no return, a threshold of some sort. Something has broken, perhaps an illusion or your attachment or adherence to the status quo.
- You recognise that there is something about the situation that you have in the past denied or ignored. The situation is now untenable. You can see the issue clearly – perhaps for the first time.
- The choice is now very clear, binary – commit and move forward or go back. However, if you are truly in step-5, going back will feel impossible – even if it is preferable or less confronting in some way.
- A burning platform that demands commitment – a decision must be made one way or another.

When we commit, the moment of truth that triggers the commitment may be invisible, and the change that it provokes may also initially be invisible to others because it's often an internal process. But we can feel it. We literally see the situation before us with new eyes. Something is different, cracked or dissolved. In that moment, we are not the same person any more. It's almost like an internal re-calibration, where the past splits from the present and future.

Couples who marry and end up divorced can often point to a moment where they knew the marriage was over. Perhaps it was the realisation that their partner was never going to support their ambitions, or the recognition that they were having the exact same fight they always have or that their partner was never going to make them and their family a priority. Something either happens or the wishful thinking simply comes to an end, and they see the relationship for what it really is – over.

The same can happen in a friendship; the process is often very similar. Initially we only see our new friend's great qualities and amazing attributes. Eventually, we get a glimpse of a different person, but we put it down to stress or work challenges. Human beings tend to provide a fairly sizeable amount of latitude in relationships that matter to them. But sometimes, something happens, or the friend says something or does something that becomes 'the straw that breaks the camel's back', and in that moment we know the friendship has run its course.

In our professional life, the commitment step is the same. Something about the current reality becomes insufferable, and change becomes necessary. I remember when I committed to leave the business I was working for before I started Complete. I vividly recall standing in my garden at home in Romsey. Things had been getting worse and worse over the previous months. I was vacillating about what to do. With hindsight, I had been working my way through step-2, step-3 and step-4. I had been telling myself for weeks that, as dysfunctional as the business was, things were familiar and there were plenty of resources. We did good work. But in that moment, none of my fabricated justifications mattered. I just knew it was over and I needed to get out. I was also well aware of the isolation of my position. I knew it was up to me to take action and exit the business. I could almost feel myself pull away and separate from my past. The decision was made; the change was done. All I had to do now was execute that change externally.

This pulling away from the past is an important part of step-5. We see this separation enacted and ritualised in various rites of passage around the world.

Rites of passage

The break with the past at these moments of truth are so significant to most cultures that many have developed ritualised ceremonies to mark such transitions. I've always been personally fascinated with rites of passage and how they take so many different forms in different parts of the world – some simple, some highly complex. In Western teenage culture, the prom ritualises the transition from high school to college. In some African tribes we see the 'jumping the cow' ritual to prove bravery and physical prowess. In some cultures the rite of passage is more religious, such as the Jewish bar mitzvah, where the boy becomes a man. Native American fathers take their sons into the wilderness where they are left alone to experience their 'vision' (a glimpse of their future purpose or calling) or simply to survive the night. Historically, if the boy returned (and they didn't always) the boy was considered a man and helped by the elders to fulfil his vision.

> As you go the way of life,
> You will see a great chasm. Jump.
> It is not as wide as you think.
>
> Advice given to native American boys at their initiation

At the first sign of menstruation, girls born into the Nootka tribe of the Vancouver Islands were taken by an elder woman far out to sea, where she would be left in the ocean, bleeding and naked. If she managed to swim to shore, then she had proven herself as a woman.

Many ethnologists and anthropologists have built their career around documenting these cultural rites of passage. All such examples testify to the fact that step-5 is one of the most significant moments of change in all societies. An individual crosses the threshold from the known world of childhood into the unknown world of adulthood.

Anthropologist Arnold van Gennep was the first to discuss the concept of rites of passage in his book of the same name published in 1908. He suggested that rites of passage were subdivided into three sub-categories: rites of separation, transition rites and rites of incorporation. These may appear as phases in one overall rite of passage or be individual rites. The purpose is to allow the individual to face death in some terrible or scary situation. The person faces their fears, therefore cheats death and experiences resurrection as they are reborn as a new member of the group. We can see this in the native American tradition as well as some hazing rituals in university fraternities and secret societies.

Anthropologist Victor Turner took van Gennep's model and emphasised the separation rites, suggesting that there was a limbo where the person's identity was temporarily suspended between separation and incorporation. And, of course, Joseph Campbell's The Hero's Journey is itself a rite of passage as the hero moves from the known world to the unknown world and returns to offer something new and better. It is step-5 commitment and crossing the threshold that heralds the willing, conscious, albeit nervous step into the unknown.

Rites of passage herald a significant change. There is no going back. There is no return to childhood – even if we want to. Such rituals mark the transition by public acknowledgement, and they explicitly recognise the change.

Although rites of passage have often been passed down through generations and cultures to help individuals transition from one group to the next (adult to child, single to married, civilian to the military), many of the modern adventure activities are tapping into this urge to 'face death' and survive. Take bungee jumping, base jumping or white water rafting as examples. In many cultures, especially Western cultures, rites of passage have died out or been highly stylised or homogenised to the point where they have lost their true meaning. Adventure sports have, to some extent, filled that void. There are now very few times in a modern life where we do actually face death, move to the edge and physically experience the fear and push past to recognise ourselves as someone else, altered in some way by the experience. Marriage may be a transition from single to married, and we may pledge our commitment in front of our friends and family, but the statistics on divorce tell us it's not the type of pledge or commitment it once was. In addition, there is no fear to surmount, although the threat of alcohol-fuelled indiscretion or chaos on a stag or hen night may create a moment of anxiety. But marriage for the vast majority of people is a happy occasion. And yet, human beings still crave that visceral moment of truth, the choice to jump or not jump.

Even a cursory look on YouTube of video footage of first-time bungee jumpers allows us to see the whole process up close and personal. In many ways, it's a living demonstration of the Kubler-Ross grief curve. First, the denial, "Oh this is going to be a blast." The bravado as the individual is put into the gear. The silence as the weight of what's about to happen becomes apparent, followed by the anger and how it doesn't matter if they don't do it. It's not that big a deal anyway. Bargaining follows, as they ask a million questions of the guy securing the ropes and look for ways to evade or minimise the fear. "What if I jump backwards – will that help?" Then there is just flat-out fear and panic. The recognition that there is no escape without looking foolish in front of the camera. All bravado has disappeared. A calm descends as the jumper accepts their fate. We can almost see a switch being flicked in their head; they walk to the edge of the platform and jump. Screams of joy, facilitated by a flood of adrenaline, follow. The integration occurs over the next few days as they quietly muse, "I can't believe I did that."

There is something very liberating about commitment. We jump or we don't jump. That's it. For many people, these experiences act as anchor points in their life in much the same way that ancient rites of passage did for people of other cultures. They act as a permanent reminder of the person's ability to reinvent themselves and create a new future. They commit to doing something they are terrified of and live to tell the tale. They faced death and survived; it's a moment of immortality and rebirth at the same time. The creation of a new identity. Besides, if it wasn't genuinely hard and terrifying then it wouldn't have the powerful impact that is necessary to propel us forward.

How does it feel to be at step-5?

There is usually a ramp up of anxiety prior to the commitment of step-5. This is essentially the last push. What follows is a short period of isolation and a moment of feeling profoundly alone. The key thing to remember here is that when we are in step-5, we *are* alone. No one else can really help or push us into a decision – it's up to us.

There's a fork in the road: one way leads to a re-engagement with the resistance and delusion of earlier steps and the other leads to commitment and, ultimately, progress. When we choose commitment, we often feel a sense of solidity and resolve. It feels right. It may not be pleasant, and it may not be comfortable, but it's right.

Often there is also a feeling of liberation. It can be a relief to reach this point. After all the waiting, we can finally lay down the resistance and accept the situation honestly and bluntly. Of course, the liberation and exhilaration rarely last, because commitment is one thing but execution is another. But we do need that rush of energy we get when we cross the threshold to propel us to step-6.

Everything up to step-5 is designed to build towards the moment of truth. It's like a pressure cooker, and once the decision is made the pressure is released and a serene peace can descend – at least for a while. It's almost as though we are coming to terms with a separation of some sort, a separation from some part of ourselves, our past or present that must change.

This sense of separation from the situation, at least internally, is crucial because it represents a moving away from something that is simply not working anymore. And yet, for the impending change to stick and really take us to a new place, we also need to move towards something better.

If we are simply trying to get away from someone, something, an environment or a situation, the risk is that we only change the external circumstances. If so, nothing changes on the inside, and the change will not sustain. We will start to feel the same pain again. If we don't have any idea of what we are moving towards we will lose momentum, progress will stall and we may, like Icarus, fall back down to earth. Crossing the threshold successfully requires us to move away from our old Self and seek our new Self. If we don't realise this, we will discover the truth of the old adage that "wherever I go, there I am".

The only time the commitment changes anything is when we recognise that we are the thing that needs to change. Real commitment is a commitment to be a different person in some way. We can change the environment or the people we interact with, but unless something happens inside of us, nothing is ever going to really change.

Ultimately, step-5 is about the 'I' change. We are called to recognise that something about us must change in order to make way for something new. If we don't change on the inside, the new environment will morph into a worse version of the situation we just left.

There's a lovely story about two travellers that illustrates this reality perfectly. The first traveller has been walking for days, and he comes to the outskirts of a town. As he reaches the crest of a hill just above the town, he encounters an old woman at the side of the road selling fruit and water. The man stops to buy a couple of apples. "Tell me," he asks the woman, "what are the people like in the town down there?" The old woman looks up and asks, "What were the people like in the last town you visited?" "Oh, they were terrible." the man exclaims. "They were rude and impatient. That's why I left." The woman adds, "Well, I'm sorry to have to tell you but the people in this town are much the same." The first traveller sighs in frustration and walks off towards the town.

An hour or so later a second traveller reaches the top of the hill outside the same town and also stops at the old woman's stall to buy some water and apples. "Tell me," he asks the woman, "what are the people like in this town?" The old woman looks up again and asks, "What were the people like in the last town you visited?" "Oh, there were wonderful." the man effuses. "They were kind and generous. I was sad to leave." The woman adds, "I'm sure you will find the people in this town much the same." The second traveller smiles, thanks the old woman and walks off towards the town.

Wherever you go, there you are!

The real journey is the 'I' journey, the interior journey. For a commitment to stick and the change to be realised, there has to be an 'I' change. Without it, any 'WE' or 'IT change is unlikely to sustain.

State change vs level change

Real commitment tends to be a visceral experience rather than a rational experience. The heightened anxiety and sense of loneliness of step-5 amplify the senses. It can be very intense, and it's certainly something we feel rather than think.

However, this visceral component can muddy the waters because crossing the threshold is not just about "feeling the fear and doing it anyway". Step-5 requires you to feel the fear and change your Self, and by this I don't just mean change your state, I mean change who you are. This means changing your level not just your state. The confusion between the state change and level change is the main stumbling block to truly crossing the threshold.

It was Jean Piaget, a Swiss psychologist known for his work on child development, that first alerted the world to 'levels' of development. He wrote beautifully about how all children progress through various levels or phases of development that are facilitated by their rapid brain development. Ken Wilber and many other developmental academics have taken the idea of levels of development further and clarified that it isn't just children who progress through well-defined levels of development; adults do too. It's therefore possible to be euphoric and believe that you have made a commitment when all you've really done is change state and become more skilful at your current level (i.e., nothing significant has changed, only your emotional state and only temporarily).

Some years ago, I was approached by the CFO of a major multi-national consultancy. She said, "We need your help with one of our leaders. We don't know whether to promote her or fire her."

"That's very interesting." I said. "Why do you say that?"

"Well," the CFO said, "she's one of the largest fee earners in our London office, but we have five grievance procedures around her."

"On no, don't tell me Margaret, you gave her a coach, didn't you?"

"Yes" the CFO said, "I did."

"And the coach taught her some skills, didn't she?"

"Yes." the CFO said.

"It's just made her a more effective bully, hasn't it?" I said.

"That's exactly what's happened." the CFO said. "Before, she used to get really angry and rant at her staff. Now she's learnt how not to be that angry, but she still bullies them, just in a much more subtle way." the CFO said.

"Well," I said, "that's because she hasn't learnt the difference between state change and level change. It's good to manage your anger, but if that isn't part of you levelling up and becoming a more emotionally intelligent human being, then all that happens is you make people more skilful bullies."

In that moment the CFO appreciated that there is a world of a difference between standard skills-based coaching and coaching that is specifically designed to help leaders level up and become more mature human beings. This distinction requires us to appreciate the difference between vertical development, which adds levels of ability to a human being, and horizontal learning, which adds knowledge or state change and simply addresses an individual emotion at any given time without understanding that there are levels to emotional intelligence that go way beyond simple state management.

Levelling up or level change is a game changer; state change is not.

We can move from cheerful to grumpy, scared to euphoric – that is a state change. State change has long been confused with level change. Ken Wilber has written extensively about this confusion in his 850-page tome about the future of all the great traditions.[1] As Ken points out, most religions were founded when the only thing available to them was state changes. These religions were born thousands of years ago, long before Piaget pointed out the importance of levels of development. So, most religions used state change to try to provoke a spiritual experience or pursue 'enlightenment'.

Most religions have practices that create an altered state of consciousness through prayer, chanting or even whirling like a dervish where the individual spins around so much they enter an altered state. These experiences, or something similar, can also happen at a meditation retreat. I have personally seen 'trainers' run breathwork classes that teach people to hyperventilate until they dropped their CO_2 levels so much they induce vasospasm in their own brain, while the trainer claims they are having a spiritual experience, when all that was really happening was a dangerously uncontrolled alteration of intracellular calcium in the smooth muscles of the blood vessels in their brain, causing reduced blood supply and an altered state of consciousness.

Of course, such state experiences can feel powerful – profound even. I remember as a medical student I took part in a group meditation chanting exercise where 50 people sat in a room, chanting in a low sound, which when combined with everyone else created this gentle thumping reverberation in my chest cavity that generated a deep sense of connectivity with those around me in a quasi-spiritual experience. It was a state change, and once it was over it was over. There was no paradigm shift in my level of comprehension of myself, the world around me or the meaning of reality. I did not change as a human being. I was not more insightful or more mature, but I did have a state change.

Luckily for me, I recognised the difference between state and level change early on in my career. But those who fail to make this distinction run the risk of imbuing state changes they experience with inflated meaning. When they alter their state of consciousness, they can start to believe they are somehow better, smarter or more enlightened, when all that really happened is they consciously shifted how they felt in that moment. They may feel extraordinary, and those who practise may feel closer to God, but it's a state change not a level change. Nothing about that individual's interior 'I' has really shifted.

Until Piaget explained the importance of levels of development, most people didn't even understand there was such a thing as level change. At step-5, many confuse state change for level change and believe they are making progress when they are actually still stuck at step-5, albeit euphorically!

When someone truly commits, they experience both – a state change *and* a level change. They have crossed a threshold and are different in some way, like the person who jumps off the cliff in a squirrel suit or the person who loses their virginity. Something is different, and there is no going back. They can't un-jump or get their virginity back. At step-5, the change has started but hasn't yet really take hold. All that has happened is a change in commitment. The real work of change is yet to come. And before any work starts we need to prepare, which is exactly what step-6 is about.

Cultural metaphors

Joseph Campbell called step-5 "crossing the threshold". Here, the hero stands at the threshold of a new adventure and they are being invited into a new unknown world. Doubts have been expressed at step-4, the initial fear when approaching the moment of truth at step-5 has subsided and the hero is now free to enjoy a few moments of peace and quiet before crossing. In the movies, as in life, there are many thresholds to cross.

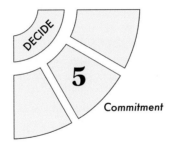

The Matrix: This film has probably encapsulated the greatest metaphor for the threshold moment. After Neo decides to stay in the car, Trinity removes the tracking worm that he believed was a bad dream and takes him to Morpheus. Morpheus talks to him as though he can read his mind: "Let me tell you why you are here. You're here because you know something. What you know you can't explain, but you feel it. You've felt it your entire life. That there's something wrong with the world. You don't know what it is, but it's there. Like a splinter in your mind, driving you mad. It is this feeling that has brought you to me." This is the famous red and blue pill scene. Although Morpheus explains to Neo what the matrix is, he adds that no one can be told what it is, they have to see if for themselves, and offers him a choice. Once made there is no turning back. Take the blue pill and the story will end. Neo will wake up in his bed and can believe whatever he wants to believe. Or take the red pill and he "stays in wonderland" and Morpheus will show him "how deep the rabbit hole goes". Neo takes the red pill. He's committed to the truth – no going back. Morpheus' reference to the rabbit hole continues the nod to *Alice in Wonderland* which started when Neo was asked to "follow the white rabbit". This reference reinforces the cultural power of the metaphor by anchoring it to other well-known cultural metaphors.

The Lord of the Rings: Frodo and Sam cross the threshold when they agree to leave the Shire. Before leaving to travel on ahead, Gandalf warns Frodo to never put the ring on. Having picked up Merry and Pippin as they travel out of the Shire, Sam says, "This is it. If I take one more step it will be the farthest away from home I have ever been." Frodo reassures him. He reminds him of what Bilbo used to say: "Remember it's a dangerous business, Frodo, going out your door. You step onto the road, and if you don't keep your feet there's no knowing where you might be swept off to." A second threshold moment occurs when the hobbits glimpse the unknown world they are about to enter when they have a close encounter with the Ringwraiths, who are hunting for the ring. The four hobbits realise for the first time what may be ahead of them as they cross the threshold at the ford of Rivendell, leaving the known world of the Shire behind them.

Star Wars: There are many mini-threshold moments in Star Wars. For example, Luke committing to training as a Jedi is a threshold moment, but Luke encountering the strange new world in the Mos Eisley cantina is probably the most iconic threshold moment in the entire series. As viewers, we cross the threshold into the cantina a few moments before Luke does. We see the whole array of, literally, alien creatures from all over the universe before Luke does. After we adjust to the weirdness, we then see Luke's reaction as he crosses the threshold and enters the cantina. Luke has to grow up fast as his life is immediately threatened.

Harry Potter: Hagrid takes Harry to the back of the Leaky Cauldron pub and taps the wall, which moves. Harry then crosses the threshold and enters the world of magic for the very first time in the wizardly mysteries of Diagon Alley.

The Wizard of Oz: Dorothy crosses the threshold as a result of the tornado picking up her house in the monochrome world of Kansas and literally dropping her and her dog Toto in the strange new full-colour world of Oz. The switch from black and white to colour is a metaphor for crossing the threshold. When she lands, she immediately meets the threshold guardians, which are the Munchkins, and Glinda, the Good Witch of the North.

The transition from step-5 to step-6

After crossing the threshold not much is different, and everything is different. The hero has made a decision and is in a new world, but the real journey has only just begun. In a leadership setting, this new world requires a completely new way of operating. This is about changing your mindset from 'predict and control' to 'sense and respond'. In the old world, many leaders invest an incredible amount of time scenario planning, predicting every future eventuality, building contingency plans for each and trying to control the outcome. But in a world that is now changing so rapidly, where knowledge is doubling every year, where machine learning, AI and pandemic-induced digital transformations are disrupting everything, this 'predict and control' approach is woefully inadequate as a way of managing the future. Many organisations waste extraordinary time and resources perpetually forecasting and re-forecasting. A much wiser approach to the uncertainty is to develop sensory capability.

Predicting is a fool's game; just look at the impact of COVID-19. Everyone watched the news with vague interest about a virus that was spreading in China. Very few people saw the global ramifications. Even 18 months on from those early reports, it was impossible to predict what would happen health wise, never mind the economic fallout. What's needed is much greater agility, so we can adapt and respond to the world as it unfolds. And such agility requires the ability to sense instantaneously how things are changing and respond accordingly.

As we move from the commitment to change in step-5, we start to prepare for change in step-6. A critical part of this preparation is to prepare a new mindset for a new world. This means much greater levels of openness and curiosity. We need to pay better attention to the signs and signals so that we can interpret them more accurately. We must sense the winds of change. Look for proof that the choices we continually make move us in the direction we desire. We must avoid digging in. We must stop self-justifying, blaming and casting doubt. We must hone our change capability for this new world. Sense the impact of our choices and respond continually to that sensory data.

In this new world, we must become truly response-able. Own up to our own short-comings, have the humility to admit we may be wrong and change who we are, how we relate and what we are doing all the time. The leadership winners of the future will be those who can sense and respond with great agility.

Questions to ask yourself

If you are unsure if you are in step-5, it can be helpful to ask yourself some questions:

- Am I ready to change?
- Do I want to change?
- Do I want to discover how far I can go?
- Has the frustration reached a point where I am prepared to do whatever it takes to really succeed?
- Do I really believe I can develop, heal, change my life, or was I just kidding myself?
- Do I trust my guide and their stories of change?

Use the answers to strengthen your resolve and pique your interest at what's going to be needed for the change journey ahead.

Note

1 Wilber, K., (2017). *The religion of tomorrow: A vision for the future of great traditions.* Colorado: Shambhala.

6 Step-6

Prepare for change

Sit in a room and read—and read and read.
And read the right books by the right people.
Your mind is brought onto that level, and you have a
nice, mild, slow-burning rapture all the time.

(Joseph Campbell)

At step-6, we are no longer in limbo; we have decided, and what we must do now is prepare for what that decision will bring. We are in the new world, but we have yet to learn the ways of the new world. Step-6, then, is the prequel to the main event of the next phase and the trials and tribulations that lie ahead. Step-6 in many ways is a mini-respite from the intensity of what just happened. We are packing our bags for the climb, for the adventure we have decided to take, and we are looking around for what we may need. The resources we seek are both internal and external.

To succeed in our journey, we must prepare to learn *and* develop. We can't develop if we don't first learn. As such, there will be an acquisition of skills, knowledge and experience (learning), but we must also prepare to deploy those new skills, knowledge and experience to move up to another level (development). Learning alone does not step change capability; it's the daily deployment of that learning and the fine tuning of that learning that converts learning into development. We must convert knowledge into wisdom, theory into practice. A critical part of that preparation is to deeply understand the difference, and that is a step-6 activity.

We initially explored the difference between horizontal learning and vertical development in step-3. Both are important on the change journey. They ensure the change sticks and capability is enhanced with each revolution of the Change Wheel. Step-6 is where we operationalise that difference as we come to understand that the difference between theory and practice is nothing in theory and everything in practice.

The first step of practice is to identify what additional learning we need, and then we must practise in order to convert that learning into vertical developmental progress.

DOI: 10.4324/9781003170402-7

How do I know if I'm at step-6?

In step-6, we are excited to get going, but we realise we need time to prepare. We have made the commitment to change and are now assessing ourselves and our environment to work out whether we have the skills and resources to execute the change successfully. Indications that you might be in step-6 include:

- A realisation that you are ill-equipped for the journey ahead.
- A recognition that you need access to more resources, either people, tools, skills, knowledge or inner resolve.
- A recognition that you don't yet have enough energy for what lies ahead.
- A willingness to prepare yourself, literally and metaphorically.

In our personal life, step-6 may include the recognition that we are missing key information or a different perspective that might help us break through and overcome our current challenges. Step-6 is the point where couples may seek out counselling to address the problems in their relationship. One or both parties recognise that something is wrong, or something has changed, but they may be unsure what it is or, more importantly, how to get the relationship back on track. They realise that perhaps they need additional information, insight or third party objectivity to illuminate a path for them that they can't see because they are too involved. If the commitment made in step-5 was not that the relationship was entering a new phase but that the relationship was over, then step-6 is about preparations for change including research on alternative accommodation, how to manage shared childcare, etc. Step-6 is everything we do between the internal commitment to change at step-5 and the external execution of that commitment in step-7.

In our professional life, step-6 can also take many forms. The performance review process may highlight learning gaps or professional shortcomings that must be addressed. When assessing where we are in our career development, it may become clear that we lack the technical or leadership capabilities to progress. Step-6, therefore, often involves leadership assessment and what we may need to improve our chances of promotion. This is also the moment when many leaders or senior executives embrace the idea of coaching.

Step-6 is about taking the time to consider what capabilities we need, what resources (internal and external) we may be missing to make the changes needed to succeed at the next level. As such, high-quality assessment of our current level of development is critical if we want to prepare ourselves well for the journey ahead. We need to know exactly where we are now, what resources we already have and what resources we need to acquire to ensure success.

Behaviours needed to master step-6

There's an old adage that if we "fail to plan then we plan to fail". At step-6, we need to plan what behaviours we'll need to develop at step-7. Fortunately, of the thousands of potential behaviours leaders may need, Harry Schroder, from the University of Florida, and Tony Cockerill, from the London School of Economics, identified which ones really matter in driving organisational success. They studied businesses that were experiencing a huge *number* of unpredictable changes, large and small, as well as organisations that were experiencing many different *types* of changes. Their research pin-pointed the behaviours that really matter and their practical applications.

Schroder and Cockerill found[12] that there were only 11 leadership behaviours or "letters in the behavioural alphabet", which means all the thousands of potential behaviours are either one of these eleven or combinations of these eleven "letters". This is akin to the four base pairs in our DNA that make up all of our genes. These eleven "letters" are organised into four distinct sequential clusters, with three behaviours in each cluster and two in the last cluster as illustrated by Figure 6.1.

Step-6 is where we have commited to change, looking ahead and imagining life in the new world. In doing so, we envisage the journey and what we need for that journey to ensure we arrive at our chosen destination.

Imagine

The 'imagine cluster' describes the key three behaviours needed to execute the changes at the beginning of the journey. Information needs to be gathered, and the idea of change must be constructed before we can actually change anything. The three behaviours in the imagine cluster are:

1 **Seeking information** – are we able to gather the information we need to change ourselves? What's missing? What do we need to learn?
2 **Forming concepts** – once we have gathered the right information, how well can we marshal it into a workable idea and map the journey of change that lies ahead?
3 **Conceptual flexing** – once we have created a basic idea of change, how well can we develop additional ideas and not become overly stuck on just one path ahead? Can we fine tune our approach and flex our thinking as we encounter the reality of the journey?

Preparing for change is all about gathering resources. We may need inner 'I' resources, such as greater courage, increased insightfulness, better reflectiveness, more openness or appreciation; we may need others or 'WE' resources, engaging the help of a 'Sherpa' or experts for a specific part of the journey can make all the difference. These 'WE' resources may include our partner or business colleagues who will be involved in the change process or people in our network that we may need to draw on. Thinking about our network and reaching out to the right people who can guide us on the journey is vital. Many leaders are quite resistant to asking for help. This can impair their ability to drive change. Some of the best change agents in history take the exact opposite approach, exhibiting insane curiosity and polymathic tendencies. One study of the world's most influential scientists, for

IMPLEMENT	IMAGINE
Maximise operatoinal efficiency and enable organizational change to deliver commercial performance and customer value	Take a broad and deep view of the commercial context that ensures vision and strategy create competitive advantage
Being Proactive	Seeking Information
Continuously Improving	Forming CoNcepts
-	Conceptual FleXing

IGNITE	INVOLVE
Connect with people to release their commitment, enthusiasm and support for ideas, plans and strategies that take the business forward	Fully engage and develop individuals and teams to build trust, nurture potential and get the best out of people
Transmitting Impactfully	Empathic Connecting
Building Confidence	Facilitating Interaction
Influencing Others	Developing People

Figure 6.1 The eleven letters of the 'behavioural alphabet'.

example, revealed that 15 of the top 20 were polymaths.[3] Clearly, polymaths can be very effective in delivering change.

In addition to 'I' and 'WE' resources, we will also need 'IT' resources for the journey. 'IT' resources vary widely depending on what sort of change we are trying to achieve. Climbing Mount Everest requires very different equipment compared to changing our commercial strategy, building deeper levels of trust in a team or growing our own capability.

How does it feel to be at step-6?

Left to our own devices, it can feel unsettling to be at step-6. There is a simultaneous sense of urgency and uncertainty. The urgency comes with knowing we have committed to change, but we are not yet living that change. We may have left the known world, but we are not yet in the new world, and we are often not sure how to get there or whether we have what we need to get there.

That said, it can also be exciting. Depending on how long we were stuck in earlier steps, there may also be a sense of relief that finally we are moving forward.

There is a renewed sense of possibility, hope and curiosity about the future that we may not have felt for some time. When curiosity trumps fear or uncertainty, there is an openness to the possibility of change, to our own discovery, potential insight and the journey ahead. This could also be called the growth mindset or the art of the possible.

Appreciation

Although learning is crucial at step-6, we don't always deploy what we learn. In fact, research has shown that we often need to hear something seven times before it really lands and we *use* the information.

One of the ways to accelerate our progress and shorten the information-to-deployment cycle is to cultivate the art of appreciation. We must first learn to appreciate in order to appreciate what we learn.

Most of us are unfamiliar and unskilled in the art of appreciation. Why? Because most people have spent years judging themselves, creating a belief that they are, in some way, not enough. Not smart enough, not rich enough, not resourceful enough, not good looking enough, not successful enough, not thin enough – the list is endless. This is a widespread belief. We are brainwashed into believing we are in some way inadequate and unworthy. Such faulty code is baked into our brain from an early age, without our permission, and then directs our life forever until we wake up to the fact that the faulty code is faulty and unhelpful.

Everyone has baggage or faulty code – even those who were brought up in a secure, loving and stable home. Most children reach adulthood and don't really feel that great about themselves. Many children journey through the phases of:

1   I'm not OK, you're OK to
2   I'm not OK, you're not OK to

3   I'm OK, you're not OK before they finally reach the
4   I'm OK you're OK stage.[4]

Our belief that something is missing or something is wrong with us blinds us to our own brilliance. We often fail to see how genuinely astonishing we really are. The human body and human systems can do amazing things, but most people don't really appreciate that. And they certainly don't appreciate the skills and the capabilities they already have.

As Marcel Proust said, "The real voyage of discovery is not in seeking new landscapes, but in having new eyes." In other words, instead of focusing on what is missing or what we lack, which keeps us locked in negativity and drains our energy, perhaps it's time to flip the equation and practise the art of appreciation so we acknowledge and honour what we are already.

I remember sharing the Proust quote with a 55-year-old CEO. He told me how the quote reminded him of his four-year-old grandson. His grandson had come to stay for the weekend, and on Sunday morning the boy climbed into bed with him. He snuggled up to his 'grandpa' and promptly fell back to sleep. As this CEO watched his grandson sleep, he witnessed the magical moment when the little boy woke up again. The joy and sheer delight on the boy's face when he realised he was awake and had another day available to play was a real wake-up call for the CEO. The CEO thought, "Shit, when was the last time I felt like that?"

He realised that he'd lost the simple joy and appreciation of being alive. In that moment, he was able to see his life with new eyes. The journey of discovery was not in new landscapes but in those new eyes that his grandson had shown him he needed.

There is a related concept to this Proust quote in Zen Buddhism called the beginner's mind. The idea is that we should approach everything in life with an attitude of openness, eagerness and freedom from preconceptions. The idea is not that we are a complete beginner in all situations, rather that we see each moment of our life with fresh eyes. It's that state of appreciation, curiosity, awe and wonder that allows us to absorb learning superfast. Appreciation is not just a better place to operate from because it feeds our spirit and gives us energy, it's extremely useful as a skill when preparing for change. Remember, first we must learn to appreciate in order to appreciate what we learn. If we can't appreciate things in general, then we are likely to need to hear something seven times before we can action that learning. Appreciation significantly shortens the learning-to-deployment timeframe.

The change journey, regardless of the type of change, will require new learning. The faster we can learn the quicker we can make progress, and appreciation is rocket fuel for our progress.

Appreciation skill

Human beings habituate to things very quickly. It's easy for us to start taking things for granted. If we don't take the time to consciously focus on the things and appreciate the moment, we will almost certainly ignore what's of value in our lives. One of the positive unintended consequences of COVID-19 was that many people felt a renewed sense of gratitude for health workers, delivery drivers and many relatively low paid workers in society. We also found a new level of appreciation for some of the simple pleasures in life, like spending time with those we love.

The appreciation skill is designed to make us much more conscious of the many things in our life that we should give thanks for on a daily basis. The process may seem simple or even trite, but it's an antidote to self-judgement, which is a massive drain on our energy. Learning to appreciate ourselves helps create the foundation from which we can better appreciate others, as well as the ups and downs of life.

Appreciation exercise

Make a list of all the things you appreciate about yourself. These things are true about you whether you have a good day or a bad day. Learning to appreciate yourself enables others to see the good in you too.

To make this exercise easier, think about what you appreciate about yourself across six distinct areas:

- Mentally – What do you appreciate about your mental abilities?
- Emotionally – What do you appreciate about yourself emotionally?
- Physically – What aspects of your physical attributes or abilities do you appreciate?
- Socially – What do you appreciate about your social skills and how you interact with others?
- Professionally – What do you appreciate about your professional skills and capacity?
- Spiritually – What do you appreciate about yourself spiritually, ethically or morally?

Psychologist Sonja Lyubomirsky from the University of California at Riverside found that people who took the time to count their blessings, even just once a week, significantly increased their overall satisfaction with life.[5] Psychologist Robert Emmons from the Davis campus of the same university also found that gratitude

MENTALLY	PHYSICALLY	PROFESSIONALLY
Thoughtful	Healthy	Dedicated
Quick witted	Eat well	Knowledgable
-	-	-

EMOTIONALLY	SOCIALLY	SPIRITUALLY
Supportive	Interested in others	Inner calm
Sensitive	Outgoing	Connected
-	-	-

Figure 6.2 Example of Appreciation.

(which is the favourite cousin to appreciation) improved physical health and increased energy levels and, for patients with neuromuscular disease, relieved pain and fatigue. Emmons added, "The ones who benefited most tended to elaborate more and have a wider span of things they're grateful for." [6]

You may decide to practise appreciation while you are in the shower in the morning or when you sit down for a coffee or for lunch. You may decide to reflect and appreciate your day before dinner and share these thoughts with those around you to consolidate the habit. Or keep them to yourself. Once you get into the rhythm of self-appreciation, you will be better able to appreciate others, even those you don't naturally warm to. This, in turn, will also allow you to better find the positives in even the toughest situations or events.

Cultural metaphors

Step-6 is the preparation. The hero must ready themselves for the change ahead. This might include making their way to a certain location or finding resources or help for the journey. Most of the enduring films that follow Campbell's mono-myth narrative arc spend some time at step-6 preparing their hero for the trials that await at step-7 and beyond. This is a very relatable part of the story because most of us realise that we can achieve very little without putting the work in and preparing for the journey.

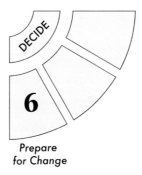

Prepare for Change

The Matrix: Before Neo fully enters the Matrix, he engages in an agent training programme with Morpheus. This is a construct room designed to teach freed operatives the rules of the new world. Morpheus accompanies Neo to explain how the training programme works and shows him what he will need to know and use when he finally enters the Matrix. They walk around a crowded urban street, like the one Neo will encounter in the Matrix, where Neo bumps into people in largely dull coloured clothes, except for the woman in the red dress. Morpheus asks if Neo finds her distracting, which he does. Morpheus asks him to look again, and she turns out to be the threat that Morpheus is trying to teach Neo to be aware of. The metaphor is that if you stop paying attention, the Matrix will sedate you and you will disappear. In this new world of the Matrix, Neo will need all his inner resources, namely his wits about him.

The Lord of the Rings: Frodo Baggins is an everyman hero. He lacks the wisdom of Elrond, the bravery of Aragon or the powers of Gandalf. But he does possess inner resources, namely common sense, a good heart and the determination to do his best, and as Gandalf often points out "hobbits are tougher than they look". On his near year-long quest to destroy the ring he inherited from his cousin Bilbo, Frodo relies on the 'WE' resources of Samwise Gamgee as well as Merry and Pippin. The main 'IT' resource available to Frodo is the ring itself, and early on he wears the ring at critical moments to make himself invisible and save his own life. But he learns this 'IT' resource can have dangerous consequences, and he battles with its addictive powers until he realises that this is not something he should rely on.

Star Wars: Luke prepares for his life ahead by going through training at the Jedi Temple on Coruscant. The key 'IT' resource he acquires is his lightsabre. The inner 'I' resource Luke needs is to be able to feel the Force, but he's also trained to resist interrogation, the temptations of the dark side of the Force and mind probes.

Harry Potter: Harry's preparation for his new life largely takes place in Diagon Alley. He gathers all the provisions he will need for Hogwarts. Central to the journey ahead is the key resource for all wizards – a wand. Harry tests many until he finds the one for him: a wand made of holly with a phoenix feather core. Harry is kitted out with the clothes he will need; he buys 'every-flavour beans', bubble gum, 'chocolate frogs' and 'cauldron cakes', all provisions for the train ride. He purchases a pet owl, Hedwig; he acquires a whole range of books including one on magical theory by Adalbert Waffling. He meets his 'WE' resources on the Hogwarts' Express – Ron Weasley and Hermione Granger, who become Harry's best friends and allies. In addition to these 'IT' resources, Hagrid reminds Harry that he will need 'I' resources: specifically, an open mind, an open heart and wizarding courage.

The Wizard of Oz: Dorothy acquires a few 'IT' resources for her adventure on the yellow brick road. She is given a pair of silver slippers, a reference to silver (slippers) replacing gold (yellow brick road) as a monetary standard at that time. It was MGM who changed Dorothy's footwear to ruby slippers for the film. But the story majors on the 'WE' resources Dorothy needs for her journey. She gathers three key companions, who themselves are on their own journey to become whole again. The Tinman needs a heart, the Lion needs to find courage and the Scarecrow needs a brain. Dorothy realises she will also need inner 'I' resources of hope and optimism for her journey. The iconic song "Somewhere Over the Rainbow" is a dream of a better tomorrow and what lies ahead of them.

Despite being written in 1900, The Wizard of Oz has endured as a cultural metaphor because it's an allegory for humanity. Its author, L Frank Baum, was writing about the conditions in America at the turn of the 20th century. The Scarecrow represented the farmers who had seen crop prices drop by 50 per cent, and people thought they were too simple (without a brain) to do anything about it. At that time, it was felt that factory and railroad workers were oblivious to the famer's plight, hence the

Tinman without a heart. And politicians, represented by the Lion, were without the courage to change things.[7]

The transition from step-6 to step-7

The transition from step-6 to step-7 is all about momentum. Once we are confident, we have the provisions and resources we need and we are pregnant with expectation and ready for the journey to begin in earnest.

And the journey of a thousand miles starts with the first step. The truth is we have taken many steps already, but until we get some way down the path and experience the adventures and challenges that lie ahead, it may feel like we haven't really moved. The transition from preparation to action is no more complex than putting one foot in front of another. Once we start moving, the trepidation we may have felt melts away.

Questions to ask yourself

If you are unsure if you are in step-6, it can be helpful to ask yourself some questions:

*   Do I have what I need?
*   Am I ready?
*   Have I planned properly?
*   Do I know what awaits me?
*   Do I know what the timescales are and how to assess my progress?
*   Can I see the milestone(s) ahead?
*   Have I understood the rules of development?

The answers should foster greater determination. You may experience a sense of peace, although it is likely to be short lived. You have made the leap. You have prepared. You are ready.

Notes

1 Schroder, H.M., (1989). *Managerial competence: The key to excellence.* Dubuque, IA: Kendall Hunt.
2 Cockerill, A.P., (1989). The kind of competence for rapid change. *Personnel Management,* **21**, 52–56.
3 Ahmed, W., (2019). *The polymath: Unlocking the power of human versatility.* New York: John Wiley & Sons.
4 Harris, T.A., (2012). *I'm OK, you're OK: A practical guide to transactional analysis.* London: Arrow Books.
5 Lyubomirsky, S., (2007). *The how of happiness.* New York: Penguin.
6 Wallis, C., (2004). The new science of happiness. *Time Magazine.*
7 Houlberg, L., *The Wizard of Oz: More than just a children's story.* Florida State University Writing Resources English Department. [Accessed 19 April 2021].

7 Step-7

Trials and tribulations

We don't even need to risk the adventure alone; the heroes of all time have gone before us, the labyrinth is fully known, we have to only follow the thread of the hero path.

(Joseph Campbell)

It's all been leading to this.

This is where change really happens.

The change we seek may be small. We may develop a single capability, or we may choose to change our entire life. The change may be a change in us. A change in how we think or feel. A change in who we are, the stories we tell about ourselves and the meaning we have been creating, based on our current level of development. We may change how we relate to situations and events. Our relationship with our Self or with the people we travel with on our journey. We may change our relationships with loved ones, with strangers, the world or the world of ideas. We may have decided to change what we're doing or why we're doing it. At step-7, anything and everything is up for grabs.

Step-7 takes us into the development phase of the leader's journey, where the real work of growing up finally happens. The work may occur in the psychiatrist's consulting room, in the boardroom, while talking to a customer or simply on our couch when we're home alone. We may be at step-7 for a minute, an hour or a lifetime. Whether our work here is momentary or monumental, it is definitely work. It requires effort. The work may start with some small simple experiments. Small tweaks in our way of being. Minor adjustments in the way we operate or relate with others. But if the work works then we are changed forever.

At step-6 we've done all the planning, we've accumulated all the 'I', 'WE', and 'IT' resources we need for the journey. Step-7 is where we deploy these resources, roll up our sleeves and get stuck in. This is where we find out who we really are and what we may be capable of. If we fail to convert what we learn then we're doomed to keep repeating our experiments until the penny finally drops – if it ever does. If we get stuck, then step-7 ceases to be our salvation and becomes our swamp. In that case, years of effort can evaporate; progress fades like the colour in a photo bleached by the light of a window. In some cases, we may even regress.

DOI: 10.4324/9781003170402-8

How do I know if I'm at step-7?

Step-7 is a time for action. We must find the value in difficult moments and focus on the skills that can lead to our development. Indications that you might be in step-7 include:

- A recognition that the work has begun including the pleasure of the toil.
- An appreciation of, and willingness to engage in, full scale experimentation.
- A glimpse of the size of the challenge – the work just got real.
- Excitement and awe of what's now required and how everything was leading to this point.

Change is here. We have prepared and now it's time to buckle down to the work, effort and practice of change. On a personal level, a leader may have realised (at step-2) that they were not enjoying their life that much. Something's missing; they feel restless but don't know why. Perhaps they tried a few things: a hobby, the gym or socialising more but nothing made any difference (step-3). Maybe a sabbatical from work might help, but that just felt a little like running away from the issue. Perhaps it dawned on them that they had to lean into this discomfort (step-4). Change was needed (step-5). Maybe they started reading some personal-development books, but that didn't help much either. Luckily, they bumped into a skilled developmental coach who offered to help. The coach prepares them for change (step-6). That involved some fierce conversations and introspection, but the leader now feels they understand their restlessness a little more. And they start to sense a greater level of calm and resilience surfacing. This is the work of step-7. The leader is doing the work to properly address some deep-seated issues, learning and using tools, applying new strategies and, as a result, witnessing the first results of change.

On a professional level, a leader may have committed to the creation of a new taskforce or the implementation of a new IT system to streamline efficiency and improve the customer experience. Step-7 would, therefore, include all the change work needed to deliver that outcome and make sure it sustains. The team will need to stay vigilant about what's happening and why, what's working and what's not so that alterations can be made in real time toward the objective. Such improvements in their professional life may involve making sure the new IT team work well together and have the technical ability to get the job done.

Whether the step-7 work is personal or professional, there's an awareness that the change may require change in ourselves ('I' change), our relationships ('WE' change) or what we do ('IT' change). We should point out that moving from any one of the steps on the Change Wheel to another step is a change. But step-7 change is fundamentally different and specifically developmental. Step-7 change delivers sustainable improvement by increasing our sophistication and step changing our capability. And the key to increased sophistication and developmental progress is choosing the right action to action, the right focus to focus on. Poor choices mean we will fail to deliver any sustainable change, so we must tread carefully. It's very easy to get lost on the journey of change.

There are two options. We either start from where we are or we get input and start where the biggest impact can be made.

Start from where you are

We know from experience of working with thousands of leaders across multiple geographies that the change that changes *everything* is 'I' and 'WE' change. But we also recognise that it's next to impossible for many leaders to appreciate this.

There are two reasons for this. First, for most leaders, their predominant experience of change, successful or otherwise, is within the 'IT' domain. Most leaders are 'IT' addicted – by necessity. Most understand that they have been hired to deliver 'IT' changes and if they don't, they'll be fired. As a result, it's difficult to pay attention to anything other than the clear and present danger to their professional future. As the world speeds up and becomes more complicated, it's very easy to fall into the trap of just focusing on the short-term and obsessing about the immediate tasks (i.e., this year's plan). There are so many operational issues to sort out, and most leaders feel compelled to address this quarter's numbers, the almost ubiquitous need to reduce the cost-base and the pervasive need to improve the operating model. Inevitably, many leaders are effectively forced to trade off tomorrow in order to deliver today. Many are simply more comfortable dealing with today rather than contemplating tomorrow. This is partly because the ability to think strategically and architect the future is significantly more difficult and demanding than firefighting operational problems. Why? Because thinking strategically requires us to handle much greater levels of complexity (an 'I' capability). The future needs us to be super comfortable with uncertainty and make choices when often there's scant evidence to support any choice.

This 'IT' addiction is exacerbated by the fact that of the three domains of human experience it's much easier to implement and measure changes in the 'IT' domain. The rational, objective world of 'IT' is observable. We can see if our actions produce results. We can see if our marketing strategy is improving sales. But even though 'IT' change is easier and more quantifiable, we are still not that great at driving operational adaptations. The statistics on change are woefully consistent. In 1995, renowned change management thinker John P Kotter revealed that only 30 percent of change initiatives are successful.[1] Ten years later, Malcolm Higgs and Deborah Rowland reported that, "Only one in four or five change programs actually succeed."[2] In 2006, McKinsey & Co. surveyed 1,546 business executives from around the world and confirmed a stubborn consistency. Only 30 per cent of change initiatives were considered a success.[3] From the Gartner Group to Harvard Business School to McKinsey & Co. and beyond, all the independent research into the effectiveness of change initiatives over the last few decades has demonstrated a 70 per cent failure rate. In fact, Towers Watson bumped that figure up to 75 per cent when the ability to sustain change was factored in.[4]

The results are clearly not great, but 'IT' change is doable and quantifiable, at least 30 per cent of the time. Leaders can point to their activity and effort to change the operation. Ultimately, most leaders become somewhat skilled at 'IT' change or getting stuff done. But is such change capability moving the dial enough? Is such 'IT' addiction going to step change Kotter's stats or deliver sustainable results?

What's the alternative to obsessive 'IT' focus? We believe that much of the change leaders seek in the 'IT' can be delivered by not focusing on 'IT' and instead focusing on 'I' and 'WE'. But how can we see 'I' change? How do we know if personal transformation is sustained? And when we consider the level of complexity created by complex human beings interacting in a complex way with each other, it's easy to understand why cultural 'WE' change is perhaps the hardest change of all and certainly much harder than strategic 'IT' change. The 'WE' dimension really is the final frontier for human development.

But given that most leaders suffer with an 'IT' addiction, this is where we start with leaders or teams helping them to develop their change capability. We initially help them address their most pressing 'IT' change. We do this because we know from experience that once the leader gets results, they will also begin to understand that the 12 steps and 4 phases apply to 'I' and 'WE' change as well as 'IT' change. This insight opens up the possibility of real sustainable transformation.

Once some 'IT' results are under their belt they begin to appreciate that the potential richness of a three-dimensional life may have disappeared. Many have become one dimensional, often without even realising it. They have become 'human doings' trapped in a life of endless tasks, targets and metrics from which they feel they can't escape. It also begins to dawn on them that their 1D approach is the reason the statistics on successful change are so woeful.

When we take a 1D approach to a 3D problem, any changes we make in the 'IT' world can easily result in an exacerbation of the 'I' and 'WE' issues. For example, a few years ago Ken Wilber was asked by the then Ukrainian President Yulia Tymoshenko to offer some guidance on how to rebuild the country. Ken and I discussed the challenge and agreed we should convene an international conference and invite some brilliant thinkers to explore all the political, commercial and economic issues at play. At that time, one of the many issues in the Ukraine was security. It was clear that we would need to protect the hotel where the conference was to be held. We were advised that the way to do this would be to erect a fence around the hotel and put some sentries on the fence and give then AK47s – so gates, guards and guns. This may well be the 'IT' answer to the security issue, but it makes the 'I' problem worse. The 'I' problem is fear. If we asked the academic community to walk past a lot of people with guns, they were likely to be so intimidated they would decide not to attend. And of course, no amount of gates, guards and guns solves the relationship problems between the Ukraine and Russia or the Ukraine and the West. So, the 'IT' answer exacerbates the 'I' and 'WE' problem.

We need to approach all change by considering which dimension we're predominantly 'working on' right now and what the implications are for the other dimensions. To do this we use *The Complete Leadership Frame* (see Figure 7.1). This

COMMERCIAL PERFORMANCE
- Drive revenue profit and EBITDA
- Develop offer, products & services
- Build scorecards, KPIs & metric tracking
- Create competitor radar
- Control operational risks
- Run performance & talent mgt systems
- Manage the business system

MARKET LEADERSHIP
- Clarify vision
- Set ambition
- Uncover purpose
- Identify strategic pillars and initiatives
- Establish effective governance

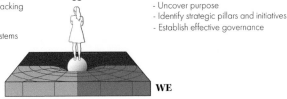

I

IT

WE

PERSONAL PERFORMANCE
- Energy, resilience and well-being
- Quality thinking
- Maturity and sophistication
- Personal brand (purpose, PoV etc.)

PEOPLE LEADERSHIP
- Drive culture transformation
- Develop company values
- Build leadership teams
- Cultivate deep relationship ecosystems

Figure 7.1 The Complete Leadership Frame.

enables us to map what we are working on and describe the relationships between all the critical factors at play.

In our leadership frame, we see the leader standing at the centre of her world. Front and left are the short-term commercial performance issues ('IT'). Front and right are the longer-term market leadership issues ('IT'). Over her right shoulder, and out of normal vision, are the people leadership issues in the interpersonal world of 'WE', and over the left shoulder are the personal issues in the inner subjective world of 'I'.

The Complete Leadership Frame is, therefore, not a theoretical model but a description of reality. Nothing exists outside this model and every situation, challenge or desired change falls into one or a combination of all four quadrants. Once we start planning and actioning change in all four quadrants, we vastly improve our chances of success.

It may come as no surprise, therefore, that exceptional leaders are those leaders who are capable of changing themselves (their interior 'I'), as well as inspiring others to do the same and who are capable of changing their relationships with others in the 'WE' domain. Ironically, the increased speed and agility that many leaders seek and the paradigm shift that could create massive competitive advantages are rarely found in the 'IT' domain. That speed, agility and capability emerge almost exclusively from change in the 'I' and 'WE' domains. In the rare circumstances where there is a disruptive 'IT' advantage, it can usually be traced back to a transformation in 'I' or 'WE'. The disruption came out of the individual genius of a single mind or from the collective hive mind and the wisdom of a crowd.[5] Vertical development of the 'I' and 'WE' dimensions will step change capability to deliver an 'IT' transformation.[6]

Leadership really starts with the 'I' domain. Instinctively we know it. We may feel we have no choice but to ignore it because 'IT' change is more pressing and easier to measure, but we know that, at best, such 'IT' focus can only ever deliver a temporary uplift.

When we work with leaders all over the world, I often ask them to name which leader, alive or dead, has had, over the last 50 years, the biggest impact on the world. After some debate, Nelson Mandela always tops the list, even in China and Mexico. What's interesting about the example of his life is that for 26 years he couldn't *do* anything! There wasn't much 'IT' activity going on and scant 'WE' work beyond the odd inmate or a few uninterested guards. Mandela spent 26 years developing his 'I' interior, working on himself year after year. When he was finally released, the power, maturity and sophistication of his 'I' was awe inspiring. He left prison with absolutely no hostility towards his captors because he realised that if he didn't leave his resentment at the gates of the prison then he would still be imprisoned by his own anger. That maturity, insight and inner strength is what made him the standout statesman and world leader he was. And it was only possible by Mandela's conscious, deliberate and consistent 'I' development.

Start where the biggest impact can be made

Over the last 25 years coaching CEOs and leaders across the globe, we've found that early insight into the power of the 'I' dimension can ignite change and fast track transformation. That can be achieved by quantifying the 'I'. As I said earlier, 'IT' change is often considered easier and more relevant because it can be measured. But by monitoring a leader's physiology at work for three days using heart rate variability (HRV) technology, we *are* able to quantify key, commercially relevant aspects of the 'I' dimension. We have been tracking leaders' physiology in this way for over two decades and probably have one of the largest C-suite biology databases in the world.

Measuring a leader's physiology enables us to precisely pinpoint where they should start their change effort for maximum results. There are thousands of conversations we could have with a leader, but this data allows us to identify some quick wins as well as fundamental changes the leader may need to make to their lives. For example, energy levels are a key component of this diagnostic assessment. If a leader is completely exhausted, it doesn't matter how smart they are or how brilliant their strategy is, they won't be able to deliver anything. Why? Because they are too tired and don't have the stamina to follow through. Changing a leader's energy level, therefore, starts with quantifying how much energy they actually have. Not how much energy they subjectively believe they have, but how much they objectively have. The HRV data gives us that data. Tracking their biology also reveals whether a leader has too much adrenaline, too little adrenaline or whether their adrenaline levels are high at the wrong point of the day or the night. We can also tell, just from a leader's biology, whether they are struggling with motivation or endurance; we can discern critical insights about the quality of their sleep cycles, whether their body clock is disrupted, whether the amount of effort they are making is adequately matched by the quality of their recuperation and many more precise insights that are important to delivering commercial outcomes. Such diagnostic precision is critical if we want to help a leader make change that really matters, fast, such as developing boundless energy levels.

The Complete App

If you would like to increase your energy levels (step-2–4) and you've committed to doing so (step-5) you may want to download the Complete App (step-6) which is a resource that can help you increase your energy levels (step-7 and beyond). You can get the App in the App Store or Google Play. One of the ways of tracking your progress in the cultivation of boundless energy is to do the interoception questionnaire on the Complete App.

Interoception is the technical term for increased awareness of bodily sensations. This questionnaire will tell you which of the eight dimensions of interoception may be getting in the way of increasing your energy levels. Specifically, it measures your ability to:

1   Notice – do you even notice your bodily signals and energy levels?
2   Distract – do you tend to ignore or distract yourself from uncomfortable signals?
3   Worry – do you tend to worry too much about bodily sensations?
4   Focus – can you sustain concentration on bodily signals?
5   Comprehension – do you understand the signals your body is giving you?
6   Comfort – are you able to soothe yourself when your body is in pain?
7   Listen – do you listen to your body?
8   Trust – can you trust the information your body gives you?

Even reflecting on your energy levels can help to unconsciously manage your energy more effectively. But if you want to significantly increase your energy levels then you need to dig into the many programmes and practices on the Complete App. For example, you can start by focusing on your breathing. Just by paying attention to your breath, you will start to notice how disordered your breathing pattern normally is. As you 'wake up' to the problem with your breathing (step 2), accept that only you can change the way you breath (step 4) and commit to making that change by practising every day (step 5), you can then schedule that Practice on the App (step 6). If you then do the work and practise that skill (fully explained in the App), you will make the change and create much more coherent breathing, gaining access to greater energy reserves (step 7). This illustrates the point that whenever you start a new practice you rapidly go through all the preceding steps prior to commencing that practice. This means that every time you practise, you are building your change capability by rapidly moving through the steps of change.

Controlling our breath is incredibly important for our health, wellbeing and performance. When we get upset or agitated, the first thing to 'go' is our breathing. For example, if someone is frustrated their breathing tends to become a series of mini breath holds or what is known as 'glottic stops'. We basically close our glottis, which is the place in our throat where are vocal cords are located. Closing our glottis shuts off our lungs and builds pressure in our chest, which means we hold the frustrated tension in our body.

But our breathing is not just disordered when we are frustrated; it's also disordered when we are panicking, anxious or angry. Pretty much all our negative emotional states involve a different sort of disordered breathing pattern. When our breathing is erratic, the electrical signal our heart generates becomes chaotic. This chaotic cardiac signal is sent to every cell in our body and can influence all our other bodily systems. The net result is that we start to 'leak' significant amounts of energy. Learning how to regain control over our breathing is a fundamental skill in preserving energy and mastering emotions.

Every single emotion can be differentiated by its unique biological or energetic signature. In the Complete App, we provide 2,000 different emotional states for users to explore, and with each emotional state we experience a slightly different state of consciousness. Many people, when they reach step-7, become fascinated with different emotional states, different states of consciousness and exploring how they feel in each one.

Traditionally, the whole subject of emotions has been dismissed as irrelevant to business. Many leaders mistakenly believe we should 'leave emotions out of business'. It's not possible to remove emotion from business and it's not advisable either. What people who suggest this probably mean is that it's advisable to remove uncontrolled emotions from business, rather than leave emotions out altogether. If so, I would agree. But we mustn't throw the baby out with the bath water. Emotions are critical to business, and we need to understand them and harness them not ignore or try to delete them.

For example, passion is the number one predictor of performance across all dimensions of performance, including health. If we are passionate about something, we do it better. A business that lacks passion will not do as well. Few leaders would ask their people to remove passion from their work. Similarly, most companies in the world conduct annual engagement surveys. And what is engagement if not an emotion? Employees may feel engaged or disenfranchised. Companies track such things because they recognise that high levels of engagement improve commercial outcomes. We should actually track employee emotions every day – this is what the Complete App enables organisations to do.

Charting our progress

Step-7 is all about action and experimentation – doing the work of change. But we need a framework that stops us getting side-tracked by interesting detours and distractions on what 'might work'. Knowing where to start, what dimension of change we are seeking ('I', 'WE' or 'IT') in what line of development (Figure 3.1) can certainly help. Together, they can help to create a change road map, like a product road map. Some of the critical questions to ask would be:

• How many changes am I engaged in right now?
• Which domain are they focused in – 'I', 'WE' or 'IT'?
• Of all the possible lines of development, where should I focus to accelerate change? (Refresh your memory by reviewing Figure 3.1).

- What level of sophistication am I operating from on my key lines of development?
- What skills do I need to learn, practise and master to vertically develop up that line?
- How can I quantify my progress?
- If I'm stuck, am I avoiding the work or not doing the practice? Do I need to re-engage?
- How is my emotional state during the change?
- Am I developing capability to better manage my emotional state so I can accelerate?

How does it feel to be at step-7?

Ideally, step-7 should foster curiosity and excitement. There is a wonder that emerges as a result of doing the work of change. Openness and the willingness to experiment in a spirit of curiosity is vital at step-7.

That said, step-7 is work, the trials and tribulations, so how we feel can fluctuate wildly as we toil and travel our way through the dramas of our life.

When our efforts bear fruit and we witness our own change, it can be thrilling. There is something deeply satisfying when we catch ourselves being different. Perhaps a recognition that we didn't act the way we might have acted before the work, or we didn't make our usual quip or feel a certain feeling. There is also an appreciation of how our altered behaviour or mindset led to a better outcome for everyone. We made that happen. Our efforts. Our determination to stick with the process and do the work. This witnessing of our own metamorphosis in real time is often accompanied with a burst of energy and enthusiasm for the change process. Optimism is often high as we wonder what else we could successfully change and what the positive ramifications of that additional change might be. The first time we feel the impact of successfully navigating step-7, it can feel intense – like a lightning bolt, a revelation. Change is possible. The implications of that can be visceral, a deeply felt sense of having found some magic key that unlocks untold doors. Often, we can almost feel the internal recalibration of what we believe we can accomplish. We can feel full to overflowing with such positive emotions – we are literally 'full-filled'.

Finding a consistent way to bring about change in our personal and professional life is itself a game changer. Considering the amount of failed change and the cost of that failed change; becoming a change warrior with proven change capability can radically alter the trajectory of any career.

That said, there is no fast track or quick fix in step-7; we can't delegate the work to others or outsource change. We can't even rely on our mentor, guide or coach. It's up to us. Our coach can encourage and point the way to appropriate skills and tools, but it is up to us to use them. We must do the work of change ourselves, otherwise we will not make progress. This may even be the main reason there is so little genuine adult development in the upper echelons of business. Too many other priorities, endless to-do lists and perhaps a touch too much hubris to engage in something as mundane as 'practice'.

But if we want the rewards that change can deliver, we've got to keep at it. Becoming a better, more capable and sophisticated human being is our primary task. It is our life's work.

Courage will get us started, but awareness, patience and perseverance are what will see us through. We need more perspiration than inspiration. We need to pay attention. What is our experience of the practice? Do we gain any insights? Do we know the parameters of our experimentation? Depending on the outcome, do we need to tweak our efforts to ensure a better result? For example, we all have a pre-ferred learning style that influences how we take on information and use it. Do we have development recipes that work for us?

Educational theorist David Kolb suggests there are four learning styles: accom-modating, converging, diverging and assimilating. Accommodators are 'hands-on' and want to learn by doing. Convergers are better able to deal with abstract ideas but still like concrete results; they understand theories but want to test them out in practice. Divergers use personal experiences and practical ideas to formulate the-ories that can be applied more widely. Assimilators are the ones that are most com-fortable working with abstract ideas and concepts. They extend their understanding by developing new theories of their own. This sort of typology can be helpful, but in truth there are hundreds of 'descriptive' typologies that characterise an individual's ability to learn. We suggest you just keep experimenting with the process of change and use what works for you rather than limit yourself to one 'type' of learning style or one type of experiment.

Of course, if the effort is not going well and you don't glimpse flashes of the future then it is easy to become discouraged. You may feel you're doing the work, practising the skills, but nothing's happening. This is the most dangerous point in the development journey because it can lead to indifference and ultimately regression.

Lack of diligence

As with the other steps, there is a bumping up against reality in step-7 that, unless managed, can cause regression. In this case, it's the lack of diligence.

It's easy to give up on change if we are unable to appreciate the benefits. All of our earlier resistance can come roaring back at this point with an avalanche of doubt. "What's the point? I've never been able to change this before." "This is a waste of time." "I've got better things to do than these stupid practice sessions." "I knew this wouldn't work."

Working with a coach can be crucial at this stage to vent our frustrations and share our doubts while fostering diligence. A good coach can re-energise us and keep us going. Find effective ways to practise without practising (i.e., build our practice into our daily lives so we can protect ourselves against the virus of indif-ference and frustration). It's common, after an initial flurry of enthusiastic activity, for life to get in the way; other priorities squeeze out our best intentions and our practice is forgotten.

As a coach to some truly exceptional leaders and athletes, I often found that many intellectually understood the benefits of practice and the outcomes that could be achieved but still struggled to keep going. I decided to come up with a way of helping leaders to practise without actually practising. This may not be as odd as it sounds. Human beings engage in all sorts of practising without realising they are practising. For example, many people are very proficient at feeling bad about themselves. They rehearse negative emotions almost continuously and, therefore, get very good at it. This got me thinking of what else we do without thinking much about it. I realised that we do lots of things without thinking. For example, we get dressed every day. We don't practise getting dressed, we just do it. When you look closely at our lives, we do hundreds of things every day without thinking, and we repeat these activities day after day. Our daily lives are highly ritualised. I started to wonder if it's possible to create practice rituals where people rehearse the skills we taught them as easily as though they were just getting dressed. When studying human habits, it became clear that most of the rituals in our lives occur at the transition moments of our day, when we move from one activity to another. In these moments of transition, we develop a little ritual to help us through that transition.

For example, the first ritual of most people's day is the 'getting up' ritual. This transitions us from being horizontal, in bed, to being upright. Some people's rituals involve an alarm, some not. Some people wake up and sit up in bed, some people wake up and get straight out of bed. Some people go to the bathroom; some go to the kitchen to put the kettle on. Everyone has their own rituals, and this is pretty consistent every day. Similarly, we may have a specific breakfast ritual that enables us to transition from lower energy sleepy state to a higher energy 'refuelled' state. We will have various 'getting ready for work' rituals.

I decided to see if we could use these rituals to get people to practise a positive emotion. We called this 'Positive Energy Practice' or the PEP skill. The idea is that we practise by inserting the rehearsal of positive emotions into our existing routines or habits. PEP is based on the idea of habit stacking. Rather than seeking to establish a new habit of practising a skill like mastering your emotions, just piggy-back on an existing habit and 'habit stack'.[7]

So, if you always have a shower in the morning, habit stack a couple of minutes spent mastering your emotions into that activity. Choose an emotion that you would like to start your day with and create it for yourself in the shower. Not only do you get to practise your emotional mastery, which is building vertical capability in your emotional line of development, you get to start your day feeling a positive emotion. You might add a couple of minutes at the end of your shower practising the breathing skill from the Complete App. Habit stacking is a great way to build practice into your life. This is how we help people to practise without practising – rehearsal just becomes part of their daily activity. Life just becomes practice. We are what we practise, so if every shower triggers a feeling of joy as warm water runs over you then you will become familiar with the experience of joy. If every plate of food triggers a feeling of gratitude, if every time you fire up your PC you feel thirty seconds of patience, then all these positive emotions become part of your daily experience.

My favourite example was when I was coaching the creative director of a TV company and she said she had thought of a great PEP – opening a door! I asked her what positive emotion she had stacked into that small ritual of opening a door, and she said, "excited anticipation". She explained that she didn't know whether what she would encounter on the other side of the door would be a triumph or a disaster. So, for about ten to thirty seconds, she would be in a state of excited antici-pation. She probably walked through fifty doors a day, so she very rapidly learnt what it was like to feel excited anticipation. She mastered that emotional experience quickly and was able to turn that emotion on in other situations too.

In addition to such informal practice, we also encourage people to 'landscape' their week. This means review their week ahead and schedule in time to practise. The Complete App makes this easy because you can set up time to practise using your mobile phone, where you can easily schedule reminders for a certain moment of the day or week. Landscaping helps you identify where you could really do with the skills you are practising and deliberately inserts some time before that event to practise. For example, it might be useful to create a boost of extra confidence before a performance review or facilitate coherent breathing before entering a negotiation.

Step-7 is the work – it's where the rubber of the change we've committed to at step-6 meets the road and where our lives really come alive. Step-7 is where we experience the trials and tribulations of change. This is where we meet and beat many of the difficulties of our life. We learn to use tricks and hacks to help us move along and master the skills we need to make progress. PEP and landscaping are two of those hacks.

Cultural metaphors

Step-7 is when the hero must train, learn new skills that they need in this new, unknown world. In some movies, the film jumps straight to the ordeal that the hero must face. They may show us, often in flashback or flash forward, that the hero, in the thick of the action, doesn't have some skills they need to succeed or confront the various challenges they face. In most stories there are two great ordeals. These represent step-7 and step-8 (more on step-8 next). In most films we see the hero, who is not yet a master, battling with the initial ordeals, but most commonly these tests are preceded by the director showing us a representation of the waking up of phase 1 (steps-1–3) and the owning up phase (steps-4–6) including crossing the threshold (step-5), all of which prepares us for the main part of the drama of step-7.

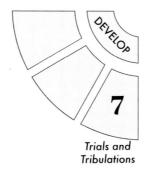

Trials and
Tribulations

The Matrix: Having taken the red pill and entered the Matrix, Neo meets the crew of the Nebuchadnezzar. Morpheus, seeing Neo's skill in the training ground, becomes convinced that he is the One. Much of the first film's narrative is concerned with Neo wrestling with the possibility that he may be the saviour, or the One. In the first film, when Neo meets the Oracle she tells him he isn't the One. In the second film, after he has successfully overcome many trials, such as somehow redefining the physics of the Matrix to dodge the bullets, she tells him he is the One. But that still isn't the end of his test. In all three films, Neo faces many challenges such as sacrificing himself to save Morpheus in the first film; facing the choice given to him by the Architect, in the second film, to reboot the Matrix or save Trinity; or escaping the subway, in the third film, where Neo is trapped. The subway station is called Mobil Avenue, which is an anagram of 'limbo'. The third film is where Neo's greatest ordeal really takes place, but more on that later.

The Lord of the Rings: Having left the Shire, Frodo and his three hobbit companions face the Ringwraiths on their way to meet Gandalf at Bree. They hide under the tree roots as the Black Rider looms over them. At Bree they meet Strider, who later turns out to be Aragon (another ally), and he helps them escape the Ringwraiths again. Frodo experiences many trials on his journey including what looks to be a mortal wound. He is rushed to Rivendell where he is reunited with his friends and allies. These companions bond to become the Fellowship of the Ring. The tribe then go through their own trials in the Mines of Moria: meeting Gollum, fighting off the orcs, defeating the cave troll and losing Gandalf as he fights off the balrog and appears to fall to his death in the chasm. Eventually they reach Lothlorien, home of the elves, where the wise Galadriel tells Frodo what he must do to complete the quest. She is basically describing the second ordeal that still lies ahead and the work of step-8.

Star Wars: In the space opera of the Star Wars story, spread across many films, there are numerous cycles of the Change Wheel. Luke, as the main hero, faces many calls to adventure, refusals, threshold crossings, trials and ordeals to overcome before he and his companions return. This is largely because George Lucas was deeply inspired by the work of Joseph Campbell. The two men spent a lot of time together. At one point in the story, Obi-Wan Kenobi starts to train Luke as a Jedi. Obi-Wan gives Luke a lightsabre and asks him to block the shots emitted from a floating training drone, in a scene reminiscent of early samurai films. As Luke struggles, Obi-Wan gives him a helmet that cuts off his vision. This is a critical metaphor that's repeated throughout the whole franchise. Obi-Wan is basically trying to teach Luke to turn from the dark side, which is his over reliance on intellectualisation, his worldly attachments in the 'IT' domain and the negative emotions that such cognitive bias and attachments trigger. Luke must stop over thinking everything and trust himself. Or, more specifically, trust the midi-chlorians inside him. Midi-chlorians are the microscopic life forms inside Luke akin to the bacterial, viral and fungal DNA inside all human beings. Obi-Wan exhorts Luke to "feel the Force". A metaphor for trusting your feelings.

Harry Potter: Like all the other cultural metaphor based on Campbell's 12 steps of change, Harry Potter also has to work his way through a host of trials and tests throughout the books and films, from his initiation at Hogwarts to his enlightenment, triumph and resurrection. Harry's first initiation test comes at the sorting ceremony when he aligns himself to the house of Gryffindor, even though the Sorting Hat suggests he could be great if he joined Slytherin, the wizard equivalent of the dark side. Harry's journey includes defeating a giant snake and a young version of Voldemort, the Potter equivalent of Darth Vader, in *Harry Potter and the Chamber of Secrets* (book two). In *Harry Potter and the Prisoner of Azkaban* (book three), Harry defeats the Dementors, who are very similar to the Ringwraiths of *The Lord of the Rings*. And in *Harry Potter and the Goblet of Fire* (book 4), Harry has to obtain a golden egg, save his friend Ron from the merpeople in the school lake and reach the centre of the maze in the Triwizard cup.

The Wizard of Oz: Dorothy encounters many trials on the yellow brick road as she looks for the emerald city. Most of them are at the hands of her nemesis, the villainous Wicked Witch of the West (the equivalent of Darth Vader or Voldemort). Dorothy's trials include fire, attacks from trees, sleep-inducing poppy plants, flying monkeys and the witch herself. These trials that Baum writes about are a social commentary, expressing Baum's views about the real challenges facing American society from 1890 until the book was published in 1900. The sleep-inducing poppy plants are, of course, a real-life reference to opium, which was commonplace at the time Baum wrote the book. In fact, the US passed legislation to control the distribution of opium and coca five years before Baum died.[8] The flying monkeys are widely regarded to be a reference to Native Americans. Baum's racist views are well documented, following two controversial editorials where he suggested the safety of the white settlers depended on the genocide of Native Americans.[9] The first of these was written just five days after the murder of Lakota Sioux holy man Sitting Bull.

The transition from step-7 to step-8

When the work works, at step-7, there can be a real sense of achievement. This can provide momentum which may, particularly in the first few revolutions of the Change Wheel, lift the leader right over step-8 and drop them into step-9, where consolidation takes place. What makes someone genuinely embrace step-8 is a deeper awareness that they're on a journey of development. For example, a leader may have been working on their emotional resilience and may have developed a much greater level of resilience. The deeper question is why they lacked resilience in the first place. Have they just papered over the cracks? Is the change they've achieved permanent? Have they really dug out all the roots of the problem? Is there more to do? The key to the transition from step-7 to step-8 is deep reflection.

In the movies, the hero reflects on their progress, and it starts to dawn on them that there is a deeper ordeal to be faced, a greater demon to be slayed. Battles have been won, but the ultimate battle remains. In real life, there may be a recognition that some issues have improved but some deeper issues remain stubbornly intransigent. The leader's insight on this may be triggered by the observation that they seem to be making three steps forward followed by two steps back. There have been leaps and lapses. It can help to make a note of these insights or situations, as they may provide guidance for effective exploration of step-8.

Questions to ask yourself

If you are unsure whether you need to go deeper and into step-8, it can be helpful to ask yourself some questions:

- Has my development slowed?
- Have I stopped changing or making progress?
- Am I just rebadging change?
- Have I sorted most of the surface challenges I faced?
- Are things going a lot better? Am I moving faster?
- Do I understand how all the changes I have made fit together?
- Am I confident of my progress?
- Have I cleaned up my system and now realise that there may be a couple of deeper issues to address?

Use these insights to decide if you are happy with the change that you've achieved so far. If you are, you may be able to skip forward to step-9. If you feel that you are banging your head off the same wall, then step-8 may be calling.

Notes

1 Kotter, J.P., (1995). *Leading change: Why transformation efforts fail.* Boston, MA: Harvard Business Review.
2 Higgs, M. and Rowland, D., (2005). All changes great and small: Exploring approaches to change and its leadership. *Journal of Change Management,* **5**(2), 121–151.
3 Vison, M., Pung, C., and Gonzalez-Blanch, JM. (2006). Organizing for successful change management: A McKinsey Quarterly Global Survey, 4. June 2006.
4 Towers Watson, (2013). *Only one-quarter of employers are sustaining gains from change management initiatives, Towers Watson survey finds.* Available from: www.towerswatson.com/en/Press/2013/08/Only-One-Quarter-of-Employers-Are-Sustaining-Gains-From-Change-Management.
5 Watkins, A. and Stratenus, (2016). *Crowdocracy: The end of politics.* Kent: Urbane Publications.
6 Watkins, A., (2016). *4D leadership: Competitive advantage though vertical leadership development.* London: Kogan Page.
7 Clear, J., (2018). *Atomic habits: Tiny changes, remarkable results.* London: Random House.
8 Warner, M., (2016). *The power of the poppy: Exploring opium through "The Wizard of Oz".* National Museum of American History.
9 Ritter, G., (1997). Silver slippers and a golden cap: L. Frank Baum's "The Wizard of Oz" and historical memory in American politics. *Journal of American Studies,* **31**(2), 185–187.

8 Step-8

Deep work

In the cave you fear to enter you will find the treasures you seek.

(Joseph Campbell)

Step-8 is the only step that can be skipped over, at least for a couple of revolutions of the Change Wheel. Often the vertical gains made at step-7 have expanded our capability enough to facilitate the change that is being sought. As a result, it's possible to skip past the deep work and move straight to step-9. However, skipping past the deep work can't go on forever. Once we've mastered the key skills and moved up the vertical ladders across the multiple lines of development in the 'I', 'WE' and 'IT' domains, we will hit an inevitable developmental ceiling. Eventually we must lean into our fears, look at our shadow and venture out to where even angels fear to tread. This is every leader's and every hero's ultimate ordeal.

Even with the skills of step-7 locked in, there is a recognition that we still have to use those skills. The things that make us angry often still make us angry. We may have developed greater emotional resilience and are able to retrieve the situation or alter course, but we still don't necessarily understand the message that anger brings to us and why it keeps re-appearing. The mission of step-8, for those willing to accept it, is resolution over reconciliation, transformation over toleration.

What is it that's triggering the anger? What's it all about? These are the types of questions that start to bubble up. Often, as we prepare to do the deep work, we become vaguely aware of something on the outskirts of our consciousness: an enclave on the edge of our awareness that starts to merge with the metropolis of our mind. We can't quite grasp it. There's something there calling us to go deeper. To quote *Star Trek*, we are compelled "to explore strange new worlds."

To use that deep enquiry to resolve and transform, we must discover what we have not yet seen. We must fully understand its significance and the hold it has over us. We must find the treasure we really seek. And that treasure lies in the innermost cave.

Although the significant life changes made possible by thorough engagement at step-7 may be enough for many, and these changes are accessible *without* the deep work, it's not possible to reach advanced levels of development without doing the deep work. Our shadow is the collective aspects of Self that we can't see or we have

DOI: 10.4324/9781003170402-9

disowned, repressed or ignored. It's possible that we got a glimpse of our shadow at step-2, when our reality was challenged. Our tendency to disown and repress what lies beneath our awareness is often what's behind the resistance we experience at step-3. Once we have been around the Change Wheel a few times and have exhausted the advances we can make while avoiding step-8, we may begin to recognise our shadow is holding us back. It might be time to address it once and for all.

How do I know if I'm at step-8?

By step-8, it may have become apparent that we are up against stronger forces in favour of the status quo than we anticipated. Something in our understanding of Self is missing and is impairing our ongoing development. We've hit a developmental ceiling, and only the deep work will allow us to break through. Indications that you might be in step-8 include:

- A sense there is something deeper that requires your attention.
- A nagging suspicion that *you* might be the problem.
- A recognition that, although you have learnt a lot through step-7 and progress has been made, the breakthrough you feel is imminent still seems to elude you.
- A willingness to explore parts of your life and your Self that you may be unfamiliar with.

The willingness not to skip past step-8 and knuckle down to the deep work may come into focus when, despite the work of step-7, life keeps becoming painful. For example, when someone experiences their third divorce they may start to wonder if there is something else going on that they just aren't seeing. Making relationships work isn't easy. The first divorce could be put down to a poor choice, marrying too young or growing apart. A second divorce is harder to rationalise away. Surely, enough learning took place in the first marriage to prevent the demise of the second. Of course, it may just be bad luck. There comes a point in our life as an adult human being that we are all called to ask, "Is this me?" If that moment has not arrived prior to this, the third divorce is surely that moment. A red flag that something is going on that perhaps the individual has not been willing to look at until now.

On a professional level, step-8 may finally be addressed if someone is repeatedly ignored for a promotion or keeps getting the same challenging feedback from multiple different sources. The undeveloped will dismiss the feedback. Those who have worked at step-7 will manage the pain of the feedback from a point of greater clarity, and from that clarity they will start to see a deeper message emerging that must be dealt with.

Many people need several revolutions of the Change Wheel before the penny finally drops. Eventually, they listen to what's being said and consider it objectively. Could it be true? If there is even a glimmer of recognition that the feedback might be accurate, then step-8 becomes possible. I worked with a very senior leader in a large multi-national who felt that he wasn't getting the recognition he deserved for his efforts. He was doing the job of a senior leader, but his job grading was that of a senior vice president (SVP) not an executive vice president (EVP). Some of his peers on the global leadership team, who were less capable than he, were EVP. He just couldn't get over this. To him it felt disrespectful and was massively undermining his morale, his sense of self-worth and even his wellbeing. I was asked to coach him because his anger at not being an EVP was causing him to be aggressive with people. In his coaching programme we got to step-7 and helped him manage his anger much more effectively. This created the opportunity in step-8 to look much more deeply at why he wasn't being promoted to EVP. We had captured some behavioural 360 data to support the fact that he was incredibly goal focused and would push extremely hard. As a result, he would always deliver the results, but it would often come at the expense of his 'WE' relationships and those around him. It was this latter point that was blocking his promotion. He had to hear this message from me, his line manager and HR business partner several times until he could finally accept that he was not easy to work with, and he had to own that part of himself at step-8 before he could move forward. He has now committed to becoming a champion for psychological safety. He has had to take on board some pretty robust feedback, use his step-7 skills and the deep work at step-8 to ensure he's not crushed by that feedback. He has since been made up to an EVP, and he's even more committed to becoming the leader he is capable of being.

The work of step-8 is like entering a dark cave. At first, we have no interest in entering. We perceive there's nothing in there for us. We have acquired the skills we need at step-7, and we have no need to enter the cave. When it finally becomes obvious that we must enter our innermost cave and face our demons, acknowledge all of who we are, including our shadow and those aspects of ourselves that we don't like or are unhelpful, we go in hesitantly. There is little light in the cave, and everything looks distorted. The modest illumination from the cave entrance is like the flickering light from a bedside lamp creating more shadows and childhood monsters. We enter with all our biases, our pre-conceived ideas of who we are, created by the conditioning process (more on that in a moment). Without a guide, we can get lost in the cave recesses forever. Our own personal purgatory.

The early work of the cave is to decondition our mind. Our thoughts and beliefs have been created by many programmes embedded in the deep recesses of our mind. Most are laid down before we learn to speak. The code starts to go in from the day we are born. It's essentially brainwashing. Some of this brainwashing is helpful, some is profoundly unhelpful. While this conditioning is an automatic survival and learning mechanism, the code itself alters everything we see, hear, feel, touch and experience. The main purpose of the code is threat detection and survival. The scripts of these programmes are deeply embedded in the emotional nuclei of our brain, in our amygdala, our hippocampus and our anterior cingulate cortex.

The core operating principle is pattern recognition. We encounter too much data to store the raw data, so we store the relationships between data points rather than the actual data points themselves.[1] The early programmes are around learning how to learn, and they allow infants to assimilate vast tracts of information very quickly. The speed at which this code is laid down is phenomenal. But problems arise; just like the hasty preparation of Tutankhamun's burial chamber, the code on the wall contains transcription errors, only some of which we cross out. The result is that a great deal of the code we use as an adult is faulty.

For example, let's look at what scares us. The only fears we are born with are the fear of falling and loud noises (both related to predators). Everything else we fear, someone has taught us. The problem is that all the information that creates these learnings, faulty or otherwise, is embedded into our brain before we have critical facility. Our neocortex, specifically the frontal lobes, which are responsible for that critical facility, are not fully developed until our late teens or early 20s. As a result, we just soak up all this learning without ever assessing it for accuracy or validity. This code, a great deal of which is inaccurate, then drives our beliefs and assumptions, and we don't even realise it.

The purpose of the deep work, certainly in the early part of the cave, is to find and eliminate this faulty code. Why? Because it creates shadows, including our shadow. The shadow is the unhelpful or difficult side of who we are that led us to that third divorce and stopped us getting the promotion. We never see our own shadow. Others can often see it clearly, but when we turn to look the shadow turns, too. As such, it is often just out of our field of vision. We need to go into the inner-most cave so we can identify these shadows and heal the wounds that created them.

Before we enter the cave, there is often a cameo appearance of each of the last five steps. First, there is a renewed resistance to the deep work (step-3). This can be so effective that a leader may decide that the uplift from step-7 was enough and will push on through to step-9. There is nothing inherently wrong with this decision. Significant progress can be made from embodying the change of step-7. However, the divorce papers on the third marriage or missing the promotion may be enough to move quickly through step-4 and step-5 – overcoming resist-ance and committing to change, respectively. It's time once again to cross the threshold – this time we are called to enter the innermost cave and do the deep work. Preparation for change, step-6, may involve seeking out a skilled guide for the deep work. This is critical. Many developmental coaches that can help leaders level up in the clear light of day can't help in the cave. You may need a new devel-opmental coach. Someone who has been into the cave many times and can see in the dark. Once in the cave, it's dark and murky and it's incredibly easy to get lost. Plenty of people do – wandering aimlessly trying to figure out what faulty code is important and what is irrelevant.

We all arrive at adulthood with vast quantities of faulty code, even if we enjoyed a happy and secure upbringing. It's impossible not to have faulty code because the code was written when our critical brain wasn't even active. As a result, the code was never audited, revised and upgraded. We were effectively hypnotised by the information we received in the first seven years of life. Some of that information, such as "don't play with matches", is helpful and stops us getting burnt; some of it is just plain wrong and ends up creating fears, limiting beliefs and patterns that hold us back.

That said, no one has the time or inclination to ferret around in the innermost cave indefinitely. There are plenty of people who spend a lifetime in the cave entrance, navel gazing and pontificating about what they found and how enlightened they've become, having never really ventured into the cave. But we don't need to overwrite every piece of faulty code. We just need to identify the pieces that are still negatively impacting our adult life and overwrite those. The code that leads to three divorces or constant rejection for promotion or whatever the resulting dysfunction might look like. We need a skilful guide that can get us into the cave, identify the key pieces of faulty code, support us to heal those errors and get out of the cave as fast as possible.

If you've ever played an online game like Bubblewitch Saga, coloured balls line the top of the screen in various patterns and constellations. The idea of the game is to shoot various coloured balls into the constellations to collect them. If a red ball hits the top of a collection of red balls, all the red balls underneath fall. That's a bit like deep work. We could faff about fixing one piece of faulty code here and one piece of faulty code there, which would be like collecting one red ball at a time. Or we can go for the high scoring approach and use a skilled guide to help identify the piece of faulty code that holds a whole bunch of other bits of faulty code in place. Heal that piece, and all the bits underneath fall away. Like the cluster of red balls in the game, hit the right red ball at the top of the cluster and the 30 balls below fall. Such an approach is faster and much more effective because not all faulty code is equal. There is some that has very little negative impact and there are other scripts that are truly debilitating. Find that. Heal that and get out. We need to know what we are looking for, ideally before we go in, and that requires a skilful guide.

Once in the cave, we will still need all the skills we developed at step-7. We may be facing our demons, fears and confusion, but we will not be alone. The right guide will be our companion in the darkness and hopefully will shed light and dispel fear (more of the role of the coach in Chapter 13).

Albert Pesso's five basic needs

If we all reach adulthood with faulty code, how do we know which bits of code are causing our problems? What do we go looking for?

Psychotherapist Albert Pesso created a beautiful theory that can help to narrow down our search. Pesso's work is another example of a meta-frame. This meta-frame allows us to identify where our faulty code may be located and why.

Pesso identified five basic human needs that must be met during our maturation in order for us to develop properly. These specific needs must first be met literally, then metaphorically and then developmentally. If any of these three steps fails, it can result in faulty code or a limiting pattern that can impair our behaviour and performance for the rest of our life, or until we become aware of the limiting pattern and correct it. Without that awareness, our limiting patterns can define how we interpret reality and, therefore, how we think and behave today. It's often these limiting patterns that facilitate the three divorces or block the promotion opportunities. It is largely agreed that what we learn as a two-year-old is actively influencing our adult life. The evidence comes from many fields including psychology, evolutionary biology and neurophysiology. As an adult we believe we are rational, logical human beings, when actually we're walking, talking reactions to long forgotten lessons and events.

Pesso's five needs are:

1   Home/Place
2   Nourishment
3   Support
4   Protection
5   Boundaries

Interestingly, these limiting patterns can be created either by an unmet need or an excessively met need. Thus, someone whose early experience was relatively rootless with the family constantly moving house may develop a limiting pattern around home. Alternatively, if they grew up in a deeply connected and loving home, they may struggle to establish their own home that measures up to their early experience. Either way, the resulting faulty code or limiting pattern is wired into their psyche. This, in turn, influences the way they see the world and what they believe, which leads to limiting behaviour, thinking or emotional patterns that impair everything from the ability to maintain relationships to their ability to lead a team, division or business.

Home/place

If there is a literal or metaphorical absence or excess of home then a pathology can occur that creates faulty code that can then negatively impact the individual's ability to create their own place in the world.

Everyone's first literal home is in the womb. Once an infant is born, their literal home becomes their cot and eventually their bedroom. This is a literal place where they exist. If for some reason that literal home is disrupted, then it can lead to a pathology around home. For example, this may happen to a child in a family that is constantly on the move, perhaps where a parent works in the armed forces or is an executive who is moved to a new location every few years. In this instance, the child can struggle to meet this basic need and never quite feel at home anywhere. Conversely, if home life is wonderful and enriching, it may infantilise the children for much longer because they simply can't create anything approaching the magic of their parents' home. In this case, home again can become a pathology that creates faulty code.

Some years ago, I coached a senior executive in one of the big accounting firms. The reason he wanted to talk to me was he literally didn't feel at home in the business. He felt like a square peg in a round hole. He was unclear why he felt so restless. He had a good job, but he felt like he just didn't fit in. When I first met him, he was overly attentive. He would spend the first five minutes of every meeting trying to make me feel at home: "Would you like some water? Sparkling water? Tea perhaps? Are you warm enough? Are you comfortable here or would you prefer to go to the local coffee shop?" There was an almost endless list of questions as he tried to make me feel at home. He was projecting his own limiting pattern onto me and assuming, like him, I may not feel comfortable or 'at home' at work. This was such a prominent and persistent part of our interaction that it alerted me to the possibility that he had a home pathology and this was probably at the root of his current discomfort. So together we went into the cave and explored his early childhood.

He had grown up in a wonderful family and had an exceptional home life, so much so that nothing he could create felt like it could measure up. The resulting pathology could be seen in every area of his life. He was late to leave home, late to get married and late to have children. His drive to feel at home was the motivation behind his incessant questions when we first met and the source of his current dilemma at work. He was very socially skilled at making people feel at home, but he wasn't always getting the job done. He simply never felt at home at work or indeed in his life or many of his relationships.

Once we identified the faulty code and worked on laying down some new neural patterns and experiences, it enabled him to feel comfortable in his life, and his relationship with his wife and child flourished. He left that firm where he had felt massively uncomfortable and joined a smaller firm that was more aligned to his values – he found a better home! He found his place in the world, and he has remained with his new company for many years. Prior to fixing the faulty code, his constant attempts to create his own place in the world had been getting in the way of his ability to create his own home with his own family. It had been stopping him from feeling genuinely comfortable in his own skin. Effectively, he overwrote the faulty code and dissolved the limiting pattern that had, up until that point, being directing his life choices without his awareness.

Even if the need for a literal home is met well enough, there is still a metaphorical need that must be met. We all need to feel at home or like we have a place in our parents' heart. If this metaphoric step fails, we generate attachment disorders, which have been extensively studied by John Bowlby and many others over the years.[2] Attachment disorders can be profoundly disabling, preventing people from forming any healthy relationships with others. Or they can manifest more mildly but still be debilitating and block us from fully developing as adults. It's quite common, for example, for people to talk about being the black sheep of the family. Many experience imposter syndrome or a sense of being an outsider. A good developmental coach will recognise that such self-belief may be driven by a place pathology and the code created by an early childhood experience where they felt like an outcast in their own home.

If the child is lucky and their literal and metaphorical need for home is met, they take on their need to find their place in the world as a developmental task. Many people fail at this third step and struggle to make their own way in the world. They are unsure of their identity and who they are beyond their parents' influence. The gap year favoured by many students the world over or the Duke of Edinburgh Award scheme are both modern attempts to help young adults discover this for themselves. If the search for identity fails, then individuals may be late to leave home and establish their own home.

You may have a home/place pathology:

1   If you lived in a number of different homes growing up.
2   If your parents divorce and you lived between two homes.
3   If you only lived in one home and find yourself comparing your adult home life to your childhood homelife.
4   If you consider yourself to be the black sheep of the family.
5   If you always felt like an outsider in your home, perhaps even to the point that you wondered if you were adopted.
6   If you were significantly different from your siblings or peer group for some reason.

Nourishment

A developing baby's first literal nourishment is from the placenta in the womb. Everything they need to grow and develop is provided by the placenta. Once the child is born, that literal nourishment becomes the baby food they are spoon fed by their parents. A child who grew up in a home where there wasn't always food to eat or where the child was overfed may develop a nourishment pathology. This may manifest in later life as an eating disorder such as anorexia or bulimia. Obesity can often be sourced back to faulty code around nourishment.

If a child is literally nourished properly, they then need to be metaphorically nourished by their parents in order to develop. A parent's job is not just to literally feed their child; they must also feed their sense of self-worth, personal responsibility and resilience, for example. Again, too much or too little nourishment can create faulty code.

Too little and the child may grow into an adult that is always doubting themselves. They have an underlying sense that they are never enough in some way. They are constantly running negative thought loops in their head such as, "I'm not good enough", "I'm not sexy enough", "I'm not slim enough", "I'm not bright enough", "I'm not earning enough money" or any number of perceived deficiencies. This impacts their ability to learn how to nourish themselves because they were always starved of that nourishment in their formative years.

Too much metaphorical nourishment can lead to delusions of grandeur. Simon Sinek talks about this in his popular presentation on millennials in the workplace.[3] In an effort not to be like their own parents and be more nourishing, he argues that parents of millennials have gone too far the other way: where they were never really nourished and encouraged by their parents, they now overly nourish their own offspring with disastrous results. If a child is overly nourished metaphorically and told how amazing, special and talented they are just for managing to get out of bed in the morning, they develop an inflated sense of their own abilities and their own importance. They believe they are amazing, special and talented and become distressed and confused when they find a job and their boss doesn't agree. They never learn to take nourishment on as a development task and figure out how to nourish themselves. Instead, they simply rely on an endless stream of false nourishment from over attentive parents and come to expect and need that same external nourishment from others in the form of likes and shares on social media, often deeply hurt when others don't recognise their obvious brilliance and don't lavish them with the praise they came to expect from their parents.

If we experience an absence or excess of either literal or metaphorical nourishment then we don't take nourishment on as our own developmental task. We never learn how to nourish ourselves.

You may have a nourishment pathology:

1   If you regularly went to school hungry.
2   If you suffer from an eating disorder or have otherwise wrestled with body issues all your life.
3   If you are obese and can't ever seem to shift it.
4   If you feel you were starved of affection as a child.
5   If you comfort eat.
6   If you find it a lot easier to care for others than care for yourself.

Support

Initially, a baby is literally supported in the womb. Once born, the baby is literally supported in the crook of their parents' arm. The baby is literally supported as they are carried around and they are supported in a push chair, baby backpack or papoose. As the baby progresses to a toddler, the parent will hold their hand and literally support them as they learn how to walk. If there is too much or not enough literal support then faulty support code may be created.

If the literal support needs are met, the child will seek metaphorical support from their parents. The parents will need to support their child's emerging identity rather than undermine it. They will need to support their efforts to achieve, helping with homework, offering supportive advice if the child experiences bullying etc. Parents may literally support their child financially through university and metaphorically by emotionally supporting career choices. Too much support also fuels the dysfunction that Sinek discusses. A pushy or overbearing parent that solves all their child's problems can prevent that child from developing tools and strategies for supporting themselves. Those who experience too much or too little support, either literal or metaphorical, never really learn how to stand on their own two feet. Those with too much are always looking for someone else to solve their problems. In a relationship, they may be looking for their 'other half' or they may resonate with Jerry McGuire when he said, "You complete me." They are looking for that support from someone else because that's what they came to expect as a child. Someone else would fix it, solve it or make it better. Children from wealthy families often have this pathology because they have never learnt how to support themselves. Their parents have overindulged them with gifts or provided an endless credit card that prevents them from developing as a fully mature adult human being and learning how to support themselves – financially and otherwise.

Those with too little support can often stumble through life. Ironically, they can be quite clumsy. They fall into relationships or fall into a career without any real conscious choice.

You may have a support pathology:

1   If you felt that you had to grow up fast.
2   If you were a carer for a parent and the roles were often reversed.
3   If you felt as though you were left to your own devices.
4   If you were smothered by an overinvolved parent who wanted to solve all your problems.
5   If you were always in a relationship and never on your own as a young adult.

Protection

Again, a baby's first experience of literal protection is the amniotic sack in the womb. After birth, the child is protected by their parents. Safety gates are installed on stairs and electrical sockets are covered to prevent little fingers from getting electrocuted. Washing powder pods and matches are put away out of the reach of children to protect them. Too little protection can lead to excessive risk-taking behaviour as an adult. Too much protection from a mollycoddling parent can prevent the child from learning and they can end up overly fearful, anxious or cautious as an adult.

If the literal need for protection is addressed, then the child still needs metaphorical protection. This includes helping a child understand key principles like 'stranger danger'. They may also protect you by withholding information that, as a child, you don't need to know. For example, there may be financial issues or family relationship dynamics that you're too young to understand. Your parents may protect you from harmful imagery, literally, such as stopping you watching the Texas Chainsaw Massacre as a six-year-old or parental control on internet searching, or metaphorically protecting you from harmful imagery by distracting you from thinking about certain topics that you don't have the emotional or cognitive abilities to process and assimilate. Parents may protect children from themselves. Children can be naïve in certain situations and not understand the risks they may be exposed to. Children who have been physically, sexually or emotionally abused will often develop protection issues.

If the protection fails, then the child develops faulty protection code and may never really learn how to protect themselves. This can manifest in later life as always getting into scrapes or finding that they have been taken advantage of in some way. People who frequently end up in toxic relationships have a protection pathology that prevents them from recognising the danger signals before it's too late.

You may have a protection pathology:

1   If you had a lot of accidents as a child – numerous broken bones.

2   If you were exposed as a child to things that were not age appropriate or that you didn't want to be exposed to.
3   If you frequently feel as though others take advantage of you in some way.
4   If your parents never let you do anything, always protecting you from 'dangers'.
5   If your relationships are too 'one-way', where you do all the giving and the other person does all the taking. This may be a very mild form of abuse (you of yourself or the other person of you).

Boundaries

As a baby develops in the womb, there is a literal, physical boundary of the abdominal wall that separates the baby from the outside world. There is also a literal boundary between the baby and their mother. Once the baby is born, the literal boundaries may include a play pen or their cot, which stops them from going places they shouldn't.

If the need for literal boundaries is met, the parent needs to establish the metaphorical boundaries to help children learn what's acceptable and what's not acceptable. Some of these boundaries may be tied up with protection protocols while some may reflect the values of the parent or the culture. These boundaries allow the child to understand the rules of life: how to be a proper human being, as defined by the parent within their culture.

If there are too few boundaries, the child never learns the rules and can behave inappropriately as an adult. If there are too many boundaries, the child can end up as a fearful adult never willing to try anything new or seek out new experiences.

It is often quite easy to spot someone with a boundaries pathology – especially one that was formed from too little boundary setting as a child. They are the people who just don't seem to appreciate social conventions. Often, they work in sales and are brilliant because they just don't hear the word "No". They will push past the point that most people would stop. Such an approach can be useful in sales, but it can be disastrous in relationships and can be a liability in business. I remember working with someone who had a boundaries pathology. He was great fun to be around, but he over promised and under delivered. He also had no sense of what was OK in a work setting. I remember him telling me that he had met with a very senior leader in a FTSE 100 company. The leader, a female, seemed tense to him, so he decided to give her a shoulder massage! Boundary pathologies are also common amongst the population of prisons.

You may have a boundaries pathology:

1   If you frequently do or say things that shock or confuse others.
2   If you have been accused of riding rough shod over other people's needs or desires.
3   If you have routines and set rules for things that you never waver from.
4   If you have gotten yourself into hot water because of inappropriate behaviour.
5   If you are maverick and reject social conventions, or you feel that you tend to slavishly follow the rules even though most other human beings don't.

Fixing the faulty code

What's so useful about Pesso's meta-frame is that it helps us work on the deep limiting patterns that stop us from finding the real treasure in the innermost cave. Even reading the short descriptions above and considering the questions, it's likely that you feel more resonance with one description over another. You may experience a sense that your deep work is around home/place, for example, or boundaries. This resonance can then act as a starting point for the deep work.

If we can identify the key pieces of faulty code that are driving some of our most dysfunctional and unhelpful beliefs and behaviour, we can overwrite the code and dissolve the limiting pattern. This will help us navigate to the depths of the innermost cave and find what we are looking for.

There are many techniques that can help an individual work on their shadow and limiting patterns to ultimately overwrite the faulty code buried deep in their psyche. In psychotherapeutic terms, overwriting the code can lead to the development of a new neural pathway or, in technical terms, 'structure'. It is possible to create a new neural structure without actually having the full-blown experience that created the faulty code or structure. So, once that structure has been identified you can artificially create the conversation that you should have had (literally, metaphorically or developmentally) with the key person that could have helped you develop healthy code.

Even though the structure you create today is artificial, it can still work to overwrite the faulty code because your mind can't tell the difference between the real world, where an experience caused faulty code to be written, and the imaginary world, where you may have artificially created a new experience to replace the old faulty experience. In essence, we can use our imagination to create new code that drives new behaviours, replacing the dysfunctional behaviours that might have been present our entire life.

Working with shadows and limiting patterns is deep and delicate work, particularly in vulnerable people. It should not be undertaken lightly and should definitely not be undertaken by someone who doesn't have the skills, maturity and sophistication to do this work. Depending on whether you have ever looked at the deeper aspects of your Self or not, some of what follows may not make that much sense to you. Don't forget we are now in the cave; the light is dim; things are a little confusing. I will try to shed some light, but if you are more confused don't worry; exit the cave, continue onto Chapter 9 and maybe come back to this chapter at a later date to see if the content makes more sense then. In addition to creating new neural patterns using structures to overwrite code, as outlined above, there are many other techniques that can be helpful in the innermost cave. Here are three to give you a sense of what the deep work entails:

- 3-2-1 Skill
- Rotating Chair
- Repeating Question

3-2-1 skill

The 3-2-1 skill is a process designed to help you take complete ownership of those aspects of your Self that you may have disowned, rejected or simply couldn't see. The first step of the technique is to objectify the aspect you are struggling with. This means seeing the issue from the vantage point of an observer – what's called the third-person perspective (hence 3). To complete this step, we suggest you write a description of the problem as though you were a journalist reporting the issue to the world. The issue may be just an inner aspect of who you are or it may be part of you in relation to another person but reporting on it in this way allows you to see more of the issue in a different context.

The second step is to get closer to the problem by interacting with it. If the aspect of you that you are dealing with is manifesting in a relationship, then write down a dialogue between you and the other person. If the problem is an inner aspect of who you are, or a conflict between two aspects of who you are, then you can still write a dialogue between the two aspects of you. Documenting the dialogue facilitates second person perspective taking (hence 2). To create a realistic dialogue, you must switch from one 'voice' to the other and see the issue from both vantage points. In constructing this dialogue, you may achieve a better understanding of both perspectives and find something that both vantage points can agree on. Or, at the very least, you may become much clearer about the disowned perspective or oppositional 'voice'.

The final step is to completely internalise the issue in a healthy way by integrating it with what's already healthy within you. The goal is to take back the rejected part as part of you. If you own it and internalise it, then this is your first-person perspective (hence 1). To integrate the disowned part successfully you must understand the message this shadow or projection provided. What is the shadow telling you? If you can understand the message, then it has served its purpose. One of the ways to accelerate integration is to objectify what is aggravating you and rather than see it as separate, change the name of that aspect and put your own name over it. For example, if you are aggravated by John's indecision, consider your own indecision. Sometimes the thing that annoys us most about someone else is really just that same aspect in ourselves that we have disowned and need to re-integrate. Sometimes what we can see so clearly in someone else is a mirror or 'projection' of our faulty code. It is a message to help us integrate that disowned part back into ourselves.

Rotating chair

The rotating chair technique is also designed to reveal a fundamental truth about our deeper selves. It zooms in on the '2' of the 3-2-1 technique and works that perspective. The rotating chair technique is best done, initially at least, with a skilled developmental coach or practitioner. Start by setting up two chairs facing each other. You sit in one chair and your coach sits in the other. The role of the coach here is to hold the space so you can have a dialogue, out loud, with the disowned part or shadow. First, tell your 'other' what your problem is with them. The other, in this case, can be the coach or someone else who is representing the problem or it may be an imagined other that represents a hidden part of you. Once you feel you have said the key thing you wanted to say, stand up and switch seats so you can sit in the other chair and take on the persona of your other. Then reply as the other to the initial statement you shared. You then rotate positions in a Q&A session between the two parts that are in conflict until the conversation comes to a natural close and some insight or fundamental truth has revealed itself. This truth is what allows integration.

The benefit of this approach is that by physically moving position and deliberately taking on the persona of the other, you get to appreciate the perspective that you may have been previously rejecting. This may sound odd but with a skilled guide it works extremely well. In fact, when you understand how to do this process, you can do it yourself without a guide or coach even needing to be present.

Repeating question

The repeating question technique is designed, like the other two techniques mentioned above, to help you get closer to the treasure in the innermost cave. It zooms in on the '3' of the 3-2-1 technique and works that perspective. The repeating question technique seeks to peel back the layers of beliefs and forensically identify a fundamental truth about your deeper Self. This process starts by noticing something simple that is causing concern. Initially it could be something superficial. Perhaps you are uncomfortable with public speaking. This is a common problem and can be a significant problem for some leaders who need to communicate and inspire those around them.

Start by identifying the surface problem: "I'm uncomfortable with public speaking."

Then ask yourself: "What's the value of this discomfort to me?"

Look into the darkness and see if you can peel back a layer to uncover something deeper than you first thought. Initially you may believe there is no value, but look again.

Whatever that first answer is, ask yourself the same question again: "So what's the value of this discomfort to me?"

Write down what emerges. It may be something like: "It forces me to stop what I am doing and slow down to think."

Then ask yourself the same question again: "So what's the value of this discomfort to me?" Look into the darkness again and see what emerges. It might be something like: "If it forces me to think, then I will create a better answer."

Keep going and ask yourself the same question again: "So what's the value of this discomfort to me?" Look into the darkness again and see what emerges this time. Maybe what emerges is "If it's about better answers then maybe the discomfort is helping me to create greater impact."

Keep going if you don't think you've got to your final answer and ask yourself the same question again: "So what's the value of this discomfort to me?" Look into the darkness once more and see what emerges. Maybe it might be something like: "If it's about creating greater impact then maybe that will help me realise that I can create such an impact." If this answer seems to show that you are onto something, keep going. Peel back another layer and maybe what emerges this time when you repeat the question is that what this is really about is building your self-confidence and trusting that you have a voice and it is worthy of listening to. Usually when you get to the truth you can feel it. Again, the first few times you use this technique it may need to be done in the presence of a skilled developmental coach or guide, who can keep posing the repeating question for you. But ultimately, like the 3-2-1 and rotating chair exercise, you can do this on your own. Once you discover the real meaning to the discomfort, you have effectively received the data that this discomfort was seeking to transmit, the discomfort has served its purpose and it will often disappear because it is no longer required.

When we ask ourselves the repeating question for the first time, our standard rote answer will almost always pop out to justify our position. But if we keep asking the same question, after each new response we will come up with deeper and deeper insights until the real reason or truth shows itself. Every experience has a meaning and a message for us. The skill is hearing that message and putting it to good use to overcome the faulty code that is preventing us getting to the treasure in the innermost cave.

Remember, a lot of this faulty code was created when we didn't have a sufficiently developed neocortex to process information and critique the code that was written into us by our parents, siblings, friends, teachers, media, religion or culture. This code gets baked deep into our system and largely determines how we see ourselves all the way into adulthood, even though a lot of it is wildly inaccurate.

How does it feel to be at step-8?

How it feels in step-8 depends on whether we enter the cave or skip past onto step-9 on this revolution of the Change Wheel. If we go into the cave, then how we feel depends on whether we go in alone or whether we have a really good coach or guide with us. If we do go in, then how we feel depends on how deep we decide to enter the cave. Just because we enter the cave doesn't mean we go in all the way and discover the treasure we seek. There's still lots of value in venturing into the cave, dealing with shadows and limiting patterns and disowned aspects of Self, even if we don't find the ultimate treasure.

Having said all that, when we are in the cave we are entering into an unknown, the unexplored recesses inside ourselves. That can cause anxiety. That's why the metaphor of the innermost cave is so useful. We are literally going into the darkness of our own psyche. Not darkness as in evil or negative per se but simply a place we have never explored or shed any light on before.

Paradoxically, there can be something empowering about making that choice to do the deep work. To boldly go and face whatever demons may or may not be there. The demons are the shadows, projections and disowned parts of the Self. But finding that faulty code and overwriting it once and for all, meeting our demons and slaying them, is not why we enter the cave. We can certainly heal our Self in the cave but that's still not why we enter. We enter for the treasure. And the greatest treasure, more significant than healing, more significant than integration of disowned aspects of who we are, is the person we are truly meant to be. The treasure is us. The most magnificent version of us that we were scared to accept might exist. The larger, more compassionate, more brilliant version of us.

This is what Marianne Williamson is referring to in her famous quote:

> Our deepest fear is not that we are inadequate. Our deepest fear is that we are powerful beyond measure. It is our light, not our darkness that most frightens us. [4]

But we must go through the darkness to reach the light. And to find our greater Self we must kill off the old version of ourselves. The one riddled with doubt, fear and insecurity. The version that says we can't. What we find is not a version that says we can but a version that *knows* we can. If we succeed in the ultimate treasure hunt and find the real treasure, then we are changed forever. If we know all this before we enter the cave, we can often feel a strange mix of excitement and trepidation in step-8.

Step-8 can feel intense. As mentioned earlier, before we enter the cave there is often a mini-rerun of all the steps from the resistance of step-3 through to the skills accumulation of step-7. This includes the emotional rollercoaster of those steps' associated feelings. It is common for someone at the cusp of deep work to feel overwhelmed, unsure, nervous, anxious, angry, excited, elated and thrilled – all within minutes of each other.

The main emotional tools we will need to ensure the deep work is a success are openness, non-attachment, courage, determination and trust.

We must be open to all the experiences of the cave so we can understand them quickly and keep moving. We need to be open to boldly go wherever the process takes us. Non-attachment simply allows us to watch what comes up for us rather than entering the cave with preconceptions about what we might find. If we enter with expectations of ourselves, of our coach, of the outcome then this will slow us down and prevent progress. Courage and determination in the face of darkness and the trials and tribulations of the cave are vital. And perhaps most of all trust in ourselves and our guide. Remember, we have acquired these skills and many more at step-7, and we can use them in the innermost cave to support our exploration. Deep work can be hard. It can be uncomfortable, intense and highly emotional, but it is never fatal.

Fear

There's an emotion or mindset in each of the steps up to this point that has the potential to derail progress. In step-8, that emotion is fear.

Human beings, especially those who have achieved a certain level of success, have spent a great deal of their life cultivating their public image. In many instances it's a mask that is designed to project competence and confidence, and there's little or no incentive or motivation to look behind it. So, no need for the cave.

What tends to happen, therefore, is that leaders will cycle through the Change Wheel a few times. As long as they master the key techniques in step-7, they will make significant progress, even with minimal or no deep work. But eventually that progress will grind to a halt. Often something big will happen. Perhaps that third divorce or an end to promotion prospects. But something will dislodge the mask and it might start to slip. At this point, leaders have two options. They can refuse to consider that something else lives behind the mask of the public image and regress back to the distraction techniques of step-2 and the resistance of step-3. Or they can feel the fear and enter the cave anyway. If they choose the first option, their development is over. If they choose the second, they just may unlock new levels of capability, creativity, cognitive sophistication, joy and meaning.

Most people never venture into the innermost cave to do the deep work. They might read a bunch of books and pontificate about various theories, but knowing something intellectually and knowing something experientially, in the fibre of our being, are two radically different things.

Part of the fear is that the cave will be dark, scary and lonely. We are social animals. We need social connection. If we go in the cave, we won't know who is in there and how they might help us. This often amplifies the fear and stops people crossing the threshold into the innermost cave.

But part of the lesson is learning to deal with the darkness and create our own light. Essentially, once we face our demons, understand them and integrate them so they are no longer 'shadow', the light goes on and we see that often the darkness and loneliness were of our own making. Having entered the cave and found the treasure with me as her coach, a female leader from a big tech company told me, "This has been one of the best weeks of my life. I see things so clearly now. I'm not scared anymore."

There is an adage that states, "the only way out is through". The only way out of pain is through pain; the only way out of the innermost cave is through the innermost cave. We can't go around it. We can't delegate it. This is the work only we can do.

Joseph Campbell put it beautifully when he said, "The cave you fear to enter holds the treasure you seek." Face the fear. It's the only way to get the treasure. Besides, it is never as bad as we imagine, and the sense of freedom and liberation that comes from deep work is always worth it.

Delusion and pseudo-enlightenment

It's also worth pointing out the dangers of delusion and pseudo-enlightenment. One of the risks at step-8 that prevents people from really embracing the deep work and taking it seriously is a mistaken belief that they've already done it! Perhaps they have flirted with the innermost cave and they may have even identified and healed a piece of faulty code, but it's not a crucial piece. The experience is enough for them to think they have done the work and know what they are talking about. But their understanding of the cave remains thin. It's a superficial understanding, and it's certainly not led to the profound change that occurs when someone has slain their dragons, healed a key piece of crucial faulty code and found the new version of themselves.

All that's happened is that they now understand the deep work a little better. Maybe they have read a ton of books on Theory-U, shadow work and depth psychology.[5] This enables them to present a persona of enlightenment and Zen-like acceptance. However, they have not slain their demons or integrated their shadow; they simply know they are there and have chosen to accept them. That is very different from genuine healing or the transformation that occurs if they had actually entered the cave and found the treasure.

This pseudo-enlightenment is widespread in the personal development industry. People who dedicate their life to a philosophy or theory and can and often will tell everyone that will listen all about it. But they are not a living demonstration of it. Those who have really done the deep work are different; they don't need to tell people how different they are.

Cultural metaphors

Step-8 is the journey into the belly of the whale, where we encounter maximum danger. The level of danger experienced in the trials and tribulations of step-7 pales compared to the danger at step-8. In the darkness of the cave, at step-8, everything is simplified; the ordeal becomes a simple matter of life and death. In this regard, the journey into the innermost cave is the apotheosis of many stories. This is the ultimate ordeal, the true test. This is where the highest point of development occurs, at least in this cycle of the Change Wheel. For a hero to break through, they must kill the old version of themselves to find the new version. This is where we experience a death and a resurrection. This is where we touch the divine. Our resurrection, rebirth or elevation enables us to discover the highest version of ourselves. This is the ultimate boon, the goal of the entire quest, our holy grail. We find the treasure we've been seeking all along and we are purified by it. This is our destiny.

The Matrix: In the third film in the trilogy, *The Matrix Revolutions*, the hero, Neo, once he is released from limbo (the Mobil Avenue subway station) fights his nemesis, Agent Smith. Over the course of the three films, Neo and Agent Smith have been converging. Despite being a computer program, Agent Smith gained the ability to operate outside the Matrix by assimilating part of Neo. He does this initially through a character ironically called Bane. In *The Matrix Revolutions* and the run up to the final battle, Bane blinds Neo in an oedipal twist, but Neo develops 'second sight', which enables him to travel to the Machine City, a metaphor for the inner-most cave. He warns the source that one of their rogue programs, Smith, is virally infecting the entire Matrix grid. The Machine City enables Neo to jump back into the Matrix to face Agent Smith in a final battle. Neo sacrifices himself by allowing Smith to assimilate him. Neo had instructed the machines to surge his body with energy in the real world, causing the connection between him and Smith to be broken. This destroys them both, including all of Smith's clones. The death of Neo and Smith reboots the entire Matrix and saves the human city of Zion at the same time. Peace descends, with the machines allowing the co-existence of the real world of humans. This is the revolution of the third film's title.

The Lord of the Rings: We said that non-attachment is a key asset when entering the innermost cave. *The Lord of the Rings* presents us with a wonderful depiction of what happens to a hobbit when he becomes completely attached. Gollum was a Stoor hobbit called Smeagol before he discovered the ring in the River Anduin. He was immediately corrupted by its power and killed his cousin Deagol to make sure he had the ring for himself. He became obsessed with his "precious", and his attachment to it twisted his body and mind until eventually he both loved and hated the ring. Gollum is also a metaphor for the emotional, physical and spiritual distor-tion that comes with being in the darkness for too long.

Gollum represents a couple of archetypes: the shapeshifter and also, in many ways, Gollum is Frodo's shadow. Gollum eventually dies in the fires of Mount Doom, liberating Frodo who is taken by three mighty eagles to the Undying Lands. In the discovery of the treasure in the innermost cave, the hero is often reborn. Many narratives depict the emergence of the new version of the hero as a sort of immortality. The old version of the Self has died, and a new version is resurrected. Once Frodo lets go of the ring, and his shadow Gollum dies in the process, he is indeed transported to the Undying Lands.

Star Wars: There are many moments in the Star Wars films that explore the motif of the 'cave', allowing the character to have a moment of introspection and potentially evolution. In the original trilogy, Luke faces the cave many times, and even in the recent trilogy created by Disney the main character Rey is also called to the cave to confront her fears. In first film, in their attempts to escape the Death Star, Luke, Leia, Han Solo and Chewbacca fall down a garbage chute and end up in a trash com-pactor. The trash compactor scene is an early cave ordeal that hints at the deeper cave experiences in later films. The water in the compactor is seen as a common meta-phor for our unconscious. Luke is then pulled under the water by an unseen foe, the dianoga monster. The troupe manage to survive the attack thanks to their faithful droid turning off the power. In another scene, when Luke was being trained in Jedi skills by Yoda, he is asked to enter a nearby cave. Luke asks what's in the cave. Yoda replies, "Only what you take with you." Upon entering and descending deeper and deeper into the cave, he is confronted by Darth Vader. A lightsabre battle ensues between the two, in which Luke cuts the head off Darth Vader. It then rolls between his feet where the mask explodes, revealing Luke's own face inside. His realisation here is that it is easy for anyone to start on the path of good but be swayed by distractions. He questions whether we end up becoming what we fear most simply by not being mindful of these distractions. In another famous 'cave' scene, Luke is asked to kill Vader by the Emperor and take his place. This is the 'sins of the father' motif that is repeated throughout the films. Luke refuses to kills his father, and the Emperor tortures him with lightning. Rather than Luke killing his father to avoid turning to the dark side, Vader sacrifices himself to save his son, Luke.

Harry Potter: Harry's apotheosis occurs when he realises that part of his nemesis Voldemort's soul is locked inside him. The darkness of Voldemort was coded into Harry when he was a baby. The faulty code is what marks Harry with his scar and it also enables Harry to speak with snakes. The only reason Harry doesn't die as an infant is because his mother sacrifices herself to save Harry's life. Her love was stronger than Voldemort's darkness. Harry survives and follows his journey until eventually he faces the moment of his own sacrifice. Professor Snape reveals that "when the time comes the boy must die", meaning that there must be a death for the man to emerge. Harry realises that this is his path to becoming 'the chosen one' and fulfilling the prophecy. So, in the *Deathly Hallows* book, Harry goes to the Forbidden Forest to surrender to Voldemort so no one else would die for him. Of course, he is really killing the part of Voldemort within himself. This sacrificial protection is a common theme in many stories. It immortalises the chosen one, who 'dies for our sins' or 'dies so that we may live'. This echoes Harry's own mother's sacrifice.

The Wizard of Oz: Dorothy's approach to the innermost cave occurs in the Wicked Witch's castle. The witch threatens to drown Dorothy's dog Toto if she doesn't give up her ruby slippers. If the witch gets the slippers, she will become the most powerful force in Oz, and Dorothy will lose the ability to get home and the quest will be over. Dorothy refuses. The witch sets fire to Scarecrow, and Dorothy grabs a bucket of water to douse the fire. She accidentally splashes the witch, who then melts into a puddle on the floor. Dorothy is rewarded with knowledge. She grabs the witch's broomstick and expects that the Wizard of Oz will send her home to Kansas. He reneges on his promise because, as Toto reveals, he is not all powerful and to be feared, he is just a meek old man. The treasure Dorothy discovers in the 'cave' is the knowledge that adults and authority figures are just the same as her and their pretence of power is illusory.

The transition from step-8 to step-9

When we have done the deep work, we know it on a molecular level. We are forever changed.

In the innermost cave, we not only reboot our Self but we reboot our purpose. The treasure that Campbell spoke of creates ripples that change the future. There is a great deal of discussion about purpose in business, not just from a corporate perspective but also many leaders increasingly realise that they need to understand their own personal purpose, particularly to avoid exhaustion in a post-COVID world. In addition, their own purpose needs to be aligned with the business's purpose and objectives. Given that an individual's purpose is significantly expanded in the innermost cave, if leaders skip past step-8 because it's where they fear to tread, how can they expected to reboot their purpose?

If we have the courage to do the deep work, we will emerge from the cave with new information and a deeper understanding of who we really are. As we transition from step-8 to step-9, the primary focus is to rest and consolidate before we return to the fray.

One way to think about step-8 is the discovery of buried treasure. We are born with the treasure bright and sparking inside us. All that is required is a good guide and the courage and curiosity to discover it. For most people, the treasure is hidden by layer upon layer of faulty code, limiting patterns, beliefs and assumptions. We can't see the bright and sparking treasure that lies beneath. If our efforts at step-8 remove enough of the debris, we can spot and then excavate that gift. As we come to know our new Self, we begin to understand that treasure and what it might mean for the rest of our lives. Often, deep meaning and purpose are unlocked at step-8 through the deep work.

Questions to ask yourself

If you are unsure if you are in step-8, it can be helpful to ask yourself some questions:

- Is the change achieved on the journey so far permanent?
- How do I make sure my levelling up and development is permanent?
- How do I sustain the new me?
- Do I understand the message of my shadow? Am I aware of my 'projections' and how my limiting patterns are preventing my development?

Deep work is a breakthrough, and the change effected alters everything that comes after so long as the embodiment of step-9 consolidates the wins of step-8.

Notes

1 Pribram, K.H., (1971). *Languages of the brain.* New Jersey: Prentice Hall.
  Hawkins, J. and Blakeslee, S., (2005). *On intelligence: How a new understanding of the brain will lead to the creation of truly intelligent machines.* New York: Henry Holt.
2 Bowlby, J., (1988). *A secure base.* London: Routledge.
3 Sinek, S., (2016). *Simon Sinek on millennials in the workplace.* Available from: www.youtube.com/watch?time_continue=4&v=hER0Qp6QJNU&feature=emb_logo.

4 Williamson, M., (1992). *A return to love: Reflections on the principles of a course in miracles.* New York: HarperCollins.
5 Scharmer, C.O., (2007). *Theory U: Leading from the future as it emerges.* Cambridge, MA: SoL, the Society for Organizational Learning.
Chopra, D., Williamson, M. and Ford, D., (2010). *The shadow effect: Illuminating the hidden power of your true self.* New York: HarperCollins.
Neumann, E., (1990). *Depth psychology and new ethic.* Colorado: Shambhala.

9 Step-9

Embodying the change

The privilege of a lifetime is being who you are.

(Joseph Campbell)

At step-9, we emerge from the innermost cave. We've done the work and gained the treasure, a new version of our Self. We are healed by the elixir. We have removed critically relevant faulty code that has been inadvertently impairing our life.

Once the work is done, embodying the change becomes the goal.

If we chose to skip past step-8 and avoid the deep work or only skirt the entrance of the cave, there is still an embodiment of the step-7 changes at step-9. Once we are regularly deploying the step-7 skills consistently to a point where it becomes habitual then we are changed. Our capability has increased, and we have stepped up a level. But without the deep work of step-8, the faulty code which still exists deep inside us may still have us under its spell.

The following description of step-9 will mainly focus on what happens when someone *has* done the deep work of step-8. Remember, the way we are taught and socialised, together with how our biology evolves, means that it is impossible to arrive at adulthood without some faulty code. The key is finding the critical pieces of code that are unconsciously impairing our life, causing us to make a series of poor decisions, getting us stuck in habitual dramas or leading us to sub-optimal performance.

There may only be a handful of inaccurate beliefs or limiting patterns that if discovered and healed could step change our lives and deliver a profound evolution. Hence the importance of a skilful guide to ensure we locate and heal those pieces instead of endlessly stumbling around in the dark of the innermost cave trying to heal everything. No one needs to be stuck in deep work for years, although many types of therapy encourage this, often for self-serving pecuniary reasons. If people are stuck in the cave, or frankly at step-7, then we must conclude that the work they are doing is not working!

It is also worth pointing out that there is a tragic irony between those who engage in the deep work of step-8 and those who choose to skip past the invitation. Often seasoned leaders will resist the work of the innermost cave, either because they dismiss it as irrelevant or it doesn't fit with their commercial addictions and

DOI: 10.4324/9781003170402-10

'IT' focus. Invariably such leaders view the deep work as soft, namby-pamby, self-help bullshit. So, they crack on with the concrete change tools of step-7 and avoid step-8.

The irony is that the deep work is not soft. It is likely to be the most emotionally gruelling developmental work they will ever undertake. The soft or easy option is actually to ignore it. The second irony is that by skipping over step-8, they must stay vigilant in the change process and actively choose to use and deploy the tools. Had they found the courage to do the deep work of step-8, they wouldn't have to think about being different – they would just *be* different.

The amount of effort and energy required to constantly bring about change in a business when you haven't done the deep work (because you effectively stopped at step-7) is significantly higher than the energy and effort expended by someone who has had the courage to do the deep work. To reiterate, the objective is not to find and heal every piece of faulty code, it's to find and heal the pieces that have a significant negative impact – right here, right now. We're talking about an exploration that may take a few hours. That seems like an unbelievably good trade for the liberation, capability and vertical uplift genuine deep work can facilitate.

How do I know if I'm at step-9?

Where change at step-7 requires deliberate hard work and is conscious, change at step-8 is largely a consequence of the experiences in the innermost cave, although some active work may be required. At step-9, we recognise the difference between what we've achieved in step-7 and step-8. In step-7, we learned skills and practised those skills so we could use them when needed to bring about positive change or better outcomes. Before step-7, we might get angry in a meeting, which would hamper progress. Once we developed emotional resilience skills at step-7, we were able to shift out of that anger, recalibrate ourselves quickly and avoid making the type of comment or doing something that might have previously derailed the meeting. Once we've done the deep work of step-8, we tend not to get angry in the first place. We see things differently. The healing has changed who we are on a very deep fundamental level and we know it. Indications that you might be in step-9 include:

- A realisation that you have changed – permanently.
- You experience the world and others differently.
- You know that you are not the person you were, and that's a good thing.
- You've caught yourself acting, thinking or behaving differently a few times and recognise the internal shift as transformational.

The real test of whether someone has fundamentally changed at step-8 and consolidated that change at step-9 is if their relationships with others change. For example, someone may have changed themselves to such an extent that the thing that used to drive them nuts about their partner and always led to a fight no longer causes a fight. Prior to this, if neither party had done any development or deep work there may be a bundle of faulty code that creates a shared pathology. This shared pathology can trigger attraction, in a sort of "you've got the same problems as me" stance. There is a compatible dysfunction. Partner A does X and partner B always reacts with Y, which ends is a blazing row. The two then endlessly engage in this co-dependant dance. Such dynamics can go on in some relationships for years, until one person does some deep work.

Let's say partner B enters the innermost cave and changes. When partner A does X, partner B no longer reacts the way they used to react. Partner A doesn't know what to do. Something has changed, and this could transform the relationship for the better if the change is understood. If the change is misinterpreted as a lack of care or indifference, the change may break the relationship.

Alternatively, partner B may have grown up and realise that they no longer wish to be in a co-dependent dance with partner A. They need partner A to grow up too. If partner A decides to do some deep work on themselves, the relationship tensions can be resolved. One of the reasons there is such a high divorce rate in many countries is that one partner grows up and the other doesn't. The change causes a gap in maturity, and if the couple don't 'mind the gap', the probability of separation is significantly higher. Matched development is a much better predictor of relationship longevity than how much people claim to love each other at any given point in time. Similarly, at work the relationships that endure are either those where each person's developmental level is similar or they mind the gap effectively.

Embodiment

The work of step-9 is to consolidate and stabilise the new version of your Self. This doesn't just happen; effort is required. Embodiment hinges around your sense of Self, and at step-8 your identity has fundamentally changed. You are a different person now, and it will take some time to get used to this new version of you. One of the key skills at step-9 is your sensory ability. Can you sense in what way you are different and reinforce the new pattern? All of our identities are rooted in our biology.[1] Thus, if we produce testosterone we are likely to identify as a male, and if we produce oestrogen we are more likely to identify as a female. This is not absolute because identity is a very complex phenomenon. For example, there are rare medical conditions where people can't recognise their own hand as 'theirs'. Conversely, people with phantom limbs perceive they have an itch in their foot even after their leg has been amputated. There are experiments where it is possible to induce a sensation of being 'touched' on the hand when actually it's a fake hand that has been touched rather than your actual hand. This suggests that our 'sense of sense' is not confined to our physical body, it embraces our 'emotional body' and our 'conceptual body', too.[2]

Nevertheless, our ability to sense this new version of ourselves starts with our ability to sense our own biology. This is called interoception, as we mentioned in step-7. If this new version of us operates at a higher or lower energetic level, we need to be able to notice that. If this new version of who we are starts each day from a new emotional set point because we are living on a different emotional planet, then we need to be able to notice that too. Sensing the parameters and boundaries of this new Self is vital. If we start to drift away from our new biology, our new emotional set point and our new identity, then our ability to embody the new version we worked so hard to uncover may be compromised.

In most cases, step-9 is just a case of not back sliding. The new version of who we are has emerged; the work of step-9 is to prevent a regression and build confidence in this new Self. If we consolidate this new version of ourselves, soon enough it will start to feel authentic. It should happen naturally because that's the process. Once we've overcome our resistance to change, at step-4, and progressed through step 5, we still haven't changed a thing. We are essentially still *talking the talk*.

Once we have committed to change and we start preparing for the work ahead, we may start reading a few books or attending a few workshops in an attempt to make progress. We might tell others all about what we've learned, even if the other person isn't interested. At step-6, we move from *talking the talk* to *talking the walk*. We basically know what we need to do. We've committed to changing ourselves, but we still haven't started the work of change. At step-6 we may contract a severe case of 'aboutism'. We know about the stuff, but we have limited, if any, experience of that stuff. There is intellectual understanding. But nothing has changed – yet.

Until we do the work at step-7, we are at risk of jumping around from one book that "you really have to read" to the next "awesome" book that "changed my life" to the latest workshop that "Oh my God – you have to do it". Our aboutism is often tinged with smugness and a soupcon of sanctimoniousness. We feel we know just a little bit more about everything than everyone else. The irony is that we only know just enough to be dangerous but nowhere near enough to be effective. And we may actually be speaking to someone who is light years ahead of us on the development journey but who doesn't feel the need to broadcast it. This moment on our journey can be encapsulated by the phrase "those who don't know say, while those who know don't say".

At step-7, once we've done some real work, developed some skills and worked out how and when to deploy those skills for maximum result, we are *walking the talk*. We are regularly practicing the things that make a difference. We can teach the developmental skills we have developed to others and are often highly motivated to do so. Our ability to teach is massively enhanced once we have found the treasure in the innermost cave. We know that these skills have changed our life and want to share that knowledge.

At step-9, the compulsion to teach stops. We are now *walking the walk*. We are a living embodiment of the change we used to teach. Any teaching we may offer at this point is by example. We've emerged from the innermost cave of step-8 a new version of ourselves. We are a much more grounded, more serene version of ourselves than the person we were at step-7. We know we are different and don't feel the need to broadcast the fact. A lot of the stuff that used to trouble us doesn't anymore. It's not deleted, we are still aware of it, but it doesn't drive us or upset us anymore. This is non-attachment, and it can be hugely liberating.

This can be a liberation from even the most difficult of life's experiences. For example, some people have had terrible things happen to them. The statistics on abuse alone are horrifying. But if we perpetually focus on the terrible moments of our life, engaging in endless treatment cycles, this can keep us trapped and bound to the trauma itself. What's required is development, so those who have experienced severe life events can do the deep work around those situations, heal the wound, fix the faulty code and move on with their lives. The abuse doesn't disappear; those affected are still fully aware of what happened to them, but they are no longer defined by it and it doesn't influence their life or the choices they make. It simply becomes something that happened to them on their journey. It isn't who they are, and it certainly doesn't limit who they can become and what they can achieve. In this regard, I can speak from personal experience.

As part of the stabilisation in step-9, when we've emerged from the deep work of step-8, we often need to rest. We have, in truth, done some of the most intense work of our lives. The deep work can be a profound, life-altering experience, and we need time to adjust to our new normal and new way of being. We've got the treasure – the new version of ourselves.

Purpose

Joseph Campbell said that every man and woman's purpose is to find their purpose. Our purpose flows from our identity. The work we do on ourselves at step-7 helps us to see more clearly who we are, which is why we say at step-7 that the two most important days of our life are the day we were born and the day we find out why. Therefore, the discovery and precise articulation of our purpose can be a game changer.

However, at step-8 our identity can change completely. The deep work helps us to resolve some of the faulty code and the unhelpful programming that took place without our permission. By the time we are adults, we have mountains of the stuff and collectively it influences how we see ourselves, what we believe about ourselves and what we believe we are capable of. This conditioning essentially creates a bunch of lies and limiting beliefs about who we are. If purpose flows from identity, when our identity changes and we are reborn, rebooted or re-shaped in the innermost cave we may come to realise that our purpose is upgraded too. Something deeper, more profound, and inclusive can emerge. Something that transcends and includes our step-7 articulation.

The stillness and tranquillity of step-9 allows our new identity and new purpose to settle. At step-9, our purpose doesn't change but as we rest in the sunlight, how we think about it does. When we are *walking the walk* we become less attached to the whole idea of a purpose. We don't feel the need to explain it. We simply accept it as a part of who we are. Our focus at step-9 is living our life on purpose. This is a shift from meaning to experience, from head to heart, from being guided by our intellect to trusting our soul. We filter our reality less through the lens of our identity; we now become more interested in directly experiencing reality.

As we rest, we begin to objectify our journey up until this point and join the dots of our previous experiences. From this new enlightened and expanded vantage point we are better able to follow the breadcrumbs of our life and recognise the

patterns. Those patterns usually point to how to live our life according to our purpose. Embody the changes, consolidate them and integrate them.

Step-9 is the last step in the develop phase. We have developed. We have found
meaning. We have done the hard work, and we are forever changed by our efforts in
step-7 and step-8. We understand our journey. We understand what it has taught us
and why. We have taken the useful lessons and discarded the rest. We have scrubbed
out the lines of faulty code that were impeding our progress, and we have our north
star. We know who we are, and we are clearer about where we are going and why.

How long we spend at step-9 is not fixed. It may be a few days; it may be a
few months. It's a period of renewal. As we look back, we become aware of our
journey's connection to the future and what might be next. Step-9 is what Gandhi
was talking about when he said, "Be the change you want to see in the world."

The 'story of you'

Step-9 may also include time spent honing the new story of you. Everyone has a
story: it's the retrospective narrative we use to explain our lives to ourselves and
others. The story we used to tell is no longer accurate. In truth, it never was. Often it
was simply the verbalisation of our faulty code either to ourselves or others.

We are no longer that person, so taking the time to create a new story of you can
be liberating. Whether you share that new narrative or not isn't that important, but
coming up with a new story of you is really important.

How does it feel to be at step-9?

There's a sense of relief, pride, achievement and possibly quiet inner celebration at
step-9. We did it. We did the hard work of step-7 and mustered the courage to face
the demons at step-8. And we are still alive. And we have the treasure.

Having overcome the final ordeal in the cave, we may feel, possibly for the first
time ever, a surge of self-acceptance, a peacefulness and maybe even forgiveness at
step-9. One of the big boons is a letting go of the drama and turmoil that used to
fill our days. The angst that used to invade our thoughts dissolves away. Even those
who have done us wrong are often forgiven in step-9. Remember, forgiveness is a
gift we give ourselves. The only person to suffer when we carry around anger and
hate toward someone else is us. The other person is not impacted at all. Their cortisol levels are not sky high. We don't forgive somebody to let *them* off the hook. We
forgive them to let *us* off the hook. So we can stop beating ourselves up about what
was or was not done, what was said or not said. It's gone, it's over. Through the deep
work of step-8, much of the 'charge' of an event or hatred for a person disappears
from our system. It's like we're able to step back, see the bigger picture in some way
and thank them for their part in our journey – even if that part was horrific. That's
the quality of forgiveness. The negative charge disappears from our system, and we
are no longer driven by our emotional reactions to our memories. There is a real
sense of equanimity and contentment that comes from such forgiveness.

It is also great for our health.

Dr Fred Luskin, director of the Stanford Forgiveness Project, brought a small group of people together as part of a project he called HOPE (Healing Our Past Experiences). Participants were from either side of the Northern Ireland 'Troubles', and everyone had lost loved ones in the fighting. Even though their loss was already decades old when the project was run (2000), the emotions, including grief and hate, were still raw. The first breakthrough came when both Protestants and Catholics recognised that the grief they felt was the same as the grief the other side felt. When the week-long project ended, participants reported that they felt less hurt, less anger and less depression. In addition, they experienced a 35 per cent reduction in physiological symptoms of emotional stress such as irregular sleep patterns, unusual appetite, low energy levels and fewer physical aches and pains.[3]

The peacefulness of step-9 is often experienced in contrast to the compulsive seeking that is characteristic of step-7 and earlier. The compulsion stops, largely because the compulsion was a drive to find a solution, to fix something, even though we were rarely sure what. Now things are fixed, so the chasing subsides. At least for now.

As we rest, there is often a renewed sense of wonder and excitement about what it all may mean for us. How is this change going to play out? How will it impact our relationships? How will the ripples of this experience radiate out into the rest of our life?

Complacency

There is always an emotion or mindset that can keep us stuck at any step and prevent us from moving forward on the Change Wheel. At step-9, that stumbling block can be complacency.

Having done the deep work of step-8, we have in many ways found what we were searching for. Up until step-9, we often feel a little bit of a fraud. Imposter syndrome is the result of not really knowing who we are. We're never really sure that the mask we've created and the public image we present is really us. Of course, this is understandable because of all the faulty code and conditioning. Effectively, we spend the first seven years of life being hypnotised by our parents, siblings, carer, nanny, nursery teachers and the culture we live in. That accumulated 'noise' builds a picture for us about who we are. The resulting conditioning means that we behave like a marionette – someone or something from our past is always pulling our strings or pressing our buttons. And on some level, we know it.

This is why family can be such an intense cauldron. Most of our faulty code was created in that cauldron. Why do you think Christmas is so bittersweet for so many people? Even though the children are now over 40, get them together and everyone is pulling everyone else's strings and pressing their buttons. The older siblings squabble, and the youngest tries to defuse the situation with humour. Each member is 'playing their part' in the repeating family drama.

At step-9, following the deep work of step-8, at least some of those strings are cut. When the string is cut in this way we stop 'playing our part'. We stop acting and reacting in the way we have in the past. As a result, the endless drama stops. There is often a deep sense of relief coupled with a sense of coming home. We have finally found ourselves. We're not perfect and we're never entirely 'fixed', but the manic searching for answers has stopped, and we feel at peace with who we are. Often for the first time.

So much so that complacency can creep in. The drama and angst that dogged someone's life prior to step-8 has gone. Imagine a point where anxiety or depression just disappears! That can and does happen when people do the deep work. This can feel genuinely miraculous for those who had come to believe such states were permanent and unavoidable. The relief can be overwhelming. So much so that the eradication of these states is viewed as enough of a prize to stop forward momentum.

Cultural metaphors

The embodiment of the treasure receives scant, if any, attention in most films. It's a difficult moment to convey on film because, essentially, it's an inner transformation which we have to infer from the hero's outward actions. And we can only see how the hero has changed when they return to the known world. The hero's embodiment only becomes obvious in steps 10 and 11. One of the most brilliant depictions of embodiment comes in the film *Razor's Edge* (the 1984 remake). The main character, Larry Darrel, having witnessed horrors in World War One, sets out on his journey and is transformed by his experiences. Ultimately, he is able to embody the advice from the Katha Upanishad that: "The path to salvation is narrow and as difficult to walk as a razor's edge." This insight is beautifully portrayed when Larry returns home and visits his boyhood friend Gray, who is suffering with a migraine. Larry's compassion is palpable, and he is clearly a very different man from the one who set out on his journey of self-discovery many years earlier. This scene not only captures the essence of embodiment, but it also confirms that step-9 counts for nothing if the change remains within us. We may have slain the dragon, but no-one knows. We may have emerged from the cave with the treasure, but we must return for the change to be useful to the world. So, once we have rested and fully embodied what we have discovered, we must begin the long journey home.

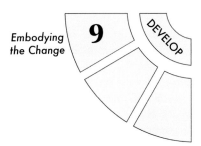

The Matrix: Towards the end of *The Matrix Reloaded*, the third film, Neo meets the Architect, who reveals there have been five previous iterations of the One. This pivots the entire narrative away from a linear concept of change to a cyclical view, in keeping with Joseph Campbell and the views expressed in this book. This awakening to the cyclical nature of existence resets the life and death struggle in the innermost cave in the context of eternity. The purpose of Neo's sacrifice is to deliver sustained peace between the machine world and Zion. Peace is the treasure Neo achieves in his fight in the innermost cave with Agent Smith. It's also his destiny as the One. When Neo is stuck in limbo (Mobil Avenue train station) prior to his ultimate battle with Agent Smith is when he comes to understand the cyclical nature of existence and the importance of balance. Neo asks the Ramachandra character he meets in the train station (the father program) whether he believes in karma. Ramachandra replies "Karma is a word. Like love" and suggests it's not the word but the concept of what the word points to that matters. This suggests that there is a greater reality to be considered in the cyclical nature of existence. And the inner and outer worlds are inextricably linked.

The Lord of the Rings: Not every journey has a simple and happy ending. The treasure that Frodo delivers after destroying the ring in Mount Doom is that Sauron will never be able to take physical form again; he wanders as a spirit in Middle Earth like Saruman. But Frodo himself never completely recovers from the physical, emotional and spiritual wounds he suffers during his quest. However, two years after the ring is destroyed, Frodo and Bilbo Baggins as ring bearers are granted passage and sail to the Undying Lands of Valinor, the earthly paradise where Frodo can embody peace and light.

Star Wars: Despite Luke destroying the Death Star, killing his sister's tormentor and delivering peace throughout the galaxy, he subsequently expresses regret for the killing of so many people on the Death Star. Luke's initial triumphant return subsequently matures into a deeper understanding and compassion for the sanctity of all life.

Harry Potter: After his fatal battle with Voldemort, Harry wakes up in hospital where Dumbledore tells Harry about his parents and explains he's not alone in the world. He has always had the ancient magic of his mother's love and sacrifice to protect him. Voldemort's killing curse on Harry didn't work. It only destroyed the dark side within Harry.

The Wizard of Oz: Dorothy left Kansas to find a better life. After Toto pulls back the curtain, Dorothy realises that sometimes even powerful people are not who they pretend to be. It's not until Dorothy gets home that she truly appreciates the treasure she found when she faced her fears. She discovered the self-confidence necessary to embody the knowledge that to do anything, you must stop trying to be the person you think everyone expects you to be and simply be yourself.

The transition from step-9 to step-10

The transition from step-9 to step-10 begins when we recognise that change is a journey. Life is a journey. What's the point of doing all that work and finding the treasure if we do nothing with it?

Often there's a subtle shift from the past to the future. At first, when we reach step-9, we are often tired from the effort of step-7 and step-8. As we rest, our energy returns and we review the process and look back, clarifying our future as we do so. Then, finally, even if we would like to stay, we know that we have finished the tough develop phase and we must now move into the deliver phase.

The work may have felt intensely personal and it almost always is. But there is a growing sense that the next part is not about us but about what we can do for others and perhaps even humanity.

Questions to ask yourself

If you are unsure if you are in step-9, it can be helpful to ask yourself some questions:

- Am I ready to return?
- What do I tell people about what has happened to me?
- Do I know how to be in the world in this new way?
- Do I know what awaits me?
- Has the world that awaits changed?
- Am I still 'fit for purpose'?
- Do I need to do something else now I have a much deeper understanding of my purpose?

Step-9 is the calm before the next storm. Here begins a dawning realisation that the effort must result in something more than a greater sense of peace and clarity. We must return home and put our treasure to good use. The quest was not just our quest – it was humanity's quest.

Notes

1 Watkins, A., (2021). *Coherence: The science of exceptional leadership and performance*. (2nd Ed.). London: Kogan Page.
2 Watkins, A., (2014). *Coherence: Secret science of brilliant leadership*. London: Kogan Page.
3 Lipton, B.H. and Bhaerman, S., (2009). *Spontaneous evolution*. New York: Hay House.

10 Step-10

Return

You are the Hero of your own Story.

(Joseph Campbell)

Step-10 is a largely metaphorical one. Unlike the movies, where Frodo returns to the Shire or Dorothy returns to Kansas, the return of step-10 is often just Monday morning. There are no fireworks. No bunting. No parade around the office with cheers and cake. In reality, the assimilation of what we've learned and the taking stock of step-9 is often almost inseparable from step-10 – the return.

That said, the return is a deliberate stepping forward to return to the world. It might just be the showing up for work after an intense workshop, but there is always a recognition that we can't stay at step-9 forever, regardless of how pleasant it may feel. We have to return and implement what we've learnt, otherwise what's the point of the effort?

Step-10 is the first step of the final phase of the journey. We deliver the treasure to the world, and that treasure is the reborn version of ourselves. We are changed, because we have embodied and consolidated this new version of ourselves at step-9; we can now 'be the change' we seek to see in the world. But this change is only useful if it delivers something better. Our return is the first step towards delivering that better future, and from this point forward we show up differently.

How do I know if I'm at step-10?

It may take some time for others to notice, but at step-10 we know we are different. We know we can't go back: we can only go forward and live our life as this new person. At step-8, we emerge from the cave knowing we are different, but at this point there is rarely a desire to broadcast that news. It simply doesn't feel necessary. Besides, it's often very difficult to know or explain exactly what happened. One of the quirks of the deep work is that we may enter the cave full of the angst and drama that has driven our life and the minutia of the challenges that fill our waking minutes. Once we've done the work, much of that evaporates like a snowball on a hotplate, so much so that we find it difficult to even recall what we used to get so anxious about. It can be really hard to explain what happened in the innermost

DOI: 10.4324/9781003170402-11

cave, and we are not even sure what faulty code was overwritten. But we know it was, and we have been permanently changed as a result. At step-9, we settle into this new version of ourselves. Authenticity builds and we start to develop the narrative that clarifies the change to us and to others. At step-10, we recognise that we need to share the narrative so others can appreciate the change. We need to update the world on who we are now, so they don't keep operating on old data and faulty assumptions about us. Indications that you might be in step-10 include:

• A recognition that the development is over, at least for now, and it's time to re-engage with the world.
• A realisation that what you have been through can change lives.
• A willingness to share your insights for the benefits of others, either proactively or in response to others' curiosity.

On a personal level, the return might be the return to a relationship, or to the family following an adventure, a period of change or an intense experience. In truth, people close to us including friends and family may never really know we are doing the work. Alternatively, they may have been with us through the change experience, but the return is more a metaphorical return and re-engagement with the world we left behind when we crossed the threshold at step-5.

The same is usually true in a business setting, where the leader simply returns to work. There may be a physical return, where the leader returns from a Harvard leadership programme or a week-long off-site experience. But often the return is just the next day after an inner transformation. We may reconnect with renewed vigour. We may want to mark our return with a celebration. We may just quietly get on with our job, preferring a more low-key return to our role. Which version of the return we choose will depend on many situational factors, the nature of our transformation and what we are returning to.

The purpose of the leader's journey, doing the work and transforming ourselves was not to impress anyone on our return. We do the work because it needs to be done. We need to develop because we're either stuck, or something is wrong, or the world is changing around us, and if we don't change it will overtake us. So, we set out on the adventure of change and once we cross the threshold we dig in, experiment and, if we're fortunate, find the treasure in the innermost cave. We become who we are meant to be.

The point of the return is we can now get on with our lives. Whether we want to trumpet our elevated wisdom, increased innovation capability, our greater humility or simply let people know we have had a change of heart depends on what we plan to do with the new version of ourselves.

The return journey can last some time, but often step-10 may be nothing more than a few seconds. Given that, it would be easy to underestimate its importance. The journey back to our previous world can contain some of its own unique challenges. There may be a few tests of our commitment to the new version of our Self. The time spent on the journey can be an important buffer that allows us to further consolidate, rest more, restore more energy, improve our story or simply figure out who to communicate this new version to. It can also be a time to plan and prepare. The return can have echoes of step-6, step-7 and step-9.

Working with your purpose

When we discover a new version of who we are, our personal purpose may also evolve, as we previously suggested. We return clearer about who we are; armed with new purpose and vigour we need to be clear about how to work with our purpose. This can involve checking three things about three things: how we describe our purpose to others, how we further enhance our purpose back in the world and how our purpose is changed when the rubber hits the road and we meet reality back in the world.

1   **Definition**: At step-8, we discovered the treasure that changes who we are. As a result, our purpose changes, and with a good developmental guide we can emerge with our purpose boiled down into a few extremely powerful words. It's not the three or four words themselves that create the power but what those words point to. One of the words is a verb and the first word is always "I". So, a leader's purpose may be "I provide" or "I work things out". Written out of context, these phrases look dull or inane. But if they have been fought for and embodied, they can represent a profound truth about who we really are, what our core operating principle really is, and as such they can be truly life changing. The reflection on the return journey is, if my purpose is "I provide", to clarify whether the word 'provide' means providing in the sense of 'giving', 'looking after', 'setting conditions', 'delivering' or something else.

2   **Direction**: Purpose is not the same as direction, although the two concepts are often confused. Having defined your purpose at step-8, it can help to then clarify how that purpose is applied – that is, its *direction*. Direction helps set the limits to your purpose. A purpose without direction can be overwhelming. One aspect of this is to identify what is included in and excluded from your purpose. For example, if your purpose is "I provide", then what do you provide and what do you not provide? Energy, ideas, support, attention, focus? You may also consider broadening the application of your purpose for even greater fulfilment. Another way to give direction is to consider when and where you use your purpose. So, if it is "I care", when do you care and why? Where do you care most strongly – is it all the time, just one part of your life or particular kinds of situations or people? Why do you care more in some contexts than others?

3   **Process and practice**: A more detailed description of the steps within your purpose can help you live your purpose and improve the flow through the steps to get a better result. This is what sportspeople do to stay at the top of their game. For example, professional golfers will know every element of their golf swing and how small adjustments can change the shot they take. Typically, the process of your purpose will be the same regardless of context. Ask yourself: what do you do when you use your purpose? What triggers it to come into

focus? What do you do first and how does it proceed? For example, "I discover" could have the following steps: 'curiosity–question–explore–notice–pinpoint–unearth–analyse–conclude–integrate'. Now you know the process, what steps can you practice to get more out of your purpose? Going back to your direction, could you apply it more easily in some contexts?

4   **Leading**: As a leader, your purpose will manifest, either helpfully or unhelpfully, in the 'I', 'WE' and 'IT' dimensions (i.e., personally, interpersonally and operationally). How does your purpose affect your feelings, relationships and what you do day-to-day? For example, if your purpose is "I see clearly", on days when you can't see clearly you may become extremely frustrated, causing you to create interpersonal tensions and maybe even behave badly. If seeing clearly is what you are all about, when others fail to see clearly what effect does that have on you and your relationship with them? If you are now all about seeing clearly, the power of this may be predominantly manifesting in the objective world of operations. When others are confused by operational signals, you're crystal clear. This might explain why you become irritated when there is a lack of data. It may be that as a leader you add significant value by being able to clearly see the vision of the future when others are still stuck in the short-term.

5   **Living:** When you return to your life it may become clear how you can live your purpose more expansively with a greater level of fulfilment. Consider all the different aspects of your life – work, career, partner, family, friends, home, leisure, health, wealth – how productively can you apply your new purpose? Where will your life feel 'on purpose' and where will it feel 'off'? What can you do back in the world to feel more purposeful and fulfilled? How can you live your purpose more fluidly and powerfully? Your purpose should be a guiding compass for the decisions you are making in all areas of your life. Look at the decisions you make in the world and decide how much they are likely to be influenced by your new purpose. How will it, for example, affect your work performance and the quality of your relationships outside work? How will your new purpose affect whether you consider the day to be a good day or a bad day?

6   **Powering Up:** You can think of your new purpose as your personal elixir, the source of your 'magic'. It's unique to you and comes to life through you. So how will you power up your purpose? How will you maximise its impact and use it to further drive your development? Reflecting on the process of your purpose may reveal steps that can be sped up or reconfigured for greater effect. Could you power up a single process step so it's more intuitive and takes less time? Another way to power up your purpose is to consider how it helps you with a development challenge. For example, if pushy and aggressive people are difficult for you to relate to, try reframing this as an opportunity to apply your purpose.

7   **Meaning:** As you return, you can reflect on understanding of the role of your purpose (i.e., the 'purpose' of your purpose). This involves considering the extent and nature of its impact on the world so you can broaden and deepen

it. Try asking yourself – how does my purpose serve others? What difference does it make to my community, to humanity? If your purpose is "I create movement", what kind of momentum could you create? Who for, and why? You could also explore the 'legacy' of your purpose. What lasting impact will your purpose have? What would you like to be remembered for if you lived your purpose fully?

8   **Integrating:** As you become more developed and live your purpose more fully, you will notice that it has a downside. Exploring and embracing the 'shadow' of your purpose will enable you to be more at peace with who you are and to live your purpose more fully. Consider the following questions. Your return is a great time to consider when your purpose doesn't serve you well, that is, what is its downside? When does it get in the way of your success or happiness? How does it feel when you cannot use your purpose, or you have to do the opposite, and how do you deal with that? For example, if your purpose is "I take charge", how do you feel about situations when you are unable to do so or when you have to surrender control? For someone who takes charge, reflecting on the nature of 'surrender' can be a useful source of self-discovery. Similarly, if your purpose is "I facilitate", how do you feel about the concept of 'non-facilitation'?

9   **Evolving:** We have seen that our purpose may change from step-7 to step-8 as we discover who we really are in the innermost cave. In fact, with each revolution of the Change Wheel your purpose may evolve repeatedly. Each version tends to transcend and include the previous one, becoming a more sophisticated expression of who you are. Imagine the timeline of your life. Looking back, what have been the significant turning points and experiences that fundamentally changed you? What does that imply about previous versions of your purpose? How have they transcended and included each other? Moving to the present and looking forward, how are you developing now? What are the implications for your purpose? How is it evolving, and what might the next version be?

If step-10 is momentary, there will be no time for this sort of reflection. Therefore, some of this work may need to happen once you are at step-11, but it's really part of the step-10 process.

Follow your bliss

Follow your bliss … If you do follow your bliss, you put yourself on a kind of track that has been there all the while, waiting for you, and the life that you ought to be living is the one you are living. When you can see that, you begin to meet people who are in your field of bliss, and they open doors to you. I say, follow your bliss and don't be afraid, and doors will open where you didn't know they were going to be.

(Joseph Campbell)

Step-10 is likely to be when we first become fully aware of what Campbell was talking about when he suggested we follow our bliss. When we are a living embodiment of the change we have sought and our efforts are aligned with our purpose, then doors open; weird synchronicities occur where we meet exactly the right person at exactly the right time. As we return and prepare for the next step, the right resources start to show up to facilitate our success. This is because we are radiating a different energy, so we attract different things. Our energy is cleaner. Living in this more flow-like state becomes even more pronounced the more revolutions of the Change Wheel we experience.

How does it feel to be at step-10?

Often there is a sense of excitement, wonder and awe at what we've achieved. We are rightly proud of our effort and how we've changed. There is also a growing sense of satisfaction and fulfilment at having made it this far. At the same time, even if we've broken through to a whole new level, we know that we need to deliver on that breakthrough and that is still ahead of us.

At step-9, we may have taken a meta-view of the journey, looking back and reflecting on our own experience of that journey. In step-10 we take a meta-view of the journey itself. We can see that there are four phases: discover, decide, develop and deliver. We also know that there are three steps in each phases. We can map our own journey through those steps and phases. We often don't realise this until step-10 when we return to the world.

The previous phase was not in the known world, so the juxtaposition is now obvious. Returning to the world allows us to see that we were in a different place at each step of the Change Wheel. For most leaders this is experienced as an internal 'I' space versus an external 'IT' space. When we are developing, we are exploring and evolving in an inner world. When we return, we take the new person we have become back to the outer, objective world. At step-10 we start to clearly see the connection and relationship between the inner and outer worlds. This assists us in our appreciation of the guide that the Change Wheel provides. Step-10 starts to close the circle, and in the closing of the circle we realise there is a circle, whereas before we might have thought of it as simply a pathway or journey to a chosen destination. When we return, we begin to glimpse that the destination is actually going to be where we started! But because we are different, everything is different. To paraphrase T.S. Eliot's wonderful poem 'Little Gidding', we never stop changing, and when we have changed, we find ourselves back where we started only to know ourselves for the first time. Because we are different, everything is different.

Failure to mark the return and disillusionment

In the movies, crossing the threshold into the unknown world and the return are literal. We see the main characters literally leaving home and travelling to a new world. Later in the film we see them return to great fanfare and celebration. The hero has returned.

In real life, especially in business, that doesn't happen. As I mentioned at the start of this chapter, there is often no formal return. No celebration; it's just Monday morning. If we have genuinely engaged with the Change Wheel, we may recognise that the most transformational journeys we can ever take happen intern-ally. For example, changing how our minds create meaning from experience liter-ally changes our entire world. This is an inner change not a surface change in what we are doing. More often than not, the 'unknown world' we set off to explore is not literally a new planet somewhere beyond the Pleiades, it's the exploration of Self. And this inner exploration happens as we live our lives in the known world that we operate in every day. Most people we coach are doing their day job as we guide them through the Change Wheel. There is rarely, if ever, a trek up a mountain to sit in a cave. The cave that holds the treasure is metaphorical.

As such, there is rarely a literal departure or literal return. We know we have done the work and we are changed. The more perceptive of our colleagues may start to notice that something is different, but often we have not left our desk; we are still in the same position in the same environment as we were before our transformation. This means we can often fail to recognise the importance of the return and the value of creating a buffering moment to signal, at least to ourselves, that this is the first moment of the rest of our lives.

If a leader has done the work of step-7 and step-8 and embodied that change in step-9, they are fundamentally changed. A completely new leader walks into their office on that Monday morning even though they will look the same on the out-side. The job title is the same and they sit in the same chair in the same office in the same building, but they have changed. It is important, therefore, to acknowledge that difference and celebrate the return properly. It doesn't have to be loud and it doesn't have to involve anyone else, but the leader must recognise the journey they have been on, appreciate the treasure they now possess and quietly celebrate that accomplishment, otherwise it's importance and relevance can slip away in the day-to-day pressures of work. If we don't effectively acknowledge our own trans-formation, we risk disillusionment setting in as we wonder why we even bothered changing in the first place.

In the sunshine of step-9, embodiment can feel good. Similarly, the reflection and celebration of step-10 can also feel good, especially in the early days of the return. But if we haven't marked the return and acknowledged its importance, once the day kicks in the thought of another revolution of the Change Wheel might feel daunting. If this cycle of the Change Wheel included step-8, then the risk of being intimidated or inhibited at step-11 is massively reduced. Without formal recogni-tion that we have changed and have now returned at step-10. we may even begin to question that anything is different at all. Celebration or acknowledgement of the return, therefore, helps to solidify the difference by inviting us to consider what this is going to or could mean for us in our current position. What we must always do at step-10 is figure out the bigger implication to that new delivery based on what we've been through and experienced.

Cultural metaphors

In the movies, step-10 often features more significantly than it does in real life. The return home may be euphoric and triumphal or quiet and moving, depending on the movie. There is a joy and relief at the return but also often a recognition, perhaps only by the hero, that this is not the end of the story. Life will never be the same again.

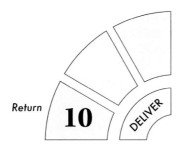

The Matrix: The return moment in the Matrix is metaphoric rather than actual. Neo extinguishes Smith by allowing Smith to infect him. Victory is achieved by breaking the cycle of suffering that flows from living in a dualistic world. Neo has understood his own role in this duality. He recognises that merging with Smith breaks the dance of duality. Neo is happy to let go of his own identity. This free will choice mirrors the same free will choice made by Morpheus who walks out into the machine swarm to prove the war is over. Likewise, Trinity chooses to go to the Machine City with Neo and dies in the process. Salvation from the Matrix is there for those who choose it actively, not passively. They must know themselves and on their return take hold of that truth within and make their personal choice based on their journey. The emphasis is on the personal capacity to transcend and the inner revolution. In the final battle between Smith and Neo, when it's clear that Smith has won, he asks Neo "why do you persist?" Neo replies, "Because I choose to." The last line of the whole Matrix trilogy also highlights the point about choice. Seraph asks the Oracle, "Did you always know?" She replies, "No, but I believed." So even the all-seeing Oracle says truth is not achievable without faith. This is the marriage of sense and soul,[1] science and spirituality, machine and man. We need to discover the world within to change the world outside us.

The Lord of the Rings: When Frodo initially returns to the Shire, there is a clear realisation that further adventures await. He may be changed, but more cycles of the wheel lay ahead. We see the hobbits enjoying a drink in the local pub. At this point, it's clear that Sam is going to ask his childhood sweetheart to marry him and Pippin and Merry are going to carry on much as before. But Frodo already knows that he no longer belongs in the Shire, and he will be leaving again soon. Ultimately, after Frodo has destroyed the ring, he returns not to the Shire but to the land beyond duality – the Undying Lands of Valinor.

Star Wars: Because of the expansive nature of the Star Wars films there are multiple journeys and returns for Luke and many of the other characters. Through Luke, Anakin Skywalker is reborn and the Sith are destroyed. The Empire is resoundingly defeated, and Luke returns triumphant having enabled the Rebel Alliance to restore freedom to the galaxy. In a subsequent revolution of the Change Wheel, Luke detaches himself from the larger galaxy to focus on uncovering the secrets of the Jedi and rebuilding the Order, but he fails and the Jedi are destroyed. Luke, being the last Jedi left, goes into hiding. He lives in the ancient Jedi temple on Ahch-To, his whereabouts unknown to the rest of the galaxy. He is rescued by Rey, who is eager to learn the ways of the Force. Rey and Yoda remind Luke who he once was and what he can be again. They encourage Luke to end his seclusion, which he does, and so Luke experiences another return. His elixir this time is his insight into his own weaknesses and the meaning of his failures.

Harry Potter: After Harry defeats Voldemort and returns to a world without his nemesis, he learns that a part of Voldemort's soul lives on in him. Harry realises he must sacrifice himself to purge the darkness. As Campbell points out, to complete any adventure a returning hero must survive the impact of the world. In Harry's case, the crossing of the return threshold occurs after the dream sequence in King's Cross with Dumbledore. This is where Harry comes back from the dead. This scene is the beginning of the make the return rather than the actual return. At this point, Harry still has to fight Voldemort and defeat him once and for all. Once he does this, he completes the return and becomes the master of the two worlds, life and death. This is where the hero can now live as he chooses. In Harry's case, this means marrying Ginny Weasley and having three children.

The Wizard of Oz: On the road back from Oz, and as part of the celebration of the return, the Wizard gives the scarecrow a diploma, the lion a medal for bravery and the tin man a ticking heart. These are all symbolic rewards, and it's not the gift that makes the difference but how these gifts make them feel. Dorothy's return is a little more complicated. Initially, when it is time for Dorothy to receive what she thought was her reward – a trip home to Kansas in a balloon – her dog Toto jumps out of her arms to chase a cat. Toto, who really represents Dorothy's instincts, knows that she can't get back to Kansas in a balloon. And as Dorothy runs after her dog the balloon rises out of reach, taking the Wizard away as its only passenger. So, Dorothy stumbles as she tries to return, revealing that the transition isn't always smooth. Fortunately, Glinda reappears and explains that Dorothy always had the ability to return right from the start by using her magic slippers. This beautifully illustrates the constant juxtaposition of the known world with the inner world of transformation. Glinda kept this information from Dorothy to enable her to experience the lessons that she needed to drive her transformation.

The transition from step-10 to step-11

The transition from step-10 to step-11 is the pivot from rocking back to rocking forward; from reflection to action; from neutral to the forward gears. Energy rises as our excitement to step into life increases. We're clearer about what we want to achieve as a result of our work. We have a much deeper appreciation of our new purpose. We may quickly go through our final checklist like a pilot shortly before take-off, but the transition to step-11 is all about the take-off. This can be a double-edged sword for many people because the journey to step-11 can give them an insight into the meaninglessness of their day-to-day work, and that can be brutal. But that's partly the point of step-10 – to find new meaning in what may have become somewhat meaningless. With this new sense of meaning we can re-engage with the world regardless of how troubled the world might appear.

This pre-take-off ritual may include a quick stock take of the resources we have versus the resources we need to execute effectively. In that regard the transition can feel a little like step-6. But this time there is much more self-assurance, momentum and urgency. Even as we rock forward and get stuck in, there is often a growing realisation that while we have returned, at some point in the future we are going to leave again. This realisation, albeit not yet shared with others, can feel like an inner secret – another journey and adventure await.

Questions to ask yourself

If you are unsure if you are in step-10, it can be helpful to ask yourself some questions:

- What do I tell people about what has happened to me?
- Do I know how to be in the world in this new way? Do I know what awaits me?
- Has the world I left changed? Can I still connect with those that need my help?
- Am I ready to step up?
- Am I ready to lead?
- Am I confident in how I change the future?
- Has the level of thinking subsided so I am ready for action?
- Is the readiness to deliver ever present?

There is a consolidation to the return, another breather before moving forward to step-11, where you will deliver at a whole new level.

Note

1 Wilber, K., (1999). *The marriage of sense and soul: Integrating science and religion.* New York: Broadway Books.

11 Step-11

Delivery at the new level

I don't believe people are looking for the meaning of life as much as they are looking for the experience of being alive.

(Joseph Campbell)

Step-11 is when the change effort becomes visible. There may have been glimpses at step-9 and step-10, but step-11 is when we are cooking on gas. The capability uplift that the change facilitated is now manifest, enabling us to move at incredible speed. Step-11 is literally the embodiment of a true step change!

How do I know if I'm at step-11?

Step-11 is really the culmination of all the effort that has gone before. It is the point where we become a living, breathing demonstration of our vertical development. Indications that you might be in step-11 include:

- You can perform at a whole new level. It's irrefutable.
- You can deliver things that you simply weren't capable of before – genuine breakthroughs.
- You can go further, faster.
- You are aware that these new abilities seem almost magical to the previous version of you.

In your personal life, step-11 is where you and your partner are getting along better. There are fewer arguments, and the relationship with your children has improved significantly. There is more enjoyment in the home and less tension. There's a deeper connection and a growing sense of meaning and fulfilment.

In your professional life, step-11 could mean a promotion based on a demonstrated ability to deliver at this new level. When we deliver at the new level, the consequences can ripple far and wide and change our lives in the 'I', 'WE' and 'IT' dimensions. In one European retailer, turning over €6 billion in revenue, we took the Exec group on a team journey and transformed them over the course of 18 months. This enabled them to deliver at a whole new level. We saw a step change

DOI: 10.4324/9781003170402-12

in engagement across the workforce of 65,000 people in four countries. We asked the CEO, prior to the engagement survey, how much of an improvement he was hoping to see in engagement levels, to which he replied one per cent, because the Group improvement was 0.9 per cent over the previous 12 months. We saw a 16 per cent improvement. This was so dramatic that the independent agency that measured the data checked four times. They had never seen such an improvement in such a short space of time. Whist the CEO was pleased with this cultural transformation in the 'WE' domain, he reserved judgement until the trading figures were in. As he said: "It's great that colleagues are more engaged, but it doesn't count for much if we're not doing better as a business." When the trading figures came in three months later, we saw a €109 million jump in profits. This proved to the team that when you change the 'I' and the 'WE' domains it can also delver a transformation in the 'IT' domain. Up to this point revenues had been flat and profitability was unstable.

This step change was a result of us taking the team on a journey, which consisted of eight days a year developing them as individuals and as a team. This represented a return on investment of approximately 1,600 times. This reveals how much more can be delivered when significant change is really delivered. The CEO commented: "What's great is that we're taking the broader team with us and that's around 65,000 people. The change in our top team is cascading throughout the business and to our millions of customers as well." With our careful guidance of the leadership team through each step of the Change Wheel, this team achieved 10 years development in just 12 months. Such a transformation is not an isolated occurrence.

More recently, we worked with the leadership team of another £1 billion business. The new CEO, who took over in 2018, recognised that: "The business hadn't been performing and the key to unlocking its success would be a strong leadership team. I knew I couldn't fix things all by myself. I needed a guide to help me and to engage the team, to give us the tools and techniques to help us manage ourselves and our team." The team developed significantly during the first 18 months of work, enabling them to increase revenue by 17 per cent despite a global pandemic. The share price over the same period increased by 254 per cent, making it the highest performing share in the FTSE 250. The CPO commented: "We have made considerable progress, which can be seen from our financial results. The techniques that we are learning have guided us through the pandemic." Recognising that such step change in not a one-off phenomenon, the CEO concluded: "We're moving on, we are seeing new things. We're now recognising that the team is a thing in its own right, and we will continue to invest the time, space and external impetus to keep us growing."

The journey, which, at the time of writing, we are facilitating with 25 different multi-national corporations' top leadership teams, requires us to use our suite of developmental assessments. These can precisely quantify what the developmental challenges are, across the 'I', 'WE' and 'IT' domains of the business, that need attention. This directs the change effort and enables us to focus on the areas of improvement that will deliver the biggest impact for each person, the team and the entire organisation. One of the reasons so much of the change effort with leaders and teams fails to deliver is because the quality of what is assessed and measured doesn't focus the effort in the right way.

Unfortunately, far too much emphasis is still being placed on descriptive leadership assessments as a way of determining development need.

Such instruments come in three main forms:

1   Typologies like Myers Briggs Type Indicator (MBTI) or the Enneagram
2   A personality test like Hogan
3   A strengths finder like the Gallup Strengths Finder

Descriptive assessments are rooted in the science of individual differences that became popular at the start of the 20th Century. Initially, such tests emerged from the murky waters of eugenics and intelligence testing but then they focused more on cognitive performance designed to better assign troops to duty during World War Two. After the war, the industrial psychology movement, particularly in the USA, expanded such testing to the workplace. Much of the evaluation of individuals focused on aptitude and suitability for job roles. Over the last seventy years, the thrust of all this assessment work has been to describe the abilities of an individual. This is despite the fact that descriptive tests cannot predict success. The leadership literature provides a very clear signal that there is no one type of leader, one leadership personality or one set of skills that always succeeds. Nevertheless, most organisations are still locked into this outdated idea of descriptive testing.

We believe that assessing the developmental level of a leader is much more useful and developmental assessments will, over the next five years, replace descriptive assessments as the preferred methodology. This is largely because developmental assessments are much better at predicting who will succeed when promoted. For example, when deciding who is needed to manage the complexity of a specific problem, it doesn't really matter whether they are introverted or extroverted, agreeable or disagreeable or whether they have one set of strengths over a different set of strengths; the ability to solve any problem, especially complex problems, comes down to whether or not they have reached the level of development where their mind can cope with that complexity and the interdependencies that complexity creates. The ability to solve any problem doesn't rest on personality, typology or strengths; it rests on whether those involved have developed the sophistication of mind to solve the problem and do the job.

We see this error of judgement all the time in industry. I clearly remember, some years ago, witnessing a large multi-national promoting their CFO to the CEO role because all the descriptive tests suggested he was a strong candidate. He knew the business. He was very financially literate, good with the analysis and could manage the Plc reporting process and all RemCo issues with ease. The Chairman was confident that he had appointed the right man. My concern was that he may be an expert CFO, but his identity was wrapped up in his role as an accountant. I felt he would struggle to let go of his expertise as a numbers guy and enable the leadership team to achieve its goals. He was a good CFO, but I doubted he had the maturity to cope with the much broader role of a CEO. This is exactly what happened. He did the CEO role as though he was still the CFO. He ran the company off a spreadsheet, rarely left his office and micromanaged his CFO successor. Consequently, the company dropped out of the FTSE 100 for the first time in years as their performance faltered.

In today's rapidly accelerating and disrupted world, descriptive assessments may generate talking points but commercially they are not that useful. Every leader and team are different and understanding a leader's level of sophistication is way more important than aspects of personality. Our diagnostic tools offer quantifiable measurement of individual and team starting positions on the developmental journey. They also provide a way of measuring the change that is being delivered at step-11.

A critical part of delivering change is the ability to accurately measure whether meaningful change has occurred. How do we really know if we're different? How do we know if we have more energy? How do we know if we're much better at emotional regulation? How do we know if our team's performing at a new level? How do we know if we are more mature? How can we tell if the high potential individual has stopped being a bully or whether they have just become a more sophisticated bully? Without quantifiable measures it can be incredibly easy to rationalise, justify and imagine we have changed. We're all very good at retrospectively claiming that our efforts have delivered results. Such is our propensity for self-justification. But we need to be significantly more discerning about what we are measuring when we are looking at individual and team change to determine if that change is real or imagined.

Retesting using accurate diagnostics allows us to quantify the change, stabilise it, understand it and therefore continue to drive it. We must get better at assessing inner individual and team development and become professionally fascinated with the idea and quantification of progress. The perception of change is not the same as a change in perception. We might like to believe something is different, but is it? Alfred Korzybski once said, "The map is not the territory", meaning our perception of the world is being generated by our brain and can be considered as a 'map' of reality written in neural patterns. But reality is not that map. A map of New York is not New York; to know New York we must got there and experience it through our senses.

Our forensic assessment of individuals and team and their developmental level gives us an accurate map, but we must engage with a leadership team to really know how accurate that map really is. When we define a specific developmental level, it's important to understand whether the individual or team is at the start of this new level, in the middle of the level or on the cusp of exiting that level. Within every level there are multiple sub-levels and understanding this requires skills and experience. To help a team navigate its way through all the steps of change on the Change Wheel, we need to understand the details of every step; not just the entry and exit criteria, but the mini steps within a step, the dynamics at play and what determines progress at that step.

Step-11 is about action. As such, there's a very strong behavioural focus at this step. Of the eleven letters of the behavioural alphabet identified by Schroder and Cockerill, step-11, delivery at the new level, often shifts the focus from the *Imagine* cluster of behaviours to the *Involve*, *Ignite* and *Implement* behaviours. At step-6, the

IMPLEMENT		IMAGINE	
Maximise operatoinal efficiency and enable organizational change to deliver commercial performance and customer value		Take a broad and deep view of the commercial context that ensures vision and strategy create competitive advantage	
Being Proactive		**Seeking Information**	
Continuously Improving		**Forming CoNcepts**	
-		**Conceptual FleXing**	
IGNITE		INVOLVE	
Connect with people to release their commitment, enthusiasm and support for ideas, plans and strategies that take the business forward		Fully engage and develop individuals and teams to build trust, nurture potential and get the best out of people	
Transmitting Impactfully		**Empathic Connecting**	
Building Confidence		**Facilitating Interaction**	
Influencing Others		**Developing People**	

Figure 11.1 The eleven letters of the 'behavioural alphabet'.

Imagine cluster is particularly important as we prepare to do the work. It may also be used at step-10 as we prepare to deliver at the next level. At step-11 we need to start working with the other letters in the behavioural alphabet (Figure 11.1).

Involve

At step-11 we may have done the work then discovered the treasure, we may be embodying this new version of our Self and returned home, but we still need to involve others if we want to deliver at a new level. There are three behaviours that are critical in the involve cluster:

- **Empathetic connecting** – are we able to really listen to other people's perspectives? Can we understand what they mean rather than what they say? Can we reflect back to them and create in them a sense that they are seen and feel understood? If we want to work with them to deliver a new level, do they feel we are empathic, and do they feel connected to us?
- **Facilitating interaction** – how well can we facilitate genuine interaction between team members to build an aligned view in the team? Can we teach a team to build on each other's comments rather than pretend to hear each other only to dismiss each other's points of view and flip into broadcasting our own view?
- **Developing people** – how good are we at supporting an individual's progress around the Change Wheel so they can develop? Can we personally coach, mentor or stretch others?

Ignite

Once we've fully engaged others in the need to deliver, connected with them, built bonds between them and helped them mature, then the next step is to ignite their confidence and influence them to action. There are three behaviours that are critical in the ignite cluster:

- **Transmit impactfully** – can we fire up others by getting our point across clearly and in a compelling way? Will people remember our message?
- **Building confidence** – do we create self-belief in others that they can deliver results? Do we proactively celebrate success with our colleagues and create a sense of optimism?
- **Influence others** – do we build sustainable mutually beneficial alliances and win/win relationships? Are we good at persuading people to action by promoting benefits and advantages?

Implement

Once everyone is fired up to deliver, there are two behaviours that are critical in the implementation stage:

- **Being proactive** – do we assign roles and responsibilities and build delivery plans? Do we ensure delivery happens by overcoming barriers, bureaucracies and inertia?
- **Continuous improving** – do we set and measure appropriate goals to improve performance? Do we manage quality by routinely tracking key performance indicators?

How does it feel to be at step-11?

It feels fantastic.

There's an almost effortless joy at step-11 as we really embrace and own our change by recognising what we're capable of and delivering it. This is the culmination of all our effort, but that effort is now visible. Emerging from step-8 and the innermost cave, we know we're different, but step-9 and step-10 are still largely internal steps. Step-11 is when we unleash our new capabilities on the world and everyone can see the transformation in us, born of our progress round the Change Wheel.

Everyone who crosses the threshold at step-5 does so with some aspiration or hope. "If only I could…" Step-11 is where that hope becomes a reality. "If only I could stop smoking." "If only I could get that promotion." "If only I could become CEO." Step-11 is when we achieve that aspiration. We are finally a non-smoker or have the job we dreamed of. It can be deeply fulfilling because the thing we wanted is now here. There's a deep sense of excitement and joy.

There's also pride in what we've accomplished and a growing sense of excitement that we have somehow cracked the change code. We are a living demonstration of the change we sought. This can massively accelerate our self-confidence and may also pique our curiosity in what else might be possible.

Satisfaction

At every step there is a risk that we get stuck at that step or regress. This danger is usually an emotion or mindset. At step-11, the danger is deep satisfaction.

Mick Jagger once complained "I can't get no satisfaction" even though he tried and tried. At step-11, our desire for satisfaction is satisfied. We've literally arrived at the destination we always wanted to get to. We're absolutely smashing it and loving life. But there is a seductive nature to this step. If we're not paying attention, it can easily morph into step-1 – comfort zone. Things may be going so well at step-11 that we may become complacent and just stop trying or thinking or wondering. We may even become so comfortable that we let go of our professional fascination with measuring progress. This usually only ever happens in the first cycle of the Change Wheel. Once we recognise the cyclical nature of change, we become much more mindful of moving into step-12 rather than simply skipping past it to languish again in the comfort zone.

Cultural metaphors

Most films don't hang around to show what the hero's life is like after he returns. It's usually considered too boring compared to the drama of the trials and tribulations, the battles with demons or the triumphant return. The delivery is, therefore, almost always metaphoric, an ideal or a change in the grand order. We don't tend to see heroes back in the known world because it may make them look mundane. The exception to this rule is in sequels, prequels, trilogies or, indeed, a series of movies. Then what the hero delivers in the first film is clearly a stepping stone for the next revolution of the Change Wheel.

The Matrix: At the end of the first film, Neo defeats Agent Smith and returns with new powers such as the ability to fly and disrupt the physics of the Matrix, reinforcing the belief that he is the One. But in *The Matrix Reloaded* and then *The Matrix Revolutions*, Neo's 'delivery' becomes more metaphoric. It's the delivery of peace between the machine world and the human world, and in that peace stability and order is restored. Harmony and balance preside, and from this point another cycle of development can begin. Not a reloading of the Matrix, because Neo rejected that choice, but a better version based on more evolved principles. This inspires another evolution of the Change Wheel. As the final scene starts, we see the delivery of change roll into the streets. We see Sati, the little girl, wake up as a black cat crosses her path. Sati represents love, and she has built a new Mega city in honour of Neo's sacrifice. At the end of the trilogy the Architect, who is seen as the father of the Matrix, speaks to the Oracle, who is it's mother. He says to her: "You played a dangerous game." To which the Oracle replies: "Change always is."

The Lord of the Rings: The film trilogy is really one unbroken story, so there are many battles, caves and returns with increased powers gained by Frodo on his journey. However, the main 'delivery' happens at the end of the third film and it's a metaphoric delivery of peace after the ring has been destroyed. There is only scant information about Frodo's life once he reaches the Undying Lands. He lives for a further sixty years or so before he dies.

Star Wars: Like the other great movie franchises, Luke experiences several cycles of the Change Wheel. But in the recent reboot of the franchise, *The Force Awakens*, the heroic lineage and mantle very clearly passes to Rey. This is reinforced by Rey's meeting with Luke on the remote planet of Ahch-To. As such, Rey goes through all the same steps as Luke did from her humble beginnings on the desert planet of Jakku. Luke moves from the hero to mentor. And that is his delivery in the reboot.

Harry Potter: In the first film of the franchise, *Harry Potter and the Philosopher's Stone*, Voldemort uses Professor Quirrell's body to stay alive, like a parasite. When Quirrell tries to grab the philosopher's stone, he touches Harry and dissolves into ashes, leaving Voldemort without a host body, but he still escapes. Harry returns to Hogwarts and wakes up in the infirmary. He has new knowledge and insight. Harry can function and deliver at a whole new level, but it's clear there will be many cycles of the Change Wheel before Harry's journey is complete. So, with each new film there is a return and a step change in what Harry is capable of until eventually he liberates himself through sacrifice in the final film.

The Wizard of Oz: After Dorothy clicks her heels and says three times "There's no place like home", she wakes up safe and sound in her bed in Kansas. In the movie, the implication was that the entire film had been a dream. However, in the original book she lost her slippers over the desert on her way back to Kansas, proving she really had been to Oz. As with most other films, the 'delivery' was metaphoric rather than literal and the story really ended with the return rather than any details on how Dorothy performed as a result of her ordeal. It seems that real life and cultural metaphor differ significantly in their focus. Films naturally focus on the drama and the transformation process rather than the life after transformation and how the leader delivers.

The transition from step-11 to step-12

Step-11 is about today. Delivery today. Success today or the short-term. Step-12 is about tomorrow and what's next. The transition from step-11 to step-12 begins with this recognition that if we become entranced by today, we will never discover tomorrow. This short-term addiction is an extremely common trap in business. Many leaders spend most of their time focused on this year's plan, the operational performance, cost cutting, organisational structure, risk management and the battle for quarterly performance. If we don't lift our eyes up from the here and now, from the tyranny of the moment, then we will never start to dream of tomorrow. But today and tomorrow are connected. If we fail to truly realise that, today becomes dry and ultimately unsatisfying. So, eventually, even the most hardened short-term addicts may start to wonder if there is something else.

Eventually questions begin to bubble up, hopefully as a result of the joyful contentment of step-11. In our satisfied reflection of past and present we start to wonder about the future: "If I could achieve this, what more could I achieve?" In this regard, the comfort of step-11 is profoundly different from the comfort of step-1. Step-11 comfort is tinged with openness and optimism and the possibility of more. In contrast, the comfort of step-1 is insular, an echo chamber of complacency and ignorance. Step-1 comfort is tinged with an ensnaring hint of negativity, which shackles you to the moment.

In the warmth of step-11 achievement, we can start to dream. As delivering at the new level becomes our default, we are called to consider what's next. What other treasures might we find in our next adventure? The excitement moves us forward to step-12.

Questions to ask yourself

If you are unsure if you are in step-11, it can be helpful to ask yourself some questions:

- Do I understand the new level I am operating at?
- How do I bake my new insights into the system, so it doesn't require me to be present for the system to change?
- How do I let my change be its own teaching?

The answers to these questions can help to fully embody step-11 and trigger the final push to step-12.

12 Step-12

Inspire

A hero is someone who has given his or her life to something bigger than oneself.

(Joseph Campbell)

We can sit around and hope for change to emerge, but that change may be glacial. Or we can understand change and facilitate something much faster and more efficient. At step-12, the last step of the Change Wheel, we understand all twelve steps and all four phases, and evolution becomes revolution. The difference between evolution and revolution comes down to time and intensity. It's an evolution when that change is hard to even notice because it's so slow. Revolution, on the other hand, is a fast, intense, game-changing transformation, and it's revolution that comes into sharp focus at step-12. We have the blueprint for change. We have lived through and survived each of the four phases and every one of the twelve steps. We have also reaped the rewards and are, therefore, inspired to keep going.

When we've spun the Change Wheel a few times, it's possible to develop something called vertical autopoiesis. Essentially, once we realise the cyclical nature of change and the relationship between all the steps, we develop change competence. With every new spin of the Change Wheel, we become increasingly unconsciously competent, and then it's almost impossible not to keep cycling, keep expanding, keep growing, keep progressing and keep evolving. Not out of a compulsion; the change simply gathers its own momentum, like a spiritual gyroscope.

How do I know if I'm at step-12?

Step-12 is the last step of the deliver phase and the end of one complete revolution of the Change Wheel. Of course, once we appreciate the nature of the steps and the phases of discover, decide, develop and deliver, we recognise that it's not the end but the beginning. Indications that you might be in step-12 include:

- You're inspired. Your change has created a desire to repeat the cycle, this time on a higher level. You feel as though you finally have the knowledge and tools to bring about whatever change you want. This is what meaning feels like.

DOI: 10.4324/9781003170402-13

- You realise how you show up now and could show up in the future. You also understand how this can inspire others to change or to start their own change journey. This can be deeply satisfying as you are a living demonstration of what's possible.

In your personal life, step-12 might include the conscious creation of a shared vision for your family. Someone's relationships at home may have improved as a result of them delivering at a new level. This may bring deep satisfaction and joy to the family experience, but in step-12 there is a tilt to the future. We are all happier; this is a nicer, more enjoyable way to live – what can we do as a family now? Often, the sense of having been on a change journey will inspire that person to nurture their family on a similar journey, individually and collectively, so that everyone can grow and develop. Isn't that the true nature of parenthood?

In your professional life, step-12 is similar in that there is a conscious appreciation for what's been delivered. A leader may be stunned as they review individual and collective accomplishments across the whole organisation. If you review your accomplishments, the swell of pride may provoke a desire to tell the story to a much wider audience, not in a self-congratulatory, arrogant way but out of a desire to celebrate and acknowledge everyone's contributions. This helps people own the change and use their success to stoke positive feeling and inspire a revolution.

At step-9, we look back and assess our own personal change journey, what we experienced, what we learnt and how we changed as a result. At step-10, we look at the dynamic of the journey itself and begin to appreciate the relationship between the steps and phases and how to deliver change. At step-12, we add in the accomplishments at step-11. Given all that, how can we not keep going?

Step-12 is where we would conduct an achievement audit – a conscious looking back on what has been achieved across the dimensions of 'I', 'WE' and 'IT'. This is a systematic quarter-by-quarter assessment and documentation of results so that everyone involved in the change journey can fully appreciate just how far they, their team and business have come. Why is it that in business, mistakes are dissected for learning but our successes are rarely even catalogued? The argument is usually time. We don't have time; we have to keep going; we have a new laundry list of objectives to achieve.

We need to call out our successes to solidify and stabilise step-12 so we can see, feel and genuinely acknowledge the results of our efforts. It is also crucial for inspiration, of self and others.

There are three components to inspiration:

- Expansion
- Future focus
- Momentum

When we inhale, we take in air and our lungs expand. In the same way, step-12 – inspire is about recognising what we have taken in as we've journeyed around the

Change Wheel. We have taken in knowledge and learning; we have sought to deploy that learning and convert it into development. That effort has paid dividends as we've delivered at a new level. We are a very different person, and the question that often follows is: "What now?" Step-12 is a good place to be but there's a recognition that it's transitory. The future is the focus. Buoyed with knowledge, a sense of accomplishment from step-11 and a realisation that further adventures are possible or even desirable, we develop momentum towards the next revolution of the Change Wheel and we 'go again'.

At step-12, we may inspire ourself or others to change. We may discuss how what we achieved at step-11 was made possible by the change we experienced at step-7 and step-8 and expanded as we embodied that change in step-9. The clear step change in our performance can trigger curiosity in others. They may want to know what secret we've stumbled upon and how they can access it. Part of our ongoing development involves encouraging others to wake up and embark on their own journey of change. If we can help others to be inspired by a new, expanded version of themselves and what that might look like, we will help increase change capability in the whole organisation.

At step-12, we are looking forward to where we must go next. The diagnostics and measurements of step-11 are crucial to help us reset our focus. Genuine progress is all that matters. Imagined progress simply leads to hubris and arrogance.

How does it feel to be at step-12?

Whereas there was a relaxed, joyous, confident energy to step-11, at step-12 the energy shifts and increases significantly. There's a growing excitement about possibility, especially after the achievement audit. If we have achieved all this and are demonstrating the benefits of change so visibly in step-11, what else is possible? The energy increase at step-12 is vital. If energy doesn't increase, there's a real risk that the warm confidence of step-11 drifts us into the comfort zone of the next turn of the Change Wheel, and we get stuck at step-1. This is a slippery slope to complacency. This risk of complacency diminishes with every revolution of the Change Wheel, but it remains a risk, nevertheless.

With each revolution of the leader's journey, we vertically develop; we literally become more of who we are: more capable, more intelligent, more energetic, more mature, more emotionally resilient, more sophisticated, more informed and more healed. And those capabilities mean that we can go further, faster and travel lighter through life. This is what 'en-lightened' really means. We are able to move at speed unencumbered by angst, guilt or a propensity to get stuck in any negative emotion for too long. We can achieve more with less energy. Our reserves are full. That's what 'full-filled' means. All we need to decide now is the focus of our next great adventure and how we might use our treasure and our magic for best effect.

We are inspired. We've taken everything in from our journey around the cycle and now we're ready to give back to the world in some way. This inspiration is not only in relation to what we can achieve in the future and what we might now turn our formidable attention to but how we can inspire others to engage in the work of change. Part of the reason change initiatives can be so soul destroying is because they promise the world and deliver very little. This disappointment robs us of energy and inspiration. And yet, as soon as we have completed one revolution of the Change Wheel successfully and we understand the mechanics and the experience of it, we have a proven path to results, a template, a meta-map that can be applied to whatever realm of change we seek.

Intention is our compass at step-12 as we direct our new capability towards things that really matter to us.

As good as it gets

Each step of the Change Wheel has an emotion or mindset that can prevent progress on to the next step. At step-12, the risk is, as we have said, complacency. If we believe we have arrived and there is no more adventure to be had then we create a self-fulfilling prophecy. Good really is the enemy of great, as Jim Collins pointed out many years ago.[1]

Of course, in our journey as a human being such a conclusion creates a type of death. We should never slip into the mistaken belief that we have reached our limit — this is as good as it gets. This is always an error, regardless of whether we are already a world class performer or just starting out. There are always more levels to unlock; more expansion to explore; more ways in which we can level up. And whilst we shouldn't become trapped in an endless insatiable search for something better, and we should appreciate all that we have and all that we are, it is our nature to evolve. Life would be pretty boring if we felt there was nothing left to learn, no more adventures to be had. So, remain open to those additional expeditions, regardless of age, and pursue them with grace and determination.

Cultural metaphors

Arriving at step-12 is like arriving at the train station ready for your next great adventure. You've delivered what you needed to deliver, and now you're ready to *"seek out new life and new civilisations, to boldly go where no man has gone before"*. Remember, step-12 can be metaphoric or literal. As Proust said: *"the real voyage of discovery is not seeking new landscapes but having new eyes."*

The depiction of step-12 in films is usually reduced to a single moment, or even a single frame of the movie, where the hero looks wistfully into the distance. The look alludes to the future and unfinished business. It's possible that whenever there has been an insight, a change, and a delivery of something new, we may be at step-12 ready for the next cycle of our journey. One of the reasons that the great movies cited in this book have stood the test of time is because they are sources of inspiration to many. Their narratives speak to us exactly because they follow the twelve steps and four phases of the Change Wheel. They are allegories for our lives. Their existence can inspire a curiosity in us about our own journey.

Inspire

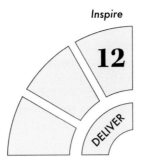

The Matrix: In the running battles between Neo and Agent Smith across the three films, there's a conversation where Smith has Neo in a head lock as a subway train rushes towards them. Smith says: "You hear that, Mr Anderson? That's the sound of inevitability. That's the sound of your death. Goodbye, Mr Anderson." He is alluding to the fact that humans are mortal while he, a program, is immortal. Ironically, Neo escapes the train and Smith is 'killed'. Later, in the final fight sequence of the whole trilogy, Smith asks why Neo keeps fighting. Smith says: "Do you believe you're fighting for something? For more than your survival? Can you tell me what it is? Do you even know? Is it freedom? Or truth? Perhaps peace? Could it be love? Illusions, Mr Anderson. Vagaries of perception. Temporary constructs of a feeble human intellect trying desperately to justify an existence that is without meaning or purpose." This conversation is designed to inspire the viewer to consider the meaning of their own existence and their own journey. A moment later, as Neo let's go and sacrifices himself, Agent Smith says: "Wait. I've seen this. I stand right here, and I'm supposed to say something. I say, 'Everything that has a beginning has an end.'" Neo agrees with him, having already made a pact with the Source to end the destructive replicating virus that Smith has become. Neo smiles at Smith, which causes Smith to suddenly realise that his statement about the cyclical nature of existence, where everything that has a beginning has and end, also applies to him. Sacrifice leads to peace and harmony, and Neo is immortalised by the human and machine worlds. Sati makes a new city for him in the Matrix, and Zion remembers him.

The Lord of the Rings: There has been much debate about the core theme of *The Lord of the Rings*. Tolkien stated in his letters that he was really writing about death and immortality and the human desire to escape one and achieve the other. It's suggested that the tale has been significantly influenced by Norse mythology, with its tone of inevitable disintegration, where even the Gods must die, and the cyclical nature of existence. Tolkien himself may have been influenced by this, his love of the old English poem Beowulf, in which he was an expert, and his Catholic belief in the redemptive nature of suffering. Many of the sub-themes in the book – good and evil, fate and free will, gain and loss – are part of the journey. But the point of inspiration is to provoke the reader to consider what it means to be alive. One of the greatest treasures of being alive is to experience love. In the appendix to the book, the immortal elf Arwen chooses mortality so she can marry her love Aragorn. Tolkien directly connects immortality to love by suggesting that it may be worth sacrificing immortality for love. Or maybe there is immortality in love. There was certainly love within the Fellowship. He also points out that when love becomes corrupted into attachment, a hobbit becomes a Gollum, twisted and misshapen. The theme of immortality is not only connected to love but also to free will. Frodo's made a free will choice to bear the ring and bring it to Mordor. Arwen freely chose love over immortality. This tells us that love and choice are inextricably linked to our own immortality. It's up to the reader to decide whether, in the end, Tolkien was writing an elegy or a eulogy.

Star Wars: A simple young farm boy gets a magic sword from an old wizard so he can defeat evil, rescue a princess and save the world. George Lucas wasn't the first person to have this idea. We've all had the same idea as we grew up. It's a perennial developmental myth designed to teach us the rules of social order and interaction. Sometimes the heroes are cowboys or Indians; sometimes the hero is a samurai; sometimes the heroes are more parochial, like doctors and nurses: the sword being the surgeon's knife. Lucas, being a good friend of Joseph Campbell, knew all that. But instead of telling a story consistent with the anti-heroes of his day, he recreated a story that was rooted in the Flash Gordon series of his childhood; however, Lucas modernised the story by embracing diversity and inclusion. He had knights, dragons, motorcycles, ray guns, teddy bears, pirates, gladiators and gangsters – the whole shebang. As such, it deals with the entirety of life. So if there is inspiration, it's in the richness and diversity of life itself.

Harry Potter: According to JK Rowling, one of the main themes of Harry Potter is death. The books start with the death of Harry's parents. There are numerous deaths throughout, so the reader must come to terms with the loss of a loved one. In the first book, *Harry Potter and the Philosopher's Stone*, Harry, on understanding that Voldemort wanted the stone to extend his cursed life, suggests: "If you're going to be cursed forever, death's better, isn't it?" Dumbledore suggests: "To the well-organised mind, death is but the next great adventure." By book seven, the main point is made as Harry approaches his own death: "Every second he breathed, the smell of the grass, the cool air on his face was so precious." JK Rowling is pointing out that death's lesson is to create a profound appreciation for life. Voldemort literally means 'flight from death', according to the author. So, as Harry Potter matures, he accepts death, in contrast to his nemesis who is trying to flee from death.

The Wizard of Oz: Produced before many of the other grand epics cited in this book and delivered as a single film, *The Wizard of Oz* really is a cultural scene setter for what great movie narration looks like. In many ways, it delivered its purpose and inspired future generations of movie makers to create more compelling stories that spoke to the issues that audiences were dealing with. The film deals with issues of childhood, self-sufficiency, virtue, the importance of friendship plus the fight between good and evil. But tying it all together are the steps of the journey. There are clearly subtle cultural references, as we highlighted in earlier chapters, that relate to the economic conditions and social struggles that Frank Baum observed. The subtext is political allegory. Some might argue that his devices resonate with the in-jokes in a modern Pixar animated movie. But we mustn't forget that Baum originally wrote the book to entertain his children and to inspire them with Dorothy's mantra that there is "no place like home".

The transition to a new change cycle

There are no optimal time frames for the time spent at each step. It's individual. But once commitment is made to the change process, it can move swiftly. The space between entering the innermost cave of step-8 and step-12 can be years or minutes.

We may choose to rest at various steps, especially from step-9 onwards. The three steps of the delivery phase are largely enjoyable. The hardest parts of the change process are behind us at that point. Resting and enjoying these steps is perfectly acceptable. But there will come a point, once a full revolution of the Change Wheel has been made, that we recognise it's time to leave. A new adventure awaits.

> *A good life is one hero journey after another. Over and over again, you are called to the realm of adventure, you are called to new horizons. Each time, there is the same problem: do I dare? And then if you do dare, the dangers are there, and the help also, and the fulfilment or the fiasco. There's always the possibility of fiasco. But there's also the possibility of bliss.*
>
> (Joseph Campbell)

Questions to ask yourself

If you are unsure if you are in step-12, it can be helpful to ask yourself some questions:

- What next?
- Do I understand what lies beyond this ability to inspire?
- How do I move from delivering at a new level to inspiring others to deliver at a new level?
- Have I drifted into the passivity of deep understanding of meaning?
- Do I know how to create new energy?
- Has the known world that awaits changed?
- Am I still 'fit for purpose'?
- Do I need a new purpose for a new cycle?

The answers to these questions will determine your next step. Consolidate the wins that you have just achieved; rest a while. Or perhaps you will dive right back in and choose a new change to action.

Note

1 Collins, J., (2001). *Good to great: Why some companies make the leap … and others don't*. New York: Random House.

13 The leader as coach

Having coached exceptional people in business, politics, sport and education all over the world in the last 25 years, I can testify to the importance of a good map. Without a map that details the twelve steps and four phases of change, then change itself often fails. Looking back at when I've failed to help leaders, it's often been because I forgot to check the map, or misread the map entirely. The map offered in this book differs from the many and varied articulations of Joseph Campbell's original hero's journey map because I've adapted it for our modern world and for leaders working in organisations and the journey they now follow. We have thoroughly road tested this map with leaders from all walks of life and in all geographies, markets and levels of society. I hope the Change Wheel we offer here will become as vital to you as a leader as it has become to us in our work with thousands of leaders all over the world.

Given the accelerating pace of change in the world, we must, as leaders, find a way to get so comfortable with change we can lead it effectively. We must learn to love change, understand its anatomy and physiology. We must facilitate it, promote it and successfully deliver it time and time again. The complexity, volatility and speed of change in modern business demands we become change champions, competent in the components of change. The leader's journey and the Change Wheel offer a tried and tested meta-frame that describes the process of change so that a leader can facilitate their own change as the hero in their own story. But a leader can also take the form of an archetype – the mentor to help others.

This chapter is designed to assist the leader in their role as mentor or coach, helping and supporting others around the Change Wheel so that, individually and collectively, the business and the people in the business can embrace change and reap the rewards it offers. We will define carefully what a coach needs to look for at each step of the Change Wheel and clarify how the role of the coach changes with each step on the leader's journey.

In our work at Complete, we use this Change Wheel when working with everyone, from CEOs and senior C-suite executives to five-year-old children in schools. This chapter is also relevant to the entire coaching community. This meta-frame can be exceptionally useful in helping clients achieve their goals faster.

DOI: 10.4324/9781003170402-14

Step-1: Comfort zone

Whether you are a coach or acting in a coaching role, the chances are if someone is in step-1 they won't even be talking to you. They are unlikely to be receptive because they don't feel there is anything wrong with the status quo. Remember, the comfort zone is comfortable. Nothing great is happening but neither is anything bad happening. No wake-up has occurred.

Questions the coach might ask at step-1 in order to start the waking up process might include:

- Are you missing something? Can you be sure that there isn't something better out there for you?
- Are you open to ideas about what that something better might be? Do you have any ideas or suggestions not of about what that something better might be or might look like for you?
- Is there something that other people aren't telling you? Are you sure? Do you ever get the sense that people are holding back information from you? Perhaps they don't want to offend or upset you? Could this be true?
- Be honest. Are you stuck in a rut? You may have ten years' experience but is it one year repeated ten times? Are you still learning, or are you running on auto-pilot?
- Are you sure you're right and others are wrong? Could there be a different way to look at the status quo?
- Are you open to change?

By answering these questions, the coach can gauge the coachee's receptivity to step-2 – challenge to reality. If you as the coach identify a willingness to consider change, then it may be possible to nudge them into step-2.

If not, then more work might be needed to prepare the ground for the challenge of step-2.

At Complete, we tend to start coaching leaders who are already at step-2. They've had a wake-up call of some sort. That's often what triggers the phone call to us in the first place. The leaders we meet at step-1 have usually been put forward for coaching by their boss without their consultation or are leaders who have heard of us and are meeting us out of politeness to a colleague or peer but who are comfortably certain they have everything covered. The process of waking someone up in their comfort zone is always the same, whether you are a leader seeking to wake up a fellow executive or an external coach seeking to help a C-suite leader understand that change is either necessary or coming whether they want it or not.

The coach must disrupt the executive's life in some way. There needs to be some cognitive dissonance, some challenge to shake them from their comfort zone. The goal is to help the individual experience some type of wake-up moment that their comfort zone may not be all that comfortable after all.

There are three types of wake-up calls, across the three dimensions of 'I' (being), 'WE' (relating) and 'IT' (doing). An 'I' wake-up call tends to be intimate and dramatic. This is the wake-up call that occurs in the moment that a doctor tells us that if we don't lose weight and become more active, we will be dead in a year. It's the threat of a heart attack or stroke that forces a reckoning. A 'WE' wake-up call may be the news that our partner is talking to a divorce lawyer or the overheard conversation where our child says they don't even know us. It's the breakdown of a friendship or working relationship. And finally, the 'IT' wake-up call might be plummeting sales figures, a profit warning or a drop in engagement scores.

If you, as mentor or coach, can see the writing on the wall but the person you are speaking to doesn't, then there is an opportunity to alert them to the fragility of their position in the comfort zone. This can be done by pointing to impending pain should the status quo remain, triggering curiosity around what might take its place or holding the mirror up to the person so they can see how their actions and behaviour may be causing issues. It may be possible to plant seeds, use data, share opinions, stories and feedback to help wake them up.

The idea is to theoretically disrupt the executive before life events disrupt them for real. It may seem calculated or even cruel, but given the opportunity most people would rather have been disrupted *before* they lost their job so they could have had the opportunity to rectify behaviour or improve results. Most people would rather have been disrupted *before* the divorce papers were served or their kids left home without a backward glance. There is hope and compassion in this active disruption.

Of course, most people also don't enjoy that conversation when they are blissful in their ignorance. They don't want to hear of impending doom. And that's where the coaching relationship becomes so important.

In his seminal book *Influence: Science and Practice*, author Robert Cialdini talks about the six basic principles of psychology that direct human behaviour. Every one of them is relevant in the coaching relationship:

- **Authority**: People follow the lead of credible, knowledgeable experts who hold positions of authority.
- **Social proof**: People will look to the actions and behaviours of other people to determine their own actions and behaviours, especially when uncertain.
- **Reciprocity**: People feel obliged to give back to people who have given them something first.
- **Liking**: People prefer to say yes to and work with people they like.
- **Consistency**: People like to be consistent with the things they have previously said or done.
- **Scarcity**: People want more of the things they can have less of.

In a leadership role, these influencers will play out, although encouraging a sub-ordinate or fellow executive to consider their current attachment to the comfort zone is always going to be easier for an internal leader than for an external coach because a relationship already exists. The authority, social proof, reciprocity and, hopefully, liking are already present. Scarcity is also more likely to be present in internal relationships because the executive already knows how busy their colleague or leader may be. Therefore, when someone offers to help, we are more likely to appreciate the fact that they have taken an interest in our journey or development. Internal coaches will also have some degree of consistency established in their relationships.

An external coach must find their own versions of Cialdini's influencers. Authority can come from the strength of the recommendation that gets the external helper through the door, or it may come from their expertise in the discipline they are being asked to help with. Academic standing imbues many business schools with quasi-authority, although it's questionable whether academic status still means they are at the cutting edge in the fast-paced corporate world. In my own experience of being that external coach, my qualification as a medical doctor delivered a certain amount of authority in the early days, but much less so now. My degree in psychology, PhD in immunology, my appointment as a visiting Professor in Business at Kingston University and the fact that I have written ten books, including four on leadership, count for more now.

Social proof often comes from being referred by an executive peer, possibly in another company or division. If that promotor is themself a chief executive or senior C-suite leader in a FTSE 100 company, there is likely to be even greater influence. Of course, social proof can also come from a proven track record. If the coach has worked with other companies in the leader's industry or region or bigger companies or companies with more complex problems then that can also help to assure the leader that the coach's input is valid and can be trusted. A track record can also be enhanced using case studies. If clients are prepared to go public on how much a coach has helped them, that's one of the strongest social proofs available. With a good track record, people are more likely to listen to what the external coach has to say. This is often quite different to a leader who is coaching others, as their standing in the company will already tick that social proof box.

Reciprocity can often be delivered in a number of ways. The way that makes sense to me as an external coach is offering real value. I also enjoy connecting brilliant people to each other. For example, I am currently coaching an exceptional CEO who is expanding his company, and as part of that process his company is being rolled into a SPAC (special purpose acquisition company). This creates complex financial dynamics that he must manage. So, I connected him to one of the best CFOs I know in a completely different company who, after I explained the situation, was more than happy to offer some guidance. People like helping each other, and I'm no different. Reciprocity may also be as simple as being able to describe their life, the challenges they are likely facing and provide some early insight or quick wins even before they have committed to work with the coach. If these can help their daily life or a business issue they might be wresting with at the time, that helps with reciprocity and it also builds trust that the coach can actually help.

Liking is vital in coaching relationships. It's not enough to have something unique to offer that can step change the outcome and really make a difference; the coach has to be easy to relate to. No one wants to spend time in a coaching journey with someone they don't like. For both the internal and external coach, humour and likability can be a real asset in relationship building. Consistency plays more of a role in a coaching relationship once the executive commits to their change journey.

Scarcity is a trickier quality to use as an external coach. I have seen other coaching companies use this by suggesting they will only work with a set number of clients and then refuse a client to create the perception of scarcity, only to miraculously find space or 'manage to squeeze them in'. Unfortunately, some people will deliberately use Cialdini's model to manipulate or fabricate influence. I am a strong believer that this is a bad idea because people are not stupid and can often sense the manipulation, and it will always be destructive to the relationship. Far better to be authentic and let the coaching speak for itself.

The role of the coach at step-1 is to help the person understand that they may be about to fail without realising it. The recipient of this message may then start to understand that the comfort zone isn't all that comfortable after all. This may actually be the calm before the storm.

When landing this point, it's vital to explain it in a way that is meaningful to the recipient and helps build the relationship, fostering trust, even if that executive doesn't currently believe they have a problem. I've seen so many consultants just pump the client for information so they can simply describe their world back to them without adding any value. This is the classic move of consultancy, where they "steal your watch and tell you the time".

The best coaching solutions require a breadth and depth of knowledge so they can provide real value to the individual that is uniquely tailored to them, and the start point on the journey is to compassionately invite the individual to consider whether the comfort zone is all it's cracked up to be or determine if they might be stuck at step-1.

Cialdini's principles of influence help us to understand what is required in that early relationship building in order to foster a willingness to listen and even consider that something better is ahead. The job of the coach, whether an internal leader as the coach or an external coach, is to gently but firmly nudge the individual toward step-2.

Step-2: Challenge to reality

Once someone is in step-2 they know about it. As a leader seeking to help one of your executives around the Change Wheel, you will know they may be ready because they will be experiencing some sort of pain. They may be struggling at work or in their personal life.

Questions the coach may ask at step-2 in order to help the individual appreciate where they are and that change may be required include:

•   Why you? What's happening in your life right now?
•   What does this painful experience really mean? What else could it mean? Could there be a larger, more significant message here?
•   Do you understand what is really going on? Can you see similarities or patterns in your current challenge to past challenges? Is there a common denominator?
•   Are you blinded by the pain, struggle or discomfort?
•   Could you be missing the message? Are you stuck in or attached to your pain?

- Are you even open to the possibility of change?
- Are you holding onto the past?
- Is it possible that you are choosing victimhood and blaming everyone else for your woes? If so, might there be a more constructive approach?

When coaching someone in step-2, it's important to remember that the wake-up call or challenge to reality must register with the individual who is struggling. The wake-up call has to be framed in the world view or value system of the person you are seeking to assist. For example, if the leader at step-2 is struggling with a specific team, they are only going to decide to do something about that team if the coach can land the message in their language. If the leader is operating at the orange value system, then the challenge to reality will need to be felt, experienced or understood from that orange world view. In this case, the conversation may need to focus on how much this dysfunctional team is hurting profit and the wider cost to the business. If the leader is operating from the earlier red value system, then the challenge to reality, data shared and the message conveyed will need to focus on how the dysfunctional team is threatening their power and status. Revisit Figure 2.2 for a reminder of the messaging at each value system.

Part of step-2 is helping the individuals we're coaching to appreciate the situation they are in. The challenge is compassionately designed to help them understand their difficulty in the context of their journey, encourage them to lean into it and do something about it. The coach's role at step-2 is to share and explain the data to support and consolidate their challenge to reality so that it acts as more than just a source of pain but a springboard into change. Once in step-2, the individual is in pain; they recognise there is a problem and they are usually feeling all the associated fear and discomfort that comes with that. The coach's job, therefore, is to offer reassurance that this is a normal and universally experienced part of the change process and, perhaps more importantly, that there is a proven path through. The coach needs to help the recipient develop their ability to objectify their issue, build psychological safety and purge the 'comfort in discomfort' that the recipient might be feeling.

Archetypes at step-2

Step-2 is where the mentor, coach, guide or wise wizard usually shows up. It's important to distinguish the wise wizard from the trickster archetype who may also show up here. The trickster can be a catalyst for change, if they are helpful, but more often they are a force for chaos at step-2. A coach who tells the leader they can transform their life but is actually just a skill builder is a bit like a trickster. They have tricked the leader into believing their coaching will work, when in fact they are depleting the leader of time, money and willingness to change. They can leave the leader in a swamp of cynicism and with the mistaken belief that change isn't possible or coaching is a waste of time. Neither is true. Change is possible and coaching can be transformational in the hands of a skilled mentor, wise wizard or developmental coach rather than a trickster.

Paradoxically, a trickster may motivate the leader by increasing their frustration at their lack of progress, which can lead to forward momentum. Another unintended consequence may be that the leader becomes much more discerning about who they seek as a guide in the future. As such, tricksters do have a role to play in the drama of change, if only to inspire real support from a mentor or wise wizard.

All the five films cited in this book feature a wise wizard: Morpheus in *The Matrix*, Gandalf in *The Lord of the Rings*, Obi Wan Kenobi in *Star Wars*, Dumbledore in *Harry Potter*, and Glinda the Good Witch in *The Wizard of Oz*. Testimony to the importance of this role in the Change Wheel.

Step-3: Resistance to change

Step-3 is where the resistance becomes more visible. The leader as coach may have heard positive noises from the person they are seeking to support. They may fully accept their challenge to reality and recognise there is a problem, but that doesn't count for much if they are unwilling to do anything about it. Professor Robert Kegan has written very eloquently about most people's immunity to change.[1]

The role of the coach is, therefore, to add value early on. Give the individual something that they didn't have before. Often that can be as 'little' as a friendly ear or sounding board. The realisation that the person is not alone and there is a guide or helper willing to travel the journey with them can help to combat the resistance. When the coach can explain to the person that pain is useful, it can help diffuse the resistance. Remember, pain is a signal heralding change, not a permanent address. Helping someone feel less alone can be incredibly powerful. Knowing they have a travelling companion with knowledge and a desire to assist in the journey is often enough to make their situation feel less daunting.

Questions the coach may ask at step-3, in order to precisely diagnose the cause of the resistance and bring it into the light, may include:

- What are you scared of? What's holding you back from facing these challenges head on and working through them?
- What's your fear?
- What might be stopping you from developing?
- Are you using past performance to predict future performance? Are you sure that's accurate? Might your past simply guide you to a better outcome in the future?
- Are you struggling to let go?
- Might you be rejecting offers of help because you are scared that you can't actually change?
- Are you hiding?

The objective of the coach at step-3 is to help uncover the fear and create activation energy to overcome the 'immunity to change'.[1] This is a process of trust building while at the same time maintaining pressure in the face of the resistance.

Change at step-3 is still largely theoretical. The person being coached may fully accept that change is needed, but then comes the realisation that it will require some type of effort on their behalf. And that throws up all the typical points of resistance. "I don't have time." "I'm not sure I can." "Actually, it's not that big a deal. I'm not even sure I want to change." "It's not me that's the problem, it's Frank." Maintaining pressure is about leaning into these statements and excuses to probe for veracity. "So, it's Frank's fault – how is that assumption working out for you?" The objective is to offer up different angles and perspectives that invite the person to reconsider their justifications and assess how accurate or helpful they really are. Remember, the only way out is through. As Winston Churchill once said: "When you are going through Hell, remember to keep going." What they need to get through is to understand their fear, and it's the coach's job to help the individual identify that fear. Recognise that resistance is futile because it's the resistance that's keeping them stuck, while simultaneously reassuring the individual that it's normal and there is an antidote for it so they can move into step-4.

Resistance revisited

The person being coached may not display very much obvious resistance. This can be especially true if the leader is coaching a subordinate. The person being coached will, because of that relationship, make all the right noises about being happy with the coaching process. As a result, a leader or an external coach may glide over step-3, falsely assuming that the recipient is committed to the coaching process. The coach assumes it's not much of an issue and the person is ready for change, or they believe that once they get to the guts of the change process and the individual is learning and using new skills, they will experience the change for themselves and much of the residual resistance will disappear naturally.

This is valid – up to a point. A reluctant participant in the change process can be transformed into an advocate when they experience some positive results. But if that work doesn't work, the coach will almost certainly have to back track to step-3. There are three reasons the work doesn't work:

1   The person on the change journey didn't make a real commitment at step-5.
2   The coach didn't adequately address their resistance at step-3.
3   The quality of the coach is insufficient to bring about real development.

As a result, sometimes it is necessary for the coach to retrace their steps and revisit step-3 for a second time. If this happens, showing the person the Change Wheel can be especially effective because they can better appreciate the nature of change and the steps that must be taken on their change journey. Their resistance is given context, which allows them to accept it as a normal part of the process.

If you don't meet or witness strong resistance, don't assume it's not there. Resistance comes in a myriad of forms that can be quite deceptive. Pay attention and make notes about the lack of resistance. It may be that the person is simply hiding their true feelings and resistance. Both parties will find out the truth when they reach step-7. If the individual is not making progress, the coach will almost certainly have to revisit step-3 in order to progress authentically.

Archetypes at step-3

Step-3 is where the threshold guardians are likely to show up. These may take the form of the internal resistance noted at step-2, or they can also take the form of other people in the individual's life who are advocating for the status quo. The funny thing about change is that it's viewed agnostically by others until that change either impacts them or somehow shines a light on their own shortcomings. Then there can be a concerted effort to prevent that person from crossing the threshold and starting the change journey in earnest. We see this in life all the time. A colleague who pushes for developmental coaching to further their career, or someone who decides to lose weight or get in shape. At first, no one pays much attention. But once that person starts the developmental coaching and makes headway or begins to lose weight, the pressure mounts. The back-handed comments, the suggestions that they are 'such a teacher's pet' or 'so boring now' or the encouragement to miss a coaching session because everyone is too busy or the invitation to go out for a meal or enjoy a nice piece of chocolate cake. This pressure comes from the guardians who are keen to stop the person at the threshold from making real change. These people are almost always the people who should also be doing developmental coaching or losing weight and getting in shape themselves. The individual's efforts to change remind them, albeit subconsciously, that they too should be doing something about their own situation.

Step-4: Overcoming resistance

Step-3 is the peak of resistance; at step-4 the resistance is subsiding either out of boredom – the individual being coached is simply sick of making no progress – or it subsides because they start to trust their coach. The person may have thrown everything at the coach in an effort to gain approval for the status quo and no change. It's not worked. The coach has kept up the pressure for change. The coach may have helped facilitate a greater understanding of the role of resistance and its value to the journey. Or resistance may have subsided simply because the passage of time has lessened the fear.

When we listen to our fear and allow that fear to stop us, there's always a cost. The role of the coach at step-4 is to bring that cost into awareness. It may have served a useful purpose, but it's now holding them back. This more balanced view of the cost and purpose of fear brings a greater awareness of resistance as a phenomenon. This more nuanced understanding of fear can be especially useful once someone has cycled around the full revolution of the Change Wheel and then embarks on more change. Resistance is *always* present. But when it's fully understood, resistance itself transforms from a roadblock into a springboard.

Questions the coach may ask at step-4 in order to speed up the move towards commitment include:

- What will help you move faster?
- How well have you really let go?
- Do you really want to change?
- What's still holding you back?
- Are you really listening to your guide or coach?
- Are you curious enough about what your future could look like?

The role of the coach at step-4 is essentially to instil courage and build confidence to prevent backsliding or resistance flaring up. Step-4 tilts to the future. The objective is to encourage the individual to really consider what's possible now that the resistance brakes are off. What's going to come next? This is where the courage comes in – it's required for the commitment in step-5.

Step-4 is the preparation for commitment, whereas step-6 is the preparation for change. These are subtle differences that require the coach to encourage the person to envision their future. Imagine a new world, a new version of themselves coupled with ongoing reassurance that this new vision is possible – if they chose it. But the individual must actively choose it or not choose it. This is not a passive process.

Coach's resistance

The journey out of step-3 and step-4 can also be negatively impacted by the coach themselves. When a coach is too attached to a certain model or framework, they can be blinded to the needs of the person they are supposed to be helping. Their refusal to flex and find a coaching approach that resonates with the individual can slow the journey down.

Or as a leader you may be charged with coaching a senior executive that you don't particularly like or respect. Something about them rubs you up the wrong way. This, too, can slow progress. It also offers an invitation for enquiry for the leader. What is it about this person that causes the angst? Often, we become irritated by the traits of others that are, in fact, reflections of our own failings. This suggests that the coach has done insufficient work themselves in step-8. These sorts of challenges for a coach are red flags that, when used properly, can lead to greater personal growth, development and more effective coaching.

For an external coach, their resistance may stem from the fact that the client pays for their input, and the danger is that if they are too direct or tell the leader what they think they want to hear as opposed to what they need, their honesty may cost them the contract. This is always a mistake; for coaching to make the type of difference that it can make to an individual's life, personal and professional, the coach themselves needs courage and they must always be authentic to the process and hold that person's feet to the fire when necessary, as well as their own.

When handled maturely on the part of the coach and the coachee, progress to step-5 becomes easier.

Archetypes at step-4

The main new character or archetype that appears at step-4 is the herald. They signal the winds of change now that the resistance is subsiding. They appear to help with the preparation for the moment of truth in step-5. The herald may appear at step-2 as part of the wake-up call, but they are much more effective in the lead up to crossing the threshold. In many films, the herald's role is fulfilled by other characters for reasons of simplicity. In the Matrix trilogy, for example, Morpheus, Trinity and the Oracle all play the role of herald at some point as they herald change.

Step-5: Commitment

Done effectively, step-4 has guided the person seeking change to their moment of truth. They can see before them a self-imagined future that is exciting and appealing. The coach must now step back. Only the individual seeking change can make the commitment to change and jump from the ledge into the new, unknown world. The coach can't make that choice for them. If they do, or worse, they push the person into commitment, cajole or threaten them, it won't work. This is relevant to all coaches, whether a leader is taking on the role or an external coach. But it's especially important when the leader is the coach that there's no coercion – this will damage their professional relationship and will stall the change process. If the leader applies undue influence, the individual being coached will feel the pressure to conform and acquiesce to what the leader wants. All the leader can do is encourage them to make a decision; they can't make it for them or force them into the decision.

Questions the coach may ask at step-5 to encourage genuine commitment include:

- Are you ready to change?
- Do you want to change?
- Do you want to discover how far you can go?
- Has your frustration reached a point where you are prepared to do whatever it takes to really succeed?
- Do you believe you can develop, heal, change your life?
- Do you trust me to guide you?

Seeking to exert undue influence over someone at step-5 will almost always backfire. If the change doesn't go well or doesn't yield the desired results, the guide will always be blamed. As the coach, the leader must give the person space to make that choice themselves. They must commit or decide not to commit but the choice is theirs and theirs alone.

The person on the change journey is truly on their own at step-5, certainly at that point of choice. It is their moment of truth, as they alone can cross the threshold and then meet the coach again on the other side of the commitment.

Archetypes at step-5

It's rare for any new archetypes to enter the narrative at this step. The hero is on their leader's journey; the coach is encouraging from the side lines but has stepped back to give them space. The herald predicted this moment of truth. Given that this is the biggest threshold moment of the journey, the threshold guardian may reappear – not to stop the process, however; just to heighten the importance of the moment. Essentially the leader has a choice to make, and this mustn't be contaminated by the introduction of distracting characters.

It is possible that the shadow or villain, who is really present from the start of the journey, may deliberately seek to sabotage the decision and stop the hero from crossing of the threshold. In *The Lord of the Rings*, the Ringwraiths appear for just this reason.

Step-6: Prepare for change

Once the commitment is made in step-5 and the leader has transitioned into a whole new world, then preparation for change starts in earnest. At step-6, the coach's role is to explain the maps, tools and resources that will be available to the leader during the change process. The objective is to instil confidence for the journey ahead and also build confidence in the coaching partnership that is developing.

Questions the coach may ask at step-6 to ensure the individual is preparing for change include:

* Do you have what you need?
* Are you ready?
* Have you planned properly?
* Do you know what awaits you? Are you ready for the challenges ahead?
* Do you know what the timescales are and how to assess your progress?
* Can you see the milestone(s) ahead?
* Have you understood the rules of development?

The coaching role at this point is to help the individual assess what resources they already have and what they need to ensure success. The objective is also to work out the fastest route for the individual based on their stated change or desired outcomes.

Sequencing is key for the coach at step-6. In the coaching work we do at Complete, sequencing means the coach considers which of the eight lines of development is going to deliver the biggest positive impact. Although in theory we could start with any one of our assessment instruments, the optimal choice depends on what the person being coached is trying to achieve. In reality there is almost always some stabilisation at the start of the Change Wheel, where we focus on increasing physiological performance so that the person feels better, younger and has access to more energy. It is, after all, very hard to bring about the change required if we're exhausted all the time.

The coach's role is, therefore, to work with the individual to create a plan of action for change that's going to deliver the best results for that person in a sequence that not only makes sense to the individual but also makes sense in terms of what might be holding them back. The coach must also be mindful of possible blocks on the journey, what detours are likely and how the coach can best get the individual back on track. Seek to anticipate issues before they arise. This plan often involves consulting other stakeholders to ensure the goals for the journey and the coaching programme are appropriate.

Archetypes at step-6

Having crossed the threshold, this is often where the whole cast of archetypes appear. There are allies, companions, knights, warriors, fools, rogues, shapeshifters and many others. Their role is often setting the scene for the trials and tribulations the hero is yet to face. The focus of step-6 is mainly on the resources for the leader's journey rather than the obstacles. But just as the leader is preparing themselves, so are the forces that will oppose the change planned which occurs at step-7. Some of the characters that show up at step-6 have already appeared in another form earlier on, but here is where they broaden their remit. For example, in the film The Matrix, Trinity was a herald at step-4; at step-6 her role changes to include the companion, lover and maiden warrior. Of course, the allies represent the metaphoric version of the leadership team. And every leadership team has its unique set or characters. Some are rogues who believe rules are meant to be ignored, broken or reinvented. They may be portrayed as outlaws with a talent for deception, trickery and swash-buckling adventure, such as Han Solo in StarWars or Sirius Black in Harry Potter. Some are more rough diamonds cast as the barbarian archetype, such as Gimli in The Lord of the Rings. Some are understudies to the leader themselves. These would be the CFO or COO in an organisation. In cultural metaphor, these are the mythic warrior archetype. In The Lord of the Rings, this role is taken by Legolas.

Step-7: Trials and tribulations

Step-7 is where the work gets done through the trials and tribulations. It is the point where the rubber meets the road in terms of change. The coach's role at step-7 is to provide the maps, tools and techniques that will help the individual make change and elevate performance. But the individual must use those maps, tools and techniques. This is the stage of practice and action. Again, no one can do the work except the person in the change.

Questions the coach may ask at step-7 to help navigate the challenges of change include:

- Has your development slowed?
- Have you stopped changing or making progress?
- Are you just rebadging change or gaming the change?
- Have you sorted most of the surface challenges you face?

- Are things going a lot better? Are you moving faster?
- Do you understand how all the changes you have made fit together?
- Are you confident of your progress?
- Have you cleaned up your system and realised that there may be a couple of deeper issues to address?

The person progressing through change will need to practise the skills and deploy them consistently. The role of the coach, therefore, is to check in with them regularly to find out how that process is working. How are they getting on with their homework? Are they doing the necessary practice to develop proficiency? How does it feel? The coach must explain the learning cycle to the individual so that they recognise that change, learning and development are non-linear. It can feel frustrating. It can feel as though we are going backwards sometimes. All these things are normal.

The coach must hold the individual's feet to the fire and hold them accountable for doing what they've committed to doing. These new skills take time to learn, practice and master. There are no quick fixes or magic bullets, but the effort will yield results if they just stick with it. At step-7, the coach's only objective is to ensure the work works. Paying attention to what the person is telling them so they can offer additional guidance on every experiment and technique and help interpret their results to ensure progress is maintained, skills understood and objectification of progress is developed as well as ownership of that progress. Coaches must be skilled at supporting, encouraging, challenging, cajoling, entertaining, role modelling, reflecting back and inspiring the individual to stick with the practice.

It is imperative that the person being coached understands and appreciates the transformational nature of step-7. But that transformation will not materialise without the individual's focused effort and commitment to the tools. Not just learning and understanding them for the purpose of developing 'aboutism', but really using them day in, day out. An individual who embraces the learning at step-7 and uses it consistently transforms learning into development, and with that they step change their capability forever.

This recognition of value at step-7 can also speed up any subsequent revolutions of the Change Wheel significantly. We all want change in one form or another. What separates the change champions from everyone else is their appreciation of the effort required and their willingness to embrace that effort – time and time again. Step-7 is the work. Do the work, reap the rewards; don't do the work, don't reap the rewards. It's very simple. The role of the coach is, therefore, to articulate that choice and support that effort so the individual can reap those rewards. The individual must understand the value of the work – otherwise they will find ways to avoid it!

Archetypes at step-7

At step-7, all members of the cast vie for attention. It's where the battles between the leader and the shadow – sometimes known as the villain – get going in earnest. The shadow is ever present at all steps of the journey, but in step-7 the early skirmishes erupt into all-out war. Step-7 is also when the trickster most frequently appears in both positive and negative forms. Their main role is to keep the story moving and ensure progress. Tricksters, such as Merry and Pippin in *The Lord of the Rings* or Dobby in *Harry Potter*, keep things moving along. They may be accompanied by another common archetype – the shapeshifter. These characters blur the lines between adversary and ally. Gollum fits the bill here in *The Lord of the Rings*, and Gilderoy Lockhart does the same in *Harry Potter*. In business, tricksters and shapeshifters are the mavericks, innovators, integrators and polymaths usually lurking one or two levels below the leadership team. They are the 'weirdo geeks' in marketing or IT that no-one understands but who can accelerate progress more than virtually anyone. In *The Matrix*, the Merovingian has embraced all the rogue programs or tricksters to prevent them from being deleted. Business has only recently fully woken up to the importance of diversity. Diversity is vital not because it enables some puerile gender and racial tick boxing but because it pulls in all the various archetypes. which all hold value, thus facilitating wisdom. And it's wisdom that facilitates real progress.

Step-8: Deep work

Doing the deep work at step-8 is always optional. If successful, step-7 can deliver transformational change and vastly improve an individual's life; then they may opt to skip past step-8. This is perfectly acceptable and real change can still be achieved, but without embracing step-8, a developmental ceiling will *always* be reached.

It's the coach's job to decide if the individual is ready and willing to explore the deep work of step-8. A good coach will be able to identify when there is a need or a significant opportunity to enter their innermost cave and do the deep work. A good coach will also be able to articulate the sizeable benefits available from this add-itional work. The deep work may not even take that much time, but a coach should never enter the cave if they are not skilled in the cave, and they certainly can't take someone beyond the level of their own development.

Questions the coach may ask to help establish the need for deep work at step-8 include:

- Is your change permanent?
- How do you make sure it is?
- How do you sustain the new you?
- How do you become a living example of what you now know?
- Do you understand how to interrupt your 'projections'?
- Do you still sometimes react in ways you don't like?
- Are there still parts of you that confuse you or don't make sense to you?
- Would you like to be able to resolve your shadow? Would you like to become more of you without so much constant effort?

The key difference between step-7 and step-8 is depth. At step-7, an individual could learn how to control their breathing and regulate their emotional reaction to events and situations. They could become so good at this that the moment they get angry, they could regulate their breathing in seconds and choose a more constructive emotion a few seconds after that. These skills have game-changing potential. But what if you just got rid of the anger in the first place? Step-8 gets rid of the anger. The coach's role at step-8, therefore, is to explain the difference and gauge if the individual needs to enter their innermost cave and could gain from that effort, considering the types of changes they want to achieve. Step-8 is not for the faint-hearted; it's often emotionally intense and challenging work, and it requires real skill on the part of the coach.

As such, both parties must be prepared to go into the darkness. The coach must know what they are doing. If they don't, they risk serious and maybe permanent damage. They must know when to encourage the individual to go deeper and if that deep work is likely to yield significant rewards. The coachee must be willing to stick with the emotional intensity to get to their truth. Remember, this is the domain of faulty code and limiting patterns and beliefs that were constructed in infancy. The objective of deep work is to uncover and overwrite the pieces of faulty code that are still negatively impacting the individual's life in the present. But it has to be their choice. The coach can't force or coerce the individual to do the deep work. It has to be something they see value in.

But for those that become really fascinated by their own transformation and curious to know how deep the rabbit hole goes and how far they can go, then step-8 takes the transformation to a whole other level. At step-8, the individual slays their demons rather than simply muzzling them!

Archetypes at step-8

At step-8, the main archetype is the shadow or villain. The shadow archetype represents the embodiment of all the disowned characteristics of the person on the change journey. Sometimes the villain is a manifestation of internal demons. Sometimes the demon is genuinely an external force. Voldemort in *Harry Potter* and Agent Smith in *The Matrix* are both ultimately inner demons. Sauron, Boromir and Gollum in *The Lord of the Rings* are external villains, although Gollum is both external and metaphorical in representing what a hobbit becomes when consumed by the need for power and overwhelmed by attachment. Gollum is mainly a shapeshifter, at times manifesting as a villain. At step-8, the coach is helping the person on the coaching journey to seek out their own shadow, the parts of themselves that are unhelpful or ignored so they can be integrated into the whole Self, thus healing them and dissolving their negative influence.

Step-9: Embodying the change

At step-9, the individual is either embodying the skills of step-7 or the deep work of step-8. The coach, therefore, offers advice to help the individual consolidate what they've learnt and prevent future backsliding.

Questions the coach may ask to help facilitate step-9 include:

- Do you know how to be in the world in this new way?
- Do you know what awaits you?
- Has the world that awaits you changed?
- Are you still 'fit for purpose'?
- Do you need to do something else now you understand your purpose?

The objective of the coach at step-9 is to seek to tease apart the theoretical knowledge from the lived experience and encourage the individual to recognise any gap between the two. Have the skills and techniques of step-7 been learned but not deployed? It's only when they are used consistently that they become embodied by the individual. It's the coach's job at this step to identify whether there has been learning and development or just learning. Learning is great, but the application of that learning is the game changer. If the individual has experienced some backsliding where improvements were made but then diminish, then it may be time to revisit step-7 or step-8.

Archetypes at step-9

At step-9, this is where, after the treasure has been secured, the leader is very close to the members of his fellowship. His allies and his trusted companions are by his or her side. This is the time for real intimacy between Frodo and Samwise Gamgee in *The Lord of the Rings*, or Han Solo and Luke Skywalker in *Star Wars*. In business, this is where the leadership team has stepped up to a new level and can feel the difference because they are embodying it. With each new level of team development, the energy within the team increases and the speed with which they can make a decision and align behind that decision also increases. This is because the depth of trust has significantly improved, and the amount of self-serving egoic political playing diminishes.

Step-10: Return

At step-10 there is a return to the familiar, known world, following the work of change. In truth, this isn't like the movies. There is rarely a grand return or celebration in the real world of business. It's simply a time of reflection and decompression as the individual takes stock of the journey.

At this step, the coach will explain what the individual might encounter as they return to the known world. Often the individual feels different, forever changed, and yet the world may not notice. This can be both a blessing and a curse.

Questions the coach may ask to help with step-10, the return, include:

- What do you want to tell people about what has happened to you?
- Do you know how to be in the world in this new way? Do you know what awaits you?

- Are you ready to step up?
- Are you ready to lead?
- Are you confident in how you change the future?
- Has the level of thinking subsided?
- Is the readiness to deliver ever present?

At step-10, it can be useful to look back on the change process. The coach can remind the individual just how far they've come; how much resistance there was at the start and how they overcame that resistance; their unwillingness to do the practice but how that eventually paid off. This is often the first time the individual is truly aware of change being cyclical. This is a powerful insight because it gives them a road map for change. It doesn't even matter to them if the outside world recognises their change or not. They know they are different and have gained confidence in that difference.

Archetypes at steps-10 to -12

There are rarely, if ever, any new archetypes in the delivery phase of change. There may be flashbacks or flashforwards to future cycles of change, but for this revolution everyone that needed to appear has appeared. All archetypes have served their purpose and played their role in the transformation.

Step-11: Delivery at the new level

Step-10 and step-11 are joyous places. As such, the coach celebrates with the individual and encourages them to appreciate how the changes have manifested in their life. The change effort is paying off, and they are delivering at a new level.

Questions the coach may ask to help the individual appreciate this new capability include:

- Do you understand the new level you are operating at?
- What new gifts and insights have you noticed at this new level?
- What are your new superpowers?
- How do you embed your new insights into the system so it doesn't require you to be present for the system to change?
- How do you let your change be its own teaching?

The work has worked. The role of the coach is to encourage the individual to appreciate how far they have come and recognise the causal impact of the work they embarked upon and the results they have achieved.

Whereas step-10 is looking back at the Change Wheel, step-11 is looking back and taking stock of what's been achieved as a result of the change effort. The coach is seeking to ensure that the individual is able to clearly appreciate the connection between their efforts and their ability to deliver at a new level.

In a way, step-11 is its own version of embodiment; not embodying the change in the individual but embodying or understanding the relationship between that change and the world and how that change has positively impacted the world. The individual can see and appreciate their role in the change and what change itself can accomplish. This is truly exciting because it is the fulfilment of the hope and also a nod to what is now possible.

Step-12: Inspire

The coach's work is almost done at step-12. All that is left is to encourage reflection on what the future may hold.

Questions the coach may ask to facilitate inspiration at step-12 include:

- What next? Are there more cycles on the horizon?
- How do you move from delivering at a new level to inspiring others to deliver at a new level?
- Do you understand what lies beyond this ability to inspire?
- Have you drifted in the passivity of deep understanding of meaning?
- Do you know how to create new energy?
- Do you need a new purpose for a new cycle?

With step-12 comes a renewed sense of responsibility. That responsibility might manifest in a number of different ways. The individual may realise they are in the wrong place and make a career move; they may become inspired to share the journey and the Change Wheel with others so they can experience the joy of completing a revolution. Change is not easy, but when we understand the meta-narrative that underpins all change it becomes much less daunting and more doable. There is less fear, mis-steps or wrong turns.

Part of the inspiration at step-12 is, "wow that was amazing – let's go again." There is a deep sense of self confidence and fulfilment at having cracked the change code. And the possibilities that generates are endless. What next? The coach's job is to enquire about what might be next to generate greater excitement and energy for the next adventure.

Step-12 is not just inspiration around what the individual can now achieve but also how to ignite the same curiosity and determination in others. Change is possible. It is not to be feared but embraced and used to make the world a better place.

Note

1 Kegan, R. and Lahey, L.L., (2009). *Immunity to change: How to overcome it and unlock the potential in yourself and your organization.* Boston, MA: Harvard Business Press.

Index

accountability compass 63, 64, 65–67; crossing the threshold and 63

achievement, sense of: in trials and tribulations (Step-7) 108

agility 99; transition from commitment (Step-5) to preparation and 82–83

Ally, archetype of hero's journey and 3; description of 4

ambivalence, change and 1

anger: in deep work (Step-8) 111–112; disordered breathing and breathwork for 101–102

Antonovsky, Aaron 8

anxiety 31–33; in commitment (Step-5) 77–78; disordered breathing and breathwork for 101–102; *see also* mental health

application of the boon, hero's journey and 3

appreciation: appreciation exercise 91–92; example of 91; in prepare to change (Step-6) 89–92

Archetypes: at challenge to reality (Step-2) coaching 176–177; change process and 4, 6; Change Wheel and 4; at commitment (Step-5) coaching 181–182; at deep work (Step-8) 186; descriptions of 3–4; at embodying the change (Step-9) 187; at overcoming resistance (Step-4) coaching and 181; at prepare to change (Step-6) 182–183; recognition of as transformative 6; at resistance to change (Step-3) coaching 179; return (Step-10), delivery (Step-11) and inspire (Step-11) 188; at trials and tribulations (Step-7) 184–185

attachment theory: cortisol and 34–35

be the change 138, 143

beginner's mind 90

behavioural alphabet 88; focus on Involve, Ignite and Implement in delivery at the new level (Step-11) 157, 157, 158; in prepare for change (Step-6) 87

blame, business change and 22

bliss, following 147–148

bodily awareness, Complete app for improving 101–102

boon (reward), hero's journey and 3

boredom 59

breathwork and breathing 79; Complete app for 101–102, 105–106; glottic stops and 101; negative emotions from disordered 101–102

Bubbleswitch Saga (game) 115

business change: need for emotions in 102; resistance to and distraction from 44–45; wake-up calls and 22

call to adventure, hero's journey and 3, 21; Campbell on 55; challenge to reality (Step-2) and 21, 27–28, 38; resistance to in Step-3 53–54

Campbell, Joseph 2, 5, 43; on acceptance 73; biography and educational path of 2; on call to adventure 21, 55; on fear and encouragement 111; on following hero's path 95; on following your bliss 147–148; *Hero with a Thousand Faces* of 2, 4; intensive self-study of during Great Depression 5; on life's challenges as opportunities 57; PBS interview with Bill Moyer of 6; on purpose 137; on reading 85; surfacing of meta-frames of 5–6; on what makes a hero 143, 163

catabolic hormones 29–30

cave. *see* innermost cave metaphor

challenge 37; Campbell on life's challenges as opportunities 57; hardiness/resilience and 8, 36, 37 challenge to reality (Step-2 on leader's journey) 55; archetypes in 175–177; biological consequences of pain of 29–30; call to adventure and 21, 27–28, 38; cultural metaphors/films depicting 37–39; leaders as coaches and 175–177; mental health impacts when stuck in 30–33; observable pain as sign you are in 27–28; pain as signal to heed for change and 29–33, 39–40; personal pain as sign you are in 28–29; prolonged discomfort as sign you are in 27, 30; questions to ask yourself 39–40; transition from to resistance to change (Step-3) 39; transition to from comfort zone (Step-1) 18–19; value-based wake up calls and motivational drives and 22–27, 24, 26, 40; victimhood and 33–37, 37; wake-up calls as indication you are in 21–22

change process: archetypes and 4, 6; challenge to reality (Step-2) and 37; change as journey 141; change competence 12; change road map creation 102–103; Complete Leadership Frame and 98–99, 99; Holmes and Rahe Stress scale and 7–8; need for awareness of what Step you are working on in 98; need for experimentation in at Step-7 103–104; need to understand steps/ stages in hero's journey for 5–7, 171; negative view of 1–2, 11; overcoming resistance (Step-4) as critical to 57; pain as signal to heed for 29–33, 39, 40; requirement for new learning in 90; statistics on change initiative success and 97; see also 'I' (being) change; 'IT' (doing) change; 'WE' (relating) change; Change Wheel; leader's journey

Change Wheel: archetypes and 4; complacency risk and 165–166; deep work (Step-8) as only one that is skippable 111–112, 125; four phases of as corresponding to human development and 8–10, 9; illustration of 9; improved change and capability with each revolution of 85; at inspire (Step-12) 163, 165–166; insufficient application as preventing progress in 62; leaders as coaches around 171; physiological diagnostic assessment to determine where to start on 100; questions for resistance to change (Step-3) and 55; resistance and distraction in 44–45; shift

from victim to owner as most important revolution in 37; wise wizards and 177

change, dislike of 1; Joseph Campbell as roadmap to transforming 2

choice, victimhood and 34

clarity, for overcoming resistance (Step-4 of leader's journey) 64, 65

coaching for leaders 47, 49, 51–54, 104–105, 171; Change Wheel and leader's journey as time-tested maps for 171; for diligence building for trials and tribulations (Step-7) 104–105; see also leaders as coaches

Cockerill, Tony 87, 88, 156

comfort zone (Step-1 of leader's journey) 55; addiction to 11–12; conscious desire to evolve drive and 12–13; illusion of 11; insularity and complacency of 14–15; known world in films and 16–18; leaders as coaches in 172–175; professional clues to being stuck in 13–14; questions to ask yourself in 19; survival and exploration drives and 12–13; transition from to challenge to reality (Step-2) 18–19; trap of narcissism in 15–16, 33; see also under leader as coach

commitment: hardiness/resilience and 8, 36, 37

commitment (Step-5 of leader's journey): 'I' change for 77–78, 80; anxiety, loneliness and liberation as feelings in 75–78; crossing the threshold in 73–78, 80–82; cultural metaphors/film examples of 80–82; discover phase of Change Wheel and 73; indications you are in 73–75; leaders as coaches at 181–182; questions to ask yourself 83; rites of passage and 2, 75–76; state vs. level change in 78–80; transition from to preparing for change (Step-6) 82–83; transition to from overcoming resistance (Step-4) 69–70

complacency: in comfort zone (Step-1) 14–15; risk of in inspire (Step-12) 165–166; as stumbling block of embodying the change (Step-9) 139–140

Complete App for energy/breathing/body awareness 101–102, 105–106

Complete Leadership Frame 98–99, 99

confusion, shapeshifters and 6

control 37; hardiness/resilience and 8, 36, 37

cortisol 29–30; attachment theory and 34–35

COVID-19 82; renewed gratitude/ appreciation from 91

crossing the threshold, hero's journey and 3; accountability compass and 63; at commitment (Step-5) 73–78, 80–82; at overcoming resistance (Step-4) 60, 63

cultural metaphors of hero's journey: challenge to reality (Step-2 on leader's journey) and 37–39; of comfort zone (Step-1) 16–18; of commitment (Step-5 of leader's journey) 80–82; of deep work (Step-8) 128–130; of delivery at the new level (Step-11) 159–160; of embodying the change (Step-9 of leader's journey) 140–141; of inspire (Step-12) 166–169; of overcoming resistance (Step-4 of leader's journey) 66–69; of prepare for change (Step-6) 92–94; Razor's Edge (film) as embodiment and 140; of resistance to change (Step-3 of leader's journey) 53–54; of return (Step-10 of leader's journey) 149–151; of trials and tribulations (Step-7 of leader's journey) 106–108; see also Matrix, The (film)

cultural rites of passage 2, 75–76

curiosity: in prepare to change (Step-6) 89; at Step-7 103; transition from commitment (Step-5) to preparation and 82

decide phase of Change Wheel 8–10, 9; Step-4 as start of 57, 59, 62, 67, 69

deep work (Step-8 of leader's journey): anger and shadow in 111–112; cultural metaphors/film examples of 128–130; delusion and pseudo-enlightenment as feeling in 127–128; faulty code fixing 113–115, 133; faulty code fixing via Pesso's meeting of 5 basic human needs 115–122; fear as feeling in 114, 126–127; fixing faulty code with three skill examples 122–125; indications that you may be in 112–115; innermost cave exploring for treasure in 111, 113–114, 122, 124–131, 134, 186; irony of skipping for leaders 133–134; leaders as coaches at 185–186; potential need for rest post-deep work (Step-8) 137; questions to ask yourself 131; transition from to embodying the change (Step-9) 130–131; transition to from trials and tribulations (Step-7) 108–109

dehydroepiandrosterone (DHEA) 30

deliver phase of Change Wheel 8–10, 9, 142

delivery at the new level (Step-11) 159–160; behavioural alphabet focus on Involve, Ignite and Implement 157, 157, 158; cultural metaphors/film examples of 159–160; descriptive leader assessment vs. developmental level of leader assessments 155–156; engagement surveys and 153–154; engagement surveys and high performance in 153–154; indications you are in 153–154; leaders as coaches at 188–189; pride and joy as feelings in 158; questions to ask yourself 161; satisfaction as feeling in 159; transition from to inspire (Step-12) 161; transition to from return (Step-10) 151–152

delusion, in deep work (Step-8) 127–128

denial, in comfort zone (Step-1) 15

departure stage, hero's journey and 3

depression 31–33; see also mental health

develop phase of Change Wheel 8–10, 9; embodying the change (Step-9) as last step in 138, 142; highest point of development at deep work (Step-8) 128; trials and tribulations (Step-7) as start of 95

development needs: instruments for determining 155

diligence, to avoid regression 104–105

discover phase of Change Wheel 8–10, 9; commitment (Step-5) and 73; resistance to change as last step in 54, 57

distraction: resistance to change and 43–44, 57, 59, 127; as sign you are in challenge to reality (Step-2) 22, 28–29; tricksters and 6

doubt 73; overcoming resistance (Step-4) and 61–63; transition from commitment (Step-5) to preparation (Step-6) and 81

drugs, mental health and 33

Eliot, T.S. 148

embodiment 135–137; Razor's Edge (film) as 140

embodying the change (Step-9 of leader's journey): complacency as stumbling block of 139–140; as consolidation of Step-8 change and stabilisation of Self 131, 134–138, 143–144; cultural metaphors/film examples of 140–141; finding purpose and 137–138; forgiveness and peacefulness as how it feels to be in 138–140; indications you are in 134; interoception in 135–136; as last step in develop phase of Change Wheel 138; leaders as coaches at 186–187; a new 'story of you' in 138; questions to ask yourself 142; relationship changes as indication you are in 134–135; *talking the talk to talking the walk* in 136; transition from to return (Step-10) 141–142; transition to from deep work (Step-9) 130–131

Emmons, Robert 91–92

emotions 102, 105; Complete app for positive emotions 105–106; emotional pain as signal to heed 29–33; emotional self-management as skill for mental health 31–33; need for in business 102; negative emotions and breathing and 101–102; practicing positive 105; *see also* by specific emotion; mental health

energy levels: Complete app for improving 101–102; vital energy increase in inspire (Step-12) 165

engagement surveys 102; delivery at the new level (Step-11) 153–154

evolve, conscious human desire to 12–13

excitement: at return (Step-10) 148; at trials and tribulations (Step-7) 102–103

expert mindset: *vs.* openness 60–61; as stumbling block in Step-3 50–51

explanatory style, three P's of (permanence, pervasiveness and personalisation) 35–37, 37

exploration drive 12–13

Eye of Spirit, The (Wilber) 6

fairy tales 2, 6

faith, overcoming resistance (Step-4) and 61–63

faulty code 89; fixing of in deep work (Step-8) 113–122, 133; need to find and fix the pieces causing significant negative impact 133–134; Pesso's meta-frame of meeting basic human needs for 115–122

fear 73; Campbell on 111; in deep work (Step-8) 114, 126–127; in resistance to change (Step-3) 47

films 4; of comfort zone (Step-1) 16–18; of commitment (Step-5) 80–82; of deep work (Step-8) 128–130; of delivery at the new level (Step-11) 159–160; of embodying the change (Step-9) 140–141; Herald archetypes in 181, 183; of inspire (Step-12) 166–169; Mentor

archetypes in 53–54; of overcoming resistance (Step-4) 67–69; of prepare for change (Step-6) 92–94; *Razor's Edge* 140; of resistance to change (Step-3) 52–54; of return (Step-10) 149–151; *Rocketman* 63; of trials and tribulations (Step-7) 106–108; Trickster archetypes in 185; wise wizards in 177; *see also* Harry Potter (film); Lord of the Rings, The (film); Matrix, The (film); Star Wars (film); Wizard of Oz, The (film)

follow your bliss 147–148

forgiveness, in embodying the change (Step-9) 138–139

Frankl, Viktor 34

futility, as indication you are in Step-4 57–59, 178

Gallup Strengths Finder 155

gender, hero's journey and 3

German fairy tales 2

Ghandi, Mahatma 138

glottic stops 101

Granger, Katheryn 60–61

gratitude 91, 105; health and 91–92

Guide as archetype. *see* Mentor, archetype of hero's journey and

hardiness 8, 36, 37; *vs.* victimhood 36, 37; *see also* resilience

Harry Potter (film): challenge to reality (Step-2) and 38; comfort zone (Step-1) and 18; commitment (Step-5) and 82; deep work (Step-8) and 130; delivery at the new level (Step-11) and 160; embodying the change (Step-9) 141; inspire (Step-12) and 168; overcoming resistance (Step-4) and 68; prepare for change (Step-6) and 93; resistance to change (Step-3) and 54; return (Step-10) and 151; trials and tribulations (Step-7) and 108; Trickster archetypes in (Sirius Black/Dobby) 183, 185; Villain/internal demon archetypes in (Voldemort) 186; wise wizard in (Dumbledore) 177

health, gratitude and 91–92

Herald, archetype of hero's journey and: in challenge to reality (Step-2) 37; description of 3; in films 181, 183

Hero with a Thousand Faces, A (Campbell) 2; conscious applications of by artists, artists and filmmakers 4

hero's journey 2, 95, 143, 171; boon (reward) in 3; change process and

Holmes and Rahe Stress scale 7–8; inevitability of 7; irrelevance of gender in 3; need to understand steps/stages in for change 5–7, 171; need to understand underlying structure of 6–7; ordinary world in 3, 17–18, 37–38, 68; overview of stages and archetypes in 2–4

Hero's Journey, The (Campbell): rite of passage into unknown world and 75–76

Higgs, Malcolm 97

Hinduism 2

hitting rock bottom 59

Hogan personality test 155

Holmes and Rahe Stress Scale 7–8, 22

Holmes, Thomas 7–8, 22

hope: in delivery at the next level (Step-11) 158, 189; in prepare to change (Step-6) 89

HOPE (Healing Our Past Experiences) project 139

horizontal learning: in commitment (Step-5) 79; in prepare for change (Step-6) 85

hubris: from imagined progress 165; in resistance to change (Step-3) 47, 49, 58

human development: four phases of Change Wheel and 8–10, 9; instruments for determine needs in 155; levels of development 48, 78–80, 111; vertical development in resistance to change (Step-3) 45–46, 48, 51–53; see also vertical development

human needs, 5 basic 115–122

humility, as indication you are in overcoming resistance (Step-4) 58, 61

hyperventilation 79–80

'I' change (being): at commitment (Step-5 of leader's journey) 77–78, 80; Mandela's development of 100; at overcoming resistance (Step-4 of leader's journey) 67, 69–70; at prepare for change (Step-6) 87, 89; at resistance to change (Step-3) 45–47, 48, 51, 53; as start of leadership 99; at trials and tribulations (Step-7) 97–100, 102; wake-up calls of 172–173

immaturity, in comfort zone (Step-1) 15

indifference 104

initiation stage, hero's journey and 3

innermost cave metaphor: emerging from in embodying the change (Step-9) 133–137, 141; exploring for treasure in deep work (Step-8) 111, 113–114, 122, 124–131, 134, 186; in return (Step-10) 144, 147

inspiration and being inspirational: in inspire (Step-12) 163–166

inspire (Step-12 of leader's journey): achievement audit in 164–165; cultural metaphors/film examples of 166–169; inspiration and being inspirational as indications you are in 163–169; questions to ask yourself 169; risk of complacency in 165–166; transition to a new cycle 169; transition to from delivery at the new level (Step-11) 161; vital energy increase as feeling in 165

insularity: in comfort zone (Step-1) 14–15; in resistance to change (Step-3) 47, 49

interoception 101; in embodying the change (Step-9) 135–137; see also bodily awareness; Complete App for energy/breathing/body awareness

invincibility, in comfort zone (Step-1) 15

'IT' change (doing): 'IT' addiction of leaders and 70, 93, 97–98, 133–134, 161; at overcoming resistance (Step-4 of leader's journey) 67, 69–70; overcoming resistance (Step-4) 67, 69–70; at prepare for change (Step-6) 87, 89; at resistance to change (Step-3) 45–47, 47, 51, 53; at and tribulations (Step-7 of leader's journey) 97–100, 102; wake-up calls of 172–173

John, Elton 63

Joyce, James 2

Kegan, Robert 45, 49, 177

known world 16

Kobasa, Suzanne 8, 36

Kolb, David 104

Kotter, John P. 97–98

leader's journey: 12 steps of 8–10, 9; blame and 22; development coaches for 47, 49, 51–54; films and 4; instruments for development needs 155; meta-frame of as guidance 6–7; physiological diagnostic assessment to determine where to start on 100; resistance and distraction in 44–45; time frames of leader's journey 125, 127, 134–135, 138, 140, 144–145, 163, 169; as updated, integrated version of Campbell's work 8; see also challenge to reality (Step-2 of leader's journey); comfort zone (Step-1 of leader's journey); commitment (Step-5 of leader's journey); deep work

(Step-8 of leader's journey); delivery at the new level (Step-11); embodying the change (Step-9 of leader's journey); inspire (Step-12); leader as coaches; overcoming resistance (Step-4 of leader's journey); prepare for change (Step-6 of leader's journey); resistance to change (Step-3 of leader's journey); return (Step-10 of leader's journey); trials and tribulations (Step-7 of leader's journey)

leaders: 'IT' (doing) addiction of 70, 93, 97–98, 133–134, 161; coaching for 47, 49, 51–54, 104–105, 171; Complete App for energy/awareness of bodily sensations for 101–102; descriptive leader assessment vs. developmental level of leader assessments 155–156; dislike of change and surprises in/of 1–2; irony of skipping or dismissing therapy by 133–134; Joseph Campbell as roadmap for 2; leadership behavioural alphabet 87, 88, 157, 157–158; Nelson Mandela as leader with biggest impact on the world 100; see also performance

leaders as coaches 171; challenge to reality (Step-2) coaching 175–177; Change Wheel and leader's journey as time-tested maps for 171; comfort zone (Step-1) coaching 172–175; commitment (Step-5) coaching 181–182; deep work (Step-8) coaching 185–186; delivery at the new level (Step-11) coaching 188–189; embodying the change (Step-9) coaching 186–187; innermost cave metaphor and exploring for treasure in deep work (Step-8) and 111, 113–114, 122, 124–131, 186; inspire (Step-12) coaching and 172–176, 189; overcoming resistance (Step-4) coaching 179–181; prepare for change (Step-6) coaching 182–183; resistance to change (Step-3) coaching 177–179; return (Step-10) coaching 187–188; trials and tribulations (Step-7) coaching 183–185

leadership behavioural alphabet 88; focus on Involve, Ignite and Implement in delivery at the new level (Step-11) 157, 157, 158; in prepare for change (Step-6) 87

learned helplessness 34–36, 61; see also victimhood

Learning and Development (L&D) 44

learning styles 104

letting go 59, 61, 63, 73, 138

levels of development 47, 78–80, 111; Piaget on 78–80

life events: stress and illness from vs. resilience 7–8

'Little Gidding' (poem, Eliot) 148

loneliness, of commitment (Step-5) 75, 77–78

long-dark night 59

Lord of the Rings, The (film): comfort zone (Step-1) and 17; commitment (Step-5) and 81; deep work (Step-8) and 129; delivery at the new level (Step-11) and 160; embodying the change (Step-9) and 141; inspire (Step-12) and 167–168; overcoming resistance (Step-4) and 68; prepare for change (Step-6) and 93; resistance to change (Step-3) and 54; return (Step-10) and 150; trials and tribulations (Step-7) and 107; wise wizard in (Gandalf) 177

Lucas, George 4

Luskin, Dr. Fred 139

Lykken, David 35

Lyubomirsky, Sonja 91

Man's Search for Meaning (Frankl) 34

Mandela, Nelson 100

map, need for a good one 171

Maslow, Abraham 73

Matrix, The (film): challenge to reality (Step-2) and 38, 40; comfort zone (Step-1) and 17; commitment (Step-5) and 81; deep work (Step-8) and 128–129; delivery at the new level (Step-11) and 159–160; embodying the change (Step-9) 140–141; Herald archetypes in 181, 183; inspire (Step-12) and 167; overcoming resistance (Step-4) and 68; prepare for change (Step-6) and 92; resistance to change (Step-3) and 51–54; return (Step-10) and 150; Shadow/villain archetypes in 186; trials and tribulations (Step-7) and 107; Trickster archetypes in 185; wise wizards in (Morpheus) 177; see also cultural metaphors; films

maturity, overcoming resistance (Step-4) and 64, 66–67

McKinsey & Co. 51, 97

meditation chanting 80

mental health: emotional competence as skill to develop for 31–33; stigma in 30

Mentor, archetype of hero's journey and 4; description of 3; in films 53–54;

resistance to change (Step-3 of leader's journey) and 42, 47, 50–51, 53–55; in resistance to change (Step-3) 43, 47, 51, 53–54; see also leaders as coaches

meta-frames 8; as allegory of human condition 7; Campbell's surfacing of 5–6; leaders journey/Change Wheel as 6, 171; Pesso's on 5 basic human needs/fixing the faulty code 115, 122

Meyer Briggs Type Indicator 155

monomyths 2

motivation: overcoming resistance (Step-4 of leader's journey) and 64, 66; survival and exploration drives 12–13, 47; value-based wake up calls (Step-2) and 22–24, 24, 25–26, 26, 27

Moyers, Bill 6

mythology, comparative 2; Wilber's theory of emergence, differentiation and integration stages in 5–6

myths, Campbell on: as clues to spiritual potentialities of life 5; meta-frames and 5–8, 171

naivety, in Step-1 (comfort zone) 15

narcissism, trap of: in Step-1 (comfort zone) 15–16, 33

Native American culture 2, 75, 108

needs, 5
    basic human 115–121

negative emotions, breathing and 101–102

Northern Ireland, Troubles of 139

observable pain in others: as sign of wake-up call/challenge to reality (Step-2 of leader's journey) 27–28

Olympic Games 60–61

openness: vs. expert mindset 60–61; need for in inspire (Step-12) 165; in prepare for change (Step-6) 89–90; transition from commitment (Step-5) to preparation and 82

ordinary world, hero's journey and 3, 17–18, 37–38, 68

overcoming resistance (Step-4 of leader's journey): accountability compass for 63, 64, 65–66; clarity for 64, 65; cultural metaphors/film examples of 67–69; faith and doubt in 61–63; indications you may be in 57–59; leaders as coaches for 179–181; maturity and 64, 66–67; motivation and 64, 66; openness vs. expert mindset 60–61; ownership and 59–60, 63, 66–67, 69; proactivity/

follow-up for 64, 65–66; psychological death in 63; questions to ask yourself 70–71; skill/ability for 64, 65; soul searching in 59; as start of decide phase of Change Wheel 57, 59, 62, 67, 69; three dimensions of 'I,' 'WE' and 'IT' (being, relating, doing) 67, 69–70; transition from to commitment (Step-5) 69–70; transition to from resistance to change (Step-3) 54

ownership, resistance to change and 59–60, 63, 66–67, 69

pain: biological consequences of in Step-2 29–30; as signal to heed for change 29–33, 39–40; see also observable pain in others; personal pain; prolonged discomfort

parasympathetic nervous system 30

passion, as predictor of performance 102

pattern recognition 137–138; in deep work (Step-8) 113; see also faulty code

PBS interview, Campbell and 6

peacefulness, in embodying the change (Step-9) 138–140

performance 99; controlling breath for 101; DHEA as performance hormone and 30; faulty code as affecting 115, 133; at inspire (Step-12) 165; leader as coach and 177, 182–183; mental health and 36; passion as predictor of performance 102; professional performance reviews 27, 36, 86, 106, 155–156; in return (Step-10) 146; tracking of key indicators of 158; see also 'IT' (doing) change

permanence, explanatory style and 35–37, 37

personal pain, as sign of wake-up call/challenge to reality (Step-2) 28–29

personalisation, explanatory style and 35–37, 37

pervasiveness, explanatory style and 35–37, 37

Pesso Albert 115–116, 122

Piaget, Jean 78–80

polymaths 87, 89

Positive Energy Practice (PEP skill) 105

positive emotions: Complete app for 105–106

practice, benefits of 104–105

predicting, transition from commitment (Step-5) to preparation (Step-6) and 82–83 prepare for change (Step-6 of leader's journey): appreciation cultivation as indication you are in 89–92; behaviours needed for 86–87, 88, 89; conversion of learning into development 85, 95; cultural metaphors/film examples of 92–93; leaders as coaches 182–183; professional performance review as indication of 86; questions to ask yourself 94; recognition of missing key info as indication of 86; transition from to trials and tribulations (Step-7) 94; transition to from commitment (Step-5) 82–83

professional life: in inspire (Step-12) 163–164

professional recognition: deep work (Step-8) and 112–113

progress charting 102–103

projection, victimhood and 36–37, 37

prolonged discomfort, as sign of wake-up call/ challenge to reality (Step-2) 27, 30

promotions: deep work (Step-8) and 112–115, 127; delivery at the new level (Step-11) 153, 155, 158

Proust, Marcel 90, 166

Prozac 32

pseudo-enlightenment, in deep work (Step-8) 127–128

psychological death 63

puberty 1

purpose: Campbell on 137; finding in embodying the change (Step-9)) 137–138; working with in return (Step-10) 145–147

Rahe, Richard 7–8, 22

Razor's Edge (film), embodiment and 140

reading, Campbell on 85

recognition, deep work (Step-8) and 112–113

regression, lack of diligence and 104–105

relationships: in deep work (Step-8) 112; in delivery at the new level (Step-11) 153; in embodying the change (Step-9) 134–135; in inspire (Step-12) 163–164; in return (Step-10) 143–144; in teenage years 2; in trials and tribulations (Step-7) 95–96; see also 'WE' (relating) change

religion 79; comparative 2; The Troubles in Northern Ireland and 139; Zen Buddhism 90, 128

resilience 111; 3C's of (Commitment, Control and Challenge) 8; emotional 33; from stressful life events 7–8

resistance resources 8

resistance to change (Step-3 of leader's journey): assessing of coaches/ consultants 51–53; cultural metaphors/ film examples of 53–54; development coaches for 47, 49, 51–55; expert mindset as stumbling block in 50–51, 59–60; hubris, fear and insularity in 47, 49, 58; indications you are stuck in 43–45; leaders as coaches in 177–179; mentor/guide/helper archetypes and 43, 47, 50–51, 53–55; questions to ask yourself 55; rationalisations for 44–45; three dimensions of 'I,' 'WE' and 'IT' (being, relating, doing) 45–47, 48, 51, 53; transition from to overcoming resistance (Step-4) 54; transition to from challenge to reality (Step-2) 39; vertical development in 45–46, 51–53

rest, potential need for post-deep work (Step-8) 137

return (Step-10 of leader's journey): cultural metaphors/film examples of 149–151; disillusionment from failure to mark return 148–149; excitement, awe and flow-states as feelings in 148, 151; following your bliss in 147–148; as getting on/re-engaging with our lives/ world 144–145, 152; leaders as coaches at 187–188; questions to ask yourself 152; showing up differently in 143–144; transition from to delivery at the new level (Step-11) 151–152; transition to from embodying the change (Step-9) 141–142; working with purpose in 145–147

return, hero's journey and 3

rituals 105; Positive Energy Practice (PEP skill) as 105; rites of passage 2, 75–76

road of trials, hero's journey and 3

Rocketman (film) 63

Rowland, Deborah 97

satisfaction, in delivery at the new level (Step-11) 159

scepticism: as indication you are in Step-4 58, 63

Schroeder, Harry 87, 88, 156

Seligman, Martin 34–36

shadow work 37; 3 techniques for fixing faulty code with 122–125; in deep work (Step-8) 111–114, 122–124, 127–130, 132

Shadow, archetype of hero's journey and: description of 4; in films 186

Shapeshifter, archetype of hero's journey and 6; description of 3–4
short-term success, addiction to 161
skill/ability: for overcoming resistance (Step-4 of leader's journey) 64, 65
soul searching, for overcoming resistance (Step-4) 59
spiritual experiences and spirituality 79–80; appreciation/gratitude and 91; myths as clues to 5
Stanford Forgiveness Project 139
Star Wars (film) 4; comfort zone (Step-1) and 17–18; commitment (Step-5) and 81–82; deep work (Step-8) and 129–130; delivery at the new level (Step-11) and 160; embodying the change (Step-9) 141; inspire (Step-12) and 168; overcoming resistance (Step-4) and 68; prepare for change (Step-6) and 93; resistance to change (Step-3) and 54; return (Step-10) and 160–161; trials and tribulations (Step-7) and 107; wise wizard in (Obi Wan Kenobi) 177
Step-1. see comfort zone (Step-1 of leader's journey)
Step-10. see return (Step-10 of leader's journey)
Step-2. see challenge to reality (Step-2 of leader's journey)
Step-3. see resistance to change (Step-3 of leader's journey)
Step-4. see overcoming resistance (Step-4 of leader's journey)
Step-5. see commitment (Step-5 of leader's journey)
Step-6. see prepare for change (Step-6 of leader's journey)
Step-7. see trials and tribulations (Step-7 of leader's journey)
Step-8. see deep work (Step-8 of leader's journey)
Step-9. see embodying the change (Step-9 of leader's journey)
stigma, mental health and 30
'story of you', new in embodying the change (Step-9) 138
stress: catabolic hormones and 29–30; change process and Holmes and Rahe Stress scale 7–8; cortisol and 34–35
success: short-term success 161; statistics on change initiatives and 97
survival drive: comfort zone (Step-1) and 12–13; resistance to change and 47
synchronicity 69, 148

teenage years, change in 1–2
tension, glottic stops and 101
the road back, hero's journey and 3
therapy, irony of skipping/dismissing of by leaders 133–134; see also deep work (Step-8 of leader's journey)
threshold guardians, hero's journey and 4; description of 3
time frames of leader's journey 125, 127, 134–135, 138, 140, 144–145, 163, 169
Towers Watson 97
trauma cycles 136–137
traveller story 78
treasure, personal. see innermost cave metaphor
trials and tribulations (Step-7 of leader's journey) 133–134; 'I' and 'WE' vs. 'IT' change in 97–100, 102; Complete App for breathwork and positive emotions and 101–102, 105–106; Complete Leadership Frame and 98–99, 99; cultural metaphors/film examples of 106–108; indications you are in 95–96; leaders as coaches at 183–185; learning styles and 104; physiological diagnostic assessment to determine where to start change 100; questions for change road map creation 102–103; questions to ask yourself 109; regression from lack of diligence and 104–105; signs you are in 103–104; as start of development phase of 95; starting from where you are in 97–100; transition from to deep work (Step-8) 108–109; transition to from prepare for change (Step-6) 94
Trickster, archetype of hero's journey and 6; as archetype in challenge to reality (Step-2) 176–177; description of 4; in films 185
Troubles of Northern Ireland 139
Turner, Victor 75
Tymoshenko, Yulia (Ukrainian President) 98

Ukraine 98
universal metaphor 5
unknown world, hero's journey and 3
Upanishads 5, 140

value-based wake up calls (Step-2) 40; motivational drives and 22–27, 24, 26; see also challenge to reality (Step-2 of leader's journey); wake-up calls (Step-2)
van Gennep, Arnold 75

vertical development: in commitment
(Step-5) 79; in prepare for change (Step-
6) 85; in resistance to change (Step-3)
45–46, 48, 51–53
victimhood: as deafening wake-up calls
33–34; *vs.* hardiness 36, 37; as obstacle
in challenge to reality (Step-2 of leader's
journey) 33–37, 37; projection and
36–37, 37; three P's of explanatory style
and (permanence, pervasiveness and
personalisation) 35–37, 37

wake-up calls: of 'I', 'WE' and 'IT' change
172–173; in business 22; in challenge to
reality (Step-2) 21–22; need for intensity
in 39–40; observable pain in others as
sign of 27–28; personal pain as sign of
28–29; prolonged discomfort as sign of
27, 30; victimhood as deafening
33–34; *see also* challenge to reality (Step-
2); value-based wake up calls (Step-2)
'WE' change (relating): at overcoming
resistance (Step-4 of leader's journey) 67,
69–70; at overcoming resistance (Step-
4) 67, 69–70; at prepare for change
(Step-6) 87, 89; at resistance to change

(Step-3) 45–47, 49, 52, 54; trials and
tribulations (Step-7 of leader's journey)
97–100, 102; wake-up calls of 172–173
Wilber, Ken 5–6, 78–79; international
conference with Tymoshenko (Ukrainian
President) 98; on three dimensions of
"I," "WE" and "IT" (being, relating,
doing) 45
wilful ignorance: in Step-1 (comfort zone)
15
Williamson, Marianne 126
wise wizards 176–177
Wizard of Oz, The (film): comfort zone
(Step-1) and 18; commitment (Step-5)
and 82; deep work (Step-8) and 130;
delivery at the new level (Step-11) and
160; embodying the change (Step-9)
141; inspire (Step-12) and 168–169;
overcoming resistance (Step-4) and
68–69; prepare for change (Step-6) and
93–94; resistance to change (Step-3)
and 54; return (Step-10) and 151; trials
and tribulations (Step-7) and 108; wise
wizard in (Glinda the Good Witch) 177

Zen Buddhism 90, 128

Christianity and the University Experience

ALSO AVAILABLE FROM BLOOMSBURY

The African Christian Diaspora: New Currents and Emerging Trends in World Christianity, Afe Adogame

Christianity Today: An Introduction, George D. Chryssides

Christianity and the University Experience

Understanding Student Faith

MATHEW GUEST, KRISTIN AUNE, SONYA SHARMA AND ROB WARNER

B L O O M S B U R Y
LONDON • NEW DELHI • NEW YORK • SYDNEY

Bloomsbury Academic
An imprint of Bloomsbury Publishing Plc

50 Bedford Square	1385 Broadway
London	New York
WC1B 3DP	NY 10018
UK	USA

www.bloomsbury.com

First published 2013

British Library Cataloguing-in-Publication Data
A catalogue record for this book is available from the British Library.

ISBN: HB: 978-1-78093-601-7
PB: 978-1-78093-784-7
ePub: 978-1-78093-639-0
PDF: 978-1-78093-621-5

Library of Congress Cataloging-in-Publication Data
Christianity and the university experience : understanding student faith /
Mathew Guest . . . [et al.].
pages cm
Includes bibliographical references and index.
ISBN 978-1-78093-784-7 (pbk. : alk. paper) – ISBN 978-1-78093-601-7 (alk. paper) –
ISBN 978-1-78093-639-0 (epub) – ISBN 978-1-78093-621-5 (pdf)
1. College students – Religious life. 2. Universities and colleges – Religion.
I. Guest, Mathew, editor of compilation.
BV4531.3.C49 2013
274.1'083088378198 – dc23
2013005954

Typeset by Newgen Imaging Systems Pvt Ltd, Chennai, India
Printed and bound in Great Britain

Contents

List of figures vi
List of tables vii
Foreword, by Christian Smith ix
Acknowledgements xi

Introduction 1

1 Historical, cultural and scholarly contexts 11

2 What makes a Christian student? 27

3 Institutional variations in the university experience 53

4 Is the university a force for secularization? 83

5 The challenges of being a Christian student 113

6 Organized Christianity on the university campus 137

7 Social differences among Christian students: Age, class, ethnicity and gender 165

8 Broader implications 195

Appendix: How many Christian students are there in England's universities? 211

Bibliography 219

Index 239

List of figures

3.1 Students process into Durham Cathedral on graduation day 58

3.2 The Emmanuel Centre, housing chaplaincy services for the University of Leeds and Leeds Metropolitan University 61

3.3 Promotional material for the international students club, University of Leeds 70

3.4 View of Canterbury Cathedral from the University of Kent campus 72

3.5 University of Kent Carol Service, organized by the Chaplaincy 73

3.6 The Multi-Faith Centre, University of Derby 74

3.7 Entrance to Senate House and University Chapel at the University of Chester 76

3.8 Stained glass cross by Cloisters, University of Chester 76

4.1 Percentage of Christian students by general church attendance profile within each of the five university types 106

5.1 The Halo nightclub (converted church), Leeds 123

5.2 Poster for club night at Halo, Leeds 124

6.1 The University of Kent chaplaincy tea towel 143

6.2 A lone worshipper in the worship space in the Emmanuel Centre, Leeds 144

List of tables

2.1 General orientation to religion or spirituality among all student respondents and among self-identifying Christians among them 33

2.2 Responses from Christian students to the question 'Which of the following most closely expresses your understanding of Jesus?' 34

2.3 General church attendance profile of self-identifying Christian students based on combining frequency of churchgoing during vacations and during term-time 39

2.4 Key indices of Christian identity, presented according to our fivefold typology of Christian students 50

3.1 The fivefold typology of England's universities 56

4.1 Proportion of students who say that, since starting university, they have become more religious, less religious or say their perspective has generally stayed the same 89

4.2 Church attendance by denomination both before and during university among undergraduates self-identifying as Christian 91

4.3 Frequency of church attendance both during term-time and during university vacations among undergraduates self-identifying as Christian 94

4.4 General church attendance profile among Christian students cross-tabulated with the denomination attended before coming to university 96

4.5 'What do you think about sexual relations between adults of the same sex?' comparing Christian students with those of 'no religion' 101

4.6 Responses among Christian students and students of 'no religion' to the question 'People who are terminally ill should be legally permitted to take their own lives if they choose to' 102

4.7 Christian students' perception of whether they have become more or less religious since being at university, cross-tabulated with university type 104

4.8 Indicators of religious decline and religious intensification among Christian students at the five different types of university 107

5.1 Responses to the drinking culture among undergraduates, comparing Christians with those of 'no religion' 123

5.2 Responses from Christian students to the question 'Which of the following best expresses your view on the relationship between science and the Bible?' 130

6.1 Proportions of CU-involved Christians compared with non-CU Christians who affirmed different sources of religious authority were 'very important' 150

6.2 Responses from CU-involved Christians compared with non-CU Christians to various moral issues 151

7.1 General church attendance profile of self-identifying Christian students, by age 167

7.2 General orientation to religion or spirituality among self-identifying Christians, by age 168

7.3 Responses to the statement: 'Men are more naturally equipped to be leaders in society', by gender 180

7.4 'Have you done any voluntary work during the past 12 months in any of the following areas?', percentage figures for Christian students and students of 'no religion' 189

A1 General orientation to religion among undergraduates studying at universities in England (2010–11) 214

A2 Responses to the question 'to what religion or spiritual tradition do you currently belong? Please choose the one that fits best' among undergraduates studying at universities in England (2010–11) 214

Foreword

by Christian Smith

Christianity and the University Experience is an important milestone in the advance of our sociological knowledge of the religious and spiritual lives of university students in the United Kingdom. It nicely presents the findings of the first study of its kind in the United Kingdom, not 'filling gaps' of social-science knowledge but blazing a trail of scholarship in an important area of study. Many people wonder or are concerned about the religious commitments of university students. What is actually going on in their lives when it comes to faith and practice? Is religion declining or absent among university students? Or is something else unexpected happening? Most of what people 'know' on the topic, however, has been impressionistic – based on guesswork, anecdotal experience and generalizing inferences. That is because reliable knowledge grounded in careful social science research has been scarce.

'Christianity and the University Experience' helps to change all that. Offering evidence, insights and explanations about a previously largely un-researched phenomenon – Christian university students in the United Kingdom – this valuable book draws on new, primary evidence collected by a skilled team of researchers to shed new light on this significant matter. With this book, previously mere common assumptions, speculations and stereotypes can now be subject to the scrutiny of hard evidence provided by the application of robust sociological methods and smart analysis and interpretation. The authors bring us inside the world of Christian university students, revealing for readers the empirical reality happening on the ground among them. The findings provocatively challenge more than a few common assumptions on the matter, and should prove to be the stimulus of important discussions, fruitful debate and further research. The gift this book offers, in other words, is the solid empirical light it sheds on the issue, leading us to evidence-based rather than speculative, prejudiced or ideologically driven beliefs and arguments.

More generally, this book cultivates in readers the reflective consideration of numerous important questions, such as, how to even properly study such a population, how to historically and socially contextualize university students of faith, and the variability in experience that different Christian university students in the United Kingdom can and do have, especially along the lines of social class, race, ethnicity and gender. In 'Christianity and the University Experience', we also learn more about some of the challenges and difficulties Christian university students face at this level of their education, and the kinds of on-campus and nearby-campus organizational resources and supports that help sustain them. Readers of this book will have the opportunity to rethink – based on solid empirical data – questions of secularization in modern, educated societies, the nature of the university experience for many students and the possible future of religion in the United Kingdom.

We in the United States have been fortunate enough to have the research resources to study the religious and spiritual lives of American teenagers and emerging adults very well. The more we have learned here, however, the more we have wished to see similarly solid sociological studies conducted in other countries, in order to facilitate the kinds of comparisons that only a multiplicity of similar research projects can provide. I am gratified that 'Christianity and the University Experience' takes a major step in providing exactly that, and I commend it enthusiastically to anyone interested in religion, Higher Education and young people in the United Kingdom and beyond.

Christian Smith, University of Notre Dame (Indiana, US), is the Principal Investigator of the National Study of Youth and Religion (US) and author of *Soul Searching: The Religious Lives of American Teenagers* (Oxford University Press, 2005) and *Souls in Transition: The Religious and Spiritual Lives of Emerging Adults* (Oxford University Press, 2009).

Acknowledgements

This book is the major published outcome of the 'Christianity and the University Experience in Contemporary England' project, funded by the Arts and Humanities Research Council and Economic and Social Research Council as part of the Religion and Society Programme. We are most grateful to these funding bodies for creating this invaluable opportunity, and to those steering the Programme – Linda Woodhead, Rebecca Catto and Peta Ainsworth – for their on-going and unfailing support and encouragement. Linda's tireless advocacy for the entire Religion and Society Programme has been exemplary and hugely important for returning debate about religion to the public domain.

Throughout the three-year life of the project we have been assisted by a wide range of individuals and organizations without whom such an ambitious endeavour would have been impossible. We have benefited from sage advice and on-the-ground wisdom shared by our advisors and stakeholders group: Andii Bowsher, Sue Bennett, Peter Brierley, Harriet Crabtree, Richard Davey, Adam Dinham, Sophie Gilliat-Ray, Stephen Heap, Sister Teresa Kennedy, Kat Luckock, Rebecca O'Loughlin, Vaughan Roberts, Tim Rudge, Maeve Sherlock, Hugh Shilson-Thomas, Jonathan Smith, Pamela Taylor, Hilary Topp, Rich Wilson, Paul Weller and Christopher Woods. To all of these we extend our thanks.

Our team meetings were for the most part held in Leeds, given its geographically convenient location. Each time we were well accommodated in the Emmanuel Centre, and we thank the staff at the University of Leeds Chaplaincy. We are also grateful to the Multi-Faith Centre at the University of Derby for hosting our advisors' meetings.

As we have promoted our findings on the 'conference circuit', our thoughts and ideas have been greatly enriched by dialogue with academics and students who share our interests in student religion. Feedback and discussion were enjoyed at a variety of events and conferences, located at Christ's College Cambridge, Durham University, King's College London, St Catherine's College Oxford, Trinity College Dublin, University of Chester, University of Derby, University of Edinburgh, University of Exeter, Goldsmiths University of London, University of Kent, University of Lancaster, University of Newcastle, University of Warwick and Woodbrooke Quaker Study Centre, Birmingham.

International engagement was enjoyed at the annual SSSR conferences in Milwaukee (2011) and Phoenix (2012), the Nordic Sociological Association conference (University of Oslo, 2011) and at the ISSR conference in Aix en Provence (2011). Special thanks are due to the BSA Sociology of Religion Study Group for their collegial support through the duration of the project.

Invaluable conversations were had with Christian Smith and Amy Wilkins, who shared methodological insights based on their own, US-based, projects in similar areas. Extensive advice on the design and administration of our questionnaire survey was generously given by David Voas of the University of Essex, and guidance on the analysis of statistics and weighting process from James Brown of the University of Southampton. Sylvie Collins-Mayo, Adam Dinham and Paul Weller have been supportive and generous, offering insights based on their own, related research projects.

More practical, but equally invaluable, assistance was provided by Angie Harvey and Paul Smith as we were putting the manuscript together; our collective IT limitations were addressed by Stefan Wilczek, who helpfully designed the project website.

Our sincere thanks also to all of the universities that took part in our study, and especially those university managers and administrators who worked with us to secure access to the students within each. Our five case studies were made much more accessible and the experience of studying them much more enriching because of the guidance offered by our on-site contacts, and we are particularly grateful to Matt Ward, Peter Geldard and Stephen Laird, who went well beyond the call of duty in helping us understand their respective university contexts. Most of all, we thank the staff and students who took part in this research. They cannot be named, for obvious reasons, and they are disguised with pseudonyms throughout this book, but they know who they are. We could not have done this without their help and generosity.

Our families, friends and partners have been supportive and understanding as this project has gradually taken over more and more of our lives; without their patient forbearance, this book would not have been possible.

Introduction

In December 2012, as this book was being written, a news story appeared in the British press about a controversy triggered by a Christian organization at the University of Bristol. According to *The Times*, the Bristol Christian Union had 'tried to ban women speakers at its meetings unless they are accompanied by their husbands'. The student-led society, traditionally associated with a firmly Evangelical brand of Christianity, had previously only allowed male preachers to speak at its evangelistic events. A proposal calling for equal opportunities for men and women triggered an internal revolt among those uncomfortable with the prospect of women speakers, and a compromise policy was drawn up by its leadership. The compromise amounted to allowing female speakers, but only in certain contexts, not including as a main speaker for 'mission weeks',[1] although, according to a statement issued by the CU president, 'a husband and wife can teach together' on these occasions. The statement triggered a range of protests, by women's groups, the Students' Union and even criticism from the Evangelical Universities and Colleges Christian Fellowship (UCCF), the national organization to which the Bristol CU is affiliated. Soon afterwards, the Bristol CU amended its position, affirming its willingness to extend 'speaker invitations to both men and women' to all events 'without exception'.

This episode was not an isolated incident. In recent years, Christian Unions have featured in a number of public conflicts on university campuses, chiefly over issues of equality and tolerance, and especially concerning gender, sexuality and the treatment of other religious groups. In 2006, the Christian Union at the University of Birmingham had its bank account frozen and its membership suspended by the University's Guild of Students over its equal opportunities policy, with CU members claiming the underlying issue was their refusal to mention gay, lesbian, bisexual or transgendered people in their charitable constitution. The following year a similar conflict erupted at the University of Exeter over the rights of gay people, and controversies have occurred at Oxford, Edinburgh and other UK campuses in subsequent years. The consequent media coverage has illuminated the potential tensions that can emerge between freedom of religious expression and gender and sexual equality. These stories also highlight the capacity of universities to generate forms of religion that sit uncomfortably alongside dominant social norms concerning tolerance, equality and the status of men and women. There is something countercultural about the religion we often find on university campuses. Such underlying tensions are by no means restricted to Christianity; in recent years universities have been identified by the UK government and various other public bodies as a major source of recruitment to extremist forms of Islam. Several of the British Muslims guilty of recent acts of terrorism were students at British universities, some exposed to teaching by militant individuals invited to be visiting speakers by student-run Islamic Societies. As a consequence, the university campus has come under scrutiny as a context of religious 'radicalization'. Calls for a centralized interventionist response have inevitably come into conflict with those keen to preserve freedom of religious expression as well as the time-honoured status of the university as a guardian of free thinking.

Such fractious developments highlight the newly heightened visibility of religious matters on UK university campuses, not just as an issue of conviction for religious students, but for non-religious students as well. Indeed, if a measure of a group's social significance is to be found in the excitability of its opponents, religion on campus appears alive and well. This is evidenced in the prominence of a 'new atheist' agenda in recent years, the growth of student Atheist Societies, and the 2009 establishment of the National Federation of Atheist, Humanist and Secular Student Societies (AHS), an umbrella association for student groups sceptical about religion to mirror the various national networks representing Christian and Muslim students. The expansion of such networks in recent years – for example the British Sikh Student Federation was established in 2008; the Union of Jewish Students in 2010 – suggests university campuses have witnessed not just a rise in countercultural religion but a heightened mobilization of religion as a marker of identity for students across the religious spectrum.

This is a book that takes these developments seriously and asks what they reveal about the status of universities as contexts of religious expression. Its specific focus is students who identify as Christian at universities located in England. As such, the book investigates the status of the most influential, embedded and culturally complex religious tradition in the British Isles. As revealed in the National Census in 2011, the majority of individuals in England and Wales (59%) still identify themselves as Christian, and while this figure is in decline (down from 72% in 2001), it indicates a persistent cultural resonance between the Christian tradition and the life of the nation. But how does this resonance become manifest within universities and within the lives of students? Sociologist Peter Berger (1999) has presented universities as carriers of modernity, vehicles for the furtherance of a certain way of looking at the world, one that – in Western Europe and the elite United

States at least – has little use for religion (Berger, Davie and Fokas, 2008). This is a common and influential understanding, and rests upon the idea that knowledge, at least legitimate knowledge, is contaminated by association with religious concerns (Guest, 2012). As universities are in the business of furthering and conveying knowledge, their work is best achieved when religious matters are excluded, kept in their place – that is in the private realm – and certainly outside of the classroom. Berger's portrayal of the university is not without substance: there are indeed institutions governed by these assumptions, but it would be a mistake to say the matter ends there. Indeed, the recent developments described above suggest universities are contexts in which religion is a vital and powerful presence. Public disputes between university Christian Unions and Student Unions over issues of inclusion and tolerance point to pockets of conviction and well-mobilized activism. While Berger may be right about the secularizing bias among Western European academics, we should pause before projecting the same perspectives on to their students.

Intrigued by this problem, the authors of this book undertook a three-year project aimed at discovering what distinguishes university students who identify as Christian and how their experience of university affirms or undermines their Christian faith. The project, entitled 'Christianity and the University Experience in Contemporary England' (or CUE), was conducted between 2009 and 2012 and this book reports on its main findings. Our argument, unpacked in detail throughout the course of the subsequent chapters, is that Christian students – much like UK Christians in general – comprise a sizeable and diverse population of individuals. They are unified neither by doctrinal assent nor moral conviction, and engagement in the institutions of the church is uneven and often tentative. While the most visible are conservative in doctrine and ethics and conversionist in their orientation to the world, many more occupy the liberal centre ground that has much in common with mainstream British culture. University shapes their identity, not primarily via intellectual challenges to their faith, but chiefly via existential challenges that arise from a disruption of familiar life patterns and the dominance of particular forms of organized Christianity within different campus contexts. To summarize, *it is first and foremost the subjective and relational experience of university that engages their faith*, with a variety of different consequences.

This is not an argument about long-term change. While we have a strong interest in how universities may influence Christian students in a way that has long-term consequences, a longitudinal comparison – assessing change by comparing the lives of students at two specific points in time – is not what we are dealing with here. Excellent longitudinal work has been carried out in the United States, particularly in association with the National Study of Youth and Religion, led by Christian Smith, which has generated some insightful conclusions, based on large data sets collected at different points in the life-course (Smith and Denton, 2005; Smith and Snell, 2009). While we have learned a lot from this work, and continue to pursue longitudinal issues based in our own data, the present book has a different set of ambitions. It focuses on a single point in time, taking a snapshot of Christian students studying at England's universities in order to discover what distinguishes them as a population. What kinds of beliefs and values do they share, and how are these similar or different from non-Christian students? How do they practise their Christianity: do they pray, read the Bible or do volunteer work? If so, how often, and what significance do these practices have for their lives? This is, if you like, the descriptive dimension to the book; we are painting a picture, one that has not been painted before and which will therefore illuminate a significant sub-group within contemporary Christianity in the United Kingdom, helping us understand better how this religion functions within a largely secularizing context.

There is a second dimension to the book, one concerned with the way in which these Christian students interact with their university environment. How do they engage with the peculiar set of circumstances that face them upon embarking on their career as an undergraduate student, and how does this appear to impact upon their Christian identity? This is why the title of this book refers to the university experience. Previous studies of the ways in which higher education impacts upon religious identity have tended to focus on factors like academic study or exposure to cultural pluralism. We take a different approach, exploring this process of interaction in terms of a more holistic approach to university life. In short, we take seriously the combination of factors that mark different types of university as distinctive, and build on this in forming an understanding of different configurations of student experience. As will be argued throughout this book, these configurations illuminate why Christian students respond to university life in the ways that they do. In this sense, we are advocating the pluralization of the university experience; that is, as a variable impacting upon Christian identity, university does not function as a singular, homogenous phenomenon, but follows a variety of distinctive institutional patterns.

It is worth making a few comments in this introduction about focus and method. One obvious question one might have upon taking up this book and reading about the research upon which it is based, is why Christianity? This appears counter-intuitive on two counts. Why restrict a study to one religious tradition, considering the increasing religious diversity of the UK context? Given recent political interests, wouldn't Islam qualify as a more interesting, more urgently relevant focus of interest, especially given concerns about the radicalization of students within universities? Also, given research into young adults that suggests an at best loose adherence to conventional boundaries of religious belonging (Collins-Mayo et al., 2010; Day, 2011; Hopkins et al., 2011), is there not a strong argument for bypassing traditional categories like 'Christianity' in favour of a general analysis of 'the religious' (as opposed to the secular), or perhaps of 'the spiritual'? Aside from reasons of conceptual focus and author expertise, the relationship between UK universities and Christianity has a long and rich history. Christianity is the most culturally influential tradition in this country, and hence accounting for its presence within universities is a challenge that has enormous relevance to understanding the nature and significance of highly influential institutions – universities – and a sizeable sub-group within the nation's population – the students who occupy them. The evidence we have collected says a great deal about the continuing cultural significance of Christianity within the contemporary United Kingdom.

A second question might be, why England? Why not study Christianity within universities across the United Kingdom? Since devolved governments were established in Wales, Scotland and Northern Ireland, all with powers of governance over education, the institutional trajectories of each have become more distinct. The Scottish Parliament abolished university tuition fees for Scottish and EU students (but not for students from England) in 2008, instigating a change likely to have a marked impact on the demographic constituency of its universities' students. The federal university of Wales has undergone a significant re-structuring, with several institutions facing an uncertain future. These changes complicate existing distinctive features that arise from the histories of universities within the three provinces. For example, Scotland's ancient universities maintain a strong relationship with the Presbyterian State Kirk, one not replicated in England, Wales or Northern Ireland. What these various factors together point to is a structural fragmentation and reconfiguration along national lines. In focusing upon England alone – where the majority of UK universities are situated – we are dealing with a single system, albeit one that is increasingly complex.

A third question relates to our selection of universities and their capacity to be representative of England's Higher Education sector as a whole. As we discuss at length in Chapter 1, these universities have emerged from a complex history, and appear to us today as a wide variety of educational establishments. For example, Durham University – one of the three universities leading this project – is the third oldest in England, established in 1832, and has become one of the leading research universities in the country, being recently admitted to the prestigious Russell Group of elite, research-led universities alongside the likes of Oxford and Cambridge. Its coverage of traditional academic subjects and long-standing elite reputation is reflected in its high proportion of privately educated undergraduates, while the city's ancient Cathedral and the nearby colleges create a sense of tradition, antiquity and privilege. Contrast this with the University of Derby, which was formed out of pre-existing local colleges and granted university status in 1992, maintaining a long-standing focus on vocational training. Two-thirds of its students are from the local region in the industrial Midlands, with around 5% from outside the EU and even fewer from private school backgrounds. Derby's emphasis on widening access to higher education is reflected in the high proportion of its students who are from lower socio-economic backgrounds. Such differences – the product of both historical and contemporary factors – also influence how religion in general, and Christianity in particular, are expressed within different student bodies. Durham was founded on ecclesiastical bases, has a leading Theology and Religion department, multiple college chapels and chaplains, and holds matriculation and graduation ceremonies in its eleventh century Norman Anglican Cathedral. A sense of Christian context and history is enhanced by the use of Christian festival names for university terms (Michaelmas, Epiphany and Easter) and the multitude of churches nearby. Derby, on the other hand, has a much more multicultural student body, as well as a purpose-built Multi-Faith Centre, which caters to those of all faiths, incorporating several adaptable worship spaces and male and female washing areas for use before Muslim prayers. The university offers halal food, publishes a multi-faith calendar and factsheets on religious holidays, and includes a mandatory equality and diversity online training module for staff. These two examples represent just two orientations to religion affirmed within England's diverse HE sector. Others may be described as practically indifferent or wilfully dismissive, still others as positively affirming, some universities even embracing Christianity as integral to their identity and mission. So how do we capture this diversity?

Our analysis of universities across England has allowed us to develop a typology, outlined in detail in Chapter 3, structured around key differences in the ways universities function as contexts for the expression of religious identity. It comprises five clear categories: traditional/elite universities; inner-city red-brick universities; 1960s campus universities; post-1992 universities; and universities belonging to the Cathedrals Group, a collection of church founded institutions that have an explicitly Christian ethos. The universities that eventually agreed to take part in the CUE project, listed by category, were: Cambridge, Durham, University College London (traditional, elite universities); Leeds, Newcastle, Sheffield (inner-city 'red-brick' universities); Kent and Salford (1960s campus universities); Derby and Staffordshire ('post-1992' universities); and Canterbury Christ Church, Chester and Winchester (from the 'Cathedrals Group'). These universities reflect the diversity of the English Higher Education sector in all major respects, including with respect to history, institutional ethos, student demographics and the character of the immediate locale, all of which are highly likely to shape the patterns of religious expression associated with each university.

Our large-scale survey of university students across these 13 universities provides us with a wealth of data, and with 4,500 students completing it, the survey constitutes the most ambitious study of religion among university students in the United Kingdom to date.[2] As this book unfolds, we will draw from our survey findings in mapping the broad contours of student Christianity – what these students say they believe, what moral values they hold and how they express their Christian identity in practical terms. The survey also provides us with valuable information about the social background of Christian students, including their gender distribution, school background and the economic circumstances of their parents. This allows us to trace connections between different variables, not least the relationship between social class and religion, something that is understandably magnified by the university experience (this relationship is explored in detail in Chapter 7). But the survey only takes us so far. It provides us with clues about the expression of Christian identity within universities, but only limited qualitative detail. We might develop a metaphor that likens the Christian student's progress through university to a journey. Much of the questionnaire data may be viewed as co-ordinates on a map representing student identity. We, as academics, have defined the dimensions of the map, where the contours lie, the different roads featured, their direction and connectedness to one another and to the various places depicted on the map. In asking respondents questions we invite them to place themselves on the map, but they can only place themselves in relation to our predefined co-ordinates. This has its advantages; it allows us to measure identities in relation to these co-ordinates and in relation to one another, and this facilitates a systematic analysis. It also enables us to count how many Christian students follow particular routes, and how many appear to take the journey alone. However, we must formulate assumptions about what respondents might mean by relating to the map in the way that they do, and these meanings cannot be explored beyond these assumptions. In short, we have to assume they represent common meanings, and any underlying nuance remains inaccessible. This is why we incorporated into the project extended interviews with Christian students at five case-study universities. Interviews might be likened to an invitation to respondents to describe their journey through the same terrain, but with little or none of the constraints imposed by the map. While similar language and categories might be used, the respondent is not constrained by them, and can decide upon their own route through the territory; they may redefine the lay of the land, or adopt a completely different perspective on it, if they wish. In simple terms, we learn a lot more about how Christian students negotiate the university experience, because we can get beyond preconceived categories and explore these students' lives in much greater depth, including allowing them to tell us their stories in their own words.

Our interviews have been essential in challenging preconceived assumptions about the nature of religion, of Christianity and of Christian students. We conducted semi-structured interviews with 75 Christian students based in 5 universities, 1 from each of the categories described above, and another 25 with university figures instrumental to the management of religious identities in their respective institutions, such as equality and diversity officers, CU presidents and chaplains from various denominational backgrounds. Through these fascinating conversations, we were able to explore how students experience university, and how this experience influences their Christian faith. We were able to hear stories about their experiences, about academic learning that provoked a rethinking of their beliefs, about opportunities for evangelism that arose out of social engagements with non-Christians, about tensions between different on-campus Christian organizations and how this challenged assumptions about morality and the Christian life. Most of all, what our interviews reinforced was our emerging impression that university for Christian students is not primarily a context characterized by a cognitive undermining of faith. It is, rather, a context that presents challenges, but also opportunities, and these foster a sense of empowerment rather than disillusionment among many Christian students. The majority of students view university as having had a benign influence on their religious identity, even while the process of negotiating this experience is often portrayed as difficult. In the following chapters we will set out the evidence for this, and describe how this process takes place. Chapter 1 places UK universities within their historical and cultural contexts, paying attention to how such contextual factors shape the presence of Christianity within them. Chapter 2 offers an extended description of what distinguishes Christian students as a demographic group, drawing from our national survey. Chapter 3 complicates the picture by outlining a fivefold typology of England's universities, using our case studies as illustrations, and focusing on how these types foster different orientations to Christianity. Chapter 4 asks whether universities can be viewed as a force for secularization, and draws from our survey evidence in offering a response that adds nuance to existing interpretations. Chapters 5 and 6 both focus on the experiences of Christian students, drawing from interviews to explore how university presents challenges to their faith and how they and their Christian organizations contribute to life on campus. Chapter 7 places the case of Christian students in a wider theoretical context by asking how Christian identities relate to other indices of identity, such as ethnicity, gender and social class. In this way we place religious identity within a broader matrix of factors that shape life within England's universities.

Any team-authored volume presents unique challenges for the task of authorship. All four authors take full responsibility for the content of this book: it is the product of three years' empirical research in which we all played an important part, numerous team meetings, seminars and conferences at which we discussed our ideas at length, and an extended writing process during which all four of us read one another's drafts and offered critical comment. The practicalities of academic life have also required a clear division of labour in the production of the book's text, and it is useful to detail that here for the sake of transparency. While all four authors have contributed to every chapter, Guest was primarily responsible for the Introduction, Chapters 1, 2, 3, 4, and the Appendix, Sharma for Chapter 5, Warner for Chapter 6 and Aune for Chapter 7. The conclusion was drafted by Warner and then revised and edited into the final version by the whole team.

The lived reality of contemporary Christianity in the United Kingdom is under-researched and commonly misunderstood. Indeed, the misconceptions surrounding the relationship between religion and education are mirrored by a widespread ignorance about what Christians actually believe. We hope that this volume will go some way towards addressing these issues. We have no illusions that this will be the last word on the matter, and look forward to emerging conversations about our arguments and our evidence. Like many of the students we spoke to and learned so much from, we hope to provoke an on-going dialogue, not to claim an indisputable truth.

Notes

1 Mission weeks are a series of outreach events held annually by university Christian Unions, typically focused on attempts to bring non-Christians to the Christian faith.

2 More detailed information about the survey is provided in the Appendix.

1

Historical, cultural and scholarly contexts

Introduction

While secularism and scepticism are nowadays more often associated with university education, religion, and Christianity in particular, has enjoyed a long and complex relationship with university life. This has mirrored changing understandings of scholarship, of the status of theology and of science, and of the public function of the university. It has also developed in reaction to the shifting needs of a diversifying student body, which in turn reflects the complex religious profile of the United Kingdom. This changing relationship, driven from above by academia and government policy, and from below by popular student engagement and religious organizations, shapes the opportunities and boundaries that frame orientations to Christianity among students today. In the pages that follow we offer a brief history of how the emergence of UK Higher Education has been caught up in wider cultural responses to Christianity, and discuss the complex Christian heritage of England's universities. The intention is to offer the historical and cultural context relevant to the task of understanding how universities function as sites of religious expression. We conclude by considering the existing scholarship that has focused on religion within university contexts, and note how this work informs our own approach.

Religion and UK universities in historical perspective[1]

The origins of the UK university are bound up in religious controversy. Archbishop of Canterbury Thomas Becket famously fell out of favour with his monarch, Henry II, over the privileges owed to the church. Henry sought to weaken the independence of the clergy, while Becket fostered a haven of scholarship at Canterbury. This association of learning with independent thinking meant that, following Becket's murder in 1170, Henry recalled the English clerks based at the University of Paris. Upon their return, they sought a new geographical base. Proximity to London, two large monasteries, and an Augustinian Priory, St Fridewide's, that had already attracted scholars by its impressive literary holdings, meant Oxford was an obvious choice (Armytage, 1955, pp. 34–8). By the end of the twelfth century the University of Oxford was established as a centre of learning. By 1207, some of its clerks had migrated to Cambridge, establishing the two 'ancient' universities of England that remained the nation's only universities for another 600 years. In the intervening period, Scotland established its own: St Andrews at the start of the fifteenth century, then Glasgow (1451), Aberdeen (1495) and finally Edinburgh (in 1583), the latter distinguished by being a civic, rather than religious foundation; the leaders of the city, not the church, brought it into existence and it was the Crown that gave it authority to confer degrees. This contrasted with all of the other 'ancient' universities, which retained significant links with ecclesiastical authority. Up until the mid-1800s, Oxford and Cambridge only admitted students who were members of the Established Church of England, and this was also the case for Trinity College, Dublin (established 1591) for the first 300 years of its existence (Graham, 2002, p. 6). Moreover, religious testing (e.g. requiring prospective students to subscribe to the Thirty-Nine Articles of the Church of England) was the norm in the ancient English and Scottish universities until well into the nineteenth century, before widespread discontent buttressed by political and theological liberalism forced a more open policy, steered through parliament by Prime Minister William Gladstone in 1871 (Bebbington, 1992).

The nineteenth century witnessed the end of the Oxbridge duopoly in England, first with the founding of University and King's Colleges in London and then with Durham University in the north east in 1832. The latter two were established as Anglican foundations, while University College has explicitly secular origins, originally denied a university charter on account of its admission of Jews, Roman Catholics and Non-conformists (Graham, 2002, p. 7). University College London (UCL) achieved an early reputation as a centre of dissent, both as an institutional protest against Tory ascendancy (the Conservative Party emerging predominantly out of Oxford and Cambridge) and against Anglican control (Armytage, 1955, pp. 171–2). Indeed, the formal creation of the federal University of London in 1836 occurred in part as a parliamentary compromise response to protests that such a 'godless' place be granted the power to award degrees, which were, according to disgruntled figures in Oxford, 'badges of a Christian education' (Bebbington, 1992,

p. 260). With the formal power to award degrees conferred, not on UCL, but on an umbrella University of London, the matter was apparently settled. This federal system also departed from the Oxbridge tradition in admitting 'external' students, that is those studying while living at home, sometimes at some distance from London, rather than in residence on college premises. This opened up higher education to a much wider constituency, including those in mechanical and industrial occupations, and added momentum to a broadening of the student body that included the admission of women from the 1880s onwards.

Soon afterwards came the establishment of the six 'civic' universities within major industrial centres. The Victoria University of Manchester (now part of Manchester University) was the first of the so-called 'red brick' universities to be established, in 1880, followed by Birmingham in 1900, Liverpool in 1903, Leeds in 1904, Sheffield in 1905 and Bristol in 1909. None of these were entirely new institutions, but were granted university status by Royal Charter following the merger and development of pre-existing colleges, often specializing in medicine, engineering and technology, in reflection of the burgeoning industrial age they were established to serve. For example, the University of Sheffield emerged out of the Sheffield School of Medicine, Firth College, established in 1879 by a local steel manufacturer to provide arts and science education to the under-resourced Sheffield area, and the Sheffield Technical School, founded in response to the need for greater skills training among those working in local industry. The first clause in the original charter of the University of Liverpool, setting out the objects of the new university, made reference to 'technical instruction as may be of immediate service to professional and commercial life' (Kelly, 1981, p. 52). Industry drove expansion, and as a result, by 1932, there were 11 universities in England (with 3 additional university colleges: Exeter, Nottingham and Southampton), 4 in Scotland, 1 in Wales and 3 in Ireland, together recruiting well over 62,000 students (Robinson, 1944, pp. 85–8).

While traditionally confined to this original group of six, the label 'red brick' is commonly ascribed to other universities established between the turn of the twentieth century and the 1960s. This number includes the independent universities of Cardiff and Swansea, supplementing the higher education in Wales that had originated at St David's, Lampeter in 1822, later incorporated into the federal University of Wales. Scotland saw the founding of the University of Dundee (originally a college of St Andrew's) and in Belfast, Queen's University was established in 1908. In England, this period saw the emergence of universities in Exeter, Hull, Leicester, Nottingham, Reading and Southampton. The University of Newcastle Upon Tyne began as a college of medicine, affiliated to the University of London from 1834 and then to the University of Durham from 1851. Its subject coverage gradually expanded into the physical sciences and engineering, and the University finally achieved independent status in 1963 via an Act of Parliament.

The 'red bricks' share a number of common features. Most are situated in urban centres, many in former industrial towns, and as such present students with a particular kind of environment: often multicultural, densely populated and commercially vibrant. These universities are also, for the most part, either located in buildings scattered around city centres, or else are based in clusters forming inner-city campuses, only a stone's throw from the city centre itself. This enhances the universities' linkages with the urban environment, and can foster a greater integration between town and gown. In this sense they contrast with Oxford and Cambridge, which, while also set within major cities, retain an elite and aloof reputation that perpetuates boundaries between university and local communities. Notable exceptions to the 'red-brick' pattern are the Universities of Birmingham and Nottingham, which occupy some of the earlier established university parks, situated at some remove from their respective cities. The 'red-bricks' marked a number of innovations in the university sector, one of the most significant being the prioritization of disciplines more consonant with science and industry than with the classical disciplines of traditional scholarship. This arguably fostered an internal secularization of universities, as the discursive subtleties of theology and other 'humanities' gave way to the more utilitarian logic of post-Enlightenment science.

The Robbins Report and 1960s expansion

During the 1960s, higher education apparently grew faster than any other major industry, excepting electronics and natural gas. Between 1962 and 1968, the number of students in full-time higher education in Britain grew from 217,000 to 376,000, the increase during these 5 years greater than expansion over the preceding quarter of a century (Layard and King, 1969, p. 13). Key to this development was the 1963 Robbins Report, which issued predictions and recommendations for higher education that shaped the sector for the remainder of the decade and beyond. The committee chaired by Lord Robbins was convened by the Conservative Government in 1961 for a number of reasons. Post-war economic growth in Britain had precipitated a rise in demand for university places, as advances in industry required more skilled and educated workers, and as rising standards of living made university a viable option for an increasing proportion of the population. The post-war baby boom also meant that, by the 1960s, a larger than previous proportion of the population was of university age, leading to an inevitable rise in demand in absolute terms. The existing university system was deemed to have fallen short in providing insufficient opportunities for this aspirant generation, measured simply by the ratio of individuals leaving school with two 'A' levels to the number of university places available. The Robbins Committee was formed to address this problem, alongside a series of other administrative and structural issues facing the higher education sector in a transformative decade, not least the status of the colleges of advanced technology and of education, and the need for greater co-ordination across different parts of the sector and with central government as its primary funder.

The positive reception of the Robbins Report by government, universities and the public reflected a new consensus that universities should enhance a larger segment of the population rather than serve an elite few, and that inclusion be based on merit alone. Its most significant recommendation endorsed an overall expansion of the higher education sector, resulting in increases in university places and the establishment of brand new universities. Those founded in the wake of the Robbins Report share significant family resemblances. First, and most obvious, is their campus context; while Leeds and Manchester occupy buildings interspersed among civic and commercial outlets within their busy city centres, the likes of Kent, Lancaster, York and Warwick are located in purpose-built, scenic university parks beyond the urban sprawl. In terms of the student experience, this makes for a more bounded sense of community and for some an almost utopian separation from the non-university world, and with the better equipped sites now boasting a range of convenient food and service outlets, students may complete their degree with minimal need of leaving the safe confines of the campus. However, what for some is a welcome haven is for others a stifling and insular environment too distant from a more 'authentic' life experience. Purpose-built campuses, especially those at some distance from the nearest town, can foster a rather closeted existence, and it may be in such contexts that student societies acquire a particularly powerful role in shaping the undergraduate experience (as they also do within Oxbridge colleges, for different, albeit related, reasons). Campus universities can remain relatively untouched by the cultural diversity characteristic of those based in inner-city contexts, and we might expect this to be an important variable in understanding patterns of cultural and religious tolerance among the student population.

Second, the 1960s campus universities are children of their time, and their contemporary ethos and institutional identity remain informed by the organizational structures put in place at their foundation. For example, as part of a progressive effort to mirror the industrial and cultural present – rather than the traditional, scholastic past – the universities of Essex, Keele, Sussex, Warwick and York were established without an academic department of theology. Lancaster University retained an academic interest in religion, but did so by founding the first department of Religious Studies, self-consciously defined over and against theology as the dispassionate study of religion as a purely academic endeavour, rather than one shaped by, or in service to, ecclesiastical institutions. Applications for its first chair of Religious Studies were invited from candidates 'of any faith or none' (Smart, 1967), reflecting a more confident public agnosticism and the loosening of ties between university and Christian tradition. An exception within this group of new universities was the University of Kent, whose location in the historic city of Canterbury fostered stronger links with The Church of England: its Visitor is the Archbishop of Canterbury, students graduate in Canterbury Cathedral and the university has always had a department of Theology (Beloff, 1968, p. 137). These universities have retained the services of chaplains, and student religious societies have remained vibrant, but religion remains outside of their professed institutional identity, absent from their systems of governance and at best subdued within their public discourse.

Further expansion and restructuring

The 1960s also witnessed the establishment of the first 'polytechnics', institutions of higher education which grew out of the former colleges of technology and were viewed as complementing the older, more traditional universities by offering practical, vocational training and stronger links with commerce and industry. Over time, the polytechnics began to teach a wider range of subjects, many branching into the social sciences and humanities and inviting obvious comparisons with the more established universities. Nevertheless, the polytechnics were very different institutions, not least in remaining under the financial control of local authorities, whereas universities had autonomy from local and central government and hence more freedom to define their own priorities.

This situation changed in 1992 with the Further and Higher Education Act, which removed the binary system that separated the universities and polytechnics, instead establishing a unitary system for higher education based around subject-defined funding councils. The polytechnics, along with all colleges of higher education, were given the right to apply for university status, something most now have. As a consequence, during the early 1990s the number of universities in Britain doubled from around 50 to 100 and the number of enrolled university students increased dramatically. The status of the former polytechnics also changed, as with university status they could appoint professors, award degrees, join the Committee of Vice Chancellors and Principals and compete for funding from the newly created funding councils alongside their more established colleagues (Graham, 2002, p. 11). Nevertheless, given their history and shared priorities – including the provision of vocational qualifications, widening access to students from under-represented groups, and the centrality of student learning over research – the former polytechnics are still often grouped together as the 'post-1992 universities'. This has some justification, although also risks masking important differences among this large collection of institutions, not least in terms of subject specialisms, target demographics and form of course delivery (including now, an increasing market for distance learning). One sub-group is particularly relevant here, as it reflects a peculiar set of relations with Christian churches.

The Council of Church Universities and Colleges (CCUC), or 'Cathedrals Group', as it is commonly known, has 15 members: 14 universities in England and 1 in Wales. Each is a former church college of teacher training, a breed of institution that historian Callum Brown claims was important in 'sustaining religiously committed teachers in Britain' during the 1960s and 1970s (Brown, 2006, p. 226), although the history of many goes back to the nineteenth century. Each university and university college within the Cathedrals Group was established as a church foundation by the Anglican, Roman Catholic or Methodist Church, and continues to have a strong relationship with its founding denomination. This connection to organized Christianity has implications for systems of governance, collective identity, student welfare provision and chaplaincy, as well as fostering a shared understanding of what university education is for and what its mission might be within broader society. The fact that many Cathedrals Group institutions have retained teacher training as a core priority reflects their emphasis on vocational and public-service-oriented programmes of study. On its website, the Cathedrals Group states that it 'supports the Churches' continuing role in Higher Education through the Church Universities and Colleges as a means of developing the historic partnership between the Churches and the State and of contributing to the public good and the well-being of society'.[2] Hence, in contrast to the ancient universities, where institutional links to ecclesiastical bodies are largely expressed in tradition and ceremony, and the 1960s campus universities, which tend to marginalize religion in a campus environment, the Cathedrals universities openly foster a positive engagement with the Christian churches in a way that is allowed to inform their identities and priorities as public institutions.

Twenty-first-century challenges

The United Kingdom's Higher Education sector has been radically transformed over the past 150 years. The number of enrolled students has increased dramatically and structures of funding have evolved as expansion of the number of universities and students requires the securing of finance beyond central government. The shrinking pot of government funding has become a resource over which there is fierce competition between universities, and this money is increasingly distributed according to criteria that prioritize research excellence. The Research Assessment Exercise (RAE) – now reconfigured as the Research Excellence Framework (REF) – has since 1986 assessed research quality at each higher education institution at roughly five-year intervals. The results directly inform the distribution of research income across the sector and indirectly shape universities' public appeal, reputation and status, not least through ascribed rankings in increasingly ubiquitous league tables published in national newspapers and student guidebooks. Also significant in this respect is the National Student Survey (NSS), which since 2005 has invited all final year students in higher education in England, Wales and Northern Ireland to rate the quality of their degree programmes. Widely published and increasingly used to construct university rankings, the NSS results have become essential to universities in maintaining strong reputations, especially those teaching intensive institutions for whom student fees, rather than research-related income, is the predominant source of revenue. This regime has fostered a more outputs focused, audit-driven culture within universities, with centralised processes of review and administrative accountability shaping research and teaching (Strathern, 2000). As previously stable income streams have become more contested, universities have responded with a marketization of educational product, investing in course advertising, school outreach, public relations and liaison with private business on an unprecedented scale in order to remain viable. Part of the same process has seen the gradual shrinkage in centrally available funding for students, including the abolition of mandatory payment of tuition fees via local education authorities, and the increase in fees between 1998 and 2012 from a standard £1,000 to up to £9,000 *per annum*, provoking questions about the accessibility of higher education, particularly among applicants from less privileged backgrounds.

If marketization is one dominant trend, another is a measured diversification, as different universities attempt to steer their activities in a way that capitalizes on their strengths and maximizes their chances of success. Expansion of the higher education sector has seen diversification in alignment with different target audiences, and the aggregation of universities of a similar core ethos into campaign groups that are thereby better equipped to negotiate current challenges and engage policymakers. Hence the sub-division of the sector into six mission groups: the Russell Group (comprising the 24 larger, research intensive universities); the 1994 Group (the 12 smaller universities which prioritize research); the Million+ Group (25 former polytechnic colleges with ambitions to achieve research strength); the Alliance Group (22 former polytechnics with an emerging track record in research); the Cathedrals Group (the 15 church foundations); and GuildHE (the remaining former polytechnic institutions).[3] This categorization is driven by the current status and ambitions of different universities, accorded in relation to targets set by central government and their own managers. It also represents a structural hierarchy, on two counts. First, it is the research intensive universities that are awarded the most funding by the UK government and which – generally speaking – have less difficulty attracting students, and therefore student fees, than the more teaching-oriented institutions. Second, there is an enduring order of prestige within the sector, framed mainly with reference to the Russell Group, which continues to shape popular and academic perceptions of the status of different universities. The latter is determined by a combination of league table positions – increasingly pervasive in matters of student recruitment and academic status – and age-old reputations that endure in the popular imagination.

A more recent aspect of diversification relates to the opening up of the higher education sector to private providers. Unlike the United States, the vast majority of UK universities are in most respects public bodies. This is not to say that they are, or ever have been, entirely state-funded public service providers analogous to the hospitals of the National Health Service or the British state schooling system. Indeed, up to the First World War universities were funded by a combination of long-standing endowments, student fees and local initiatives; it was only after the establishment of the University Grants Committee in 1919 that a structured system of limited state funding was instituted on a national scale (Collini, 2012, p. 29). However, as a consequence of an exponential rise in student numbers from 1945 onwards, including many from non-elite backgrounds, the state emerged as the dominant funder, so that by the 1960s universities had acquired the image of a public service commonly associated with the various wings of the post-war welfare state, albeit one available to a necessarily limited cohort. That being so, continuing university expansion has proved no longer compatible with the resources at the state's disposal, and while marketization within existing universities has been one consequence, another is the establishment of private higher education. For many years the only independent university in the United Kingdom was the University of Buckingham, established in 1976 (and granted its Royal Charter in 1983) following the example of similar institutions in the United States, whose independence from the state was associated with an enhancement of academic freedom and creativity. To date, Buckingham remains the nation's only fully fledged private university, although in 2010 law and business specialist BPP was granted university college status, and further private providers were ushered into the UK sector following the Coalition Government's education reforms, intended to diversify in-sector provision and expand student choice. Significantly, the recent increase in tuition fees at public universities makes some private providers highly competitive, so in weighing the options in economic terms, we might expect more applicants, and hence more providers, to gravitate to the private model.

A further dimension relates to globalization, markedly visible within universities in the growth of international students, whose financial contribution in student fees configure them as a target market, while their presence on campuses has a significant cultural impact, not least in terms of religion. As we will discuss in later chapters, the influx of students from different parts of the globe can have a massive influence on the relative vitality of different Christian traditions, as well as triggering the establishment of brand new groups within campus contexts. Universities constitute a fascinating site in which the global flows associated with late modern economics and culture are arguably intensified, with the regular turnover of students securing constant change and an ever-new injection of new energies and influences. Their attraction of academic staff from across the globe also emphasizes this international cultural dimension, subverting conventional boundaries associated with nation, language and academic disciplines. Such peculiarities warn against taking universities as in any way representative of the broader British picture; while illuminating possible trajectories of future generations in one respect, universities as spatial, institutional phenomena are highly distinctive, and offer an experience within an individual's life that will, most likely, not be repeated.

A third trend is especially relevant to this book as it coincides with our conceptual focus: the university experience. For good or ill, the codification of the 'university experience' has emerged as a major preoccupation of UK higher education policymakers in recent years. Therefore, formulation of our approach in this book demands special care, lest it be caught up in discourses not of our own making and possibly not in keeping with our intended argument. Duna Sabri has traced the emergence of the 'student experience' in government policy documents, particularly since 2009, noting its association with the conceptualization of students as 'customers' and the treatment of their reported levels of satisfaction as key indicators of the 'success' of higher education (Sabri, 2011). As such, as Sabri argues, a 'reified "student experience" is wielded as a criterion for judgment about what is, and is not, worthwhile in higher education' (Sabri, 2011, p. 659). Related to this is the valorization of student choice, claimed by policymakers to be instrumental to current efforts to improve higher education provision. Sabri cites the influential Browne Review of 2010 that states: 'We want to put students at the heart of the system. Students are best placed to make the judgment about what they want to get from participating in higher education' (Browne, 2010, p. 25). The trend in policy discourse identified by Sabri reflects the recent marketization of higher education and the elevation of the power of the student as consumer, whose act of choosing one university over others will presumably function as a driver of quality in the sector. Within this discourse, the 'student experience' is a powerful notion, and 'evokes radical reorientation, challenge to vested (academic) interests, consumer power and the quest for value for money' (Sabri, 2011, p. 661). It remains to be seen whether Christian students in particular present a reflection of or challenge to this set of assumptions.

The above changes, summarized as the interconnected processes of marketization, diversification and the elevation of the student as consumer, illustrate how England's universities echo broader developments in contemporary Western culture. The advancement of consumerism and superior influence of the neo-liberal economics of the free market have been cited by numerous authors as characteristic of late modern society (e.g. Carrette and King, 2005) so it is not surprising to find similar influences extending into universities. The repositioning of students as customers with consumer demands heightens their status as self-directed individuals, while disempowering academics whose expertise is sometimes required to defer to perceived market needs. In competing for student applicants, universities find themselves increasingly governed by organizational norms derived from private business, with managers prioritizing the virtues of calculability and efficiency as they steer the provision of educational product (Ritzer, 1996). Taken together, it is possible to theorize these developments in terms drawn directly from Max Weber's sociological studies of modernization: as a form of intensified rationalization, taking norms of bureaucracy and systematization to a heightened level, while ultimately framed by a perception of ubiquitous and incontestable market forces (cf. Gerth and Mills, 2009, pp. 196–264). If we pursue this argument in keeping with Weber's vision of modernity, we might conclude that universities also function as forces of disenchantment, although as we argue in Chapter 4, this would be to beg too many questions and do a disservice to the evidence at our disposal.

What is clear is that these developments have provoked widespread dismay on the part of academic staff, and triggered a debate about the proper purpose and nature of universities. Indeed, recent years have seen a burgeoning literature offering critical – sometimes scathing – comment on the various innovations that have characterized British university life of late. Tara Brabazon's *The University of Google* (2007) offers a passionate diatribe against the devaluing of higher education brought about by an uncritical, modish embrace of e-learning. The technology of the digital revolution has, she argues, been hijacked by capitalist agendas driven by a need to cut costs and maximize efficiency, with little serious consideration for the quality of students' education. Stefan Collini's acclaimed book *What Are Universities For?* (2012) critiques the increasing tendency to reduce the value of higher education to a process of equipping young people with the skills to contribute effectively to the global economy. Proceeding from a perspective shaped by the disciplines of the humanities, Collini probes the complex issues of the purpose and benefits of universities, getting beyond the unstable reforms of the present by placing higher education in a broader historical and cultural context. Further critical discussions have emerged from the perspective of Christian theology, sometimes echoing Collini's vision of universities as contexts for human flourishing (Higton, 2012), while other scholars place calls for positive transformation within a broader debate about what a distinctively Christian university might look like (D'Costa, 2005).

Notwithstanding the urgency and persuasiveness of these critiques, they highlight the persistent capacity of the university to generate critical discussion about itself. While this might seem a banal and obvious point, it is striking that academics attacking the current state of the university are employed by those very same institutions. Freedom of scholarship remains an unassailable tenet, much more so than in the United States, where partisan ideologies can legitimately impose moral and religious demands upon university employees (Riley, 2005, pp. 193–4). This is in part a consequence of the peculiarly public status of UK universities – both autonomous and state-bound at the same time, steering a complex intermediate course between the private universities of the United States and the continental European model that maintains universities as 'direct instruments of government policy' (Collini, 2012, p. 5). As Collini acknowledges, in Britain, while largely funded from the public purse, and with ever more conditions attached, 'successive governments have (so far) respected the principle of the autonomy of universities . . . largely leaving them to determine their own internal affairs, including their academic programmes' (Collini, 2012, p. 5).

The reason why this is important to emphasize here is because of the implications of this enduring characteristic for the kind of culture fostered by universities among staff and students. In spite of the pessimistic nostalgia evoked among romantic academics who long for a time when state interference was barely heard of, universities remain, by comparison with many other forms of commerce, industry and public service, strikingly autonomous. The sector is admittedly diverse in this respect, and elite status may be inversely proportional to an encroaching culture of managerial control, but an experience of research and teaching relatively free from external oversight and preserving the self-directedness of individual scholars, remains commonplace.

This leads us to the final section of this chapter, which focuses on ways in which we might understand the relationship between the experience of university and the culture of university students, particularly those seeking to embody a religious identity. While this broad question has been relatively unexplored in the United Kingdom, on the other side of the Atlantic it has generated an abundance of literature, much of it based on extensive empirical research. In the following paragraphs we attempt to bring insights emerging from that literature into conversation with the circumstances of the United Kingdom.

Understanding Christianity and the University Experience

Debates about the interaction between religion and higher education have long been framed by assumptions about the secularizing power of educational institutions, in turn attributable to the common association of knowledge and learning with rationalism, empiricism and post-Enlightenment science (Guest, 2012). Additional factors have also been cited, such as the heightened exposure to cultural and religious pluralism in university contexts, and the newly embraced opportunity to reject traditions associated with one's parents, commonly attributed to the transition through youth and young adulthood (Hill, 2009). In this sense Western higher education is persistently understood as a powerful force for secularization (Berger, 1999; Wuthnow, 1988), and its expansion a catalyst for the acceleration of the secularization process. This understanding is lent scholarly credence by studies that have offered empirical evidence of how students have moved away from home-based religious traditions towards more liberal, humanistic perspectives over time (Hastings and Hoge, 1976), and of how colleges have had a tendency to liberalize the perspectives of religious students (Hunter, 1987). As Mayrl and Oeur summarize, it became generally understood that the 'expanded horizons and exposure to new ideas that college provides were thought to lead students to question and ultimately abandon their traditional religious beliefs' (2009, p. 264). Recent studies have questioned this interpretation, providing empirical evidence that challenges the association between university and a liberalization of belief (Mayrl and Uecker, 2011; Uecker et al., 2007). Among other scholars, an apparently opposing trend has emerged, whereby university campuses are characterized as hotbeds of religious vitality, with the majority of students apparently showing great interest in matters of religion (Cherry, DeBerg and Porterfield, 2001; Ivan, 2012; Lee, 2002), or moving away from traditional religion but showing an interest in 'spirituality' (Bryant, Choi and Yasuno, 2003). Much like the influential debates about secularization, discussion of the relationship between religion and higher education has sometimes become organized around bearers of bad news and resistant optimists.

Successfully avoiding this unhelpful bifurcation, recent research has focused on delineating in more detail precisely *how* university shapes religious identities. What is it that distinguishes the experience of higher education and what happens when religious identities are exposed to its influence?

Indeed, the nature of this very exposure is an important dimension of this question; are we right to assume that the acquisition of new knowledge will necessarily trigger cognitive dissonance among students who hold religious convictions based around tenets seemingly at odds with this knowledge? Will creationist students always struggle with the theory of evolution, either accommodating their beliefs to this new set of ideas or fiercely resisting it and rejecting its legitimacy (Berger, 1980)? The 'conflict model' implicit in this argument, while popular within the mass media, apparently commands only limited support among US college students (Scheitle, 2011a). The relationship among different forms of knowledge or truth claims is apparently more complex than this model might suggest. Working with a qualitative study of college students, Tim Clydesdale (2007) found that before embarking on their college education, students typically placed their religious identities in an 'identity lockbox', leaving them relatively unexamined and unquestioned during their first year. Religion was treated as something good to have, but chiefly as a resource to draw upon later in life; in effect, the relationship between religion and college was distinguished by a *lack* of interaction. Other research has theorized similar patterns in terms of compartmentalization, the strategy of handling religious ideas and non-religious ideas (especially those in potential tension with religion) entirely separately, as discrete aspects of life that are not brought into conversation (e.g. Sabri et al., 2008).

The work of Clydesdale and others alerts us to the dangers of assuming apparently logical ideational tensions (miracles vs scientific empiricism, creationism vs evolution, etc.) will necessarily be experienced as tensions by individual students. Religious identities cannot be simply reduced to a matter of propositional belief, conceived as coherent and cerebral, and hence vulnerable to cognitive dissonance (also see Guest et al., 2013). Recent research suggests teenagers and young adults have only limited understanding of the doctrinal content of the religious traditions they affirm (Smith and Denton, 2005). Matters of 'belief' are not of primary importance to them (Savage et al., 2006), or at the very least, are configured as 'believing', an active, embodied performance of identity, rather than an assent to a given set of official truth claims (Vincett et al., 2012). The form taken by religious and spiritual identities in the contemporary West, perhaps especially among young adults, is often more fragmented, more conflicted and more open-ended than our theoretical tools might lead us to understand. As such, we might find that cultural and religious pluralism serves as a source of inspiration to evolving, self-directed identities, rather than a threat to established plausibility structures (Berger, 1967). We might also expect such identities to be less vulnerable to the secularizing power of higher education than more conservative forms of religion, which depend on the maintenance of a clearly defined moral order.

Even then, we need to be open to the possibility that conservative religious students will develop strategies for circumventing such challenges to their faith, whether through selecting only benign subjects to study, forming sectarian-style support structures among like-minded students (Bramadat, 2000), or developing cognitive abilities that allow apparently incompatible knowledge-claims to be engaged concurrently without the primary (religious) ones being undermined.

Just as religious identities cannot be simply reduced to a matter of propositional belief, so the experience of university cannot be simply reduced to what happens in the classroom. Reviewing the abundant literature on religion in higher education, Mayrl and Oeur identify one major problem as a tendency to decontextualize students: to treat the university experience as an essentially singular phenomenon, papering over important differences between institutions and failing to explore the ways in which 'specific institutional contexts interact with the religious engagements of undergraduate students' (2009, p. 271). This is not simply a matter of recognizing that universities may fall into different types, distinguished by different cultures and fostering different patterns of religious expression (Hill, 2011; Small and Bowman, 2011), but that the relationship between the religious identities of their staff and students and the identity of the institution in which they work is not a straightforward one. The *official public life* of many American colleges and universities is nowadays fairly secular, but it is secular *in spite of* the mostly religious perspectives of academic staff (Gross and Simmons, 2009) and students (HERI, 2004). In other words, there can be a qualitative difference between the culture of the institution as presented in its public discourse, and the culture of its constituent members. Furthermore, these two cultures can exist in tension, but with beleaguered religious identities thriving as a consequence, as reflected in Jonathan Hill's finding that Roman Catholic students in the United States increase their religious participation when attending Evangelical colleges (Hill, 2009). Institutional cultures can function as a force against which to react, as well as a social order with which to conform.

Adopting the language of our overall title, the 'university experience' is a phenomenon that extends well beyond the teaching and learning processes associated with particular degree programmes. In addition, it draws in the challenges (including economic ones) of being away from home, exposure to new forms of cultural and religious difference, unprecedented levels of personal independence, the opportunities generated by new friendship networks, fresh avenues for extra-curricular pursuits and the possibilities of personal advancement and empowerment these bring, and many other dimensions that feed into this complex amalgam that makes for a powerful, life-changing experience.

Conclusion

The above account illustrates the peculiarities of the UK university context. For complex historical reasons, Christianity features heavily, though not straightforwardly, in the life of these institutions of higher education. It would be accurate to say that for most, it is an ambient, rather than salient institutional feature, colouring architectural contexts and ceremonial rhetoric, with more proactive agencies such as chaplaincies very much occupying the margins of university life, catering to a select minority and enjoying very limited power and influence on the larger campus. Departments of Theology and Religious Studies exhibit a parallel shrinkage as STEM subjects[4] are prioritized and economically stretched undergraduates migrate to more obviously vocational degree programmes. There are exceptions of course: Oxbridge chaplains remain numerous and central to college life; Theology has its centres of excellence that are prized and well-resourced by their universities; Cathedrals Group institutions retain their distinctively Christian ethos, enshrined in mission statements and structures of governance.

The national UK picture has been set out here in broad brush strokes. Chapter 3 will explore these dimensions in more localized detail, as we try and develop a typology of universities and offer some cases studies to illustrate how they differ. Before that, we continue in our attempt to offer the broader picture by presenting general findings from our survey of Christian students at England's universities. Just what is it that distinguishes this group?

Notes

1   While our analysis in this volume is confined to universities in England, the survey in the present chapter covers the United Kingdom as a whole so that the Higher Education sector may be set within its broader historical and cultural context.

2   http://cathedralsgroup.org.uk/AboutUs.aspx (accessed 21/8/12).

3   These figures are of course subject to adjustment as different universities change their affiliation to different mission groups over time.

4   STEM refers to science, technology, engineering and mathematics, subject areas whose funding for university teaching has been ring-fenced by the current UK government whilst heavy cuts have been applied to other subjects.

2

What makes a Christian student?

Three Christian students

When we met Grace she was a final year student on a degree course in Theology and Religious Studies. She had come to university from a small town in which she was a regular attendee at the local Anglican Church, although her parents are not Christian and she did not describe her upbringing as Christian either. This church – that she refers to as 'middle of the road . . . the Book of Common Prayer and a few hymns and that's it' – she contrasts with her experience at university, which has impressed her with its diversity of Christian activity. She has embraced this diversity in her own life: after initially attending a Catholic church, she took part in CU events and then spent her first year attending a Café Church convened by the university chaplaincy team, which she found helpful for her faith as it encouraged lots of discussion, something she also benefits from during seminars she attends as part of her course. Discussion among friends about troubling items on TV news counts for her as 'time spent focused on Christianity'. After building a number of friendships through Café Church she decided to expand her horizons further and started attending St George's, an Anglican Evangelical church highly popular with students in her university city. Grace likes the fact that this church teaches the Bible, but not like it is taught in her lectures; whereas the latter are delivered from a position of perceived neutrality, she sees the sermons at St George's as 'teaching with faith'. Given her on-going practice of embracing ever new opportunities to live out her Christian faith – from chaplaincy events, volunteering for a Brownies group and raising money for a cancer hospice – it is not surprising that Grace views her experience of university as having enhanced her Christian identity. As she says, 'there's just so many opportunities . . . I think my Christianity has sped up. It's become more important I think than it was before.'

Grace is capable of engaging with a wide range of available activities and organizations and drawing from them as positive resources, even when they do not entirely reflect her own values. This is apparent in her participation in CU events; after initial scepticism and wariness of the ideas she was encountering, she has achieved a discriminating perspective that allows her to appreciate the positive and disregard the aspects she finds uncomfortable. As she says,

> . . . I don't agree with a lot of things that they as an organization say, but I like the speakers they have. A lot of my friends are in the Christian Union, the worship's quite good and sometimes you just have to ignore the things that they believe and just have a good time . . . Just because you're there when they're saying it, doesn't mean that you believe it too.

Grace's attitude is characterized by a tendency to draw from a range of different resources in a way that places personal preferences above denominational or inherited loyalties; what is driving her Christian life are the choices she is making, and these empower her to move between contexts and experiences as they enrich and provide meaning for her at different times. There is also here a striking tendency to prioritize relationships and experiences over matters of belief or doctrine, and this is reflected in her lack of interest in matters of sexual identity (something dominating public discussions associated with most mainstream churches), and in her discomfort with Christian attempts to convert others to their faith. Hers is a Christianity that is vibrant and active, and at its heart is the expression of Christian commitment via relationships and conversations.

Jerome was in the second year of a degree in Sports Therapy when we met him. Aged 21, and originally from southern Africa, his family had moved to London in 2002, before later moving to Milton Keynes, where he stays during university vacations. Raised Roman Catholic, Jerome started to question his Christian faith during his teens after several encounters with priests he felt were imperious and judgemental when his Mass attendance began to slacken; for Jerome, these individuals fell short of the unqualified acceptance and welcome he sees as central to the Christian message. Following some encouraging conversations with a close friend who had recently converted from atheism to Christianity and meeting Christians at university who were strongly committed but not judgmental of others, Jerome's faith was restored. In fact, he feels it has enriched his life as a student while the university experience has enriched his Christian faith, in spite of several serious obstacles Jerome has faced since he started life as an undergraduate.

Located at a subsidiary site at some remove from the main university buildings, Jerome has found it difficult to join a Christian community as the student societies operate chiefly on the main campus. An initial encounter with one Christian student group left him uneasy because of its evangelistic tone: '. . . in my opinion, it's good to talk to people and let them know what your faith is like but not try and force it on them . . .' He is also uncomfortable and feels insecure in the local area and this has prevented him and his house-mates from making many other friends, enjoying much of a social life, or participating in a nearby church. These factors have led him to abandon any quest for a local Christian community and instead he focuses on church when at home during the university vacations. While his term-time experience of university has been troubling, his faith has become a major resource in coping with this, enhanced by contact with his uncle, who has held some Bible study meetings with him:

> [My faith's] strengthened a lot since I came to university because I went through a bad patch and started getting depressed and slightly upset when I was back in Milton Keynes, but since stepping away from that . . . it has helped me . . . look at myself and think why am I getting upset? Why is my faith faltering? And it's helped me settle all these doubts inside me so it has helped and it has strengthened . . . [my faith]. I feel it's stopped me from turning away from Christianity.

Two major aspects of the university experience are cited by Jerome as key to the reinvigoration of his faith. The first is his course in Sports Therapy, which has generated many opportunities to engage in volunteering, including in association with the London Marathon for Guide Dogs and the Modern Pentathlon, and Jerome has realized a major motivation of his is to help people: '. . . that's the reason why I'm doing this course . . . it's all optimised towards volunteering . . .' This experience has 'opened his eyes' and he now aspires to do more volunteering work with charities that help disabled children. The second aspect is the culture of student social life he has encountered, including heavy drinking and sexual promiscuity. He has found himself calling upon the moral teaching of his childhood in resisting these temptations, his upbringing helping him 'restrain myself during the whole year that I haven't been in my parents' house, so it has helped me as a person during the entire time of being away from home'. His abiding sense of right and wrong he sees as a dependable guide through the challenges of social life at university, informing his decisions about who to mix with and how to behave around other people. The public expression of his faith has been made easier by the culture of his university, which he contrasts with life in London, where he encountered lots of different religious perspectives and lots of people with a combative way of discussing religion. His experience of university has rather been one in which discussion about religion has been lively but positive, with other students markedly reluctant to be forceful in their opinions. As he commented, 'it's easier to express yourself . . . at university than . . . at home'.

When we interviewed Eva, she was a 19-year-old in the 2nd year of an undergraduate Politics degree. She had completed our questionnaire and ticked the box next to 'Christian' and afterwards agreed to be interviewed. However, her Christian identity was much more elusive than that affirmed by Grace and Jerome. She had been confirmed in the Church of England when she was 11; she explains this as something interesting to do with friends at the time, but still cites it as a reason to claim 'Christian' as her identity. She also says that, if she were to choose a particular label, she would say she is 'mainstream Protestant', and yet her engagement with organized church life has been sporadic and limited. She wasn't raised in a churchgoing family, hadn't been attending church before university and wasn't attending as a student either. Moreover, her ambivalent perspective is one that she holds consciously, and she is open about her uncertainty with respect to all matters of faith and ultimate reality. On the one hand, she is aware of following traditional Christian morality as an automatic consequence of living in a culture historically influenced by the Christian Church: '. . . I suppose I do live by some of the Ten Commandments but they've kind of trickled into normal life these days, everybody follows that.' On the other, she is conscious of feeling a vague attachment to the traditions of the Anglican Church, which she occasionally attended when a pupil at a Church of England school, and which offers a restrained, English traditionalism that she likes. She contrasts this with the Evangelical churches she has occasionally encountered, including while at university, whose effusive and tactile style – what she calls 'happy clappy' – she has found intrusive and uncomfortable. As she comments: 'I'm quite happy to go to old fashioned churches and sit there, and I used to go to church actually with school like at Easter. We'd go to [the local] cathedral and to Christmas services. I love carols . . . you sit there, you listen, you leave, not have someone come up and hug you.'

Eva admires people who have strong religious identities, as their conviction contrasts with the apathetic attitude to religion she sees as typical nowadays, but she remains sceptical about traditional ideas of God. This she puts down, in part, to her father's death in a car accident when she was an infant, the thought of this triggering her incredulity that an all powerful God could take away someone's husband and father. That being so, she shows no evidence of graduating to an atheist or secularist perspective: she is keen to have a religious wedding, and maintains a less conventional but clearly articulated set of beliefs. Reflecting on her childhood habit of praying to one of her deceased relatives, she describes her perspective: 'I don't necessarily believe in God, I believe in people, the good that they can do, and if you believe, not necessarily everyone, but people that are close to you, like I believe in them . . . I believe that they've got the power to help me if I need help.'

During the interview, there was very little evidence that Eva's experience of university had influenced her orientation to Christianity, aside from the occasional visits to Evangelical churches that reinforced her perennial traditionalism. Her politics degree had only triggered thoughts concerning religion in a recent module on Political Morality, which had included discussion of the Iraq War and former Prime Minister Tony Blair's culpability for the deaths of the conflict's victims. Blair's well-publicized Christian faith had been addressed in class, specifically the question of its consistency with a decision to go to war, although Eva remains of the view that one need not be religious to have a clear sense of morality. Other than this, the Christian dimension of her identity has been relatively unengaged by university life, perhaps unsurprisingly given the very limited extent to which she has made it a part of her social self as a student.

The destabilization of Christianity as a category

The ways in which Grace, Jerome and Eva live out their Christian identity at university reflect patterns we observed across many other students. The differences between them, while shaped by their unique lives, illustrate common approaches to the expression of Christianity within university contexts, and common strategies for making sense of Christian faith within the context of the university experience. What they share is an affirmation of Christianity as their religious tradition of choice. They also share a tendency to view their Christian identity as something primarily shaped by and expressed in social relationships, rather than in assent to doctrine or belief. It is also, for all three, something that is evolving in dialogue with their life experience, not fixed or firmly established, and as such has developed in response to their experience of being university students. This experience, though, is varied and multifaceted, and the extent to which Grace, Jerome and Eva see this new set of experiences as a challenge to or an affirmation of their existing orientation to Christianity very much depends on the circumstances in which they find themselves. 'Christianity' as a category of identity reveals itself as a contentious phenomenon that is, when observed within the lives of individuals, highly resistant to closure or definition. So, given these observations, how might we begin to make sense of it?

This question constitutes the central focus of this chapter, which will attempt to unpack what is distinctive about Christian students within

England's universities. Despite common perceptions, it is not at all clear what unites those who self-identify as Christian in British society generally, and the examples above illustrate the radical differences that can be encompassed by this apparently singular tradition. 'Official' criteria – those formally issued by churches or Christian organizations – have historically focused on ritual markers or a rite of initiation (e.g. baptism), and/or doctrine, gauged by professed individual assent. Doctrinal commitment is also often ritualized (as in the rite of confession and absolution central to the Anglican and Roman Catholic traditions), although in recent times, Protestant groups have increasingly defined their distinctiveness via formal, discursive expressions of identity, variously entitled 'statements of faith', 'doctrinal statements' or a 'shared basis of faith' (the UCCF 'doctrinal basis', to which all affiliated university Christian Unions subscribe, is discussed in Chapter 6). The resulting point-by-point documents are used both to remind members of expected standards, and present the group's identity to the outside world, not least in stressing its finer distinctions from other, doctrinally divergent, Protestant movements.

The tendency of Protestantism to fragment into ever-new configurations has long been observed (Bruce, 1989; Martin, 1978; Niebuhr, 1962), and sociologists of religion have often delineated Christianity according to different organizational types, acknowledging the Christian religion in its ecclesiastical, sectarian and denominational forms (Troeltsch, 1931; Wilson, 1967). Roy Wallis's influential reworking of the church-sect typology offered a means of correlating organizational structures with forms of belief, emerging in a fourfold framework of church, sect, denomination and cult which, in capturing variations within Christianity and outside of it, presents a valuable theoretical tool for comparative analysis (Wallis, 1976). Such models continue to help us understand certain forms of Christian religion, not least sectarian groups whose defence of group boundaries lends itself to this kind of organizational analysis. However, for most self-identifying Christians the current, twenty-first-century predicament demands a different approach. In the present-day popular imagination Christianity retains a set of clear doctrinal and ritual dimensions for some, but is characterized more by loose associations and vague ideas among others, and the secularization process, while variously conceived, has undoubtedly rendered organized forms of Christianity in Britain increasingly obsolete, socially marginal and to some degree redundant among the grassroots populace. And yet other evidence points to a continuing cultural resonance for Christianity as a collection of identity resources bound up in the history, traditions and moral sensibilities of the British people (Guest, Olson and Wolffe, 2012), most basically demonstrated in the majority identification with Christianity among the UK population (affirmed in the 2001 census, and reaffirmed, if at a lower level, in the 2011 census). With church attendance levels at an all time low, but categories of atheism, agnosticism and 'no religion' failing to capture the imagination of the vast majority, the ideas and traditions of Christianity hover within an uncertain realm, neither socially salient nor culturally meaningless. Moreover, as James Beckford has argued with respect to contemporary religion more generally, this process has not simply rendered Christianity a nebulous residue of the past; rather, it has loosened the ties that bind religious categories to their former meanings, effectively creating the conditions for new forms of identity to emerge (Beckford, 1989; Lyon, 2000).

The present-day pattern is one of reconfiguration at the popular level, and while this process is not unconfined by established tradition it is also characterized by an unprecedented blurring of boundaries, informed by a common cultural experience of cultural and religious pluralism. 'Christianity' is a category that is being rethought and reconfigured in ways that challenge conventional definitions we might have once considered normative. Let us take another, more striking piece of evidence by way of an illustration. In our questionnaire survey of university students, we asked separate questions about the religious tradition students belong to on the one hand, and about more general orientations to religion on the other, and in so doing are able to separate Christianity from the idea of being 'religious', a strategy that is highly illuminating (see Table 2.1). Of all those students who self-identify as 'Christian': 40.4% see themselves as 'religious', 31.2% as 'not religious but spiritual', 15.4% as 'not religious *or* spiritual', while 13% are unsure. Interestingly, answers to the same question among those students subscribing to the other major religious traditions in England – Buddhism, Hinduism, Islam, Judaism and Sikhism – also display a significant diversity of responses, suggesting that notions of being religious, spiritual and neither are common across the board, that there is a significant lack of agreement about which is the most appropriate notion to associate with each tradition, and that there is a sizeable proportion of individuals within each who are secular, or at least

TABLE 2.1 General orientation to religion or spirituality among all student respondents and among self-identifying Christians among them (weighted)

	Religious (%)	Not religious, but spiritual (%)	Not religious or spiritual (%)	Not sure (%)
All respondents	24.9	30.8	33.1	11.2
Christians (N = 2,248)	40.4	31.2	15.4	13.0

sufficiently non-religious to distance themselves from the idea of being either religious or spiritual. In other words, the boundaries of religious community do not coincide with the boundaries of individually affirmed religious identity. It is especially noteworthy that Christian students encompassed a broader spread of responses to this question than students from any of the other religious traditions, suggesting 'Christianity' is the least stable as a category of identity.

Self-identifying Christian students also exhibit a striking range of orientations to doctrinal issues typically understood as central to Christian faith. Perspectives on the status of Jesus provide an instructive example (see Table 2.2). Here, the response most commonly associated with the official or orthodox position of the Church – Jesus as 'fully God and fully human' – is chosen by 35.4% of Christian students. The less recognized variations on Jesus' status each attract only minimal support, aside from the 12.9% opting for Jesus as 'God disguised in human form', which could be attributed to confusion over doctrinal language (this wording may well appear to convey a more plausible conception than the paradoxical 'three in one' idea to many young people in the contemporary West). The other highest figures appear next to the 'not sure' response (18.9%, comparable to the 20.2% who gave the same response to our survey question on God), and the staggering 24.1% favouring the description of Jesus as a 'human being who embodies divine virtues'. Almost a quarter of Christian students favour an understanding of Jesus that makes no claim to his divinity, instead emphasizing his humanity and virtuous life.

TABLE 2.2 Responses from Christian students to the question 'Which of the following most closely expresses your understanding of Jesus?' (weighted)

Understanding of Jesus	Percentage of Christian students (%)
God disguised in human form	12.9
Mostly God, partly human	3.1
Fully God and fully human	35.4
Mostly human, partly God	5.5
A human being who embodies divine virtues	24.1
I am not sure	18.9
Total	(N = 2,229)

In fact, examining survey responses to questions on God, Jesus, Mary and the Bible, between a quarter and a third of Christian students gravitate towards responses that do not affirm a divine or supernatural dimension – Jesus as a human being with divine virtues, Mary as an inspiring example, deferring to science rather than biblical authority. Even the question on the nature of God saw 29% of Christian students either opting for the vague 'impersonal life force' response or saying they were decidedly unsure, with a further 6.5% of Christians claiming there is definitely no God. Their tendency is towards the immanent rather than the transcendent, with authority found in endeavour that is identifiably human. Furthermore, there is a significant degree of uncertainty among Christians about what these core doctrines mean. This is patently clear in the consistent measure of around one fifth of respondents opting for 'not sure'. These are not a discrete group – we are not faced with a significant sub-group characterized by doctrinal uncertainty across the board[1] – but represent selective expressions of uncertainty by different individuals about different topics. Whatever the issue, 20% of Christians are unsure about it. This reflects recent research that has highlighted low levels of religious literacy among the UK's younger generations (Savage et al., 2006), the legacy of a complex constellation of factors connected to secularization. Our data suggest that this tendency extends well into the Christian population; alternatively, an expression of uncertainty could be taken as an indicator of doubt in the veracity of the doctrine in question (cf. Francis, 2001), less an issue of knowledge, more one of plausibility. At the very least, one needs to ask whether a purely cultural Christianity – free from the trappings of supernatural belief – is shaping how a wide range of students conceive of their Christian identity.

On one level these patterns are not surprising. Since the 2001 census results confirmed a majority identification with Christianity among the UK population, the relationship between Christianity and British identity has been newly examined. This inevitably evokes H. Richard Niebuhr's famous study of the proper relationship between Christ and the culture in which Christians find themselves (Niebuhr, 1951); using more sociological language, is Christianity best understood as set apart from culture, as rejecting culture, or as a force intent on transforming culture? When does Christianity become a vehicle for wider cultural values and is it ever meaningful to separate the doctrines, ideas or values we associate with Christian faith from the cultural contexts in which we find them expressed? The situation is complex, and the destabilization of Christianity as an identity category renders these questions much more open to negotiation than they have been in the past.

As Christianity in the United Kingdom has seen its institutions erode and shrink, its often subterranean, popular expression has become more profoundly caught up in meanings ordinarily consigned to the cultural realm.

In popular parlance, the claim to be 'Christian' is often taken to mean a churchgoer, follower of Jesus' teachings, or observer of the Mass, but it is also taken to indicate being British, being a loyal British citizen, being a morally responsible person or being committed to a residual Christian observance that extends to key rites of passage and/or life crises (Bradley, 2007; Brown, 2009; Brown and Lynch, 2012). These typically vague expressions of identity often retain vestigial associations with biblical or liturgically based ideas, as well as with national identity, the royal family and British historical heritage, but the notion of a shared religious orientation or set of beliefs distinguishing all those claiming the Christian label is no longer sustainable, if indeed it ever was. Historians have long been sensitive to this nuance (e.g. Hempton, 1988; McLeod, 2007); social scientists have typically been less subtle, perhaps because an acknowledgement of such blurred boundaries threatens to undermine the precision of measurable variables, although in recent years more concerted attempts have been made to separate out different forms of Christian nominalism (e.g. Voas and Day, 2010). That being said, the cultural and ideological complexity of the self-identifying Christian contingent is, while often alluded to and acknowledged, rarely systematically examined using fresh empirical evidence. The following paragraphs attempt to do just this, asking if the category 'Christian' has become destabilized, then what does it now mean for the university students who affirm it?

Developing a typology of Christian students

Drawing from our survey data, it is possible to map Christian students in relation to their perspectives on a range of doctrinal and ethical issues. This reveals a complex picture, suggestive of limited pockets of doctrinal traditionalism, large segments positioning themselves close to the social (liberal) norm on moral issues and significant levels of uncertainty on moral *and* doctrinal issues. But how do these patterns take us further in understanding the constituency of the Christian student population? One way in which to answer this question is to divide Christian students into meaningful sub-groups, in order that more precise and detailed patterns can be identified. But how should we do this? Which criteria would best suit this purpose? Aside from general tendencies leaning towards the permissive/ open on the one hand, and the conservative/traditionalist on the other, the doctrinal and ethical orientations of Christian students do not appear to coalesce into obvious sub-groups with clear boundaries. And, anyway, how might these aggregated quantitative data be reconciled with the complex subtlety in evidence in our interviews with students? Denominational affiliations are also not helpful here. As discussed in more detail later on, among Christian students who attended church before university, less than half continue to attend a church of the same denomination during their time as students (something illustrated in the three students described earlier). Denominational attachments are apparently not beyond significant rethinking as circumstances change, evoking recent research into young Christians that argues denominational affiliation has become secondary to a pan-Christian identity, driven predominantly by individually held conviction rather than institutional loyalties (Vincett et al., 2012, p. 281).

What we are faced with is a perennial methodological problem, one that arises when handling a large quantitative data set, valuable for the picture it paints of a large population, alongside a small, but much more nuanced body of qualitative data, that may well undermine, and certainly challenge, the inevitable simplicities that emerge when dealing with aggregated survey findings. One approach, which offers a meaningful strategy for generating Christian sub-groups *and* begins to capture the significance of change that occurs at university, is based on an examination of the practical expression of Christian commitment. What unites Grace, Jerome and Eva is the fact that their commitment to Christianity is oriented around a church or number of churches as an identity resource. For Grace this takes the form of present-day participation, for Jerome it is the shaping influence of family-based tradition derived from his upbringing, for Eva it is an attachment to the traditions embodied in an established Church that has coloured her life experience, even as it stands in the background at the present time. One's relationship to the church as an institutional entity matters, and whether configured in positive or negative, active or occasional, terms, it has a major place in framing one's expression of Christianity itself.

This approach has a strong basis in previous research. A number of studies have argued for a strong correlation between church involvement and distinctively Christian beliefs (e.g. Gill, 1999; Voas and Crockett, 2005), suggesting that, as church attendance declines, a parallel decline in assent to core Christian ideas can also be discerned (Gill, Hadaway and Marler, 1998). One explanation associates enduring socialization into Christian ideas with enduring involvement in Christian institutions (Bruce, 2002; Wilson, 1966). In a thoroughgoing examination of available survey data from the British context, Robin Gill has established that there are 'broad patterns of Christian beliefs, teleology and altruism which distinguish churchgoers as a whole from nonchurchgoers' (1999, p. 197). This set of distinctive features is not absolute, Gill goes on to argue; the attitudes and beliefs that characterize the Christian community overlap significantly with the non-Christian population. The distinctiveness of Christian individuals is a relative difference – Christianity and British culture are overlapping, not discrete, social entities – but churchgoing is confirmed as a major independent variable that is predictive of these differences. In simple terms, going to church *does* make a difference, overall, to the kinds of priorities and values people have. This is a useful corrective to contemporary scholarship that tends to associate our 'post-Christian' context with a form of popular spirituality that functions independently of the boundaries of Christian tradition (Heelas, 1996; Heelas et al., 2005; Rose, 1998, p. 19). Self-identifying Christians – even those with only tenuous links with the churches – nevertheless embody a set of perspectives that are often profoundly shaped by the traditions and conventions they sometimes vehemently reject.

Our own study offers a way of exploring this further, but through a very particular kind of case study. The experience of going to university is distinctive in many respects, but one of the most important is the way in which it places students simultaneously within two different contexts. The majority who move away to university experience the campus environment during term-time and return home to parents, old friends and the familiarities of a previous life during Christmas, Easter and summer vacations. The growing number who attend university within their local area do not undergo such a dramatic transition, but nevertheless forge for themselves a new set of experiences and social networks that sit alongside, while often highly distinctive from, their pre-existing life circumstances. One way in which to ascertain how this change influences Christian students in particular is to ask how their churchgoing habits differ between the 'home' environment and the term-time, university environment. This allows us to probe how Christian identities are formed at a moment of transition by asking students about habits of involvement both *internal and external to the university context*. As numerous studies have demonstrated (e.g. Brierley, 2006a; Gill, 1993), patterns of church attendance can tell us a great deal about the changing status of Christianity; this is especially true when *different degrees* of activity in *different contexts* are taken into account.[2]

In the following discussion, we offer a profile of Christian students based on their self-reported church-going habits during vacations and during term-time. We categorize church attendance levels into measures of frequent (weekly or more), infrequent (fortnightly, monthly or occasionally) and never, and then gauge the extent to which students maintain different degrees of church involvement within these two contexts. Aggregating these measures generates five descriptive categories that capture 95.9% of our Christian respondents, together forming a typology that provides us with a general profile of church attendance across this population. This typology is made up of (i) consistently frequent church attenders; (ii) students who attend church frequently during vacations but either infrequently or not at all during term-time; (iii) infrequent vacation attenders who are also infrequent attenders during term-time; (iv) infrequent vacation attenders who do not attend church at all during term-time; and (v) consistent non-attenders. The respective size of each category as a proportion of all Christian students is given below in Table 2.3.

For the sake of abbreviation, we refer to the five types listed in Table 2.3 as: *active affirmers, lapsed engagers, established occasionals, emerging nominals* and *unchurched Christians*. Over a quarter of Christian students maintain frequent churchgoing habits both during vacations *and* during term-time, while over 30% never attend church in either context. The remaining 45% consist of infrequent attenders who continue in this habit, and around a quarter whose church-going habits change between the two contexts. This fivefold typology may be described as a spectrum of church-going intensity, as the five categories progress in a linear fashion from those most frequently attending regardless of context, through to those who never attend whatever context they are in, although it would be a mistake to equate this with a measure of religious strength, for reasons that will become apparent. What this categorization can be used for is the identification of a clear and strong set of correlations with variables associated with Christian practices like prayer and Bible reading, as well as Christian belief and moral conviction. In other words, orientations to churchgoing that combine vacation and term-time practice break down into coherent sub-groups of Christian students.[3]

TABLE 2.3 General church attendance profile of self-identifying Christian students based on combining frequency of churchgoing during vacations and during term-time (weighted)

Church attendance profile	Category	Percentage of self-identifying Christian students (%)
Consistently frequent attenders	Active affirmers	25.9
Frequent vacation attenders who attend infrequently or not at all at university	Lapsed engagers	9.0
Consistently infrequent attenders	Established occasionals	13.9
Infrequent vacation attenders who opt out at university	Emerging nominals	16.2
Consistent non-attenders	Unchurched Christians	30.9

This can be illustrated by returning to the three students we introduced at the start of this chapter. Grace, by virtue of engaging in regular church involvement during vacations and term-time, is an *active affirmer*. Jerome, active in a church in Milton Keynes during vacation visits home, has not engaged in church life during term-time due to practical difficulties in finding a suitable church, and so may be categorized as a *lapsed engager*. Eva, with no regular church involvement in either context, is, in our terms, an *unchurched Christian*. Moreover, their relative proximity to church life has a direct, although not simple, relationship to the way they live out their Christian identities during their time as university students. Grace's faith is enriched and developed via her active engagement with a variety of organized forms of Christian activity, including churches, in whose life she has enthusiastically participated, and voluntary work that she has undertaken as an expression of her Christian commitment. As such, her Christian identity is vibrant and dynamic, a learning experience that draws in a diversity of resources. Eva's attachment to Christianity has a tenuous and unsettled connection with institutional church life, consisting in a nostalgic and very occasional participation in Christian rites of passage alongside a sentimental attachment to the aesthetics of Christian tradition. It is unsurprising, then, that her orientation to religious matters is characterized by ambivalence, uncertainty and a rather heterodox set of convictions. Jerome falls between the two, in emerging from a strongly observant Catholic family and a clear sense of his Catholic identity, but who has withdrawn from any organized expression of his Christian faith during university term-time. The practical circumstances that have led to this selective pattern have not, apparently, fostered in Jerome a growing disinterest in or scepticism towards Christianity though. Rather, the experience of not having an institutional context for his faith appears to have inspired him to a more concerted attempt to respond to the challenges of university life in a responsibly Christian fashion. Withdrawal from church has helped him develop a more independently robust set of perspectives that, he believes, have strengthened his faith.

These three individuals represent very different examples of Christian student. They also illustrate three of our sub-categories, which, while by no means clear-cut or internally uniform, nevertheless represent parallel patterns of church involvement and orientations to religious and moral issues. These patterns can be illustrated with reference to a wide range of data; in the following discussion, we primarily focus upon the responses given by Christian students to the open-ended question that concluded our questionnaire: 'In your view, and in your own words, what does it mean to be a Christian?' Respondents offered a wide-ranging set of answers to this question, some of which were highly considered and some extensive. A content analysis of these writings, alongside other survey and interview data, informs the following description of each of our five categories of Christian student.

Active affirmers

Active affirmers are consistently frequent churchgoers, that is they maintain enthusiasm for involvement in church both at home *and* during term-time. As such we might expect them to be firmly socialized into Christian language and ideas, and affirm a committed personal faith. They have backgrounds across the denominations but include high proportions of those with experience attending Evangelical and Pentecostal churches (70% of whom fall into this category).

Responses from *active affirmers* as to the meaning of being a Christian are unmistakably theological, and many have an intellectual quality: precise, indicative, dispassionate sentences offering a clear and comprehensive definition. The following excerpt taken from a questionnaire response serves as a striking example:

> A Christian accepts Christ as personal saviour and saviour of humankind; that Christ is one with God and sent as 'son' to redeem sinners by the Grace of God. A Christian walks by this faith as guided by the Holy Scriptures (Bible), and lives by the help of God's Holy Spirit, which enables and supports the Christian. Being a Christian also means knowing God through Christ personally and having the courage to share the good news of the redeemed life so that others may come to know God through Christ as well.

It is interesting to note the crisp diction, the considered use of 'scare' quotes for 'son' and the initial capitals used for God, Bible and Holy Spirit, all presumably conveying a series of theological claims. This quotation is not untypical among *active affirmers*, and reflects a theological confidence and fluency commonly associated with certain forms of Evangelicalism. This tradition's predilection for 'doctrinal statements' may have rubbed off on these students, who rehearse familiar theological propositions. Underlying this would appear to be a quest for legitimacy, and a desire to operate within a given set of ideas and connotations that are easily recognizable to like-minded Christians. Unlike the other categories, there is very little expression of uncertainty or equivocation, and pithy, personal expressions of subjective commitment are overshadowed by a more discursive, theologically textured account of faith. *Active affirmers* wrote more on average in answer to our question than any other category.

Many responses suggest an underlying theology of substitutionary atonement, and for these students this is at the core of their faith. Indeed, the essential importance of accepting Jesus' sacrifice on the cross is sometimes contrasted with matters of church, ritual and leading a good life, which are at best secondary to what Christianity is all about – 'everything else is just extras to this'. In keeping with this essentialist tendency, while many responses are lengthy and developed, they are also fairly circumscribed in terms of the ideas they support. Statements are more likely to develop an understanding of key doctrines than reflect on what these ideas might imply about proper conduct within students' everyday lives.

Occasionally, evocations of these doctrinal reference points are clothed in more informal, subjective language that permits a more relational dimension, as is the case with Grace, who we discussed at the start of this chapter. For another student, a theology of atonement lies behind their understanding of what it means to be a Christian, but this is expressed in a way that foregrounds an experiential component more in keeping with the relational language commonly associated with individuals of the Y generation (Collins-Mayo et al., 2010):

> [Being a Christian involves] a living relationship with God, that spills out into my life in the way I love and relate to others. A new identity in Christ in which he doesn't see my sin, but Jesus' righteousness and even though I slip up, I'm covered by his grace and he amazingly wants to use me in his purposes in spite of the times I mess up. Certainty for the future, forgiveness for the past, and direction and companionship for the present.

Other respondents echo the wariness towards 'outward' expressions of Christianity in affirming the importance of being personally transformed: 'being a Christian means that you are changed on the inside, not controlled from the outside. It means that your heart has been changed by the presence of God.' In this sense, there is a tendency to associate an authentic Christian life with that which is internal and experiential, rather than according merit to that which conforms to externally imposed expectations. This is found as a pervasive trope among all of our categories to varying degrees, but for *active affirmers* it is most likely to be expressed in a way that does not exclude the invocation of what are taken to be core Christian doctrines, most often concerning substitutionary atonement, Jesus's sacrifice on the cross, and the reality of his resurrection from the dead.

It is undoubtedly true that an Evangelical set of ideas underpins a lot of what is said among *active affirmers* about the meaning of being a Christian. This is the only category that includes unequivocally positive references to evangelism, although even here these are few and far between. There is also a marked emphasis upon passive verbs: Christians 'accept' Jesus as saviour, they 'have been saved by God's grace', are 'shaped by the Spirit's work'. Notions of surrender and obedience feature, of 'handing my life over' to God. However, it would be misleading to ascribe an Evangelical identity to the entirety of those within this category. For one thing, there are various flavours of Evangelicalism and the tension between subjective experience and biblical/doctrinal authority that has recently characterized the British movement (Warner, 2007) is also evident among our *active affirmers*, with some citing doctrinal formulae and others a more essentialist notion of divine relationship. Some, like Grace, attend Evangelical churches – perhaps among other, very different, places of worship – but affirm a set of values that is quite different from the Evangelical doctrinal norm. Moreover, there remain responses that defy simple categorization, either because of their brevity or enigmatic phrasing. Finally, the importance of following Jesus' example, and a general belief in God and Jesus, feature here as within the other categories, although the sense of a widespread developed doctrinal understanding is more in evidence here than in any of the other groups by a significant margin.

Lapsed engagers

The *lapsed engagers* attend church frequently while at home but infrequently or not at all during term-time. As such they represent a decision to disengage from church life when they are most engaged in university life, and yet they return to frequent churchgoing habits once they are in a different context. Given they are the category most likely to say they have become less religious since being at university, we might take this as evidence of a significant level of individual-level secularization triggered by the university experience, although the example of Jerome discussed earlier cautions against simplistic generalizations. *Lapsed engagers* include a disproportionately high number of Roman Catholics, but also fairly large numbers of Anglicans, non-conformists, and those attending independent Evangelical and Pentecostal churches. As might be expected among regular church attenders (even if this attendance lapses at university), *lapsed engagers* often refer to matters associated with the ritual and tradition-based life of the churches, but these references are vague and largely undeveloped. A concrete experience of church remains, but for most, it remains in the background.

Understandings of what being a Christian means among *lapsed engagers* include many references to traditional Christian language, but the essence for most lies in living a good life and following the example of Jesus. There is a significant emphasis upon dependency upon God and forming a relationship with Him that provides comfort for the individual, reflecting what for some appears to be a very personal, private, intimate understanding of faith. This is echoed in a stress on personal attitude, being 'pure of heart and mind' as one respondent put it. It is also affirmed in an emphasis upon love, both love of God and love of our neighbour, which is cited as essential to being a Christian among the majority of students within this category. According to one respondent, being a Christian means:

To love God so much that you want to do everything to please him. He loves you and wants to be with you and there is no need for the confinements or labels we put on ourselves such as rituals. These can be meaningless and if you don't mean it it does nothing. It's not a matter of ticking boxes to get into heaven, it's about a wonderful gift of freedom to enjoy life while loving Him.

The elevation of subjective experience as a major site in which a vital relationship with God is worked out may reflect the presence of students influenced by the charismatic tradition, or by the broader emphasis upon the subjective found across religious developments in contemporary Britain (Heelas et al., 2005). Here, as elsewhere, it is set against the 'empty' religion of rituals and blind conformity, which represents an inauthentic faith and a suspicion towards forms of religion that depend on institutional structures. Evangelical language also appears among these students, citing the importance of being 'born again' and 'accepting Jesus as your saviour'. Allusions to the inevitably sinful nature of humankind and even to the devil also appear among a few, although for most an essentialist sense of devotion to God and living a 'good life' remain centre stage. This emphasis upon right action is also common among *established occasionals* and *emerging nominals*. How one behaves and conducts one's relationships are cited measures of the Christian life, rather than habitual churchgoing or simply 'swallowing the party line'. In some cases the very act of serving others appears definitive, such as with the respondent who said 'To me being Christian means helping others, being considerate, being the best person you can be.' For another student, it is the positive impression made on others that is decisive: 'if a stranger can then turn and say "Oh, that person was very nice, really happy and positive" and felt a joy just being in their presence, then that person is a true Christian.'

Established occasionals

Our third category encompasses those self-identifying Christian students who attend church occasionally during vacations, and occasionally during term-time. In not changing their habits between the two contexts, we have labelled them 'established', assuming that occasional attendance has become for them an accepted and desirable mode of Christian practice. This is an interesting category: logically it could be interpreted as one step towards detachment from church, and yet at the same time includes students who have developed and informed understandings of Christian faith, to which they affirm a strong commitment. It is the category that includes the most Christians who have volunteered for political causes within the previous 12 months, its members are most likely to have at least 1 close friend who follows a religion other than Christianity, and it is the category most likely to affirm the importance of the traditions of the church as a source of religious authority. This latter feature is illuminated by the denominational constituency of the *established occasionals*. They are more likely than all other categories to have an Anglican background, although Roman Catholics make up a slightly larger proportion of this sub-group. As such, it is tempting to ascribe a provisional association with what some might label 'mainstream', 'moderate' or 'liberal' Christianity, traditionally defined as a 'mode of believing' that takes seriously academic learning, refuses to adopt fixed positions on matters of doctrine and its interpretation, and which extols the value of engaging seriously with contemporary culture, including issues of moral and political urgency (Gee, 1992; Harris, 2001). To what extent does this image match the understanding of Christian faith affirmed by our *established occasionals*?

The emphasis upon following a moral code of behaviour is certainly present, especially expressed as following Jesus' example or the 'golden rule' – treating others as we would like to be treated – although this is tempered by a stress on the importance of individual reflection:

> [Christianity] is a personal relationship with God, who (through Jesus Christ and the Holy Spirit) has provided us with teachings, which encourage one to live one's life in a moralistic fashion. However, these morals and their interpretation are something each person must come to terms with separately, and so one person's Christianity (or religion, or belief) is different from another's and should not be imposed upon them.

As with our other categories, there is an evident wariness of having religion imposed by an external authority or constrained by externally defined rules, personal experience remaining a sovereign arbiter and guide in arriving at a legitimate interpretation of the Christian life. For some, this principle is explicit and its affirmation unabashed – 'Christianity is about freedom of choice and no rules are imposed and it's up to the individual to do as they wish' – whereas for others it is more subtly expressed. As such, there is an acknowledgement that faith is changeable, adaptive and evolving, one's relationship with God is 'something that I must try to further understand as I try to grow in faith and nurture'.

Descriptions of the Christian life reflect a high degree of theological fluency for many *established occasionals* (much more so than the *lapsed engagers*); the language of creation, grace, redemption and, for a limited number, atonement, feature in what are occasionally florid, almost poetic, accounts. There is a tone of positive proclamation in some of these, suggesting a mode of being that is being celebrated as well as embraced wholeheartedly:

> [Christianity is] to adopt a way of life that is led by the spirit and taught by Jesus, one where walking with God in your everyday life brings peace, joy

and security and a sure knowledge of salvation and freedom, to share love and hope with all and to see others not as man sees but as God sees. It means everything and is the anchor for my soul in a very troubled world.

Loyalty to traditional Christian ideas remains at the centre for many *established occasionals*, and vague commitments to 'belief in God' are often set alongside references to prayer, sacrifice and, occasionally, specific Bible verses. However, again this commitment is often tempered by personal experience – 'I don't follow all the traditions and rules laid out by the church as I find some contrary to my personal beliefs, but I do believe in God and most religious beliefs of Christianity.' Others support their selective engagement with a more theological rationale, preferring to follow Jesus rather than the entirety of the scriptures, for example. *Established occasionals* appear firmly located within a set of traditional Christian reference points – references to other religions or the vague language of 'spirituality' are almost entirely absent – and yet the *implications* of this framework for living a Christian life are by no means fixed. While not echoing the association with political and moral causes commonly associated with 'liberal Christianity', they remain oriented to faith in a way that allows personal experience to guide belief, and which foregrounds the importance of living a 'good life' as the primary fruit of this process.

Emerging nominals

The *emerging nominals* are respondents who maintain occasional church attendance during university vacations, but stay away from church during term-time. Given this ambiguous status, it is perhaps unsurprising that many affirm a tentative and selective adherence to traditional Christian ideas and practices, which are presented as restrictive. There is very little evidence of cynicism or disillusionment towards Christianity, and only a small minority reduce their faith to a matter of culture or upbringing, but many *emerging nominals* have nevertheless arrived at a point in their lives when certain aspects of the Christian faith no longer make sense to them. For some this is rationalized as a kind of essentialist position focused on love for God and love for one's neighbour, as reflected in the respondent who commented:

To me, being a Christian means to love God, Jesus and all life around you. While I do not believe or follow everything that the Bible teaches, I feel that this does not matter so long as my faith and love for God is true.

Another reinforced an essentialist understanding by distinguishing religion from faith, the latter representing what lies at the heart of Christianity:

I am a Christian and I have faith that there is a higher being, yet I do not follow the Bible. Christianity is a religion but to be a Christian you do not need to be religious, you simply need to have faith.

Many present the Bible as a less than dependable source of Christian truth – '. . . the Bible among other things can be restrictive' – and do not take church attendance to be a necessary part of being a Christian, instead supporting an approach that accords greater significance to personal conduct. As one student put it, 'It is a personal matter. For me it's about believing in forgiveness and the good in people.' For many, their aim is to ensure sound Christian values are embodied in their everyday lives, and this is more important than following the Bible or attending church. At the same time, though, the resources of the Christian tradition remain important, and the frequency with which theologically developed ideas ('Trinity', 'soul', 'afterlife', 'Jesus as saviour') and Christian rituals ('Holy Communion') are positively cited suggests a reluctance to relinquish the familiar symbolic reference points of a Christian upbringing. Being a good person is paramount, but it is telling that several articulated this in terms of being a 'Good Samaritan' or following the example of Jesus. In stressing the importance of belief in God and sound moral conduct, *emerging nominals* reflect many *unchurched Christians* (see below), although their engagement with Christian ideas is more concerted and their sense of dependence on Christianity as their *particular* source of meaning more profound. While affirming an understanding that foregrounds a humanitarian sentiment, one student also demonstrates a conscious choice for Christianity over other religions:

Christianity is the only religion in which God transposes himself into the human condition and sacrifices himself for the well-being of humanity. I think that sums it all up as to why I chose to be a Christian and not belong to other religious groups.

Christianity represents an ultimate framework for life, and at its heart is the love and compassion demonstrated by Jesus. As one student stated, 'Everyday I live in this world to make sure I testify to love like Jesus did.' Even those who do not mention Jesus focus on everyday conduct as a standard by which their Christianity is expressed: 'Acting like a Christian is what makes you a Christian.'

Unchurched Christians

Respondents we have classified as 'unchurched' do not attend church during term-time or during vacations, and most did not attend before university either. As such, it is unsurprising that when describing what Christianity means to them, they use traditional Christian language only in a rather vague and general way. The requirement to believe in God is often mentioned, perhaps alongside following Jesus or reading the Bible, but more doctrinally specific or developed theological ideas are almost entirely absent. Much more prominent are the *moral associations of the Christian life*, and qualities repeatedly stressed are generosity, fairness, kindness, acceptance and honesty. For example, evoking the 'golden rule', one respondent suggested that being a Christian entailed being:

> A good person who thinks of others and always puts themselves in the other person's position, therefore not doing anything to cause another human being harm.

Conversely, respondents often included comments on what Christianity *ought not to be*, focusing on habits of closemindedness, prejudice, judgementalism and forcing religion 'down people's throats'. When specific in their criticism, it is the institutions and traditions of the Church that come under attack; there is a distinction drawn between the essence of Christianity and its formal institutional expression, often presented as hypocritical and corrupt. The unchurched respondents are also likely to emphasize the similarities rather than differences between Christianity and other world religions, often presenting the former as one possible pathway through life, but not the only one ('Christianity is just one of many methods of appreciating "whatever else" there is to life'). They are also likely to distinguish between churchgoing and being a Christian, the latter sometimes developed into a privatized faith, as with the respondent who emphasized 'an open minded belief in god that I do not have to prove. I know that I am a Christian but I tend to keep my religious beliefs to myself'. Another stressed the relational as an integral part of having a personal Christian faith: 'It means to follow Jesus' and God's teaching in your own way. It means to have faith in the religion and believe that God is always there to talk to.' Another invoked God as a 'friend' or 'part of you', someone who is 'always there, in your mind, in the background'.

Personal experience is often cited or implied as a dependable guide to life, with Christianity either reduced to a vague set of moral principles or viewed in an openly selective way, respondents embracing some aspects but not others. There are also a good number of the 'unchurched' who expressed an altogether more cynical perspective, some going as far as to retract their earlier affirmation of Christian identity and/or offer a damning indictment of a worldview they view as blinkered, absurd or dangerous. Others were happy to retain the ascription, but reduced it to a nominal connection to family or British culture, or a consequence of being baptized, or, like Eva, affirmed a nostalgia for Christian tradition that accompanied a more inchoate sense of religiosity. Connections to Christianity forged early in life, especially via baptism, were also, however, often presented as inauthentic given their association with experiences that predated their ability to consciously choose their own path. The unchurched Christian students strongly affirm their individualism, both indirectly through their diversity, and directly in their support for the sovereignty of individual freedom of belief.

Taking stock of Christian students

The qualitative evidence cited above reinforces the argument that social distance from the church can be correlated with a cognitive distance from traditional Christian ideas. Subtle nuances notwithstanding, the more persistently and regularly engaged students are with a church, the more likely they are to affirm doctrinally orthodox beliefs. Conversely, the more disengaged they are from church life, the more likely they are to affirm heterodox ideas and scepticism about Christian tradition. There is also a discernible tendency for disengagement from church to be accompanied by a foregrounding of moral responsibilities over theological language, but this is less straightforward and less obviously linear. This pattern is reinforced further by evidence from our survey, including other forms of Christian devotional practice and trends in professed beliefs and values. Table 2.4 summarizes these statistics in order to demonstrate the strong relationship between proximity to church and other indices of Christian identity; however, it also offers some evidence that should caution us from drawing simple conclusions about this relationship.

As can be seen in the first section of statistics cited, indices of Christian practice, doctrinal traditionalism, moral conservatism and integration into Christian friendship circles, can be associated in a clear linear fashion to our five types, increasing with levels of regular involvement with church. The second section illustrates the same point but in the other direction: doctrinal liberalism, atheism/agnosticism and moral permissiveness are associated in a clear linear fashion, this time increasing with levels of disengagement from church. However, it is important to emphasize that this typology is not intended to imply a simple spectrum of religious strength or commitment. We are not suggesting that those self-identifying Christian students who attend church most are the most religious, and those who never attend are the least. The example of Jerome discussed earlier illustrates how examining life beyond term-time churchgoing reveals a complex relationship between Christian practice and Christian identity. Rather, churchgoing is the axis by which we are mapping Christian students, but the relationship between intensity of involvement and conformity to Christian ideas and values is not entirely straightforward.

TABLE 2.4 Key indices of Christian identity, presented according to our fivefold typology of Christian students

	Active affirmers (%)	Lapsed engagers (%)	Established occasionals (%)	Emerging nominals (%)	Unchurched Christians (%)
% who pray frequently	94.2	72.0	59.5	31.6	12.7
% who read the Bible frequently	75.6	27.1	13.0	2.3	1.1
% involved in organized Christian activities at university	72.9	27.9	19.6	3.0	1.5
% who believe in a personal/ 3in1 God	97.2	86.5	77.8	54.4	29.6
% who view homosexual relations as 'always wrong'	65.1	25.0	19.9	7.5	4.3
% with 3 or more close Christian friends	68.9	45.3	45.5	33.4	23.2
% who view Jesus as a human being with divine virtues	4.8	12.7	27.4	30.1	40.3
% Atheist or agnostic	1.2	8.0	13.8	30.1	59.3
% who have no problems with the student drinking culture	12.3	27.0	33.4	41.0	54.5
Most prevalent tradition (in terms of church background)	Evangelical/ Pentecostal (28.5)	Roman Catholic (36.2)	Roman Catholic (27.7)	Roman Catholic (30.9)	None (67.2)
% who see the traditions of the church as an important source of authority	64	60.5	68.5	65.4	51.4
% who are the only practising Christian in their family	12.1	4.5	6.8	5.8	10.3

For example, as outlined above in our discussion of the qualitative evidence, theological literacy is much stronger among *established occasionals* – those who attend church infrequently during vacations *and* term-time – than it is among *lapsed engagers* – those who attend frequently outside of term-time. Moreover, while 62.4% of those who say they have become more religious since university are *active affirmers*, the remaining 37.6% are spread across the other categories, cautioning against overstating the connection between church attendance and an intensification of faith at university. Furthermore, the final section of Table 2.4 cites evidence from two variables that upset this linear relationship. First, the proportion saying the traditions of the church are important sources of authority actually peaks among the *established occasionals*, with *emerging nominals* scoring higher on this than the *active affirmers*. This is likely to reflect trends in denominational background – more Bible-focused Evangelical/Pentecostals among the *active affirmers*, more traditional Anglicans and Roman Catholics among the middle three categories. However, the levels of assent to this position across the more disengaged categories (including the *unchurched*) are still fairly high, suggesting it would be a mistake to characterize this spectrum chiefly in terms of a growing scepticism towards the authority and traditions of the churches. Whether nostalgic, habitual or heart-felt, many of these practically disengaged Christians do not wish to relinquish the centrality of church tradition. Second, the figures for the proportion of respondents saying they are the only Christian in their family present a curious picture. The middle three categories all occupy the same c. 5% territory; the *active affirmers* have 12.1% claiming this status, tempting an inference that these are Evangelical converts. But 10.3% of the *unchurched* also claim this, suggesting not only a pocket of *unchurched Christians* who are conscious and deliberate in their Christian commitment, but who also cannot be said to owe this commitment to a vestigial or nominal attachment to family traditions. There are a significant number for whom Christianity is not expressed in any conventional fashion, but who can also not be easily categorized as a secularizing fringe.

This chapter has addressed the difficult task of offering a coherent account of how Christian students embody the Christianity they affirm. Our fivefold typology draws together patterns of church involvement and moral/doctrinal values, and will be drawn on throughout this book as a framework for understanding how the experience of university shapes the lives of these students. Having set out what makes up their Christian identity, then, it makes sense in the following chapter to turn to the universities themselves, specifically how patterns of institutional difference come together in influencing the management of religion among the student body.

Notes

1 There were some Christian respondents who opted for 'not sure' on all four of these questions, but they amounted to only 68 cases within our unweighted sample.

2 Peter Brierley's work on church attendance has revealed much more than levels of weekly Sunday churchgoing, and his 2005 English Church Census uncovered the increasing significance of mid-week services, fortnightly and monthly attendance, and attendance at Cathedrals (Brierley, 2006a).

3 It is also possible to defend this typology using more sophisticated statistical techniques. Using multiple linear regression analysis, the fivefold general church attendance profile is demonstrated to be a strong predictor of patterns of doctrinal and moral values among Christian students. Indeed, it is a stronger predictor than church attendance levels taken independently as measures of vacation *or* term-time observance, and is stronger than an aggregate measure of Christian activity more generally. In other words, patterns in the moral and doctrinal orientations of Christian students are most strongly associated with their combined term-time/home configuration of church involvement, reinforcing our fivefold typology as a meaningful sub-division of Christian students.

3

Institutional variations in the university experience

The university experience

Surveying the significant body of literature on religion and higher education, Mayrl and Oeur suggest that many previous studies 'have the unfortunate tendency of decontextualizing the students that they study' and call for greater consideration of the different institutional cultures that shape how religion is engaged within university contexts (Mayrl and Oeur, 2009, p. 271). In this book we respond to this critique in two ways: first, by grounding our analysis of Christian students in the historical and cultural context of higher education in the United Kingdom (as we did in Chapter 1), and second, by developing an institutional typology of England's universities, the latter being the concern of the present chapter. Our principal question: do different types of university handle Christianity and Christian students in different ways, and if they do, how is this reflected in the lives of the students themselves?

We approach the 'university experience' as a phenomenon that is variable by institutional factors, and this requires us to categorize universities, grouping institutions that have common features into meaningful sub-groups. While a challenging task, we are by no means the first to attempt this. Quite aside from the self-directed division of universities into their own 'mission groups' (see Chapter 1), sociologist of religion Sophie Gilliat-Ray (2000, pp. 141–59) formulates a culturally and historically sensitive classification, affirming a relationship between history and institutional ethos on the one hand, and orientation to religion on the other (also see Weller, 2008, pp. 135–54). She classifies universities into three types: (1) older or collegiate universities, with a Christian foundation; (2) civic universities and 1960s universities, with a secular ethos; and (3) 'new' post-1992 universities with a pluralist, multi-faith approach. These three types are situated within a narrative of the development of universities, reflecting shifts in wider society from the dominance of Christianity towards secularism and more recently towards the acknowledgement of religious pluralism (Weller, 2008). Through the process of researching England's universities for this book, it became apparent that this tripartite model papers over too many important distinctions. For example, as demonstrated in Chapter 1, inner-city red brick institutions – the civic universities cited in this typology – have a very different provenance to the universities established during the 1960s, and the campus contexts of the latter foster a very different environment for the expression of religion. Moreover, the Cathedrals Group universities present a very distinct sub-set of the post-1992 group, embodying a decidedly Christian ethos rather than one in keeping with ideas of religious pluralism, which is affirmed in some post-1992 universities, but is muted in favour of a more secular ethos in others.

In light of this, we have chosen to work with five categories, reflecting the four factors that appear most salient in shaping orientations to religion within the current university environment: history, institutional ethos, student demographics and the character of the immediate locale. Referring to the historical overview offered in Chapter 1, these five categories are: traditional, elite universities; inner-city 'red brick' universities; 1960s campus universities; post-1992 universities; and universities belonging to the Cathedrals Group. These offer a range of student experience, reflecting previous research that suggests these different types of university handle religious diversity in very different ways (Gilliat-Ray, 2000; Weller, 2008), while offering a more subtle framework for exploring associations between types of university and the ways Christianity is fostered, embodied and challenged within each. The differences between these five types are summarized in Table 3.1.

Each of the four criteria used to distinguish these university types remain important in understanding their differences, although they are important in different ways and to different degrees. Noting the founding period offers a short-hand for matters of historical background and tradition, and specifically offers insights into the kind of vision inspiring the origins of each institution; clearly it makes a huge difference that the University of Bristol was founded at the turn of the twentieth century within a context of thriving industry, and not during the mid-1960s as part of the nationwide response to the Robbins Report, like the universities of Lancaster, Sussex or York. Each period carries its own assumptions about the norms and values of British culture, and these shape the formation of their universities, sometimes in strikingly enduring ways. For example, some of the 1960s campus universities were founded on an explicitly secular basis, embodying a set of assumptions about what properly belongs within the public life of that institution. In our attempts to recruit universities for the 'Christianity and the University Experience' project, we received negative responses from some of these universities that suggest this set of assumptions is alive and well, at least among university managers, 45 years after their institutional inauguration. The 'institutional ethos' is an approximate attempt to capture the priorities kept at the forefront of these universities' activities as providers of higher education. This is easier in some cases than others, and the post-1992 category (by far the largest) includes a diversity of provision that exceeds all of the others; however, the focus on employability and vocational skills is sufficiently widespread to justify this characterization. The 'student demographic' column represents an attempt to chart the ways in which each category attracts students from different backgrounds, focusing here on four key indicators: gender, ethnicity, age and full-time/part-time status. We also include the proportion of state school entrants as this serves as a reasonable indicator of a university's appeal to those from more constrained economic circumstances. As is clear, it is the post-1992 universities (including, and especially, the Cathedrals Group) that attract the highest proportion of part-time students, reflecting their emphasis upon vocational courses likely to attract mature students, who also appear in high numbers for these two types. The most ethnically diverse are the traditional elite universities – although this may be skewed by high numbers of international postgraduates, who are included in these figures[1] – and the most 'white' are the Cathedrals Group, by some considerable margin. Finally, geographical location provides some clues as to the spatial aspects likely to shape the student experience; the historic small town offers a different environment to the large city, and campus and accommodation arrangements are also influential. In terms of the aspects of the student experience most likely to shape orientations to religion in a campus environment, we believe these four dimensions capture the key factors essential to the present analysis.

Five illustrations

Any typology is by definition based on generalizations that may fail to capture the specific features of individual cases. There is no such thing as the pure traditional elite university or prototypical post-1992 university, and so we work with approximate models and in so doing identify common clusters as the building blocks for a nation-wide analysis. We also recognize that painting the 'bigger picture' based on national trends risks missing more localized expressions of Christian identity, which offer more complex, subtle case studies, and thereby often do a better job of capturing the quality of relationships between Christian students and their university contexts. This thinking lies behind our decision to gather extensive qualitative data from five case-study universities, one from each of the five types described above.[3]

TABLE 3.1 The fivefold typology of England's universities. (Demographic data is for the 2010–11 academic year, statistics generated on the basis of figures available from the Higher Education Statistics Agency)[2]

Type of university	Founding period	Institutional ethos	Student demographic	Geographical location
Traditional elite universities	Early nineteenth century or earlier	Academic research led. Often collegiate. Full range of traditional academic disciplines	51% female 48% white 68% aged under 25 17% part-time 59% state school	Mainly medium-sized towns, strongly associated with the university located in their midst
Inner-city red-brick universities	Early twentieth century	Wide range of subject coverage, traditional and applied/industry-related research	54% female 65% white 74% aged under 25 16% part-time 77% state school	Large cities. University buildings scattered around the urban centre

1960s campus universities	1961–7	Progressive and modern. Campus-based and collegiate: contemporary translation of Oxbridge model. Some focus on business management	53% female 54% white 68% aged under 25 21% part-time 88% state school	Located in purpose-built parks on the margins of medium-sized towns and cities
Post-1992 universities	Various, university status granted 1992 or after	Prioritization of teaching and student experience. Education for employment; humanities subjects marginalized. Widening access key emphasis	57% female 64% white 60% aged under 25 32% part-time 96% state school	Various, out-of-town parks and inner-city locations
Cathedrals Group universities	Late nineteenth century, university status granted 1992 or after	Emphasis on training for public service professions alongside strong humanities coverage. Education for life. Explicit basis in ethical and religious values	68% female 82% white 58% aged under 25 34% part-time 97% state school	Mostly historic towns, but also some large cities

These particular university contexts will provide the substance of the argument that frames the rest of this book, and we introduce them in this chapter. As institutions they both exemplify the trends outlined in Chapter 1, while also introducing more local factors that frame how Christianity is expressed.

Traditional and elite: Durham University

Established in 1832, and as such the third oldest university in England, Durham University is located in a small historic city in the northeast. For historical reasons, not least Durham's Norman Cathedral (Figure 3.1) in which all new students matriculate and all leaving students graduate, Christianity is woven into the fabric of the university: its architecture, traditions, calendar, ceremonies and social life. Its reputation and history draw a large postgraduate and a large international student population.[4] In keeping with its elite reputation, it has one of the highest proportions of students recruited from independent schools (40%) in the sector.[5]

The university does not collect data on the religious affiliations of its students. Nevertheless, the influence of Christianity – and in particular the Church of England – is apparent through Durham's collegiate structure. Students are allocated to a college, the basis of residence and social life (although not academic teaching) for most students for a large portion of their degree. Nine college-based chaplains serve the university, all attached

FIGURE 3.1 *Students process into Durham Cathedral on graduation day. With permission of Durham University.*

to a specific college or two, and the older colleges have traditional chapels, which attract small but committed congregations. In addition, there are denominational chaplains from Catholic, Methodist, Orthodox, Baptist and Quaker traditions, all attached to local religious communities, although the dominance of Anglicanism is apparent (all college chaplains are drawn from this tradition). Some colleges have strong religious links; for instance, St John's has independent status and incorporates Cranmer Hall and the Wesley Study Centre, offering clergy training programmes and other ministry-related courses for Anglicans and Methodists respectively.[6] St John's also publicly characterizes itself as a Christian institution and so tends to attract a high proportion of Christian undergraduates.

For Christian students, opportunities to meet other Christians are plentiful. The Durham University Ecumenical Christian Council (DUECC) coordinates university-wide worship and study groups aimed at fostering dialogue between different Christian societies. The Christian Union has a strong presence, offering numerous activities including Bible study, mission and outreach; its evangelistic tone provokes a mixed reaction from other students, including Christians of different theological perspectives. Other Christian groups include the Methodist and Catholic Societies, Christians in Science, as well as groups such as 'Speak' that focus on faith and social justice.

For students of other faiths, provision is more limited, an ongoing concern for the Students' Union (SU). There was recently a debate over whether the CU's doctrinal statement was incompatible with SU equal opportunities policies, and this has to some extent hampered the interfaith work the SU have recently wished to conduct. A small space has been made available for Muslim students to pray and there are Jewish, Baha'i and Islamic societies, but these are small compared with the Christian groups. There is also a Humanist and Secularist Society, whose membership has grown, its co-founder believes, partly as a counter reaction to the Christian culture of some of the colleges.

The city of Durham is home to a vibrant Christian community. Apart from the Cathedral, within the city centre and its local surroundings there are around 20 active churches, some with sizeable student congregations. The most popular are Evangelical churches, of various denominations and worship styles, from a conservative Evangelical independent church with strong links with the CU, to a more moderate Evangelical Anglican church popular with local families, to a lively charismatic church which is part of the 'new church' Ichthus network (Kay, 2007). In addition, students attend services at Catholic and Methodist churches, some at more liberal Anglican churches and others in college chapels. The availability of Christian activities in Durham and the way Christianity is woven into the institutional spaces students inhabit means that it is easy and common for students to sustain unusually high levels of Christian commitment during their university years.

The inner-city red-brick: The University of Leeds

Situated in the northern county of West Yorkshire, Leeds is by population the third largest city in the United Kingdom. A major commercial centre, it has a large service sector and is a busy, urban metropolis with a vibrant culture. It also has a vast student population of around 60,000, with over half attending the University of Leeds. Established to train students to meet the demands of an industrializing society, it initially concentrated on science subjects but soon expanded, eventually including, after some debate in the 1930s because of its non-religious foundations, theology and religious studies (Brown et al., 2002, p. 5). Today, the university attracts students from across the world (with 19.8% of its students coming from elsewhere in the EU or further afield).

The Leeds Students' Union publicly states its aim to provide an inclusive environment for students of all faiths and none, describing the university as a 'multi-faith campus'.[7] Its Freshers' Week features non-alcoholic social events, catering especially for religious students who might feel excluded by alcohol-based activities. The SU is openly supportive of faith societies, exemplified in its Faith and Cultural Development Coordinator post, and there are around a dozen 'faith' societies, including Pagan, Baha'i and Buddhist Meditation, although the three largest are the CU, the Jewish Society and the Islamic Society. The CU runs a weekly meeting for worship and preaching, Bible study groups, a girls' group and five-a-side football. Its 'street light' initiative involves giving water and shoes to students after nights out, providing opportunities for evangelism. The Catholic Society (CathSoc) meets after Sunday evening mass for social events such as barbecues, hiking and quiz nights. It runs the charitable St Vincent de Paul Society and students fundraise, distribute food to the homeless and visit the local elderly population.

The chaplaincy is predominantly Christian, partly because some other religions have good provision elsewhere (for instance, Hillel House for Jewish students and the Church of Jesus Christ of Latter-Day Saints has its Institute for Religion close to the campus). The Anglican Chaplaincy, the Emmanuel Centre, is housed in a former church (see Figure 3.2), while the Catholic Chaplaincy has a chapel and offices close by, and both serve Leeds Metropolitan University as well as the University of Leeds. Muslim students have access to a prayer room on campus and their request for a chaplain is under discussion. The chaplaincy has around 15 chaplains or faith advisors and regular activities include the popular midweek mass, the Just Act social action group and a staff prayer group. Café Church is a Sunday event attracting a range of Christians, mainstream or liberal Protestant especially, and is seen by some as a third Christian student society (alongside the CU and CathSoc).

Churches in Leeds are plentiful: the chaplaincy's guide to churches lists 36 places of Christian worship from across the denominational and theological

FIGURE 3.2 *The Emmanuel Centre, housing chaplaincy services for the University of Leeds and Leeds Metropolitan University. With permission of Universities in Leeds Chaplaincy Trust.*

spectrum.[8] The most popular with students is a large city-centre Anglican church with an Evangelical flavour and a busy programme of student activities, closely followed by several Evangelical New Churches.

According to the university's annual student census, during the 2010–11 academic year 71.8% of (non-EU) international students affirmed a religious identity, compared to 54.2% of home and EU students. Overall, the proportion of all students who were Christian was 41.5%, while those of no religion or belief made up 43.2%. Muslims amounted to 7.3% and Hindus 2.7%, Jews 1.4%, Buddhists 1.4%, Sikhs 0.7% and Seventh Day Adventists 0.2%. Among international students, the proportion of Muslims was much higher (28.7%); proportionately speaking, there were also considerably more Hindus and Buddhists but significantly fewer Christians and people of no religion.[9]

The legacy of the 1960s: The University of Kent

Opened in 1966 in the wake of the Robbins Report, the University of Kent was established originally as a purpose-built campus 2 miles from Canterbury and now has several smaller local campuses. The university describes itself as 'the UK's European university', with campuses in Brussels and Paris,[10] and attracts high numbers of international students (23.9% of its total student body). Religion is treated as an important strand within the university's commitment to equality and diversity, and religious students can apply for special provisions if an exam falls on the day of a religious festival. Conversely, however, the terminology for university terms has moved away from a church calendar model towards the more neutral autumn, spring and summer, and Easter now sometimes falls in the middle of the spring term. There are three full-time chaplains (Anglican, Roman Catholic and Pentecostal), funded by their respective denominations, but with an activities budget provided by the university. The university benefits from Canterbury's illustrious religious history and the decennial Anglican Lambeth Conference – gathering together representatives from across the global Anglican Communion – takes place on university premises.

Kent has half a dozen well-established campus-based Christian groups: the Catholic Society, the Anglican Christian Focus group, the CU, the Christian Performing Arts Society, the New Life Pentecostal group and the Chinese Christian Fellowship. There are also several new African Pentecostal groups, attracting growing numbers. A recent chaplaincy survey on student involvement in Christian societies revealed an active membership of 450–500, with a further 250–300 nominal members; the Anglican chaplain estimates that around 80–100 are involved in campus-based Islamic activities. The Campus Christian Council brings together representatives of different Christian student groups. There is an active SU, known as the Kent Union, and while some religious societies are affiliated, others (for instance the Catholic Society, the CU and Christian Focus) are not, partly owing to a desire to maintain autonomy from the SU's administrative procedures. The SU's requirement that societies charge a membership fee was seen as a barrier to participation by the Catholic chaplain, who believes students should not have to pay to practise their religion on campus.

Chaplains estimate that Catholic Society membership is particularly strong, with mass three times a week, and a weekly 'club night' in the Catholic Chaplaincy Centre (which offers a 'home from home', with a friendly social space and bar). Membership is significantly greater than that of the CU, which has declined in recent years, partly because of the growth of the Pentecostals. The Catholic Society also owes its popularity to the large numbers of overseas students from countries where Catholicism is relatively strong (France, Germany, Italy, Poland, Spain and African nations), and the chaplain regularly holds masses in different languages, with themed dinners afterwards.

The University is distinctive in hosting three different church services each Sunday – Anglican, Catholic and Pentecostal – all of which are led by the chaplains, who estimate that approximately the same number of students worship on campus as attend nearby churches. Off-campus churches also run activities for students, the most popular being New Church (notably Vineyard and New Frontiers) and Independent Evangelical. Students of other faiths are supported by the Buddhist Society, Hindu Society, Sikh Society, Islamic Society and Jewish Society, and there are Buddhist, Jewish, Quaker and Muslim chaplains supplementing the full-time provision of the three mainstream Christian representatives.

The Post-1992 University: The University of Derby

Situated in an East Midlands city with a strong transport manufacturing industry, the origins of the University of Derby lie in a range of nineteenth-century training colleges; it gained university status in 1992, the only institution to make a direct transition from Higher Education College to university. It has since grown rapidly. Half of its students are from the local region, with only 10% from beyond the British Isles (including 6% from outside the EU).[11] Because many commute to the university from home or undertake part-time paid work, fewer are involved in student societies than at many institutions. Reflecting its higher than average proportion of students from lower socio-economic groups, only 2% of its students come from private school backgrounds.

Situated in a prominent location on the university's main Kedleston Road site, the university's Multi-Faith Centre was formally opened in 2005 as a flexible space to engage students, staff and the local community in mutual understanding of each other's faiths (see Figure 3.6). Although not uncontroversial, it quickly became a space welcomed and used by a spectrum of religious groups, including the CU and Islamic Society.[12] It is a key partner in running the EU-funded Belieforama training programme on religious diversity and anti-discrimination, and has convened a youth inter-faith forum (attracting local young people and some students), inter-faith football and a regular programme of talks and spiritual activities. The Multi-Faith Centre is home to the chaplaincy, which is integral to the university's pastoral and support services provision. Its team of 15 include Buddhist, Jewish, Muslim, Sikh, Hindu, Baha'i and Unitarian advisors, as well as Christian chaplains from different denominations. Islamic Prayer (for which purpose-built washing facilities exist), Catholic Mass, Taizé Prayer and a Fair Trade Lunch (the latter attended mostly by Christian Union members) take place there each week, and there is also a philosophy group run by the Russian Orthodox chaplain. The university has a religion and belief equality scheme in place, and has committed to conducting impact assessments for religion and belief (an analysis to check whether any group is adversely affected by proposed changes, followed by actions to redress any negative impact). It offers *halal* food, publishes a multi-faith calendar and factsheets on religious holidays, and staff take a mandatory online training module in equality and diversity. Freshers' Week features non-alcoholic social events and the SU coffee shop is alcohol-free and has a *halal* section.

Derby is described by one chaplain as a city 'ghettoed by faith', where different religions occupy different areas and where Christians divide into two sectors ('independent Evangelical' and 'traditional'). The university, this chaplain believes, mirrors this separation, despite attempts by the chaplaincy and Multi-Faith Centre to bridge divides. There is just one Christian student society, the Christian Union, made up mostly of Evangelicals. Its main weekly meeting involves worship and a talk, and there is a fortnightly prayer breakfast and Bible study groups. Chaplains are keen to provide for non-Evangelicals and non-Christians, and provide one-to-one pastoral support to a range of students. The CU introduces students to local churches, and consequently several large Evangelical churches (New Church, Pentecostal and Church of England) have a large regular student contingent, with smaller churches and older denominations attracting fewer. The Catholic chaplain estimates a student attendance of around 100 at the Sunday evening Mass in the city centre, and its post-service group, for young professionals, is attended by a large group of international students.

The SU has only one affiliated faith society, the CU; the Islamic Society is affiliated to the Federation of Student Islamic Societies (FOSIS). The SU has run faith-based events such as Diwali celebrations and supports the Islamic Society's Islamic Awareness Week. There has been no conflict between the CU and the SU, and the SU stress that, so long as they abide by SU inclusion and diversity policies and operate democratic elections for committee members, students are free to lead the societies as they wish.

A breakdown of the student body in 2010–11, based on student self-identification, revealed a Christian population of 46.6%, 38.3% were of 'no religion', 7.4% Muslim, 3.7% Sikh, 1.5% Hindu, 0.7% Buddhist, 0.1% Jewish and 1.7% 'other'.[13]

The Cathedrals Group: The University of Chester

Although only granted full university status in 2005, the University of Chester was founded in 1839 as a Church of England teacher training college and expanded its provision during the nineteenth and twentieth centuries, becoming an affiliated college of the University of Liverpool in the 1920s, and subsequently a university college in the 1990s. Its Anglican foundation shapes its mission to be an 'open and inclusive environment guided by Christian values'[14] and while its governance is now more ecumenical, most of the 13 foundation governing members are required to be practising Christians.[15] Like Derby, a greater than average proportion of Chester's students come from state schools and lower socio-economic backgrounds. Typical of Cathedral's Group universities, two thirds of Chester's students are female, a trend not unconnected to its popular teacher training, nursing and midwifery programmes.

Reflecting its Christian foundations, the University of Chester is more explicit than our other four case-study universities about the Christian focus of its faith provision. While chaplains at some universities are viewed primarily as part of student support and welfare services, at Chester their *religious* role is recognized and appreciated by university management. Chaplains support the faith development of staff as well as students, lead the annual Founder's Day Service and sit on the University Senate. The chaplaincy holds daily ecumenical services at the Chester campus, weekly services at the smaller Warrington site and promotes a range of activities including book clubs, retreats, a spiritual mentoring programme, charitable activities and the (student-led) Christian Union. The weekly Wednesday evening service attracts 30–40 people each week and there is a weekly Catholic mass. A university-wide service takes place each term. As well as chapels at Chester and Warrington campuses, the university provides faith spaces, which those of any faith or belief can use. There are separate facilities for men and women, including washing facilities, particularly important for Muslim students. The six chaplains named on its website are all Christian, but they can connect students to a team of advisors from a range of faith traditions.

The Christian Union is the only faith-based SU-affiliated society. Unlike the situation at some universities, the Chester CU appears to adopt a more theologically moderate perspective (for instance, on issues of sexuality). Its relationship with the Students' Union is congenial and it is one of its largest societies. Figures available on the religious adherence of students enrolling in 2010 indicate that the proportion of students belonging to religions other than Christianity is low (2.9%), while more than half (52.9%) affirm a Christian identity, a higher figure than all other universities for which we have figures, while 38.1% claim to be of 'no religion'.[16]

Most of the local churches attended by students are Evangelical (Church of England, Independent or New Church), with some attending a Roman Catholic Church; according to one chaplain 'students flow between the churches to a significant degree, but the churches work together acknowledging that the moving is beneficial for the students'. Some Christian students are involved in the citywide Light Project, an evangelistic initiative involving around 50 local Christian projects and churches.

Five patterns of engagement with Christian faith: Comparisons

All of the above universities remain within the same higher education system, and hence are responding to the same shifts in government education policy, the same funding regime, and are relating to the same geographical context, broadly speaking. However, they differ in their history, institutional ethos, student demographics, and the character of their immediate locale, all of which make for overlapping, but distinctive, models of the university experience, especially in terms of the way that Christianity is framed. Each represents a different localized culture, shaped by a variety of factors, and it is worth sketching this out in more detail in order to achieve an account of the university experience that allows for a subtlety reflective of the evidence available.

The perception of Durham amongst its staff and students reflects a sense of Christian fabric that is ambient, but obvious, entrenched, but rarely achieving power within the structures of the university. Part of this impression is grounded in architectural factors and the visibly ecclesiastical flavour of the city itself, but it also arises from some of the organizational characteristics of the university. There are a large number of chaplains and most are Anglican, but this has to do with collegial arrangements that owe their continuity to long-established endowments and local trusts, rather than university policy endorsed by senior management. The Anglican Cathedral remains a prominent spatial reference point, and the tradition of holding graduation ceremonies there is a relatively recent one, suggesting a willing embrace of ecclesiastical links. However, Durham is a very small city, its cathedral a huge and dominant feature at its centre. There are obvious motivations for making use of the building that have to do with its aesthetic and historical appeal (especially for visiting parents), symbolic status in marking the unity of city and university, and its size (the university has no other assembly halls that approach its capacity). Indeed, the sense that the cathedral is embraced for practical, historical and aesthetic reasons, rather than religious ones, is emphasized at each graduation ceremony, when, in his welcome speech, the Dean of the cathedral emphasizes the secular nature of the occasion.

On the other hand, there is a strong perception that Christianity occupies a vibrant and prominent place among Durham students that is atypical of the HE sector. The close proximity of several thriving churches, some well connected to university life, the provision of worship at college chapels, and the lively student-led Christian societies, all contribute to an impression – shared by several of our staff and student interviewees – that students could easily engage in an organized Christian activity every night of the week. One SU officer suggested the 'insular' Durham environment (often described as 'the Durham bubble') contributes to the polarization that frequently emerges among the CU, other Christians and non-religious students. Reinforcing this is the close-knit community life of the Durham collegiate system, and while for some this is claustrophobic, for others it is a cherished source of identity, generating close friendship circles, localized Christian subcultures and formal positions of responsibility. The opportunities to practise Christianity in Durham and to facilitate this provision as a student generates an environment in which the secularizing patterns commonly associated with life in the United Kingdom are somewhat muted. Thus, the proportion of practising students *appears* to be unusually high, and this provokes strong counter reactions among non-religious students, some of whom echo 'new atheist' arguments against the Christian hegemony they perceive in the public life of the nation. Shortly before the start of the 'Christianity and the University Experience' project, a group of Durham students revived what became the Humanist and Secularist Society, in part as a response to what was perceived to be the strongly Christian aspect of student culture and the many long-established, but unquestioned, Christian traditions that punctuate student life (Latin grace before formal meals, the pastoral role of college chaplains, naming university terms after the Christian calendar, etc.). In talking to the president of this society, we found that proposals to name it the Durham Atheist Society were abandoned because of a perception that Durham students would not feel comfortable aligning themselves with an openly atheist agenda, given associations with 'extremism' and the Christian environment of the university.

Nevertheless, the Durham Humanist and Secularist Society recruited around 60 members, with 150 to its mailing list, within its first 4 weeks of existence, and its rapid momentum illustrates the kind of polarized response that the student experience at Durham appears to provoke when it comes to Christianity. Occupying a defined and public secularist position becomes more important because it constitutes an attempt to mark out an identity in distinction from a perceived norm. Beyond the ambient features mentioned earlier, this norm is often discursively mobilized in very specific terms, reflecting the conversionist Evangelicalism of the Christian Union. The Durham CU appears to be closely aligned with the basis of faith affirmed by its parent body, the UCCF: its events and members affirm a theology centred on substitutionary atonement, evangelism as a means of converting non-believers to a personal commitment to Jesus, and the elevation of biblical authority above all other, and especially priestly and tradition-based, sources. Together these foster a style of Christian commitment that leans towards separatism and makes for occasionally strained relationships with chaplains, the Students' Union and other Christian societies deemed 'unsound' in their theology. Within the general student culture such expressions of Christianity are often viewed as intolerant, judgemental and intrusive, and while the student-led annual 'mission week' has incorporated more subtle forms of engagement with the non-Christian population, it remains firmly wedded to an understanding of evangelism focused on personal conversion, rather than social justice or public service. A broader vision of Evangelical Christianity is promoted in some of the larger local churches, so that these form nodes in a complex network of Christian activity pulling in sometimes very different directions. Their apparent complementarity – representing various shades of conservative and charismatic Evangelicalism, with accompanying variations in perspectives on women's leadership and the nature of mission – arguably enhances the vibrancy of student Christianity by catering to a wide range of orientations, as well as expanding the options available should students wish to switch churches mid-term.

Several of the staff we interviewed who had experience of other universities remarked that Durham was atypical, both in the demographic constituency of its students (more upper middle class, independent school educated) and in terms of the Christianity expressed amongst the student body. It certainly has a strikingly visible Christian subculture, although the fact that much of this is shaped by the college system and size of the city suggests Oxford and Cambridge may follow similar patterns, and studies of Christian Unions in these contexts do reveal similarly conservative pockets of Evangelicalism (Dutton, 2008; Goodhew, 2003). Furthermore, the close connections between social elites and the conservative Evangelical tradition suggest we may expect to find parallel pockets of Christian enthusiasm in other traditional elite universities. Our survey results reflect significant similarities between Durham, Cambridge and UCL with respect to the values of their students, with Durham students coming out as most conservative on some measures but not on others.

Interestingly, one of the local church pastors at Durham had also worked in student ministry at the University of Leeds, and was able to draw an instructive comparison, with reference to the importance of 'sound doctrine' as a marker of identity among Durham's Christian students:

> That is a thing that you would never come across in Leeds. The word 'sound' was not even on people's register, whereas around here it's the buzzword. Are they sound? Is that speaker sound? Is it a sound book?

Several years have passed since this individual worked at Leeds, and yet it remains an environment in which doctrinal identities appear secondary to other markers of difference among Christian – and non-Christian – students. This is partly a consequence of the cultural and religious diversity of the student body, which has generated a tradition of catering to student needs across the major faiths. At the same time, the emerging provision has its hub at the central chaplaincy building, and this seems to prevent any problematic fragmentation between different religious sub-groups or along religio-cultural lines. The chaplaincy emphasizes its purpose as a service-provider for people of all faiths and none, and in serving students and staff, constitutes an integrated pastoral support network across the University of Leeds and Leeds Metropolitan University. The former is a large and internally diverse university, and its inner-city location, where students from all parts of the institution mix alongside locals as they pass by commercial outlets on their way to lectures, enhances a sense that this diversity is integral and normative, as it is to the city of Leeds itself.

This embrace of diversity is also embedded in the university's regulatory structure. The Students' Union goes to great lengths to embed systems of governance and consultation that incorporate the perspectives of all minority groups, whether defined by faith, ethnicity, age, sexuality or student status.[17] Its Equality Service (which ensures the university meets equality legislation requirements for public bodies) has put in place an action plan with targets for the promotion of equality of religion or belief, including flexible provision for students needing to organize study and examination commitments around religious festivals or designated periods of worship or prayer. The university has recently introduced religion into its equal opportunities monitoring of students, and within processes of staff recruitment.

Student events that have a Christian flavour remain prominent and popular, but they often serve wider agendas to do with cultural integration and mutual understanding. For example, the highly popular International Students Club is organized by Christians but attracts students from across different faiths, fostering a sense of community among students studying at a distance from their home country (see Figure 3.3). The Bible discussion groups organized by the international chaplain serve a similar function, providing a context in which those wishing to explore their faith and those wishing to learn more about Christianity may do so alongside one another, while special provision is offered to those wishing to explore the Bible in their mother tongue. In this sense the pastoral service offered via the chaplaincy enables students struggling with an alien environment to adapt and integrate, assisted by an experience of engagement with Christian texts and ideas. Interfaith activities also feature prominently, including the SU's recent collaboration with the Lokahi Foundation's initiative Campusalam. Founded in 2007, Campusalam encourages and supports dialogue between students of faith, nurturing their ability to make positive contributions to their university campuses. The Walk in my Shoes scheme pairs students of different faiths for interfaith discussion, and the 'Under: Stand: Up' comedy event was run jointly by the Islamic Society, the Jewish Society and the CU. Owing in part to its well-organized and well-connected faith provision, which addresses Christian concerns alongside those of other faiths, the University of Leeds presents a lively, vibrant and diverse context for Christian students that mirrors its inner-city location.

Cultural diversity is also a major feature of life at the University of Kent, although in this case it is characterized by different strands of Christianity, rather than a range of world faiths, as in Leeds. Non-Christian faiths are represented among the student body, but only in small numbers, and the high proportion of non-UK students draws heavily from West Africa and continental Europe, resulting in high numbers of Roman Catholic and Pentecostal students. Given that student-led Christian groups tend to gather

FIGURE 3.3 *Promotional material for the international students club, University of Leeds. With permission of Universities in Leeds Chaplaincy Trust.*

for worship on campus, rather than in the city of Canterbury, this makes for a vibrant Christian presence that is unusual for a 1960s campus setting. This has not always been the case, and when Kent was established in 1966 it followed the secular model favoured by some of the other universities founded at that time. Originally there was no chapel, no chaplains, and plans to name constituent colleges after religious figures like Augustine were abandoned in favour of more modern 'saints' like Charles Darwin, T. S. Eliot and John Maynard Keynes. However, this tendency was short-lived, and by the close of the decade a chaplaincy team had been established;[18] by the 1990s, this had evolved into a threefold full-time team of Anglican, Roman Catholic and Pentecostal representatives.

Its international constituency has fed into a vibrant Christian subculture among the Roman Catholics and Pentecostals, but this has come at the apparent expense of other groups. The fact that the energy driving these groups comes from outside the white middle-class British contingency appears to have diminished the conservative Evangelicalism associated with the Christian Union. The CU at Kent has, according to the Anglican chaplain, declined significantly in recent years, regular participants down from around 100 to 20 during the last 10 years or so. Evangelistic initiatives remain, but are noticed for their ineffectiveness, in spite of concerted efforts by the students. The Evangelicalism most visible at Kent is Pentecostal or 'new church', with active West African-inspired groups on campus and a popular Vineyard Church in town. However, on-campus involvement is hampered by a schismatic tendency among Pentecostals who fragment along doctrinal lines, the original Pentecostal gathering on campus losing students to more recently established groups, such as Salem Campus Fellowship, Believers Love World and the Redeemed Christian Church of God. All of these function as outposts of larger international networks, which play a part in resourcing and recruiting for such groups, including via the internet. The international constituency of the student body also has implications for the levels of social capital available to student-led Christian endeavours. With many non-UK undergraduates arriving as part of the EU-wide Erasmus scheme and staying no longer than a year, the annual student turnover makes for an international and transient population. Within such an environment, it is not surprising that the most successful Christian endeavours are both located on campus (where perennial resources are well embedded) and resourced by full-time chaplaincy staff.

Like several other 1960s campus universities, Kent's original collegial system has over the years developed into little more than an on-campus residential arrangement, with teaching and social facilities centralized. Unlike Durham, it is not the colleges that have proven instrumental in maintaining Christian provision, but the cross-university efforts of the three full-time chaplains and wider chaplaincy team, which conceives of itself as serving the entire student body. Even while it is the sponsoring denominations that pay the chaplains, they receive an operational budget, offices and a chapel, and sit on the social welfare committee of the university. Chaplains are also seen as valuable advocates for students of all religious persuasions, promoting the cause of Muslim students requesting non-alcoholic social events and halal food on campus, for example. As such they play a kind of vicarious role analogous to that often assumed by Anglican bishops in the House of Lords (Davies and Guest, 2007, p. 63), functioning at an institutional level as champions of religious conscience as well as contributors to student welfare provision.

While architecturally and historically located within a secular stream of university development, its proximity to Canterbury and strong chaplaincy

FIGURE 3.4 *View of Canterbury Cathedral from the University of Kent campus. With permission of the University of Kent.*

tradition has fostered a dimension to the university's identity that is distinctively Christian, if largely ambient rather than salient (see Figure 3.4). Like at Durham, graduation ceremonies take place in the local cathedral but within a decidedly non-religious ceremony. However, in the same venue, the annual university carol service is also extremely popular, with around 5,000 students applying for 3,000 ticketed places, and key members of university staff – including the chancellor and vice-chancellor – as well as the President of the Students' Union, taking on reading parts in a traditional Christmas service (see Figure 3.5). One chaplain commented to us that, in his judgement, this was 'the only thing that brings the whole university together'. In this sense, Kent manages to foster a culture of student Christianity that enables the coexistence of vibrant West African-inspired Pentecostalism and an institutionally embedded Christian traditionalism that spans the main denominations.

This contrasts markedly with the University of Derby, which of our five case studies has embraced a religious diversity agenda most visibly. As a post-1992 university developed from a number of established local colleges, Derby does not have the collegial structure of Durham or the campus context of Kent, and its high proportion of part-time and mature students makes for a more fragmented student culture. Relatively free from historical loyalties and faced with a student population with diverse needs, it has elected to develop an identity of its own, with the affirmation of cultural and religious diversity a key guiding principle. This is embodied most vividly in its purpose-built Multi-Faith Centre, which houses offices for chaplains and faith advisors, alongside multi-purpose spaces that can be used for worship or other meetings,

FIGURE 3.5 *University of Kent Carol Service, organized by the Chaplaincy. With permission of the Chaplaincy at the University of Kent.*

dedicated Muslim prayer rooms, 'quiet spaces', and a unique design that manages to avoid symbolic associations with any particular religious tradition while projecting a sense of openness, light and welcome (see Figure 3.6). The Catholic chaplain affirmed his institution's ethos in saying '. . . the way that Derby is set up, it's secular in its environment but it's very proactive when it comes to providing facilities for religious expression.' A Students Union officer considers its approach more 'neutral' although also suspects that Christian students are particularly vulnerable to ridicule for their faith, something echoed in some of our interviews with students.

This prominent multi-faith provision is also distinctive for being wholeheartedly endorsed and driven by the university's management. This is in no small part

FIGURE 3.6 *The Multi-Faith Centre, University of Derby. With permission from the University of Derby Multi-Faith Centre.*

a response to the demography of the student population, which includes a disproportionately high number of part-time and mature students, as compared with the average for the sector and for post-1992 universities. Many of these students live locally and work to support themselves, resulting in a student population that is more time poor and less generationally unified than on many campuses; as a consequence, student-led extra-curricular activity is relatively limited, and faith-based provision steered largely by the Multi-Faith Centre and chaplains, working collaboratively and with the support of university managers. This appears to be vibrant and respected on campus, but there is also recognition among chaplains that their student demographic means many will focus their religious lives on the local parish churches, chapels or mosques they attended before they were students. In turn, this can lead university-based provision to focus particularly on the welfare needs of international students, or those whose faith identities are most visible. In this sense Derby highlights the difference that student demographics can make to university-based religious expression; for the many students living at home, the experience of university is very different from those who have moved away and relocated, with the relative independence and insecurities that brings.

Chester differs from all four of the above universities in many respects. While sharing its post-1992 status with Derby, it has a very different set of institutional priorities and a stronger sense of a coherent identity than Durham, Leeds, Derby or Kent. Moreover, it is a sense of identity that appears to be well integrated into its structures as an organization, not just on account of its formal links with the Church of England but also because of concerted efforts on the part of current managers to sustain a distinctively Christian ethos. While the Christian aspect of Durham as an institution is widely treated as a survival of its past history, in Chester its Christian foundation remains relevant to its current identity. Typically of church foundation universities, Chester pays its chaplains, rather than depending on external church funds, and this creates time and resources as clergy are not stretched by off-campus duties, while also projecting a clear message about the university's priorities. This message clearly gets out to parents and prospective students, and the Dean of Students suggested to us that Chester had developed a reputation for offering a caring, dependable environment analogous to the appeal commonly associated with the United Kingdom's church schools. He attributes this to the Christian ethos of the university, but also to a pastorally sensitive culture that has developed out of its history as a teacher training college:

> . . . I suspect, and it is only anecdotal talking to parents, that a lot of the parents see a church university, it's a bit like a church school, it's a good place to go because you'll be cared for and of course the support work stuff here is good so they tend to see that as a package. And in the same way that faith schools are seen in a particular light . . . we're a church university and we have a deep and abiding care for people which translates into everything we do. But there's another voice, which says this is an old teacher-training establishment and teacher-training establishments notoriously are good at caring . . .

This captures an elusive kind of Christian identity, a set of values that extends beyond the ecclesiastical brickwork (see Figures 3.7 and 3.8) and into a culture that channels notions of care, altruism and community mindedness into its constituent relationships. This is not to say that all students and staff buy wholeheartedly into a shared Christian ethos, and the Dean of Chapel[19] commented to us that he had never come across an undergraduate applicant for whom the university's church foundation status was decisive, but it clearly affects the culture of the university in a way that is viewed positively by many students. As one interviewee put it, '. . . there is a gentle Christian ethos in the background and in the sort of ways that they look after the students . . . you do feel that the students are cared for here . . .' Some of the most striking expressions of this ethos may be unconnected in some students' minds with the Christian faith, such as the strong tradition of volunteering that is made an institutional priority (see Chapter 7). And yet Chester also retains similar kinds of architectural and ambient signals of Christian identity characteristic of Durham, albeit in a less magisterial form, and concerted attempts by chaplains and senior management to vocalize this Christian identity make for a more immediately visible and live sense of institutional commitment that appears to filter into the experiences of the students. Some university managers view this as a unique selling point: within the now ruthlessly competitive, financially driven culture of

FIGURE 3.7 *Entrance to Senate House and University Chapel at the University of Chester – this demonstrates the close proximity of the Anglican chapel to the centre of the University. With permission of Rob Warner.*

FIGURE 3.8 *Stained glass cross by Cloisters, University of Chester – an example of Christian iconography embedded in the campus. With permission of Rob Warner.*

UK Higher Education, Cathedrals Group universities may claim to be the only institutions motivated by a clear set of moral and religious values.

This has made for a model of chaplaincy that is more holistically integrated into the life of the university, the Dean of Chapel describing its mission as threefold: 'ministry to students, ministry to staff and ministry to the institution'.

The public-service-oriented degree programmes also generate a role for the chaplain in terms of a curricula contribution, for example helping to develop notions of spiritual care within nursing courses or encouraging lecturers to reflect on what kinds of values are implicit in the material they teach. The chaplain also sits on University Senate and is directly line-managed by the Vice-Chancellor, reflecting the centrality of a clerical contribution to the governance of the institution.

If a pastorally minded, community-oriented Christianity is at the forefront of the University of Chester's priorities, modes of governance and approaches to managing students, at the grassroots undergraduate level, a similarly collegial experience appears to typify the lives of Christian students. Unlike at Durham, while firmly Evangelical, the Chester-based Christian Union has an enduringly positive and collaborative relationship with both the Student Union and university chaplains, and Roman Catholic students appear solidly integrated, suggesting an inclusive ecumenism that sits uncomfortably alongside the more stridently Protestant position commonly affirmed by the UCCF. This consensual, co-operative pattern is reinforced by the local church culture, which includes a broad range of Anglican and independent Evangelical churches, some of whom collaborate together in catering to student needs. Staff attribute this pattern to a former associate chaplain, who as an Evangelical clergyman won the trust of the CU, but also managed to 'curb their excesses' and foster a positive set of relationships that has become established as an enduringly collaborative culture among its members. The positive relationships with the chaplaincy, which can then support the needs of the CU at university level, thereby curtail any silo tendencies among more strident sub-groups within the Christian student body. The large numbers of students studying for theology or Christian youth work degrees may also make it difficult for more narrowly dogmatic perspectives to achieve momentum among the students. The emerging, more moderate, tendency is reflected in the CU's rather 'left-wing' take on Christian values, characterized by the chaplain as a kind of popular, if selectively expressed, 'universalist theology', which places them in a rather uncomfortable relationship with the UCCF. The university experience for Christian students at Chester is affirmative and embedded in the institution, and while moderating tendencies are fostered, even among Evangelical parties, levels of practical engagement and observance appear noticeably vibrant.

Space and identity

Universities, as public institutions, are, in one respect, expected to embody a certain neutrality when it comes to matters of religion. The religious identities of students are often treated similarly to matters of culture or ethnicity, as representing a measure of difference within the student body that shapes their needs and perspectives. As such, there is a general consensus, at least among university managers and education policymakers, that universities 'do not – or at least should not – exhibit partiality toward a person based on his or her beliefs any more than the colour of a person's skin' (Dinham and Jones, 2010, p. 13). This is the liberal perspective that frames higher education policy – especially salient in the discourses of equal opportunities, ethnic diversity and multiculturalism – and shapes many of the governing values of contemporary British culture. Given the instrumentalist language of the 'student experience' (Sabri, 2011), it is unsurprising that such values are most explicitly mobilized within attempts by universities to provide for students with specific needs. Thus, religion is negotiated as an element of student life through top-down responses, with universities accountable for the adequacy of associated provision and motivated to better this provision by the dynamics of the higher education marketplace. This is the theory, and one apparently enshrined in recent policy documents (Browne, 2010).

In practice, even clothed in the language of 'neutrality', approaches to the management of higher education reflect a variety of value-laded perspectives, universities treating religion as a positive aspect of student formation, a reality of human life that ought to be engaged and catered for, a sensitive political hot potato to be avoided at all costs, or as irrelevant to the proper life of a university, ideally focused on rational thinking and the (secular) pursuit of knowledge. The impossibility of absolute 'neutrality' is illustrated in this final perspective, which is sometimes elaborated and justified by academics and managers as a 'neutral position', while at the same time clearly excluding – or marginalizing – religious language and practice from the public life of their universities. Taking Christianity as our focus complicates this set of circumstances further, for the Christian faith is historically embedded in the life of the United Kingdom and its public institutions, and as such enjoys structural advantages that often translate into perennial resources, as exemplified in the case studies discussed in this chapter, especially Durham and Chester. Even when originating structures have sought to exclude religion, as at Kent, Christianity has gradually regained an integral place within the life of the institution. This is in part attributable to geographical and historical contingences, and in part to institutional orientations that represent deliberate strategies implemented by university staff and communicated among students. This is most striking in the case of Chester, which typifies the Cathedrals Group universities in seeking to develop and maintain an institutional culture that has Christian values at its heart. In retaining a clear institutional identity, Chester is, however, unusual, and the cases of Leeds, Derby and even Durham suggest orientations to Christianity that are far more ambivalent and less amenable to a singular description.

In addition to matters of shared ethos and formal chaplaincy provision, the above comparison also reveals how the configuration of university spaces can have a major influence upon how Christian students negotiate their way through the university experience. Geographer of religion Peter Hopkins (2011) writes of religious students' experiences of 'campus geographies'. He argues that the location of worship spaces on campuses influences whether students experience their religious identities as validated or marginalized. The designation of sacred spaces within universities can be highly visible or spatially sidelined, effectively promoting or concealing opportunities for religious expression (e.g. Reimer-Kirkham et al., 2012; Weller et al., 2011). Chaplaincy premises can be ambiguous resources in this respect: sometimes occupying a prominent and symbolically powerful position on campus, but also often internally arranged in a way that neutralizes religious symbolism in the interests of inter-faith inclusion. The Multi-Faith Centre at the University of Derby is one example, a building of interrelated spaces designed to reflect how faiths are practised and lived in relation to one another. Gilliat-Ray suggests that these purportedly 'neutral' sites of religious and/or spiritual activity can be viewed as generic by virtue of the opportunity they present for people to explore their own 'sometimes muddled beliefs (or lack of them)' (2005, p. 364). She observes that the combined use of such spaces by people of all faiths and those who do not affiliate with a faith makes them politically and spiritually appropriate in societies or institutions characterized by religious diversity and religious uncertainty. The Leeds chaplaincy is a peculiar example, in occupying a former Anglican church (hence externally resonant of Christian identity), which is internally reconfigured into a series of neutral, sparsely decorated meeting rooms, used for a range of university functions, including teaching. At its heart is a Christian worship space, retaining some of the stained glass of the original church building (see Figure 6.2). Hence, as a functional meeting space it integrates a variety of university activities into the work of the chaplaincy, while retaining a dominant Christian identity that is prevented from being overbearing by a selective and subtle use of Christian symbolism. This is an example characterized by the deliberate design of a bespoke space; on-campus spaces can also be enhanced or marginalized as a consequence of geographical circumstance. Like other universities established in the 1960s, the University of Kent occupies an out-of-town campus: an attractive grassy park within which sits a conglomeration of concrete functional buildings typical of the era in which they were constructed. The campuses at York, Lancaster, Essex and Warwick are similar in offering a campus environment somewhat separate from the towns and cities closest by. While the Kent campus is situated at a distance from the city centre of Canterbury, it is perched on a hill, and the enormous Canterbury Cathedral is clearly visible from the campus as a dominant feature of the landscape (see Figure 3.4). At Kent, it is impossible to escape the ecclesiastical traditions that shape the culture of the local area.

Clearly, university spaces do not lend themselves to a simple or singular description, and this shapes the ways in which religious matters are negotiated. Lily Kong argues that 'while the sacred is often constructed, and gathers meaning in opposition to the secular, place is often multivalent, and requires an acknowledgement of simultaneous, fluctuating and conflicting investment of sacred and secular meanings in any one site' (2001, p. 212). Universities are spaces in which multiple political, historical, social and religious meanings come together to define their contexts, which can be difficult to navigate, perhaps especially for students who have a clear sense of their own identity. The complexity of university spaces presents a challenge to those Christian students who seek to locate their identities within a clearly defined terrain, either as evangelists, carers, theologians or simply responsible Christians living out their faith in a way that is faithful to their convictions. On the other hand, those who successfully identify opportunities to embody these roles – especially when built on a range of inter-subjective encounters and community activities – appear to thrive in the vibrant contexts of university life. The case of Grace, introduced in Chapter 2, is a prime example.

The migration of international students and the practices they bring from home contribute to this complex plurality of university life. Thomas Tweed (2006; also see Peach, 2002; Peach and Gale, 2003) contends that new religious traditions can transform religious and cultural landscapes in Western contexts. We observe this in the presence of African Pentecostals at Kent and the Multi-Faith Centre at Derby. As a result of globalization, religions (and hence cultures) with differential boundaries between public and private, secular and sacred, have triggered a reconsideration of the role and practice of religion in public spaces (Reimer-Kirkham et al., 2012, p. 209), perhaps particularly in universities. Because of global flows of people and the changing demographic profile of students, universities are increasingly required to manage the varied spatial and temporal needs of different cultural and religious groups. The migration of students, from overseas and within the United Kingdom, also affects local geographies of religion, with the membership of churches and faith groups that surround universities benefitting from the influx of new students each year.

The spatial intersection of home, university and religion reflects feminist geographer Doreen Massey's consideration of space as a product of interrelations (2005, p. 1012). Space is porous and never a rigidly bounded entity. She understands identities as simultaneously produced inside, outside and between spaces, which are also spheres of multiplicity and difference. The fluidity of spaces allows us to understand how religion is lived and practised beyond the 'officially sacred' (Kong, 2001). Religious Studies scholar Robert Orsi argues 'lived religion cannot be separated from other practices of everyday life . . . Nor can sacred spaces be understood in isolation from the places where these things are done', including work, home, streets, schools and universities'

(Orsi, 2003, p. 172). Seeing religion as lived, rather than simply as a set of beliefs, undermines binaries of public/private, secular/sacred. Students' religious identities are not separate from their experience of university. Although some have argued that these remain in the background during this time (see Uecker et al., 2007), students' religious identities are not simply left at home, but shape the context and lived experience of universities, even when the expression of religious identities changes in response to the university experience (Sharma and Guest, 2013). Because universities cater to a geographically transient student population, they are sites of intersection and encounter, meeting points where the local and global converge and the material and symbolic can take on new meanings. Religion at universities is affected by broader social and political influences, while also being 'situated amid the ordinary concerns of life, at the junctures of self and culture, family and social world' (Orsi, 2003, p. 172).

This chapter has sought to chart the institutional plurality of England's universities with respect to their accommodation of Christianity and Christian students. It has proposed a fivefold typology of English universities based on history, institutional ethos, student demographics and geographical locale. All of these factors are important in framing how Christian students react to university life, but they generate an understanding of institutional cultures and geographies that is driven by structures and resources, largely determined by provision offered by universities. Student culture is a different matter altogether, and the life of undergraduate students, while contextualized by these structures, also reflects a degree of agency and opportunity that allows for dominant ideas and norms to be challenged and reconfigured, as well as embodied and internalized. The following chapters focus on the perspectives of Christian students themselves, exploring how they respond to their experience of university.

Notes

1 Postgraduate as well as undergraduate students are included in these figures as the purpose here is to paint a general picture of the culture fostered within each university type, including the crucial part played by its entire student body. The only exception is the figures for state school entrants, which are generated from HESA's available data provided by new first year undergraduate students.

2 This typology does not quite capture all of England's universities. A clear exception to all categories is The Open University, established in 1969 and distinguished by its open access policy (students on almost all courses are admitted without their former education taken into account). With over 250,000 students, the OU is the largest higher education institution in the United Kingdom, although its high number of distance (including overseas-based) learners means it fosters a very different kind of student experience to the rest of the sector. As such, it is not included in our analysis.

3   By size of student body, our five case studies vary considerably, as does the sector as a whole. According to 2010–11 figures, Durham had a total (both undergraduate and postgraduate) of 16,355 students; Leeds had 32,435, Kent 18,950, Derby 17,600 and Chester 15,400. These are all significantly close to the mean average size of university within each of their five types, with the exception of Leeds (the average size for red bricks is 24,760) and Chester (the average size for Cathedrals Group universities is 7,652) (figures extracted from HESA tables).

4   *Durham University: Facts and Figures* retrieved at www.dur.ac.uk/about/facts (accessed 22/4/13).

5   Unless otherwise stated, all demographic statistics for universities are drawn from tables published by the Higher Education Statistics Agency and refer to the 2010–11 academic year.

6   The neighbouring St Chad's College was also originally established for training Anglican clergy. While it no longer offers this, a Christian ethos remains, owing in part to the fact that this college, like St John's, is also officially independent of the university.

7   www.leeds.ac.uk/info/20016/campus_life/100/clubs_and_societies (accessed 21/8/11).

8   www.leeds.ac.uk/chaplaincy/events/worship/Student%20Guide%20to%20 Churches%202011.pdf (accessed 21/8/11).

9   Figures made available by Revd. Matt Ward, Anglican chaplain.

10 www.kent.ac.uk/european/index.html (accessed 31/8/11).

11 www.derby.ac.uk/statistics/student-statistics (accessed 8/1/13); 'University of Derby – Religious Preference 2010–11' (document supplied by University of Derby).

12 The CU was initially concerned that it would lead people to 'false gods', while the Islamic Society objected to the funding it had received from the Millennium Commission, which had in turn received funding from the National Lottery (Weller, 2008, pp. 139, 144–7).

13 University of Derby – Religious Preference 2010/11 (Excel Spreadsheet). Figures supplied by University of Derby. 15,310 students were questioned.

14 www.chester.ac.uk/about/the-university/our-mission-values (accessed 26/8/11).

15 Information provided by the University of Chester.

16 Of 1,106 students, the full figures are: Christian Church of England: 374 (33.8%), Christian Roman Catholic: 139 (12.6%), Christian (other): 72 (6.5%), Other Faith: 32 (2.9%), No religion: 422 (38.2%), Declined: 67 (6.1%) (internal document, made available to Rob Warner).

17 That is both mature and younger students, undergraduate and postgraduate, full and part-time.

18 Interestingly, according to the Roman Catholic chaplain, this change of direction occurred in response to pastoral needs among the student body following a car accident. The chaplaincy team were then depended upon to provide support and counsel to vulnerable or distressed students.

19 This is the title given to the chaplain in charge at the University of Chester.

4

Is the university a force for secularization?

Introduction

Writing in 1992, historian David Bebbington argued that throughout the course of the twentieth century, British universities have become increasingly secularized, chiefly on account of broader social trends rather than as a result of conscious intervention by the state. He contrasts this with the mid-nineteenth century, when Christianity was an 'integral part' of universities in Britain: the training of Anglican clergy was central to their purpose, students were required to take theological tests prior to admission and the universities were regarded as 'branches of the established churches of England and Scotland' (Bebbington, 1992, p. 259). Since then, massive expansion of the Higher Education sector – numerically, demographically and in terms of curricula – has been accompanied by an increasing institutional detachment from matters of religion that mirrors social changes in the nation at large. The reader might be forgiven for thinking that, nowadays, while universities like Canterbury Christ Church and York St John incorporate a Christian ethos that reflects their names, many other institutions retain at best a perfunctory inclusion of Christian concerns. Renewed attempts by universities to accommodate the needs of religious students (see the previous chapter) point to a more widespread and deliberate engagement, especially after the Equality Act of 2010. However, these may be interpreted cynically as an attempt to fend off government interference and preserve a positive public image, or as a tokenistic extension of reforms intended to enfranchise minority groups, whether defined by ethnicity, disability, sexuality or religion. More explicitly secularist perspectives are also in evidence. While not represented among our own case studies, some universities maintain an orientation characterized by Dinham and Jones as 'hard neutrality', seeking to 'protect public space from religious faith' as an unwelcome intrusion into a secular context (2010, p. 17). However, even when managers and institutional structures press a distinctly secular agenda, it would be a mistake to assume a straightforward correlation with the culture of students.

Relating the current state of England's universities to contemporary cultural trends inevitably raises the issue of secularization. The current chapter revisits some of this debate's major aspects in light of our findings on Christian students, asking whether universities in England can be understood as forces that advance the secularization process. To be sure, in so far as they mirror wider cultural developments – not least increasing cultural pluralism, social differentiation and the elevation of individual over collective achievement – it would be naïve to assume universities do not play *some* role in secularizing successive generations, but their *specific* impact remains unclear. Moreover, as we argued in the previous chapter, it is not our view that universities and their educational influence can be understood in singular terms – even within the same national context – not least because of the complexity of the relationship between the institution and the culture fostered within it. Hence the later section in this chapter examines how different types of university provide evidence of differential patterns of secularization, reflecting their institutional character and context.

The debate as it stands

Universities have often been conceived as institutions that magnify secularizing forces evident in broader social contexts (Bell, 1974; Berger, 1999, p. 10; Hilliard, 2010, pp. 79–82). In particular, higher education has been associated with the advancement of secular rationality, although other dimensions to secularization are equally, if not more, salient. Universities' tendency to foster social mobility can be viewed as a fast-track to heightened individualism, and the often diverse cultures of campus life constitute an accelerated exposure to cultural and religious pluralism. Of course, these are sweeping generalizations and depend in large part on a Western European model of higher education, just as, as some have argued, dominant secularization paradigms have depended upon a Western European understanding of modernity (Davie, 2002; Warner, 1993). Studies emerging from the United States and Canada have presented a more complex picture, with universities characterized variously as liberalizing students' religious identities (Hunter, 1987), generating conditions that allow intensification of religious interests (Bramadat, 2000; Ivan, 2012; Lee, 2002), and presenting a life experience in which religious matters are temporarily relegated while other life concerns are prioritized (Clydesdale, 2007). This body of research helps us to question critically the theoretical assumptions that often underpin understandings of how universities shape religion, and in so doing assists in the clarification of research questions. However, this extensive scholarship has for the most part emerged from the United States, and the extent to which its insights might apply to the United Kingdom remains unexplored.

Sociologist Grace Davie has argued for European exceptionalism; the condition of religion in Europe is consequent upon specific and local factors in the interaction between religion and society, rather than serving as the template for a global religionless future (Davie, 2002). In calling for explanations that pay greater attention to historically and culturally contingent factors she commands broad support (e.g. Brown, 2009; Martin, 2005; McLeod, 2007); however, emerging arguments remain understandably shaped by theoretical assumptions about the nature of modernity, and as such rest on several key ideas that bridge regional boundaries. For example, interpreting a public world shaped by rationalization and bureaucracy, Max Weber argued that modern Europeans inhabited an 'iron cage', from which the spiritual or religious was largely excluded (Gerth and Wright Mills, 2009). Considering the increasing bureaucratization and centralized regulation of UK universities described in Chapter 1, we might expect higher education to share in the secularizing trajectories of industry, the civil service and national health provision. Religion – once central to so many aspects of public life – becomes increasingly marginalized as it loses its functions to secular providers. Indeed, according to Weber, it was not only public life and the world of work that functioned within a religionless 'iron cage', but also the university (Weber ET 1948, new edition 1991). He considered the university a necessarily agnostic environment. Religion was an important subject for academic study and a primary arena of sociocultural expression and value formation. However, he considered religious consolation to be outside the university's remit. Universities today remain in the business of generating and conveying knowledge, but this is knowledge that is often so governed by post-Enlightenment science that it has increasingly marginalized or de-legitimized notions of religious truth, especially within research-intensive universities. Hence the well-established Western tendency to conceive of education as something *in tension with* religion, reflecting US sociologist Daniel Bell's influential characterization of the 'knowledge class' as a cohesive group who are necessarily antagonistic towards religious concerns (Bell, 1974). While some European universities today reflect a more subtle approach to religious matters, many operate within a hermeneutic of suspicion and a methodological agnosticism: hence the anxiety among some pious parents that university may necessarily be corrosive of faith, above all in departments of critical Theology.

Steve Bruce (1996, 2002, 2003, 2011) has built upon Weber's approach to argue that the decline of Christianity in Western Europe is not driven by a crisis of truth, but rather by a growing indifference to religion in all its forms. Religion has shifted from being a universal quest for ultimate reality to a devout pastime for the minority who still find religion relevant. From Bruce's perspective, God is coming to be seen as a social construct that faces cultural obsolescence, and for those who embrace it, an increasingly privatized phenomenon. The secularizing power of modernization is a theme that pervades Bruce's work, and its theoretical genesis can be detected in his early research into the changing status of the Student Christian Movement (SCM) and Intervarsity Fellowship (IVF, now the Universities and Colleges Christian Fellowship, or UCCF) (Bruce, 1980), cases studies addressed in detail in Chapter 6.

For Peter Berger, the key contributor to the decline of religion in Western Europe was the rise of pluralism: religious choice, particularly among the proliferating sects of Protestantism, fractured and destroyed the sacred canopy of Medieval Europe (Berger, 1967). Berger described the former givenness and pervasiveness of religion, when everything in public and private life was conducted with reference to the authority of the Church and under the inescapable gaze of the Eternal Judge of all. With the death of Christendom, the sacred canopy was shattered and the innate cultural plausibility of religion began to erode. Berger later recanted of these conclusions, arguing that the international evidence demonstrates the enduring resilience of religion in the context of globalized modernities and religious pluralism (Berger, 1999). Other sociologists have presented evidence at a more localized level that lends weight to Berger's revised thesis, such as Christian Smith, who associates the vitality of US Evangelicalism with contexts that foster conflict and tension; it is strong 'not because it is shielded against, but because it is – or at least perceives itself to be – embattled with forces that seem to oppose or threaten it' (Smith, 1998, p. 89). Universities often present a culture of interconnected experiences characterized by a heightened cultural pluralism that some students are unlikely to encounter beyond campus life. The increasing internationalization of UK universities – in terms of staff and students – suggests this tendency will intensify with time. The question this raises is whether on-campus pluralism undermines student religion or enables vitality or even growth.

Pluralism is often associated with the appeal of choice, of choosing one's religion rather than having it endowed, attributed or inheriting it from one's family or community. Davie (2007) has, in recent years, proposed that Western European religion is now typically vicarious in form; the established and official churches are treated like a public utility, available at the point of need, but otherwise most people are content to let someone else get on with keeping religion going. This builds on her previous notion of 'believing without belonging' in proposing a residual grassroots sympathy with inherited religious traditions, alongside a general disinclination to get personally involved, at least not on a regular basis. There is certainly good evidence supporting this contention in Britain, not least the high levels of Christian identification but much lower levels of regular church involvement (Guest et al., 2012). However, things may be changing with succeeding generations. Davie observes that young European adults now show signs of being less inclined to atheism than their parents, and increasingly open to diverse religious beliefs and practices. She concludes that while the model of 'religion of birth' remains popular in Britain, and indeed is often dominant in rural areas, the cities are increasingly characterized by an orientation to religion based on choice (Davie, 2007).

This shift in the primary loci of contemporary expressions of religion has profound implications. Measuring the demise of increasingly obsolete public forms of religion – the Sunday service and sermon – should not be conflated with the question of whether the religious impulse itself can be shown to be dying. If there is sufficient evidence of religious resilience in diverse expressions of personal and small group spirituality, counting Sunday attendance as a definitive measure of contemporary religiosity will miss the point: religion may have gone underground and be evolving in hidden ways, despite the continued decay of religious institutions. In light of these developments, we might ask: do Christian undergraduates tend to privilege subjectivized religion rather than the doctrine and teachings of the Church? Do they describe their personal faith in 'born again' terms, or is there more emphasis on continuity and sharing their parents' faith? Is there evidence for durable religious identities that continue to find expression in personal spirituality, even when congregational involvement is infrequent? If there is a shift in religious orientation at university, it may not simply be characterized by deconversion or disengagement, but by a reconfiguration of identity along more subjectivized and relational lines. Collins-Mayo et al. (2010) describe the religious orientations of Generation Y (those born from 1982 onwards) in these terms, suggesting the faith of these young people is not, typically, in religion as such, but in having happy and fulfilling relationships with friends and family (2010, p. 19). If Christian students combine this relational emphasis with a positive orientation to Christian ideas, beliefs or traditions, then we might expect students exposed to such a generational culture at university (intensified by numbers and proximity) would emerge more profoundly socialized into it. An emerging question would be whether Christian students embody a primarily relational faith – grounded first and foremost in relationships – or a faith more akin to an atomized individualism. With economically straightened times, increase in the cost of a UK degree and consequent increase in the number of students working part-time alongside study, we might expect a growing utilitarian individualism among students. As students become more selective and more pragmatic in their priorities, individualistic rather than community-based religion may seem the most resonant and practically expedient mode of engagement.

Just how we can demonstrate that Christian students reflect or challenge the arguments that emerge from the literature on secularization will of course be determined by the evidence we have available, and one continuing challenge is isolating 'university experience' as an independent variable. As we discussed in the previous chapter, university does not lend itself to a singular analysis, and yet it appears to function along the lines of institutional cultures rather than be amendable to the disaggregation of salient variables such as degree subject or classroom exposure to new ideas. It is in light of this discussion that we spend the latter section of the chapter examining how different patterns of religious change may be discerned within each of our five university types: the traditional/elite universities, inner-city red-bricks, 1960s campus universities, post-1992 universities and members of the Cathedrals Group. The latter also allows us to explore how distinctive are universities that affirm an explicitly Christian ethos. Before that, we explore the evidence relevant to the questions of secularization and subjectivization across universities in England.

Self-reported change

In a project such as this, which has a single phase of data collection, longitudinal comparisons are, strictly speaking, impossible. However, we can get a sense of how students' orientations to Christianity have changed since they arrived at university by asking them about their lives before they were students, and inviting them to compare this to the present. This method depends on self-reporting, which can be notoriously unreliable, especially when religious issues are concerned, as individuals may feel pressured to overstate their religious observance in order to fulfil expectations others may have of them (cf. Hadaway, Marler and Chaves, 1998). However, in this case, questionnaires were completed privately and anonymously, and respondents were contacted by email and were not recruited from within particular church communities, hence going some way towards minimizing this possibility. We asked our survey respondents whether they felt they had become more religious since being at university, less religious since being at university or whether their perspective was more or less the same as it was before. As can be seen in Table 4.1, a large majority reported no change, that is they had a perception of stability with respect to their religious identity since starting university. It seems the notion of university as a hive of Evangelical or new atheist conversions is without foundation. In fact, of all the Christian students who completed our survey, only 2.5% said they had an experience during their university career when they had made a decision to follow or abandon religion.[1] Dramatic changes in either direction are rare indeed.

TABLE 4.1 Proportion of students who say that, since starting university, they have become more religious, less religious or say their perspective has generally stayed the same (P = <.001) (All students: N = 3,936; Christian students: N = 2,060)[2]

	Less religious		Perspective stayed the same		More religious	
	All students (%)	Christian students (%)	All students (%)	Christian students (%)	All students (%)	Christian students (%)
First years	6.8	8.9	84.0	80.5	9.2	10.7
Second years	13.7	14.1	74.9	70.0	11.4	15.9
Third years	14.2	12.5	73.1	68.4	12.8	19.1
Total	11.4	11.9	77.6	73.2	11.0	15.0

But what about change over time? While we do not have figures for how students might have responded to the same question before and after their university career, we can break down responses to this question by year of study, and hence investigate whether those students who have spent longer at university have a different perspective. As we asked this question of all students responding to our survey, we can also show how different Christian students are from the overall pattern. The results are given in Table 4.1.

Several observations are worthy of note. First, for all cohorts, a significant majority are claiming stability; self-identifying as a Christian does not challenge that trend, regardless of a student's year of study. Students as a whole include a higher percentage of individuals claiming stability than do Christian students, with Christians about 5 percentage points more likely to have their identity change in one direction or the other since embarking on their university education. Second, in terms of their overall perspective, Christians become increasingly unlike the general student population as their university career progresses. Time and experience erode the large proportion claiming a stable religious perspective. Third, this change is most striking among those who consider their religious identity to have become *stronger* since starting university. Between years 1 and 3, Christian students claiming religious decline rise in proportional terms by 7.4 percentage points; those claiming religious intensification rise by 8.4 percentage points. This is not a massive difference, but it does seem to rule out any overwhelming secularization among Christian students, at least as far as their own perception of their lives is concerned. Interestingly, the pattern for all students moves in the opposite direction: those becoming less religious increases by 7.4 percentage points, those becoming more religious by just 3.6 percentage points. Self-reported identity change therefore paints a picture overwhelmingly characterized by stability; divergent patterns at the fringes suggest that, overall, the experience of university secularizes students, but that those identifying as Christian are slightly more likely to cite religious growth. Of course, our survey does not pick up students who have abandoned their Christian identity during university but before completing the survey. In theory, those most dramatically secularized by university could be invisible to us, owing to the fact that they would not, by definition, affirm their identity as 'Christian' any longer. However, the qualitative evidence we have gathered from interviews with staff and students does not support this, and if changes in religious identity occur at university, all of the evidence points to them being, for the most part, gradual rather than dramatic.

Patterns of church attendance and denominational affiliation

The most common evidence cited within the secularization debate relates to involvement in religious institutions – in the Christian context, frequency of church attendance. This is especially revealing in our own data when correlated with denominational identities. In order to allow for a useful analysis, we have reduced the long list of denominational options that appeared on our questionnaire to five main categories. Anglican and Roman Catholic are self-explanatory, and deserve their own categories given the large proportions of Christian students aligning themselves with these traditions. 'Historic Protestant' refers to all of the traditional non-conformist Protestant denominations, which each claim a relatively small portion of the Christian population in the United Kingdom, including Baptists, Methodists and the United Reformed Church, but also the Presbyterian Church of Scotland.[3] The fourth category comprises all independent Evangelical churches, 'new churches' and Pentecostal churches, capturing all forms of church that can be described as unquestionably Evangelical in their theology. A final, 'other' category captures churches that do not comfortably fit into any of the above, including the Orthodox churches, which constitute a small but distinct sub-population of Christians within the UK context.[4]

Respondents self-identifying as 'Christian' were asked if they had attended church prior to university. Just over 70% said they had, while the remainder had not. We then asked those who had said yes about the denomination they had spent the longest time attending, following this up with a separate question of 'what church denomination do you attend while at university?' Comparing the two sets of answers allows us to form an initial picture of patterns of churchgoing and how they change among Christian students once they are established within the university context (see Table 4.2).

Among self-identifying Christians, the general pattern is of church attendance dropping off once at university, with each denomination achieving much lower levels of engagement in the second column than in the first (the proportion attending Roman Catholic and Historic Protestant churches more than halves in each case, while the Anglican proportion drops by almost 5 percentage points). The only notable exceptions to this pattern are the Evangelical/Pentecostal churches, which increase their proportionate share of the student churchgoing market by almost 2 percentage points.[5] In other words, it is only the denominational groups that are *definitively Evangelical* in their theology that appear to attract a higher proportion of students during term-time than they did among this same group of students before they started university. The pattern is even more striking once we exclude the non-attendees. The proportion of Evangelical/Pentecostal attendees then increases from 15.4% pre-university to 27.4% during term-time, the exact same term-time proportion as Anglican attendees (with Roman Catholics down from 29.3% to 21.4% and Historic Protestants down from 19.9% to 12.9%). Hence the market share for Anglicans and Evangelical/Pentecostals increases significantly, with

TABLE 4.2 Church attendance by denomination both before and during university among undergraduates self-identifying as Christian (weighted)

Denominational category	Church attendance pre-university (%)	Church attendance during university (%)
Anglican	17.5	12.8 (– 4.7)
Roman Catholic	20.8	10.0 (– 10.8)
Historic Protestant	14.1	6.0 (– 8.1)
Evangelical/Pentecostal	10.9	12.8 (+ 1.9)
Other	7.6	5.1 (– 2.5)
None	29.2	53.3 (+ 24.1)

almost 55% of all term-time church attendance taking place in these kinds of churches, although the increase among the Evangelical/Pentecostal attendees is by far the most dramatic.[6] While this does not take into account the relative strength of Evangelical churches in the students' pre-university locations, the general pattern indicates that Evangelical/Pentecostal churches appear especially vibrant in university towns.

This trend is even more apparent if we assess patterns of church attendance at the level of the individual, that is by asking how individual students with different denominational backgrounds change their churchgoing behaviour once they start university. In general terms, of all self-identifying Christians who attended church before university, 45.3% continue to attend a church within the same denominational category at university, 15.5% switch to a different denominational category, while 39.2% opt out of churchgoing altogether. It is the Historic Protestant denominations that are least successful at retaining their attendees in proportional terms, with only 30.5% of students who attended one of these churches also attending one during term-time. As we are conflating several different denominations here, the actual percentage attending the exact same denomination as before university is almost certainly much lower still. What is especially noteworthy is that over 40% of all those attending Historic Protestant churches before university choose not to attend *any* church after they have arrived. By virtue of being a single identifiable grouping, the Anglicans may be said to have fared even worse, with 45.4% continuing to attend an Anglican church, and 44.6% attending none. The Roman Catholics retain 43.8% of pre-university attendees with 48.3% opting out of church altogether once they arrive at university, constituting the denomination with the largest dropout level at university. The Evangelical/Pentecostal group achieve far greater levels of consistency, with 69.3% of students attending such churches before university also attending the same kind of church when they get there, with only 13.9% dropping out of church altogether. The most consistent category, though, are the non-attendees, 87.7% of whom continue to stay away from church once they get to university. Few self-identifying Christians who come from an unchurched background, it would seem, are converted to *any* kind of churchgoing after they reach university.

This deserves further comment, as it evokes the common perception that university-based Christianity is most vibrant among Evangelicals (Dutton, 2008; Guest et al., 2013). Our evidence suggests that Evangelical churches – emphasizing the authority of the Bible, a conversion-based model of faith, and prioritizing evangelism and mission – are most successful at *retaining* (although not necessarily *recruiting*) active members within the university context. They also constitute a significant voice among Christian students. However, their significance rests on their resources – supported by the national networks of UCCF – and social capital, *not* on a dominant share in the Christian student population. Measured by term-time involvement in Evangelical/Pentecostal churches, Evangelicals make up 12.8% of self-identifying Christian students; add to this those Evangelicals attending Anglican and Historic Protestant churches,[7] and we still only achieve a total of around 20%. We asked a sub-section of our questionnaire respondents whether they would self-identify as Catholic, Mainstream Protestant, Evangelical or Pentecostal, allowing them to choose as many options as they liked or none. Those who selected 'Evangelical', 'Pentecostal' or both amounted to 24.6% of the total. Therefore, by the most generous measure, Evangelicals make up less than a quarter of Christian students, while at the same time undoubtedly speaking with the loudest, and clearest, voices. In Chapter 6, we return to this issue in examining the theological and social profile of those students involved in Christian Unions, in order to assess whether those involved in Evangelical associations sustain a particularly active faith life.

Aside from denominational factors, there are interesting patterns to be found by examining students' frequency of church attendance in different contexts. For example, turning back to the figures in Table 4.2, the largest change relates to the non-attendees, with the 29.2% of Christians claiming they did not attend church prior to university increasing to 53.3% during university term-time. In other words, *over half of self-identifying Christian students do not attend church during university term-time.* Something about university disinclines students from retaining their pre-university pattern of church attendance. At first sight, this may appear solid evidence for the secularizing influence of going to university; however, closer inspection of the evidence reveals a more complex picture. Interesting comparisons emerge in relation to the *frequency* of church attendance during *term* and *vacation* times respectively (i.e. when students are at university, and when they are staying at home away from university life). 32.6% of Christian undergraduates claim they 'never' attend church during vacations, while over 50% claim they never attend during term-time. The full figures are given in Table 4.3, and suggest not a complete and inexorable cessation of pre-university churchgoing habits, but the development of two different levels of engagement: one for term-time, one for vacations. Many students appear to maintain different churchgoing habits depending on whether they are at university or home for the holidays.

Frequent attendance (defined as once a week or more) is more common during vacations, and occasional attendance markedly so, the latter perhaps suggesting attendance at rites of passage or family gatherings. The intermediate options of once a fortnight and once a month appear to be relatively unaffected by the transition between university and home. Of course, we do not know how durable home-based habits of churchgoing are,

TABLE 4.3 Frequency of church attendance both during term-time and during university vacations among undergraduates self-identifying as Christian[8]

Frequency	Church attendance during term-time (%)	Church attendance during vacations (%)
More than once a week	10.9	9.6
Once a week	17.9	25.2
Once a fortnight	3.4	4.8
Once a month	2.7	3.2
Occasionally	14.6	24.6
Never	50.5	32.6

and evidence of differential levels of church engagement between term-time and vacations may indicate not an enduring underlying Christianity muted or set aside during university terms, but levels of family pressure that encourage church attendance out of obligation during the holidays, an obligation only abandoned or modified when the student has the free choice to do so, i.e. when not under the watchful eye of their parents. In adjudicating between these two interpretations, we might refer to the case of mature Christian students (aged 25+), whose relative independence from parental constraint will presumably reveal a more freely chosen set of churchgoing habits. Our figures for such students reveal levels of frequent (i.e. weekly or more) churchgoing during vacations and during term-time that are much closer together (31 and 30% respectively) than they are among younger students (35.8 and 28.5%). Hence the geographically and socially significant transition between term-time and vacation residences may well inflate churchgoing levels in a way that will not be sustained in the longer term, although the evidence is far from conclusive.

A more illuminating picture emerges if we return to our fivefold typology of Christian students outlined in Chapter 2. Just over a quarter of Christian students (25.2%) fall into the *lapsed engagers* and *emerging nominals* categories, and hence show indisputable signs of disengagement from church during university term-time. We could take this as evidence of a 25% erosion rate supportive of university as a secularizing influence; however, this would be stretching the evidence, especially given that over a third of these students maintain frequent churchgoing during university vacations. Their disengagement may have more to do with the specific circumstances of their university, rather than an emerging disinclination towards church in general. However we relate this evidence to secularization generally, the precise constituency of those adopting each of our five orientations to church involvement sheds considerable light on the dominant contours of change *within* the Christian student population. It is worth noting some striking correlations with pre-university denominational identity, which we can take as a useful benchmark against which to measure change at university. The full set of figures can be found in Table 4.4, which details the patterns of change in churchgoing practice among students associated with different denominational categories. First, 28.5% of *active affirmers* went to an Evangelical/Pentecostal church before coming to university. Anglicans, Roman Catholics and those who attended Historic Protestant churches each claim just below 20% of this group also. However, the high figure for the Evangelicals is even more striking than it might first appear; examined the other way around, as a proportion of each denominational group, we find that over 70% of students who attended an Evangelical/Pentecostal church fall into the *active affirmers* category, making it by far the most likely denominational grouping to produce students who continue in their committed churchgoing after they reach university. Second, the largest group among the *lapsed engagers, established occasionals* and *emerging nominals* is the Roman Catholics. Only 22.5% of Roman Catholic students are consistently frequent attendees. The reasons for this are likely to be complex, drawing in factors of on-campus provision or the lack of it, a more entrenched norm of occasional attendance among self-identifying Catholics, and the potentially alienating dual Protestant hegemony of lively Evangelical churches and well-resourced Anglican chaplaincies, which shape the public image of university-based Christianity. It could also be attributed to a higher measure of 'birth Catholics' who are non-practising, compared to nominal Protestants, the former typified by a stronger set of ethnic, cultural and familial reasons to retain a Christian self-ascription. Whatever the reason, it is worth noting that in general terms, among those associated with a specific denominational grouping, it is Roman Catholic students who seem most disengaged from regular church attendance at university. Third, 75% of those who did not attend church before coming to university are also consistent non-attendees once they get there, adding further substance to the picture of the *unchurched Christians* as a clearly defined sub-group. Those disengaged from church are, for the most part, consistent in their complete withdrawal from organized Christian gatherings.

We have not discussed students who become *more religious* at university, and this is because, while there is a small contingent claiming to have become more religious, the evidence in practical terms implies an even smaller proportion. The number of Christian students engaging in *more*

TABLE 4.4 General church attendance profile among Christian students cross-tabulated with the denomination attended before coming to university (P = <0.001; Cramer's V = .344) (weighted)

General church attendance profile		Pre-university denomination						
		Anglican (%)	Roman Catholic (%)	Historic Protestant (%)	Evangelical/ Pentecostal (%)	Other (%)	None (%)	Total (%)
Active affirmers	% within general church attendance profile	19.6	17.5	20.9	28.5	10.7	2.8	100
	% within pre-university denomination	30.9	22.5	39.3	70.2	37.3	2.6	27
Lapsed engagers	% within general church attendance profile	20.1	36.2	18.1	16.1	7.0	2.5	100
	% within pre-university denomination	10.9	16.0	11.7	13.6	8.4	0.8	9.3
Established occasionals	% within general church attendance profile	24.4	27.7	17.4	7.1	9.6	13.8	100
	% within pre-university denomination	20.8	19.2	17.5	9.4	18.1	7.0	14.5

Emerging nominals	% within general church attendance profile	21.3	30.9	13.5	1.7	8.3	24.3	100
	% within pre-university denomination	21	24.9	15.9	2.6	18.1	14.3	16.9
Unchurched Christians	% within general church attendance profile	8.7	11.3	7.0	1.4	4.3	67.2	100
	% within pre-university denomination	16.4	17.4	15.6	4.3	18.1	75.3	32.2
Total	% within general church attendance profile	17.1	21.0	14.4	11.0	7.8	28.8	100
	% within pre-university denomination	100	100	100	100	100	100	100 (N = 2,140)

frequent churchgoing at university than they do during vacations amounts to less than 5% of all Christians. These 90 respondents represent what we might call the 'intensified Christians', that is self-identifying Christians whose churchgoing habits are reported to increase during term-time when compared to university vacations. Fifty-four individuals (or 2.4% of Christian students) claim in vacations, their church attendance is infrequent whereas in term-time it is frequent; 27 individuals (1.2%) claim they never attend church during vacations but attend infrequently during term-time; and 9 individuals (0.4%) claim that during vacations they never go to church but during term-time they attend frequently. Demographically, there is little to distinguish this sub-group from our overall population of Christian respondents. In terms of their Christian lives, more of this group claim a dramatic conversion experience, and far more say they have become more religious since university (44% compared to 14.7% of all Christian students), neither of which are surprising. A newly found religious enthusiasm is also reflected in higher levels of assent to orthodox understandings of God and Jesus, and higher numbers engaged in frequent prayer and Bible study. A higher proportion of the intensified Christians have recently done religious volunteering, and twice as many engage in university-based organized Christian activity (including Evangelical staples like the Alpha course and Bible studies, but also university chaplaincy events), reflecting more enthusiastic levels of church involvement. Almost half (44.8%) attend an Anglican church during term-time (compared to 12.8% of the overall sample), reflecting the major role Anglican churches play among the student Christian population within university towns. The intensified Christians also include a disproportionately high number attending traditional/elite and inner-city red-brick-universities, the former category making up over 40% of this sub-group (compared to only 18.7% of all Christian students). Broken down by individual university, these students are almost all studying at the universities of Cambridge and Durham, suggesting an institutionally intensified faith may be connected to the expanded opportunities for Christian activity at collegial universities. This last point will be explored in greater detail later in this chapter.

In summary, Christian students include a larger proportion of active, institutionally committed individuals than the Christian population in the broader national context. The proportion of self-identifying Christians who attend church on a weekly basis in England is roughly 10%;[9] the proportion of Christian students who attend weekly or more is around 30% (28.8% during term-time, 34.8% during vacations, 25.9% maintaining weekly attendance within *both* contexts). Pockets of term-time vitality appear closely associated with on-campus Evangelical organizations and Anglican (most likely Anglican Evangelical) churches, phenomena explored in more detail in Chapter 6. At the same time, a quarter of Christian students withdraw from previous churchgoing habits once at university, including an approximately 40% share of those with backgrounds in Anglican, Roman Catholic and non-conformist churches. Of course, we do not know whether this withdrawal will be enduring, although the analysis based on age groups cited above suggests this scenario is more likely than a significant resurgence post-university. Taking these figures together, we find a net positive vitality among university-based Christians, that is, there appear more Christians active in their faith than disengaging from it. Future research will need to explore whether these parallel patterns endure or take a different course in the years following their university career.

Testing the subjectivization thesis

Beyond measures of church involvement, the secularization debate has evolved to include consideration of the emergence of particular forms of religion out of the late modern context. Scholars who take issue with a hard-line secularization thesis have interpreted the associated rise of individualism not as a symptom of religious decline but of a transformation of religion into a more subjectivized form. Citing Joseph Tamney's work on congregations in the United States, Heelas and Woodhead point to the Durkheimian foundation of the subjectivization thesis, that 'people are more likely to be involved with forms of the sacred which are "consistent with their on-going values and beliefs". . .' (2005, p. 78). Given the recent well documented 'subjective turn' in Western societies (Bellah et al., 1996; Taylor, 1992, 2002, 2007) – distinguished by an emphasis upon the interior, experiential, subjective dimensions of life – we may well expect the religious movements most resilient to secularization to affirm these aspects over (or at least alongside) more traditional authorities and sources of meaning. Indeed, this is the thrust of the argument in Heelas and Woodhead's influential book *The Spiritual Revolution* (2005), backed up with evidence of a growing holistic milieu and a congregational domain whose most vibrant communities affirm the centrality of personal experience *and* holy scripture, most obviously charismatic Evangelical churches. As argued in Chapter 2, the Christian students who took part in our study exhibited *some* evidence of embodying a subjectivized form of Christianity, not least in their tendency to attach importance to personal experience and relationships in their religious lives and in their suspicion towards conversionist evangelism, specifically the right of people to preach authoritative and definitive truth to those who have a different perspective. In this section we will press this evidence a little further, in order to ascertain in more precise terms the extent to which the subjectivization thesis can be applied to Christian students.

One repeatedly referenced body of evidence is the increasing use of the term 'spiritual' over 'religion' in the self-descriptions of Westerners. This was incorporated into our survey, which found among all respondents (Christians and non-Christians), 'spiritual but not religious' was indeed a more popular self-ascription than 'religious' (30.8% compared to 24.9%). However, among those preferring to call themselves 'spiritual but not religious', less than a third (27.5%) distance themselves from organized religion by choosing the 'no religion' option in the following question on religious belonging. The 7.9% choosing 'other' are an eclectic group, but there are far more among them affirming some form of Christian commitment than any connection with alternative spiritualities.[10] In other words, 'spiritual' is not an unambiguous indicator of scepticism about or alienation from organized religion, but is a descriptor that may be – *and most often is* – embraced alongside a clear identification with one of the major world religions. Hence the sizeable number of Christian students (31.2%) who affirmed 'spiritual' rather than 'religious' as their preferred self-description. But what do they mean by this?

The answer is: probably lots of things. 'Spiritual' is commonly used by progressive-minded individuals wishing to distance themselves from traditional religion, but also by Bible-focused Christians wishing to distance themselves from religion as a human construct, and by others who see in the word 'spiritual' a means of capturing a vibrant relationship with God that surpasses what they see as 'empty ritual'. The label 'spiritual' in and of itself does not capture a clearly defined grouping, and this is reflected in our survey data. Christian students who favour this label over 'religious' cross the denominational boundaries in fairly even proportions, so we cannot even isolate this notion to the unchurched and the Evangelical/Pentecostals. Moreover, Christian students who say they are 'spiritual but not religious' are not markedly different from Christian students generally when measured by a wide range of identity markers. 'Spiritual Christians' are almost twice as likely to see God as an 'impersonal life-force' (15.6% rather than 8.5% of all Christian students) and significantly more likely to view Jesus as a human being with divine virtues (34.2% rather than 24.1%). However, they are actually less likely to be atheist or agnostic, and levels of personal prayer, Bible reading, volunteering, belief in a personal/3 in 1 God and belief that homosexual relations are 'always wrong', to take just a few examples, are remarkably similar in both populations. If 'spirituality' among Christian students highlights a distinctive turn to the subjective, then it is so for a relatively small population whose subjectivization is very partial and highly selective.

And yet there is strong evidence to suggest Christian students have been affected by the subjective turn in their orientations to moral issues, which reflect a cultural relativism that elevates personal sovereignty over external regulation. Survey data on two issues – homosexual relations and assisted dying – illustrate emerging patterns. A conservative perspective on homosexuality has come to be seen as a major identity marker among many Christians, the factor that marks them out as different from the liberal cultural consensus. This view is supported by our evidence to a degree, but needs careful qualification (see Table 4.5). Certainly when compared with students of 'no religion', Christian students are far more likely to say that homosexual sex is in some sense wrong (35.7% rather than 5.7%), and almost half as many say it is 'not wrong at all' than the 'nones'. However, taken together, those affirming 'not wrong at all', 'rarely wrong' and 'not sure' still make up a majority – 64.2% – of the Christians, suggesting a liberal tendency significantly more popular than the conservative position. The picture is complicated further when compared to national attitudinal data. The impression that then emerges is not of unusually conservative Christians, but of unusually liberal non-religious students, a trend partially attributable to generational differences. Figures from the British Social Attitudes Survey from 2010 have 19.9% stating 'always wrong' to the same question, with 43.6% saying 'not wrong at all'; broken down by age category, the older generations are more conservative, although a clustering around the 55% mark saying 'not wrong at all' distinguishes all age groups between 15 and 54. Furthermore, the BSA figures broken down by religion suggest Christian students are more liberal on this issue than Christians (of whatever stripe) generally, with the proportion of our surveyed Christians opting for 'not wrong at all' coming roughly midway between those of no religion in the general population and the average for all Christians in the general population. In sum, on this issue, Christian students appear slightly more conservative than the general population, slightly more conservative

TABLE 4.5 'What do you think about sexual relations between adults of the same sex?' comparing Christian students with those of 'no religion' (weighted)

	Christian students (N = 2,233) (%)	Students of 'no religion' (N = 1,474) (%)
Always wrong	25.1	2
Sometimes wrong	10.6	3.7
Rarely wrong	8.7	5.2
Not wrong at all	44.2	84.6
I am not sure	11.3	4.4

than their age group in the country at large, but more liberal than Christians generally. Non-religious students, by contrast, take a much more permissive view, with only 11% voicing any kind of objection; the vast majority view homosexual sex between adults as 'not wrong at all', distinguishing them as markedly more liberal than any age group within the general population.[11]

On assisted dying (Table 4.6), Christians are much more likely to take an opposing view than the 'nones'. However, far more – 50% – take an affirmative position, even if this is much lower than the 85% of the non-religious who do. Non-religious students reflect a more permissive attitude on this than the general population of Britain, although not radically so – the 2005 BSA survey included several questions on this issue, with the highest measure of approval around the 80% mark, but much lower measures for questions that propose euthanasia in the hands of patients or relatives, rather than a professional doctor, and measures of disapproval range much higher in percentage terms than the Christian students' responses here. This is also the ethical issue on which Christian students are most likely to express uncertainty, perhaps reflecting the live debate about this topic in British public life.

Christian students appear, on the whole, to be more conservative or traditionalist on a range of ethical issues than students of 'no religion'. However, they are not unified. Those who are most conservative appear radically at odds with the dominant attitudinal trends of their generation, but not with the general population of the country. Those who affirm more liberal positions are much closer to the liberal norm among non-religious students, although the non-religious appear generally more decisive; for example, on

TABLE 4.6 Responses among Christian students and students of 'no religion' to the question 'People who are terminally ill should be legally permitted to take their own lives if they choose to' (weighted)

	Christian students (N = 2,233) (%)	Students of 'no religion' (N = 1,475) (%)
Strongly disagree	11.8	1.2
Disagree	13.3	1.6
Agree	34.6	44.6
Strongly agree	14.9	39.8
I am not sure	25.5	12.8

homosexual practice, abortion and assisted dying, the Christians who are unsure what they think outnumber the unsure non-religious students 2:1.

Therefore, it is possible to identify a liberal, permissive tendency among Christian students that commands more support than conservative or traditionalist positions on moral issues. It seems that many students favour the rejection of traditional forms of morality shaped by religious authorities, and instead privilege respect for personal choice over moral absolutism. This reflects the subjectivizing tone evident in Christian students' attitudes towards evangelism, documented in Chapter 2; they affirm a strong resistance to associating Christian identity with an entitlement to speak authoritatively into the lives of those who have different perspectives or cultures. In this sense, the 'ethic of civility' that James Davison Hunter identified among US Evangelical students during the 1980s (Hunter, 1987) is discernible as a predominating influence shaping orientations to the Christian life among students at England's universities. For some this resembles a kind of tentative, polite relativism, prioritizing the maintenance of healthy relationships over any sense of definitive truth:

> Sometimes people will use Christianity as a sort of overarching way of getting across views that I don't necessarily agree with. I'm a bit hesitant with evangelism because, I don't know . . . I might be wrong for all I know. I'm not about to go and tell someone else, stop believing your way of approaching God and start believing in mine, even though we're probably most likely both of us wrong in the exact details. (Jessica, Durham)

Such reluctance to speak in the imperative is even apparent among active members of the Evangelical Christian Unions; asked what they would contribute to their university's 'mission week', one of our interviewees responded:

> . . . I don't know, bake cakes or give out cakes . . . I'm not actually sure of the general activities. I'm probably not going to take part because I don't always agree with evangelism which is the whole idea of it, so I'm very cautious with that sort of thing because I don't think anyone has a right to try and impose their faith on anyone else. (Martha, Chester)

While not expressed in the language of 'spirituality', among the majority of Christian students there is a tendency to speak about their faith in *subjective* and *relational* – rather than doctrinal – terms. Indeed, this shapes how they negotiate the challenges of the university experience, as we will explore in the following chapter.

Differential patterns across universities

While overall patterns suggest parallel processes of vitalization and withdrawal, alongside a tendency towards subjectivization, Christian students appear to fare differently within different types of university. The institutional variations charted in the previous chapter do seem to matter, at least in some cases they do. The survey results for self-reported change among Christian students are given in Table 4.7, broken down into each of our five university types.

The most striking pattern here is the overwhelming sense of stability in evidence across all five categories; for a clear majority of each, most Christians say their perspective on religion has stayed the same since they started university. Only a small minority claim they have become more or less religious, and for most categories these proportions are fairly similar – between 10 and 15% for each – although the overall pattern points in favour of an intensification, rather than a diminishment of religious identity. The only category that breaks with the dominant pattern is the traditional/elite universities, for whom a much lower proportion of Christians claim a stable transition, and much higher proportions claim to have become less religious *and* more religious (18.9% and 25.6% respectively). That both ends of the spectrum are heightened to a degree quite unlike all other categories suggests that traditional/elite universities generate a peculiarly unstable environment for Christian students, who appear more likely to become more religious, but also more likely to become less religious, when they study at universities like

TABLE 4.7 Christian students' perception of whether they have become more or less religious since being at university, cross-tabulated with university type (P = <0.001) (weighted)[12]

	Less religious (%)	Perspective has stayed the same (%)	More religious (%)
Traditional/elite	18.9	55.5	25.6
Inner-city red-brick	11.8	77.0	11.2
1960s campus	11.5	77.3	11.2
Post-1992	10.0	77.8	12.3
Cathedrals Group	7.4	76.3	16.3
Overall figure	11.9	73.1	15.1

Durham, Cambridge and University College, London. One response to this would be to cite the relatively high proportion of independent school entrants into traditional/elite universities as the key explanatory variable. With chapel attendance a core (often obligatory) aspect of school life in many private schools, one might expect that the freedoms of the university experience would trigger a more dramatic response among students with this kind of background than those from state schools in which religion is often marginal. Perhaps some discover at university a richer version of school chapel life that they willingly embrace, while others seize the opportunity to abandon a prior obligation. If this is the case, then the distinctive pattern at traditional/elite universities would have to do with their demographic profile rather than their institutional cultures. However, our evidence does not support this. Multiple regression analysis confirms that levels of church attendance both during vacations and during university term-time are only weakly related to prior schooling. Going to a traditional/elite university (rather than any other type) is a much stronger predictor of church attendance levels after controlling for prior schooling. Hence there is something peculiar about this category of university that seems to encourage unusually high levels of religious instability within the lives of Christian students.

A similar pattern is found when we compare types of university by levels of church attendance. Are our five types – the *active affirmers, lapsed engagers, established occasionals, emerging nominals* and *unchurched Christians* – evenly distributed across our five categories of university? Or are particular forms of Christian engagement disproportionately more prominent in certain kinds of university, suggesting a relationship between institutional type and Christian response? The distribution of each of our five types within each category of university is set out in Figure 4.1. In proportional terms, *active affirmers* – that is, Christians who attend church frequently both at home and during term-time – outnumber all of the other categories 2 to 1 within the traditional/elite universities. For the 1960s campus universities, the largest group is the unchurched, who make up 45.3% of self-identifying Christians, with *active affirmers* a much lower 20%. The unchurched also make up the largest group among Christians studying at inner-city red-bricks and the post-1992 universities, where numbers of *established occasionals* are also higher, especially in the latter. The Cathedrals Group presents a curious mix, with very high proportions of *active affirmers and unchurched Christians*, perhaps reflecting a high provision of Christian activities alongside their appeal to nominal Christians attracted to a kind of university associated with pastoral support, community building and moral responsibility.

If the proportions of *lapsed engagers* and *emerging nominals* are taken to be evidence of secularization (as self-reported disengagement from church following the start of the university career), then the most

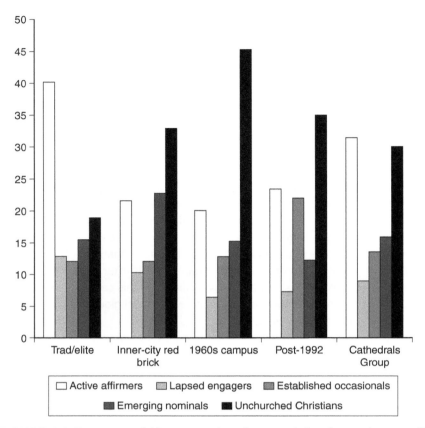

FIGURE 4.1 *Percentage of Christian students by general church attendance profile within each of the five university types.*

secularizing universities are the inner-city red-bricks, which may lend weight to a correlation between urban multiculturalism, religious pluralism and secularization, although the fact that the traditional/elite universities are only slightly behind them counts against this. Various other measures, taken from our survey data, allow us to add nuance to the emerging picture (see Table 4.8). For example, the affirmation of an atheist or agnostic Christianity (i.e. ticking Christian as their religion but also affirming they do not believe in or are unsure about God) is much higher among Christians at red-bricks than those at the traditional/elites, but it is highest overall among the 1960s campus students. Looking at the converse trends, measures of a vibrant Christian presence appear to place the traditional/elite universities ahead of all others by far, with far more saying they have become 'more religious' since university, and far more attending church frequently both during term-time and during university vacations. The proportion with three or

TABLE 4.8 Indicators of religious decline and religious intensification among Christian students at the five different types of university (weighted)

	Trad./ elite (%)	Red-brick (%)	1960s (%)	Post-1992 (%)	Cathedrals (%)	OVERALL (%)
% become 'less religious'	18.9	11.8	11.5	10.0	7.4	11.9
% of lapsed engagers/ emerging nominals	28.6	33.3	21.8	19.6	25.0	26.2
% of atheist or agnostic Christians	20.6	30.8	31.2	27.0	23.5	26.8
% become 'more religious'	25.6	11.2	11.2	12.3	16.3	15.1
% of 'active affirmers'	40.2	21.7	20.0	23.5	31.5	27.0
% with 3+ close Christian friends	39.8	37.6	47.4	43.9	45.0	42.2

more Christians among their five closest friends reveals a rather different pattern, with 1960s campus and post-1992 universities scoring highest. The possibility that this supports the argument that close-knit religious sub-groups emerge most within contexts where they are a beleaguered minority may be thrown into question by the almost equally high score for the Cathedrals Group universities, although of course these patterns may be emerging for quite different reasons in each university type. The full figures for comparison are provided in Table 4.8.

Conclusions

At the close of this chapter, we return to the opening question, 'Is the university a force for secularization?' From the point of view of Christian students, as we have seen, this is predominantly not the case. However, it is not difficult to see how university is a life stage that indirectly enhances and even accelerates many cultural processes of secularization. University is the first great social disruptor in the lives of most undergraduates, in which they are taken away from their childhood friends, schoolmates and family. Since the vast majority of Christian students have their faith identity in common with at least one parent, distance from the environment in which they were socialized into their faith represents a major shift. This alone would give cause for some students to drop out of churchgoing in term-time, as they step for the first time beyond the parental gaze.

Thrown onto their own resources, students are empowered to enact personal autonomy in every aspect of their university experience. This elevation of personal choice confirms existing cultural norms, but inscribes them upon the individual student's experience. This has a subjectivizing impact, legitimating the instilled cultural preference for personal judgement and the authority of personal experience, over the authority of the Church.

While this shift has not, according to the evidence we have collected, triggered a mass exodus from the churches, the differential patterns of church involvement on the part of a large minority suggests university provokes a significant unsettling of the faith lives of Christian students. To be sure, personal faith is not repudiated or scorned in the vast majority of university contexts, but it is taught to know its place within a wider context that is secularized and pluralistic, affirming the autonomy of the individual and the inappropriateness of intruding upon the opinions of others in all matters to do with religion, unless their opinions violate contemporary mores. Private spirituality may find a quiet space within the secularized university, but as the churches have grown weaker, the iron cage of rationality and bureaucracy has grown stronger. The university does not have to be assertively secular for its prevailing culture and bureaucratic processes to have a marginalizing impact on the significance of faith and the authority of religion. The student who enters university essentially indifferent to religion is unlikely to encounter significant opportunities to reappraise instinctive attitudes that are increasingly culturally normative.

However, as argued in the previous chapter, the university experience is not a singular phenomenon, and disaggregating our data by university type reveals some intriguing patterns worthy of further note, patterns that suggest that in some cases, the institutional variations charted in Chapter 3 foster quite distinctive cultures of Christian activity. First, the relative instability of Christian identities at traditional/elite universities compared to the other four types invites an interpretation centred on the public tone and visibility of Christianity at these institutions. As mentioned earlier, this is a particularly striking tendency at Durham and Cambridge, both collegial universities with multiple chaplains, active college chapel congregations, and both situated in small cities off the beaten track in which Christian symbolism is highly prominent, not least in the numerous local churches and historic architecture. Christianity features as part of the cultural background, and as such is difficult to escape. They are also both universities in which the Christian Union is numerically strong, well resourced and dogmatically Evangelical; Christianity as a student phenomenon is commonly associated with this particular brand of Christian faith and the churches and organizations that promote it. Qualitative evidence suggests this phenomenon plays a large part in both empowering *and disempowering* Christian students. As one Durham student commented:

> The predominating churches here are Evangelical, so, the ones you tend to see on the street are Evangelicals . . . handing out pamphlets, giving out teas, and standing outside of club nights and doing a lot of apostle-like work, but a lot of people find that can be a bit too much. So, generally, when I've had conversations of faith with people it's because I've been trying to clarify their anger with what they see to be Christianity.

The significance of Christian Unions is discussed in much more detail in Chapter 6; for now it is worth noting that the Evangelicalism they often represent functions within the public culture of places like Durham and Cambridge as a destabilizing influence on Christian students generally, triggering enthusiastic activism and disillusioned withdrawal in apparently equal measure.

A different picture emerges of the Cathedrals Group universities, which are the closest we have in the United Kingdom to the determinedly Christian universities of North America (Riley, 2005). While not applying religious criteria of admission or the more closely policed community rules characteristic of the latter, the Cathedrals Group institutions nevertheless manage to communicate a religio-moral ethos that is commonly recognized and welcomed by staff and students alike. As such we might consider whether these universities function as 'moral communities', effectively fostering the Christian identities of students by providing a cohesive environment in which those identities are publicly affirmed. The 'moral communities' thesis is that the religious lives of individuals are sustained within contexts that legitimate associated language, motives and behavioural norms (Hill, 2009, p. 517). As discussed in Chapter 3, Cathedrals Group universities have a stronger claim to offer this kind of community than any others in England, integrating Christian expectations into norms of governance, fostering a clear Christian ethos of support and community mindedness, supporting and resourcing chaplaincy as a central aspect of university life. The data reported above does not support the contention that Cathedrals Group universities generate higher levels of Christian commitment per se, although their Christian ethos does seem to encourage a more benign culture than that among Christian students at traditional/elite institutions. The high proportion of *unchurched Christians* seems to reflect the high number of entrants from Christian families, and the relatively high proportion of *active affirmers* reflects high levels of church involvement. The relatively high measure of Christians with three or more close Christian friends also suggests a strongly cohesive Christian culture that contrasts with the more fractious contexts of the traditional/elite universities.

However, self-reported measures of religious change and abstracted survey data only take us so far. Working with data from two waves of the National Study of Youth and Religion, Pearce and Denton find that, when they asked young Americans whether their religious identities had changed between 2002 and 2005, most said that they had not. A pattern of relative stability was dominant; however, this simple assessment failed to capture the variety of orientations to and embodiments of religious identity in evidence within the project's qualitative interviews. Many of the young people taking part in the study fell between these extremes (Pearce and Denton, 2011, pp. 11–12). In order to avoid over-simplifying the rich data we have on Christian students in England's universities, we turn in the following chapter to a discussion that draws more extensively on our qualitative evidence, focusing on how Christian students make sense of the university experience when their faith lives and student lives collide.

Notes

1 While seemingly paradoxical, this statement makes absolute sense within the context of a population of self-identifying Christians, of whom less than three quarters see themselves as religious or spiritual. Hence, the notion of becoming or ceasing to be 'religious' alongside the retention of a Christian self-ascription remains a meaningful one (see chapter 2).

2 Students who answered 'not sure' (only 3.2% of the total sample and 2.5% of Christians) are excluded from the analysis as the very low N numbers rule out correlations of statistical significance.

3 While our focus is on universities in England, the undergraduates studying in these universities do, of course, come from a wide range of countries, including from other parts of the United Kingdom.

4 This is an inevitably imperfect typology, and what is gained in a reduction of categories to a number suited to calculations that have statistical significance may be lost in analytical nuance as markedly different church groups are categorized together. However, such strained grouping is kept to a minimum by keeping Anglicans and Roman Catholics separate, and the Evangelical/Pentecostal group has its own coherent theological rationale. The Historic Protestant category has most potential to be problematic, not least as it includes denominations with very different structures of governance and with a reasonable variety of theologies across the Protestant spectrum. We acknowledge that there are a sizeable proportion of Evangelical Christians within Anglican churches and some non-conformist ones, especially the Baptists. However, in our view the strengths of the typology by far outweigh its weaknesses.

5   Cross-tabulation shows the correlation between pre- and term-time denomination to be statistically significant to a P value of < .001 (Cramer's V = .512). Hence, despite appearing very small, the increase in the Evangelical/Pentecostal share is noteworthy.

6   While direct comparisons are problematic, one can get a sense of how the culture of churchgoing among students compares to the national picture in England by comparing the data here with Peter Brierley's English Church Census from 2005 (Brierley, 2006b, Table 12.2.2). Grouping Brierley's figures into our own five denominational categories, we find the churchgoing population made up of 28% Anglicans, 28% Roman Catholics, 19% Historic Protestant churches, 21% Evangelical/Pentecostal and 4% Other. Hence, the overall emerging university term-time picture suggests a movement closer to the Anglican norm, a significant shrinkage in the Roman Catholic share, an almost as severe drop among Historic Protestants, and significant growth in the vitality of the Evangelical/Pentecostal churches.

7   Peter Brierley found in 2005 that 34% of Anglican churchgoers were evangelicals (2006b, 5.15). With this as our guide, approximately 4.3% of our Christian students would be evangelicals attending Anglican churches. Working with the same method, the proportion of evangelical students attending Historic Protestant churches would amount to a very small number, around 3% of the total.

8   It will be noted that the proportion claiming to 'never' attend church during term-time is different from the proportion who answered in this way when asked about their denomination of choice (50.5% rather than 53.3%). This is probably due to a questionnaire design issue; the 'never' figure for the denomination question was calculated post hoc, as the proportion who did not answer the question, while the 'never' proportion for the church attendance question reflects the number of respondents who chose this specific response. As the figures are not terribly dissimilar, we do not consider it damaging to our analysis, but on balance, the figure in Table 4.3 has the stronger claim to be the more accurate one.

9   While a full set of up to date, accurate figures are not available, a rough calculation can be attempted using the most recent statistics that cover the English national context. The figure of 10% is based on the 2011 census figure for England and Wales of 59% of the population self-identifying as Christian, and the 2005 English Church Census figure of 6.3% attending church on a weekly basis (Brierley, 2006a). Proportions were then calculated based on the 2012 population of England (56,100,000).

10 We provided an open response box on our questionnaire for those opting for 'other' on the religious belonging question, so that respondents could describe their religious identity in their own words. Some respondents here preferred to affirm denominational specificity rather than 'Christianity' as such (e.g. Roman Catholic, Orthodox or Quaker), while others took the opportunity to distance themselves from institutional categories in favour of a personal relationship with God and/or Jesus. As such, among the 'others', it was possible to infer a clear Christian identity among a larger proportion than those for whom clearly identifiable traditions of 'alternative spirituality' (e.g. Wicca, Pagan) applied.

11 According to the BSA data for 2010, the age group with the highest proportion saying sexual relations between two adults of the same sex are 'not at all wrong' are the 25–34-year-olds, with 59.3% favouring this option (figures taken from www.britsocat.com).

12 This table excludes the 'not sure' responses, which make up only 2.6% of the total and suggest no significant variations between university-type.

5

The challenges of being a Christian student

In previous chapters we discussed the mutual relationship between the ethos of universities and undergraduates' lived experiences of religion, remarking on how they can shape one another. Undergraduates who transition from home to university confront numerous challenges. Until recently, studies conducted in the United States declared that an undergraduate education 'secularizes', leading students to abandon their faith (Hunter, 1983, p. 132; also see Caplovitz and Sherrow, 1977; Feldman and Newcomb, 1969; Hadaway and Roof, 1988; Sherkat, 1998). However, academic study is not necessarily responsible for students' declining religious practices. Sociologists Uecker et al. found that activities such as church attendance decline 'because of factors that influence the lives of all emerging adults', which include 'the late-night orientation of young adult life and organized religion's emphasis on other age groups' (2007, p. 1683). Christian students' university experience is not merely about academic study and its impact on religious identities, but also social activities, friendship networks, housing arrangements, employment and extra-curricular experiences, which can all affect students' religious engagement.

This chapter takes a multifaceted view of the university experience, examining key challenges to students' faith. We explore (a) how these challenges affect Christian students, and (b) how their Christian identity appears to be drawn upon as a resource in responding to these challenges. Transitioning to a new environment can be difficult and lead students to utilize their religiosity, formed before university, to cope with the unfamiliarity of student life. Links to home are maintained and emulated in the churches they attend and the family-like support they provide. We discuss social challenges, particularly the student drinking culture. Student social activities typically involve alcohol, with the night-time economies that surround universities endorsing drinking as a form of entertainment and leisure. Christian students sometimes see themselves 'not fitting in' with these activities, and so Christian communities on and off campus become sites of refuge. The challenge of learning is another theme. In lectures and seminars, students have opportunities to debate and reflect on their beliefs. For some this results in stronger religious convictions and a broadening of religious perspectives – for others, the stagnation or erosion of faith. Like Uecker et al. (2007) and Mayrl and Uecker (2011), we found that students' religious faith is only marginally and occasionally influenced by academic learning. Rather, it is the challenges of fitting in and of navigating their way through different student social groups that affect them most. University offers a 'make or break' point, presenting students with opportunities to give up or renegotiate their religious identities during this time of newfound autonomy. Despite the challenges of university life, many students are resilient and hold on to religious values, carving out 'a faith of their own', a theme addressed at the close of this chapter.

The following discussion draws particularly on our qualitative interviews as they illuminate the lived complexity of being a Christian at university. We focus specifically on the experiences of *active affirmers*, those who are committed to and frequently involved in churches and other organized Christian activities during university term-time. Their concerted expression of Christian identity within the public contexts of university life means patterns of engagement between faith and the university are most visible and most developed among these individuals. This is not to say that other Christian students did not face similar challenges, but they are magnified within the lives of *active affirmers*, whose experiences represent what happens when Christian identity seeks social and public status within university contexts.

The challenge of change: Coping with the home-to-university transition

The majority of students taking part in this study were brought up in households where one or more parents or close relatives were Christian; 90.5% of students who identified as Christian were not the only practising Christian in the family. Family is central to religious socialization and parents are key in the passing on of religious beliefs and values (Crockett and Voas, 2006; Pankhurst and Houseknecht, 2000). University, on the other hand, was a site of heightened transition with many students living away from home for the first time, exploring new friendships and social situations and being exposed to new learning environments. For many, Christianity offered, on the one hand, a sense of continuity between home and university, and on the other, a focus of discontinuity, as students changed pre-university habits, beginning to practise their faith infrequently or not at all.

Students who were *active affirmers*, maintaining an enthusiasm for church and Christian involvement both at home and during term-time, relied on religion as a portable resource (Beckford, 1989), which was drawn upon in handling the upheaval of starting university. Undergraduates arriving at university cultivated a sense of continuity by developing relationships to places and people that were reminiscent of where they had come from. In 2010–11 the United Kingdom's Higher Education Statistics Agency (HESA) reported that 79% of full-time undergraduate students lived away from home, a proportion reflected among our interviewees. Young people with strong Christian ties depended on religious resources, such as prayer, Bible study and church, to help them adjust to the unfamiliar experience of student life. Dave (Leeds) reflected on what his faith meant to him during his first few months at university:

> It's great but there will come at least one point in that first semester where you just think, 'I want to be home, I want to be in my bed, with my family, with my mum bringing me a hot drink and giving me a hug, and I don't want to have to cook my own meals and I don't want to have to wash my own clothes', and when I had that moment I was like okay, my family aren't here, they live a couple of hundred miles away and it's 30 quid to get down to see them on the train. So right, I've got God, I can pray to Him, so I would say it's a great thing to have, and I'm thankful that I am a Christian and I've found it really useful in the transition when it came to that point.

Students' religiosity, formed within their familial contexts, helps them to orient themselves, enhancing their ability to cope with the novelty and loneliness of the university experience. In their US study of religion and youth, Smith and Snell (2009) report that family members are an important influence on young people's religiosity during the ages of 18–23. Our findings encourage us to see family as broader than this: students report that away from home, relationships that adopt a form or function analogous to family are also important for similar reasons. *Active affirmers* were attracted to church or campus faith groups because of family-like relationships or close friendships with other students. Sven, a Norwegian student at Leeds, said of his church: 'it's a family away from home . . . It's people you can be accountable to, people with the same heart as you. It is really important when you go out of your home and start building your own life'. Church communities function as surrogate families, providing students with comparable relationships to those they have at home, acting as a stabilizing structure during a time of transition. Megan (Kent), a second year student, described the emotional support she received at church: '. . . there's always people there who are happy to hug you if you're upset, celebrate with you when you're happy.' Ruby (Kent) explained that her church was 'family-orientated' and because she was a student was invited to be part of a local family's gatherings. She said, 'I go to an Evangelical Anglican church that is really family-orientated. I've got a host family that look after me here, an old couple who are really lovely, cook me dinner, that kind of thing and there's a really good student ministry.' Like a normatively imagined family, churches can become associated with a particular set of relational norms and practices that are vertical and hierarchical, based around relations of paternalism and dependency.

Intra-generational relationships are equally, if not more, important to young people's religious identities (Hopkins et al., 2011; Sharma and Guest, 2013). Churches and student faith groups were particularly significant, as Wendy (Derby) explained:

> Most of my friends are in the Christian Union, but I've only got a few friends that aren't [Christian] and they're either flatmates or people who I sit with in class. I think having a lot of close Christian friends has benefited me. When I was in school, there were only two people in the whole school who were Christians and it was a big school, whereas [at university] I know it's massive and I don't know everybody, but I know a lot more Christians than I did. I'm not the only one. It's reassured me that what I believe in is not false, that I can actually believe it. Other people believe it as well.

Sociologists of religion have privileged vertical relationships (i.e. parent to child) in the study of religious socialization (e.g. Voas and Crockett, 2005). However, drawing on research into siblings and friendships (e.g. Mauthner, 2005; J. Mitchell, 2003; Pahl, 2000), which have also been found to shape identity and value formation, we can see how students model, embody and convey religion through lateral relationships. In addition to intergenerational links, religious perspectives are informed by significant people, places and practices that are 'intra-generational', suggesting a transmission of religion *between* young people (Hopkins et al., 2011), and a heightened experience of religious identity within student contexts. William (Durham), who was involved in Christian groups at university, explained it like this: 'I think church and many Christian organizations, like the Christian Union, are very community centred and lend themselves towards strong friendships and a large proportion of my friends are Christians [as a result of] that.' Reinforcing this correlation between institutional involvement and the social cohesion of Christian networks, our survey revealed a direct relationship between consistency of church involvement and number of close Christian friends. Among *active affirmers*, 68.9% said that three or more of their five closest friends were also Christians, compared with 45.5% among *established occasionals* and 23.2% among *unchurched Christians*. There is a strong association between active church involvement and having a close friendship group who share similar beliefs. Some of the students we interviewed went a step further and lived with other Christian students. Such living arrangements, whether sought out or stumbled upon, gave students support, a common ground on which to build friendships, and served as a site of intra-generational religious transmission. They also provided a sense of continuity when returning to student life after university vacations. Lewis (Leeds), who had met and maintained friendships with a group of Christians during his degree, described his experience:

> I'd say most of my friends or most of my close friends now I've met through Christianity, through the Chaplaincy and socially it's shaped my experience quite a lot . . . it's allowed some kind of continuity or somewhere to come back to. When I first got to [university] in my first semester, I didn't find a church. I looked in the first couple of weeks and didn't really find anywhere and then gave up. But then I came back in the second semester and I found Café Church at the Chaplaincy and I don't know, I don't want to say it's somewhere to call home because that sounds terribly cheesy! But that's the kind of place I'm coming from, I suppose . . . and it's provided me with a university family, people I live with.

Valentine argues that '"family", defined in the broadest sense, still remains a form of relationship that most people strive to create for themselves and are still attached to' (2008, p. 2102). She contends that the ways that people 'do family' and foster emotional ties often take place both within and beyond the family unit (Finch, 2007). Student faith groups are one such place where students' imaginaries of family extend, effectively cultivating intimate ties that become 'home'. Living in a shared house at university can result in family-like ties and non-material benefits, such as intimacy and relationships (Kenyon and Heath, 2001). Lewis' living arrangement provided these advantages, blurring familial and friendship boundaries (Pahl and Spencer, 2010). Churches and student Christian communities are spaces in which young people 're-extend' their family while away at university (Warner and Williams, 2010). In these spaces students develop strategies for 'doing family' in ways that refer – whether as a point of similarity or contrast – to their home experiences. As with religion, family can function as a portable set of associations (Morgan, 1996), flowing into new relationships and spaces, including Christian collectives (Sharma, 2012) and new living arrangements, affecting students' religious formation and experience.

Students' Christian faith, however, did not always continue to be lived and practised in the same way while at university. Although there were students for whom religiosity eased the transition between home and university, for others university offered an opportunity to renegotiate emerging identities. Hannah and Kimberley described their experiences:

> I was brought up a Christian, and I have maintained that. When I was in school I went to a really good church and had a really good group of friends there, but since I've been at university I've missed that quite a bit . . . [At university] my closest friends are all non-Christian . . . In first year, I lived in Halls and had a really good group of friends and none of them were Christians, so I found the first few months I wanted to get involved with everything that my friends were doing, and I didn't go very regularly to the CU and I never really started going to church until second year. (Hannah, Leeds)

> When you're at university, there's other issues and other factors and church is far away and you don't have a car and no one is in the house saying, 'Come on, we've got to go to church.' Sometimes I say to my boyfriend, 'Oh I've got to go to church today, I should have gone.' He'd say, 'Why are you going to church?' And I'm like 'Yes, okay, I just won't go.' I don't know, it's weird, but then when I'm at home, I always go. (Kimberly, Durham)

As we discussed in Chapter 4, it is commonly assumed that university will be a secularizing experience, where students' commitment to religion erodes or is abandoned. In our research, a significant majority of students, Christian and non-Christian, viewed their religious identities as stable over the course of university, although some Christians, including many in our *active affirmers* group, reported becoming more religious during their university career. Although young people experiment with new social situations and relationships, and these can take precedence, as they did for Kimberley and Hannah, this does not mean that their faith is entirely rejected while they negotiate their emerging identities among the diverse social options available. Rather, students can approach their faith in ways comparable to the strategies for coping with college life that Clydesdale (2007) found in his US-based study of 125 undergraduates. Clydesdale argues that, during the course of their first year, 'students place their religious identities—along with their political, gender, race, and civic identities—in an "identity lockbox" before entering college, essentially leaving them unexamined and unquestioned' during this transitional period (Clydesdale 2007 cited in Mayrl and Oeur, 2009, pp. 264–5). Similarly, Christian beliefs and values were important to the students we interviewed, but religious practice or community involvement often took a backseat. Yet, as Hannah told us, this can be picked up again later on. She began to engage in church again in her second year. In this sense, *lapsed engagers* and *emerging nominals* presented a form of Christian engagement that was 'broad rather than deep' (Mayrl and Oeur, 2009, p. 263) – these students typically believed in God and prayed infrequently but their participation in church services and campus religious organizations was limited or absent altogether. The shift in students' religious identities was a non-linear and heterogeneous process, influenced by a range of experiences and locations in which they were situated.

The social challenge: 'Fitting in' to student life

Although Christian practices and communities often eased the transition between home and university, and students found other non-Christian contexts in which to belong, a significant theme among students we interviewed was the challenge of 'fitting in'. Christian students were aware of how their religious identities could marginalize them and made moves to negotiate these circumstances in both explicit and more subtle ways. The student drinking and clubbing culture, evident on most university campuses, was particularly difficult for those students who saw this as morally inconsistent with their religious values. Weller, Hooley and Moore's research into students and staff members' experiences of religion and belief in UK universities reports that 'the almost ubiquitous presence of alcohol and the relative lack of alternatives increases their isolation and can lead to them feeling excluded', especially during induction activities (2011, p. 8). Some of the students we spoke to utilized emerging opportunities to be a Christian example rather than excluding themselves altogether (cf. Moran, 2007, p. 427). Sally (Chester) spoke about being a role model for her faith:

> The university lifestyle is to go out and get as completely trashed as you can and don't really care much about anyone else really. But it challenged me, because I knew I would be living in a house with most likely non-Christians, which I am. I'm living with four non-Christian girls. So it's challenged me in how that's actually a really good opportunity, that I can be a [Christian] witness.

For Sally and others, it was important that their peers saw them abstaining from alcohol and being supportive and helpful if one of their friends had too much to drink. Offering their support created an opportunity to share their faith. Young people who were active in Christian ministry on campus discussed outreach activities such as providing toast and tea to students returning home from an evening out. Christian students who were Evangelical were also sometimes interventionist and sought opportunities to share their faith verbally with others.

> I'm Evangelical so I believe it's really important to tell people about God, but only on their terms . . . So, I always pray that it will be natural and

that it will just come up in conversations . . . I used to rush off home after lectures, because I'd always have something else I wanted to do, and there was one point where some friends said, 'we've got an hour before the next one', and because I lived five minutes away I used to dash home and get something done and come back, but they said, 'we're going to the sofas', so I went with them instead of dashing home, and we had these amazing conversations about God, and that morning I'd been praying for opportunities, and after this, when we were in the next lecture I thought, you've answered the prayer, thank you Lord. (Sean, Derby)

Given their common reputation as places of secular rationality and social indulgence, universities are frequently perceived by Evangelical Christians as prime sites for mission and ministry. Mission activities are often a priority for Christian Unions, who view the university campus as a 'mission field' in which Christian students can 'win others for Christ'. Evangelical groups are generally the most prominent Christian groups on university campuses and can therefore have a significant influence on how student Christianity is externally perceived (Guest et al., 2013).

However, the Christians in our study were not predominantly active in evangelism, and those who were affirmed a more socially subtle form of outreach than the interventionist and direct conversion tactics associated with the 'street preacher' stereotype. A majority of students expressed some discomfort with evangelism, and this applied to Evangelical as well as non-Evangelical Christians. Some were wary about confrontational approaches to evangelism because of their potential to alienate Christians from their university friends. Dave, who was in his first year, said that he had heard 'a few horror stories from people' who said that the Christian Union wanted them to 'go around and knock on people's doors in halls'; as Dave said, 'I've got to live with these people for a year, that wouldn't be a great start.' Proselytizing about one's faith could cause discomfort and unease with other students. Christian students generally preferred other students to approach them, perhaps asking them about 'wearing a crucifix' or why they 'went to church'. Michael (Durham) said, 'I think it's difficult to ask someone, "Do you believe in God? Are you a Christian?" . . . When you're living around people, you notice and as you learn about people you become more comfortable to ask this kind of question.' Aware of the decline in practising Christians and general scepticism towards religion in mainstream British society, living faith through actions – rather than combative conversation – was a way to achieve respect among non-Christians and learn about others' perspectives on religion. Sean, Sally and Michael's approach to sharing Christianity with others can be likened to the idea of 'friendship evangelism', the strategy of being respectful and sensitive to the suspicions of non-Christians, with evangelism taking place over time as relationships develop (Guest, 2007; McPhee, 1978; Schneider, 1989). For students we interviewed, such practices opened up possibilities for religion to be laterally conveyed, but they took cues from others' behaviour before they ventured into conversations about religion. Navigating the terrain of universities presented tensions, especially concerning how Christianity might be perceived in relation to other religions. Dave went on to talk about this:

> One of the unfortunate things about being a Christian in a Christian country is the fact that people who aren't Christians feel able to get away with mocking your religion in a way that they couldn't publicly do with Islam or Sikhism or Hindus because it's considered racial abuse. Instead they take the Mick out of your mate because he's a Christian and believes in some random geezer . . . I mean there's a lot of Muslim girls and it's quite easy to see them around campus because they're wearing the head scarf, and so it's quite easy to spot how many people [there are] who are able to publicly show their faith like that without receiving any hassle.

A recent survey conducted by the National Union of Students (NUS) found that 62% of students who belonged to a religion said that their university was a place where they could freely practise their faith (Barker, 2010, p. 12). However, as Dave also explains, being open about one's Christian identity can lead to being ostracized. Graham (Derby) explained that he did not talk about his Christianity 'to people at university because it would be very awkward and I would be instantly challenged with opinions I can't answer'. Like Dave, he went on to say that 'Christianity is something that is perfectly fine to mock; atheism is something that you poke a bit of fun at, but not too much, and Islam is something that you can't criticise at all.' Discourses of diversity promoted on campuses can conceal tensions that may exist among and between groups and in the organizational life of universities (Ahmed, 2007). The ways in which students handled these dynamics was complex, seen in the above students' responses, applying varied and tentative approaches to faith, and further exposing tensions between religious identities that are public or private. In order to pre-empt experiences of marginalization and because of their moral framework, some Christian students, particularly those in our *active affirmers* group, made deliberate moves to live only with Christians and not drink or go to nightclubs, consciously managing their social life according to what they saw as Christian moral principles. This could, however, prevent them from learning about their university peers and limit their socializing to Christian contexts. For example, students at Durham described the abundance of activities that were available to Christian students, which could involve a Christian activity every night of the week. Some leaders of prominent student churches in Durham were aware of this, and so encouraged students to meet non-Christians and participate in non-Christian events in order to vary their student experience.

Drinking among students

In the United Kingdom, many universities are located in or nearby city centres where bars and pubs thrive. Valentine et al. report that 'the last decade has seen alcohol play an increasingly important role in urban regeneration, with the development of the nighttime economy achieved through promotion of the hospitality industries' (2010, p. 8). Corporate branded bars and clubs target a range of consumers, including students who are 'offered a host of promotional nightlife discounts such as happy hours and cheap entry prices', with well-known pubs, bars and clubs catering particularly to the student market (Chatterton and Hollands, 2002, p. 98). However, these spaces provide few options for those who observe abstinence, such as some Christians and many Muslims (Valentine et al., 2010). Excessive alcohol consumption is arguably the number one behavioural concern among university students in the United Kingdom. It is also one of the most cited factors in the alienation of religious students from student social life; with so much of the organized on-campus events centred around drinking, those with moral reservations about alcohol often find themselves with no place to go. While this problem has prompted most attention with respect to the lives of Muslim students, given their much more univocal reservations about alcohol consumption, it also creates problems for Christian students, although not, it would seem, to the same degree. We asked our survey respondents how they responded to the student drinking culture, and the results are given in Table 5.1.

It is perhaps unsurprising that twice as many Christians as those of 'no religion' say they are against the drinking culture and let others know, and twice as many say they are against it but keep their opinion to themselves. What is less expected is the almost equivalent proportion acknowledging 'some problems' with the drinking culture, but who do not see it as a 'serious problem'. This position attracts 36.5% of Christian students and 37.5% of students of 'no religion'. Students who have no problem at all with the drinking culture make up 48.5% of the 'nones', but not too far behind are the Christians, with 34.8%. Over a third of all Christian students have no problem at all with the student drinking culture, suggesting a generally more permissive perspective in keeping with the cultural norm.[1] This may be the most striking finding with respect to perspectives on moral issues: on the student drinking culture, while Christian students are much more likely to disapprove, the majority (over 70%) either see no serious problem, or see no problem at all (Figures 5.1 and 5.2).

TABLE 5.1 Responses to the drinking culture among undergraduates, comparing Christians with those of 'no religion' (weighted)

	Christian students (N = 2,233) (%)	Students of 'no religion' (N = 1,475) (%)
I am against it and let others know	9.9	4.6
I am against it but keep my opinions to myself	18.9	9.4
I have some problems with it, but do not see it as a serious problem	36.5	37.5
I have no problem with it	34.8	48.5

FIGURE 5.1 *The Halo nightclub (converted church), Leeds. With permission of Universities in Leeds Chaplaincy Trust.*

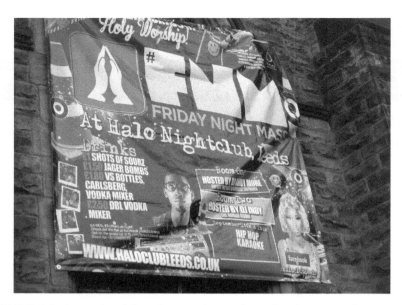

FIGURE 5.2 *Poster for club night at Halo, Leeds. With permission of Universities in Leeds Chaplaincy Trust.*

While the majority of Christian students appear aligned with the more relaxed approach to social drinking that typifies young people in Britain more generally, those Christian students who see a problem are likely to be those who are most involved in the life of the churches. Using our categories, 53.2% of Christians who agreed with the two more conservative responses above are *active affirmers*. In this section, we focus on this particular sub-group.

Among students we interviewed, *active affirmers* found the drinking culture somewhat concerning. The drinking culture constituted an uncomfortable dimension of student life, particularly among those keen to express their faith in social and/or public spaces. Students told us that drinking could often become an expectation rather than a choice and some went along with alcohol-related activities in order to 'fit in'. Researching the geographies of public and private drinking environments Holloway et al. found that three reasons for drinking that were significant among 18–24-year-olds were 'getting drunk, losing one's inhibitions and family/peer pressure' (2009, p. 825). Morton and Tighe found that undergraduates' drink in order 'to socialise, [for] pleasure, to feel intoxicated, [for] enjoyment of taste, [the] cheap cost of alcohol and student alcohol promotions' (2011, p. 296). Other research with university students presents alcohol consumption as a coping mechanism used in the negotiation of difficult social situations (Kuntsche et al., 2006). This is not surprising given that university is a transitional time where students face competing challenges related to course work, housing arrangements and the maintenance of friendships. Students may resort to drinking to cope with the pressures of student life.

In addition to health-related reasons, the student drinking culture is problematic for *active affirmers* because it can encourage young people to engage in behaviour they later regret. Brandon (Chester) said, 'It's very difficult because as a culture, especially when you first come to university, you'd go drinking because you can, but it's very easy six months later to look back and go, I wish I hadn't done that.' Brandon's experience is not dissimilar to findings from an NUS study on student drinking at three English universities. It found that 61% of student drinkers felt embarrassed by their own behaviour after drinking on occasion with 12% feeling this 'all the time' or 'frequently' (Brito and Whittaker, 2010, pp. 4, 13). International students we interviewed were genuinely perplexed by the drinking culture that takes place on university campuses. Adrian (Leeds) from Greece told us about his approach to drinking which was at odds with other students he observed. He said, 'I'm not someone who likes to go out every week. I go out when I feel I did good work or when someone has something special. I don't go out just to feel happy; I cannot understand people who do that.' A study of cross-cultural contact at a British university found that university marketing material for 'home' students showcased the 'vibrant nightlife and 24 h party culture', whereas for international students they emphasized 'quaint old England', omitting information about the dominant drinking culture (Andersson et al., 2012, p. 506).

Among *active affirmers*, home and international, drinking for 'fun' was viewed as worrying, their concerns including the risk of physical injuries, embarrassing behaviour and regrettable sexual situations. These students countered the drinking culture by placing themselves in non-alcoholic contexts, where they felt comfortable and accepted for their non-drinking stance. This usually meant social activities and outings with friends from church or a Christian student group. Such contexts were a refuge for those who had not encountered alcohol, or were living away from home for the first time and in challenging housing situations where flatmates were more indulgent. Some students found solace with students of other faith traditions who did not drink. Alicia (Derby) spoke about her friendship with a Muslim flatmate:

I live with six girls including me, one of whom is a Muslim, a practising Muslim and the other four of whom have no faith. So, me and Shazia have formed a small group of people that don't go out. I will go out but I will go out once every couple of weeks whereas they go out repeatedly. So, me and Shazia have formed a small group of people that tend to be up earlier than everyone else and tend not to be hung-over in the morning.

Together Shazia and Alicia formed a close friendship through similar beliefs and values. Their faith can be viewed as a form of protection against 'the unquestioning hegemony of drinking', which is often accompanied by intolerance towards those who practise abstinence (Andersson et al., 2012, p. 506). Although university campuses often emphasize pluralism and inclusivity, particular norms dominate, not least in the context of leisure spaces, where there are few options for religious students unwilling to embrace the drinking culture (Andersson et al., 2012). Universities in Britain are attempting to address this issue. It was reported that London Metropolitan University plans to create alcohol-free areas on campus out of 'cultural sensitivity' towards 'young women from traditional Muslim homes' (Bingham, 2012). After consulting staff and students, such initiatives have been undertaken in order that students' experiences are not tarnished by an alcohol-centred social life.

The common perception is that drinking is 'what students do' and so this informs the stereotypical image of student life. Christian students often deliberately avoided engaging in such activities and developed negative perspectives on their fellow students. Joel, who was in the third year of his undergraduate degree at Chester, said that he and his friend, 'we're both like, "I hate students." We didn't like fitting into the stereotypical look of going out every night, getting wasted and just being really rowdy'. Joel's Christianity and involvement in religious activities gave him an alternative social life. Audrey (Durham) expressed her view on student drinking: 'I don't think there's anything wrong with drinking; but I do believe it says in the Bible not to get drunk and so I don't do that.' Echoing observations that Menagi et al. (2008) found among a sample of American Christian undergraduates, religious dispositions were treated as a protective barrier against alcohol use. For both Joel and Audrey, their faith gave them, and other students, an ethic by which to say 'no' to the student drinking culture. It gave them a moral framework by which to negotiate social contexts that appeared in tension with their beliefs, uncomfortable and alienating. In contrast, some student faith groups offered pub nights as a way to congregate after a Bible-study, yet these opportunities left some students feeling conflicted about whether this demonstrated an inappropriate Christian example or if it showed other students that Christians could be 'cool' too. Such groups, by including drinking as part of their social repertoire, can co-opt consumer, media and popular cultures to convey Christianity as 'cool', on-trend and progressive (McCracken, 2010). However, there is a concern about whether matters of faith can be easily packaged in secular notions of what is considered fashionable, 'cool' or appealing to today's youth especially when framed by the experience of corporate branded urban pubs and nightclubs. Stephen (Chester) told us about a Christian student group meeting he attended: 'I can't really judge them but they just seem to be on one hand worshipping and praying and then two hours after that's finished they would be drunk or living a different sort of standard I wouldn't have expected.' As such, the dilemmas presented by alcohol were challenging for Christian students, but were also important in shaping their faith and their personal sense of responsibility. The ways in which students negotiate their Christian identities amid social and religious contexts at university are multifaceted, and for some students their academic study added another layer of complexity.

The challenge of learning

Across the universities we surveyed, Education, subjects allied to Medicine, and History, Philosophy and Theology, were the most popular subject areas among Christian students. The popularity of certain courses reflects the reasons they enrol on such degrees, which for many were related to their future goals – 'to make a difference' through teaching, caring for others or taking up roles in ministry. We were interested in how academic study affected Christian students' faith, and discovered that students handled the relationship between their faith and academic study in a variety of ways (also see Sabri et al., 2008). Among the students we interviewed, a small minority gradually moved away from a previous faith position. As explored elsewhere (Sharma and Guest, 2013), in addition to the culture of student life, friendships with non-Christians and not finding a faith community, academic study triggered a change in their relationship to Christianity. Students who took courses in Theology or Religious Studies were often deeply moved by them, and for some this prompted a shift in faith position. Sara (Durham), a Catholic student, said that studying the sociology of religion inspired her to give up her Christian faith:

> I did a module in Shamanism, which has been the best decision I think I've made because it's just a brilliant module and really opened my eyes to, well, a lot . . . At the moment I don't class myself as a Christian anymore. Over the past couple of years I've decided that I don't want that to be a part of my life anymore, and I don't regret it was a part of my life before. But, being at university, even though it's quite a step out, you're allowed to be your own person and it is nice being away and knowing your own mind, and being able to figure that out as an individual.

For Sara, studying a particular field prompted her to reflect upon and reconfigure her Christian faith, leading to a gradual change of identity. While this process was difficult, she was encouraged by the curriculum, which offered her a way to work through her beliefs and make her own mind up about them. Ben (Leeds), who was studying philosophy, said that this had 'steered him away from his faith'. He said, 'If you want to get a good result on an essay you can't just argue from an atheistic or theistic point of view, you have to balance it out. I always found the atheist arguments were a lot stronger.' After great heart-searching during this course, he took up a different position from the one he had held upon arrival at university. Other students found that course material on religion fuelled their faith. Raj (Kent), who was seeking to become an ordained minister after university, discussed his experience on a Religious Studies course:

> We did a module this year, The Death of God: Christianity and Modern Society, and some of the things we were doing, you know it was hard to sit there and listen to these people in the class and to these scholars saying these things and then going you know what, 'no' and putting your hand up and getting involved in seminars and going you know what, this is total rubbish and then going away and thinking well you know it enriches your own faith . . . a faith that you don't think about, that doesn't change, is no good to anybody.

Lectures and seminars can be places where academic subjects are experienced as empowering or exclusionary, marginalizing some expressions of religious identity while affirming and galvanizing others (Hopkins, 2011). In Raj's experience, his faith was empowered and 'enriched' because of the questions raised on his course. Courses like these provided opportunities to discuss religion and belief in constructive and critical ways. However, there was some concern among local church leaders that these courses might undermine or distort students' Christian beliefs, so they made efforts to provide support for students who might experience a crisis of faith. Such support included pastoral guidance, prayer or a parallel curriculum of talks or discussion groups that would function as a means of conveying legitimacy upon certain kinds of knowledge over others. Students who took Theology or Religious Studies courses were often struck by how different their academic study of theology was from the theology they were taught in church. Joel (Chester) told us:

> [University has been] very challenging and it challenged a lot of preconceptions I had about Christianity . . . It probably came because of Theology . . . being opened up to other people's opinions that were different from what I had in my church . . . [Theology] has made a difference because I think I understand why I believe certain elements of faith and Christianity . . . Some of the modules I've taken have enabled me to see where those beliefs come from and to see them in a positive way rather than the cynical way which I brought at first.

Some students arrived at university expecting to integrate their faith and academic study (cf. Sabri et al., 2008, p. 52). Yet, as they experienced the course material they became aware of the ways in which it challenged them to interrogate their faith, and, for some, this became an anxious and unsettling process. Joel's experience reflects this, as manifest in his sense of inner conflict, but he eventually integrated sources of reason and scholarship with teachings from his church and the Bible. Unlike Joel, other students we interviewed sought to keep academic study separate from their faith, prioritizing their churches and private Bible study in their faith development. Wendy (Derby), a Psychology student, responded to class-based teaching about evolution with unqualified scepticism: 'they've got it so wrong'. Scientific perspectives did not sway her religious beliefs and she felt that her courses should be more open to religious points of view. Among our survey respondents, only a small minority of Christian students perceived a tension between scripture and evolution. The relationship between the Bible and science as sources of knowledge is an important aspect of the encounter between Christianity and universities, as illustrated in the form of Christianity – common in the United States – that positions itself in firm opposition to 'the world', viewed as embodied in institutions of public education. This is a significant factor in understanding the relationship between Christian commitment and academic study, as positions on this issue may be expected to frame student orientations to learning, as well as to universities in general and what they represent. In the United States, scepticism about evolution among Evangelical Christians has contributed to a strong separatist tendency, influencing the establishment of openly Evangelical and fundamentalist universities, and a rise in the popularity of home schooling (Numbers, 2006; Rosin, 2007). The structures of education in the United Kingdom, where public funding for (regulated) faith schools means there is less call for private Christian provision, make these responses less practically viable and cultural factors seem to discourage their emergence. In our survey we asked our respondents: 'Which of the following best expresses your view on the relationship between science and the Bible?', providing a range of options associated respectively with creationism, intelligent design, a compatibilist view that reconciles the Bible and Darwinian evolution and a perspective that elevates scientific investigation over theological traditions when asking certain kinds of questions. The results are given in Table 5.2.

Shown here, a fifth of Christian respondents expressed uncertainty, opting for the 'not sure' response. The 'hard' Evangelical response, affirming biblical literalism and an oppositional stance towards mainstream science, commands support of 9.3%: a small minority, but not an insignificant one. Support for intelligent design is lower, reflecting the more modest profile of this debate in the United Kingdom compared to the United States (Guest, 2009). Hence we have a sub-population of c. 15% affirming a clear scepticism towards the theory of evolution. A large proportion opted for the compatibilist

TABLE 5.2 Responses from Christian students to the question 'Which of the following best expresses your view on the relationship between science and the Bible?' (weighted)

Understanding of the relationship between science and the Bible	Christian students (N=2,229) (%)
The Bible disproves Darwinian evolution – Genesis should be taken literally as God's revealed account of the six-day creation	9.3
Intelligent design is a theory that makes better sense of the biblical data than Darwinian evolution	6.0
Genesis tells us the truth about God's act of creation; Darwinian evolution captures the mechanics of creation	30.9
In matters of scientific investigation, science must take precedence over theological traditions, which ask different questions	33.4
I am not sure	20.3

position, seeking to maintain support for both evolution and the Bible as truthful, reliable accounts offering complementary perspectives on the same phenomenon. More students, though, wish to elevate science above the Bible as a source of authority when it comes to asking 'scientific' questions, comfortable distinguishing between biblical and scientific knowledge. Wendy's perspective, it appears, is very much a minority one, with most Christian students finding no serious tension between science and the traditions of their faith.[2]

Nonetheless, attending university can test one's faith, and not just via learning and teaching, but also as provoked by the views expressed by other students who are sceptical about religion in general, or Christianity in particular. Megan (Kent) explained how other students on a drama module perceived it as 'rubbish' to put on plays about God. Other students felt pigeonholed as the spokesperson for all Christians. Hannah (Leeds), a Maths student, said her peers interrogated her about the Catholic Church and its history of sexual abuse. She said, 'Sometimes you get it quite bad, the whole Catholic priest thing that came out, it's really bad, all the cases of paedophilia; it's terrible and you feel how can I say that Christianity's good when they're countering you with something like that?' While students described issues of religion raised among their peers, it was evident that religion, for most, was not a source of intellectual or personal engagement instigated by those teaching their courses. Students told us that matters of faith were mainly unexplored in classroom contexts or in exchanges with their lecturers and professors. From a university lecturer's perspective, Fairweather (2012) has written that despite teaching ethnography of faith communities to British undergraduates, his course has rarely provided students with opportunities to engage with these communities in a way that focuses on their actual lived experiences of faith. He argues that social sciences in the United Kingdom have inherited a model of academic engagement that privileges secular objectivity, inhibiting forms of knowledge that extend beyond the purely rational, and discouraging any interrogation of the religious experiences of students. A dominant theme among students we interviewed suggested they did not experience cognitive dissonance between their faith and academic study. In order to understand this further, we return to Clydesdale's notion of the 'identity lockbox'. He argues that young people in their first year of college do not see university as 'an opportunity to examine oneself and one's place in the larger world' rather most 'keep core identities in an "identity lockbox" during their first year out and actively resist efforts to examine their self-understandings', including through academic study. He contends that this preserves their mainstream identities from 'intellectual or moral tampering that would put them out-of-step with the communities that shaped them or hinder their efforts to pursue the individual achievement they have always envisioned for themselves' (2007, p. 4). Similarly, students in our study exemplified how faith, as an intellectual, personal or social inquiry, was not interrogated in their classes. This may seem surprising, but the recasting of faith identity in non-cerebral terms, as a combination of experience, participation and personal spirituality, seems to have rendered Christian identity fairly immune to intellectual crises generated by academic study. Very few of our interviewees cited academic work as a challenge to their faith, and survey data revealed no significant correlations between degree programmes and patterns of religious expression. We found that students' faith remained as an absent presence, embodied but in the background, and mainly engaged with and preserved in other, non-academic contexts, such as campus religious organizations, churches and among friends.

More important than intellectual engagement is social experience. Universities are spaces often of ethnic and religious diversity and because of this several Christian students we spoke to experienced a broadening of their religious views. Edward (Chester) told us, '[University] definitely broadened [my faith] in the sense you meet a lot of people from different backgrounds, different denominations, different beliefs within the Christian faith, which is eye opening.' While Chloe (Kent) explained, 'When you're at home you're in a sheltered church and that's what you know, but at university there's loads of different beliefs, types of worship and ideas about doctrine or God. So yes, it's opened [my] eyes in that way.' Like Lefkowtiz, in her study of university students in the United States, we found that transitioning from home to university 'can allow for more religious exploration' and exposure 'to other beliefs and religious traditions' (2005, p. 41, 51). Although students were not usually intellectually engaged in matters of faith on their courses, they were aware of religious diversity on campuses, and this largely generated positive sentiment about their own and others' faith traditions.

Making faith their own

For the students in our study, Christianity created a sense of continuity between home and university, but was also an focus of discontinuity, whereby students' sense of agency shaped religious preferences and constructed an alternative Christian experience. On account of their greater autonomy and changing religious environments, students were presented with opportunities to define their Christian identities on their own terms. Beth said '[at university] my faith kind of became my own and so it is kind of *my* faith, not a faith imposed on me by my family, [for example] choosing my own church.' While church was one way of distinguishing their Christian identities, the experience of living with others also shaped their religious formation. Audrey (Durham) explained:

> It was really nice to choose my own church . . . I guess at home everyone knows me as the daughter of my mum and dad, whereas here . . . I got to choose where I went, I got to make all my new friends, and people know me for being me . . . It's made me grow and develop a lot. Back home it was easy because you're living in a Christian household, where Christian views are upheld, and it's a place of grace and love and everything; whereas coming and living here, you're learning to live with people you've never lived with before; you're learning to build really good, strong friendships with them . . . you've got to then work out how you apply what you believe into a completely new situation, with a new set of circumstances, a new set of people, and it's really good, because actually I guess it's made me think about what I actually really believe.

Students we interviewed took up opportunities to develop their Christian identities *apart* from their parents. Beth and Audrey were 'making their faith their own', and hence merging the two transitional projects of faith development and the pursuit of independence distinctive of early adulthood.

George (Kent), who was a mature student, explained that 'coming to university was a testing time at times but it also has given me self-confidence in who I am and what I believe'. University could offer a liberating context in which to consolidate positions that students were once hesitant or unsure about. Oliver (Durham), who was in his final year, remarked on university as a key transitional experience 'I think there is a large group of people that come from home, were brought up in a Christian home but then university defines a point when . . . it is make or break . . . now [your faith] is your choice.' This process can foster the emergence of a new identity with or without faith. Pearce and Denton (2011), who draw on data from the National Study of Youth and Religion in the United States, offer a similar portrait of young people, whereby their faith can be rich and dynamic arising out of this period of personal development as well as something they are defining, practising and living out in their own ways. In our research, Tori (Leeds) who grew up going to church with her grandmother, lived with non-Christians, enjoyed going nightclubbing with friends and was involved in campus ministry. Kristina (Kent), a student who was originally from Germany and was brought up Lutheran, enacted her faith through volunteering and being responsible and more open to others. Most evident in our study was students' 'faith-in-action, faith-in-relationships' (Orsi, 2003). Some students lived out their faith through their essays and assignments. Sean (Derby), who was studying music technology, composed worship music in his course studio sessions, while Andrew (Durham) wrote a blog about being a Christian studying geography. Others, like Oliver, were involved in social action groups and selling fair trade goods at a local church. Janet (Leeds), said that getting together to share a meal with other Christians was important and generated fellowship. And those like Peter and Lewis (Leeds), who lived with other Christians, were grateful to be able to pray together. In his US study, Clydesdale found students focusing on 'daily life management', including relationships (with romantic partners, friends and authority figures), personal gratifications (e.g. substance use and sexual activity), and their economic situation, 'with its expanding necessities and rising lifestyle expectations' (Clydesdale, 2007, p. 2). Our students were not dissimilar. As noted, for the most part, faith remains in the background of students' academic study, but in other realms of student life faith is mobilized, disassociated from or renegotiated in order to establish a sense of ease and belonging with others, something that Audrey mentions above. The primary challenge for Christian students is not academic study but the everyday management of life and relationships. Students' Christian identities are drawn upon and shaped according to the personal and social circumstances in which they find themselves. In this sense, religious identity emerges as a perpetually negotiated phenomenon, socially reactive and adaptive, and universities are one contextual lens through which to observe this multifaceted process.

Conclusion

In this chapter we have discussed the impact of the university experience on Christian students, particularly those most involved in church life, who we are calling *active affirmers*. Significantly, our analysis challenges research that conceives young people and religious change in the linear terms associated with the secularization of public institutions (e.g. Hunter, 1987; Jensen, 2000; Penning and Smidt, 2002). First, the interaction between the university and students' religious identities is much more multifaceted and is a two-way exchange, not merely a linear progression on a scale of intensification to diminishment. As we argue elsewhere, 'Christian identity among students at university simultaneously serves both an anchoring function, in channelling connections to pre-university life, and a perspectival function, in filtering new experiences and, as such, often challenging and reconfiguring pre-existing assumptions and values' (Sharma and Guest, 2013, p. 61). Second, the impact of the university experience was less challenging for students who sought out Christian community and friendships. They averted challenges to their faith such as the affects of the student drinking culture by deliberately seeking out 'moral communities' on campus, Christian groups and organizations that protected them from situations they did not wish to engage. Thus, religion is not static or left at home, but functions as a portable resource, generating a sense of continuity between university and home and illustrating how religion operates as a dimension of human movement and relationality (Tweed, 2006). As a result, attending churches that were similar to the ones they attended at home or that offered a vibrant student congregation provided role models, spiritual sustenance and opportunities to uphold existing religious commitments. Third, living with others affirming religiously diverse perspectives increased openness to religious diversity, and in the case of some students who lived with fellow Christians, the lateral transmission of faith was of major significance. The time spent at university is not restricted to achieving a qualification, but offers important opportunities to make new friends and take part in a range of social and non-academic activities (Holdsworth, 2006, p. 496). Exploring and reconstituting one's faith in the ways addressed above also plays a significant part.

Universities were mainly perceived as spaces of tolerance and diversity, where students gained a sense of confidence in their Christian identities and felt their faith was more accepted than it had been during previous experiences at school or work (also see Hopkins, 2011). Contrary to some previous research (e.g. Sherkat, 1998; Wuthnow, 2007), academic study did not necessarily lead to a liberalization of religious beliefs. One possible explanation might refer to the move universities have made away from secular assumptions towards a positive engagement with religion as a marker of identity (Dinham and Jones,

2010, p. 7). Campus cultures, seeking to be inclusive of all, become more protective of religious traditions, reflecting wider cultural norms of religious tolerance and diversity (Mayrl and Uecker, 2011). This generates more opportunities for Christian students to engage with religious groups that hold similar or complementary beliefs and values, whether as an affirmation of cultural inclusivity or critical response to it. It is in these groups, particularly for *active affirmers*, that their faith is most actively preserved, 'undercutting the "cultural broadening" effect' of university (Mayrl and Uecker, 2011, p. 202). It is to these groups that we now turn our attention.

Notes

1 Cross-tabulation analysis reveals only a very weak relationship between type of university and orientation to the drinking culture among students in general and among Christian students in particular, so this apparent permissiveness is not attributable to the different circumstances of different universities.

2 This contrasts markedly with the situation in the United States. Bryant characterizes evangelical students' experiences in the classroom as provoking challenges to their faith so that students feel they have to '"sell out" (particularly in the sciences) in order to be successful' (Bryant, 2005, p. 23).

6

Organized Christianity on the university campus

Introduction

The previous chapter examined the challenges that Christian students face at university and traced their responses to these challenges as individuals. The present chapter turns this issue the other way around, asking how Christian students engage with the university experience on a collective basis, by belonging to and becoming involved with formal organizations defined in Christian terms, and in more informal networks of fellow believers. Our evidence suggests the proportion of Christian students taking part in organized groups is relatively small. In our survey, we asked Christian respondents: what 'church-based and/or student-based Christian activities are you usually involved in during term time?' offering them a list of possibilities and also an open response box for any we might have been unaware of. Only 27.1% said yes, they are usually involved in such activities; the majority appear largely unengaged in organized Christian activity. The fact that those who *are* involved are, for the most part (75.2%) *active affirmers*, confirms that involvement in such activity is strongly associated with involvement with church life. In numerical terms, organized Christianity is very much a minority pursuit. And yet the religious convictions of Christian students become most visible on campuses through organized and collective endeavour, as illustrated in the controversy surrounding the Christian Union at the University of Bristol, recounted in our Introduction. Organizations like the CU, the Student Christian Movement (SCM), denominational societies like Cathsocs and Methsocs, and the networks surrounding university chaplains, offer students a focal point for their faith, as well as resources, professional guidance, and an experience of community among like-minded peers. So what is the significance of these organized expressions of Christian identity, and what does their changing status indicate about the place of Christianity within England's universities? This chapter takes the most influential of these organized expressions of university-based Christianity and examines their significance for the Christian students who took part in our study.

The changing context of chaplaincy

While chaplaincy in the more ancient universities and church colleges has a long tradition, provision of this kind expanded geographically and diversified only after the Second World War. From 1954, The Church of England General Assembly set aside funds for chaplains in the modern universities, while the Chaplaincies Advisory Group oversaw national co-ordination of provision and training. Expansion accelerated after the Robbins Report of 1963, when student numbers increased dramatically and, as the decade unfolded, the Church of England, Roman Catholics, Methodists and Baptist churches all appointed individuals to oversee the work of the increasing number of clergy administering university chaplaincy on behalf of their respective denominations. The 1960s presented the ideal circumstances for the consolidation of professional chaplaincy as a clerical vocation: army chaplains were recognized as having provided a valuable service during the Second World War and the emerging professions of social work and counselling shaped expectations of what clergy ought to be able to provide by way of pastoral support (France, 1968; Gilliat-Ray, 2000, p. 28). The massive expansion of students in line with the post-Robbins establishment of new universities highlighted a new pastoral field, especially among young people living away from home for the first time, and presented a strong rationale for church-sponsored intervention. By the 1980s, most universities had chaplaincy provision, and chaplains were expected to have a sound understanding of the social and cultural contexts in which they were working. Chaplains' responsibilities included the pastoral guidance of individual students and staff, and facilitating outreach to different groups across campus.

Because Anglicans have been the denomination most closely associated with university chaplaincies, the mid-twentieth century saw, in particular, the establishment of many well-organized Catholic and Methodist student societies. Catholic Societies (Cathsocs) have continued to affirm the centrality of the Mass in their student activities, although this often extends into the provision of a more extensive calendar of religious and social events. McGrail and Sullivan (2007) found that Catholic students enrolled at universities often experience indifference or hostility to their faith, having come from schools where their faith was facilitated and institutionally supported. Such experiences can be countered by the safe haven found within the Catholic chaplaincy, whose appeal can extend beyond Roman Catholic students.

Catholic chaplains advised our research team that the numbers of British Catholic students attending these activities have declined in recent decades, just as Catholic church attendance has fallen. According to a Kent chaplain, the boost to Cathsocs from Southern European students has also diminished, as more Spanish and Portuguese Catholics distance themselves from traditional religious practices. The growing numbers of Eastern European and African students tend to make Cathsocs particularly cosmopolitan. Some present themselves as pockets of vitality, especially at universities where the chaplain has a large presbytery to accommodate events, and is keen to foster links between Catholic students and his parish. In Durham and Kent, for example, this extends to the provision of student lodgings in the presbytery and a popular calendar of theological discussion and prayer, weekend trips away, and social events (Kent's Catholic Chaplaincy even has a bar area, with bar managers elected each year from within the Catholic Society). On one level, socialization appears to have remained much more effective in Catholic than Protestant contexts; however lapsed in beliefs, behaviour and rituals, those brought up Catholic retain a sense of specific religious identity, and Catholic international students in particular readily gravitate to their Cathsoc. For these reasons, and despite declining British numbers, Cathsocs have thus far proved much more durable than their Protestant denominational equivalents. Lisha (Kent) told us what her university Cathsoc meant to her:

> When I came to university I found the Catholic Society was really helpful – seeing a few people that are genuine and love God, coming to Mass and worshipping and sometimes talking about God and discussing different theological issues. It's been really good and I'd say university and meeting people that believe in God and help you on your journey has been really important.

Because Catholic chaplains frequently say Mass on campus, Catholic chaplaincies function for some Catholic students as a church might to a Protestant student. This was the case for Ethan (Leeds), an Austrian student. Asked about his church attendance, he described how he attended Mass at the Catholic Chaplaincy each week. Ethan explained that his university life and his Catholic life were 'separate'. Studying and socializing with his (non-Christian) friends, who he met through his first year hall of residence, he sees Mass, using a petrol station analogy, as like 'filling up'. Asked what he meant by this, he replied:

> If you are Catholic and you trust in God then one of the key issues is that you trust He can help you, the Lord can help you in any case . . . If you go to church once a week you can tell Him what problems you have and

just different issues. It helps you in some cases if you can address these issues to God.

Methodist Societies (Methsocs) have faced a more dramatic denominational shift of policy. In the 1950s, the Oxford University Methsoc, known as the John Wesley Society, had over 500 members. During the 1960s, the growth in campus universities led to an expansion of Methsocs, which were student-led and usually affiliated to Student Unions; in that decade the total number exceeded 80, although Methodist chaplains advised that not more than around 60 were large enough to be sustainable. In line with the severe decline in Methodist congregations since the 1960s, by the end of the century fewer than 10 viable groups remained. In 2011 at least 15 Methsocs remained in traditional/elite, inner-city red-brick and 1960s campus universities. Methsocs no longer present themselves as societies for Methodist Christians, but have been repositioned as student faith communities welcoming those of all traditions. At the same time, Methodist chaplaincies have evolved from providing chaplains for students to chaplains for the entire university community. Methodists now fund chaplains in almost every university, many on a very part-time basis, usually working in ecumenical and increasingly multi-faith teams. There has then, at least partly because of funding cuts, been a double reorientation of Methodist work at British universities; away from a focus on undergraduates to the entire university community, and away from a denominational to a primarily ecumenical orientation.[1]

Gordon, who grew up in the Methodist Church, was an active member of Durham's Methsoc, an evidently active group involving Bible studies and social events. He attended two Methodist churches in the city, where students were part of the music group, did Bible readings and welcomed people arriving at church: 'we really feel like we're completely immersed in that community', he said, 'it's not like being sort of long-term visitors'. He had come out as gay, and while his parents had taken some time to come to terms with it, he had made supportive, close friends at Methsoc. Both church and Methsoc were important, he said, because they kept him 'anchored' in his faith in a society where 'secularism is sort of endemic' and the pressures and tasks of life threaten to crowd out faith.

Many chaplaincies intend in part to provide a safe haven for students alienated from various aspects of the university experience. Students from rural environments may find the chaplaincy community a resource to help them cope with this life transition. Some will find there a religious ethos similar to their pre-university experience of traditional Anglican, Roman Catholic or Free Churches. This religious environment is more familiar not only than the ethos of the wider student body, but also compared with the more exuberant and extrovert, dogmatic and evangelistic approaches of some Evangelical and Pentecostal organizations.

Living at home and commuting to university or studying and working part-time have become more common undergraduate lifestyles in recent decades, both as a result of widening access to those less inclined or able to live away from home, and in response to the increasing costs to students and their families of university education.[2] The resulting rise in time-poor students who are less engaged with campus life means that some are not aware of the chaplaincy and many have less time to engage in activities that are non-essential to their study or economic livelihood. As a result, chaplains have needed to become more creative with their provision, perhaps holding services during the week rather than on Sunday in order to accommodate students' study schedules. Of course, among home-based, mature and part-time Christian students, many are likely to continue to participate in their pre-university church; engaging with campus-based religion is unlikely to be a priority.

The internationalization of British universities has given further impetus to the model of chaplaincy as a safe haven. First, as a student support service, it responds to significant needs among international students navigating their way through new learning environments, social contexts and cultural differences. Along with local churches and student-led religious societies, chaplaincies have served as a significant pastoral resource, helping students and sometimes whole families settle into a new community. Some overseas students, as discussed in Chapter 7, are surprised by the more secular and hedonistic aspects of undergraduate life in the United Kingdom. Chaplaincies often provide a space in which students can express their faith openly, including prayer and worship or informal conversations about common beliefs. The ability to access a community of faith on campus not only helps students' transition to a new place but also provides a moral framework within which they can continue to live. For the students who express concerns about the drinking culture that pervades university social activities, chaplaincies can offer an alternative context in which to meet friends and like-minded peers. For many of these students, the chaplaincy is their church, and regular on-campus services enhanced experiences of community and common identity, although it should be noted that this pattern is more common among Catholics and mainstream Anglicans than among Evangelicals, who often prefer to participate in a local church in addition to campus-based gatherings such as those organized by the Christian Union.

As the number of international students has increased, so have the number of faith traditions found on university campuses. The range of different Christian traditions and the prominence of non-Christian faiths has grown, as has the number of students openly defining themselves as atheist, agnostic or secularist (hence the establishment of the National Federation of Atheist, Humanist and Secular Student Societies in 2009). Many chaplaincies have accordingly transformed over the years from spaces that are mainly Anglican to ecumenical and more recently to multi-faith spaces (Figure 6.1). While in most universities chaplains work collaboratively, Anglican chaplains are usually either in a position of overall authority, or are informally treated as such by university management. For example, at the University of Sunderland, an Anglican chaplain provides leadership to a 'multi-faith team' that includes an 'Islamic imam, Jewish rabbi, Methodist minister, Roman Catholic priest and Sikh guru among others' (Fagbemi, 2011, p. 24). This is largely to do with religious and cultural history, Anglicans' responsibility to minister widely, and the preferences of universities to structure their personnel into sections with departmental heads (McGrail and Sullivan, 2007).

The chaplain's role has, over the past 50 years or so, become more complex and more specialized. In a context where most chaplaincies cannot expect the majority of students and staff ever to attend their services, they have reinvented themselves in many ways:

- as places of inclusive and open spiritual exploration;
- as centres with a strong ecumenical emphasis;
- as embodiments of social cohesion through the celebration of international diversity and commonality;
- as safe havens for students of many faiths and none;
- as leading expressions of multi-faith awareness and affirmation;
- as places and people serving the whole university community, often providing counselling as well as religious activities.

The model of the parish priest is no longer an obvious or adequate template for priests working in contemporary university contexts. Chaplaincy has become a site for innovation and experiment in public and plural faith, a focus of adaptation as chaplains reach out to those beyond the normal boundaries of the church. For some clergy, particularly the more overtly heterodox in doctrine and ethics, chaplaincy has been a welcome refuge from parish ministry. On the other hand, one chaplain spoke to us of repeated encouragement from a bishop to 'take a proper parish' as the prerequisite to further ecclesiastical preferment. Chaplaincy has therefore assumed an ambiguous relationship with more conventional forms of parish ministry, and some selection panels have had difficulty in making appointments of suitable candidates who understand the particular complexities of this kind of work.

Bearing in mind these profound and continuing transformations in the role and activities of chaplaincies, our study discovered that students who do find

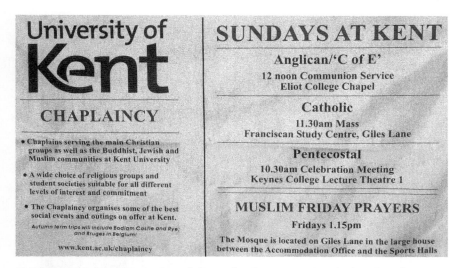

FIGURE 6.1 *The University of Kent chaplaincy tea towel, distributed to new students, illustrating the diversity of provision for students of faith. With permission of Fr Peter Geldard, Dean of Chaplains and Catholic Chaplain, Eliot College, University of Kent.*

a spiritual home in this environment speak with great warmth and appreciation of their chaplains. Peter (Leeds) discussed the 'profound' impact that the chaplaincy had on him, where he could have 'worshipful conversations' with others about their faith and Christian journey. Grace (Leeds) said, 'There's so many opportunities in the chaplaincy that I think my Christianity has become more important than it was before.' Raj (Kent), who participated regularly in events at the Anglican Chaplaincy, told us that the chaplain had been very important to his reflections on going into ministry. Naomi, who was involved in the Chaplaincy at Chester, told us that there was 'an active chapel community. We meet on Wednesday evenings and the aim is to give people opportunities to experience different forms of worship, so we have quite a varied programme'. She said the 'experience of seeing and being involved in different worshipping styles has been very good, and it does make you think more about why we do what we do'. Echoing this affirmation of diversity often distinctive to chaplaincy contexts, one student described his chaplaincy community as having helped him become 'holistically Christian'.

While these accounts from interviewees suggest a vibrant and valuable role for chaplaincy at university, the bigger picture – as reflected in survey findings – suggests those regularly involved are a small minority. Among Christian students, just 2.7% said they were usually involved in university chaplaincy during term-time. When asked whether the chaplaincy was central to their Christian experience at university, 8.7% agreed. This latter

FIGURE 6.2 *A lone student in the worship space in the Emmanuel Centre, Leeds. With permission of Universities in Leeds Chaplaincy Trust.*

figure is significantly higher and demonstrates that the chaplaincy's reach extends significantly further than its regular participants, and the fact that patterns of involvement varied by ethnicity (see Chapter 7), illustrates the capacity of chaplains to incorporate into their work a wide variety of social networks. The fact that only a minority described the chaplaincy as *central to* their university experience does not mean that most found the chaplaincy unimportant. Indeed, our qualitative evidence from among students and chaplains themselves suggests that chaplaincy often functions as an integral, if somewhat ambient, aspect of university life, an aspect of the broader institutional context that, like the Church of England in the nation as a whole, is welcomed and appreciated by the population, but turned to actively only in times of crisis or major life transitions. Grace Davie (2000) has argued this in relation to religion in Britain – that it is 'vicarious', performed by a small number (for instance, priests, religious broadcasters and church choirs) on behalf of a larger mass of the population. Chaplains appear to play a similar kind of role, although it is difficult not to describe the level of regular student involvement in chaplaincy activities as modest.

What is inescapably disconcerting, given the immense scale of transformation in the practice of chaplaincy, is the lack of contact with those Christian students who are disconnected from church; only 1.5% of *unchurched Christians* have any involvement with organized Christian activities during term-time, none of them with university chaplaincies. If the chaplaincy is a first-fruit of the church of tomorrow, then that church may have a bleak future, as it shows every evidence of maintaining diminishing points of contact with the majority of young adults, not only among those of no faith, but also among those who continue to call themselves Christian.

The Student Christian Movement

The Student Christian Movement (SCM) is the oldest undergraduate Christian society in the United Kingdom, founded in 1889 as the Student Voluntary Missionary Union. SCM's contribution to global Christianity has been indisputably immense (Boyd, 2007). Until the mid-1960s it saw itself as 'church ahead of the Church', leading the way in commitment to global mission and its extension to global social justice, pioneering ecumenical co-operation in ways that shaped the founding of the World Council of Churches and also informed later developments in ecumenical chaplaincy in the United Kingdom. SCM Press became a leading publisher of German theologians and biblical scholars, introducing much of their pioneering work to the English-speaking world. At the same time, SCM retained a Christocentric emphasis on spirituality and Bible study informed by theological scholarship, articulated by such leaders as William Temple, Stephen Neill and Leslie Newbigin. According to Boyd, in 1935, out of a total student population in Britain of 72,000, no less than 11,500 were in membership with SCM (2007, p. 28). In its heyday, SCM was a remarkable influence not only among students, but upon the wider Church, with a pervasive influence in society and across the globe. As Adrian Hastings noted, SCM in the 1930s was 'easily the principal organ of the ecumenical movement' (Hastings, 2001a, p. 24). However, Hastings also charted the decline of the movement such that by the end of the 1960s it was 'left almost without message, constituency or even material resources' (Hastings, 2001b, p. 543). There then followed a period that could be designated 'kingdom without church' in which some leading participants embraced a neo-Marxist secular Christianity, and became more distanced and even alienated from the Christian churches. By 1982, there were just 40 SCM groups left, but a significant fundraising campaign raised £1 million to spend on regional workers. However, despite a small increase in student participation, SCM were unable to sustain this income and by 2011 had just three paid staff, based in Birmingham. Hilary Topp, the current National Coordinator of SCM, advised our research team that in 2011 there were 15 affiliated groups, not all of which were called SCM groups, and some of which were new start-ups, plus 45 affiliated chaplaincies.[3]

After decades of decline, SCM now presents itself as committed to an open and enquiring faith, as an exploratory expression of Christianity for the twenty-first century rather than the final receding echo of nineteenth- or twentieth-century liberalism. Linkage with Greenbelt, the annual Christian arts festival that was Evangelical in origin but is now well-established as liberal, experimental and inclusive, has doubtless helped SCM to reconnect with contemporary expressions of broad and questing Christianity. The dedication to global social justice is accompanied by a reaffirmed commitment to active participation in the life of the Church.

Like UCCF, SCM defines itself as 'student-led', but with a fundamentally different emphasis; while UCCF's central organization and basis of faith establish parameters of Evangelical orthodoxy within which the local student committees are expected to operate, SCM's national governance is led by students. Membership of Christian Union Committees is only open to those who assent to the latest version of the UCCF basis of faith, and in some universities this applies to all members, while membership of SCM groups is open to all. What would be heterodox anarchy to the conservative organization is the lifeblood of student empowerment to the liberal. Moreover, the cultural turn towards relationality and subjective experience – highly evident among the Christian students we interviewed – could even indicate that the SCM – Greenbelt axis of spiritual openness, social justice and creativity may yet be coming into its own.

Certainly the national leadership of SCM continues to express a robust and passionate optimism. However, a noble past and ambitions to continue to make a transformational impact upon church and society do not guarantee continuing cultural viability for SCM, any more than for the Historic Protestant denominations that are now in severe decline. The profile of SCM was very limited when this project began, so we decided it was not significant enough to mention in our questionnaire; we therefore do not have figures on levels of engagement among students. Qualitative data from interviewees suggests only minimal involvement but among small pockets of passionate activists. Tori, a student from Leeds, had recently taken up a role on the General Council of SCM and spent her weekends attending conferences and running campaigns. She was one of the few respondents whose Christianity had shifted from being nominal to highly active since starting university, and the political, humanitarian perspective of the SCM had become the context in which her Christian identity had become intensified.

> I just feel like in the past year I have grown so much, and that's partly me, because I tend to do before I think, so I've just thrown myself in there and my Christianity is really important to me now. When I leave I want to work either in a Christian charity or within the church, and that would have not been something I would have said when I came to university.

However, this student is an exception that proves the rule among Christian students, most of whom do not volunteer for political causes and show few signs of developing a politico-moral stance out of their Christian convictions. As discussed in Chapter 2, the *established occasionals*, the sub-group closest to affirming a form of 'liberal Christianity', prioritize living a good life, but express this in terms of vague moral principles and respecting others, rather than any more specific commitment to social responsibility or justice. Moreover, while more within this group have volunteered for political causes than all of the other sub-categories of Christian student, these volunteers still only make up 12.2% of *established occasionals*. A mobilized, active and clearly defined liberal Christianity appears evident among only a very small minority of Christian students, suggesting the SCM may struggle to recruit significant numbers in the immediate future.

Christian Unions

The largest and most visible Christian group at most universities is the Christian Union (CU). They are often one of the biggest student societies, and are usually recognized within or affiliated to their university's Students' Union (SU). CUs are self-governing student societies, affiliated to a national body, the Universities and Colleges Christian Fellowship (UCCF), that not only determines the standard doctrinal basis of faith that local CUs are expected to uphold, but also supplies regional workers, paid and voluntary, whose task is to support and train the leaders of each university CU.

CUs typically have one central meeting a week, at which a visiting speaker, who is typically required to sign the current UCCF basis of faith, delivers either a biblical exposition or an evangelistic address. They organize weekly small group Bible studies, often based in colleges or halls of residence, and often also have regular prayer meetings and voluntary activities such as staffing a student crisis centre or providing coffee late at night to students who have been partying. CUs often promote a limited number of student-friendly churches, to which clusters of Evangelical undergraduates walk on a Sunday morning long before many students have recovered from the night before. Once a year, many hold a 'mission week', with a visiting evangelist or team of evangelists serving as guest speakers. In the past, evangelistic outreach has included events such as 'Grill a Christian', at which students are invited to ask any questions they like of the guest speaker, with the intention of demonstrating the reasonableness of Evangelical faith. In recent years, CUs are more likely to convene 'lunch bars', to which all students are welcome, and at which an invited speaker will offer a brief talk on a theological question (e.g. why does God allow suffering?), before opening up the floor for questions from the audience. Throughout the year, CU students will also endeavour to run small groups for enquirers, often using *Student Alpha* or an equivalent programme from a less charismatic source, such as *Christianity Explored*. In sum, active members of CUs are likely to be very busy students, engaging in frequent prayer and Bible study, churchgoing and volunteering, with an eager concern to assist in the conversion of others.

Although from the outside it is easy and sometimes convenient to caricature CUs as uniformly 'hot Prots', Bible-bashing fundamentalists who are anti-gay and anti-women, in fact the complex diversity within contemporary Evangelicalism generally is mirrored within the CUs. Central emphases remain Bible and conversion, with an unswerving emphasis upon biblical infallibility, reformed doctrine, penal substitution and the dire consequence of eternal suffering in hell for all who do not come to personal faith in Christ. But these are emphasized to varying degrees, and for many are upheld alongside, or made subservient to, an affirming community experience of faith, in which relationality with their peers, communal spirituality and an optimistic ethos, grounded in Bible study and prayer, are pivotal to their religious identity.

Evangelical diversity creates increasing pressures for an Evangelical organization that aspires to be inclusive. UCCF states that they are 'Passionate about unity: gathering and uniting all Christians around the essential truths of the gospel'.[4] However, centre stage is a rigorously conservative definition of 'the essential truths of the gospel', articulated in such a form that the aspiration to unite 'all Christians' is premised on a very specific understanding of the term 'Christian', appropriated in sectarian terms to be more or less synonymous with conservative Evangelical Protestantism. According to such a model, penal substitutionary atonement, biblical infallibility and belief in hell as a place of eternal punishment for non-Christians, are central aspects of Christianity.

UCCF's resistance to Evangelical pluralism proved highly successful in the twentieth century. Even though many moderate Evangelical leaders privately bemoaned the organization's intolerant conservatism, no alternatives emerged that achieved national prominence. Moreover, this prominence has allowed a consistently conservative doctrinal basis to remain uncontested, issuing a model of Christian identity far more rigid and uncompromising than would be comfortable for most Christians in the United Kingdom, and arguably most Evangelicals. Even compared to the Inter-varsity Christian Fellowship, its sister organization in the United States – ordinarily associated with more strident forms of Evangelical Christianity – UCCF has been able to sustain a more homogeneous 'Evangelical canopy', an impression reinforced by its well-publicized and theologically comprehensive 'basis of faith', an eleven-point manifesto for a thoroughgoing conservative Evangelicalism.[5]

These religious and organizational trends sit uncomfortably alongside a wider cultural tide that works against the claims of exclusivist religious groups, instead favouring the language of inclusion and co-operation, driven in part by the ecumenical movement and in part by broader liberal agendas associated with equality of opportunity. These cultural shifts have informed in recent years the 'CU wars', in which several CUs, including UCL (2004), Birmingham (2006), Exeter (2006) and Edinburgh (2006), have battled eviction from Student Unions and exclusion from university premises. The disputes have centred upon CUs' affiliation to UCCF, the restriction of leadership positions to those who sign the basis of faith, the refusal to have a democratically elected leadership and the refusal to have a Students Union rep on the executive. In the case of Edinburgh, the concern was that the CU was running a course on sexuality that promoted homophobia; the University authorities concurred that the course contravened its Equality and Diversity Policy. In some cases legal action sponsored by UCCF was threatened, but compromises have been found: for example, the Edinburgh CU was permitted to continue running its course, but only from a private residence, and the Exeter CU was renamed the *Evangelical* Christian Union, to indicate its particular ethos, following an SU vote on a compromise motion proposed by a CU member. These disputes are symptomatic of a rising mood of moral disapproval towards expressions of religion that are inconsistent with the dominant cultural norms of affirming gender and sexual equality, tolerance and the avoidance of imposing religious opinions on others.

Profiling Christian Union members

10% of those who identified as Christian in our survey said they were usually involved in Christian Unions during university term-time. Of course, in any religious grouping there will be a committed core and a wider periphery. 49.4% of these CU Christians are in a Bible Study Group, compared with just 8.8% among all Christians outside CUs. 30.6% are in a Prayer Group, compared with 4.5% outside. Turning to consistency of church attendance, 75% of CU Christians are *active affirmers* – attending church frequently both during term-time and during university vacations – while this can only be said of 21.8% of Christian students not involved in the CU. In terms of denominational affiliation, those involved in CU are much more clustered than those who are not, with 80% claiming a background in the Protestant churches – spread fairly evenly across Anglicanism, the free churches and the independent Evangelical/Pentecostal churches. At university, the majority (69.9%) attend Anglican or Evangelical/Pentecostal churches, reflecting their status as centres of university-based Christian vitality, as argued in Chapter 4. Reflecting this relatively high participation in group-based Christian activities, over two-thirds of Christians in CUs have three or more close Christian friends, which is true of less than two in five of Christians outside CUs.

CU Christians' personal spirituality is highly disciplined and frequent. The number praying daily (72.1%) is particularly striking, indicating active and sustained personal engagement (contrasting with 28.3% of non-CU Christian students). These figures far outstrip levels of daily private Bible reading: 44.8% among CU Christians, 9.3% among non-CU Christian students. Although we cannot say when this change occurred, there has evidently been a relative downgrading of Bible study among Christian students, which was once the primary and essential focus of the Evangelical 'Quiet Time'.

A slightly different pattern emerges when we compare answers to our survey question on different sources of religious authority (see Table 6.1).

Unsurprisingly, CU Christians still rank the Bible the most important source of religious authority. Under the influence of contemporary experientialism and the impact of the Pentecostal and charismatic movements, this is closely followed by religious experience (although as an indicator of difference between the CU and non-CU Christians, this measure is of limited statistical significance). Reason and scholarship command around the same level of support as insights from today's world, perhaps implying equivalent hesitancy in trusting both institutions of learning and wider social norms. This hesitation is understandable when, particularly since the 1960s, Western society has been increasingly rejecting conservative Christian values, and the Evangelical tradition associated with the CU, along with Roman Catholicism, has been the most resistant to this societal transition. The tradition of the Church demands only limited support among Christian students generally, and while the even lower measure among CU Christians reflects an enduring separatist legacy

TABLE 6.1 Proportions of CU-involved Christians compared with non-CU Christians who affirmed different sources of religious authority were 'very important' ($P = <.05$; $*P = <.10$) (weighted)

	CU participants (N = 224) (%)	Non-CU Christian students (N = 2,008) (%)
The Bible	88.4	51.2
The tradition of the church	11.4	19.9
Reason and scholarship	19.3	23.7
Personal experience	54.5*	50.2*
Insights from today's world	20.8	29.7

of ecclesial scepticism, this no longer appears as distinctive of Evangelical sub-groups. Other comparisons with non-CU Christians reveal only minimal difference, except with respect to the Bible, which reflects the differences in regularity of private reading discussed above.

Of course, a professed Biblicism does not require a fully fundamentalist ideology, and CU Christians show limited sympathy with anti-Darwinian creationism. Although 15.5% hold to a literal six-day creation and 10.5% hold to intelligent design rather than Darwin, 52.7% believe that while God is the Creator, Darwinian evolution captures the mechanics of creation. Anti-Darwinism remains a persistent instinct among some Bible-centred Christians, but it has become a minority and residual conviction which cannot fairly be claimed to characterize most Evangelical Christians at British universities.

Orientations to moral issues reveal CU Christians as much more conservative than those Christian students not involved in the Christian Union, although measures of conservatism may not be as extreme as some might imagine (see Table 6.2). For example, it is striking that nearly a third now consider sex outside marriage acceptable, over a third no longer accept that gay sexual relationships are always wrong and only half (53.5%) are clearly opposed to voluntary euthanasia. On abortion, CU Christians are actually more conservative than students with a Roman Catholic background (16.2% of whom see abortion as 'always wrong'), although 24.2% is still a small minority. While CU Christians are far less relaxed about the drinking culture at England's universities than their non-CU peers, one in five do agree that

TABLE 6.2 Responses from CU-involved Christians compared with non-CU Christians to various moral issues (P = <.001) (weighted)

	CU participants (N = 224) (%)	Non-CU Christian students (N = 2,008) (%)
% who believe sex should be confined to marriage	69.1	18.2
% who believe homosexual sex is 'always wrong'	61.2	21.1
% who believe abortion is 'always wrong'	24.2	10.2
% who agree that euthanasia should be legally available	22.8	52.4
% who have 'no problem' with the student drinking culture	9.8	37.6

euthanasia should be legally available to terminally ill people who wish to end their lives. CU Christians appear more moderate than many Evangelical lobby groups in the United Kingdom and United States concerning sex outside marriage, homosexuality and euthanasia.

James Davison Hunter argued a generation ago that American Evangelical students were engaged in cognitive bargaining, as their faith came under intellectual scrutiny in higher education (Hunter, 1983, 1987). Today's Evangelical students in England reveal a process of *ethical bargaining*, in which the moral absolutism their tradition holds in common with the Vatican is brought into question by the moral values of the contemporary West. We might argue that the contemporary moral consensus appears so compellingly self-evident to most young adults that moral traditionalism becomes subject to decay.

Attitudes to gender roles are also surprisingly moderate. 66.6% of CU Christians think women should be given the same opportunities as men in church leadership. 48.7% do not think men are more naturally equipped to be leaders in society, and another 20.1% are not sure. This latter high level of uncertainty may indicate that young adults who have been formed within a conservative tradition are now coming to terms with the contemporary normativity of gender equality, not only in Western society and in particular within universities, but also in a growing number of churches and denominations. There remains a minority, no doubt vocal in some Christian Unions as in the Anglican General Synod debates on women bishops, who think men to be more natural leaders (31.3%) or do not want all church leadership positions to be open to women (22.3%). However, this perspective no longer predominates within CUs, and so the conservative minority cannot credibly claim to speak for CUs in general or for all Evangelical Christians. This transition hit the headlines in early December 2012 when, as described in this book's Introduction, the national press reported that Bristol University's CU was seeking to ban women speakers from its events.[6] In fact women speakers had always been banned at this CU, which was attempting to reach a clumsy compromise between its conservative minority and the rising tide of moderates. The proposal was that women speakers were acceptable, but that at major events they should share the platform with their husbands. Denounced by the press and under investigation by their Student Union,[7] within days there were two further developments. First, UCCF disowned this new policy as inappropriate and unsupported by the national organization, whether for theological reasons or uncertain of the implications of the Equalities Act.[8] Second, Bristol CU made a public statement on their website that they would now accept women speakers.[9] The CU attempted to sustain unity while managing change, by proposing a compromise that was unthinkable in contemporary Britain. Whether or not Bristol CU actually invite women speakers in future, they have experienced the pressures of a rapid realignment with the majority culture.

Alongside a clearly Chalcedonian Christology – the orthodox doctrine of Jesus' full divinity and humanity united in a single person – views of God have become a little more fluid. Although 97.3% of CU Christians affirm belief in a personal God or God as 'three in one', only just over half (52.7%) make specific reference to the latter. More surprising is the affirmation of Mary, the mother of Jesus, by over two-thirds (67.2%) as an inspiring example. When this figure is combined with those who consider her worthy of devotion, a remarkable 79.9% of CU students hold a positive view of Mary. Attitudes have evidently softened considerably. In the nineteenth century, anti-Catholicism was a defining feature of British and American Evangelicalism (Warner, 2007). Twenty-first-century CU Christians are migrating to more moderate and ecumenical attitudes, no longer preoccupied with the controversies of the Reformation. Although in sexual ethics they are still dissenters from the liberal consensus, in their doctrinal beliefs they are choosing to accentuate the positive.

Despite the official UCCF policy that CUs should prioritize evangelizing fellow students, CU Christians appear to share with other students some hesitancy about imposing their faith on others. To be sure, the strong community of the Christian Union and its sense of activism inspire some members to a passionate evangelism, as with Anna (Durham):

> When I came to university, I got involved with the Christian Union and we started looking at what it means to be a Christian on campus and doing Bible studies each week and the more I looked at the Bible . . . the more I realised that my identity is in Christ, I don't have to worry about what people think about me. The more I looked at the Gospel and the joy of the Gospel and the urgency that there is to tell other people about it, from then on I was like the best thing I could ever do is tell my friends about being a Christian.

Such evangelistic endeavour is often reconfigured into more creative forms of outreach than the caricature of the forceful street preacher, and CUs have become more keenly aware of how resistant the wider student culture is to visibly strident forms of religion. Anna goes on:

> The CU is for us . . . a mission team. So, we're there to serve our campus, so we do things like last week we did something called 'Hot dog hotline'. So when everybody is coming back from the clubs, from about 12 until three in the morning, we'll give away free hot dogs. So you can text in for it along with a question about Christianity.

While conversation rather than conversion is the intended norm for many well-meaning CU Christians, a public image of imposing and judgemental

Christianity hampers efforts to get beyond popular stereotypes. As Monica (Derby) commented:

> I did Mission Week and we came into the university and handed out fliers and stuff like that, and I didn't like it. It was weird. Being a student and being a Christian for me worked quite well, but whenever we met it was never at the university. We always met in different places, and so coming into the university and bringing in the Christian Union into the university was really odd for me. Like when you say that you're a Christian, you get separated from other people, and that's what I felt when we came [to the university during Mission week].

The very low figure of dramatic conversions among students and of 'intensified Christians' noted in Chapter 4 suggests efforts at evangelism among Evangelical students enjoy only very limited success, at least if a measure of success is the number of new Christians recruited. Clearly, some are unconcerned by this, preferring the less confrontational, more irenic social outreach that fosters good relationships by not contravening the rules of social etiquette that prevail among the student population.

The founders of IVF believed with certitude in hell as the inescapable destiny of all without personal faith in Christ, and this impelled them to an unavoidable duty and urgency in evangelism (Atkinson, 1932). It may be that the cultural value of respecting individual freedom of choice in religion is privileged by many CU Christians over the official CU obligation. Or perhaps young Evangelicals increasingly no longer really believe in hell.

While still relatively conservative in theology and ethics, CU Christians demonstrate a much greater degree of divergence than might be expected from both their caricature as unreconstructed fundamentalists and from the high conservatism espoused by UCCF. We are now able to profile CU members as follows: a higher than average proportion are from affluent backgrounds (as measured by parents' education and profession), a comparable proportion to Christian students overall went to independent schools (although fewer CU Christians went to faith schools) and almost all attended church before university. A similar proportion to Christian students overall (c. 90%) are not the only practising Christian in their immediate family. While a dramatic Christian conversion is not the experience of the majority, there are significantly more CU Christians than Christians generally who say there was a definite turning point in their life when they chose to follow Christianity (34.1% rather than 13.9%). Such experiences are much more prevalent – although not predominant – among CU Christians. At university, most migrate to Anglican or Evangelical/Pentecostal churches, with high levels of church attendance. They give more religious authority to reason, scholarship and insights from today's world than to church authority, but they claim to depend most heavily upon the Bible and personal experience. Their allegiance to traditional Christianity is therefore both dehistoricized and subjectivized; it is increasingly difficult to confine them with James Barr's definition of late-twentieth-century conservative Evangelicalism as a rationalist offshoot of the Enlightenment (Barr, 1977).

Half of CU Christians are in a Bible study group, one in three in a prayer group and one in five have taken part in Alpha or similar evangelistic endeavours. The vast majority pray and read the Bible more than weekly, but private prayer is the more frequently used spiritual resource. Two thirds count three or more Christians among their five closest friends, and the vast majority (89.5%) had done some kind of volunteering during the previous 12 months (compared to 57.5% of Christian students generally). CU Christians can no longer be defined as uncompromising reactionaries when nearly one-third have no problem with sex before marriage, half reject the notion that men are more naturally equipped than women to be leaders (over half support equal gender opportunities for leadership in church) and over half accept Darwinian evolution. Viewed from the liberal mainstream these proportions still indicate a strongly traditionalist conservative legacy, but today's CU Christians are showing clear signs of considerable cultural accommodation and ethical bargaining.

The university experience appears to be an amenable environment for the kind of Christian faith expressed by the CUs, providing space for regular meetings throughout the week, organized, informal and social. Indeed some students voiced the opinion that they considered university more amenable to a living faith than life for their friends who had not gone to university. Although a few CU Christians reported feeling marginalized by fellow students and the Students' Union, or by their lecturers and the university authorities, being a student has not weakened their faith identity. CU participation does not generate a hothouse of extreme radicalization, with evidence of a significant fundamentalist reorientation among undergraduates, but neither is university an environment where large numbers of this type of Christian abandon or re-conceive their faith (82.8% maintain the same frequency of church attendance between term-time and vacations; the figure for Christian students overall is 39.8%).

When roughly three out of five CU Christians hold a traditional, conservative position on sex and marriage, homosexuality and abortion, their self-appointed spokespersons may be inclined to speak with an emphatic stridency. But that would fail to acknowledge the actual diversity of conviction within today's CUs, and could alienate most other Christians. While this conservative voice may be insistent and assertive, and the CU is usually the largest and most visible group of Christians on campus, we should note that even when considering the key markers of common Christian activity the CU are still a small minority. 51.1% of all Christian students pray at least weekly, of whom less than a quarter is involved in the CU. 26.5% of Christian students engage in private Bible reading weekly or more, of whom just under half (48.4%) are CU participants. 32.3% of Christian students have recently volunteered in church-based contexts, of whom one in three is in the CU. The CU is therefore not only a minority voice among the totality of Christians, but also represents a minority among the most actively Christian students.

However, taken as a separate sub-group, those involved in the CU exhibit levels of regular practical commitment that far exceed their peers. CU Christians not only pray, read the Bible and go to church on average more often than other Christians at university, they also volunteer more. 54% volunteer with charities, compared with 37.2% of all non-CU Christians, and 81.5% volunteer in church-based activities, compared with 26.8% of other Christians. CU Christians are busy people, spending more time on nurturing their personal spirituality, more time with other Christians, and more time on philanthropic activities than any other Christian students. This reflects a huge shift in Evangelical priorities. At the beginnings of IVF, the liberal 'social gospel' was rejected in favour of the priority of evangelism. Basil Atkinson's account of IVF's priorities, published anonymously, rejected social reforms as dead works, 'to make the world a more comfortable place for the human race to go on sinning in' (1932, p. 17). At the Lausanne Congress of 1974, international Evangelicalism reaffirmed that social action was integral to Christian mission, alongside evangelism. Thereafter, many UCCF participants rejected Atkinson's repudiation of social justice, notably when two former General Secretaries of UCCF wrote their history of the organization and expressly rejected Atkinson's narrowness (Barclay and Horn, 2002, pp. 131–3). Nonetheless, the assumption still endures that CU Christians are all about evangelism, with no time for volunteering and social amelioration. On the contrary, they are the most frequent volunteers among Christian students. CUs at times have a problematic relationship with chaplaincies, Student Unions and university authorities, but their social contribution is considerable, enhancing the well-being of the university community and building bridges of voluntary care with the surrounding area, whose citizens are often alienated or annoyed by the rowdiness, drunkenness and lack of consideration for others that sometimes characterize student behaviour. The CU may promote an unfashionable, and increasingly unacceptable, social conservatism, but they also develop their members as good citizens.

Today's CU Christians are more diverse and moderate than their public image implies. Their espoused values are emphatically Biblicist and doctrinal; their lived values are often relational and experiential. They intend to be evangelistic and win others to Christian faith; in reality their efforts at conversion have very limited impact, whereas their levels of volunteering are exemplary.

CUs may irritate or embarrass, offend or alienate other Christians with their conservative values and their insistence on 'sharing their faith', but this religious environment evidently generates active citizens willing to make the time to help others. Although religious certainty, in terms of absolute and revealed Truth, is undoubtedly the main attractor of some participants, for others the main driver of active involvement is the fact that the CU provides in many universities the fullest expression of relational Christianity, providing strong peer-group support systems of belonging and mutual encouragement. Hence the following comments from students who participated in their university's CU:

> Being in the CU, it is really accepting and as soon as I actually started going regularly to CU last year [I] made so many more friends and was so much happier. (Martha, Chester)
>
> The Christian Union brings you more in contact with people from other churches and other students from other churches . . . It widely influences my friendship group. (William, Durham)
>
> The CU has a strong sense of community . . . I've made good friends there (Jane, Derby)

And yet CU Christians remain a small minority among Christian students in general. Because they meet together frequently, advertise their regular meetings and missions, and can often be seen going to church on Sundays in large groups, CU members are usually the most highly visible Christian sub-culture among undergraduates. Observers might therefore be tempted to consider them typical of contemporary Christian students, and the group where most Christian students are to be found. Our research confirms that such assumptions are entirely mistaken.

Fusion and the significance of local churches

Several other national organizations and networks serve the Christian student community, although on a smaller scale. For example, SPEAK, which has 18 groups across the country, mostly based in universities or university cities, and which describes itself as 'a network connecting together young adults and students to campaign and pray about issues of global injustice'.[10] Another, which has established itself on more of a network basis, is Fusion, which shares an Evangelical emphasis with UCCF, but offers a quite different approach to supporting Christians at university to the Christian Unions. Fusion was launched in 1997, emerging from the charismatic 'new churches' as an alternative relational agency for Christian students. Fusion now works with 500 churches across the United Kingdom, and is linked with partner organizations including Student Alpha, Soul Survivor, Tear Fund, Bible Society, Christian Aid and the Church Missionary Society. The first two are Evangelical in theology but distinctly charismatic in emphasis. The last two or three would not be acceptable to UCCF due to their theological breadth and unwillingness to assent to the UCCF basis of faith. Fusion also publicizes links with Fresh Expressions (a cross-denominational initiative in creative church planting), New Wine (predominantly Anglican charismatic churches), Assemblies of God and Elim (Pentecostal), Pioneer (new church) and the Evangelical Alliance (the older and broader pan-Evangelical organization, founded in 1846, of which UCCF has long declined to be a member). A notable exception to this support from new and Pentecostal churches is Newfrontiers, the Calvinistic 'new church' network with Brethren roots, whose allegiance for these reasons is more with UCCF, although much of its student work is direct, independent and instinctively separatist. More neo-Pentecostal than UCCF, more inclusive of theological breadth, with more emphasis on social action and justice, Fusion also emphasizes partnership with local churches, whose complaint has often been that they were marginalized by UCCF.

Fusion claimed in 2011 to have worked with over 10,000 students over the last decade, aiming to link 50,000 students to churches by 2020.[11] Having worked with 10,000 students in 10 years, which plainly averages at 1,000 new participants each year, allowing for growth and for some students on 4 year courses, 4,000 seems a reasonable estimate of the current number of undergraduates who are linked with Fusion. These numbers compare with UCCF's website claim to work currently with over 350 CUs and 20,000 students, although UCCF's own staff indicated to us in 2011 that a more accurate overall total may be nearer 10,000, with 200 affiliated CUs. Students linked to Fusion therefore may represent up to 40% of the number linked to UCCF. There is a much larger discrepancy in the organizations' annual expenditure: UCCF in 2009/10 spent £3,123,000, Fusion spent £211,000. Because Fusion is less staff-intensive, working closely with volunteers in local churches, it may prove more readily sustainable in a period of severe financial constraints for many religious charities. Even if its future growth projections are over-optimistic, Fusion may have had a wider impact, legitimating a proliferation of local church-based student initiatives, breaking down the former Evangelical student monopoly of UCCF.

The example of Fusion also highlights the significance of local churches in offering an organizational context for student Christianity that is in many locations much more influential than on-campus student-led societies. Historians of modern Christianity have often noted the vibrancy of 'student churches' (e.g. Hastings, 1987, p. 615); some of these have managed to sustain an appeal to large numbers of students over many decades now, such as the university church of St Mary in Oxford, while others owe their popularity to more recent innovations, especially since the charismatic renewal movement and the evolution of the 'new churches' (Walker, 2002). Some churches are chiefly concerned with non-student members, but attract a small number of students for various reasons to do with denominational affinity, local friendship networks or a desire to establish a base for their Christian practice beyond the student population. This latter rationale was affirmed by some of our respondents, whose quest for an authentic Christian community of which they could be a part during their university years led them away from student-centred gatherings and to more cross-generational churches that offered an experience decidedly different from campus life. For some, this choice is reinforced by existing sympathies for a theology of the parish, which serves to challenge the university experience with a call to service to and participation in the local community. Such churches can offer a means of integrating students into wider community structures and often benefit from student involvement as it channels youth and energy into what can often be ageing congregations. For some students, denominational loyalty is also an important factor, although this can be challenged when their new area of residence does not include a church that matches the tradition embraced during the pre-university years. Local availability of churches is highly pertinent in accounting for the contours of student Christianity, and students from smaller denominations, or churches that are marginal within the UK context, may face particular challenges in finding a suitable place to worship during their university career.[12]

Other churches make it a priority to appeal to the student population to a point where this becomes central to their shared ethos. These churches – often, though not exclusively, Evangelical churches – may practice youth-oriented worship, engage in student-centred ministry, establish links with campus-based organizations as a means of recruitment and offer positions of responsibility and leadership to students keen to assume them. With numbers come abundant resources, and these churches often benefit from a large staff, including internship schemes that attract students to serve for a contracted period beyond graduation. Some, such as Christ Church, Fulwood in Sheffield, offer a dedicated Sunday morning service for university students,[13] while Sunday evening services are particularly popular with students attending Evangelical churches like St Michael-le-Belfrey in York, St Helen's, Bishopsgate in London and Jesmond Parish Church in Newcastle. 'Surrogate parenting', 'host family' or mentoring schemes are used to connect students with local Christian families, constituting a significant support network beyond the institutional provisions of the campus. These lively churches are likely to appeal to students seeking a church in which they can spend time with others of a similar age, education and social background. Attending a church that includes a sizeable proportion of students also facilitates connections between church and other spheres of student life, reinforcing existing friendship networks and fostering a sense of wider Christian community among the student body. Organized on-campus expressions of Christianity, such as Christian Unions, can derive much of their momentum from social capital fomented within popular local churches. Some churches receive strategic assistance in realizing their ministry to students from external networks, as is the case with Fusion and Student Alpha, which offers free resources to churches and student societies wishing to evangelize to their non-Christian peers along the lines of the famous Alpha course (Hunt, 2004). In this sense national and local networks interrelate, and in many cases the ideological agendas of national bodies like UCCF and SCM are enabled because of the collective strength of Christian sub-groups, supported and energized by involvement in local churches sympathetic to the cause. In some towns, a single church has emerged as the local worshipping community most associated with the university Christian Union, by virtue of being viewed as theologically most in keeping with the UCCF and its doctrinal basis. Others have seen a number of student-oriented churches develop complementary styles of ministry that are mutually constitutive, as each refines its own strategy to reach their segment of the student Christian market. Such alignments generate their own localized tensions, and the fissiparousness of Protestantism can become especially unpredictable when filtered via a transient and changeable student population. The costs of developing a distinctively student-focused church also include the challenge of retaining an ever-changing population that undergoes a complete turnover every three years. Students are often highly motivated, energetic and with lots of time to give; on the down side, they very rarely stay long.

This issue of turnover raises another distinctive feature, related to the character that localized expressions of student Christianity assume over time. In talking to university chaplains and staff involved in engaging Christian students in the longer term, we found that, while certain trends appear fairly durable (e.g. the generally centrist theology of chaplains, the relative success of the more Evangelical churches), the loyalties and tone of the Christianity affirmed by students is capable of changing quite significantly between student year groups. In some locations, this amounts to incremental growth, as with the charismatic Evangelical Holy Trinity Church in Cambridge, where students make up between a third and a half of its 500+ regular congregation, and which in 2011 reported a 20–30% growth in numbers each year for the previous 5 years.[14] In others, this marks a denominational shift, as in Coventry, where Christian students from the University of Warwick flock in their most abundant numbers to St Mary and St Benedict's Roman Catholic Church, largely as a consequence of international students arriving from strongly Catholic nations. According to the Free Church chaplain at Warwick, the on-campus Roman

Catholic chaplaincy service also regularly attracts five times as many as the parallel Anglican/Free Church service.[15] Changes in the cultural constituency of the student body are clearly capable of overturning established patterns of growth and vitality. One chaplain's account that students often follow the choice of church affirmed by that year's CU president reminds us that less structural, and less predictable, factors may also exert a major influence.[16]

There are also significant geographical factors that can generate distinctive patterns of churchgoing among the student population. At Kingston University, Christian students tend to be dispersed among a large number of churches, reflecting the multi-site nature of the university, and a culturally diverse student body, many of whom commute from other areas of London.[17] By contrast, the spatially compact Durham University, enveloped within a historical city that boasts a high concentration of churches, attracts a more culturally monolithic student demographic, most of whom originate from different parts of the United Kingdom but move to Durham to study. In this context, student Christianity is fostered most effectively among a small number of well-attended Evangelical churches, most situated within a single square mile at the heart of the city. Moreover, each of these churches is highly distinctive in its professed theology, and there is little crossover of students or convergence of resources; by contrast, students at the University of Chester are served by a group of mostly Evangelical churches who work together, acknowledging a flow between churches to be healthy for Christian students.[18] Clearly, any generalized claims about the shape of student Christianity across geographical locations and over time need to pay special attention to the evidence on the ground.

Conclusions

This chapter has identified several areas of profound transformation in the university experience among Christian students. Declining student interest and support has resulted in a decline in funding for denominational societies and the long-term decline of SCM. The CUs remain relatively strong, but only encompass 10% of Christians and in practice have become more effective at nurturing a community of faith than at successful evangelism, notwithstanding their avowed missional priorities. The chaplaincies have substantively reinvented themselves, becoming resource centres for social cohesion, support for international students and the promotion of inter-faith understanding and co-operation. They have not yet worked out how to recover engagement with the vast majority of Christian students who are at present disconnected from their provision, let alone the growing number of undergraduates with no particular faith identity or interest in spirituality and religion. Local churches – especially Evangelical churches – continue to be major centres of student Christianity, although the precise contours of activity differ within different locations and over time.

The broader picture of organized Christianity on England's university campuses reveals a complex array of resources that are effectively mobilized to the degree that their histories, institutions and local Christian cultures allow. Undoubtedly their influence extends well beyond those students most regularly involved, and collaborative ventures appear to amplify emerging stocks of social capital. One student at the University of Kent described a 'prayer week' event, at which representatives from different denominations and styles of Christianity were given the chance to express their traditions in a way that was radically inclusive. The chaplaincy have extended this to inter-faith events, facilitating common ventures with Muslim and Jewish students as well as catering to the different cultural needs of students from overseas. There is a common perception that pockets of conservative Evangelicalism – perhaps concentrated in Christian Unions – commonly upset opportunities for ecumenical endeavour by refusing to share a platform with those of a different faith persuasion. Our research did uncover examples of this, but the overall picture is not so simple, and suggests student Christianity is often not as sectarian in its instincts as many sceptics make out. For example, among CU Christians, one in eight considered the chaplaincy central to their university experience. On the logic of the wider penumbra, we can expect more to find the chaplaincy helpful but not central. It would therefore be a grave error to consider the CU and chaplaincy to be necessarily and always two mutually exclusive and rival entities. Certainly in some institutions their relationship is distant, wary or hostile – one chaplain referred to 'giving up' on trying to work with the hard-line element within the CU – but there is often a significant overlap. In some contexts, co-operation and a cross-fertilization of influences are not only occurring but are fostered by a shared institutional ethos that places Christian unity above doctrinal correctness. This seems to be the case at the University of Chester, where there is a membership overlap between the CU and chaplaincy, and strong positive relations between the two.

In his early work on Christianity among university students, Steve Bruce characterized the durability of the SCM as particularly precarious due to the high turnover of the student population at different universities and its liberal Protestant ideology (Bruce, 1984). He contrasted this with the Evangelical Intervarsity Fellowship (IVF), whose doctrinal cohesiveness is used to explain its growth and continued strength through the twentieth century as the SCM declined. The evidence marshalled above appears to confirm that such trajectories have continued into the present, although a qualified conclusion is called for. The most conservatively Evangelical student organizations do appear to foster the most robust and practically committed faith identities among Christian students, while the more liberal, social justice-oriented organizations – notwithstanding pockets of innovation and vitality – show little signs of regaining comparable influence. However, our national survey reveals that these communities of organized and active Christianity – whether Evangelical or not – only reveal a small minority of the students who self-identify as Christian. The 'hidden Christians' constitute the majority, whether as quietly observant church attendees or more nominal or cultural Christians sceptical of organized centres of faith. Further research will need to explore whether these 'hidden Christians' migrate towards an ever more nominal, ever more religiously indifferent position over time, or whether our tendency to focus on conventional indicators of Christian observance has led us to miss hitherto uncharted, but significant, pockets of Christian vitality.

Notes

1 This information was provided in August 2011 by Robert Jones, long-term co-ordinator of Methodist chaplaincy in the United Kingdom. He also supplied a copy of the Methodist Report, *Higher Education Chaplaincy: Vocation or Vacation?* (2000). This significant document explores diverse models for chaplaincy, in a secular and religiously plural environment; chaplaincy has been re-oriented from a focus on students to the whole university, and from denominational to ecumenical priorities. The report also recognizes failings and shortcomings in practice, with some chaplains feeling isolated, not understood by the wider church, and experiencing the pressures of unrealistic expectations – 'Large MethoSocs filling the Sunday pews, was once seen as a tangible return for the minister's time . . . most Chaplains recognize that they are working in a radically different, and highly secular environment . . . where visible returns can be few and the work often time-consuming, demanding and arduous' (2000, p. 9).

2 In the 2000/1 academic year the proportion of full-time undergraduate students at UK universities living in the home of their parent/s or guardian/s was 17.3%; by 2010/11 this had risen to 21% (almost 300,000 students) (www.hesa.co.uk, accessed 26/9/12).

3 Information provided in interview (October 2011).

4 Annual Review 10/11 UCCF: thechristianunions www.uccf.org.uk/about-us/resources/annual-review.htm (accessed 30/8/11, p. 3).

5 See www.uccf.org.uk/about/doctrinal-basis.htm(accessed 30/8/11). The IVF basis of faith (1928) was revised in 1974, 1981 and 2005, expanding in the process from 149 to 324 words. The 1981 version was more emphatically conservative and Calvinist than its predecessors. The 2005 revision left the exclusivist theology unmodified, but introduced gender inclusive language (Warner, 2007, pp. 168–73).

6 www.thetimes.co.uk/tto/faith/article3621945.ece (accessed 24/4/13).

7   http://ubu.org.uk/news/article/UBU/A-statement-regarding-the-University-of-Bristol-Christian-Union/ (accessed 22/12/12).

8   www.uccf.org.uk/student/news/uccf-statement-on-women-speaking-in-christian-unions.htm (accessed 22/12/12).

9   www.bristolcu.org.uk (accessed 24/4/13).

10 www.speak.org.uk/about-us (accessed 24/4/13).

11 Some UCCF and Fusion data is declared on their websites (uccf.org.uk, fusion.uk.com) and much fuller disclosure was provided by their representatives at various consultative meetings during this research project.

12 Several interviews with Mormon students revealed fascinating ways in which more sectarian groups develop tightly knit networks intended to support students of a given faith in their new environment.

13 Information provided by the Church Manager, Christ Church, Fulwood, Sheffield (May, 2011).

14 Information provided by the Student Pastoral Assistant at Holy Trinity, Cambridge (May, 2011).

15 Information provided by the Free Church Chaplain, University of Warwick (May, 2011).

16 Information provided by the Chaplain, University of Winchester (May, 2011).

17 Information provided by Kingston University Ecumenical Chaplain (May, 2011).

18 Information provided by the University Chaplain, University of Chester (May, 2011).

7

Social differences among Christian students: Age, class, ethnicity and gender

Introduction

Christianity is an important aspect of identity for many students. But religious identities cannot easily be separated from those of class, sexuality, ethnicity, gender, age, nationality or (dis)ability. Each factor overlaps or intersects with others, and different factors emerge as more or less significant in different situations, where some markers of identity are also more visible or more recognized than others. Identities are also closely linked to social inequalities: to be disabled, gay, black, female or working class is to inhabit a comparatively powerless position compared with those who are able-bodied, heterosexual, white, male or middle class. To see how ethnicity, class, age or gender shape, and are shaped by, Christianity at university, is also to see how class, age-related, gender and racial inequalities structure students' lives. This chapter explores how this occurs. It starts from the sociological premise that, whatever their biological or theological bases, identities are also *socially* constructed. Social divisions involve social processes, relations and practices and are created as individuals and groups interact with them. The chapter also considers how important the identity markers of class, ethnicity and gender are to Christian students. Do students draw upon them in discussing their Christian identities – and if not, why don't they, and how does this relate to how class, gender or ethnicity are expressed in the contemporary United Kingdom? Are these markers of social identity drawn upon and constructed explicitly and intentionally by students, or implicitly and tacitly? Moreover, what is the relationship between these social identities and students' social cohesion and engagement while at university? We then discuss how Christianity helps students reinforce or challenge social divisions and inequalities.

In this chapter we focus on class, ethnicity and gender, taking them as illustrative of the ways in which social differences function and intersect or overlap.[1] Before we do so, however, we explore briefly the significance, of age differences among the students we studied.

Age

What difference does age make to Christian students' university experiences? The majority of students in our sample – 82.9% of the whole sample and 81% of Christian students – were aged 18–24; the rest were 25 and over.[2] Age makes some difference to students' expression of their faith at university, as might be expected. In many areas, however, including attitudes to gender equality, proportions of Christian friends, attitudes to science, church doctrine and religious authority, differences are small, subtle and statistically insignificant, challenging any assumptions that younger and more mature students will see the world or their faith in clearly contrasting ways. Younger Christian students are more likely than older ones to experience changes in their faith commitments. Older students' religious identities are more stable. While 83% of 25s and over say that since attending university their perspective on religion has stayed the same, the figure falls to 68.5% among 18–24s.

As Table 7.1 shows, proportions of younger and older students fitting the *active affirmer* and *unchurched Christian* profile are similar. The differences between the age groups are in three areas: (1) the *lapsed engagers* (attending church frequently at home but infrequently or not at all during term time) make up 11.2% of 18–24s but only 1.9% of 25s and over; (2) the *established occasionals* (attending church occasionally during vacations and term-time) make up 12.1% of 18–24s and 24.6% of 25s and over; (3) the *emerging nominals* (attending occasionally in vacations but not at all in term-time) constitute 18.6% of 18–24s and 9.8% of 25s and over. It is not surprising that it is the younger age groups who demonstrate more change in their religiosity at university and in their churchgoing habits from vacation to term-time. One explanation is that mature students are more likely to attend a university close to their family home, so would not experience the housing and church-related transitions common to younger students leaving home. But while there is less change in their churchgoing, they are just as likely as younger students to seek the guidance of a chaplain or the chaplaincy facilities. Differences in commitment to different sources of religious authority (the

TABLE 7.1 General church attendance profile of self-identifying Christian students, by age (weighted)

	Age 18–24 (%)	Age 25 and over (%)
Active affirmers	26.3	29.7
Lapsed engagers	11.2	1.9
Established occasionals	12.1	24.6
Emerging nominals	18.6	9.8
Unchurched Christians	31.8	34.0
Total (N = 2,142)	100	100

Bible, tradition, reason, experience and contemporary world) are, for the most part, inconsequential, although older students show more commitment to the tradition of the Church, with 69.2% viewing it as 'somewhat' or 'very' important, compared with 58.6% of 18–24s. Older students also have lower volunteering levels, which could be attributed to less free time. Generational differences observable in the general population with respect to moral and social issues are evident in the sample: for example, older students are more conservative about sexuality and abortion. Generational difference may also account for different patterns of orientation to religion: while similar proportions of younger and older respondents indicate that they are either 'religious' or 'not religious or spiritual', there is greater uncertainty among younger people: 14.5% of younger people are 'not sure', compared to only 6.6% of 25s and over (see Table 7.2).

This greater uncertainty among younger people may indicate religious attitudes still in flux, or may reflect the younger generation's discomfort with religious categories. There is greater affirmation of the 'not religious but spiritual' option among older students (40.2% vs 29.1% for 18–24s), reflecting Heelas and Woodhead's (2005) study of Kendal, where alternative and holistic forms of spirituality were especially popular among older generations rather than the young, although, as argued in chapter 4, 'spiritual' may be used to mean something quite different.

Universities attract students of all ages, and accounts of student faith that present this phenomenon as purely an issue of youth and young adults risk ignoring the wider diversification of the student body. Age is one factor affecting the transitions students experience at university. Older students

TABLE 7.2 General orientation to religion or spirituality among self-identifying Christians, by age (weighted)

	Religious (%)	Not religious, but spiritual (%)	Not religious or spiritual (%)	Not sure (%)
Age 18–24	15.9	29.1	40.5	14.5
Age 25 and over (N = 2,234)	13.2	40.2	40.0	6.6

may give up full-time employment to study or combine studying with raising a family, and many opt to attend a local university rather than moving to another location. Given that these transitions are different for older students, it is not surprising that we found that age makes some difference to Christian students' university experiences and that faith experiences also differ by age. Younger students experience more religious change as well as more doubt; older students' religious attitudes are more stable, and they are more likely than younger ones to be spiritual but not religious. The differences here reinforce our contention, explored in Chapter 5, that the university experience is shaped by the ways in which it constitutes a transitional experience for different individuals. Age is bound up with other factors like residence and family responsibilities, as well as with class, ethnicity and gender, to which we now turn.

Class

While there is some historical scholarship suggesting that church attendance in Britain has been a more middle-class than working-class activity (Davidoff and Hall, 1987), this is not conclusive (Brown, 2001, pp. 149–56). There is little research on this topic in the sociology of religion, although some evidence is available that supports a close relationship between certain types of (especially Evangelical) Christianity and middle-class identity.[3] Based on its 2007–8 survey, Christian charity Tearfund found that monthly church attendance rates were higher than average for social classes AB (professionals and middle managers) and owner occupiers without a mortgage, but lower than average for C2 and DE (manual workers and those dependent on the state) and council tenants (Accord Coalition, 2009). Also, the proportion of children eligible for free school meals (an indicator of the poorest households) is lower in church schools than non-church schools (Shepherd and Rogers, 2012).

In our survey data, Christian students appear slightly less likely than students of another faith to have attended an independent school (18.1% of Christians had done so, compared with 28.3% of other faiths); those of no religion are the least likely (16.7%) to have been educated privately. The relationship between religious belonging and attendance at a faith school is a little stronger. Nearly a third (29.3%) of Christian students had attended a faith school, compared to 13.9% of the non-religious and 15.7% of those from other faiths. Social class (arguably measurable by state or independent school attendance) correlates with choice of university, as it does in national data on all English universities (see Chapter 3, Table 3.1 for state school data for the five university types). Children of the most highly educated parents and of those employed in high status jobs were most likely to attend traditional elite and red brick universities. Post-1992 and Cathedrals Group universities had proportionately more children of skilled manual workers and of parents with low levels of formal education. 1960s campus universities occupied the middle position, with more of the children of junior managerial or supervisory fathers and skilled manual mothers, and with parents who, like those in Cathedrals Group and post-1992 institutions, had low levels of formal education. But this is not an issue of religion. The survey found there is no clear relationship between parental educational level and students' faith: there is no reason to assume that education of parents – all other things being equal – makes any difference to the likelihood of a student claiming a Christian, rather than any other religious, identity.

Neither is fathers' employment status (in relation to whether he was employed, self-employed, in education/training, unemployed, looking after the home or retired) related to religion. Mothers' employment status has a slightly clearer relationship with the students' faith, but the most significant differences relate to lower rates of female employment among non-Christian religions, a pattern found in the general population (Lindley, 2002). Little sets Christians apart from the non-religious. There are also no significant relationships between religious affiliation and parents' social grade[4] (one typical measure used to gauge social class, which we also employed).

However, when Christian students are examined alone, several things are worth noting. Children of more highly educated parents attend church somewhat more frequently. The children of the highly educated also exhibit more religious change: they are more likely to have become more or less religious than those of less-educated parents, whose perspective remains more stable. Whether these factors are directly related, or whether there is an intervening variable, is uncertain. (For instance, students with less educated parents are more likely to be at post-1992 or Cathedrals Group universities, where they are more likely to live at home, perhaps attending church with their parents, and hence would be less likely to experience the upheaval of moving to another part of the country to attend university, where they would face faith challenges without parental or home church support.) However, overall, there are no clear, strong relationships between social class and frequency of church attendance among Christians, reflecting our finding that class is not significant in determining Christians' patterns of religious involvement.

Nonetheless, our qualitative data shows that class *does* at times figure in Christian students' negotiation of the university environment, as we have argued elsewhere, and with exclusionary as well as inclusionary outcomes (Sharma and Guest, 2013). During interviews, a minority of students referred directly to social class. When they did so, it was often to describe encountering people of different backgrounds at university, to define particular universities or university towns in comparison with their home town or, occasionally, to locate themselves in relation to class. For instance, George (Kent), a mature student, explained that he had never considered going to university because 'from my parents' background, very much traditional working-class British background . . . it wasn't the sort of done thing . . . you know, you didn't go'. When his marriage broke up, he took stock and realized the job he had done for two decades 'was going nowhere'. He was inspired by a friend's son to look at some university prospectuses. His long-standing interest in collecting stamps, postcards and old photographs stimulated him to do some historical research, which led to the decision to embark upon a degree in History.

One university, Durham, attracted more comments about class than the other four case studies and its relative homogeneity with respect to class, race and religion was remarked upon, as this response by a Students Union officer illustrates:

> I think your classic Durham student is 18 to 21, white, middle class, probably – I don't know about their religious beliefs, you know, probably nominally Christian. Their upbringing probably, yeah, upper middle class. . . . I mean obviously there is a diversity, that is a massive generalisation. But at the same time . . . I was surprised when I came how many people there were that had had a very similar upbringing to . . . [myself].

However, while this view that Durham attracts the middle classes appears broadly accurate, especially judging by its lower proportion of students from state schools (60% in 2010/11, compared to 73% at Leeds, 92% at Kent, 97% at Chester and 98% at Derby), Chester and Derby in fact have a higher proportion of white students (87% and 76% respectively). Traditional elite universities are the most ethnically diverse group overall. Of our case-study universities, 72% of Durham's entire student body is white (the figure for Leeds is 70%, for Kent 60%). However, when the postgraduate population is removed from the analysis, Durham's full-time undergraduate population is revealed as 85% white.[5] It is interesting, as reflected in the SU officer's interview, that undergraduate students tend to dominate discussions of 'the student experience', and that Durham's public image exists in tension with its actual demographic profile.

If a 'typical' Durham student is perceived as white, middle class and from a nominal Christian background, subtle differences within the middle class and within the Christian constituency are at play too. This occasionally happened at other universities – for instance, the Anglican Chaplain at the University of Kent referred to the Christian Union as 'middle-class' – but it occurred mostly at Durham. One Durham church was identified as upper middle class, connected to conservative Evangelical Anglican networks in students' home towns and conservative Evangelical summer camps frequented by pupils from independent schools.[6] Such networks provided a close-knit community of support for Christian students:

> They're very kind of tight-knit communities. . . . if you become a Christian they'll make sure that you've got support . . . that you're kept in contact with so that if you're struggling you've got that support. . . . it's very networked – so for instance I'm living with two Iwerne [camp] girls this year and they'll have prayer meetings, they'll have reunions . . . a Iwerne kind of staff member will come up to Durham once a term, twice a term, to check that everyone's okay . . . that the kind of new students are being kept up with, they're being looked after. So it is very, very intense. (Lia, Durham)

This student identified another church, part of a charismatic revivalist network, as being 'for the uber cool Christians who I would say are probably middle to upper class too. People who took gap years and [. . .] kind of really attractive people'. A third and fourth church, both independent and charismatic, were identified instead as 'family' churches; the pastor of one of these acknowledged that 'we tend to get . . . more kids from comprehensives and middle middle-class, rather than the more affluent students, which is an interesting thing'. It is significant that for several Durham interviewees, class was communicated through dress, and sometimes intersected with gender and ethnicity. A Durham chaplain described the 'lads who wear the leather brogues, jeans, quite expensive nice jeans, often a pink shirt or a stripy shirt with a tweed jacket, you know, that kind of look, very Durham look'.

Overall, class, with a couple of exceptions, is a fairly insignificant variable in determining quantifiable aspects of religiosity. It is also somewhat of a 'zombie category', to use Ulrich Beck's phrase, in that it is 'dead and still alive' (Beck, 2001, p. 203). In contemporary Britain, any former divisions between working and middle classes have fragmented and class is no longer easily understood in collective terms; most people see themselves as 'middle' or 'average' (Bottero, 2004). Class is a fragmenting category, and the meritocratic assumptions of late capitalist society mean individual effort is often viewed as over-riding social-structural circumstances. However, this does not mean that socio-economic inequalities have disappeared. In our study, class is a zombie category in the sense that university students occupy a similar position in the educational system and market (in so far as they are all studying for degrees which they hope will lead to graduate-level jobs); many students do not discuss social class and do not appear to see it as an influential factor in their lives. And yet class and hierarchy still structure students' social interactions and university experience, affecting which church a student attends, how comfortable they feel in different university surroundings and which social networks they become involved with. And as students plan their futures and seek entry to graduate careers, their economic resources and social networks will help shape their futures.

Ethnicity

In our overall survey data, there is a relatively strong relationship between religion and ethnicity – for instance, Muslims tend to be of Pakistani and Bangladeshi ethnicity, reflecting their profile in the general UK population (Hussain, 2008). In comparison with gender, ethnicity is more significant: larger differences emerge between white and ethnic minority students than between men and women. Among Christians, white students are the least religious ethnic group on most measures. For instance, they were less likely than students of any other background to have attended church before university (65.5% had, compared to 87.6% of people from ethnic minority groups).

Religious change has an ethnic dimension too. Ethnic minority students had experienced somewhat greater religious change at university than white students. Among white Christian students, 10.4% say they have 'become less religious since being at university', 77.2% say their perspective has generally stayed the same and 12.5% have become more religious; for ethnic minority students, the figures are 16.5%, 60.3% and 23.2% respectively.[7]

Likewise, private practices like prayer and reading the Bible are considerably more prevalent among ethnic minority students. Non-white students are more likely (40.0%) than whites (23.0%) to be involved in one or more student-based and/or church-based Christian activities during their time at university. For both groups, church is far more significant than university Christian societies or chaplaincy groups (which attract a small minority of Christian students). Ethnic minority students are somewhat more likely to seek support from a chaplain, with 16.3% agreeing that 'The university chaplaincy and/or one of the university chaplains has been central to my experience while at university', compared with only 6.3% of white students; this is noteworthy, and we argue later and elsewhere that chaplaincies play an especially important role in easing international students' transitions into university life (Sharma and Guest, 2013, p. 5).

Racial segregation is a feature of UK church life. When African and Caribbean migrants entered British churches in significant numbers during the 1950s and 1960s, they received a mixed reception. Stylistic differences, racism and the failure of the British churches to adapt to their needs, led some to form separate, black-majority churches (Kalilombe, 1997). But this segregation was never complete, and today around half of black churchgoers attend white-majority Anglican, Roman Catholic or Baptist churches (Brierley, 2006b, p. 5.19); the proportion of black Christians who attended black majority churches was reported to be about two-thirds in the mid-1980s (Kalilombe, 1997, p. 322), so segregation appears to have reduced. The black church denominations and sects that developed were often Pentecostalist, with roots in, so Robert Beckford argues, 'the fusion between African and European religions during slavery' and 'the importation of Black American Pentecostalism to the Caribbean' (Beckford, 1998, p. 7, see also 1–13; Hill, 1971). Black Christianity in Britain today, likewise, is a reflection of black Christians' experiences as an ethnic minority (Kalilombe, 1997).

Segregation has also been observed in studies of student religion in the United States. Rebecca Kim (2006) found that second-generation Korean Evangelical students prefer to unite along ethnic grounds rather than joining mainstream or white-majority ministries, because of the desire to build community with others like themselves. She also notes evidence of 'white flight' – of white Evangelicals leaving campus ministries when 'too many' minority students join. Park's (2012, p. 8) study in the United States also reveals that 'being Protestant or Jewish was negatively related to interracial friendship' on campus: close interracial friendships are not common in the United States (reflecting patterns of segregation in housing, employment and education), but 'homophily' (the tendency for people to associate with those like themselves) is particularly pronounced among Protestant and Jewish students. Park also found that the more involved students were with student religious organizations, the less likely they were to have a close friend from a different ethnic group; it may be that religious involvement heightens existing ethnic divisions.

Given that Britain's churches are partially racially segregated, it is not surprising that we encountered some racial segregation among Christian students. Black-majority student groups such as Radical Youth, with groups at nine universities in England (and a further three due to start), have formed to provide support for a culturally diverse group of students. Radical Youth are supported by a Pentecostal church in Nottingham, but describe themselves as 'an independent student led faith group'. Responding to the transition young people have to negotiate when they enter university, they explain: 'As young people we understood the pressure, stress etc. that university can bring . . . and having the right group of people around us will help us be a better Christian.' Their objectives are: '1. To provide support that reflects the multi cultural diversity within University; 2. To offer spiritual and personal support to all students individually; 3. To offer the opportunity for prayer, discussion or/and celebration of Christian faith; and 4. To enable students to support each other by offering meeting places and events'.[8]

At the University of Kent, a Pentecostal pastor has for a long time shared chaplaincy responsibilities with Anglican and Roman Catholic clergy. Recently, a number of Protestant groups with roots in Nigeria have emerged on campus. The result, explained the Catholic Chaplain, is that while there may perhaps have been an increase overall in students attending Christian activities (for instance, one particular group attracts middle-class Nigerian students who might not otherwise have attended a campus group), 'the Protestant section has fractured', and the Pentecostal Chaplain has reported lower numbers at the services he runs on campus. An entrepreneurial style is typical of Nigerian church plants whose expansion within the United Kingdom has been notable, aided by globalization, migration and upper-middle-class Nigerians' desire to educate their children in the West and secure the social status that comes with a university degree (Hunt and Lightly, 2001, pp. 113–15; Hunt, 2002).

Our survey did not ask whether students attended black-majority or white-majority churches, although of the black ethnic minority students we interviewed, around half indicated that they attended black-majority churches; others attended Catholic or Church of England churches or had yet to find one that suited them. While the numbers are too small to generalize, in our survey Black African and Caribbean students are comparatively more likely than white students to attend a Pentecostal church. Correspondingly, white students (for whom the figures are more reliable) are under-represented in Pentecostal churches but over-represented in the Church of England. There is some evidence of interaction between white and black Christian students, for instance in Catholic societies, as discussed in Chapter 6, but white and black Christian students often do not appear to interact. Faith (Derby), a Zimbabwean student, attended a black-majority student group. Asked why she thought there was a need for both her group and the (white-majority) Christian Union, she said:

> I think it's probably because black students will come from a Pentecostal background and the white students will come from maybe Catholic and

stuff like that. So I think even the ways of life differ because they will say, 'Okay, we're okay to –' they'll go raving and maybe the black students will say, 'You can't go raving.' It's like different altogether.

The importance of moral restraint as a marker of Christian identity for Pentecostal students is evident here. Yet moral restraint was also important to many of the CU members we interviewed, and the perception that the CU was Catholic and 'party-going' was not borne out by the CU interviewees, and when the interviewer mentioned this, Faith said that she would consider attending a CU meeting. This reveals a difference between Christian groups' public image and the reality on the ground, and suggests that there is a need for more effective communication between different Christian groups within university contexts.

Two of the five African or Caribbean students we interviewed recounted incidents that could be considered racist, even if they did not use that term, or at least racially exclusionary. Nia started attending the CU some weeks after she began university but found people 'quite cliquey':

I just thought this is supposed to be church, even though it's not called church and we're supposed to be a big happy family. And if I don't feel welcome, that's not really right but I kept going, so I did try and persevere with it because I was just like maybe that's just me being a bit paranoid or something. I just couldn't fit in and I wasn't the only one. And the fact that I was basically the only black person there as well was really weird so I was just like, this is even harder.

She attended a youth inter-faith forum but reported not finding it particularly welcoming. She would like more Christian activities on campus, especially for Pentecostal students (at the time, a Radical Youth group was active on the campus but evidently Nia did not know of it), as she was concerned that 'If you speak to a lot of black kids in this Uni, a lot of them would've grown up in church so they have some belief but as soon as they come here, there's not really support for them.' She continued:

If they're not given that support and if you go to the Christian Union, you just see a sea of white faces so you immediately assume that's going to be a white church . . . it's not going to be our style, so we just don't really get ourselves involved in that. If we had a more overtly Pentecostal avenue to help people who are seeking that . . . but we've got to do it all on our own [whereas] . . . the Christian Union have a church tour so they help people find their church.

Other black students said they experienced no racism at university or church. For Lisha (Kent), a Nigerian student:

> It's so international and even if you're racist, you're going to have to hide your racism. It's so international that wherever you walk, you can see people from different places. Some people are quite open-minded. I don't really feel any racism or anything on campus. It's alright actually.

Cultural difference is an issue affecting the university experiences of black and ethnic minority international students, especially in relation to the acceptability of discussing faith. Abedi (Leeds), an African student, had been in the United Kingdom for six years. He worked night shifts in a warehouse to support his family back home and studied full-time during the day, leaving very little time to find a Christian community, although he attends a multicultural Pentecostal church on Sundays, where he is welcomed and feels at home. He was saddened by the way his faith had become more internal and 'intuitive':

> When I come to England, I realised that faith matters are personal issues. I later learnt because back at home it is not uncommon for you [to] meet a neighbour, you sit with someone, say 'Is it okay if I share with you about Jesus' and they wouldn't take it as an offence or something. But when I came here, I went to [further education college] and I was trying to inform [someone, but they were] like 'It's an offence to talk about God' and just kept saying 'It's a personal issue, please keep it to yourself' and so eventually I came to learn that it's hard in academia here. So unless I find someone who identifies, they might have an interest in Christianity, I don't bring it up.

Of course, cultural differences experienced by international students extend beyond religion. Schweisfurth and Gu's (2009) study of international students at English universities demonstrates that while the internationalization of universities in the global arena has provided many possibilities for interaction between cultures, these possibilities often remain unrealized. For instance, international students often reported that their main socializing occurs with others from similar backgrounds to them, they felt isolated from student subcultures based around drinking alcohol, or found their classroom experiences challenging and anxiety-provoking (in relation to participating in class discussions, for example). International students, Schweisfurth and Gu note, undergo not only the transition experienced by home students, but also a second, 'intercultural', transition.

Religion can often facilitate these intercultural transitions. Researching Evangelical Christians from India, China, South Korea, Japan and Taiwan attending American universities, Roman Williams found that perceiving their overseas study as a 'calling' that came from God aided their transition to life in America. Williams argues: 'A calling . . . guides action in everyday life and it superintends feelings, uncertainties, and risks associated with living in a foreign country, academic life and scientific discovery, and the public expression of faith while living abroad and upon a student's return home' (2012, pp. 23–4). Churches, chaplaincies and student Christian groups help students adjust to studying and living in a new country. At the University of Leeds, the chaplaincy's International Students' Club offers social events and Bible studies for those new to Christianity and those further on in their faith lives; students attending come from many different countries, and some are Muslim, Buddhist and Hindu. For some, their interest in exploring Christianity is generated by their academic study; the International Chaplain explained:

> Often we have students who come from [the] Far East, Japanese, Chinese, and they might be studying English literature, and there is a lot of references to [the] Bible. They don't understand what it is, where it comes from. What is this reference to Noah, or Abraham, or Moses, and then that's why they are interested.

Others are interested 'because maybe in their country they don't have a chance to study [the Bible]'. The chaplain continued: 'We have had some Muslim students and some who have even become Christians, and they said that in their own country, some of them haven't been able to tell . . . their families yet. So there might be big restrictions [concerning] . . . [Bible] study in their home countries, and when they come here they can study freely.' Another chaplain works with Chinese students, running Bible study groups in Mandarin and Cantonese. There, students share prayer requests, often concerning assignments and assessed group work. But while religion can aid international students coming to university, religion can also be a focus of isolation for students whose religious identities are not facilitated during their intercultural transitions. Abedi exemplifies both: he has found a supportive church that helps him sustain his faith at university, but only after having experienced his faith as a cause of his exclusion from the sort of full and frank intercultural communication he hoped he would find in the United Kingdom.

Overall, then, students' expressions of religious identity are, to some extent, connected to ethnic identity, with negative and positive results. For marginalized students, attending a black church or an international student group provides a source of support in a society and university where they are defined as the minority and sometimes discriminated against. Indeed, Christianity arguably functions more successfully as a resource in international and black students' lives than it does for white students, for they are generally more committed to individual and church-based expressions of faith than are their white Christian peers. For white students, attending white-majority churches or student groups also functions as an expression of ethnic identity, in this case as an expression of a whiteness that is often 'unmarked' – as whiteness is in general, with white people seeing themselves as 'nonracial or racially neutral' (Frankenberg, 1993, p. 1). So while the activities of black Pentecostals on campus may be highlighted or even problematized, the exclusion experienced by black students who attempt to join a long-standing white-dominated Christian society often go unnoticed. Moreover, Christianity may exacerbate existing cultural silences about race and racism. As Emerson and Smith (2000) argue, based on their research with American Evangelical Protestants, Protestantism's focus on individualism (seeing believers as individuals rather than defined by their social differences), relationalism (emphasizing interpersonal relationships) and anti-structuralism, means that structural constraints and social forces – such as racial or socio-economic segregation – tend to be ignored. We will return to these issues towards the end of the chapter, after considering the significance of gender for Christian students' university experience.

Gender

Turning first to the survey data, this section begins by examining whether there are gender differences in responses, before turning to attitudes to gender related issues. More females than males responded to the questionnaire survey; the proportion of respondents who are female is 61.4%. Of Christians, a higher proportion are female (64.9%). This over-representation of females – which has been accounted for in the process of weighting the data – suggests slightly greater interest in religion and Christianity among women, supporting existing research (Brown, 2001; Trzebiatowska and Bruce, 2012; Walter and Davie, 1998). As to whether there are significant gender differences in the sample as a whole, the answer, for the most part, is no. The overall pattern is gender similarity: males and females are far more similar than they are different. This finding is important, given the historical tendency in some religions to encourage men and women to adhere to different ideals (for instance, encouraging men to focus on employment and developing leadership skills, and encouraging women to concentrate on home and family). Whatever social and religious influences students may have experienced (for instance, being taught by their Catholic or Evangelical churches that only men are suitable for priesthood or church leadership, or learning at school that certain career choices are more suitable for women), few of these have translated into observable gender differences in religious attitudes or behaviour.

However, there are *some* significant differences. Among Christian students, males are more likely to describe themselves as not religious or spiritual (21.3% of males vs 11.5% of females), suggesting that definitive categories are more attractive to men, while females are more likely to describe themselves as not religious but spiritual (35.6% vs 24.4% for males). (The 'religious' proportions are similar.) Female students' greater leaning towards spirituality echoes findings from other studies, notably Woodhead's (2007) work on women's greater attraction to alternative spirituality in Kendal, northern England. Religious categories, we suggest, are slightly more fluid and their appropriation more subtle among women.

Christian males had experienced slightly more religious change, asserting slightly less often than females that 'my current religious identity is the one I have always had', and are a little more likely to assert that they had become either less or more religious since they started university. For males, university may be a somewhat more challenging environment for retaining their pre-university faith, but also an environment where faith is strengthened. Males are no less likely than females to have attended church before university, and there is no significant difference in attendance once they arrive (other than that women are slightly more likely than men to be occasional attendees – 37.1% in comparison to 29.5% of men).

While the differences are very small, Christian males (21.2%) are more prone than females (15%) to report that none of their five closest friends were Christian, suggesting that among male students, faith is somewhat more privatized. Conversely, males are slightly more likely to say that the chaplaincy or a chaplain has been central to their university experience (11.3% vs 7.0%); perhaps males are slightly less likely than females to discuss problems and emotions with friends, preferring to seek out a chaplain (also likely to be male) instead. Slightly more females had been involved in charitable activities during the past 12 months (41.7% of females, 34.6% of males). There is no significant gender difference in involvement in political, religious or church-based volunteering, mirroring the findings of the UK Citizenship Survey 2010–11.[9]

Attitudes to gender equality

Generally speaking, religion is associated with traditional attitudes to gender. McAndrew's (2010) analysis of British Social Attitudes data shows that those who believe in God, belong to a religion and attend a place of worship at least sometimes, display more conservative gender attitudes than others in the population. Youth, however, is associated with greater liberalism (Park, Phillips and Johnson, 2004, pp. 51–61). So how do the (mostly young) Christian students in our study compare? Firstly, Christian students strongly support gender equality: 80% agree or strongly agree that women should have the same opportunities as men to contribute to church leadership; only 10% disagree. Responses show a very small gender difference: males are slightly more prone to disagree or remain unsure, while females are slightly more likely to agree strongly. *Active affirmers* are the group most likely to express a traditionalist view (19.9% disagreeing or strongly disagreeing with equality in church leadership), and these students have backgrounds and current churchgoing commitments that are spread across the denominations.

The statement 'Men are more naturally equipped to be leaders in society' produced a stronger gender difference and revealed less egalitarian attitudes (Table 7.3). Two-thirds of Christian students disagree (half of them strongly) with the statement. Males are more likely than females to agree or strongly agree with the statement (32.7% compared to 17.4%); combined figures for disagree and strongly disagree are 51.2% for males but 72.7% for females.

Among Christian students, gender proves to be more significant than ethnicity, frequency of church attendance and whether or not a student attends an Evangelical church in predicting agreement with a statement affirming a natural male proclivity for leadership. Broader studies of men and women's attitudes to gender issues find a similar pattern: men are consistently more conservative than women (Crompton and Lyonnette, 2008). Male traditionalism also emerges when attitudes to homosexuality are examined. Christian males are more likely than females to consider sexual relations between two adults of the same sex always or sometimes wrong (43.2%, compared to 30.8% for females). On abortion and attitudes to sex before marriage, however, there is no significant difference, and on assisted suicide and attitudes to marrying outside the Christian faith there is barely any difference.

TABLE 7.3 Responses to the statement: 'Men are more naturally equipped to be leaders in society', by gender (weighted)

	Strongly disagree (%)	Disagree (%)	Not sure (%)	Agree (%)	Strongly agree (%)
Male	19.6	31.6	16.1	26.1	6.6
Female (N = 2,233)	39.0	33.7	9.9	15.0	2.4

Interview data: How faith influences attitudes to gender

Given the tendency for religious people to hold traditional views of gender roles, it is likely that theological beliefs and interpretations, as well as gender norms within religious communities, are partly responsible for gender conservatism. Interview data pointed to further factors, principally support for biological essentialism. During interviews, we asked students how their faith influenced their attitudes to gender and feminism (alongside sexuality and marriage). Responses fell into four main groups. Some said there had been no or little influence; the second group thought their faith required a conservative approach; the third group thought their faith required an egalitarian one. The final group blended egalitarianism and gender-traditionalism.

The first group indicated that their faith had minimal or no influence on their attitudes to gender. Some cited family or mainstream society as influences, and others had accepted the position of their church without thinking deeply about it. For students who were brought up going to church, family and church attitudes could be difficult to disentangle. Monica and Victoria were from this group. Like several who described their view that men and women should adopt different roles as 'traditional', Monica (Derby) described herself as 'old-fashioned'. She believes in equality, and sees herself as 'more laid back' than her family, but is influenced by her family's traditional approach:

Interviewer: Would you believe in gender equality within your marriage?

Monica: I don't know, to be honest. Yeah I think so. I think to some degree, yeah, everything has to be fair. I think things have to be equal, but I wouldn't kick up a fuss, be oh, you know, rights for the wife . . . In a way I'm quite old fashioned in that the man is the head of the household sort of thing, especially on my mum's side; that's how they've always been brought up, and my granddad was very much the head of the household and he had the [last] word sort of thing. . . . I think I'm a bit more laid back than my family, . . . [but] it's still a part, because if you're brought up with it, then that's how you're going to think, but I wouldn't want to go over the top and be like rights, rights, just because I'm a woman. . . .

Victoria's family raised her in the Christadelphian church. She explained that only men preach, although women take other roles in services, saying, 'I don't have a problem with [it]. I'm more than happy to have a backseat in it.' She acknowledged that others might object to this, given that in society and in the

Church of England 'there is such a push for equality'; she appears to applaud her church's traditionalist position as in some sense countercultural – counter to the mainstream church as well as to society. 'I don't see that affecting my faith at all or being a problem really', she explained, 'everyone is happy with their roles and . . . that's just how it's always been. You have had no reason to challenge it'.

Essentialism is defined by Rahman and Jackson as 'any form of thinking that characterizes or explains aspects of human behaviour and identity as part of human "essence": a biological and/or psychologically irreducible quality of the individual that is immutable and *pre*-social' (2010, pp. 16–17). This notion was present within some of our interviews, especially for students who drew on 'common sense' to defend gender-conservative views. Some students perceived that men and women were 'naturally', 'biologically' or 'scientifically' different, that gender differences should be embraced rather than denied, and do or should translate into differences in men and women's social functions. Sally (Chester) explained that she thought that men should initiate dating relationships and it was legitimate for men to protect women because of 'scientific' differences.

> I agree with the fact that men and women are equal. I do not think that one is more important or higher than [the other] . . . . But I don't think that saying things like the guy should protect the woman rather than the woman protecting the man – I don't think of that as sexist because men and women are different. Scientifically, men are normally stronger than women and that's just the way it is. And women are normally more emotional, and I don't think that it's sexist to say that . . . I think that the people that go around who are really strong feminists and say 'oh, no, who says that they're stronger and who says that they should protect?', I think it's naïve. Because I just think we need to accept that we are different, but that our differences are actually important and that we're still equal in that.

The 'biological' differences these students referred to involved men's greater physical strength and women's greater emotionalism. Feminism was perceived by some of the more conservative students as denying these differences. It is particularly interesting that the arguments students marshalled in support of essentialism were often not related to theology or the Bible. But given that in wider UK society essentialist ideas about gender circulate widely within popular culture (Gill, 2007), it is not surprising to see them featuring in students' responses.

If essentialism represents a kind of cultural 'common sense' leading some students to advocate gender conservatism, there is another, contrasting, form of cultural 'common sense' operating, one supporting gender equality. Some students who advocated equality did so because they saw it as 'logical', 'rational', or 'just common sense', speaking of gender traditionalism as 'ridiculous' or 'absurd'. Gloria (Kent) veered between stating that her feminist views were integral to her faith, and saying she felt they lay outside of it ('I think I go against my own faith really'). Her foundational view that 'I don't believe religion should be based on the fact that one sex is less equal than the other' led her to 'take some parts from a service I attend and look at some things and say, "I don't agree with what you're saying there," and take it and leave it at that'. She continued:

> To me, my faith is about everyone being equal but then it's been in the news in recent years . . . a big ding-dong about women becoming ordained. I just found it the most ridiculous argument. No one can argue that a woman can't do the job of a man. I just thought we're not talking about something that specifically requires male genitalia or anything like this . . . We're talking about a job, about leading people in their faith and how can you possibly not do that as a woman? I just think that's absurd because that goes against our faith. How can you have a faith about love and respect and then completely sideline fifty per cent of the population?

It seems that for this first group of Christian students, there are two forms of cultural common sense operating: one advocating gender difference (this is the dominant form), another, gender equality.

The second group believed the Bible teaches gender equality in worth and spiritual status, but considered men and women suited for different roles. This perspective, supporting equal worth but different and complementary roles (men as leaders and women as helpers), is often called complementarianism, by both its Evangelical advocates (e.g. James, 2002; Piper, 1991) and scholars of Evangelicalism and gender (Bryant, 2006). The complementarian group of students mostly emphasized positions in church, explaining that the Bible teaches that women should not take leadership or priestly roles. However, few supported differences in family roles. Regular churchgoers attending Evangelical (most commonly), Catholic and LDS churches dominated this group. Chloe, who attended a Catholic church, said she had become more open to the idea of gender equality since attending university, but still found it hard to accept the idea of women as priests. The role of Mary provided her with evidence for women having a prominent role ('I think that women have a very strong role in the church, because I think, you know, Mary shows that'), yet as for female priests, she was reluctant to 'ignore 2000 years of church history'.

Nia attended a Pentecostal church where women were pastors. She believed that the Bible teaches not different roles in church, but instead requires male leadership in marriage. She confessed that she would find submitting to a husband within marriage 'quite hard', but she would 'have to learn how to submit':

> I believe that women can be pastors because God's used women in the Bible to do a lot of things, like Esther and Ruth and people like that, and Deborah. I think we're equal in God's eyes but I don't think that we're exactly on the same footing. It's so hard to explain and I struggle with this a lot because I want to be independent! But for now, it's o.k. in my position as a single young lady, it's o.k. for me to be as I am . . . But as soon as I enter into a relationship, I will need to understand that the man is God's appointed head of the family. It's not that literally he's going to dictate everything . . . I don't think I suddenly become a puppet but I think when it comes to certain things. . ., you've got to listen to what your husband's saying. But I also believe that whatever God says to my husband, he will confirm to me because my husband could be wrong . . . If it's contrary to the word of God, if my husband told me I need to go and jump off a building because it's going to save my family, I'm like, 'No.' . . . [God] wouldn't say that to me because that's taking my own life. So if he's going to say some random foolishness like that . . ., I'm not going to listen, I'm just going to pray for his deliverance.

The struggle Nia described between independence as a single woman and the submissive position she will try to take on when she marries is evident; she tried to reconcile it by explaining that she will retain personal responsibility for discerning, with God's help, whether her husband's decisions are 'contrary to the word of God'. Others studying Evangelicals and marriage note the typicality of these sorts of negotiation between the traditional or complementarian approach and the more individualized approach common to contemporary Western culture (Aune, 2006); as Gallagher (2003) puts it, Evangelicals operate 'symbolic traditionalism' alongside 'pragmatic egalitarianism'.

The third group believed Christianity encouraged them to see the genders as functionally equal, and described Jesus as the champion of the marginalized, including women. Most of this group were regular churchgoers from a variety of denominations, sharing a belief that, being a Christian obligated them to defend, even promote, equality. They cited Jesus' life, as recounted in the Gospels, as their example; sometimes they dismissed the Old Testament and Epistles as of less importance or flawed because of the difficulties arising from their very different cultural contexts. For Alicia (Derby):

> My faith influences those issues because I believe that we are all equal in the eyes of God . . . To say that we're all God's children but I'm slightly better than you is somewhat idiotic. I think that a lot of stuff that is quoted

[from the Bible] in order to promote inequality . . . ignores the basic tenets of Jesus' teachings which is the last word of God from the Son of God and therefore should be given precedence over something written in Leviticus . . . I find a lot of Christianity quite hypocritical because we do pick and choose. I can't name the amount of times I've had Leviticus thrown at me and then you ask them if they are wearing mixed fibres or the last time they sacrificed two dozen turtle doves after they had their period and they look at you blankly. I don't think that because Jesus didn't have female disciples, that means we can't have female vicars . . . 2,000 years ago female disciples wouldn't have been much use because no-one would listen to them. Also, 2,000 years ago we had slavery, the Romans had a big empire and . . . they used to put people to death for crimes. We don't do any of those things anymore. I think that Jesus never at any point said that women were less than men . . . To use that as an excuse to promote inequality is wrong.

Jessica (Durham) described her exasperation with the use of the Bible to marginalize women and lesbian, gay, bisexual and transgender people. 'I guess I just think it's more about the spirit than the letter of the law,' she explained: 'Jesus only gave us two commandments. He said, love your neighbour as yourself and love God. That pretty much covers everything.' Having a feminist mother had shaped her views about gender equality:

I guess I've always had a sort of innate feeling about prejudice . . . My mum was quite a staunch feminist and she went to medical school at a time when they had a quota on women. Telling me about what life was like then for minorities and for women, it was shocking . . . To hear about this I think, well I need to take up the fight for the current thing which is currently LGBT rights. I'm not transgender myself, but they deserve rights too and I ought to campaign for that . . . Jesus would always try and stand up for minorities like Sumerian women at the well. The story of the good Samaritan, that was a minority race that the Jews hated at the time . . . He was always defending people who were unclean . . . I thought well, he certainly was a proper freedom fighter. He went against cultural norms to do what was right.

Some, like Alicia and Jessica, considered their views on gender and feminism to be theologically sound, deriving especially from the teachings of Jesus. They cited the Old Testament or the New Testament Epistles less often; here, they were quite different from the students who drew upon the Old Testament and the Epistles to defend their complementarian position.

The fourth group combined gender traditional and egalitarian views and came from a variety of church backgrounds, with some not attending church at all. Olivia (Derby) had previously attended Evangelical churches but since coming to university as a mature student had stopped going to church. She appeared to blame religion for conflicts about gender, saying: 'If it [religion] didn't exist I don't think there would be gender issues.' She continued:

> I am not a feminist. I don't think that men and women are equal. I think we're equal in value and worth but I think we have different strengths and I guess different weaknesses. Not better or worse than each other, just different . . . Given the Christian line, I do believe that we were made in God's image but different aspects of God's image. With regards to women in leadership I have no problem with that because if there isn't women in leadership then there's a whole part that the male leadership is missing out on.

Studies of attitudes to feminism in Western societies indicate that most women – around three quarters, taking an average of different surveys – do not call themselves feminists. Feminism is a label adopted by a minority, but its broad ideal of equality is familiar to and supported by most people (Redfern and Aune, 2010, pp. 4–5). 'Post-feminism', an approach that simultaneously takes feminism for granted *and* repudiates it as no longer necessary because men and women have supposedly achieved equality, has become the dominant approach to gender relations in post-industrial societies (McRobbie, 2004; Stacey, 1987). Therefore, it is important to consider how far, if at all, Christian students differ from mainstream 'post-feminist' society. Attitudes of religious people to feminism are, studies have found, predominantly negative. Just as feminists are less likely than mainstream women to be religious, so are religious people less likely to be feminist (Aune, 2011). Our research bears this out: it reveals a wariness and negativity towards the term 'feminism' and a perception that feminism has 'gone too far' in ignoring legitimate gender differences; however, it also provides evidence of Christianity being used to support, or even promote, gender equality. A substantial number of students use Christianity as a resource to inform their approaches to gender, but overall, their views do not differ substantially from the post-feminist mainstream.

Social differences, volunteering and social capital

We have seen in this chapter that Christian students' attitudes and religious practices differ, to varying degrees, by age, class, ethnicity and gender. We have also seen that attitudes to class, racial or gender inequalities vary from student to student, and can change during their time at university. Some have little awareness of gender, ethnicity or class, while for others, these are fundamental aspects of their student experience. While we have examined these factors separately, it is also clear that ethnicity, gender and class are interconnected. Many students only discussed these social differences when we asked them about them; thus, students may underestimate their potential significance and underestimate the power of social structures to delimit or advantage their current and future lives. Perhaps, as Emerson and Smith (2000) contend in the case of conservative Protestants addressing race and racism, Christians prefer to see themselves simply as Christian individuals rather than as defined by more earthly or transitory bodily markers. For students we interviewed, 'Christian' appeared to be their preferred identity marker.

At the start of this chapter we commented on the *social* nature of class, gender and ethnicity. Gender, ethnicity and class are created through interaction between individuals and groups, and in relation to social processes and social structures (for instance capitalism, patriarchy or racial segregation). In examining the significance of class, ethnicity and gender for students, this has become clear. Students live out their class, racial and gender identities in relation to a range of processes and structures, including the socio-economic position of their family, the gender assumptions of their society and churches and global patterns of migration. While it is true that students often underestimate the significance of social structures in determining the choices they make, they nevertheless participate actively in these processes, endorsing some existing social norms and seeking to challenge others. Many attend universities where they feel they will encounter others from similar social backgrounds, enabling them to fit in comfortably, as Evans (2009) found in her study of working-class young women in London. Some entrepreneurial or privileged students, for whom the idea of travelling abroad to study is part of a 'strategic and conscious pursuit of "advantage"' (Waters and Brooks, 2010, p. 218), travel from overseas to the United Kingdom to study as a means of improving their employment prospects.

How does Christianity shape students' gender, class and ethnic identities? And how do students' ethnic, class and gender identities shape how they live out their faith? We have seen how Christianity is mobilized to reinforce traditional structures of class, gender or race: at Durham, groups of students from similar class backgrounds attend churches that dovetail with their class positions; Christian Unions unwittingly reinforcing racial homogeneity because their style of worship or social interaction does not fit with, or appear to welcome, some of the black students who try to take part; and at some churches male dominance is presented as an unquestioned, even unquestionable, norm. But we have also seen how Christianity is mobilized to champion the rights of socially marginalized groups such as women or gay people. In short, Christianity appears capable both of reinforcing and challenging social norms and of being interpreted in very different ways.

How should we make sense of this? The concept of 'social capital', we suggest, offers a useful theoretical tool in taking our understanding further. Social capital is defined by Susie Weller (2010, p. 874) as:

> the resources individuals and collectives derive from their social networks. Social capital is not an 'object' but rather a set of interactions and relationships based on trust and reciprocity that have the potential to be transformative.

As Robert Putnam, one of the key proponents of the idea, explains, 'The core idea of social capital theory is that social networks have value' (2000, pp. 18–19). Social capital, for Putnam, 'refers to connections among individuals – social networks and the norms of reciprocity and trustworthiness that arise from them' 'social contacts affect the productivity of individuals and groups' (2000, p. 19). Social capital varies in terms of the kinds of connections it creates and the impact these connections can have. Putnam distinguishes between two forms: 'bonding' and 'bridging' social capital. 'Bonding' social capital succeeds in establishing close intra-group networks of friendship and mutual support based on similarity, while 'bridging' social capital looks outward: it transcends homogeneity and produces inter-group relationships with others who are different, enabling greater benefits to accrue. 'Bridging social capital can generate broader identities and reciprocity,' Putnam explains, 'whereas bonding social capital bolsters our narrower selves' (2000, p. 23).

Religion is a powerful generator of social ties and networks. It is a source of positive social capital, providing social networks that enable their members to find a supportive community, receive business advice and contacts, bring up their children successfully (Smith, 2003) and enhance their children's educational achievements.[10] Faith-based organizations are also often providers of social services (Putnam, 2000, pp. 65–79). But social capital has a 'dark side' (Field, 2008, pp. 79–100). As Reynolds (2010) argues in the context of ethnicity, young people mobilize ethnicity and culture to create social networks, but bonding within disadvantaged groups can reinforce disadvantage (Reynolds, 2010). Social capital can also aid crime, as criminals or gang members help each other to break the law and cause harm. And the close ties formed within communities can be suffocating for some, as well as excluding those who are outside or on the margins of a social network (Field, 2008, pp. 79–100).

Religion and universities are spaces where social capital is produced and reproduced. Within student Christianity there is potential for the utilization and formation of bridging social capital that unites different social groups and breaks down divisions of ethnicity or social class, for instance through inter-faith forums or within multi-faith centres on university campuses. There are also opportunities for bonding social capital: for Christian groups to act as sources of support, nurturing students' faith, facilitating the transition to university and providing them with potentially lifelong friendships and social contacts. To what extent are bridging or bonding social capital operating among the Christian students we studied?

Participants in Christian student groups may seek to reach out to others, for example in evangelistic or outreach projects, but nevertheless often associate with others like themselves. For 42.4% of Christian students, the majority of their five closest friends are Christian. Less than a third (30.9%) say that one or more of their five closest friends is committed to another faith. Evidently, students are forming close friendships with other Christians, and seeking and finding churches that often evoke the familiarities of home, as discussed in Chapter 5. These social connections appear to be enormously important to them.

Rates of volunteering enable us to examine the extent to which Christian students are socially and politically engaged, with whom, and in what ways. Table 7.4 compares responses of Christian students with those of no religion to our question about political, charitable or religious volunteering.

Overall, more than half of the Christians we surveyed had done voluntary work during the previous year, far more than those of no religion. However, rates of political and charitable volunteering are comparable; the Christians

TABLE 7.4 'Have you done any voluntary work during the past 12 months in any of the following areas?', percentage figures for Christian students and students of 'no religion' (weighted)

	Political activities (helping political parties, political movements, election campaigns, etc.) (%)	Charitable activities (helping the sick, elderly, poor, etc.) (%)	Religious and church-related activities (helping churches and religious groups) (%)	I have not been involved in any voluntary work (%)
Christians students (N = 2,233)	6.3	38.9	32.3	42.5
Students of 'no religion' (N = 1,475)	8.2	34.8	1.2	60.7

do not stand out as more *civically* engaged, just more *religiously* engaged. The major difference, unsurprisingly, is in the 'religious and church-related' volunteering category, where a third of Christians answer affirmatively and almost none of those of 'no religion' do. So while Christian students volunteer more than those of no religion, they do not volunteer significantly more when it comes to political or charitable activities: just more within the Christian community itself.

This is not to diminish Christian students' volunteering. For one thing, 'religious and church-related activities' often encompass projects that work with the wider community including, in some cases, on a global level. The examples students gave us included: helping with the Brownies, Girl Guides or Scouts; being a CU group leader; running the church children's club or Sunday School; Christian holiday clubs; stewarding at Christian festivals; working with an overseas Christian Aid project; working with homeless people; and giving out non-alcoholic drinks to students leaving the Students Union or a night club. A few mentioned being involved in mission work overseas, but this was rarely, if ever, purely evangelistic. Some students had spent whole years before university working as a volunteer for Christian youth work projects, a Christian community project, a Christian performing arts group or a Christian holiday company. Some aspired to take years out after university to volunteer. As for charitable volunteering, students described belonging to the air cadets, putting on dramas to raise awareness of domestic violence, being a university welfare rep, spending the summer at Camp America, volunteering for the Guide Dogs charity, helping at university open days, being in the university Rag society (a student-run charitable venture operating in most UK universities) and doing door-to-door collecting for charity. There were fewer examples of political volunteering, but some students were involved in environmental protests, protests against the rise in university tuition fees, boycotting retailers using sweatshop labour and promoting fair trade.

Which students are most engaged in volunteering? Christians at traditional elite and red-brick universities are involved in slightly more charitable volunteering than students at other types of institution, while church-based volunteering appears highest at traditional elite and Cathedrals Group universities. These differences are small, however, and the higher volunteering rates may be a logical consequence of there being more Christian networks and groups in these types of institutions, making it easier for students to find out about and get involved in volunteering. When the different categories of Christian student are investigated, it is the most actively engaged in church – the *active affirmers* and the *lapsed engagers* – who do most charitable (distinguished from religious or church-based) volunteering. The less engaged in church, the less likely the student is to volunteer. The link between church engagement and religious volunteering, unsurprisingly, is stronger still. This does not hold for volunteer political activities: the *established occasionals* are the most politically engaged. So it appears that close ties to a church community promote charitable activities, but not political engagement. As political engagement is often about fighting for the rights of the socially marginalized, it is interesting that it is also associated with taking a more marginal position at church.

Volunteering, especially outside of the religious community, frequently creates bridging social capital by extending students' social connections with others different from themselves: for instance, homeless people, children from disadvantaged backgrounds or older people living in residential homes. Bridging social capital is also exemplified in the inter-faith work observable on university campuses. This includes university chaplaincies and chaplains who seek to unite, and form a bridge between, students of different faiths. For instance, the University of Derby has run a youth inter-faith forum based in its Multi-Faith Centre (see Figure 3.6), which is itself a space designed

> to promote mutual understanding between people of different faiths and beliefs and to build respect between people as fellow human beings. It is an inclusive organization working with people of faith and of no particular faith orientation empowering them through their common humanity.[11]

At the University of Leeds – the largest university in our study and the one with the most sustained and organized inter-faith work – ventures organized by the Campusalam project of the Lokahi Foundation[12] led to the production of an inter-faith comedy event called Under:Stand:Up, featuring faith-focused stand-up comedy, and sponsored jointly by the university's Christian Union, Islamic Society and Jewish Society. This event was reported upon favourably by a number of students because it increased their understanding of other faiths.

Some of the students we met were involved in diverse social networks and drew upon their faith as a way of connecting to others. At Derby a social work student, Alicia, described herself as bisexual and 'very left-wing'. 'I think as I've become more Christian I've become more tolerant of other people's views,' she said. One of her closest friends in her hall of residence is a Muslim, and they became good friends because they both decided to avoid the drinking culture of their flatmates. Alicia belonged to the LGBT society, and is used to 'being the odd one out':

> I have worked in both Christian and LGBT [contexts] and have existed in both Christian and LGBT communities; . . . automatically within both communities I am the odd one out. I am in a minority. The fact that I dress in strange clothes is my own choice but it doesn't help.

She described how her distinctive style of dress made her feel 'out of place' during the CU church tour:

> I felt some way out of place . . . they're very lovely people and they were very nice and the time I went on the tour was very nice. I went to a [Christian Union] barbecue and I had very, very long multi-coloured dreads and a vintage lace dress on and I looked like I usually do which is strange. I like Goth, punk and Victoriana . . . Quite a few people came up and talked to me about my hair and then left me.

For Alicia, being at the margins of different groups is a creative place, and she seeks to build bridges between Christian and LGBT groups, promote left-wing views and to challenge social inequalities in the wider world.

Therefore, we uncovered examples of both bonding and bridging social capital among the students we studied. Overall, it is arguable that there is slightly more evidence of bonding social capital than of bridging social capital. Moreover, while bonding social capital enables many students to develop close friendships with fellow Christians, it has a less positive aspect because it reinforces homogeneity and existing patterns of segregation. Recent research in two American youth groups, one mainline Protestant and one Evangelical, presents a comparable example. Herzog and Wedow (2012) found that each youth group regarded some of its members as insiders and others as outsiders. The insiders were generally white and middle class, whereas the outsiders, who experienced varying degrees of exclusion and were often socially isolated, tended to come from more disadvantaged backgrounds. Moreover, youth ministers only partially recognized that these exclusionary dynamics were occurring. As Herzog and Wedow comment, 'evidence that religious youth groups bolster, and even create, divisions based on social and economic differences indicates that religious youth groups may serve to perpetuate aspects of broader socioeconomic disadvantage' (2012, p. 235).

Different faith, ethnic and socio-economic groups do not interact as much as they might at university, with the effect that universities remain places where students are segregated – or segregate themselves – along ethnic and faith lines. In some ways this is surprising, given universities' efforts to promote equality and diversity and social cohesion, and efforts of bodies like HEFCE and the Equality Challenge Unit to ensure respect for diversity. In other ways the persistence of relatively homogeneous social networks is not surprising. For instance, the school experiences of students are generally segregated too; as Bruegel's British study (2005) found, while friendships at primary school cross ethnic groups (especially among non-white ethnic groups in multicultural cities like London), at secondary school there is a shift away from integration and friendships become more ethnically segregated, especially for white students. Whether faith schools – promoted from the late 1990s under the Blair government and now constituting around a third of all schools – promote or hamper cohesion is vigorously debated, with some criticizing faith schools for being places where like associate with like and for being 'instruments of social and racial segregation' (Ward, 2008, p. 321), while others argue that curriculum content is crucial, and that there is no evidence that faith schools threaten social cohesion (Short, 2002). Indeed, the debate about faith schools has formed part of a wide-ranging public debate about multiculturalism, and whether policies designed to uphold ethnic diversity have in fact led to the segregation of different ethnic and religious groups (Heath, 2012). Therefore, what appears to be happening among Christian students in the United Kingdom is similar to what Herzog and Wedow argue with regard to American youth groups: 'religious youth groups appear to be a microcosm of larger insider-outsider group dynamics, and these dynamics influence how religious youth groups function. That the groups in question happen to be religious in nature does not exclude them from these typical insider-outsider dynamics' (2012, pp. 235–6).

In his study of American students' responses to diversity, David Haines argues that students have to 'navigate an environment that both encourages and inhibits interaction across difference' (Haines, 2007, p. 397). Even as universities attempt to affirm diversity by creating tailored spaces and activities for particular social groups, more subtle dynamics of social interaction – including those structured by religious interests – often reinforce pre-existing identity boundaries. This is a feature of educational and wider social life, so it is no surprise that it emerged in our study. Christian students are diverse, and their experiences of difference and inequality shape, and are shaped by, the university experience.

Notes

1 We touch on issues of nationality in our discussion of international students, but sexuality or (dis)ability as markers of identity are not addressed in detail in this volume.

2 These figures are similar to the national picture: of all undergraduate first degree students in 2010/11, 79.8% were under 25. (www.hesa.ac.uk/index. php?option=com_content&task=view&id=2411&Itemid=278) (accessed 7/1/13).

3 As Joanne McKenzie argues, the method of measuring and defining both evangelicalism and social class significantly affects the results of any investigation. The literature suggests that in the United States, the previously influential 'deprivation' theory, that evangelicalism is a religion of the socially marginal, is being countered by newer evidence associating

evangelicalism with upward mobility (Lindsay, 2007). Recent qualitative research associates British evangelicalism (but less so Pentecostalism) with the middle classes, demonstrating that middle-class and evangelical identities are closely interwoven (especially among evangelical church leaders); as a consequence, working-class members of evangelical congregations may struggle to integrate (McKenzie, 2012).

4 We used the National Readership Survey's occupational categories: (A) Higher managerial, administrative or professional, (B) Intermediate managerial, administrative or professional, (C1) Supervisory or clerical and junior managerial, administrative or professional, (C2) Skilled manual workers, (D) Semi and unskilled manual workers, (E) Casual or lowest-grade workers, pensioners and others who depend on the welfare state for their income.

5 Figures generated from the Higher Education Statistics Agency's HEIDI database (www.heidi.ac.uk/) and www.dur.ac.uk/resources/spa/statistics/undergraduate/2.10ethnicity/2.10full/102–10a.pdf (accessed 21/12/12).

6 These camps have their origin in the 1950s. They were founded by evangelical Anglican minister Eric Nash to create an environment for evangelism to young people attending the top 30 English independent schools (Warner, 2007, p. 122). Iwerne, the camp Lia names, is one of these.

7 In the figures that follow, ethnicity categories are combined into two groups, white and non-white/ethnic minority, to facilitate a statistically significant analysis.

8 http://groupspaces.com/RadicalYouth/ (accessed 22/12/12).

9 http://webarchive.nationalarchives.gov.uk/20120919132719/http://www.communities.gov.uk/documents/statistics/pdf/1992885.pdf (accessed 22/12/12).

10 Byfield's (2008) study of black British and American boys' educational achievements pinpoints possessing religious beliefs and being involved in religious communities which supported their learning as key to their success.

11 http://multifaithcentre.org/about-us (accessed 23/12/12).

12 Now named Campus Lokahi, the project 'is about exploring the idea of lokahi (harmony through diversity) on campus through research and action' (http://lokahi.org.uk/impact/projects/campus_lokahi/ accessed 22/10/12).

8

Broader implications

This book has been concerned with the ways in which Christianity is affirmed and embodied in the lives of undergraduate students at England's universities. We have, throughout, grounded our arguments in new empirical evidence, determined to describe the population of Christian students in a way that is faithful to what we have discovered, even when – perhaps especially when – these findings go against prevailing assumptions within academic debate or among the wider public. We are under no illusions that this book is the final word on the topic; indeed, there were several important avenues we were unable to pursue in the current volume which will await future endeavours, and further questions that arose as we conducted this project that others may be better equipped to address. We look forward to engaging in the emerging conversations and hope the discussions we have presented here provoke others to pursue related fields of enquiry.

Accordingly, this final chapter is composed in a more prospective tone, and in reflecting on the broader implications of our findings, we exercise the right to be a little more speculative. If the previous chapters have sought – quite rightly – to confine themselves to the evidence available, here we look beyond it, while at the same time attempting to place our arguments within a broader context. The chapter is structured around three sections, first summarizing the key findings of this research, then identifying future research priorities, and finally exploring the implications and impact of this research for organizations variously interested in the faith identities of students.

Summary of findings

Christian students' connections with the churches are highly disparate; some are very active and engaged in church life, but a large number have no connection with any church at all. The more consistently and regularly involved they are in a local church, the more likely they are to affirm doctrinal traditionalism and ethical conservatism. The stronger relationship is between regular churchgoing and ethical conservatism, reflecting the status of ethical, rather than doctrinal, identity markers as foremost among students most active in their Christian identity. In simple terms, views on homosexuality and women's leadership count for more than one's understanding of the precise nature of God or authority of the Bible.

Despite common assumptions about the secularizing impact of higher education per se, universities are not homogeneous, and different types of university have developed varying patterns of making space for religion in general and Christianity in particular. The most distinctive patterns are found in the traditional, elite universities, which are characterized by a greater destabilization of Christian identities, and in the Cathedrals Group, which exhibit a more benign and supportive moral community, reflected in higher than average levels of cohesion among Christian students, less conflict along religious lines, and a combination of high levels of Christian nominalism alongside high levels of active churchgoing Christianity.

Very few Christian students go to church more often at university. For around a quarter church involvement is significantly lower than when they are at home during vacations. However, the vast majority report no change in their faith, and Christian students are actually more likely than non-Christians to say they have become more religious at university. The faith of many Christian students is subjectivized, prioritizing personal experience and relationships with their peers, but this appears to be a cultural norm they inhabit and bring with them to university, rather than something unique to the university experience.

Contrary to common perceptions, most Christian students do not appear to experience intellectual challenges to their faith that are provoked by academic study, and this reflects the recalibration of a faith identity in non-intellectual – and for many, non-doctrinal – categories. Rather, the main challenges to their faith are found in everyday interactions and relationships with other students. For some, encounters with the heavy drinking culture or emphatic hostility to religion present the most notable difficulties. For others, the cause of alienation from their own faith is the practice of evangelism in ways that are at best embarrassing, at worst strident and judged as entirely inappropriate. It is noteworthy that, while debates about women bishops or gay relationships often trigger reactions from conservative Christians concerned that traditional Church teaching has been undermined by woolly minded liberalism, these issues, and these perspectives, were not in evidence as pre-eminent issues of faith among our student interviewees.

University-based Christianity is resourced and facilitated by a range of organizational bodies. Chaplaincies retain historical privilege and in some cases institutional advantage, but often achieve very low levels of student engagement. Denominational societies are often small, with some notable and usually Roman Catholic or Pentecostal exceptions. Politically oriented Christian societies are relatively marginal, although attract a small number of highly committed activists. CUs usually gather the largest numbers of undergraduate Christians, and command the most resources owing to the national networks and funding of UCCF. CU members are far more activist in their faith than all others types of Christian student; they attend church more often, frequently meet in small groups for prayer and Bible study, have more close Christian friends, and volunteer more often, serving both their fellow students and the surrounding community.

The more Christians are engaged in relational communities of faith, the more likely they are to be socially conservative, doctrinally orthodox and active citizens through volunteering. Non-CU Christians are often alienated by talk of evangelism, but university is not an environment that sees many conversions. Perhaps CU Christians are not going about evangelism very well, whether because their methods are viewed as inappropriate or they are too socially isolated with their busy schedule of religious activities and large number of fellow-Christian friends. Alternatively, perhaps the levels of resistance or indifference to evangelism are very high, or religious conversion is simply not on the map of post-adolescent lifestyle options for young adults today. Or perhaps CU evangelism is more important rhetorically than in practice, more spoken about as something important than integrated into daily living. Ironically, given the Evangelical tradition's early twentieth-century opposition to the social gospel, today's Evangelical undergraduates do a much better job of volunteering in social action than they do in bringing fellow students to faith. This, of course, may not be a generationally specific pattern, but may closely reflect the contrast between rhetoric and practice among adult Christians in many Evangelical and charismatic churches (Guest, 2007).

Students' expression of Christianity in universities is interconnected with identity differences based on social class, gender and ethnicity. These shape styles of Christian culture but also patterns of inclusion and exclusion. While Christians are sometimes associated with building connections between different groups (bridging social capital) they are more often found to be sustaining in-group cohesion (bonding social capital), which suggests an uncertain future for the integration of Christian students into general university life. On the other hand, of course, it may be that the university experience, particularly in larger and non-collegiate universities, to a much greater extent depends upon bonding social capital, between peer groups of like-minded undergraduates, whose integration into the totality of the student body is much like the integration of adults into a modern city as opposed to a traditional village. Close community may be a barrier to integration, but also a precondition of survival in the longer term.

Academic contexts and future research

The rise of global fundamentalisms has been widely recognized as a phenomenon of the late twentieth and early twenty-first centuries (Armstrong, 2000; Bruce, 2001; Marty, 1996; Partridge, 2001; Percy and Jones, 2002). 9/11 became the potent symbol for a rising tide of militant opposition to modernity that has found expression in almost all religions. This resurgence can be interpreted as a reaction against secularization; just as Protestant fundamentalism arose in reaction to the weakening cultural resonance of nineteenth-century American revivalism (Marsden, 1991), the globalized cultural displacement of religious conservatives in the new century has produced a defensive backlash. When some religious terrorists were found to have been highly educated, the British government expressed anxiety about Islamic radicalization in universities. In this context it is reasonable to examine whether there is evidence among Christian students of fundamentalist radicalization, a heightened social conservatism and a militant opposition to contemporary society. On the other hand, J. D. Hunter's exploration of ways in which the university experience influenced young American Evangelicals to moderate their convictions (Hunter 1983, 1987) prompts the opposite possibility, namely whether there is evidence of cognitive and ethical bargaining among Christian undergraduates, as they migrate towards the contemporary intellectual and moral consensus. The evidence of our research points much more in the latter direction; Christian students as a whole are more ethically liberal than the churches, and in particular, many Roman Catholic and Evangelical students show clear evidence of rejecting, in the case of the former, and softening, in the case of the latter, the ethical absolutism of their traditions.

This book also contributes to a new wave of research on youth and religion. This is a growing field addressing important themes, including: how young people's faith reflects – or challenges – dominant religious trends; how young people are socialized into religion and how effective this process is; how local, national and/or global contexts shape young people's spirituality; how young people negotiate their religiosity across different social contexts, including family, school, employment and media; how young people position themselves in relation to conservative or liberal/progressive forms of faith; and how social differences such as gender, ethnicity, disability or sexuality intersect with faith. In the United States the National Study of Youth and Religion has been examining these questions for a decade (see, for example, Smith and Denton, 2005; Smith and Snell, 2009), and it is from within the United States that much of this research, until recently, emerged (Flory and Miller, 2000). UK scholars are increasingly contributing to these debates. For instance, Kay and Francis et al.'s survey work has charted the erosion of, and increasing indifference to, faith among teenagers (Kay and Francis, 1996). Qualitative work reveals evidence of what Day (2011) calls 'believing in belonging' among young people, not dissimilar to Collins-Mayo et al.'s argument that most Generation Y young people place most faith in, and live out their spirituality through, 'the "secular trinity" of family, friends and the reflexive self'; theirs is a kind of 'immanent faith' (Collins-Mayo et al., 2010, pp. 32, 50). Much of this research concerns Christianity and its aftermath in the lives of young people, but increasingly Muslims are the subject of study, both in the UK (Dwyer and Shah, 2009; Lewis, 2007; Phillips, 2009) and globally (Herrera and Bayat, 2010). Collins-Mayo and Dandelion's (2010) volume *Religion and Youth* introduces many of the key debates. In the United Kingdom too, Nesbitt (2009) and Singh's (2012) studies of religious socialization and nurture of mixed-faith and Sikh youth open up points of comparison with this study. The AHRC/ESRC Religion & Society programme Youth and Religion scheme has, in this sense, enabled research on youth and education to flower in the United Kingdom.

The current volume, then, joins an exciting and growing field. It also opens up areas for further research. Published work on non-Christian religious groups within UK university contexts constitutes an expanding area including Weller et al. (2011) on religion and belief in higher education in general, Graham and Boyd (2011) on Jewish students' university experiences, and Singh (2012) on the contexts of faith development among Sikh youth. Further studies of Muslim, Hindu, Jewish, Buddhist, Sikh and other major faiths found among undergraduates would clarify whether the university experience has different kinds of impact within different religious traditions. To what extent are the parameters of identity charted in this book peculiar to Christian students, and how far do they extend among students of other faiths, non-aligned 'spiritualities' or those who profess 'no religion'? The widespread 'subjective turn' in Western culture may have encouraged a breaking down of religious boundaries so that religious syncretism is more common, or an experience-centred orientation may be emerging within, rather than outside of, different faith groups. If the shift away from doctrine among many Christian students is attributable to such widespread cultural trends, should we expect to find similarly subjectivized identities among young Muslims, Sikhs and Hindus? And what does this mean for the future of inter-faith relations?

Looking further afield, there is a need for a parallel study in different European countries, Catholic, Protestant and Orthodox, in order to enable consideration of commonality and difference between universities amidst the secularizing trajectories of Europe. David Martin expertly charted these differences in his *A General Theory of Secularisation* (1978), updated in *On Secularization: Towards a Revised General Theory* (2005), and while the parameters drawn by Martin are persuasive, there is a need to ask how universities as public institutions function as carriers of national or cross-national patterns. Does the political project of European integration over-rule or modify trajectories driven by long entrenched church-state relations, more recent post-communist discourses of liberation or established models of social welfare provision, all of which shape orientations to Christianity? Can universities be understood as agents in this process, and does the Bologna Process associated with the standardization of educational provision have an analogous, less deliberate parallel as orientations to religion are consolidated around a liberal consensus? Here the nature of the university as an institution is a key object of analysis, not just the specifics of policy or the lived perspectives of staff and students. In following US scholars Maryl and Oeur's (2009, p. 271) call for greater contextualization in the analysis of student religion, we have attempted to advance understanding of how the institutional cultures of different universities shape the experiences of Christian students. A cross-European study would take this analysis further, in mapping not just patterns of secularization and religious re-vitalization, but also patterns of institutional change in so far as they impact upon the faith identities of young adults. Similar studies in Canada and Australia, where secularization appears to correspond with the European pattern, would also expand our understanding of historical and emerging global networks of influence.

We have learned a great deal from the longitudinal studies associated with the National Study of Youth and Religion in the United States (Smith and Denton, 2005; Smith and Snell, 2009). Analysing the religious identities of young people at several different points over time presents opportunities for a much richer and much more nuanced description of the dimensions of socio-religious change. A repeat of the present study among undergraduates in five to ten years' time would enable exploration of trajectories to determine whether and how quickly the religious landscape among undergraduates in England may be changing. It would also enable us to determine whether the post-university experience is less amenable to sustained faith identities than the university context has been, and the extent to which there are patterns of accelerated secularization or, indeed, positive faith development among this generation.

A series of more narrowly focused projects would also greatly enrich scholars' understanding of patterns of faith, and would also, through active partnership with co-researchers beyond the academy, generate significant research impact. Obvious examples include:

- an in-depth study of the diverse models and present-day effectiveness among students and university staff of university chaplaincy, combined with an exploration of the perceived needs of the 'hidden Christians' this research project has uncovered, and the significance of chaplaincy as a centre of social and multi-faith cohesion and religious literacy;

- following earlier work on young Catholics (Leavey et al., 1992; Fulton et al., 2000), an in-depth study of young Catholics (and indeed older Catholics to explore the extent to which they hold similar convictions) would explore whether and how they are negotiating dissonance between their enduring Catholic identity, their rejection of Catholic moral teaching and their abandonment of regular sacramental practices;
- an in-depth study of the 'hidden Christians' we have uncovered in this study, especially those who combine an active personal spirituality with an absence from church, exploring ways in which this represents a durable and alternative way of expressing and sustaining a faith identity;
- a study of whether the increased proportion of Anglican churchgoers at university who are social conservatives endures among Christians in their twenties and thirties, generating a lasting shift to the Right among the Anglican laity and future clergy and making churchgoing increasingly an activity associated not simply with religious faith but also with social conservatism;
- an in-depth and longitudinal study of those who leave university with no faith identity, to explore whether this represents a settled and enduring secularity and indifference to religion, or whether later life stages rekindle religious or spiritual questions, appetites and aspirations.
- An ethnographic study of Christian identity as expressed and negotiated within Christian Unions and student-focused Evangelical/Pentecostal churches; the qualitative nuance afforded by this method would allow a complementary approach to our own discussion of CUs in Chapter 6.

Implications in wider contexts

This research project was greatly enriched by our stakeholder advisory group, in which we brought together academics, senior university managers, representatives of the National Union of Students and chaplaincies, and leaders of diverse Christian organizations working with undergraduates. As we presented our interim findings, the advisory group discussed together the further questions we might explore and the broader implications of our research. This chapter therefore builds upon a genuine two-way process of public engagement, in which researchers and collaborators from beyond the Academy engaged in mutually enriching co-operation both in the development of the research project and in discovering and bringing into focus its implications and impact. Before turning to stakeholder concerns, however, we examine some implications of our findings for debates about the future of Christianity in the United Kingdom.

Christian by choice

The migration of undergraduate church attendance towards Anglican and neo-Pentecostal churches (charted in Chapter 4) reflects several wider trends. First, most students tend to attend church in groups rather than individually; indeed, those who attend church have more close Christian friends than those who do not. One student observed that undergraduate churchgoing at his university is predominantly driven by 'going together'. This is entirely understandable when, for most students, their primary social network is mono-generational. Their faith is therefore both a personal choice and a voluntarist commitment to a faith community; it is not narrowly individualized.

Second, just as many students are inclined to go to church alongside their peers, they may be disinclined to go to a church where they are the only student in the congregation, even more so where they would be 20 or 30 years younger than the average age. Such an experience would tend to reinforce the public narrative of the ineluctable and rapid decline of organized religion, whereas attending in the massed congregation of a packed Anglican or neo-Pentecostal student church offers a counter narrative of vibrancy and renewed Christian hope.

Third, the cultural priority of personal autonomy elevates individual choice above familial conformity (Hammond, 1992). Students who migrate between denominations may not necessarily be consumerist in their approach to religious outlets, but they certainly embody the near universal cultural privileging of the individual's 'right to choose' (Roof, 1999; Warner, 2006). The pervasive death of both deference and brand loyalty means they have no sense of apology or awkwardness when they deem it time to try out another religious outlet (Miller, 2006; Warner, 2010a & b). Without the inertia of a complex network of intergenerational relationships, these cultural norms are more readily applied to churchgoing by students who are living away from home. Indeed, since their first job after graduation is likely to be in another new locale, this habituation will be further reinforced. When the option of having children has been deferred for most graduates to their mid-thirties, this generational capacity for high religious mobility is likely to continue for many years beyond graduation.

Fourth, since many churchgoing Christians are concerned to find a life partner with a similar faith identity, the logical place to go to church is where other young adults are found in significant numbers. Thus in London leading Anglican and neo-Pentecostal churches, notably Holy Trinity, Brompton and Hillsong Church, enjoy very high levels of attendance among newcomers to the city in their twenties.

Once students have shopped around, they are likely to continue to be denominationally mobile after university. The university experience is therefore likely to precipitate the decline of the historic free churches, and embed for churchgoers the normativity of Protestant migration into Anglican and neo-Pentecostal congregations. At the same time, although many students voiced the belief that their post-graduation churchgoing would be sustained at the highest level they had previously known, whether at or before university, it seems reasonable to suspect that Christians who opt out of churchgoing at university may find it remarkably easy to continue this approach to Sundays beyond graduation.

This pattern suggests the dynamic of change is more Durkheimian than Weberian. It is the elevation of the individual in religion, making personal choices as an autonomous religious consumer, electing whether to be part of a particular voluntarist community, that is shaping the religious behaviour of young Christians. They have been separated from the authority of religious institutions and experience diminished loyalty to inherited patterns of churchgoing. The dominant drivers of their sexual ethics are contemporary, sociocultural norms, with the exception of the social conservatives who are regular churchgoers. If there is a secularizing effect of university, it is not so much the iron cage of rationality, but rather an inking over, a legitimation by university ethos and by generational values, of the freedom of the individual to elevate personal choice above church authority and religious conformism.

Most Christians at university retain a clear and undiminished sense of their own Christian identity, even if its expression in terms of churchgoing and personal prayer, volunteering and ethics, continues to evolve. Their religion has become a religion of choice, even if it began as a religion of birth, and they choose to retain a Christian identity. Many consider being Christian to be intrinsic to their sense of self, whether they are social conservatives or liberals, whether regular or infrequent in churchgoing, prayer and volunteering.

Denominational changes

University brings about a shift in denominational market share, with severe decline for Roman Catholics and the historic free churches (see Chapter 4). Many pre-university Anglicans also never attend church during term-time, but the Anglican market share is propped up by transfers from other denominations, with additional recruitment to the independent Evangelical/Pentecostal churches. The university experience represents a consolidation of Evangelical identity for many newly recruited Anglicans. This relative resilience is good news for Anglicanism compared with the other historic denominations, and demonstrates the enduring cultural validity of this site of Christian religion, at least in its Evangelical forms. However, it also may indicate a transition towards a more ethically conservative perspective, particularly on issues concerning sex and gender. The migration of Evangelicals – new or established – to Anglican churches in university towns presents interesting prospects not just for the vibrancy of the Church of England, but for its future theological direction.

If Evangelical graduates continue with their new-found and often frequent Anglican churchgoing, this may reinforce an entrenched division on gay marriage and women's leadership. Of course, this also means that just as the balance of Anglican church involvement becomes more conservative at university, the gap between those who are active and inactive Anglicans risks becoming increasingly polarized in terms of beliefs, ethics and practice. If Anglican church attendance becomes dominated by the conservative activists, the inactive Anglican majority may feel ever more alienated from their cultural Christian home. Growth in Anglican allegiance among conservative undergraduates could result in the Church of England looking less and less like an inclusive Church for the whole nation. Cultural Anglicans could become as alienated from their church in sexual ethics as has evidently already happened for many undergraduate Roman Catholics.

Our findings indicate a strong association between ethical conservatism and churchgoing, which extends beyond the CU Christians. When the most socially liberal Christians do not attend church at university, it is not clear whether ethical conservatism predisposes people to churchgoing or whether churchgoing often inculcates ethical conservatism. Most likely these two factors are mutually reinforcing. This could indicate that self-identifying Christians who are not ethical conservatives may become increasingly disinclined to go to church at all, finding themselves increasingly marginal voices in redoubtably conservative institutions.

This Anglican transformation raises searching questions for other Protestants. The historic free churches need to consider what initiatives they might take to reconnect with Christian students. It may, of course, be too late for some traditions, many of whose congregations appear to have already entered into an aged and terminal decline. SCM has attempted to recover its role as a liberal focal point for student Christians by means of focusing on political engagement for global justice, but this may also need reappraising. Our findings indicate that most Christian students view spiritual practices and relationships, rather than political activism, as the energizing centre of their personal faith. SCM has always prided itself on being ahead of the churches; if current trends continue, the non-viability of SCM may precede and presage the non-viability of several historic denominations.

Roman Catholic students retain a much stronger sense of denominational identity than most Protestants. This reflects a much higher degree of socialization and enculturation into an enduring and distinctive Catholic identity: a non-practising Catholic is a lapsed Catholic, whereas most non-practising Protestants simply stop being 'Protestant' at all. Nonetheless, while Catholic students retain a distinctly Catholic identity, at university their churchgoing evaporates and their sexual ethics largely disregard the official edicts of the Vatican. This is well illustrated in attitudes towards abortion, traditionally viewed as a major identity marker among Roman Catholics. Our survey data reveal that students with a Roman Catholic background and students who attend Roman Catholic churches during university term-time (overlapping but not identical groups) do not appear to hold particularly strict beliefs about abortion that exceed Christians within other denominational categories. Current term-time churchgoing is more effective than pre-university background alone in fostering a conservative position on abortion. However, for neither group are levels of conservatism anywhere near the majority viewpoint, and in neither does the conservative position place the Roman Catholics apart from other denominational groups. The critical question for the Roman Catholic Church is therefore whether bridges can be built to student Catholics and their personal spiritualties and ethical convictions. Failing such a courageous initiative by the Vatican, our evidence indicates that young, liberal Catholics are at risk of becoming homeless Christians, alienated from the tradition of their upbringing and yet in denominational terms still so fully embedded in the religion of their childhood that many find themselves unable to relocate.

Pentecostals and 'New Churches' have different questions to face. Warner (2006, 2010c) has demonstrated that as Western European secularization generates a post-Christendom context, the monopoly of official religion becomes more fragile. To be sure, the cultural advantage of establishment endures, so that in England the recent decline of Anglicanism has been at a slower rate than Roman Catholicism, the United Reformed Church or Methodism. At the same time, new patterns of neo-Pentecostal growth are emerging, from small local congregations to mega-churches, both among ethnic minorities and in the majority white population. Since these highly expressive churches have a significantly younger age profile than the historic denominations, the current redistribution of market share is likely to intensify. Of course, in the British and wider Western European contexts, the recent growth of neo-Pentecostalism by no means offsets the collapse of participation in the historic denominations. Pentecostals and 'New Churches' therefore need to avoid triumphalist rhetoric; relative to the Free Churches their time may have come, but the dominant trends of Europe continue to reveal religious decline and a diminishing overall number of Christians.

Independent Evangelical/Pentecostal churches also need to determine whether they are late adopters or implacable opponents of the contemporary moral consensus. As purist traditions, with separatist instincts and a tendency to expansive vision, these Christians may be untroubled by the evident cultural and ethical chasm between themselves and most other Christians, let alone non-Christians. Nonetheless, just as all Christian students have elevated the importance and authority of religious experience, the vast majority of Christian students have now embraced a contemporary sexual ethic and strongly approve of gender equality. Pentecostal and 'New Church' traditions need to determine whether they have either the capacity or desire to accommodate expressions of inclusive liberalism and engage in this general Christian trend of ethical transition. Their history suggests the contrary, but previous purist and legalistic religious traditions have eventually been consigned to cultural obsolescence, when their high tension dissent eventually renders them culturally unintelligible to outsiders; earlier opposition to cinema, make-up, alcohol and youth culture are all examples of previous legalistic purity that has mostly become culturally obsolete.

The more these traditions welcome Christian students from different backgrounds, the more the insiders' unhesitating adherence to biblical literalism, a conservative sexual ethic and unreconstructed gender roles will come to be questioned. They will inevitably experience a gravitational pull towards the cultural, ethical and ecclesiastical mainstream, even if their instinctive and robust response is to call all others, Christian and non-Christian alike, to repent their theological and moral laxity. Their success in recruiting students from other traditions may even result in a degree of self-subversion as new recruits question the viability of long-entrenched attitudes.

The constraints upon Christian Unions

The high visibility of CUs at many universities is plain to see. With regular meetings, annual missions and zeal to evangelize, these students are far more numerous than those active in university chaplaincies, and could be taken to represent the sum or majority of Christian students (Guest et al., 2013). They are certainly the most active Christians in praying, churchgoing and Bible reading, have the highest number of close Christian friends and volunteer the most. They are more conservative in sexual ethics than any other Christian sub-group, except the Pentecostals. Their resilience is generated through a confluence of doctrinal certainties, conversionist zeal and supportive relationality in highly activist and enthusiastic communities of faith. It is too early to determine whether the impact of social networking will create new dynamics of relationality that will either subvert the conformity nurtured in CUs or provide new and enhanced opportunities for alternative expressions of faith.

Although CUs sustain exceptionally high levels of activity and prominence they only represent 10% of Christian students. Therefore university authorities and Student Unions should be careful not to confuse the hidden majority of Christian students with the minority in CUs. Furthermore, as reflected in the very low proportion of new Christian converts and 'intensified Christians', whose experience of university has included a strengthening of faith, the more confrontational evangelism often associated with CU-based Evangelicalism appears not to work in the twenty-first century. Perhaps they are actively evangelizing, but failing to persuade others to be born again. Or perhaps, despite their espoused commitment to evangelizing fellow students, in practice many pay lip service to an activity that is proving increasingly awkward, difficult and culturally alien. Our interviews included many accounts of the latter. The gap between the CU subculture, the majority Christian culture and the non- or post-Christian culture of secularized students may have become too great a chasm for enthusiastic young Evangelicals to bridge. That said, most appear to have already embraced a gentler form of outreach focused on care, friendship and service; for those who see decisive conversions as the ideal, having the opportunity to 'share about their faith' has become accepted as a more realistic, if only second best, outcome.

The challenges for chaplaincies

It would seem that a greater number of students express appreciation for chaplaincies than take an active part. Part of the chaplaincy function is to provide what Grace Davie (2000) has termed 'vicarious religion'; access is always available to a safe form of Christian faith, ritual and pastoral support. It may be the case that nothing can be done about this distancing, which reflects a widespread suspicion towards all expressions of organized and institutional religion. Nonetheless, our findings present a significant challenge for chaplaincies. Given that most Christians will not join the CU and only half are going to church at university, chaplaincies seem best placed to explore creative re-engagement with the Christian majority, on their own terms. In particular, when a significant minority of Christian students are praying privately and volunteering publicly, without going to church, chaplaincies need to continue to make every effort to connect with, and explore imaginative ways to resource these resilient patterns of personal spirituality. Online expressions of chaplaincy will almost certainly develop an increasing role, through which a questioning faith can be more at home than in a conventional Sunday congregation. Clearly chaplaincies will need to continue to explore new ways of expressing and supporting the diverse types of Christian faith. University chaplains need to be encouraged to keep on stepping outside ecclesiastical comfort zones to serve the students and staff, Christian and non-Christian alike, that conventional parish churches cannot reach.

Implications for university managers

Our findings also indicate an obligation for senior university managers to ensure that their institutions take seriously the presence among their students of widespread personal spiritualities. Reactions to equality legislation and sincere concerns for cultural sensitivity have led some institutions to accommodate better the needs of those of non-Christian faiths. However, provision is structured around conventional religious categories, and when individual students fall outside or between given boundaries, the frustrations of misunderstanding and disenfranchisement can become exacerbated further. Perhaps ironically, it is the self-identifying Christian students who can feel most alienated; the dominant discourse of multiculturalism can undermine the legitimacy of their perspective, while the voices of vociferous conservatives reinforce popular media stereotypes that dissuade more reserved, liberal Christians from any public expression of faith. Universities need to learn to cultivate religious awareness and consideration, among staff and students, not simply observe formal regulation. Valuable work is already underway, especially on raising levels of religious literacy (e.g. Dinham and Jones, 2010; Weller et al., 2011), and the management of sacred spaces on campus alongside collaborative ventures by entrepreneurial chaplaincies represent strong examples of how religious diversity may be embraced and wider mutual learning encouraged. We need to ensure that prevailing secular assumptions among baby boomers do not create an ethos of exclusion in which religious identities and personal spiritualities are demeaned or marginalized. Global universities of the twenty-first century need to learn to negotiate a student environment that encompasses both a confident secularity, religious resilience and a benign tolerance that sits as a majority disposition between the two. There is also a need to avoid allowing secularist policies to unintentionally exclude the public exploration of universal human questions, questions that are arguably essential to the healthy life of all universities (Jacobsen and Jacobsen, 2012a, p. 126). That requires an ethos in Higher Education that is far more sophisticated, adaptive and supportive of religious diversity than the dogmatic, public secularity sometimes advocated in other parts of Europe (Davie, 2006, pp. 286–90).

Concluding note: The hidden Christians

The sociology of knowledge illuminates how sociocultural frameworks make certain ways of thinking more readily accessible or even appear self-evident (Berger and Luckmann, 1966; McCarthy, 1996); we might also point to how public discourses or 'plausibility structures' can screen out inconvenient or unwelcome realities. The prevailing culture of public life in Britain, notwithstanding the continuing prominence of bishops in the political establishment, appears to have little room for religion. This is the case in politics, the media and the arts, and also in Higher Education.

The narrative of secularization has appeared to vindicate this public culture: church attendance is declining rapidly, younger adults have the lowest levels of church attendance, and therefore Christianity in particular and religion in general, with the notable exception of specific ethnic and religious minorities, can reasonably be presumed to be in terminal decline.

The data we have collected demonstrate a somewhat different reality. In conventional terms a 'practising Christian' is considered to be a communicant member of a local church. As our findings show, local churches continue to be major centres of Christian activity within university towns, but their place within the lives of self-identifying Christian students is complex. Our analysis shows that university constitutes a transitional experience, and that this experience is navigated, among Christian students, using a range of resources, deployed, embraced and engaged in a variety of ways. Churches sit alongside on-campus student-led societies, staffed chaplaincies and informal networks, often linked to national organizations that inform and reinforce patterns of identity formation through the university career. Organized sites of Christian practice are engaged selectively, contextually and sometimes as a focus of opposition rather than alignment. Moreover, a large proportion of self-identifying Christian students affirm their Christianity by not engaging in these contexts, at least not directly, and their semi-privatized religious orientation, while often considered and reflective, remains largely unrecognized by the agencies and institutions that represent the tradition they affirm.

The fact of large numbers of hidden but active Christians among university students requires a re-conceptualization within the sociology of religion. It is essential that researchers develop appropriate methods to uncover, identify and explore the living spirituality and social capital of these hidden Christians. This confirms the importance of a continuing and extensive research project on the emergent patterns of personal spirituality and the connection with public benefit through volunteering. Further research is also required to explore the extent to which these patterns of faith among undergraduates remain durable beyond university, particularly if they continue to be at least semi-detached from denominational contexts. Church attendance in a first graduate job away from home will very likely prove even more difficult to make time for than at university.

The hidden Christian majority appear disinclined to bring any attention to their personal faith and spiritual practices, and they are highly averse to evangelizing. Those who have an interest in religion at university, whether church leaders and chaplains, researchers or university managers, Student Unions or religious organizations, all have an obligation to take account of the real breadth and continuing numerical strength of Christian identity, in all its varied forms. Twenty-first-century students' ways of being Christian are more personal and autonomous, often less visible than conventional churchgoing and more distant from religious institutions and authorities, but in the context of the university experience, their religious identities appear surprisingly resilient. Accepting this finding enables us to recognize the paradox that, although many aspects of university are at least indirect contributors to the social processes of secularization, young Christians experience university as a congenial environment in which to inhabit and explore their faith.

Appendix: How many Christian students are there in England's universities?

The primary aim of this book has been to examine the distinctive characteristics of those students who self-identify as Christian, *not* to count the number of Christians among the student population. However, as we feel the latter question will be of interest to some readers, we offer some tentative reflections here on how our findings might shed light on this issue. Addressing this also allows us to say a little more about the methods used in this study.

(1) Identifying the Christian constituency

The problems of ascertaining the number of Christians at university can be reduced to two simple, interrelated issues: definition and measurement. Within the current project, the first was the less problematic, as we were, from the outset, determined to be unconstrained by preconceived or externally imposed understandings of what counts as a Christian person. The entire history of Christianity amounts to a struggle over this question, about the legitimate grounds of belief, the means of salvation and the boundaries defining who is and is not to be counted among the Christian faithful. Official criteria have largely focused on ritual markers (e.g. baptism), a rite of initiation into a church, and/or doctrine, gauged by professed individual assent. As theologians and church leaders have sought closure by formulating ever new codifications of Christian identity, social scientists have added their own definitions, driven by ambitions to demarcate the boundaries of Christianity (or its constituent sub-groups) in order to measure their social significance. Inevitably, every definition has its limitations, and in excluding individuals outside of their criteria who might nevertheless self-identify as included, they build into the emerging understanding a set of normative assumptions about who counts and who does not. In many theological definitions, this substantive bias is explicit and intended, as with the UCCF basis of faith, whose presentation of Christianity is unapologetically exclusionary; those responsible for its formulation would have no problem with the fact that it might exclude many Methodists and liberal Anglicans, not to mention Mormons and Jehovah's Witnesses. In cases such as this, the act of definition is an openly political one, set up as a claim about legitimacy and henceforth harnessed as a tool for policing the doctrinal constituency of those claiming Christian identity.

Social scientific definitions are no less problematic than theological ones; in fact, they are often more so, as inherent assumptions are sometimes unacknowledged, perhaps buried beneath the language of objectivity or scientific rigour. Recent debates about secularization in Britain have thrown such problems into sharp relief, as they have exposed how prefigured definitions of religion or religious behaviour shape what kinds of evidence are treated as reliable or relevant (Jenkins, 1999). If one assumes that Christian commitment is chiefly expressed via involvement with established, mainstream religious institutions (putting aside the contentious nature of these terms), then regular church attendance would seem an obvious measure of Christian activity. And yet if the broader evidence suggests a majority of the population identify as Christian, and yet barely a tenth of them attend church regularly, as is the case in the United Kingdom, then there would seem to be something wrong with our definition. At the very least, the situation is more complicated than this definition might allow.

In light of these problems, and of the apparently sizeable proportion of non-churchgoing – perhaps highly diverse – 'Christians' in the contemporary United Kingdom, we decided not to prejudge the category 'Christian' at all. Instead, we invited our student respondents to tell us whether they would attribute this word to themselves. This is an approach used in other studies, most famously in the national census, which now asks 'What is your religion?' followed by a series of possible options. The census question has been criticized on a variety of grounds, not least its leading nature (assuming respondents have a religion), vagueness and inability to distinguish between religion as belief, behaviour or community affiliation. As the question follows the one on ethnicity, it has also been suggested that high levels of Christian identification in the 2001 UK census data can be attributed to respondents associating Christianity with their status as white, Anglo-Saxon or indigenous (Voas and Bruce, 2004). The British Social Attitudes Survey includes a less equivocal question – 'Do you regard yourself as belonging to any particular religion?' – and our own survey question used a similar wording. However, mindful of the ways in which religious categories have become detached from notions of the supernatural in recent years, we also did not wish to exclude self-identifying 'Christians' who are unsure, ambivalent about or uncomfortable with the connotations of the word 'religion'. Recent studies suggest the boundaries of religious traditions and the boundaries of supernaturalist belief are overlapping but do not precisely tessellate, with some affirming Christianity as their tradition, perhaps engaging in conventional Christian worship, and yet remaining tentative about claims that presuppose a supernatural realm or God (Davies and Northam-Jones, 2012; Stringer, 2008). Others are uncomfortable with the notion of Christianity as a 'religion', preferring instead the term 'spiritual', with its less institutional, more open, inclusive and less clearly defined associations (Heelas et al., 2005; Lynch, 2007).

Taking these issues into consideration, we translated our aim of identifying the population of Christian undergraduates into two related questions. Asking respondents separately about their orientation to things religious or spiritual on the one hand, and about the tradition with which they identify on the other, allows for a more sophisticated mapping of meanings associated with the word 'Christian'. First, we asked survey respondents whether, 'generally speaking', they would consider themselves to be 'religious', 'not religious but spiritual', 'not religious or spiritual', or 'not sure' about this issue. Second, we asked: 'No matter how you have answered the previous question, to what religion or spiritual tradition do you currently belong? Please choose the one that fits best.' Following this was a list of the six world religions claiming most adherents in the United Kingdom, in alphabetical order, preceded by 'None', thus anticipating those sceptics wary of high religious counts where conventional religious categories are listed first with the option of 'none' appearing at the bottom. This list was followed by an option of 'Other', allowing a 'free response' statement in the respondent's own words. In focusing on 'current belonging' as an index of religious identity, we avoid the ambiguity associated with survey questions like that used on the census, and arguably discourage more nominal responses that refer to past, rather than present, affiliation. We also foreground a measure of religious identity based on community affiliation, *rather than belief or practice*, hence allowing for the diversity apparent within the UK context without losing a sense that 'Christian' is being used as a positive identity marker.[1] This approach leaves space for such affiliations to coexist with scepticism, uncertainty or ambivalence with respect to the religious or spiritual, the two questions allowing us to measure, for example, the diversity of orientations to such matters *among those identifying as Christian*. Finally, placing the question *after* the one on religion/spirituality – rather than ethnicity, for example – also anticipates any criticism that religious affiliation might be treated as a synonym for culture or ethnicity.

After the administration of the survey among a randomized sample of undergraduate students within each of our 13 participating universities,[2] the collected data was weighted to correct specifically for those factors most likely to influence patterns of religious identification. These factors were gender (in response to the substantial evidence that women are significantly more likely than men to affirm a religious or spiritual identity, see Chapter 7); ethnicity (in recognition of how pockets of religious – especially Christian – vitality in the United Kingdom are to a large extent concentrated among particular ethnic groups[3]); and the student population size of each university. The latter is particularly important as our survey universities range in size from Winchester, which has around 5,000 undergraduates, to Leeds that has over 24,000, and yet both are given equal weight in the unweighted survey data. Collectively, these weighting measures should correct for any non-response bias attributable to a skewed set of respondents in terms of gender, ethnicity or with respect to university size.[4] As a consequence, our results should be much more representative of the student population of our 13 participating universities. In turn, the extent to which these universities range across the HE sector in England in all major respects (see Chapter 3) lends weight to their status as representative of the undergraduate population across the nation.

The results produced by these two questions on religious identity are presented in the following two tables (Tables A1 and A2).

(2) The survey measure in broader context

According to our survey, 51.4% of undergraduate students studying at England's universities self-identify as Christian. Whether this is viewed as high or low depends on the kinds of comparisons made. The study closest in its religion question is the British Social Attitudes Survey, which in 2010 found 43.6% of a representative sample of the population of England and Wales aligning themselves with some branch of Christianity. For 18–24-year-olds, this drops to 28.5%, with

TABLE A1 General orientation to religion among undergraduates studying at universities in England (2010–11)

	N	% (weighted)
Religious	1002	24.9
Not religious but spiritual	1305	30.8
Not religious or spiritual	1536	33.2
Not sure	498	11.2
Total	4341	100

TABLE A2 Responses to the question 'to what religion or spiritual tradition do you currently belong? Please choose the one that fits best' among undergraduates studying at universities in England (2010–11)

	N	% (weighted)
None	1594	34.0
Buddhism	88	2.2
Christianity	2248	51.4
Hinduism	58	2.0
Islam	103	4.9
Judaism	31	0.5
Sikhism	9	0.3
Other	209	4.7

those affirming 'no religion' at 64.9% rather than 50.3% for the overall sample.[5] This reflects the 2005 data collected by Peter Brierley, which suggests that young people (aged 15–29) are declining in their regular church attendance more than any other age group in England (Brierley, 2006a, p. 139). It is noteworthy that surveys using a more ambiguous or open-ended question appear to generate higher percentages affirming a religious identity. The 2011 YouGov-Cambridge survey of over 64,000 adults across Great Britain used the census question 'What is your religion?', and found the proportion of 'Christians' increasing with age; 38% among the 18–34 age group, compared to 54% of 35–54-year-olds, and 70% of those aged 55 and over.[6] The measure for the youngest age group is the lowest, but it is still significantly higher than the BSA figure (bearing in mind the age cohorts are not precisely comparable). The obvious interpretation is that the younger generations are less inclined to identify as Christian, but that inclination increases when the definition of Christian affiliation is less definitive. This echoes studies that have found younger generations characterized by 'fuzziness' and 'uncertainty' when it comes to traditional Christian beliefs (Savage et al., 2006, p. 19; Voas, 2009); it also reflects a widely held view that younger generations affirm a resistance to labels associated with institutional or traditional authority (Furlong and Cartmel, 1997).

What about university students in particular? Do national figures suggest students are more or less likely to affiliate with Christianity than young adults generally? Here the data available is more limited. The 2001 census data for England measures Christian self-identification among students (economically active and economically inactive) as 58.5%.[7] The results of the 2011 census were only partially released at the time this book went to press, and report a drop in the general population of England and Wales self-identifying as Christian from 72% to 59%; assuming a comparable rate of decline among students, we should expect to find around 45% self-identifying as Christian this time around, although a more detailed data breakdown will reveal precise figures later in 2013.

A few universities collect data at the point of student registration. Based on the five willing to share their data with us, we find a mean average proportion of undergraduates self-identifying as Christian of 43.62%. While this is a very selective data set (roughly 6% of the English HE sector), the universities included are located in different regions of the country and span three of the categories of university used in our research (plus only one is a church foundation belonging to the Cathedrals Group, lessening the likelihood of institutional bias in favour of Christianity). They also cover all (or the vast majority of[8]) students in each institution, not a sample, and hence offer a comprehensive picture for each. The emerging figure is indeed lower than our figure of 51.4%, but not dramatically so. It is also very close to the 43.8% found by Paul Weller et al. (2011) in their study of religion among students and staff in UK higher education, undertaken around the same time as our own survey. Other data suggest a more modest figure. A survey commissioned by the National Union of Students in 2010 found that just under one-third of students (32%) in UK universities said they belonged to a religion, the same figure found in a comparable study conducted the previous year.[9] However, the proportion of Christians *within* this population shows a marked decline, down from 75% of religious students (or 24% of the total) in 2009, to 64% of religious students (or 20.5% of the total) in 2010.[10] However, without further information about the distribution of respondents by university, it is difficult to ascertain whether this low number is attributable to particular factors not universally relevant across the sector.

In summary, while our measure of 51.4% for Christians among university undergraduate students may have been inflated by the religiously indifferent opting out of our survey, most of the evidence cited above suggests this is probably not a dramatic inflation. Indeed, the figures from large-scale national surveys and particularly from official university statistics suggest a percentage measure of Christian identification between 40 and 50% is not unrealistic.

However, it is important to emphasize again what our intentions have been for this book. We are *primarily* interested not in counting the number of Christians among students, but in *examining the distinctive characteristics of those students who identify as Christian.* In this respect, if Christians are over-represented among our survey respondents, we might assume that we have achieved a broadly representative spread of students within the Christian student sub-population. We may have reason to believe that many non-Christians have selected out of the survey; we have no reason to believe any sub-set among the Christians has selected out, and indeed, as the discussion in the previous chapters shows, our self-identifying 'Christian' respondents are markedly diverse, including only 40.4% viewing themselves as 'religious',[11] and less than a third attending church on a weekly basis during term-time, undermining any suggestion that the data has been distorted by an inflated proportion of highly motivated Christian enthusiasts, particular churches or Christian student organizations. In short, the diversity among Christian students mirrors the diversity among self-identifying Christians in the nation generally.

Notes

1 Voas and Day (2010, p. 5) argue that, because of the rise in the popularity of the category of 'non-religion' within advanced Western nations and the growth in interest in matters of 'identity', self-identification is now a key measure of religious identity, more important than ritual practices such as baptism, previously prioritized in measuring levels of religious affiliation.

2 Following agreement from key university managers and administrators, 3,000 undergraduate students were randomly chosen from the student database in each university and sent an email inviting them to take part in the online survey. The only exception to this rule was Cambridge, where recruitment of respondents was via four participating colleges, which together comprised 1,340 undergraduates (of which 275 responded, i.e. 20.5%). Students were selected from across all years of undergraduate study (the single exception was a university that only granted us permission to target second year undergraduate students, on the grounds of protecting students from intrusive emails, especially vulnerable freshers and third years focusing on their final examinations). Two email reminders were sent to the students contacted, and entry into a prize draw was used as an incentive to participation. We received 4,341 responses to the questionnaire survey, which amounts to an overall response rate of 11.6%. While not as high as we hoped, the randomized sampling and post-administration weighting of the data go some way towards mitigating for any potential non-response bias.

3 The most striking example here is the black Pentecostal churches, which Peter Brierley (2006a) claims account for almost all of the net Evangelical growth among churches in England between 1998 and 2005.

4 Benchmark measures for each of these variables were identified for each participating institution, drawing from data collected by the Higher Education Statistics Agency.

5 Figures generated from the British Social Attitudes Information System (www.britsocat.com).

6 See http://d25d2506sfb94s.cloudfront.net/cumulus_uploads/.../Religion.pdf (accessed 24/3/2013).

7 Extracted from Table CT153 on CASWEB, see http://casweb.mimas.ac.uk/.

8 Some of these universities allow students not to answer this question about religion, although in these cases the number refusing to answer is always a small minority.

9 See *NUS/HSBC Student Experience Report: Internationalisation*, NUS, October 2010, p. 11.

10 See *NUS/HSBC Students Survey 2009* report, pp. 2424–30.

11 31.2% of self-identifying Christians in our sample see themselves as 'not religious but spiritual', 15.4% as neither, while 13% are unsure.

Bibliography

Accord Coalition (2009), 'Church is where the heart is', 30 January, http://accordcoalition.org.uk/wp-content/uploads/2011/06/ Tearfund-churchgoing-survey-in-word.htm (accessed 11/1/13).

Ahmed, S. (2007), 'You end up doing the document rather than doing the doing: diversity, race equality and the politics of documentation'. *Ethnic and Racial Studies*, 30, (4), 590–609.

Ammerman, N. T. (2007), *Everyday Religion: Observing Modern Religious Lives*. New York: Oxford University Press.

Ammerman, N. T. and Roof, W. C. (1995), *Work, Family, and Religion in Contemporary Society*. London: Routledge.

Andersson, J., Sadgrove, J. and Valentine, G. (2012), 'Consuming campus: geographies of encounter at a British university'. *Social & Cultural Geography*, 13, (5), 501–15.

Apple, M. W. (2007), 'Education, markets, and an audit culture'. *International Journal of Educational Policies*, 1, (1), 4–19.

Armstrong, K. (2000), *The Battle for God: Fundamentalism in Judaism, Christianity and Islam*. London: HarperCollins.

Armytage, W. H. G. (1955), *Civic Universities: Aspects of a British Tradition*. London: Ernest Benn Ltd.

Arnett, J. J. (2004), *Emerging Adulthood: The Winding Road from Late Teens through the Twenties*. New York: Oxford University Press.

Astley, J. (2005), 'The science and religion interface within young people's attitudes and beliefs', in L. Francis, M. Robbins, and J. Astley (eds), *Religion, Education and Adolescence: International Empirical Perspectives*. Cardiff: University of Wales Press, pp. 39–54.

Astley, J., Francis, L. J., Sullivan, J. and Walker, A. (eds) (2004), *The Idea of a Christian University: Essays in Theology and Higher Education*. Milton Keynes: Authentic Media.

Atkinson, B. (1932), *Old Paths in Perilous Times* (2nd edn). London: IVF.

Aune, K. (2006), 'Marriage in a British evangelical congregation: practising postfeminist partnership?, *The Sociological Review*, 54, (4), 638–57.

— (2011), 'Much less religious, a little more spiritual: the religious and spiritual views of third-wave feminists in the UK'. *Feminist Review*, 97, 32–55.

Barclay, J. M. G. (1997), 'The family as the bearer of religion in Judaism and early Christianity', in H. Moxnes (ed.), *Constructing Early Christian Families: Family as Social Reality and Metaphor*. London: Routledge, pp. 66–80.

Barclay, O. R. and Horn, R. M. (2002), *From Cambridge to the World: 125 Years of Student Witness*. Leicester: Inter-Varsity Press.

Barker, J. (2010), *NUS/HSBC Students Experience Research Report: Internationalisation and Religion*. National Union of Students and HSBC Bank.

Barr, J. (1977), *Fundamentalism*. London: SCM.

Bebbington, D. W. (1989), *Evangelicalism in Modern Britain: A History from the 1730s to the 1980s*. London: Unwin Hyman.

— (1992), 'The secularization of British universities since the mid-nineteenth century', in B. J. Longfield and G. M. Marsden (eds), *The Secularization of the Academy*. Oxford: Oxford University Press, pp. 259–77.

Beck, U. (1992), *Risk Society: Towards a New Modernity*. London: Sage.

Beck, U. and Beck-Gernsheim, E. (2001), *Individualization: Institutionalized Individualism and its Social and Political Consequences*. London: Sage.

Beckford, J. A. (1989), *Religion and Advanced Industrial Society*. London: Unwin Hyman.

Beckford, Robert (1998), *Jesus is Dread: Black Theology and Black Culture in Britain*. London: Darton, Longman & Todd.

Bell, D. (1974), *The Coming of Post-Industrial Society: A Venture in Social Forecasting*. London: Heinemann Educational.

Bellah, R. (2006) 'Is there a common American culture?', in R. Bellah and S. M. Tipton (eds), *The Robert Bellah Reader*. Durham: Duke University Press, pp. 319–32.

Bellah, R. N., Madsen, R., Sullivan, W. M., Swidler, A. and Tipton, S. M. (eds) (1996), *Habits of the Heart: Individualism and Commitment in American Life* (updated edn). Berkeley: University of California Press.

Beloff, M. (1968), *The Plateglass Universities*. London: Secker and Warburg.

Berger, P. L. (1967), *The Sacred Canopy: Elements of a Sociological Theory of Religion* (1st edn). Garden City, NY: Doubleday.

— (1980), *The Heretical Imperative: Contemporary Possibilities of Religious Affirmation*. London: Collins.

— (1999), 'The desecularization of the world: a global overview', in P. L. Berger (ed.), *The Desecularization of the World: Essays on the Resurgence of Religion in World Politics*. Washington: Ethics and Public Policy Center & Grand Rapids: Eerdmans, pp. 1–18.

— (2001), 'Reflections on the sociology of religion today'. *Sociology of Religion*, 62, (winter), 443–54.

Berger, P. and Luckmann, T. (1966), *The Social Construction of Reality: A Treatise in the Sociology of Knowledge*. London: Penguin.

Berger, P., Davie, G. and Fokas, E. (2008), *Religious America, Secular Europe? A Theme and Variations*. Aldershot: Ashgate.

Beyer, P. (2006), 'Religious vitality in Canada: the complementarity of religious market and secularization perspectives', in L. G. Beaman (ed.), *Religion and Canadian Society: Traditions, Transitions and Innovations*. Toronto: Canadian Scholars' Press, pp. 71–90.

Bingham, J. (2012), 'University to have alcohol-free areas for Muslims: a university vice-chancellor is planning to ban the sale of alcohol in parts of the campus because some Muslim students believe it is "evil" and "immoral"'. *The Telegraph*, 12 April.

Blunt, A. and Dowling, R. (2006), *Home*. London: Routledge.

Blunt, A. and Varley, A. (2004), 'Geographies of home'. *Cultural Geographies*, 11, (1), 3–6.

Bottero, W. (2004), 'Class identities and the identity of class'. *Sociology*, 38, (5), 985–1003.

Bourdieu, P. (1977), *Outline of a Theory of Practice*. Cambridge: Cambridge University Press.

Boyd, R. (2007), *The Witness of the Student Christian Movement: Church Ahead of the Church*. London: SPCK.

Brabazon, T. (2007), *The University of Google: Education in the (Post) Information Age*. Aldershot: Ashgate.

Brace, C., Bailey, A. R. and Harvey, D. C. (2006), 'Religion, place and space: a framework for investigating historical geographies of religious identities and communities'. *Progress in Human Geography*, 30, 28–43.

Bradley, I. (2007), *Believing in Britain: The Spiritual Identity of Britishness*. Oxford: Lion.

Bramadat, P. A. (2000), *The Church on the World's Turf: An Evangelical Christian Group at a Secular University*. New York: Oxford University Press.

Brickell, K. (2012), 'Mapping and "doing" critical geographies of home'. *Progress in Human Geography*, 36, (2), 225–44.

Brierley, P. W. (2006a), *Pulling out of the Nosedive: A Contemporary Picture of Churchgoing – What the 2005 English Church Census Reveals*. Eltham: Christian Research.

— (ed.) (2006b), *UK Christian Handbook Religious Trends 6 2006/2007*. London: Christian Research.

Brimeyer, T. M. and Smith, W. L. (2012), 'Religion, race, social class, and gender differences in dating and hooking up among college students'. *Sociological Spectrum*, 32, (5), 462–73.

Brito, C. and Whittaker, B. (2010), *Behind the Headlines: Social Norms and Student Alcohol Consumption, Insight into Student Drinking within Three English Universities*. National Union of Students.

Brown, C. G. (2001), *The Death of Christian Britain: Understanding Secularisation 1800–2000*. London and New York: Routledge.

— (2006), *Religion and Society in Twentieth Century Britain*. London: Pearson Education Ltd.

— (2009), *The Death of Christian Britain: Understanding Secularisation 1800–2000* (2nd edn). London and New York: Routledge.

Brown, C. and Lynch, G. (2012), 'Cultural perspectives', in L. Woodhead and R. Catto (eds), *Religion and Change in Modern Britain*. London: Routledge, pp. 329–51.

Brown, S., Francis, M., Hardy, M., Power, K., Robinson, C. and Chapman, I. Spencer. (2002), 'Religious mapping of the University of Leeds', http:// equality.leeds.ac.uk/downloads/policies/Single-Equality-Scheme-Action-Plan. docx (accessed 21/8/11).

Browne, J. (2010) *Securing a Sustainable Future for Higher Education: An Independent Review of Higher Education Funding and Student Finance*. UK Government Report.

Bruce, S. (1980), *The Student Christian Movement and the Inter-varsity Fellowship: A Sociological Study of the Two Student Movements* (PhD thesis), University of Stirling.

— (1984), 'A sociological account of liberal protestantism', *Religious Studies*, 20, (3), 401–15.

— (1989), *A House Divided: Protestantism, Schism, and Secularization*. London: Routledge.

— (1996), *Religion in the Modern World: From Cathedrals to Cults*. Oxford: Oxford University Press.

— (2001), *Fundamentalism*. Malden, MA: Polity.

— (2002), *God Is Dead: Secularization in the West*. Oxford: Blackwell.

— (2003), 'The demise of Christianity in Britain', in G. Davie, P. Heelas and L. Woodhead (eds), *Predicting Religion*. Aldershot: Ashgate, pp. 53–63.

— (2011), *Secularization: In Defence of an Unfashionable Theory*. Oxford: Oxford University Press.

Bruegel, I. (2005), 'Diversity as a constraint on social capital formation: a study of English school children'. London: London South Bank University, www. surrey.ac.uk/cronem/files/conf2005files/bruegel%20paper.doc. (accessed 19/10/12).

Bryant, A. N. (2005) 'Evangelicals on campus: an exploration of culture, faith, and college life'. *Religion and Education*, 32, (2), 1–30.

— (2006), 'Assessing the gender climate of an evangelical student subculture in the United States'. *Gender and Education,* 18, (6), 613–34.

Bryant, A. N., Choi, J. Y. and Yasuno, M. (2003), 'Understanding the spiritual and religious dimension of students' lives in the first year of college'. *Journal of College Student Development*, 44, (6), 723–45.

Burdette, A. M., Ellison, C. G., Hill, T. D. and Glenn, N. D. (2009), '"Hooking up" at college: does religion make a difference?', *Journal for the Scientific Study of Religion*, 48, (3), 535–51.

Buttner, M. (1980), 'Survey article on the history and philosophy of the geography of religion in Germany'. *Religion*, 10, (1), 86–119.

Byfield, C. (2008), 'The impact of religion on the educational achievement of black boys: a UK and USA study'. *British Journal of Sociology of Education*, 29, (2), 189–99.

Callahan Jr., R. J. (2009), 'Sensing class: religion, aesthetics, and formation of class in the Kentucky's coal fields', in S. McCloud and W. A. Mirola (eds), *Religion and Class in America: Culture, History, and Politics*. Leiden; Brill, pp. 175–96.

Caplovitz, D. and Sherrow, F. (1977), *The Religious Drop-Outs: Apostasy among College Graduates*. London: Sage.

Carrette, J. and King, R. (2005), *Selling Spirituality: The Silent Takeover of Religion*. Abingdon: Routledge.

Casanova, J. (1994), *Public Religions in the Modern World*. Chicago: University of Chicago Press.

— (2006), 'Rethinking secularization: a global comparative perspective'.*The Hedgehog Review: Critical Reflections on Contemporary Culture*, 8, (1 and 2), 7–22.

Chatterton, P. (1999), 'University students and city centres – the formation of exclusive geographies: the case of Bristol, UK'. *Geoforum*, 30, 117–33.

Chatterton, P. and Hollands, R. (2002), 'Theorising urban playscapes: producing, regulating and consuming youthful nightlife city spaces'. *Urban Studies,* 39, (1), 95–116.

— (2003), *Urban Nightscapes: Youth Cultures, Pleasure Spaces and Corporate Power*. London: Routledge.

Cherry, C., DeBerg, B. A. and Porterfield, A. (2001), *Religion on Campus: What Religion Really Means to Today's Undergraduates*. Chapel Hill and London: University of North Carolina Press.

Clydesdale, T. (2007), *The First Year Out: Understanding American Teens after High School*. Chicago, IL: University of Chicago Press.

Coles, B. (1995), *Youth and Social Policy: Youth Citizenship and Young Careers*. London: UCL Press.

Collini, S. (2012), *What Are Universities For?* London: Penguin Books.

Collins-Mayo, S. (2012), 'Choosing my religion: young people's personal Christian knowledge', in M. Guest and A. Arweck (eds), *Religion and Knowledge: Sociological Perspectives*. Aldershot: Ashgate, pp. 149–63.

Collins-Mayo, S. and Dandelion, P. (eds) (2010), *Religion and Youth*. Aldershot: Ashgate.

Collins-Mayo, S., Mayo, B., Nash, S. and Cocksworth, C. (2010), *The Faith of Generation Y*. London: Church House Publishing.

Crockett, A. and Voas, D. (2005), 'Religion in Britain: neither believing nor belonging'. *Sociology*, 39, (1), 11–28.

— (2006), 'Generations of decline: religious change in 20th-century Britain'. *Journal for the Scientific Study of Religion*, 45, (4), 567–84.

Crompton, R. and Lyonnette, C. (2008), 'Who does the housework? The division of labour within the home', in Alison Park, John Curtice, Katarina Thomson, Miranda Phillips, Mark Johnson and Elizabeth Clery (eds), *British Social Attitudes: The 24th Report*. London: Sage.

D'Costa, G. (2005), *Theology in the Public Square: Church, Academy and Nation*. Oxford: Blackwell.

—. (2011), 'The state of the university: academic knowledges and the knowledge of God'. *Pro Ecclesia*, 20 (3), 312–16.

Davidoff, L. and Hall, C. (1987), *Family Fortunes: Men and Women of the English Middle Class, 1780–1850*. London: Hutchinson Education.

Davie, G. (1994), *Religion in Britain Since 1945: Believing Without Belonging*. Oxford: Blackwell.

— (2000), *Religion in Modern Europe: A Memory Mutates*. Oxford: Oxford University Press.

— (2002), *Europe: The Exceptional Case*. London: Darton, Longman & Todd.

— (2006), 'Religion in Europe in the 21st century: The factors to take into account', *European Journal of Sociology*, 47, (2), 271–96.

— (2007), *The Sociology of Religion*. London: Sage.

Davies, D. J. and Guest, M. (2007), *Bishops, Wives and Children: Spiritual Capital Across the Generations*. Aldershot: Ashgate.

Davies, D. J. and Northam-Jones, D. (2012), 'The Sea of Faith: exemplifying transformed retention', in M. Guest and E. Arweck (eds), *Religion and Knowledge: Sociological Perspectives*. Aldershot: Ashgate, pp. 227–43.

Day, A. (2011), *Believing in Belonging: Belief and Social Identity in the Modern World*. Oxford: Oxford University Press.

'Degrees of faith: A first things survey of America's colleges and universities' (2010). *First Things*, 207, 8–12, 14–16, 18–45.

Dinham, A. and Jones, S. H. (2010), 'Religious literacy leadership in higher education: an analysis of challenges of religious faith, and resources for meeting them, for university leaders'. *Religious Literacy Leadership in Higher Education Programme*. York, UK: York St John University.

— (2012), 'Religion, public policy, and the academy: brokering public faith in a context of ambivalence?', *Journal of Contemporary Religion*, 27, (2), 185–201.

Durkheim, E. (1912 (ET 2001)), *The Elementary Forms of Religious Life*. Oxford, New York: Oxford University Press.

Dutton, E. (2008), *Meeting Jesus at University: Rites of Passage and Student Evangelicals*. Aldershot: Ashgate.

Dwyer, C. and Shah, B. (2009), 'Rethinking the identities of young British Pakistani Muslim women: educational experiences and aspirations', in Peter Hopkins and Richard Gale (eds), *Muslims in Britain: Race, Place and Identities.* Edinburgh: Edinburgh University Press.

Ecklund, E. H. and Long, E. (2011), 'Scientists and spirituality'. *Sociology of Religion,* 72, (3), 253–74.

Emerson, M. and Smith, C. (2000), *Divided by Faith: Evangelical Religion and the Problem of Race in America.* New York: Oxford University Press.

Erickson, B. (1996), 'Culture, class, and connections'. *American Journal of Sociology,* 102, (1), 217–51.

Evans, J. H. (2011), 'Epistemological and moral conflict between religion and science'. *Journal for the Scientific Study of Religion,* 50, (4), 707–27.

Evans, S. (2009), 'In a different place: working-class girls and higher education'. *Sociology,* 43, 340–55.

Fagbemi, S. (2011), 'Sunderland University', in M. Threlfall-Homes and M. Newitt (eds), *Being a Chaplain.* London: SPCK, pp. 24–6.

Fairweather, I. (2012), 'Faith and the student experience', in M. Guest and E. Arweck (eds), *Religion and Knowledge: Sociological Perspectives.* Aldershot: Ashgate, pp. 39–55.

Feldman, K. and Newcomb, T. (1969), *The Impact of College on Students, 2nd Volume.* San Francisco, CA: Jossey-Bass.

Field, J. (2008), *Social Capital* (2nd edn). London: Routledge.

Finch, J. (2007), 'Displaying families'. *Sociology,* 41, (1), 65–81.

Fincher, R. (2011), 'Cosmopolitan or ethnically identified selves? Institutional expectations and the negotiated identities of international students'. *Social & Cultural Geography,* 12, (8), 905–27.

Finke, R. and Stark, R. (1992), *The Churching of America, 1776–1990: Winners and Losers in Our Religious Economy.* New Brunswick, NJ: Rutgers University Press.

Flory, R. W. and Miller, D. E. (eds) (2000), *GenX Religion.* New York: Routledge.

France, M. (1968), 'Roles of a chaplain in a university', *The Times,* 7 September, 10.

Francis, L. J. (2001), *The Values Debate: A Voice from the Pupils.* London: Woburn Press.

Francis, L. J., Williams, E. and Robbins, M. (2009), 'Christianity, paranormal belief and personality: a study among 13- to 16-year-old pupils in England and Wales'. *Archive for the Psychology of Religion – Archiv Fur Religionspsychologie,* 31, (3), 337–44.

— (2010), 'Personality, conventional Christian belief and unconventional paranormal belief: a study among teenagers'. *British Journal of Religious Education,* 32, (1), 31–9.

Frankenberg, R. (1993), *White Women, Race Matters: The Social Construction of Whiteness.* London: Routledge.

Freitas, D. (2008), *Sex and the Soul: Juggling Sexuality, Spirituality, Romance, and Religion on America's College Campuses.* New York: Oxford University Press.

Fulton, J., Dowling, T., Abela, A. M., Borowik, I., Marler, P. L. and Tomasi, L. (2000), *Young Catholics at the New Millennium: The Religion and Morality of Young Adults in Western Countries.* Dublin: University College Dublin Press.

Furlong, A. and Cartmel, F. (1997), *Young People and Social Change: Individualization and Risk in Late Modernity*. Buckingham: Open University Press.
— (2007), *Young People and Social Change: New Perspectives* (2nd edn). Buckingham: Open University Press.
Gallagher, S. K. (2003), *Evangelical Identity and Gendered Family Life*. New Brunswick and London: Rutgers University Press.
Gee, P. J. (1992), 'The demise of liberal Christianity?', in B. R. Wilson (ed.), *Religion: Contemporary Issues*. London: Bellew, pp. 135–42.
Gerth, H. H. and C. W. Mills (eds) (2009), *From Max Weber: Essays in Sociology*. London: Rouledge.
Gill, Robin (1993), *The Myth of the Empty Church*. London: SPCK.
— (1999), *Churchgoing and Christian Ethics*. Cambridge: Cambridge University Press.
Gill, R., Hadaway, C. K. and Marler, P. L. (1998), 'Is religious belief declining in Britain?', *Journal for the Scientific Study of Religion*, 37, (3), 507–16.
Gill, Rosalind (2007), 'Postfeminist media culture: elements of a sensibility'. *European Journal of Cultural Studies*, 10, (2), 147–66.
Gilliat-Ray, S. (2000), *Religion in Higher Education: The Politics of the Multi-faith Campus*. Farnham: Ashgate.
— (2005), '"Sacralising" Sacred Space in Public Institutions: A Case Study of the Prayer Space at the Millennium Dome', *Journal of Contemporary Religion*, 20, (3), pp. 357–72.
Glanzer, P. L. and Negley, K. (Illustrator), 'The missing factor in higher education: how Christian universities are unique, and how they can stay that way'. *Christianity Today*, 56, (3), 18–23.
Gökarıksel, B. (2009), 'Beyond the officially sacred: religion, secularism, and the body in the production of subjectivity'. *Social & Cultural Geography*, 10, (6), 657–74.
Goodhew, D. (2003), 'The rise of the Cambridge Inter-Collegiate Christian Union, 1910–1971'. *Journal of Ecclesiastical History*, 54, (1), 62–88.
Graham, D. and Boyd, J. (2011), *Home and Away: Jewish Journeys towards Independence; Findings from the 2011 National Jewish Student Survey*. London: Institute for Jewish Policy Research.
Graham, G. (2002), *Universities: The Recovery of an Idea*. Thorverton: Imprint Academic.
Griffin, C. (2004), 'Representations of the young', in J. Roche, S. Tucker, R. Flynn and R. Thomson (eds), *Youth in Society: Contemporary Theory, Policy, and Practice* (2nd edn). London: Sage, pp. 10–18.
Gross, N. and Simmons, S. (2009), 'The religiosity of American college and university professors'. *Sociology of Religion*, 70, (2), 101–29.
Guest, M. (2007), *Evangelical Identity and Contemporary Culture: A Congregational Study in Innovation*. Milton Keynes: Paternoster.
— (2009), 'The plausibility of creationism: a sociological comment', in S. Barton and D. Wilkinson (eds), *Reading Genesis After Darwin*. New York: Oxford University Press, pp. 217–36.
— (2012) 'Religion and Knowledge: the Sociological Agenda', in M. Guest and E. Arweck (eds), *Religion and Knowledge: Sociological Perspectives*. Aldershot: Ashgate, pp. 1–21.

Guest, M., Olson, E. and Wolffe, J. (2012), 'Christianity: loss of monopoly', in L. Woodhead and R. Catto (eds), *Religion and Change in Modern Britain*. London: Routledge, pp. 57–78.

Guest, M., Sharma, S., Aune, K. and Warner, R. (2013), 'Challenging "belief" and the evangelical bias: student Christianity in English universities'. *Journal of Contemporary Religion*, 28, (2), 207–23.

Hadaway, C. K. and Roof, W. C. (1988), 'Apostasy in American churches: evidence from national survey data', in D. G. Bromley (ed.), *Falling from the Faith: Causes and Consequences of Religious Apostasy*. London: Sage, pp. 29–46.

Hadaway, C. K. Marler, P. L. and Chaves, M. (1998), 'Over-reporting church attendance in America: evidence that demands the same verdict'. *American Sociological Review*, 63, (1), 122–30.

Haines, D. W. (2007), '"Crossing lines of difference": how college students analyse diversity'. *Intercultural Education*, 18, (5), 397–412.

Hammond, P. E. (1992), *Religion and Personal Autonomy: The Third Disestablishment in America*. Columbia: University of South Carolina.

Harker, C. (2009), 'Spacing Palestine through the home'. *Transactions of the Institute of British Geographers*, 34, (3), 320–32.

Harker, C. and Martin, L. (eds) (2012), 'Spatializing the family: intimacy, politics, and subjectivity'. *Environment and Planning A*, 44 (theme issue).

Harris, H. (2001), 'Does liberal Christianity need defending?', *Modern Believing*, 42, (1), 47–50.

Hart, D. G. (1992), 'Christianity and the university in America: a bibliographical essay', in B. J. Longfield and G. M. Marsden (eds), *The Secularization of the Academy*. Oxford: Oxford University Press, pp. 303–9.

Hastings, A. (1987), *A History of English Christianity, 1920–1985*. London: Fount Paperbacks.

— (2001a), *Oliver Tomkins: The Ecumenical Enterprise, 1908–92*. London: SPCK.

— (2001b), *A History of English Christianity, 1920–1985* (4th edn). London: SCM.

Hastings, P. K. and Hoge, D. R. (1976), 'Changes in religion among college students, 1948 to 1974'. *Journal for the Scientific Study of Religion*, 15, (3), 237–49.

Hay, D. (1979), 'Religious experience amongst a group of post-graduate students: a qualitative study'. *Journal for the Scientific Study of Religion*, 18, (2), 164–82.

Heath, A. (2012), 'Has multiculturalism failed in the UK? not really'. *The Guardian*, 10 August, www.guardian.co.uk/commentisfree/2012/aug/10/multiculturalism-uk-research (accessed 22/10/12).

Heelas, P. (1996), *The New Age Movement. The Celebration of the Self and the Sacralization of Modernity*. Oxford and Cambridge, MA: Blackwell.

Heelas, P., Woodhead, L., Seel, B., Szerszynski, B. and Tusting, K. (eds) (2005), *The Spiritual Revolution: Why Religion is Giving Way to Spirituality*. Oxford: Blackwell.

Hempton, D. (1988), 'Popular religion, 1800–1986', in T. Thomas (ed.), *The British: Their Religious Beliefs and Practices 1800–1986*. London and New York: Routledge, pp. 181–210.

Herrera, L. and Bayat, A. (eds) (2010), *Being Young and Muslim: New Cultural Politics in the Global South and North*. New York: Oxford University Press.

Herzog, P. S. and Wedow, R. (2012), 'Youth group cliques: how religious goals can disguise discriminatory group dynamics'. *Review of Religious Research*, 54, 217–38.

Higher Education Research Institute (HERI) (2004), *The Spiritual Life of College Students: A National Study of College Students' Search for Meaning and Purpose.* Los Angeles, CA: Author.

Higton, M. (2012), *A Theology of Higher Education.* Oxford: Oxford University Press.

Hill, C. (1971), 'From church to sect: West Indian sect development in Britain'. *Journal for the Scientific Study of Religion,* 10, (2), 114–23.

Hill, J. P. (2009), 'Higher education as moral community: institutional influences on religious participation during college'. *Journal for the Scientific Study of Religion,* 48, (3), 515–34.

— (2011), 'Faith and understanding: specifying the impact of higher education on religious belief'. *Journal for the Scientific Study of Religion,* 50, (3), 533–51.

Hilliard, D. (2010), 'Australia: towards secularisation and one step back', in C. Brown and M. Snape (eds), *Secularisation in the Christian World: Essays in Honour of Hugh McLeod.* Aldershot: Ashgate, pp. 75–91.

Hinton, D. (2011), '"Wales is my home": higher education aspirations and student mobilities in Wales'. *Children's Geographies,* 9, (1), 23–34.

Hoge, D. R. and Keeter, L. G. (1976), 'Determinants of college teachers' religious beliefs and participation'. *Journal for the Scientific Study of Religion,* 15, (3), 221–35.

Holdsworth, C. (2006), '"Don't you think you're missing out, living at home?" Student experiences and residential transitions'. *The Sociological Review,* 54, (3), 495–519.

— (2009), '"Going away to uni": mobility, modernity, and independence of English higher education students'. *Environment and Planning A,* 41, 1849–64.

Holloway, J. (2003), 'Make-believe: spiritual practice, embodiment, and sacred space'. *Environment and Planning A,* 35, 1961–74.

Holloway, S. L., Valentine, G. and Jayne, M. (2009), 'Masculinities, femininities and the geographies of public and private drinking landscapes'. *Geoforum,* 40, 821–31.

Hopkins, P. (2006), 'Youth transitions and going to university: the perceptions of students attending a geography summer school access programme'. *Area,* 38, (3), 240–7.

— (2007), 'Young people, masculinities, religion and race: new social geographies'. *Progress in Human Geography,* 31, 163–77.

— (2011), 'Towards critical geographies of the university campus: understanding the contested experiences of Muslim students'. *Transactions of the Institute of British Geographers,* 36, (1), 157–69.

Hopkins, P., Olson, E., Pain, R. and Vincett, G. (2011), 'Mapping intergenerationalities: the formation of youthful religiosities'. *Transactions of the Institute of British Geographers,* 36, 314–27.

Hunsberger, B. (1976), 'Background religious denomination, parental emphasis, and the religious orientation of university students'. *Journal for the Scientific Study of Religion,* 15, (3), 251–5.

Hunt, S. (2002), '"Neither here nor there": the construction of identities and boundary maintenance of West African Pentecostals'. *Sociology,* 36, (1), 147–69.

— (2004), *The Alpha Enterprise: Evangelism in a Post-Christian Era.* Aldershot: Ashgate.

Hunt, S. and Lightly, N. (2001), 'The British black Pentecostal "revival": identity and belief in the "new" Nigerian churches'. *Ethnic and Racial Studies*, 24, (1), 104–24.

Hunter, J. D. (1983), *American Evangelicalism: Conservative Religion and the Quandary of Modernity*. New Brunswick, NJ: Rutgers University Press.

— (1987), *Evangelicalism: The Coming Generation*. Chicago: University of Chicago Press.

Hussain, S. (2008), *Muslims on the Map: A National Survey of Social Trends in Britain*. London: I.B. Tauris.

Isaac, E. (1965), 'Religious geography and the geography of religion', *Man and the Earth, University of Colorado Studies, Series in Earth Sciences No. 3*, Boulder: University of Colorado Press.

Ivan, L. (2012), 'Religious in my own way: students' religious relativism and self-actualizing values'. *Revista De Cercetare Si Interventie Sociala*, 36, 130–43.

Jacobsen, D. and Hustedt-Jacobsen, R. (2012a), *No Longer Invisible: Religion in University Education*. Oxford: Oxford University Press.

— (2012b), *Religion Matters: Higher Education in the 21st Century*. Oxford: Oxford University Press.

James, S. (2002), *God's Design for Women: Biblical Womanhood for Today*. Darlington: Evangelical Press.

James, W. (1987), *William James: Writings 1902–1910*. New York: Library of America.

Jenkins, T. (1999), *Religion in English Everyday Life*. New York and Oxford: Berghahn Books.

Jensen, L. (2000), 'When two worlds collide: generation X culture and conservative evangelicalism', in R. W. Flory and D. E. Miller (eds), *GenX Religion*. London: Routledge, pp. 139–62.

Johnson, D. (1979), *Contending for the Faith. A History of the Evangelical Movement in the Universities and Colleges*. Leicester: Inter-Varsity Press.

Jones, G. (2002), *The Youth Divide: Diverging Paths to Adulthood*. York: Joseph Rowntree Foundation.

Kalilombe, P. (1997), 'Black Christianity in Britain'. *Ethnic and Racial Studies*, 20, (2), 306–24.

Karner, C. and Parker, D. (2011), 'Conviviality and conflict: pluralism, resilience and hope in inner-City Birmingham'. *Journal of Ethnic and Migration Studies*, 37, (3), 355–72.

Kay, W. K. and Francis, L. J. (1996). *Drift from the Churches: Attitude toward Christianity during Childhood and Adolescence*. Cardiff: University of Wales Press.

Kay, W. M. (2007), *Apostolic Networks of Britain: New Ways of Being Church*. Milton Keynes: Paternoster.

Kelly, T. (1981), *For Advancement of Learning: The University of Liverpool, 1881–1981*. Liverpool: Liverpool University Press.

Kenyon, E. and Heath, S. (2001), 'Choosing this life: narratives of choice amongst house sharers'. *Housing Studies*, 16, (5), 619–35.

Kenyon, L. (1999), 'Students' transitional experiences of home', in T. Chapman and J. Hockey (eds), *Ideal Homes? Social Change and Domestic Life*. London: Routledge, pp. 84–95.

Kim, R. Y. (2006), *God's New Whiz Kids? Korean American Evangelicals on Campus*. New York: New York University Press.

Kong, L. (1990), 'Geography and religion: trends and prospects'. *Progress in Human Geography,* 14, (3), 355–71.

— (2001), 'Mapping "new" geographies of religion: politics and poetics in modernity'. *Progress in Human Geography,* 25, (2), 211–33.

— (2005), 'Religious schools: for spirit, (f)or nation'. *Environment and Planning D: Society and Space,* 23, 615–31.

— (2010), 'Global shifts, theoretical shifts: changing geographies of religion'. *Progress in Human Geography,* 34, (6), 755–76.

Koukounaras-Liagis, M. (2011), 'Can an educational intervention, specifically theatre in education, influence students' perceptions of and attitudes to cultural and religious diversity? A socio-educational research'. *British Journal of Religion Education,* 33, (1), 75–89.

Kuntsche, E., Knibbe, R., Gmel, G. and Engels, R. (2006), 'Who drinks and why? A review of socio-demographic, personality, and contextual issues behind the drinking motives in young people'. *Addictive Behaviors,* 31, 1844–57.

Layard, R. and King, J. (1969), 'Expansion since Robbins', in D. Martin (ed.), *Anarchy and Culture: The Problem of the Contemporary University.* London: Routledge and Kegan Paul, pp. 13–36.

Leavey, C., Hetherton, M., Britt, M. and O'Neill, R. (1992), *Sponsoring Faith in Adolescence,* Newtown, NSW: E.J. Dwyer.

Lee, J. J. (2002), 'Religion and college attendance: change among students'. *Review of Higher Education,* 25, (4), 369–84.

Lefkowitz, E. S. (2005), '"Things have gotten better": developmental changes among emerging adults after the transition to university'. *Journal of Adolescent Research,* 20, 40–63.

Lewis, P. (2007), *Young, British and Muslim.* London: Continuum.

Lindley, J. (2002), 'Race or religion? The impact of religion on the employment and earnings of Britain's ethnic communities'. *Journal of Ethnic and Migration Studies,* 28, (3), 427–42.

Lindsay, D. M. (2007), *Faith in the Halls of Power: How Evangelicals Joined the American Elite.* New York: Oxford University Press

Lynch, G. (2007), *The New Spirituality: An Introduction to Progressive Belief in the Twenty-First Century.* London: I B Tauris.

Lyon, D. (2000), *Jesus in Disneyland: Religion in Postmodern Times.* Cambridge: Polity.

Maher, I. (2011), 'Sheffield Hallam University', in M. Threlfall-Homes and M. Newitt (eds), *Being a Chaplain.* London: SPCK, pp. 27–9.

Marris, P. (1964), *The Experience of Higher Education.* London: Routledge and Kegan Paul.

Marsden, G. M. (1991), *Understanding Fundamentalism and Evangelicalism.* Grand Rapids, MI: Eerdmans.

— (1994), *The Soul of the American University: From Protestant Establishment to Established Nonbelief.* New York: Oxford University Press.

Marsden, G. M. and Longfield, B. J. (eds) (1992), *The Secularization of the Academy.* New York: Oxford University Press.

Martin, D. (1978), *A General Theory of Secularisation.* London: Basil Blackwell.

— (1990), *Tongues of Fire.* Oxford: Blackwell.

— (2002), *Pentecostalism: The World Their Parish.* Oxford: Blackwell.

— (2005), *On Secularization: Towards a Revised General Theory.* Aldershot: Ashgate.

— (2005), 'Secularisation and the future of Christianity'. *Journal of Contemporary Religion,* 20, (2), 145–60.

Marty, M. (1996), 'Too bad we're so relevant: the fundamentalism project projected'. *Bulletin of the American Academy of Arts and Sciences,* 49 (6 March), 22–38.

Massey D. (1991), 'A global sense of place', in T. Barnes and D. Gregory (eds), *Reading Human Geography: The Poetics and Politics of Inquiry.* London: Arnold, pp. 315–23. www.aughty.org/pdf/global_sense_place. pdf (accessed 2/1/11).

— (2005), *For Space.* London: Sage.

Mauthner, M. (2005), 'Distant lives, still voices: sistering in family sociology'. *Sociology,* 39, (4), 623–42.

Mayrl, D. and Oeur, F. (2009), 'Religion and higher education: current knowledge and directions for future research'. *Journal for the Scientific Study of Religion,* 48, (2), 260–75.

Mayrl, D. and Uecker, J. E. (2011), 'Higher education and religious liberalization among young adults'. *Social Forces,* 90, (1), 181–208.

McAndrew, Siobhan (2010), 'Religious faith and contemporary attitudes', in A. Park, J. Curtice, K. Thomson, M. Phillips, E. Clery and S. Butt (eds), *British Social Attitudes: The 26th Report.* London: Sage

McCarthy, E. D. (1996), *Knowledge as Culture: The New Sociology of Knowledge.* London and New York: Routledge.

McCloud, S. (2007), *Divine Hierarchies: Class in American Religion and Religious Studies.* Chapel Hill, NC: University of North Carolina Press.

McCracken, B. (2010), *Hipster Christianity: When Church and Cool Collide.* Grand Rapids, MI: Baker Books.

McDonald, L. Z. (2011), 'Securing identities, resisting terror: Muslim youth work in the UK and its implications for security'. *Religion, State and Society,* 39, (2/3), 177–89.

McGrail, P. and Sullivan, J. (2007), *Dancing on the Edge: Chaplaincy, Church and Higher Education.* Chelmsford, Essex: Matthew James Publishing.

McGuire, M. (2008), *Lived Religion: Faith and Practice in Everyday Life.* Oxford: Oxford University Press.

McKenzie, J. (2012), 'To what extent does the sociology of contemporary evangelicalism engage with the issue of social class?', (unpublished paper).

McLeod, H. (2007), *The Religious Crisis of the 1960s.* Cambridge: Cambridge University Press.

McPhee, A. (1978), *Friendship Evangelism: The Caring Way to Share Your Faith.* Eastbourne: Kingsway.

McQuillan, P. and O'Gorman, J. (2010), 'Religious experience among contemporary Japanese university students (searching for Kami Sama liminal experiences of some Japanese university students)'. *Modern Believing,* 51, (2), 24–41.

McRobbie, A. (2004), 'Post-feminism and popular culture'. *Feminist Media Studies,* 4, (3), 255–64.

Menagi, F. S., Harrell, A. T. and June, L. N. (2008), 'Religiousness and college student alcohol use: examining the role of social support'. *Journal of Religion and Health,* 47, (2), 217–26.

Miller, V. J. (2006), *Consuming Religion: Christian Faith and Practice in a Consumer Culture.* London: Continuum.

Mitchell, J. (2003), *Siblings: Sex and Violence*. Cambridge: Polity.
Mitchell, K. (2003), 'Educating the national citizen in neo-liberal times: from the multi-cultural self to the strategic cosmopolitan'. *Transactions of the Institute of British Geographers*, 28, 387–403.
Mizen, P. (2004), *The Changing State of Youth*. Houndmills, Basingstoke: Palgrave Macmillian.
Moody, I. (2010), 'What's in a name? The significance of John Ruskin for Anglia Ruskin University and its chaplaincy'. *Modern Believing*, 51, (4), 34–45.
Mooney, M. (2010), 'Religion, college grades, and satisfaction among students at elite colleges and universities'. *Sociology of Religion*, 71, (2), 197–215.
Moran, C. D. (2007), 'The public identity work of evangelical Christian students'. *Journal of College Student Development*, 48, (4), 418–34.
Morgan, D. H. J. (1996), *Family Connections: An Introduction to Family Studies*. Cambridge: Polity.
Morris, M. (1996), 'Crazy talk is not enough'. *Environment and Planning D: Society and Space*, 14, 384–94.
Morton, F. and Tighe, B. (2011), 'Prevalence of, and factors influencing, binge drinking in young adult university under-graduate students'. *Journal of Human Nutrition and Dietetics*, 24, 296–7.
Neill, S. and Schihalejev, O. (2011), 'Influences on students' views on religions and education in England and Estonia'. *British Journal of Religious Education*, 33, (2), 225–40.
Nesbitt, E. (2009), 'Research report: studying the religious socialization of Sikh and "mixed-faith" youth in Britain – contexts and issues'. *Journal of Religion in Europe*, 2, 37–57.
Niebuhr, H. R. (1951), *Christ and Culture*. New York: Harper & Row.
— (1962), *The Social Sources of Denominationalism*. New York: Meridian.
Numbers, R. L. (2006), *The Creationists: From Scientific Creationism to Intelligent Design* (2nd edn). Cambridge, MA and London: Harvard University Press.
Okamura, N. (2009), 'Intercultural encounters as religious education: Japanese students at a Christian university and their religious transformation'. *Religious Education*, 104, (3), 289–302.
Ontakharai, S., Koul, R. and Neanchaleay, J. (2008), 'Religious outlook and students' attitudes toward the environment'. *Journal of Beliefs and Values-Studies in Religion and Education*, 29, (3), 305–11.
Orsi, R. (2003), 'Is the study of lived religion irrelevant to the world we live in? Special presidential plenary address, society for the scientific study of religion'. *Journal for the Scientific Study of Religion*, 42, (2), 169–74.
Pahl, R. (2000), *On Friendship*. Cambridge: Polity Press.
Pahl, R. and Spencer, L. (2010), 'Family, friends and personal communities: changing models-in-the-mind'. *WP 01 Institute for Social and Economic Research*. Essex: University of Essex.
Pankhurst, J. G. and Houseknecht, S. K. (eds) (2000), *Family, Religion and Social Change in Diverse Societies*. Oxford: Oxford University Press.
Park, A., Phillips, M. and Johnson, M. (2004), *Young People in Britain: The Attitudes and Experiences of 12 to 19 Year Olds*. London: Department for Education and Skills and National Centre for Social Research.
Park, C. (2004), 'Religion and geography, Chapter 17', in J. Hinnells (ed.), *Routledge Companion to the Study of Religion*. London: Routledge.

Park, J. J. (2012), 'When race and religion collide: the effect of religion on interracial friendship during college'. *Journal of Diversity in Higher Education*, 5, (1), 8–21.

Partridge, C. H. (ed.) (2001), *Fundamentalisms*. Carlisle: Paternoster.

Patiniotis, J. and Holdsworth, C. (2005). '"Seize that chance!" Leaving home and transitions to higher education'. *Journal of Youth Studies*, 8, (1), 81–95.

Peach, C. (2002), 'Social geography: new religions and ethnoburbs – contrasts with cultural geography'. *Progress in Human Geography*, 26, 252–60.

Peach, C. and Gale, R. (2003), 'Muslims, Hindus, and Sikhs in the new religious landscape of England'. *Geographical Review*, 93, 469–90.

Pearce, L. D. and Denton, M. Lundquist (2011), *A Faith of their Own: Stability and Change in the Religiosity of America's Adolescents*. New York: Oxford University Press.

Penning, J. M. and Smidt, C. E. (2002), *Evangelicalism: The Next Generation*. Grand Rapids, MI: Baker.

Percy, M. and Jones, I. (eds) (2002), *Fundamentalism, Church and Society*. London: SPCK.

Phillips, D. (2009), 'Creating home spaces: young British Muslim womens' identity and conceptualisations of home', in Peter Hopkins and Richard Gale (eds) (2009), *Muslims in Britain: Race, Place and Identities*. Edinburgh: Edinburgh University Press.

Piper, J. (1991), 'A vision of biblical complementarity: manhood and womanhood defined according to the Bible', in John Piper and Wayne Grudem (eds), *Restoring Biblical Manhood and Womanhood: A Response to Evangelical Feminism*, Wheaton, IL: Crossway Books.

Putnam, R. D. (2000), *Bowling Alone: The Collapse and Revival of American Community*. New York: Simon & Schuster.

— (2001), 'Social capital: measurement and consequences'. *Isuma: Canadian Journal of Policy Research*, 2, 41–51.

Putnam, R. D. and Campbell, D. E. (2010), *American Grace: How Religion Divides and Unites Us*. New York: Simon & Schuster.

Puzstai, G. (2008), 'The pedagogical benefits of religiosity in Hungarian students in three countries'. *Social Compass*, 55, (4), 497–516.

Rahman, M. and Jackson, S. (2010), *Gender and Sexuality: Sociological Approaches*. Cambridge: Polity.

Redfern, C. and Aune, K. (2010), *Reclaiming the F Word: The New Feminist Movement*. London: Zed Books.

Reimer, S. (2010), 'Higher education and theological liberalism: revisiting the old issue'. *Sociology of Religion*, 71, (4), 393–408.

Reimer-Kirkham, S., Sharma, S., Pesut, B., Sawatzky, R. and Meyerhoff, H. (2012), 'Sacred spaces in public places: religious and spiritual plurality in health care'. *Nursing Inquiry*, 19, (3), 202–12.

Reynolds, T. (2010), 'Editorial introduction: young people, social capital and ethnic identity'. *Ethnic and Racial Studies*, 33, (5), 749–60.

Riley, N. S. (2005), *God on the Quad: How Religious Colleges and the Missionary Generation are Changing America*. New York: St Martin's Press.

Ritzer, G. (1996), *The McDonaldization of Society: An Investigation into the Changing Character of Contemporary Social Life*. Thousand Oaks: Pine Forge Press.

Roberts, R. (2004), 'The quest for appropriate accountability: stakeholders, tradition and the managerial prerogative in higher education'. *Studies in Christian Ethics*, 17, (1), 1–21.

Roberts, V. (1992), 'Reframing the UCCF doctrinal basis'. *Theology*, 95, (768), 432–46.

Robinson, C. G. (1944), *The British Universities*. London: Methuen & Co.

Roof, W. C. (1999), *Spiritual Marketplace*. Princeton: Princeton University Press.

Rose, S. (1998), 'An examination of the new age movement: Who is involved and what constitutes its spirituality'. *Journal of Contemporary Religion*, 13, (1), 5–22.

Rosik, C. H. and Smith, L. L. (2009), 'Perceptions of religiously based discrimination among Christian students in secular and Christian university settings'. *Psychology of Religion and Spirituality*, 1, (4), 207–17.

Rosin, H. (2007), *God's Harvard: A Christian College on a Mission to Save America*. Orlando, FL: Harcourt, Inc.

Rüegg, W. (ed.) (2011), *A History of the University in Europe, Vol. IV: Universities Since 1945*. Cambridge: Cambridge University Press.

Ryken, P. G. (Interviewee), Lindsay, D. M. (Interviewee), and Morgan, T. C. (Interviewer) (2012), 'Sailing into the storm: college presidents Philip Ryken and D. Michael Lindsay discuss the challenges in Christian higher education today'. *Christianity Today*, 56, (3), 24–7.

Sabri, D. (2011), 'What's wrong with "the student experience"?', *Discourse: Studies in the Cultural Politics of Education*, 32, (5), 657–67.

Sabri, D., Rowland, C., Wyatt, J., Stavrakopoulou, F., Cargas, S. and Hartley, H. (2008), 'Faith in academia: integrating students' faith stance into conceptions of their intellectual development'. *Teaching in Higher Education*, 13, (1), 43–54.

Savage, S., Collins-Mayo, S., Mayo, B. with Cray, G. (2006), *Making Sense of Generation Y: The World View of 15–25-year-olds*. London: Church House Publishing.

Sawicki, J. (1991), *Disciplining Foucault: Feminism, Power, and the Body*. New York: Routledge.

Scheitle, C. P. (2011a), 'U.S. college students' perception of religion and science: conflict, collaboration, or independence? a research note'. *Journal for the Scientific Study of Religion*, 50, (1), 175–86.

— (2011b), 'Religious and spiritual change in college: assessing the effect of a science education'. *Sociology of Education*, 84, (2), 122–36.

Schneider, F. (1989), *Friendship Evangelism*. Eastbourne: Monarch.

Schwadel, P. (2011), 'The effects of education on Americans' religious practices, beliefs, and affiliations'. *Review of Religious Research*, 53, (2), 161–82.

Schweisfurth, M. and Gu, Q. (2009), 'Exploring the experiences of international students in UK higher education: possibilities and limits of interculturality in university life'. *Intercultural Education*, 20, (5), 463–73.

Sharma, S. (2012), '"The church is . . . my family": exploring the interrelationship between familial and religious practices and spaces'. *Environment and Planning A*, 44, (4), 816–31.

Sharma, S. and Guest, M. (2013), 'Navigating religion between university and home: Christian students' experiences in English universities'. *Social & Cultural Geography*, 14, (1), 59–79.

Shepherd, J. and Rogers, S. (2012), 'Church schools shun poorest pupils', *The Guardian*, 5 March, www.guardian.co.uk/education/2012/mar/05/church-schools-shun-poorest-pupils (accessed January 2013).

Sherkat, D. E. (1998), 'Counterculture or continuity? Competing influences on baby boomers' religious orientations and participation'. *Social Forces*, 76, (3), 1087–115.

Short, G. (2002), 'Faith-based schools: a threat to social cohesion?' *Journal of Philosophy of Education*, 36, (4), 559–72.

Singh, J. (2012), 'Keeping the faith: reflections on religious nurture among young British Sikhs'. *Journal of Beliefs and Values*, 33, (3), 369–83.

Small, J. L. and Bowman, N. A. (2011), 'Religious commitment, skepticism, and struggle among US college students: the impact of majority/minority religious affiliation and institutional type'. *Journal for the Scientific Study of Religion*, 50, (1), 154–74.

Smart, N. (1967), 'Any religious faith or none', *The Times*, 13 May, 12.

Smith, C. (1998), *American Evangelicalism: Embattled and Thriving*. London: University of Chicago Press.

— (2003), 'Religious participation and network closure among American adolescents'. *Journal for the Scientific Study of Religion*, 42, (2), 259–67.

Smith, C. and Denton, M. L. (2005), *Soul Searching: The Religious and Spiritual Lives of American Teenagers*. Oxford: Oxford University Press.

Smith, C. and Snell, P. (2009), *Souls in Transition: The Religious and Spiritual Lives of Emerging Adults*. New York: Oxford University Press.

Speck, J. (2011), 'King's College London', in M. Threlfall-Homes and M. Newitt (eds), *Being a Chaplain*. London: SPCK, pp. 34–8.

Stacey, J. (1987), 'Sexism by a subtler name? Postindustrial conditions and postfeminist consciousness in the Silicon Valley'. *Socialist Review*, 17, (6), 7–28.

Stark, R. and Bainbridge, W. S. (1985), *The Future of Religion: Secularization, Revival, and Cult Formation*. Berkeley: University of California Press.

Stolberg, T. L. (2009), 'Student thinking when studying science-and-religion'. *Zygon*, 44, (4), 847–58.

Strathern, M. (ed.) (2000), *Audit Cultures: Anthropological Studies in Accountability, Ethics and the Academy*. London: Routledge.

Stringer, M. D. (2008), *Contemporary Western Ethnography and the Definition of Religion*. London: Continuum.

Swidler, A. (1986), 'Culture in action: symbols and strategies'. *American Sociological Review*, 51, 273–86.

— (2001), *Talk of Love: How Culture Matters*. Chicago: University of Chicago Press.

Tamney, J. B. (2002), *The Resilience of Conservative Religion: The Case of Popular, Conservative Protestant Congregations*. Cambridge: Cambridge University Press.

Taylor, C. (1992), *The Ethics of Authenticity*. Cambridge, MA: Harvard University Press.

— (2002), *Varieties of Religion Today: William James Revisited*. Cambridge, MA: Harvard University Press.

— (2007), *A Secular Age*. Cambridge, MA: Harvard University Press.

Thomson, R., Bell, R., Holland, J., Henderson, S., McGrellis, S. and Sharpe, S. (2002), 'Critical moments: choice, chance and opportunity in young people's narratives of transition'. *Sociology*, 36, (2), 335–54.

Tranby, E. and Hartmann, D. (2008), 'Critical whiteness theories and the evangelical "race problem": extending Emerson and Smith's "divided by faith"'. *Journal for the Scientific Study of Religion*, 47, (3), 341–59.

Troeltsch, E. (1931), *The Social Teachings of the Christian Churches* (2 vols). London: Allen and Unwin.

Trzebiatowska, M. and Bruce, S. (2012), *Why are Women More Religious than Men?* Oxford: Oxford University Press.

Turner, V. W. (1969), *The Ritual Process: Structure and Anti-Structure*. New York: Aldine de Gruyter.

Tweed, T. A. (2006), *Crossing and Dwelling: A Theory of Religion*. Boston: Harvard University Press.

Uecker, J. E., Regnerus, M. L. and Vaaler, M. D. (2007), 'Losing my religion: the social sources of religious decline in early adulthood'. *Social Forces*, 85, (4), 1667–92.

Universities UK (2008), Patterns of Higher Education Institutions in the UK: Ninth Report. www.universitiesuk.ac.uk/Publications/Documents/Patterns9.pdf (accessed 25/8/11).

Valentine, G. (2008), 'The ties that bind: towards geographies of intimacy'. *Geography Compass*, 26, 2097–110.

Valentine, G., Holloway, S. L. and Jayne, M. (2010), 'Contemporary cultures of abstinence and the nighttime economy: Muslim attitudes towards alcohol and the implications for social cohesion'. *Environment and Planning A*, 42, (1), 8–22.

Vincett, G., Olson, E., Hopkins, P. and Pain, R. (2012), 'Young people and performance Christianity in Scotland'. *Journal of Contemporary Religion*, 27, (2), 275–90.

Voas, D. (2009), 'The rise and fall of fuzzy fidelity in Europe'. *European Sociological Review*, 25, (2), 155–68.

Voas, D. and Bruce, S. (2004), 'Research note: the 2001 census and Christian identification in Britain'. *Journal of Contemporary Religion*, 19, (1), 23–8.

— (2007), 'The spiritual revolution: another false dawn for the sacred', in K. Flanagan and P. Jupp (eds), *A Sociology of Spirituality*. Aldershot: Ashgate, pp. 43–61.

Voas, D. and Crockett, A. (2005), 'Religion in Britain: neither believing nor belonging'. *Sociology*, 39, (1), 11–28.

Voas, D. and Day, A. (2010), 'Recognizing secular Christians: toward an unexcluded middle in the study of religion', *ARDA Guiding Paper Series*, The Association of Religion Data Archives at The Pennsylvania State University, 1–20.

Voas, D. and Ling, R. (2010), 'Religion in Britain and the United States', in A. Park Alison Park, John Curtice, Katarina Thomson, Miranda Phillips, Elizabeth Clery and Sarah Butt (eds), *British Social Attitudes: The 26th Report*. London: Sage, pp. 65–86.

Walker, A. (2002) 'Crossing the restorationist rubicon: from house church to new church', in M. Percy and I. Jones (eds), *Fundamentalism, Church and Society*, London: SPCK, pp. 53–65.

Wallis, R. (1976), *The Road to Total Freedom: A Sociological Analysis of Scientology*. London: Heinemann Educational.

— (1984), *The Elementary Forms of the New Religious Life*. London, Boston, Melbourne and Henley: Routledge and Kegan Paul.

Walter, T. and Davie, G. (1998), 'The religiosity of women in the modern west'. *British Journal of Sociology*, 49, (4), 640–60.

Ward, S. (2008), 'Religious control of schooling in England: diversity and division'. *Intercultural Education*, 19, (4), 315–23.

Warner, R. (2006), 'Pluralism and voluntarism in the English religious economy', *Journal of Contemporary Religion*, 21, (3), 389–404.

— (2007), *Reinventing English Evangelicalism, 1966–2001: A Theological and Sociological Study*. Carlisle: Paternoster.

— (2010a), 'Autonomous religious consumption: how congregations are becoming customers', in M. Bailey, A. McNicholas and G. Redden (eds), *Mediating Faiths: Religion, Media and Popular Culture*. London: Ashgate.

— (2010b), 'How congregations are becoming customers', in M. Bailey and G. Redden (eds), *Mediating Faiths: Religion and Socio-Change in the Twenty-First Century*. London: Ashgate, pp. 119–30.

— (2010c), *Secularization and Its Discontents*. London: Continuum.

Warner, R. S. (1993), 'Work in progress toward a new paradigm for the sociological study of religion in the United States'. *American Journal of Sociology*, 98, (5), 1044–93.

— (2005), *A Church of Our Own*. New Brunswick: Rutgers University Press.

Warner, R. S. and Williams, R. H. (2010), 'The role of families and religious institutions in transmitting faith among Christians, Muslims, and Hindus in the USA', in S. Collins-Mayo and P. Dandelion (eds), *Religion and Youth*. Farnham, Surrey: Ashgate, pp. 159–65.

Waters, J. and Brooks, R. (2010), 'Accidental achievers? International higher education, class reproduction and privilege in the experiences of UK students overseas'. *British Journal of Sociology of Education*, 31, (2), 217–28.

Waters, J., Brooks, R. and Pimlott-Wilson, H. (2011), 'Youthful escapes? British students, overseas education and the pursuit of happiness'. *Social & Cultural Geography*, 12, (5), 455–69.

Weber, M. (1992), *The Protestant Ethic and The Spirit of Capitalism*. London: Routledge.

— (ET 1948, new edn 1991), 'Science as a vocation', in H. H. Gerth and C. Wright Mill (eds), *From Max Weber*. London, New York: Routledge, pp. 129–56.

Weller, P. (2008), *Religious Diversity in the UK: Contours and Issues*. London: Continuum.

Weller, P., Hooley, T. and Moore, N. (2011), *Religion and Belief in Higher Education: The Experiences of Staff and Students*. London: Equality Challenge Unit.

Weller, Susie (2010), 'Young people's social capital: complex identities, dynamic networks'. *Ethnic and Racial Studies*, 33, (5), 872–88.

Williams, E. (2011), 'Research note: the relationship between rejection of Christianity and non-traditional beliefs among adolescents in Wales'. *Journal of Contemporary Religion*, 26, (2), 261–8.

Williams, R. (2013), 'Constructing a calling: the case of evangelical Christian international students in the United States'. *Sociology of Religion*, 74, (2).

Wilson, B. (1998), 'The secularization thesis: criticisms and rebuttals', in R. Laermans, B. Wilson, and J. Billiet (eds), *Secularization and Social Integration: Papers in Honor of Karel Dobbelaare*. Leuven, Belgium: Leuven University Press, pp. 45–65.

Wilson, B. R. (1966), *Religion in Secular Society. A Sociological Comment.* Harmondsworth: Penguin.

Wilson, B. R. (ed.) (1967), *Patterns of Sectarianism: Organisation and Ideology in Social and Religious Movements.* London: Heinemann.

Woodhead, L. (2003), 'Feminism and the sociology of religion: from gender-blindness to gendered difference', in R. K. Fenn (ed.), *The Blackwell Companion to the Sociology of Religion.* Oxford: Blackwell, pp. 67–84.

— (2007), 'Why so many women in holistic spirituality? A puzzle revisited', in Kieran Flanagan and Peter C. Jupp (eds), *A Sociology of Spirituality.* Farnham: Ashgate.

Woodhead, L. and Heelas, P. (eds) (2000), *Religion in Modern Times.* Oxford: Blackwell.

Wright, P. (1985), *Going Public: Report of the National Consultation of Polytechnic Chaplains.* London: National Standing Committee of Polytechnic Chaplains.

Wuthnow, R. (1988), *The Restructuring of American Religion.* Princeton: Princeton University Press.

— (2007), *After the Baby Boomers: How Twenty- and Thirty-Somethings are Shaping the Future of American Religion.* Princeton: Princeton University Press.

— (2008), 'Can faith be more than a side show in the contemporary academy?', in D. Jacobsen and R. Hustedt-Jacobsen (eds), *The American University in a Postsecular Age.* New York: Oxford University Press.

Index

Accord Coalition 168
active affirmers 41–3
Ahmed, S. 121
AHRC/ESRC Religion & Society
        programme 199
Alliance Group 18
Andersson, N. T. 125, 126
Anglican Christian Focus group 62
Anglicanism 12, 27, 30, 32, 43, 45, 51,
        59–62, 64, 66, 70, 71, 76, 77, 79,
        82n. 6, 83, 90–3, 95, 98–9, 110n.
        4, 111nn. 6–7, 116, 138, 140,
        141–3, 149, 152, 154, 158, 161,
        171, 173, 174, 201, 202–5, 211
Armstrong, K. 198
Armytage, W. H. G. 12
Assemblies of God and Elim 158
Atkinson, B. 154, 156
Aune, K. 184, 186
Australia 200

Barclay, O. R. 156
Barker, J. 121
Barr, J. 155
Bayat, A. 199
Bebbington, D. W. 12
Beck, U. 171
Becket, T. 11–12
Beckford, J. 33, 115
Beckford, R. 173
Believers Love World 71
Bell, D. 84
Bellah, R. N. 99
Beloff, M. 16
Berger, P. 208
Berger, P. L. 2–3, 23, 24, 84, 87
Bible Society 158
Bingham, J. 126
Bishopsgate Church 159
Black Christianity 173, 178, 216n. 3
bonding social capital 188, 189

Book of Common Prayer 27
Bottero, W. 172
Bowman, N. A. 25
Boyd, J. 199
Boyd, R. 145
Brabazon, T.
        The University of Google 21
Bradley, I. 36
Bramadat, P. A. 25, 84
bridging social capital 188, 189
Brierley, P. 38, 52n. 2, 111nn. 6–7, 9,
        173, 214, 216n. 3
British Sikh Student Federation (2008) 2
British Social Attitudes (BSA)
        survey 101, 102, 112n. 10, 179,
        212, 213, 215
    Information System 217n. 5
Brito, C. 125
Brooks, R. 187
Brown, C. G. 17, 36, 85, 168, 178
Brown, S. 60
Browne, J. 20, 78
Bruce, S. 32, 37, 85, 86, 162, 178, 198,
        212
Bruegel, I. 192
Bryant, A. N. 23, 135n. 2, 183
Byfield, C. 194n. 9

Cambridge University 12
Camp America 190
Campus Christian Council 62
Canada 84, 200
Canterbury Christ Church University 83
Caplovitz, D. 113
Carrette, J. 21
Cartmel, F. 215
Cathedrals Group universities 6, 17, 18,
        54, 109, 169, 190, 196, 215
    see also Canterbury Christ Church
        University; University of Chester;
        University of Winchester

Catholic Societies (Cathsocs) 62,
    138–40
Chalcedonian Christology 153
chaplaincies, challenges for 207
Chaplaincies Advisory Group 138
Chatterton, P. 122
Chaves, M. 88
Cherry, C. 23
China 176
Chinese Christian Fellowship 62
Choi, J. Y. 23
Christ Church 159
Christian Aid 158, 190
Christian constituency,
    identifying 211–13
Christianity Explored 148
Christian Performing Arts Society 62
Christian student, challenges of 113–14
    coping with home-to-university
        transition 114–19
    drinking among students and 122–7
    faith and 132–3
    fitting in to student life 119–22
    learning and 127–32
Christian students 27–31
    and Christianity destabilization as
        category 31–6
    taking stock of 49–51
    typology development of 36–40
        active affirmers 41–3
        emerging nominals 46–7
        established occasional 44–6
        lapsed engagers 43–4
        unchurched Christians 47–9
Christian Union (CU) 59, 62, 64, 65, 67,
    70, 77, 82n. 12, 108–9, 116, 120,
    147–9, 160, 161, 162, 175, 187,
    192, 197, 204
    constraints upon 206–7
    profiling of members 149–57
Church Missionary Society 158
Church of England 174, 182, 204
Clydesdale, T. 24, 84, 118, 131, 133
Collini, S. 19, 22
    What Are Universities For? 21
Collins-Mayo, S. 5, 87
    Religion and Youth 199
complementarianism 183–4
conflict model 24
Council of Church Universities and
    Colleges (CCUC) 17
Crockett, A. 37, 114, 116
Crompton, R. 180

D'Costa, G. 22
Dandelion, P.
    Religion and Youth 199
Davidoff, L. 168
Davie, G. 84, 86, 144, 178, 207
Davies, D. J. 212
Day, A. 5, 36, 199, 216n. 1
DeBerg, B. A. 23
denominational changes 203–6
Denton, M. L. 4, 24, 110, 133, 198, 200
Department for Communities and Local
    Government 179
Dinham, A. 78, 83, 134, 208
Durham University 5, 6, 12, 13, 58–9,
    66–8, 71, 75, 78, 161, 170–1
Durham University Ecumenical Christian
    Council (DUECC) 59
Dutton, E. 68, 92
Dwyer, C. 199

emerging nominals 46–7
Emerson, M. 178, 187
England 13, 17, 213, 215
English Church Census (2005) 52n. 2
Equality Act (2010) 83, 152
Equality Service 68
essentialism 182–3
established occasional 44–6, 147
Evangelical Alliance 158
Evangelical Holy Trinity Church 160
Evangelicalism 1, 8, 25, 27, 29–31, 41–4,
    51, 59–61, 64–5, 67–8, 71, 77, 86,
    88, 90–3, 95, 98–100, 103, 109,
    110n. 4, 111nn. 5–7, 116, 119–21,
    129, 135n. 2, 141, 146–63, 168,
    171, 173, 176, 178, 180, 183–4,
    186, 192, 193–4n. 3, 194n. 6,
    196, 197–8, 201, 203–7, 216n. 3
Evans, S. 187

Fagbemi, S. 142
Fairweather, I. 131
Federation of Student Islamic Societies
    (FOSIS) 64
Feldman, K. 113
feminism 182, 185–6
Field, J. 188
Finch, J. 117
Firth College 13
Flory, R. W. 198
France, M. 138
Francis, L. J. 35, 198–9
Frankenberg, R. 178

Free Church 160
Fresh Expressions 158
Fulton, J. 201
Fulwood Church 159
Furlong, A. 215
Further and Higher Education Act (1992) 16
Fusion and local churches and
    significance 157–61

Gale, R. 80
Gallagher, S. K. 184
Gee, P. J. 45
Gerth, H. H. 85
Gill, R. 37, 38, 182
Gilliat-Ray, S. 53, 79, 138
Gladstone, W. 12
Goodhew, D. 68
Graham, D. 199
Graham, G.. 12, 16
Greenbelt 146
'Grill a Christian' 147
Gross, N. 25
Gu, Q. 176
Guest, M. 24, 32, 87, 92, 116, 120, 121,
    127, 129, 134, 170, 173
Guide Dogs 190
GuildHE Group 18

Hadaway, C. K. 37, 88, 113
Haines, D. W. 193
Hall, C. 168
Hammond, P. E. 202
Harris, H. 45
Hastings, A. 145, 158
Hastings, P. K. 23
Heath, A. 193
Heath, S. 117
Heelas, P. 38, 167, 212
    The Spiritual Revolution 99
Hempton, D. 36
HERI 25
Herrera, L. 199
Herzog, P. S. 192, 193
hidden Christians 163, 200, 206, 208–10
Higher Education Statistics Agency
    (HESA) 115, 216n. 4
Higton, M. 22
Hill, C. 173
Hill, J. P. 23, 25, 109
Hilliard, D. 84
Historic Protestant 43, 90–3, 95, 110n.
    4, 111nn. 6–7, 146
Hoge, D. R. 23

Holdsworth, C. 134
Hollands, R. 122
Holloway, S. L. 124
Hooley, T. 119
Hopkins, P. 5, 79, 116, 128, 134
Horn, R. M. 156
Houseknecht, S. K. 114
Humanist and Secularist Society 59, 67
Hunter, J. D. 23, 84, 103, 113, 134, 152,
    160, 174, 198
Hussain, S. 172
Hustedt-Jacobsen, R. 208

identity lockbox 24, 118, 131
India 176
Inter-varsity Christian Fellowship 148
Intervarsity Fellowship (IVF) 86, 154,
    156, 162, 163n. 5
Islamic Society 64, 82n. 12
Ivan, L. 23, 84

Jacobsen, D. 208
James, S. 183
Japan 176
Jenkins, T. 212
Jensen, L. 134
Jesmond Parish Church 159
Johnson, M. 180
John Wesley Society 140
Jones, I. 198
Jones, R. 163n. 1
Jones, S. H. 78, 83, 134, 208

Kalilombe, P. 173
Kay, W. K. 198–9
Kay, W. M. 59
Kelly, T. 13
Kenyon, E. 117
Kim, R. Y. 173
King, J. 14
King, R. 21
King's College 12
Kingston University 161
Kong, L. 80
Kuntsche, E. 124

lapsed engagers 43–4
Layard, R. 14
Leavey, C. 201
Lee, J. J. 23, 84
Leeds Metropolitan University 68
Lefkowitz, E. S. 132
Lewis, P. 199

Lightly 174
Lindley, J. 168
Lindsay, D. M. 194n. 3
Lokahi Foundation
    Campusalam 69, 191, 194n. 11
London Metropolitan University 126
Luckmann, T. 208
Lynch, G. 36, 212
Lyon, D. 33
Lyonnette, C. 180

McAndrew, S. 179
McCarthy, E. D. 208
McCracken, B. 126
McGrail, P. 138, 142
McKenzie, J. 193–4n. 3
McLeod, H. 36, 85
McPhee, A. 121
McRobbie, A. 186
Marler, P. L. 37, 88
Marsden, G. M. 198
Martin, D. 32, 85
    A General Theory of Secularisation 199
    On Secularization: Towards a Revised
        General Theory 199
Marty, M. 198
Massey, D. 80
Mauthner, M. 116
Mayrl, D. 23, 25, 53, 114, 118, 134, 200
Menagi, F. S. 126
Methodism 17, 59, 138, 140, 142,
        163n. 1
Millennium Commission 82n. 12
Miller, D. E. 198
Miller, V. J. 202
Million+ Group 18
Mitchell, J. 116
Moore, N. 119
Moran, C. D. 119
Morgan, D. H. J. 117
Morton, F. 124

Nash, E. 194n. 6
National Census (2011) 2
National Federation of Atheist, Humanist
        and Secular Student Societies
        (AHS) (2009) 2, 142
National Readership Survey 194n. 4
National Student Survey (NSS) 18
National Study of Youth and
        Religion 3–4, 110, 133, 198, 200
National Union of Students (NUS)
        survey 121

Neill, S. 145
Nesbitt, E. 199
Newbigin, L. 145
New Church 205, 206
NewComb, T. 113
Newfrontiers 158
New Life Pentecostal group 62
New Wine 158
Niebuhr, H. R. 32, 35
1960s campus universities 6, 14–17, 53,
        54, 70, 71, 105, 106–7, 140, 169
    see also University of Kent
Northam-Jones, D. 212
Numbers, R. L. 129

Oeur, F. 23, 25, 53, 118, 200
Olson, E. 32
Open University 81n. 2
organized Christianity, on university
        campus 137–8
    changing context of chaplaincy
        and 138–45
    Christian Unions and 147–9
        profiling of members 149–57
    Fusion and local churches and
        significance and 157–61
    Student Christian Movement
        and 145–7
Orsi, R. 80, 81, 133
Oxford University 12

Pahl, R. 116, 117
Pankhurst, J. G. 114
Park, A. 180
Park, J. J. 173
Partridge, C. H. 198
Peach, C. 80
Pearce, L. D. 110, 133
Penning, J. M. 134
Pentecostals 71, 110n. 4, 173, 175,
        176, 178, 183, 205, 206,
        216n. 3
    see also Evangelicalism
Percy, M. 198
Phillips, D. 199
Phillips, M. 180
Pioneer 158
Piper, J. 183
Porterfield, A. 23
post-1992 universities 6, 17, 53–5, 72,
        73, 105, 107, 169
    see also University of Derby
post-feminism 186

Protestantism 30, 32, 60, 77, 86, 148,
    149, 160, 162, 173–4, 178, 187,
    192, 198, 203, 204
Putnam, R. D. 188

Queen's University 13

Radical Youth 173–4, 175
Rag society (university) 190
red brick universities 6, 13–14, 54,
    60–1, 98, 105, 106, 169, 190
    see also individual entries
Redeemed Christian Church of God 71
Redfern, C. 186
Reimer-Kirkham, S. 79, 80
religion and UK universities, in historical
    perspective 11–14
  expansion and restructuring 16–17
  Robbins report and 1960s
    expansion 14–16
Research Assessment Exercise
    (RAE) 18
Research Excellence Framework
    (REF) 18
Reynolds, T. 188
Ritzer, G. 21
Robbins report 14–16, 54, 61, 138
Robinson, C. G. 13
Rogers, S. 168
Roman Catholicism 12, 17, 25, 27, 32,
    40, 43, 45, 51, 59–60, 62, 64, 65,
    70, 72, 77, 82nn. 16, 18, 90–2,
    95, 99, 110n. 4, 111n. 6, 127, 130,
    138–42, 150, 151, 160–1, 174–5,
    178, 183, 197, 198, 201, 203,
    204–5
Roof, W. C. 113, 202
Rose, S. 38
Rosin, H. 129
Russell Group 18, 19

Sabri, D. 20, 24, 78, 127, 128
St Benedict's Roman Catholic
    Church 160
St Chad's College 82n. 6
St Helen's Church 159
St John's 82n. 6
St Mary Church 160
St Vincent de Paul Society 60
Salem Campus Fellowship 71
Savage, S. 24, 35, 215
Scheitle, C. P. 24
Schneider, F. 121

Schweisfurth, M. 176
SCM Press 145
Scotland 12, 13
secularization and universities 83–8
  church attendance patterns and
    denominational affiliation 90–9
  and differential patterns 104–7
  self-reported change and 88–90
  subjectivization thesis testing 99–103
Shah, B. 199
Sharma, S. 116, 117, 127, 134, 170, 173
Shepherd, J. 168
Sherkat, D. E. 113, 134
Sherrow, F. 113
Short, G. 193
Simmons, S. 25
Singh, J. 199
Small, J. L. 25
Smart, N. 16
Smidt, C. E. 134
Smith, C. 4, 24, 86, 115, 178, 187, 188,
    198, 200
Snell, P. 4, 115, 198, 200
social capital 188–9
social differences, among Christian
    students 165–6
  age and 166–8
  class and 168–72
  ethnicity and 172–8
  gender and 178–9
  gender equality attitudes and 179–80
  interview data and 179–86
social differences, volunteering, and
    social capital and 186–93
Soul Survivor 158
South Korea 176
SPEAK 157
Spencer, L. 117
spiritual Christians 100
Stacey, J. 186
Strathern, M. 18
Stringer, M. D. 212
Student Alpha 148, 158, 160
Student Christian Movement
    (SCM) 86, 137, 145–7, 160,
    161, 162, 204
Student Voluntary Missionary Union 145
Sullivan, J. 138, 142

Taiwan 176
Tamney, J. B. 99
Taylor, C. 99
Tearfund 158, 168

Temple, W. 145
The Times 1
Tighe, B. 124
traditional, elite universities 6, 54, 55, 68, 98, 104–8, 169, 170, 190, 196
	see also Durham University
Trinity College (Dublin) 12
Troeltsch, E. 32
Trzebiatowska, M. 178
Tweed, T. A. 80, 134
twenty-first-century challenges 17–23

Uecker, J. E. 23, 81, 113, 114, 134
unchurched Christians 47–9
Union of Jewish Students (2010) 2
United States 84, 113, 193n. 3, 198
Universities and Colleges Christian Fellowship (UCCF) 67, 77, 93, 146, 147, 148, 152, 154, 156, 157, 158, 160, 197, 211
University College London (UCL) 12, 149
university experience
	and understanding Christianity 23–5
	institutional variations in 53–5, 58
	and Christian faith comparisons 65–77
	Durham University 58–9
	and space and identity 77–81
	University of Chester 64–5
	University of Derby 63–4
	University of Kent 61–3
	University of Leeds 60–1
university managers, implications for 207–8
University of Birmingham 13, 14, 149
University of Bristol 13, 54, 137, 152
University of Buckingham 19
University of Cardiff 13
University of Chester 64–5, 74–7, 78, 161, 162, 170
University of Derby 6, 63–4, 72–4, 78, 79, 80, 170, 191
University of Dundee 13
University of Edinburgh 149
University of Essex 15, 79
University of Exeter 13, 149
University of Hull
University of Keele 15
University of Kent 15, 16, 61–3, 69–72, 79, 162, 170, 171, 174

University of Lancaster 15, 54, 79
University of Leeds 13, 15, 60–1, 68–9, 78, 79, 170, 177, 191, 213
University of Liverpool 13, 64
University of Manchester 15
University of Newcastle 13
University of Nottingham 13, 14
University of Reading 13
University of Sheffield 13
University of Southampton 13
University of Sunderland 142
University of Sussex 15, 54
University of Swansea 13
University of Warwick 15, 79, 160
University of Winchester 213
University of York 15, 54, 79

Valentine, G. 117, 122
Victoria University of Manchester 13
Vincett, G. 24, 37
Voas, D. 36, 37, 114, 116, 212, 215, 216n. 1

Wales 13, 17, 213, 215
Walis, R. 32
Walker, A. 159
Walter, T. 178
Ward, S. 193
Warner, R. 43, 82n. 16, 153, 163n. 5, 194n. 6
Warner, R. E. 202, 205
Warner, R. S. 84, 117
Waters, J. 187
Weber, M. 21, 85
Wedow, R. 192, 193
Weller, P. 53, 54, 79, 82n. 12, 119, 199, 208, 215
Weller, S. 188
Whittaker, B. 125
Williams, R. 177
Williams, R. H. 117
Wilson, B. R. 32, 37
Wolffe, J. 32
Woodhead, L. 167, 179, 212
	The Spiritual Revolution 99
World Council of Churches 145
Wright Mills, C. 85
Wuthnow, R. 23, 134

Yasuno, M. 23
York St John University 83
YouGov-Cambridge survey 214